The Interpretation of

St. John's Gospel
1–10

R. C. H. LENSKI

Augsburg Fortress
Minneapolis

THE INTERPRETATION OF ST. JOHN'S GOSPEL 1–10
Commentary on the New Testament series

First paperback edition 2008

Richard C. H. Lenski's commentaries on the New Testament were published in the 1940s after the author's death. This volume was published in 1942 by the Wartburg Press and assigned in 1961 to the Augsburg Publishing House.

ISBN 978-0-8066-8089-7

The paper used in this publication meets the minimum requirements of American National Standard for Information Sciences—Permanence of Paper for Printed Library Materials, ANSI Z329.48-1984.

Manufactured in the U.S.A.

ABBREVIATIONS

R. = A Grammar of the Greek New Testament in the Light of Historical Research, by A. T. Robertson, fourth edition.

B.-D. = Friedrich Blass' Grammatik des neutestamentlichen Griechisch, vierte, voellig neugearbeitete Auflage besorgt von Albert Debrunner.

C.-K. = Biblisch-theologisches Woerterbuch der Neutestamentlichen Graezitaet von D. D. Hermann Cremer, zehnte, etc., Auflage, herausgegeben von D. Dr. Julius Koegel.

B.-P. = Griechisch-Deutsches Woerterbuch zu den Schriften des Neuen Testaments, etc., von D. Walter Bauer, zweite, etc., Auflage zu Erwin Preuschens Vollstaendigem Griechisch-Deutschen Handwoerterbuch, etc.

M.-M. = The Vocabulary of the Greek Testament, by James Hope Moulton and George Milligan.

NOTE.— The translation is intended only as an aid in understanding the Greek.

INTRODUCTION

A complete presentation of the introductory material to the Gospel of St. John would require an entire volume. For more than a hundred years there has been controversy regarding the author of this Gospel, the place and the time, the origin and the purpose of its composition, the early testimonies of the fathers, to say nothing about many of the important details contained in the Gospel itself and their proper interpretation. Even the works which devote themselves to the presentation of this material find it necessary to sift and to sort, and thus omit much that now seems of little value to the student. For the purpose of a commentary, whose one aim is to penetrate the Gospel itself as fully as possible, we need only the assured introductory facts that stand out as the net result of all this effort at investigation.

One may well ask why so much learned investigation does not end in agreement concerning the vital pertinent facts. Happily, we are able to reply that the disagreement is not caused by the nature of these facts but by the character of the investigators. For some of them the results are predetermined in their own minds. John's Gospel, while in perfect harmony with its three predecessors, has marked features of its own. Instead of accepting these features and seeking to understand them, some skeptically inclined minds insert their doubts and thus nullify for themselves the evidence imbedded in the Gospel itself, as well as the testimonies of the early fathers which speak so clearly to this very day. Once started in the wrong direction, some of these men go to extravagant lengths and accept conclusions which are unwarranted when compared with the data from which they are drawn. In addition, minds that do not read the other three Gospels aright also misunderstand John's Gospel and then find only unsubstantiated hypotheses for its explanation. But hypotheses are a rather uncertain foundation on which to build a critical structure.

The observation is correct that, while John himself does not call his writing a "Gospel," the early church did not err when it considered John's composition an εὐαγγέλιον and added it to the three gospel accounts it already possessed. The word "gospel" was originally used to designate the oral message of the apostles in which they told of Jesus' words and works, and then quite naturally the same word was applied to the records which fixed this message in written form for future generations. But when it was so applied, the term meant more·than a diary or chronicle, more than a history of certified events intended only to inform. While the substance of what was understood by "gospel" consisted of these assured facts and events, their presentation always included the purpose of enkindling saving faith in the hearts of the hearers or the readers and of strengthening this faith where it already existed. This is true of all four Gospels and is directly stated by John himself in the fourth. A subjective touch with this intent appears already in the prolog, in v. 12: "But as many as received him, to them gave he the right to become children of God, even to them that believe on his name." In two other places John even interrupts his objective narrative and addresses his readers directly. When he records his testimony regarding Christ's death in 19:35 he adds the significant purpose clause, "that ye also may believe," even as he who witnessed this death believes. Then, again, when John brings his personal account to a close he writes in 20:31: "But these (signs) are written, that ye may believe that Jesus is the Christ, the Son of God; and that believing ye may have life in his name." The purpose here expressed applies to the entire document and verifies the fact that it is John's intention to compose a "Gospel" in the sense indicated. In both passages the accredited reading is ἵνα πιστεύσητε, the aorist subjunctive, and not the present πιστεύητε, which is a less accredited variant. Yet John is not thinking of his readers as still being unbelievers, so that we should translate, "in order that you may come to believe," an ingressive aorist. He writes his Gospel for believers, for people who have and who believe the other three Gospels, who thus receive this new testimony as a confirmation of what they already hold in their hearts. We must thus translate these punctiliar aorists, "in order that you may definitely believe." The present subjunctive would be simpler, "in order that you may go on believing," but the assured aorist is, after all, more positive and effective.

The fact that John writes for believers should be considered together with the obvious relation of his Gospel to the other three. John not only knew the other Gospels, he wrote his own in such a manner that entire sections of it cannot be understood by the reader unless he, too, knows the other three Gospels. The effect of this remarkable feature is that all four Gospels are a grand unit, and it is chiefly John who produces this effect. This linking of his own account with the accounts of his predecessors does not prevent John from adding much material that the other evangelists passed by. Both where he takes the other writings for granted and where he brings in matter entirely new, he writes as an independent eyewitness, one who chooses what he records according to his own principle and plan. He has most abundant resources, and he himself remarks on this fact. When John recounts events mentioned in the other Gospels he adds further information and many incidental touches of his own. This is exactly what we should expect on the part of one who knew so much at firsthand; and we ought to be thankful for every added word. Mark also has many items which indicate that he very closely follows Peter's way of telling certain events.

All that John thus adds beyond what the other evangelists offer makes many think that John intends to supplement what the others had already recorded. In a sense this is true. Yet the fact is never apparent that John treats the other accounts as imperfect or even as faulty. The brevity of all the evangelists naturally leaves much that could be added, especially by one who was himself a witness to what transpired. And this is the nature of John's additions. They supplement as the evidence of one witness supplements that of another. They also supplement as one writer's plan of selecting material amplifies what others select according to their plans.

The view is often advanced that John also "corrects" what the other evangelists wrote. But this is certainly not true. In the accounts of the other three evangelists no errors are found that another writer could correct. Every word and every statement is true. The right reading of all four Gospels reveals not a single contradiction. We are never confronted with the alternative: Shall we believe what John writes, or shall we believe what one or more of the other evangelists write? Where contradictions are thought to exist, and where corrections on the part of John are thus assumed, it is the reader who misreads John or the others, or both. These statements are made on the evidence of the four Gospel records as they stand and wholly apart from the doctrine of Inspiration. Yet all that we know about the fact of Inspiration, in particular about the promises given to the apostles by Jesus regarding the infallible guidance of the Holy Spirit, tallies with the results that appear when John is compared with the other evangelists. In the testimonies of the ancient church fathers mistakes have been discovered which we are able to correct, but none of the sacred writers made a single mistake.

John omits quite a number of features, prominent among which are the institutions of the two sacraments, which he, too, might have embodied in his record. All these omissions serve only to corroborate the accounts that had already been given to the church. They mean that John has not even one word to add on these subjects that are so vital to the church. The supposition that John's account about Nicodemus is a substitute for the institution of Baptism, and the discourse on the Bread of Life a substitute for the institution of the Lord's Supper, arises from the assumption that John should have written regarding sacraments. Both this assumption and the supposition drawn from it are ill-advised. We have no call to prescribe to John what he ought or ought not to include in his Gospel. He had far higher guidance than we at this late date can offer him.

John reports many conversations, altercations, and discourses of Jesus. The question constantly arises: Does John report these words exactly as Jesus spoke them, or does he modify them, and, if so, to what extent? This question is far-reaching. It at once involves another: To what extent is John's report of these words trustworthy? From the discourses the question branches out and takes in also the narrative sections. For if the words of Jesus may be modified, why not also the events in which they lie imbedded? We must be on our guard against the tendency to open the door to modern criticism with its subjective principles, permitting the critic eventually to rewrite

John's Gospel according to the critic's own conception.

In seeking to answer this question an appeal to the natural powers of the apostle's memory only is manifestly insufficient. He was twenty to twenty-three years old when he heard what Jesus spoke, and he was somewhere between eighty and ninety when he set these words down in writing. We know about the remarkable tenacity and the astounding exactitude of the memory of the ancients. From the day of Pentecost to his labors in Ephesus, John was associated with other apostles, and their one business was to proclaim the deeds and the words that constitute the Gospel. Constant repetition thus stereotyped much of its form. Yet if John had written immediately after Pentecost while the other apostles were still about him, if he had then depended on his memory alone, he could never have produced the reliable records that we need. To instance only one point, many of the things that Jesus said were not even properly understood by the apostles at the time they were spoken. Now, after so many years intervened, uncertainties, serious variations, and actual contradictions must certainly have crept in, considering both the extent and the profundity of all that had to be remembered, and even one unfortunate word or expression might ruin the true sense. Human memory could certainly not achieve the task of adequate and true reproduction.

We also dare not forget the change of language. Though Jesus may have used some Greek, the bulk of his words was uttered in Aramaic, and the apostles had to translate this into Greek for much of their oral preaching. John wrote his record in Greek. Now translation is a difficult task when it comes to verbal exactitude. Here, too, is where the personal factor counts heavily, for a translator has only his own fund of words and ways of expression on which to draw when it comes to a transfer of thought into another language. John was no exception — Greek was not his native tongue. We see, for instance, that he writes in his Gospel very much as he does in his Epistles. A reference to Revelation we may omit at this point.

Combining all these considerations, the conclusion can only be that, if memory alone was John's dependence, his reproduction of the words of Jesus must to an unknown extent be modified from the original utterances. Our only question would be as to what extent, and the field would be wide open to personal opinion and speculation.

Fortunately, we are not left with the possibilities of mere human memory in answering this question about the discourses of Jesus in John's Gospel. The apostles, including John, had supernatural aid in their proclamation of the deeds and the words of Jesus. The Lord himself gave them the unconditional promise· "Howbeit when he, the Spirit of truth, is come, he shall guide you into all the truth: for he shall not speak from himself; but what things soever he shall hear, these shall he speak: and he shall declare unto you the things that are to come," John 16:13. Compare Paul's testimony in I Cor. 3:13, (translation of the American Committee); the Pentecost miracle; and the promises Matt. 10:18-20; Mark 13:11; Luke 12:11, 12; 21:14, 15. This supernatural guidance and control we call Inspiration. And this is our reliance for the fact that when John wrote the words of Jesus, they are, indeed, trustworthy in every respect. We have no valid reasons for making a subtraction from this assurance. The Holy Spirit enabled John to reproduce the words of Jesus (and also all else connected with them) exactly as this Spirit desired to have them reproduced for the church of all time in the language he had chosen for this purpose. With this forever settled, it concerns us scarcely at all whether in some instances John was led to abbreviate or to condense, to rearrange or recombine, or in other ways to recast the Savior's words. The varying forms in which the other evangelists record, for instance, the Lord's Prayer, the institution of the Lord's Supper, etc., are highly instructive in this respect. We see that the Holy Spirit did not employ a stenographic, merely mechanical exactness in reproducing Christ's spoken words, but he did employ a far more vital and valuable exactness, that of inerrancy in substance and in expression. As we read John's record today, the Lord himself speaks to us through John by the Spirit of truth. Every word in its connection is able to bear the fullest stress that we today can bring to bear upon it, and not a single expression will ever fail in performing this supreme duty.

Textual criticism has done much also for John's Gospel. We have a thoroughly reliable text and are able to judge fairly the variants that remain. Two eliminations from the text must be noted, namely 5:4 and 7:53-8:11, both of which will be discussed in their proper place. John's Gospel today stands as a unit. The so-called interpolation hypotheses of the higher critics, which make of John's Gospel a coat of many colors, merit no serious attention. The source hypotheses, which reduce the Gospel to a relative unity, a compilation of a variety of material and what John himself was able to contribute, have also had their day. Among the latest efforts of this general type are those that make a distinction between the discourses and the narrative sections, stating that in certain places these are joined in "an awkward and disturbing way." On the basis of this judgment we are to conclude that the discourses existed as an earlier and separate collection or document, which eventually was worked into the Gospel as we have it today. The improbability of his hypothesis is apparent. The facts, undoubtedly, are these: John preached and taught all that is contained in his Gospel for many years and then finally put all this material into written form as one magnificent whole.

The fourth Gospel differs markedly from the other three in the fact that it indicates its author. The inner evidence for John's authorship is so convincing that it has been likened to solid granite. Every assault upon this evidence has ended in failure. The exposition of the Gospel itself is the best place for presenting the details of this inner evidence. Here we content ourselves with the following: John never names himself nor any member of his family. But this refined modesty does not prevent him from indicating his own person and making it entirely plain that he is the writer of this Gospel. In this final chapter, which was added as a supplement to the Gospel proper, the disciples of John in Ephesus add their own personal attestation to John's authority like a special seal, 21:24.

The direct indications are strongly supported by many others that are less direct. The fact constantly obtrudes itself that we are reading nothing less than the account of an eyewitness, who either saw and heard in person what we now read, or was in the most excellent position to learn at firsthand and promptly what transpired where he himself was not actually present. We are struck with the fact that, when events already recorded by the other evangelists are retold in whole or in part, new intimate and most valuable details are added, such as only an independent eyewitness could supply. We see very plainly that the writer of this Gospel was a native of Palestine and a former Jew. His perfect acquaintance with things Palestinian and Jewish is beyond question. The type of Greek which he employs is further weighty evidence. The closest examination of the Gospel reveals not a single indication that conflicts with John's authorship. Everything is clear if this apostle is the writer; very much is out of gear if his authorship is denied.

The fact that John spent the latter part of his long life in Ephesus of Asia Minor is fully established by Revelation, 1:4 and 9-11; 2:1, etc. (the seven letters to the "angels" of the seven churches). This testimony is entirely sufficient.

Probably next in importance is the testimony of Irenaeus (about 185). He was a disciple of Polycarp, the bishop of Smyrna, a disciple of the Apostle John together with Papias and others. Polycarp was baptized in the year 69 and died as a martyr in the year 155, 86 years after his baptism. The testimony of Irenaeus thus goes directly back to John through Polycarp, Papias, and others of John's disciples. In his book on *Heresies*, III, 1, 1 he reports that John, the disciple of the Lord who lay upon his breast, published the fourth Gospel while he was in Ephesus of Asia Minor. In III, 4, 4 he adds that the Ephesian church was, indeed, founded by Paul, but that John lived there until the time of the emperor Trajan (98-117). This reference to Trajan is repeated in II, 22, 25. Irenaeus seems to presuppose that John died a natural death, which accords with Tertullian, *De anima*, 50. He also regards John as the writer of the Epistles and of Revelation. Among the other evidence that corroborates that given by Irenaeus is that of Polycrates of Ephesus (about 190) in his letter to bishop Victor, and that of Apollonius (about 197), see Eusebius, *Church History*, III, 31, 2 and V, 18, 14. Some matters that Irenaeus reports regarding the teaching of the elders that were associated with John are manifestly incorrect, but the fact that these elders were in John's company and that some of them had seen Jesus we have no reason to doubt.

Contemporary with Irenaeus is Clement of Alexandria, from whose account Eusebius reports, VI, 14, 7, the fact that John as the last perceived that the other evangelists had recounted the more external parts of the story of Christ (τὰ σωματικά, his birth, travels, miracles, etc.), and that at the solicitation of his pupils, moved by the Spirit, he wrote a spiritual Gospel.

For the fact that John's Gospel soon came to be used in the writings of the early fathers we have abundant evidence, extending back to Papias, who about 130 refers to the aloes mentioned only by John in 19:39 and explains that they were used as incense. The statement that John's Gospel was published during his lifetime, is also attributed to Papias.

The testimony of Irenaeus cannot be nullified by the report of Philip of Side in the sixth century and by the note in the Syrian calendar in the fifth century that in the year 44 John was killed as a martyr together with his brother James (Acts 12:2). This calendar contains other wrong statements. We have Gal. 2:9 to prove that in the year 48 Paul met John in Jerusalem.

A good deal of controversy has arisen because of the surmise that two Johns existed. This began somewhat late, with Dionysius, of Alexandria, in the second half of the third century. He could not bring himself to believe that the Apostle John wrote Revelation and therefore sought some other author for this book. Dionysius heard that two graves were shown in Ephesus, both as graves of John. He thus concluded that there had been two Johns, one of them *not* the Apostle, and this second John, he surmised, might have written Revelation. Here is where the second John first appears — a surmise of Dionysius. Next comes Eusebius (270-340) in his *Church History*, III, 39, who quotes a statement from Papias and interprets this as indicating that there were two Johns, one the Apostle John, and the other "the presbyter John." Like Dionysius, Eusebius seeks an author for Revelation other than the Apostle John. Yet neither Dionysius nor Eusebius entertains the idea that the second John, whom they have discovered, wrote the fourth Gospel, for this Gospel was fully established in their day as having been written by the Apostle John. This cue concerning a supposed second John was taken up by modern critics, who advanced the claim that "the presbyter John" was the author of the fourth Gospel. The new hypothesis ran this course: first, this "presbyter John" was supposed to be an eyewitness of the gospel events and the actual author of the Gospel; next, he was only in a modified sense an eyewitness though still the author of the Gospel; finally, he was neither an eyewitness nor the author but only a kind of prototype of both.

Thus far, starting with Papias, at least the name "John" is retained as the author of the Gospel, which has the great advantage of coinciding, at least in sound, with that of the great Apostle John. When the fading-out process advanced, this name disappeared, and only the title by which this "John" had been distinguished remained. He was no longer "John," but he was still "the elder" — the Great Unknown, called "Elder Theologos." This title "Theologos" is affixed to him, it seems, because the caption of Revelation calls the Apostle John "the theologian." He is pictured as an Alexandrine Jew, a man conversant with Hellenic philosophy, of the type of Apollos. In drawing his picture Apollos is mentioned so often that one is led to wonder whether Apollos will not be next in having John's Gospel attributed to him. Strange to say, however, this mysterious "Elder Theologos" is said to carry forward the distinctive Pauline teaching, and

Paul's theology is made to center on the Logos — a name which Paul never employs.

The exegesis which eliminates the Apostle John from his own writings finds no difficulty in removing the external testimony for John's authorship. Although Papias designates no less than seven Apostles (John among them) as "elders," and then, when he names John a second time, again carefully calls him "elder" in distinction from Ariston, exactly as John terms himself "the elder" in his Second and Third Epistles, all this care on the part of Papias in making it plain that he knows only one John, namely the Apostle, seems to be wasted effort. We are offered a second John who is entitled "the elder John," or "the presbyter John." Though Papias uses a historical aorist ($\epsilon\tilde{\iota}\pi\epsilon\nu$) when he mentions the coming of some pupil of the Apostles into his neighborhood and then, in marked contrast, a present tense ($\lambda\acute{\epsilon}\gamma o\upsilon\sigma\iota\nu$) when he mentions John a second time, now combined with Ariston, since these two were then still alive, this is ignored by the critics, to the support of whose hypotheses Papias is quoted. We are assured that the fourth Gospel is a pseudo-composition, and yet the church accepted it without question and without hesitation included it in the canon with the other three Gospels whose authors were fully known. The writer of this Gospel, we are told, is *not* the Apostle though he poses as the Apostle; and yet the church accepts the impersonation, it thinks that it has the Gospel, and that the Apostle wrote it. The fourth Gospel is a document so great and wonderful that in all these ages the church has awarded it the palm among the Gospels, and yet the critics assure us that all trace of this master writer's name and person has been lost — was lost from the very start. Other, minor, silences are used with deadly effect against clear testimonies, but this silence is accepted without even an explanatory remark. Sober sense will

reply that it is easier to believe the testimony which
it finds in the Gospel itself and the testimonies of the
ancients that are to the same effect than the changing
hypotheses of the critics.

Throughout the second century, even in the far borders of the church, in Italy, in Gaul, in Africa, etc.,
the orthodox, the heretics, and even an occasional
pagan, in their literary remains show conversance
with John's Gospel. Clement of Alexandria, about
190, calls it a spiritual Gospel and distinguishes it
from the spurious Gospel of the Egyptians. Tertullian, born about 150, quotes a Latin translation of our
Gospel from Carthage, Africa, and knows a still earlier
translation which in his time had already fallen into
disuse. John's Gospel, as the record left by the Apostle,
was thus fully established as an unquestioned part of
the New Testament canon. Irenaeus, born in Asia
Minor about 130, a pupil of Polycarp, writes his
Heresies in distant Gaul and quotes John's Gospel
more than 60 times. Some of his testimonies have
already been noted. Theophilus, bishop of Antioch,
quotes John's Gospel in the year 180; he also composes
a harmony of the four Gospels. He is the first who
actually names John, which fact the critics turn to
account for their purpose, but in vain, for he, too, is
the first who names Paul as the author of Romans.
Apollinaris in Hieropolis, about 170, quotes John's
Gospel and appeals to it in the controversies of that
time. Athenagoras, about 176, addresses the emperor
in Rome in an apology and quotes John's Gospel.
Tatian composes his *Diatesseron,* a harmony of the
four Gospels, which begins with John's prolog and
shows how fully the fourth Gospel was accepted at this
time. Whether Tatian wrote in Greek or in Syriac is
not yet known. The earliest Syriac translations of
John's Gospel extend back to this time.

The heretical Valentinians "used in full the Gospel of John" (Irenaeus), and one of them, Heracleon, about 160-170, wrote an entire commentary on this Gospel. The Clementine Homilies, a Judaizing work opposing Paul and his doctrines, about 160, operate with passages from John. The pagan Celsus, about 178, uses passages from John in order "to slay the Christians with their own sword." The canon of Muratori (160-170) expressly lists John's Gospel. Justin, born in Samaria, founded a Christian school in Rome and about 150 in his writings refers seventeen times to the "Memoirs of the Apostles" (ἀπο μνημονεύματα τῶν ἀποστόλων), "which are composed by the apostles and by those who accompanied them." He is a great teacher of the Logos and borrows a number of expressions from the fourth Gospel. The eons of the gnostic system in 140 are certainly drawn from John's Gospel. The gnostic Marcion, who came to Rome in 138, knew John's Gospel and rejected it because it was apostolic; yet he used a section from this Gospel, possibly even two.

The battle regarding the letters of Ignatius will probably continue for many a year. The critics deny that Ignatius wrote these letters, or date them later than about 110, in order to maintain their claim that John did not write his Gospel, and that this Gospel dates from the second century. Ignatius, bishop of Antioch, when sent to his martyrdom in Rome, wrote seven letters, which have been proved genuine in the briefer of the two forms in which they have come down to us. Ignatius writes in his *Romans*: "The living water speaking within me says to me, Come to the Father. I take no pleasure either in corruptible food or in the joys of this life; I want the bread of God, which is in the flesh of Jesus Christ. I want for drink his blood, which is incorruptible love." In his *Phila-*

delphians: "The Spirit does not deceive, he who comes from God; for he knows whence he comes, and whither he goes, and he condemns secret things." Again: "He who is the door of the Father, by which Abraham, Isaac, Jacob, the prophets, the apostles, the church, enter in." In his *Ephesians* he calls Jesus "God come in the flesh." Only one who had and who knew John's Gospel could write in this fashion.

In Clement of Rome, about 96, in the *Shepherd of Hermas*, about 100, in the *Didache*, about 110, in the so-called *Second Epistle of Clement*, about 120, in the *Epistle of Barnabas*, about 130, and in a few other early writings passages occur which clearly evidence the use of John's Gospel. The critics maintain that these passages only reflect ideas and expressions current at that time that were afterward incorporated into what is now called the fourth Gospel.

Before the destruction of Jerusalem, between the years 66 and 69, the Apostle John, together with other Apostles and disciples of Jesus, moved to Asia Minor, and these made their headquarters in Ephesus, where Paul had established the most important church of this territory. Here the Apostle John wrote his Gospel in his old age at the solicitation of the Asiatic elders. The date of writing lies between the years 75 and 100, probably somewhere near 80 or 85. The three Epistles of John were most likely written after the Gospel, and Revelation last of all. Irenaeus says positively that the vision of Revelation was seen shortly before he was born near the close of the reign of Domitian who died in September of the year 96. This fixes the approximate date of the writing of Revelation between the years 93 and 96 on the island of Patmos, whither the Apostle had been banished. John died a natural death at the beginning of the reign of Trajan near the year 100 and was buried in Ephesus. "On a Sunday after the religious services, John went outside the gates of the city, accompanied by a few trusted disciples, had a deep grave dug, laid aside his outer garments which were to serve him as a bed, prayed once more, stepped down into the grave, greeted the brethren who were present, and gave up the ghost," Zahn, *Introduction*, 3, 193, etc.

Irenaeus, according to Eusebius, reports from Polycarp, his teacher and a disciple of John: "That John, the disciple of the Lord, having gone in Ephesus to take a bath and having seen Cerinthus inside, left the baths, refusing to bathe, and said, Let us flee, lest also the baths fall in, since Cerinthus is inside, the enemy of the truth."

Clement of Alexandria reports that John commended a noble looking youth in a city near Ephesus to the bishop, who then taught and baptized him. Returning some time after, John said to the bishop, "Restore the pledge which I and the Savior entrusted to you before the congregation." The bishop with tears replied, "He is dead, dead to God, a robber!" John replied, "To what a keeper have I entrusted my brother's soul!" John hastened to the robber's stronghold; the sentinel brought him before their captain. The latter fled from him. John cried: "Why do you flee from me, your father, an unarmed old man? You have yet a hope of life. I will yet give an account of you to Christ. If need be I will gladly die for you." John did not leave him until he had rescued him from sin and restored him to Christ.

Jerome reports: When too feeble, through age, to walk to the Christian assemblies, John was carried thither by young men. His only address was, Little children, love one another, (*filioli, diligite alterutrum*). When asked why he repeated these words so much, he replied, Because this is the Lord's command, and enough is done when this is done. — It has well been said that these anecdotes concerning John could hardly have been invented; they are quite unlike the later legends that betray their fanciful origin, in particular those connected with John's grave.

It has taken a surprisingly long time to determine the theme of John's Gospel together with its division or structure. Progress in this matter was slow, and such progress as was made has not always been generally accepted. Some of the best scholars who have recently interpreted John's Gospel disappoint us in this regard. The unity of the Gospel is, of course, unquestioned. Any denial of this unity ruins at the outset the work of discovering the real structure of this Gospel. Yet the full recognition of this unity has not prevented a number of serious mistakes. Thus minor parts have often been conceived as major parts. John is supposed to develop an idea, somewhat like a theoretical thesis, instead of writing a record of historical facts. Three grand facts loom up in John's Gospel. The one is that Jesus, true man, is the Son of God; the other two are the rise and the full development of faith, and the rise and the full development of unbelief. But the relation of these three has not always been clearly and adequately apprehended in the presentation which John has made. The symbolical notion of the sacred number three has been imposed on the Gospel, blurring the entire structure in the interest of a mere fancy. Even when the two grand parts of the Gospel are recognized as such, the formulation of these parts, including the perception and the formulation of the subparts, has often been inadequate and unsatisfactory.

The following outline will serve our purpose:

Prolog:　The Word became flesh, 1:1-18.

Theme:　**Jesus Christ Attested as the Son of God.**

I. *The Attestation of Jesus Christ as the Son of God in his Public Ministry, 1:19-12:50.*

1) The opening attestation as his ministry begins, 1:19-2:11.

2) The public attestation throughout the Holy Land, 2:12-4:54.

3) The attestation arousing unbelief, chapters 5 and 6.

4) The attestation in open conflict with unbelief, chapters 7 to 10.

5) The final attestation before the people, chapters 11 and 12.

II. *The Attestation of Jesus as the Son of God in his Passion and his Resurrection.*

1) The attestation in Jesus' preparation of the Apostles for the end, chapters 13 to 17.

2) The attestation in his death, chapters 18 and 19.

3) The attestation in his resurrection, chapters 20 and 21.

The purpose of John's Gospel is clearly stated in 20:31. It agrees with the general purpose of the other Gospel writers. They differ as follows: Matthew writes with the Jews in mind and shows that Jesus is the promised Messiah. Mark and Luke have the Gentiles in mind and show that Jesus is the Redeemer for whom the nations longed. John wrote when the difference between Jews and Gentiles had disappeared, after the destruction of Jerusalem and of the Temple, in Asia Minor, when the beginnings of gnostic and other heresies appeared, and thus showed that Jesus is the Son of God, and that salvation is found by faith in him alone.

CHAPTER I

THE PROLOG

The Word Became Flesh, 1-18

John's Gospel begins without a title of any kind and thus differs from Revelation, which carries a distinct title from John's own hand, and from the Gospels of Matthew and of Mark, both of which begin with titles. Luke has an introduction and an address and is peculiar in this respect. While John's prolog may be called an introduction, it is one of an entirely different type. This prolog sums up the contents of the entire Gospel. It does this by brief, succinct historical statements. Each of these is wonderfully simple and clear and yet so weighty and profound that the human mind is unable to fathom them. Amid all that has been written by the instruments of Inspiration this prolog stands out as the one paragraph that is most profound, most lofty, and incomparable in every way.

Later hands have added a caption to John's Gospel; it is like those that have been placed at the head of the other Gospels and the other New Testament writings. The oldest is simply: "According to John"; then: "Gospel according to John" and other modifications of this simple title. This was done when the Gospels and the other writings were collected and when the New Testament canon was being formed. The preposition κατά, "according to," designates the Apostle John as the writer of this Gospel. We have no linguistic or other evidence that the preposition is meant in any other sense. The contention that κατά here means: "according to the type of preaching" done by John is put forward in order to make room for the unknown author of this Gospel who is thought to have used material derived from John and who wrote at a later date. If this contention holds good, the title for Mark's Gospel would have to be: "The Gospel according to Peter," and that of Luke: "The Gospel according to Paul," for both Mark and Luke are dependent on these apostles.

John's is the paragon among the Gospels, "the one, tender, real crown-Gospel of them all" (Luther), and the prolog is the central jewel set in pure gold. The very first words show that John writes for Christian believers, for every sentence presupposes conversance with the faith. John writes as though he stands in the midst of the congregation, all eyes and ears being fixed upon him to hear the blessed Gospel words from his lips. The prolog has been divided in various ways, as one or the other of its statements has been stressed. The most natural division seems to be: 1) The eternal Word, the Creator of all, is the light and life shining into the sinful world, v. 1-5; 2) The Word came into the sinful world, awakening faith and arousing unbelief, v. 6-12; 3) The Word became flesh in the world and brought us grace and truth from the Father, v. 13-18. These three parts, however, are not coordinate blocks, laid in a row one beside the other; they are built up like a pyramid, the one rising above the other. It is all a most wonderful story, this about the Word: He shines — he comes — he appears incarnate. It is a mistake to read even the prolog, not to speak of the entire Gospel, as if John intends to show us only the eternal godhead of the Son. John attests the humanity of the Son as fully and as completely as the divinity and godhead. The miracle of the ages is that the Word became flesh and dwelt among men. Some of the most intimate human touches regarding the Savior are recorded for us by John, and yet the person to whom these human features belong is God's own Son.

1) **In the beginning was the Word, and the Word was with God, and the Word was God. This One was in the beginning with God.** Even the first readers of John's Gospel must have noted the resemblance between the first phrase ἐν ἀρχῇ, "in the beginning," and that with which Moses begins Genesis. This parallel with Moses was, no doubt, intentional on John's part. The phrase points to the instant when time first began and the first creative act of God occurred. But instead of coming down from that first instant into the course of time, John faces in the opposite direction and gazes back into the eternity before time was. We may compare John 17:5; 8:58, and possibly Rev. 3:14, but scarcely ἀπ' ἀρχῆς in Prov. 8:23, for in this passage "from the beginning" refers to Wisdom, a personification, of which v. 25 reports: "I was brought forth," something that is altogether excluded as regards the divine person of the Logos.

In the Greek many phrases lack the article, which is not considered necessary, R. 791; so John writes ἐν ἀρχῇ. But in John's first sentence the emphasis is on this phrase "in the beginning" and not on the subject "the Word." This means that John is not answering the question, *"Who* was in the beginning?" to which the answer would naturally be, "God"; but the question, *"Since when* was the Logos?" the answer to which is, "Since all eternity." This is why John has the verb ἦν, "was," the durative imperfect, which reaches back indefinitely beyond the instant of the beginning. What R. 833 says about a number of doubtful imperfects, some of which, though they are imperfect in form are yet used as aorists in sense, can hardly be applied in this case. We, of course, must say that the idea of eternity excludes all notions of tense, present, past, and future; for eternity is not time, even vast time, in any sense but the absolute opposite of time — timelessness. Thus, strictly speaking, there is nothing prior to "the beginning," and no duration or durative tense in eternity. In other words, human language has no forms of expression that fit the conditions of the eternal world. Our minds are chained to the concepts of time. Of necessity, then, when anything in eternity is presented to us, it must be by such imperfect means as our minds and our language afford. That is why the durative idea in the imperfect tense ἦν is superior to the punctiliar aoristic idea: In the beginning the Logos "was," *ein ruhendes und waehrendes Sein* (Zahn) — "was" in eternal existence. All else had a beginning, "became," ἐγένετο, was created; not the Logos. This — may we call it — timeless ἦν in John's first sentence utterly refutes the doctrine of Arius, which he summed up in the formula: ἦν ὅτε οὐκ ἦν, "there was (a time) when he (the Son) was not." The eternity of the Logos is co-equal with that of the Father.

Without a modifier, none being necessary for John's readers and hearers, he writes ὁ λόγος, "the Word." This is "the only-begotten Son which is in the bosom of the Father," v. 18. "The Logos" is a title for Christ that is peculiar to John and is used by him alone. In general this title resembles many others, some of them being used also by Christ himself, such as Light, Life, Way, Truth, etc. To imagine that the Logos-title involves a peculiar, profound, and speculative Logos-doctrine on the part of John is to start on that road which in ancient times led to Gnosticism and in modern times to strange views of the doctrine concerning Christ. We must shake off, first of all, the old idea that the title "Logos" is in a class apart from the other titles which the Scriptures bestow upon Christ, which are of a special profundity, and that we must attempt to penetrate into these mysterious depths. This already will release us from the hypothesis that John borrowed this title from extraneous sources, either with it to grace his own doctrine concerning Christ or to correct the misuse of this title among the churches of his day. Not one particle of evidence exists to the effect that in John's day the Logos-title was used for Christ in the Christian churches in any false way whatever. And not one particle of evidence exists to the effect that John employed this title in order to make corrections in its use in the church. The heretical perversions of the title appear after the publication of John's Gospel.

Philo's and the Jewish-Alexandrian doctrine of a *logos* near the time of Christ has nothing to do with the Logos of John. Philo's *logos* is in no sense a person but the impersonal reason or "idea" of God, a sort of link between the transcendent God and the world, like a mental model which an artist forms in his thought and then proceeds to work out in some kind of material. This *logos*, formed in God's mind, is wholly subordinate to him, and though it is personified at times when speaking of it, it is never a person as is the Son of God and could not possibly become flesh and be born a man. Whether John knew of this philosophy it is impossible for us to say; he himself betrays no such knowledge.

As far as legitimate evidence goes, it is John who originated this title for Christ and who made it current and well understood in the church of his day. The observation is also correct that what this title expressed in one weighty word was known in the church from the very start. John's Logos is he that is called "Faithful and True" in Rev. 19:11; see v. 13: "and his name is called The Word of God." He is identical with the "Amen, the faithful and true witness," in Rev. 3:14; and the absolute "Yea," without a single contradictory "nay" in the promises of God in II Cor. 1:19, 20, to whom the church answers with "Amen." This Logos is the revealed "mystery" of God, of which Paul writes Col. 1:27; 2:2; I Tim. 3:16; which he designates explicitly as "Christ." These designations go back to the Savior's own words in Matt. 11:27; 16:17. Here already we may define the Logos-title: the Logos is the final and absolute revelation of God, embodied in God's own Son, Jesus Christ. Christ is the Logos because in him all the purposes, plans, and promises of God are brought to a final focus and an absolute realization.

But the thesis cannot be maintained that the Logos-title with its origin and meaning is restricted to the New Testament alone, in particular to the Son incarnate, and belongs to him only as he became flesh. When John writes that the Logos became flesh, he evidently means that he was the Logos long before he became flesh. How long before we have already seen — before the beginning of time, in all eternity. The denial of the Son's activity as the Logos during the Old Testament era must, therefore, be denied. When John calls the Son the Logos in eternity, it is in vain to urge that v. 17 knows only about Moses for the Old Testament and Christ as the Logos only for the New. Creation takes place through the Logos, v. 3; and this eternal Logos is the life and light of men, v. 4, without the least restriction as to time (New as opposed to Old Testament time). The argument that this Logos or Word "is spoken" and does not itself "speak" is specious. This would require that the Son should be called ὁ λεγόμενος instead of ὁ λόγος. The Logos is, indeed, spoken, but he also speaks. As being sent, given, brought to us we may stress the passive idea; as coming, as revealing himself, as filling us with light and life, the active idea is just as true and just as strong.

This opens up the wealth of the Old Testament references to the Logos. "And God *said,* Let there be light," Gen. 1:4. "And God *said,* Let *us* make man in *our* image, after *our* likeness," Gen. 1:26. "Through faith we understand that the worlds were framed by *the word of God,*" Heb. 11:3. *"By the word of the Lord* were the heavens made. . . . For he *spake,* and it was done; he *commanded,* and it stood fast," Ps. 33:6 and 9. "He sent his word," Ps. 107:20; 147:15. These are not mere sounds that Jehovah uttered as when a man utters a command, and we hear the sound of his words. In these words and commands the Son stands revealed in his omnipotent and creative power, even as John says in v. 3: "All things were made by him." This active, omnipotent revelation "in the beginning" reveals him as the Logos from all eternity, one with the Father and the Spirit and yet another, namely the Son.

He is the Angel of the Lord, who meets us throughout the Old Testament from Genesis to Malachi, even "the Angel of the Presence," Isa. 63:9. He is "the image of the invisible God, the firstborn of every creature: for by him were all things created, that are in heaven, and that are in earth, visible and invisible, whether they be thrones, or dominions, or principalities, or powers: all things were created by him, and for him: and he was before all things, and by him all things consist. And he is the head of the body, the church: who is the beginning, the firstborn from the dead; that in all things he might have the preeminence. For it pleased the Father, that in him should all fulness dwell," Col. 1:15-19. This is the revelation of the Logos in grace. The idea that by the Logos is meant only the gospel, or the gospel whose content is Christ, falls short of the truth. "Logos" is a *personal* name, the name of him "whose goings forth have been from of old, from everlasting," Micah 5:2. And so we define once more, in the words of Besser, "The Word is the living God as he reveals himself, Isa. 8:25; Heb. 1:1, 2." Using a weak human analogy, we may say: as the spoken word of a man is the reflection of his inmost soul, so the Son is "the brightness of his (the Father's) glory, and the express image of his person," Heb. 1:3. Only of Jesus as the Logos is the word true, "He that hath seen me hath seen the Father," John 16:9; and that other word, "I and my Father are one," John 10:30.

And the Word was with God, πρὸς τὸν θεόν. Here we note the first Hebrew trait in John's Greek, a simple coordination with καί, "and," followed in a moment by a second. The three coordinate statements in v. 1 stand side by side, and each of the three repeats the mighty subject, "the Word." Three times, too, John writes the identical verb ἦν, its sense being as constant as that of the subject: the Logos "was" in all eternity, "was" in an unchanging, timeless existence. In the first statement the phrase "in the beginning" is placed forward for emphasis; in the second statement the phrase "with God" is placed at the end for emphasis.

In the Greek Θεός may or may not have the article, for the word is much like a proper noun, and in the Greek this may be articulated, a usage which the English does not have. Cases in which the presence or the absence of the article bears a significance we shall note as we proceed. The preposition πρός, as distinct from ἐν, παρά, and σύν, is of the greatest importance. R. 623 attempts to render its literal force by translating: "face to face with God." He adds 625 that πρός is employed "for living relationship, intimate converse," which well describes its use in this case. The idea is that of presence and communion with a strong note of reciprocity. The Logos, then, is not an attribute inhering in God, or a power emanating from him, but a person in the presence of God and turned in loving, inseparable communion toward God, and God turned equally toward him. He was another and yet not other than God. This preposition πρός sheds light on Gen. 1:26, "Let *us* make man in *our* image, after *our* likeness."

Now comes the third statement: **And the Word was God.** In English we place the predicate last, while in the Greek it is placed first in order to receive the fullest emphasis. Here Θεός must omit the article thus making sure that we read it as the predicate and not as the subject, R. 791. " 'The Word was with God.' This sounds, speaking according to our reason, as though the Word was something different from God. So he turns about, closes the circle, and says, 'And God was the Word.' " Luther. *God* is the Word, God himself, fully, completely, without diminution, in very essence. What the first statement necessarily involves when it declares that already in the beginning the Word was; what the second statement clearly involves when it declares the eternal reciprocal relation between the Word and God — that is declared with simple directness in the third statement when the Word is pronounced God with no modifier making a subtraction or limitation. And now all is clear; we now see how this Word who is God "was in the beginning," and how this Word who is God was in eternal reciprocal relation with God. This clarity is made perfect when the three ἦν are seen to be eternal, shutting out absolutely a past that in any way is limited. The Logos is one of the three divine persons of the eternal Godhead.

2) And now the three foregoing sentences are joined into one: **This One was in the beginning with God.** Just as we read "the Word," "the Word," "the Word," three times, like the peals of a heavenly bell, like a golden chord on an organ not of earth sounding again and again, so the three rays of heaven-

ly light in the three separate sentences fuse into one —
a sun of such brightness that human eyes cannot take
in all its effulgence. "It is as if John, i. e., the Spirit
of God who reveals all this to him, meant to bar from
the beginning all the attempts at denial which in the
course of dogmatical and historical development would
arise; as though he meant to say: I solemnly repeat,
The eternal Godhead of Christ is the foundation of the
church, of faith, of true Christology!" G. Mayer.

The Greek has the handy demonstrative οὗτος with
which it sums up emphatically all that has just been
said concerning a subject. In English we must use a
very emphatic "he" or some equivalent like "this One,"
"the Person," or "the same" (our versions), although
these equivalents are not as smooth and as idiomatic
as οὗτος is in the Greek. Verse 2 does not intend to
add a new feature regarding the Logos; it intends, by
repeating the two phrases from the first two sentences,
once more with the significant ἦν, to unite into a single
unified thought all that the three preceding sentences
have placed before us in coordination. So John writes
"this One," re-emphasizing the third sentence, that the
Word was God; then "was in the beginning," re-
emphasizing the first sentence, that the Word was in
the beginning; finally "with God," re-emphasizing the
second sentence, that the Word was in reciprocal relation with God. Here one of the great characteristics
of all inspired writing should not escape us; realities
that transcend all human understanding are uttered
in words of utmost simplicity yet with flawless perfection. The human mind cannot suggest an improve-
ment either in the terms used or in the combination
of the terms that is made. Since John's first words
recall Genesis 1, we point to Moses, the author of that
first chapter, as another incomparable example of
inspired writing — the same simplicity for expressing
transcendent thought, the same perfection in every

term and every grammatical combination of terms. Let us study Inspiration from this angle, i. e., from what it has actually produced throughout the Bible. Such study will both increase our faith in Inspiration and give us a better conception of the Spirit's *suggestio rerum et verborum.*

3) The first four sentences belong together, being connected, as they are, by two καί and the resumptive οὗτος. They present to us *the person* of the Logos, eternal and very God. Without a connective v. 3 proceeds with *the first work* of the Logos, the creation of all things. **All things were made through him; and without him was not made a single thing that is made.** The negative second half of this statement re-enforces and emphasizes the positive first half. While John advances from the person to the work, this work substantiates what is said about the person; for the Logos who created all things must most certainly be God in essence and in being.

"All things," πάντα without the article, an immense word in this connection, all things in the absolute sense, the universe with all that it contains. This is more than τὰ πάντα with the article, which would mean all the things that exist at present, while πάντα covers all things present, past, and future. While the preposition διά denotes the medium, Rom. 11:36 and Heb. 2:10 show that the agent himself may be viewed as the medium; hence "through him," i. e., the Logos, must not be read as though the Logos was a mere tool or instrument. The act of creation, like all the *opera ad extra,* is ascribed to the three persons of the Godhead and thus to the Son as well as to the Father; compare the plural pronouns in Gen. 1:26.

The verb ἐγένετο, both in meaning and in tense, is masterly. The translation of our versions is an accommodation, for the verb means "came into existence," i. e., "became" in this sense. The existence of all

things is due to the Logos, not, indeed, apart from the
other persons of the Godhead but in conjunction with
them, as is indicated throughout the creative speaking in Gen. 1. "All things came into being" since the
beginning, the Logos through whom they were called
into being existed before the beginning, from eternity.
The verb "became" is written from the point of view
of the things that entered existence, while in Genesis
the verb "created" is written from the viewpoint of
God, the Creator. John repeats ἐγένετο in the negative
part of his statement and adds the perfect tense γέγονεν
in the attached relative clause. These repetitions
emphasize the native meaning of this verb. As creatures
of the Logos "all things became."

The punctiliar tense, a historical aorist, is in
marked contrast to the durative imperfect of the four
preceding ἦν. This aorist goes back to the creative
acts of Gen. 1. These acts are fundamental; for all
creatures that came into existence in the later course
of time have their origin in the creative acts of that
wonderful week recorded in Genesis. We may thus
pass down through the centuries, even to the last day
of time, and always it will be true: ὁ κόσμος δι' αὐτοῦ
ἐγένετο, "the world was made through him," v. 10,
where this significant verb is repeated for the fourth
time.

John's positive statement is absolute. This the
negative counterpart makes certain: and without him
was not a single thing made that is made. Whereas
the plural πάντα covers the complete multitude or mass,
the strong singular οὐδὲ ἕν points to every individual
in that mass and omits none. "Not one thing" is
negative; hence also the phrase with the verb is
negative, "became without him" or apart from him
and his creative power. Apart from the Logos is
nihil negativum et privativum. Yet in both the positive and the negative statements concerning the

existence of all things and of every single thing the implication stands out that the Logos himself is an absolute exception. He never "became" or "came into existence." No medium (διά) is in any sense connected with his being. The Son is from all eternity "the uncreated Word."

The relative clause ὃ γέγονεν is without question to be construed with ἔν and cannot be drawn into the next sentence. We need not present all the details involved in this statement since the question must be considered closed. The margin of the R. V., which still offers the other reading, is incorrect and confusing. No man has ever been able to understand the sense of the statement, "That which hath been made was life in him." Linguistically the perfect tense with its present force, γέγονεν, clashes quite violently with the following imperfect tense ἦν, so violently that the ancient texts were altered, changing οὐδὲ ἓν into οὐδέν, and ζωὴ ἦν into ζωή ἐστιν. But even these textual alterations fail to give satisfaction apart from the grave question of accepting them as the true reading of the text. So we read, "And without him not a single thing that exists came into existence." The perfect tense γέγονεν, of course, has a present implication and may be translated, "that exists" or "that is made." But the perfect tense has this force only as including the present result of a past act. The perfect always reaches from the past into the present. The single thing of which John speaks *came* into existence in the past and only thus *is* in existence now. What John thus says is that every single thing that now exists traces its existence back to the past moment when it first entered existence. Thus the aorist ἐγένετο is true regarding all things in the universe now or at any time. Every one of them derives its existence from the Logos. Since γέγονεν as a perfect tense includes past origin, we should not press its present force so as to separate the past creative acts of the Logos from the present existence of the creature world.

4) From the creative work of the Logos John turns to his soteriological work. He begins without a connective and uses four brief sentences which are joined in the simplest fashion by means of three καί. **In him was life; and the life was the light of men. And the light shines in the darkness; and the darkness overcame it not.** The first two statements belong together, because the two verbs, ἦν, are identical. The third clause continues not with an imperfect but with a present tense; and the fourth ends with an aorist.

John uses the term ζωή fifty-four times. It is one of the key words of his Gospel. Used here in the first statement without the article, the quality of the word is stressed: in the Logos was "life," life in the fullest, highest sense, the eternal, blessed life of God. The emphasis is on the phrase which heads the statement, "in him" was life. This implies a contrast with all the living beings who came into existence by the creative act of the Logos. They all received life — it came to them as a gift from a higher source. They all also are capable of death, and while some escaped death (the good angels), all the rest came under death's power. The very attribute of the Logos is life, the life that corresponds with his being, forever inherent in his very essence, absolutely incapable of any hurt, subtraction, or deteriorating change. While this first statement of John's refers to the Logos only and as such reaches no farther, it is yet not to be considered abstractly, as a piece of interesting information concerning only this great being, the Logos. It is preliminary to the statements which follow and which pertain most directly to us. In fact, the very terms "Logos" and "life" look toward us and have a bearing upon us, even as all the statements in v. 4 and 5, the first as well as the rest, are made for our sakes and for ours alone.

Because John's statement that life was in the Logos follows his statement regarding the creature world, ζωή is often taken to mean "life" in the sense of the animation of all living creatures. This is unwarranted. In v. 4, 5 John predicates nothing concerning the creatures called into being by the Logos. Many of these have no life of any kind, they are lifeless and inorganic and merely exist without living. Those that are animated received their animation when they were called into existence. Moreover, ζωή is never used with reference to mere creature life; its character is always heavenly and spiritual never physical. Enough wonderful things appear in John's Gospel without our adding thereto, and we must remember that John wrote not for speculative philosophers and lofty theological thinkers but for the church at large.

Much thought has been spent on the verb ἦν, "was," especially on the imperfect tense. John writes, "In him *was* life," and not, as we might expect, "In him *is* life," i. e., ever and always, timelessly, from eternity to eternity. A strong effort is made to regard ἦν as a historical tense, referring to a fixed period in the past. One view is that John here refers to the brief period of innocence in Paradise. A division is made between v. 4 and v. 5, placing the fall of man between them. But the mere tense of ἦν is too slender a foundation on which to base such an interpretation.

Another view has "was" refer historically to the time of Christ here on earth. It is pointed out that "was" follows the two historical aorists "became" in v. 3 and even the perfect γέγονεν with its present implication. Likewise, that "was" in the first sentence in v. 4 gets its meaning from "was" in the second sentence of this verse. The latter is then regarded as pertaining to Christ's appearance here on earth. In substantiation John 9:5 is quoted, "When I am in the world, I am the light of the world." Likewise 12:46; 12:35, 36; 3:19. Of course, we are told, the light and the life did not depart with Christ's visible presence; now it is the Paraclete through whom they come to us. In spite of this argument ἦν in v. 4 is not a true historical tense. The passages adduced come within the two ἦν in v. 4, but no one is able to prove that they cover and exhaust the extent of time of these ἦν. Likewise it is impossible to prove that these two imperfects must denote the time subsequent to the two ἐγένετο in v. 3, and it is plain that these ἦν cannot be subsequent to the perfect γέγονεν.

The favorite view is that the two ἦν refer back to the entire Old Testament period. This is much nearer to the truth. Usually, however, this view is broadened to take in also all the natural knowledge of God left to the pagan world and all the moral principles that still survive among heathen nations. "There has been much foolish speculation as to how the Word of God in its divinity could be a light, which naturally shines and has always given light to the minds of men even among the heathen. Therefore the light of reason has been emphasized and based upon this passage of Scripture. These are all human, Platonic, and philosophical thoughts, which lead us away from Christ into ourselves; but the evangelist wishes to lead us away from ourselves into Christ. . . . He would not have us diffuse our thoughts among the creatures which he has created, so as to pursue him, search for him, and speculate about him as the Platonic philosophers do; but he wishes to lead us away from those vague and high-flown thoughts and bring us together in Christ . . . Therefore the light must mean *the true light of grace in Christ* and not the natural light, which also sinners, Jews, heathen, and devils have, who are the greatest enemies of the light. . . . I am well aware that all the light of reason is ignited by the divine light; and as I have said of the natural life, that it has its origin in, and is part of, the true life, when it has come to the right knowledge, so also the light of reason has its origin in, and is part of, the true light, when it recognizes and honors him by whom it has been ignited." Luther, Lenker's translation, *Postil,* 190, etc. He then proceeds to show how the light of reason, when it remains separate from Christ, becomes extinguished and dies out, how it misleads into error and the most dangerous falsehood, how, when the light of grace comes, a battle ensues, and, when the light of grace conquers, it also "enlightens the light of nature in man" and makes this what it should be. "We must follow the streams which lead to the source and not away from it."

Once it is clearly perceived that the very name "Logos," borne by the Son before the world began, is pointless save as it declares him to be God's revelation to us who need this eternal Logos, the difficulties about the tense of the two ἦν will disappear. We shall, of course, not identify these two with the three ἦν in v. 1, 2, for these three extend back only from "the beginning" into infinite eternity, while the two ἦν in v. 4 extend back from Christ's incarnation across the entire Old Testament into eternity. For John's Christian readers it was not strange that all the works of grace should have their inception in eternity and there disappear in mystery from our finite eyes. Just because ἦν goes back indefinitely, it is the proper tense. An aorist would sound historical and thus be unfit. Just as the eternal Word *was* in the beginning, so also in the beginning and in addition since the incarnation this Word *was* life, and this life *was* the light of men. John writes *was* and not the timeless *is* because he intends to make an incision at the time of the incarnation. This event and the history that follows he records in due order. It would be a misstatement to say that the Logos *became* or *was made* life either in time or before time. Looking backward, no limit can be set, looking forward, John himself sets the limit at the close of the Old Testament or at the incarnation.

As life and light are inseparably joined together in nature, so also they are joined in the domain of the spirit and divine grace. Where divine, true life is, there divine, true light is, and where light, there also life. "In Christ is the life-light, outside is the night of death." Besser. Yet "life" is placed first, and "light" second. The evangelist cannot say that in the Logos was light, and the light was the life of men. Light is that which shines out and manifests itself; it emanates from life which is fundamental and in its essence a deep, mysterious, hidden power. Divine truth is light as it shines out from him who is the Truth; but this truth is the manifestation of the life that underlies it even as Jesus also calls himself the Life.

Moreover, light is a figurative term. It recalls the sun which lights up the physical universe. So the life that is in the Logos is intended to light up the world and the souls of men. The term "light" always connotes its opposite darkness, just as "life" always suggets its opposite death. Both "life" and "light," just like "Logos," are human terms. They apply to us as we are in this world where death and darkness prevail, and where we need the revelation of the Word. In heaven these terms would either not apply at all or would apply in a meaning so wonderful that our minds now could not comprehend the concepts. "Light" equals truth, and this signifies reality, namely all the reality of God's will, purpose, and plans as they center in his love or grace and are incorporated in the Logos, who is Jesus Christ, our Lord. This divine and blessed reality is composed of many facts, each of which, in turn, constitutes a reality; and when these realities are properly voiced in human language, we call them doctrines. Our soul's highest interests are thus tied up with the doctrines of Christ, the Word. Every unreality (lie), though it is trigged up in the most captivating language, constitutes a false doctrine and by its very nature works death and destruction for the soul.

In all cases where a genitive is added to designate the domain that is to be lighted, as "the light of men" or "the light of the world," the term "light" denotes not the radiance that spreads abroad, but the luminary itself from which the radiance emanates. So the sun in the heavens is the "light" of the physical world. Without this sun we should perish in physical darkness. Without the Logos and his saving life we should likewise perish in spiritual darkness. The purpose and the task of the light is to enlighten, to bestow upon men the knowledge of the truth. "For in thee is the fountain of life: in thy light shall we see light," Ps. 36:9. This knowledge is never merely intellectual, it affects the entire being and turns all who are enlightened into children of light who are born anew of the light.

5) "And the light shines in the darkness," φαίνει, a durative present tense. Here is Luther's comment: "Christ has always been the Life and the Light, even before his birth, from the beginning, and will ever remain so to the end. He shines at all times, in all creatures, in the Holy Scriptures, through his saints, prophets, and ministers, in his word and works; and he has never ceased to shine. But in whatever place he has shone, there was great darkness, and the darkness apprehended him not." The present tense of the verb "shines" has led to the interpretation that here John speaks of the New Testament presence of the

Logos. But why impose such a restriction when **the**
general subject is still the eternal Logos, and when
"the darkness" in which the light shines is not restricted to the New Testament era? It is the very
nature of the light to shine, to send out its rays, to
illuminate, to transfer itself? Though this is true,
John is not making a remark on the abstract nature
of light in general. "The light" is the one specific
light mentioned in v. 4, the Logos with his life — it
is he that goes on shining in the darkness.

So also the phrase "in the darkness" with its
Greek article is specific, not darkness in general but
in this world of ours made dark through sin and
death. Between the later word σκοτία and the older
σκότος no difference exists. The abstract term "darkness," which expresses a quality, is here substituted for
the concrete expression "dark world" and sums up
in a single word and from one angle all the hostile
forces that exist in the fallen world. "Darkness,"
while it is a negative term like all the words for sin
and death, is, nevertheless, never used in a merely
negative way as denoting only the absence of light. If
this darkness were no more, it would be like the
physical absence of light which at once vanishes when
light is supplied, i. e., when a luminary appears. The
darkness of the world is a hostile power full of resistance to the true light of the Logos. The shining of the
light in the darkness is, therefore, always an invasion
of the territory held by the darkness, a challenge of
the power of darkness, a battle to destroy this power,
a victory robbing the darkness of its prey. It is thus
that the light shines *in* the darkness. Far from the
darkness invading the light or putting it out, the opposite takes place. Moreover, the light or luminary is
never in the least affected by the darkness — this
luminary is the eternal, unconquerable life of the
eternal Word and as such it shines and shines in

triumphant power. We see its shining in the first promise of the seed of the woman in Eden; we see its broadening, intensified radiance throughout Old Testament times; we see some of its scattered rays striking even into the dark Gentile world with which Israel came into contact; and then we see the wonderful shining like the sun in its zenith when the gospel was carried to the ends of the earth; even so it is shining now. What a wonderful fact, "And the light shines in the darkness!"

We must translate the next sentence according to the margin of the R. V., "And the darkness overcame it not." The verb καταλαμβάνειν has two meanings, "to apprehend something" in order to possess and to retain it, as in Phil. 3:12; I Cor. 9:24; Rom. 9:30; and "to pounce upon something" in order to bring it into one's power so that it shall not escape or assert itself. The analogy of Scripture is in favor of the latter meaning. This analogy embraces all the passages in which a hostile force like σκοτία is active, as for instance a demon in the case of possession in Mark 9:18; the last day as a thief in the night in I Thess. 5:4; the darkness in John 12:35; many LXX passages, like the sinner's iniquities in Ps. 40:12; the evil in Gen. 19:19; and thus constantly in the Scriptures and in other writings. We should also note that "darkness" cannot possibly "apprehend," hold and embrace "the light," it can only resist and war against it. Finally, the force of the aorist tense of the verb would clash with the durative shining of the light; this aorist would have to be a durative present: the light shines, and the darkness does not apprehend, does not appropriate it. The aorist, however, is in place when we translate, "And the darkness did not overcome the light." It made strong attempts to do so, as Jesus prophesied in John 15:18 and 16:4, as the death of Jesus attests, and the Acts report at length; but always its efforts were without success, for the light still shines on.

The A. V. translates "comprehended," which would be only an intellectual act, one that is impossible for "the darkness." The R. V. offers "apprehended," which is deeper and yet involves the same difficulty as to meaning and as to tense.

6) Verse 6 introduces the second section of the prolog which extends to v. 12. The first starts with eternity and sketches the activity of the Logos before his coming into the world. The second starts with the Baptist and sketches the Logos as having come into the world and into his own. V. 6-12 thus includes the incarnation, yet John withholds mention of it in so many words because he intends to reserve this miracle of miracles for the final section of the prolog, the climax of this mighty introduction to the body of his Gospel.

There came a man, commissioned from God, whose name was John — a few touches, and the picture of this man is complete. While the evangelist sketches the Baptist with some detail in v. 6-8, this is not done with a view to introducing to the readers a person unknown and new to them. John writes about the Baptist much as he does about the Logos. The readers know both; what John does is to lift out for each the vital and important features to which John wants the readers to give special heed. John thus presents no history of the Baptist and does not even point out his distinctive work of baptizing, either by describing this activity or by calling him the Baptist.

The very first words: ἐγένετο ἄνθρωπος, "there was (or came) a man," are in marked contrast to ἦν ὁ λόγος, "was the Word," in v. 1. The aorist is plainly historical: he came, *trat auf*, with his activity and work just like any other man. All was different in the case of the Logos. And this was "a man," a human being like other men, not an angel from the other world. Yet he differed from the mass of otherwise notable men in that he was "sent from God." The perfect participle ἀπεσταλμένος includes more than the past act of commissioning him for his special task, it covers also his standing during the entire course of that work. He was God's message bearer or ambassador. However lowly his person, his office is of the highest, with which also his name accords, "John," "God's favor." The agent with a passive verb form may be expressed, as here, with παρά. The introduction of John's name is idiomatic Greek: ὄνομα αὐτῷ 'Ιωάνης, "name for him John." We may regard "name" as a nominative absolute, and the statement regarding the name as parenthetical.

The Baptist is often treated as an Old Testament prophet who was merely standing on the threshold of the New; but he really belongs altogether in the New Testament, as our evangelist's description shows, as well as that of the other Gospels, especially also Christ's words concerning him.

7) The commission received by John is now described. **This one came for witness, that he might witness concerning the light, in order that all might believe through him.** Just as in v. 2, οὗτος reaches back and grasps all that v. 6 has said about John. The aorist ἦλθεν, while it is historical and reports the past fact, summarizes John's entire career, which was "to come for witness." It may sound Hebraic to spread out first in a phrase and then again in a clause this purpose for which John came, yet the effect is that the double mention of witnessing becomes markedly emphatic. That this is the evangelist's purpose we see in v. 8, where this witness function is mentioned for the third time.

John uses μαρτυρία, μαρτύς, and μαρτυρεῖν in their native sense, "witness" that is competent, testimony

at firsthand of what the person has seen or heard,
known and experienced himself. "For witness," without a modifier, stresses this idea. John's office was
to bear witness even as he himself describes it in
language taken from Isaiah when he calls himself "a
voice." That was his function, to speak out as a voice,
to speak "for witness." We may construe the ἵνα
clause in two ways, either as being dependent on the
verb ἦλθεν and parallel to the phrase "for witness,"
merely repeating this in the longer form of a purpose
clause; or as an appositional clause, dependent on the
phrase, then it is subfinal, merely repeating the contents of the phrase. Perhaps the latter is the better.
In either case the aorist verb is constative or com-
plexive, uniting in one point all the witnessing that
the Baptist did during his brief career. But now the
object is added to the verb in the form of a phrase:
the Baptist bore witness "concerning the light," namely
that light which appeared in the Logos of which the
evangelist has informed us in v. 4, 5. While the word
"light" is the evangelist's own designation of the
Logos, it, nevertheless, expresses exactly the contents
of the Baptist's testimony. For we must not think
that the Baptist knew nothing about the pre-existence
of the Logos whom he saw in the person of Jesus.
This is a rationalistic assumption, contradicted by
the Baptist himself in v. 15 and v. 30. In connection
with the latter passage the Baptist himself testifies
how he was made sure on this point: it was by no
natural means but by direct revelation from God who
had sent the Baptist for the very purpose of testifying
as he did. The Baptist even calls Jesus "the Son of
God," v. 33, 34. Both aorists, ἦλθεν and μαρτυρήσῃ, state
that the Baptist actually executed his great commission.

All witness is intended for faith, and so the Baptist testified "in order that all might believe through

him." This comprehensive "all" includes all who went out in the wilderness and with their own ears heard the testimony. But it does not stop with these multitudes — "he being dead yet speaketh" (Heb. 11:4), and his testimony reaches out into the wide world. Just as no limitations restricted the Baptist's saving purpose when his living voice rang out in the wilderness of Palestine, so no limitations now narrow it. That all may believe is the good and gracious will of God which is universal in extent, excluding not a single sinner; it is also called his antecedent will to distinguish it from the subsequent will which becomes effective when men finally reject the gospel and is summarized in Christ's own words, "he that believeth not shall be damned."

The evangelist does not write, "in order that all might *see* the light or *know* the light," both of which would have been good. He at once employs the cardinal term "believe," trust with the full confidence of the heart. The synonymous term "receive" occurs in v. 12. "Believe" goes beyond the figure of "light" to the reality meant by this figure, which is truth, i. e., the divine truth embodied in Jesus, the Logos, shining forth in his person, words, and works. This believing, when closely analyzed, includes knowledge, assent, and the confidence of the heart. It is never a blind trust; hence it is never, like ignorance, the opposite of science and knowledge, as so many who have no experience of saving faith suppose. While saving faith is also implicit and reaches out in trust beyond what we actually know and can know, it always does this only from the vantage ground of explicit faith, the sure ground of what we do and can know. The aorist πιστεύσωσι is best regarded as ingressive, "in order that all *might come to believe*," with the thought, of course, that once having arrived at faith, this faith will continue, even as in regeneration the life once kindled lives on and on. In this production of faith the Baptist is to be the human instrument as the phrase "through him" shows. This, of course, is because of his "witness," the very nature of which is to awaken faith, even as all true testimony ought to be believed. Faith comes only through the preached Word, and God invariably honors the preachers who truly proclaim that Word. Those who leave the Word and cry, "Spirit, Spirit!" or who invent methods that discard the gospel can never hope to have it said of them that men came to faith "through them."

8) The evangelist seems to have a special interest in defining the Baptist's person, position, and work with great exactness. We feel this especially in v. 8, and again, even more strongly, in v. 19-28; 29-34; 3:26-36; and 5:33-36. We may hazard the guess that in the evangelist's time some still thought too highly of the Baptist. Yet we find not the slightest derogation on the evangelist's part. All that he reports concerning the Baptist agrees with his noble and humble character and with his exalted mission as the forerunner of Christ. **He was not the light, but** (came) **that he might witness concerning the light.** So great was "the light" so great must it be to be "the light" indeed for all our fallen race, that no ἄνθρωπος, or any sin-born creature like ourselves, not even John, the greatest of prophets, or that other John, the foremost of evangelists, could be "the light." All that these at most can do is to testify and "witness concerning the light," and they need a special enabling even for that. Augustine writes that they are like trees and mountains upon which the sun shines, which reflect the light and show by their own brightness and beauty that a great and wonderful light, vaster and mightier than they, is shining above them. In this sense Christ himself calls the Baptist "a burning and shining light," 5:35. The evangelist is careful to follow the negative statement concerning what John was not with the

positive one concerning what he truly was, and he makes this a repetition of the clause used in 7, thus securing special emphasis.

9) After thus placing the great forerunner before us the evangelist again points to the Logos but now as incarnate and ushered in by this forerunner. **The true light, which lighteth every man, was coming into the world.** This marginal rendering of the R. V. is decidedly best. We are compelled to regard τὸ φῶς τὸ ἀληθινόν as the subject of ἦν and not as the predicate. To supply the strong demonstrative "that" as the subject (A. V.) is quite unjustifiable. This, too, is certain that ἐρχόμενον does not modify πάντα ἄνθρωπον, and that we dare not translate, "which lighteth every man that cometh into the world" (A. V.). The translation of the R. V. is rather unclear. It really makes little difference whether we regard ἦν . . . ἐρχόμενον as belonging together and forming a circumscribed imperfect (or a periphrastic future, *erat venturum*), or make the participle modify the subject τὸ φῶς. The grammars are reluctant to do the first; and it is true that John has no other example of a relative clause intervening between the two words of a circumscribed imperfect, he has only a few cases in which a few words intervene, 1:28; 3:23; 10:10 ἦν . . . βαπτίζων; 2:6 ἦσαν . . . καίμεναι Yet whichever grammatical construction is preferred, it seems quite evident that ἐρχόμενον completes the idea of ἦν. For John is not merely once more saying (v. 4) that the light *was* in existence in the indefinite past but that this light *was in the act of coming* into the world.

Here John directly identifies "the light" with the Logos and thus advances beyond v. 4, where he writes only that the life of the Logos was the light of men. "Logos" and "light" are, indeed, close equivalents, for both terms contain the idea of revelation made unto us and intended to be received by us. But here

John appends the adjective τὸ φῶς τὸ ἀληθινόν, and by using the second article he adds as much weight to the adjective as to the noun, R. 776. The adjective ἀληθινόν means real, genuine, the reality corresponding to the idea, *verus,* and is thus distinguished from ἀληθής, true, mind and word, word and deed agreeing with each other, *verax.*

The relative clause, "which lighteth every man," conveys more than an activity native to "the light"; it furnishes the evidence for this being "the genuine light." "Every man" only individualizes the comprehensive plural used in v. 4: the light "of men"; and on the other hand it corresponds with the final phrase: coming "into the world." This light is genuine because it is universal; every man, all men, the entire world of men, are wholly dependent on this one divine light. Hence also the verb φωτίζει is in the present tense, which corresponds with the tense of φαίνει in v. 5. As no restriction or limitation appears in the object "every man," so also none appears in the tense of this verb. When John writes, "which lighteth every man," he fears no misunderstanding on our part as though we might think that he means that every single human being is actually enlightened by the Logos, for both before and after making this statement he speaks of men rejecting this light and remaining in darkness. Luther has caught John's meaning, "There is only one light that lighteth all men, and no man comes into the world who can possibly be illumined by any other light." He also refers to Rom. 5:18: " 'As through one trespass the judgment came unto all men to condemnation, even so through one act of righteousness the free gift came unto all men unto justification of life.' Although all men are not justified through Christ, he is, nevertheless, the only man through whom justification comes." Augustine uses the illustration of one teacher in a city, who, then, is said to instruct all the city, meaning not that everyone actually goes to him to be instructed but that none are taught except by him.

Hebrew originals have been cited for regarding "coming into the world" in the sense of "being born" and thus as equivalent to "an inhabitant of the world." But the New Testament never uses the expression in this sense. As far as men are concerned, they never were outside of the world and thus cannot come into the world by means of birth. As far as Christ is concerned, he was already born when the evangelist writes that he "was coming into the world." This "coming" is the standard term for Christ's mission in the world, for his appearance in his office as our Savior and Redeemer. The term ἐρχόμενος is almost technical in this sense. Israel constantly expected the Coming One; and in v. 11 John writes, "He *came* unto his own," he appeared as the promised Messiah, manifesting himself as such by his word and his work, by his suffering, death, and resurrection. In v. 9, when the Baptist testified of him, he was on the point of thus coming and making himself manifest. While he came unto his own, namely unto Israel, his coming was, nevertheless, as the Savior of the entire world. Thus also ἐρχόμενον εἰς τὸν κόσμον means, "in the act of coming into the world." This, of course, involves the incarnation, yet John holds back the direct mention of this great act, saving it for emphatic mention in the final section of his prolog.

10) Verse 9 leaves us with the incarnate Logos about to enter upon his great mission when the Baptist testified of him. V. 10, 11 advance and speak of him as being fully manifest, with the tragic result that the world failed to recognize him, and that even his own refused to receive him. **He was in the world, and the world was made by him, and the world knew him not. He came to his homeland, and his home**

people received him not. The two verses are parallels. The first verse needs three clauses, for the second clause must point out why the world should have known Christ — he was its Creator. The second verse needs only two clauses, for the reason why the Jews should have received Christ is self-evident.

In v. 9 John says of the incarnate Logos that he was in the act of coming into the world. When he now proceeds and says, "In the world he *was*," the evangelist includes the entire presence of the incarnate Logos in the world. For ἦν, as distinct from the puncti-liar ἦλθε in v. 11, is durative; it spreads out the entire presence of Christ before our eyes. "The world," already in v. 9 and now three times in v. 10, means the world of men, for only for the world in this sense is The Coming One life, light, and salvation. We must not bring in the other creatures, nor dare we go back to the presence of the Logos before his incarnation. "The world" also includes the Jews, although the two are differentiated in v. 10 and 11 but only as a wider circle embraces one that is narrower.

"The world" should certainly have recognized the incarnate Logos when he appeared in its midst, for "the world was made by him," more literally, "came into existence through him," as v. 3 has already told us regarding the entire universe, πάντα and οὐδὲ ἕν. This, of course, includes also the Jews. Brute creatures might not recognize their incarnate Creator, but the world of intelligent men should certainly have recognized, worshipped, and adored him. And yet the tragic fact must be set down, "The world knew him not." The constative aorist οὐκ ἔγνω records the summary fact. We cannot see why R. 834 makes this aorist ingressive. The three clauses are simply placed side by side and are connected only with two καί, much like v. 1. Their relation to each other is left to the reader — each clause with its deep meaning being allowed to speak for itself. No effort is made to explain the tragic result. The fact is that no real explanation is possible; for the rejection of its Creator by the world is an unreasonable act, and no reasonable explanation can be offered for an act, the very essence of which is unreason. It is not an explanation to point out that "the world" means men dead and blind in sin; for the incarnate Logos bears the *gratia sufficiens* which is fully sufficient and able by means of the life and light of the Logos to overcome this death and blindness; yet when this *gratia* is applied, men not only reject it but are left far worse than before. Here lies the problem that remains unsolved.

11) When speaking of "the world" and considering the Logos its Creator, this is tragic enough. But within this greater tragic circle lies a lesser one in which the tragedy is much greater. "To his homeland came" the incarnate Logos, "and his home people received him not." Just as in v. 10 the phrase "in the world" is placed forward for emphasis, so in v. 11 the corresponding phrase "to his homeland." The neuter plural τὰ ἴδια and the masculine plural οἱ ἴδιοι form a play on words in which only the gender marks a difference. The words are strongly reflexive, R. 691, and denote what belongs to a person in distinction from other persons; what is his very own in distinction from what belongs to others. Thus the neuter plural often has the meaning of one's own home, and the masculine, in contrast with this neuter, one's own relatives. This established usage bars out the idea that these terms are only synonyms, parallels to "the world" in v. 10, and that v. 11 is only a synonymous duplicate of v. 10. Moreover, "the world" is never viewed as "the homeland" or "the home people" of Christ; quite the contrary, the term "world" always has a hostile connotation. Israel alone is "the homeland" and "the home people" of Christ. Not, however,

because he was born man in Palestine, for he was born here because this was his home. Israel was God's "peculiar people," Deut. 26:18; "a special people unto himself, above all people that are upon the face of the earth," Deut. 7:6; compare I Pet. 2:9. Thus Israel belonged to him who was before Abraham, who was God and was with God before Israel began; Israel's Temple was his Father's house, and the people of Israel his blood kin. During an era of more than a thousand years this chosen people had been under preparation for his coming and had been kept in expectation of that event. Therefore, too, John writes ἦλθεν, he "came" to his own, using the significant verb which is connected so completely with the covenant promises of the Messiah.

If anywhere in the world, the incarnate Logos, when he now revealed himself and thus came to his own homeland, should have been received by his home people. They should have embraced him with open arms and hearts, and the only danger should have been that they might jealously claim him as being exclusively their own, whom they would not share with any other nation. The very opposite occurred, "and his home people received him not." Here, as in v. 10, John writes αὐτόν, "him," although the antecedent of both pronouns is the neuter τὸ φῶς, "the light." These pronouns cannot be explained as presupposing the masculine antecedent ὁ λόγος, for this lies entirely too far back. The probable explanation is that with these pronouns John turns from the figure of the light to the reality of this figure, namely the person of Christ. That, too, is why John says in the second clause of v. 10 that the world was made δι' αὐτοῦ, "through him." All this is the strongest proof for the identity of the Logos, who also is called Life and Light, with the man Jesus Christ. Aside from its direct enunciation the incarnation can receive no more effective presentation.

Both expressions, the world "knew him not," and his own "received him not," two cases of litotes, negatives where positives are meant, are decidedly mild. "Not to know," in the pregnant sense here used, means to disown utterly, as in Matt. 7:23. The verb "know," which is here negatived, is *noscere cum affectu et effectu*, to know, recognize, and thus acknowledge and accept as one's own, John 10:14. What this form of disowning means is explained by Jesus himself in John 15:19-25, where he tells his disciples that the world will treat them as it treats him with hate and with persecution. The verb used for the treatment bestowed on Christ by "his own people" is of a different type though to the same effect: they "received him not," οὐ παρέλαβον. As compared with δέχεσθαι, which is often used regarding the welcome reception of a guest, John 4:45; Matt. 10:41, etc., παραλαμβάνειν, both with a personal and with an impersonal object, is used regarding a reception that includes full appropriation, a reception which intends permanent possession and communion. This, of course, is the reception Jesus sought when he came to his own, and this his own people denied him. They threw him out, turned him over to the Gentiles, had him made away with by a death of deepest disgrace. Note the strong contrast: he *came*, indeed, to his own; his own *did not receive* him. The verbs match, but the negative makes them clash. The aorist indicates the historical fact. The simplicity of expression is perfect, but it surely makes the tragedy thus expressed stand out only the more. "Hear, O heavens, and give ear, O earth: for the Lord hath spoken: I have nourished and brought up children, and they have rebelled against me. The ox knoweth his owner, and the ass his master's crib: but Israel doth not know, my people doth not consider. Ah, sinful nation, a people laden with iniquity, a seed of evildoers, children that are corrupters: they have forsaken the Lord, they have provoked the Holy One of Israel unto anger, they are gone away backward," Isa. 1:2-4. In vain did the Baptist call for repentance in order to prepare a true reception. When Jesus "came," they "received him not."

12)   When John writes of the world and of the Jews he allows them to take up the entire picture. It seems that he is not willing to make a coordination between these two on the one hand and the believers on the other hand. He paints the tragedy in one picture and then sets this away; then he takes another canvas and paints the salvation. **But as many as accepted him, to them he gave the right to become God's children, to those who believe in his name.** Here is the first instance of an adversative connection, namely the adversative δέ. The word ὅσοι, "as many as," "those who," does not indicate whether there were many or only a few. Far more important is the observation that ὅσοι denotes individuals, namely each and every believer omitting none. The word thus differs markedly from "the world" and from οἱ ἴδιοι, "his own people," both of which denote a body. The world as a body and the Jews as a nation rejected Christ, only individuals as individuals accepted him. But this means that "as many as" cannot be restricted to individual Jews. Since the rejection is attributed to two bodies, the lesser of which is included in the greater, the acceptance, now placed in contrast with that rejection, cannot be restricted only to individuals in the lesser body. "As many as" means both individual Jews and individual Gentiles. Moreover, while John plainly refers to the time when the Logos "came" and manifested himself, he sets no limit in the other

direction. "As many as," therefore, includes all those who accepted Jesus as the Logos since he came and manifested himself, all believers up to the time when John wrote these words and by inference all believers also after he wrote.

Still more lies in ὅσοι. First of all, that accepting Christ is an individual and not a corporate matter. Does it sound lamentable, that only single persons as individuals accept the Savior instead of an entire nation or the wide world as a whole? In reality this individual acceptance denotes universalism, "that *whosoever* believeth on him should not perish but have eternal life," — whosoever, Jew or Gentile, no matter of what nation or social and educational standing. Thus "as many as" opens the door to all men in the world. Moreover, this type of universalism comports with the very nature of true acceptance. Too often corporate acceptance is only formal. In a large body many do not assent, many others only assent, and so genuine acceptance is, after all, heavily restricted in the case of corporate acceptance. As far as the Logos is concerned, nothing whatever is lost by "as many as." We may call these the exceptions as compared with the rule indicated in v. 11. But this expresses only a superficial view. Exceptions are abnormal; they ought really not to occur. In the case of the Logos all the Jews and all the world ought to believe on him. By rejecting him these act abnormally and thus in spite of their number constitute the exception, while "as many as" act normally and thus accord with the rule.

In substance the three verbs "to know" (ἔγνω), "to receive" (παρέλαβον), and "to accept or take" (ἔλαβον) the Logos necessarily must amount to the same thing, namely to embrace by faith. It is quite evident that the simple λαμβάνειν cannot include less than the compound παραλαμβάνειν, for less was not rendered by those

who became God's children than was expected of the
Jews. The idea that the compound verb means "to
receive officially" as a King and thus solemnly to
conduct into the Temple, reads too much into the verb
as contrasted with the simple verb. Nor does ἔλαβον
need a complement in the shape of a participle to
complete its meaning, for it is sufficient to say they
"accepted," they "took" Christ, i. e., "took" him as
what he was and as what he offered himself. The
only difference between the compound and the simple
forms of the verb is that in the former the preposition expresses the purpose of full appropriation while
the latter takes this for granted. "As many as
accepted him" is placed forward as the antecedent of
αὐτοῖς, "to them," making this clause stand out in full
contrast to "the world" and "his own people" (the
Jews as a nation) more than would be the case if a
relative clause had been used, "To them, who accepted
him, he gave," etc.

All those who rejected the Logos received nothing;
they remained what they were, destitute, blind, and
spiritually dead, a condition that was the more tragic
since it might have been changed into the blessed
opposite. But to those who accepted the Logos "he
gave the right to become God's children." This is
what the others missed and lost wholly through their
own fault. John does not write: τέκνα Θεοῦ ἐγένοντο or
γεγόνασιν, "they became, or they have become, God's
children." This would be perfectly true. The objection does not hold that John would thereby say that
these persons became God's children by their own
ability. As little as ἐγένετο in v. 3 has a trace of
synergism, so little would ἐγένοντο have such a trace
of it in the present connection. And yet John writes,
"he gave to them the right," etc., placing ἔδωκεν forward for emphasis. Every time when life, pardon,
or salvation are involved, the verb "give" brings out

strongly the note of unmerited grace. The implied note of contrast is not that of synergism, as though any man might become a child of God by effort of his own or by on his part adding something toward this end. The contrast is far more obvious: the Jews, Christ's own home people, imagined they were and could be God's children without the Logos or Christ. Jesus himself had an argument with them on this very subject, John 8:42-47. They had no use for Christ because they dreamed that they could be God's children without him. That thought is what John cuts off so early in his Gospel by the wording: the Logos "gave" this right of childhood to those who received him. The two aorists ἔλαβον and ἔδωκεν occur simultaneously. The instant of accepting Christ is the instant of receiving the gift of childhood. To receive Christ is to receive life, light, and salvation.

The gift is here called "right to become God's children." Yet the infinitive γενέσθαι is an aorist and thus punctiliar and hence cannot mean that at some later time these persons would develop into God's children. This aorist infinitive expresses action that is simultaneous with that of the two preceding finite aorists ἔλαβον and ἔδωκεν — in other words, the moment of accepting Christ, which is the moment of receiving his gift, that, too, is the moment of becoming God's children, i. e., the moment of regeneration. This is called "the right," ἐξουσία (without the article, thus stressing the quality of the noun), which here means more than "possibility" and not quite as much as "power." The infinitive, "right to become," is construed as a dative, R. 1076, and is the complement of the noun. Christ's gift to those who receive him is a new relation to God, they are made God's children. Their "right" is to be such children. For this relation to God John always employs τέκνα Θεοῦ and never υἱοὶ Θεοῦ, for he always views it as the product of regeneration (τέκνα from τίκτειν). The difference between "child" and "son" is quite marked. A son may become such by adoption, so that the word for "adoption" is υἱοθεσία, i. e., placing one in the position of a son. Christ, too, is never called "the Child of God," which would leave a wrong impression, but always "the Son of God." Cremer, *Bibl.-theol. Woerterbuch der Neutestamentlichen Graezitaet,* 10th ed. by Julius Koegel, 1073 (future references indicated by C.-K.) specifies the difference: τέκνον as expressing relation or derivation *from*; υἱός as expressing relation *to*. A study of the words reveals various types of interesting usage. "Children," for instance, has the note of endearment, while "sons" often has the note of legal standing: if a son, then an heir, Gal. 4:7. Thus "son" and "slave" are in contrast, and "child" and "slave" are not placed in opposition. As regards our relation to God, the Scriptures have no sweeter name than this that we are "God's children" and belong to his household, Eph. 2:19.

The dative τοῖς πιστεύουσιν εἰς τὸ ὄνομα αὐτοῦ is an apposition to αὐτοῖς. This, however, is not intended to point out the condition for receiving the right of childhood. The fact that receiving Christ means receiving him by faith is clear from v. 7. If, nevertheless, this thought is to be repeated, the participle would have to be an aorist and without the article. For the moment one comes to faith he becomes a child of God. The articulated present participle is like a clause, descriptive of those to whom the right of childhood has been given. Its force is well rendered by Zahn, "and these are they who believe on his name," i. e., who as God's children continue thus believing. Whenever ὄνομα, "name," is used in connections like this, "name" always means the complete self-revelation of Christ in his redemptive grace. At times one or the other feature of that revelation is indicated by the context. Whether we read: "believe in him" (Christ), or: "believe in his name," makes no difference, for we know "him" only by means of his "name," i. e., his saving self-revelation. As far as the names of Christ are concerned, the special terms by which we designate his person, these are only concentrated and thus especially valuable portions of his self-revelation. Their value consists only in their rich content which reveals to us Christ's person and his work. Thus "they that believe in his name" are they whose heart's trust and confidence extends (εἰς) to the blessed revelation they have received from him. Various prepositions are used with πιστεύειν; when εἰς is employed, this points out the direction or the relation of the confidence. The idea that "to believe on the name" indicates that a certain "name" of Christ is confessed by the believer, rests on a misunderstanding. While true faith always confesses, the phrase "on the name" in no way refers to this fact.

13) Does verse thirteen speak of "God's children" and describe their spiritual birth, or does this verse speak of the human birth of the Logos, his birth from the Virgin Mary? The question is one of the text and also one of the thought. Usually the question is not raised at all, because the accepted reading of the text seems to raise no question. The incongruities, not to say impossibilities, that result are taken as a matter of course and are smoothed out in the best way possible. The best feature about the usual reading is that it does not clash with the analogy of faith, and thus in preaching on this verse no doctrinal difficulty is encountered. **Which were born, not of blood, nor of the will of the flesh, nor of the will of man, but of God,** is treated as a relative clause attached to v. 12, describing the birth of God's children as not being due to natural generation but to a generation that has its source in God, ἐκ Θεοῦ.

The accepted reading makes v. 13 the conclusion of the second paragraph of the prolog and v. 14 the beginning of the final paragraph. Whether the division for the paragraphs is made in this way or not (some divide differently), one thing is certain: καί at the head of v. 14, once we give it adequate thought, is wholly without justification. John has used this connective nine times in the preceding account, always in order to connect facts closely related to each other. Even when these facts were opposites they could be properly combined as such. Every time a new group of facts was introduced John did this without a connective, thus indicating that he was passing on to something new. Yet here in v. 14 all this would be upset. An entirely new paragraph would begin with καί. Or, to say the least, two facts wholly unrelated, strangely diverse as to time, would be linked together with "and," namely the incarnation of the Logos (v. 14) and the spiritual birth of God's children (v. 13). The latter refers to the mass of believers living at the time John wrote, the former to the time when the Logos became flesh. The two are so diverse, even as to time, that no writer, least of all John, would connect the two with "and." Regeneration and the incarnation are not even opposites, nor does John intimate any other relation between the two. This "and" should thus cause us to pause.

The second point that should make us pause and question is that with three different statements and thus with exceeding emphasis John should deny that the spiritual regeneration of God's children is not a physical operation. Evidently, this heavy denial indicates that a wrong view is being contradicted and a right view put in its place. But who in all the church supposed that regeneration was a physical act? Even Nicodemus, whose ignorance regarding regeneration Jesus rebuked, was entirely sure that a man could not be reborn by again entering the womb of a human mother, by a birth that would be physical. And then, strange to say, after this denial of regeneration as a physical birth John would add with "and" that the Logos was born physically in a miraculous manner! How can such things be?

In the third place, assuming that John felt v. 12 to be incomplete (though it is certainly complete as it stands), he could have added what he might have desired in the simplest fashion. Here is one way, "But as many as accepted him, to them he gave the right to become God's children, *and they were born of God*," etc. Again, extending the participial apposition at the end of v. 12, "to them who are believers on his name *and have been born of God*" (the perfect participle in the Greek). Or, if an inner causal relation should be John's intention, revealing that regeneration produces the τέκνα Θεοῦ, all would be clear if a relative clause with οἵτινες would have been added, "to them who are believers on his name, *such as have been born of God*." Yet in no case could the three negative phrases, denying that regeneration is a physical act, be inserted in an addition to v. 12, for this strong denial would necessarily imply that this preposterous notion had advocates among the Christians of John's time.

If we had only the accepted text, we should be left solely to conjecture, and this at best is like a guess in the dark. It is usually useless even to consider conjectures. The older reading, which removes all the difficulties indicated and others that might yet be added, has long been known. This original reading has no relative pronoun (either plural or singular) at the head of v. 13, and the final verb is singular: οὐκ ἐξ αἱμάτων . . . ἐγεννήθη. V. 13 speaks not of believers but of the Logos and of his human birth. V. 13 begins the new paragraph, the climax of the prolog.

John describes the incarnation not merely in one brief statement, "The Word was made flesh," but in two statements, the first of which is decidedly longer than the second, and thus the most natural thing in the world is for John to link the two with καί. We translate: **Not of blood, nor of the will of flesh, nor of the will of a man, but of God was he born. And the Word became flesh, etc.** The credit for first drawing attention to this reading belongs to Fr. Blass, whom Theodor Zahn followed in his various most valuable publications. We cannot enter into all the details of the ancient documentary evidence, which really belongs into works on textual criticism. We content ourselves with the following summary as being sufficient for our purpose.

The original reading appears in Tertullian, Irenaeus, and others. The gnostic Valentinians, about the year 140, changed the original singular ἐγεννήθη (without ὅ) into the plural ἐγεννήθησαν (without οἵ) in the interest of their peculiar doctrine They desired to use this passage as a description of the peculiar class of spiritual people provided for in their heretical system. In this way the verb in v. 13 became plural. The Occidentals held to the singular until the third, or possibly the fourth, century. The Alexandrians were more ready to adopt the plural and had done so by the end of the second century, but as yet without the relative οἵ. This came to be inserted in order to connect v. 13 with the believers mentioned in v. 12 and thus to shut out the Valentinian use of v. 13. This relative pronoun then found acceptance also in the Occident. For the Latins the matter of the pronoun was easier as the Latin *qui* could be used for ὅς as well as for οἵ; it was far more difficult for the Syrians, whose text had the singular verb and yet added the plural pronoun as its subject. The entire question of determining the original reading of v. 13 thus is

entirely different from the usual method of comparing
the readings of the codices in order to accept that
reading only which the best and the weightiest codices
support. This may explain why the common reading
has not been challenged more resolutely by critical commentators and text critics.

The subject of v. 13 is the Logos, who constitutes
the beginning, middle, and end of the entire prolog
and thus needs no formal mention as John proceeds
to describe his human birth. This birth was οὐκ ἐξ
αἱμάτων, "not due to bloods," i. e., the mixture of blood
from two human parents as in cases of ordinary
human procreation. "Blood" is the material substance
from which the human organism is formed. The
plural "bloods" is the more necessary in the Greek,
since the singular might be misunderstand. For the
human organism of the Logos actually began with a
bit of blood in the womb of the Virgin Mary; it was
thus that she "conceived in the womb," Luke 1:31.
The explanation of the plural from the analogy of
other Greek expressions must be dropped. Blood that
is shed in drops or in streams, animals that are sacrificed, wounds and the slain in battle, murderous acts
and the like, justify the use of the plural in the Greek
but are no analogy for the generation of a human
being. Where a real analogy occurs, as in the reading
of some texts in Acts 17:26, the singular is used in
the Greek, "hath made of one blood." When the Logos
became man, this was not due to, did not start with
(ἐκ), the blood from two parents.

From the act of procreation in which the blood of
man and woman join so that the blood of both flows
in the child's veins, John advances to the impulse of
nature which lies back of this sexual union, "nor of
the will of the flesh." The term "flesh" denotes our
bodily nature as God made it, male and female, adding
the blessing, "Be fruitful and multiply, and replenish

the earth." "The will of the flesh" is thus the natural urge and volition implanted in our bodily nature to beget and to rear offspring. Like "bloods" this "will of the flesh" includes both man and woman. It is true that our blood as well as our flesh and the will of our flesh are now corrupt because of sin and death, yet this corruption is not stressed. The human birth of the Logos is not due to our nature either as it now is or as it once was. The will to beget children, implanted in man by God, had nothing to do with the incarnation. A far higher, an entirely different will, brought that about.

Yet the decisive will in the act of procreation is that of the man not that of the woman, hence John adds, "nor of the will of man," using ἀνήρ in distinction from γυνή and thus not to be identified with ἄνθρωπος, the generic term for man as a human being including both male and female. The three phrases used by John in stating how the birth of the Logos as man was not brought about are not coordinate, merely placed side by side; nor should we subordinate the second two phrases and regard them as merely defining more closely the first phrase. These phrases are like a pyramid, one placed on top of the other. They are like three circles, the second being narrower than the first, the third narrower than the second. Thus the first phrase includes the other two, and the second includes the third. Beyond the final, most precise specification John cannot go and need not go in his negations. The Logos was born entirely without a human father. In his conception no male parent was active. The detailed history of this conception and birth John's readers know from the records of Matthew and of Luke, which John also takes for granted. Neither v. 13 nor v. 14 can be properly understood without the other two Gospels. What John here does is to restate with exact precision the vital facts contained in the full historical records of the other Gospels.

Even those who have been content with the reading of the current text, which makes v. 13 a description of our own spiritual birth, have felt that John here has in mind the other Gospel records which recount the miraculous conception and birth of Jesus. They assume that John here uses the manner of Jesus' conception and birth as a kind of type illustrating our spiritual birth as also being miraculous in a somewhat analogous manner. In a way they thus sensed what the true reading of v. 13 contains. Yet John's words offer not the least indication that he is speaking typically, comparing our spiritual birth to the physical birth of Jesus. In fact, the very idea of such a type and comparison is highly questionable. The miracle of the incarnation is too lofty to be used for the regeneration of the multitude of God's children. The type is always less than the antitype and necessarily must be, otherwise the antitype would be the type, and the type the antitype. When soberly examined, this threefold denial of a generation by blood, by the will of the flesh, and by the will of a man, sounds trivial when applied to our regeneration, regarding which it is self-evident that this is altogether only spiritual; while, when this denial is applied to the incarnation, it constitutes a most vital confession — one necessary for all ages of the church and most necessary for our own day.

The preposition ἐκ denotes source or origin, and John uses it three times in his denials as to how the birth of the Logos was not effected, and then once more with the positive phrase which states how this birth was, indeed, effected, "on the contrary, of God was he born." The incarnation of the Logos, we may thus say, was due exclusively to God. It arose from God alone as the source. John adds no other term such as "of the will of God," for this might lead to the thought that God only willed the incarnation and then used some means or other for carrying his volition into effect. All such intermediate means are excluded by the three negative phrases, which leave as their one opposite only "God." In other words, the incarnation was effected without means by the direct agency of God alone.

The verb γεννᾶν means "to beget" when used with reference to the father; also "to give birth," "bring forth" when used with reference to the mother or to both parents. The fact that John is writing of the incarnation and not of the eternal generation of the Logos is made entirely certain by the preceding negative phrases, which modify the verb, just as the final positive phrase does. The tense of ἐγεννήθη is the historical aorist, and the passive accords with ἐκ Θεοῦ, not, indeed, as the usual agent with the passive, which would be ὑπό or ἀπό, but deeper than this, as the source or origin. We might translate, "was begotten," though in doing so we would have to ward off the thought that God was in some way a substitute for the human father in the begetting of the Logos. It is better to translate, "was born," using the verb in the wider sense as including all that lies in the term "incarnation." Perhaps we may derive a little help from the figurative use of the verb. The idea of sex and of the function of sex disappears entirely when God is called the Father of his people, or when one human person becomes a spiritual father to another. Fatherhood and motherhood intermingle in this form of thought. So the Logos "was born" of man by a birth due to the miraculous intervention of God wholly apart from any paternal sex function.

14) With the closing words of v. 13, "of God was he born," the connective "and" accords perfectly: **And the Word became flesh and tented among us,**

and we beheld his glory as of the Only-begotten from the Father, full of grace and truth. What lies in ἐγεννήθη is brought out by σὰρξ ἐγένετο; by his "birth" the Logos "became flesh." While this may well be called the climax of the entire prolog, the fact should not be overlooked that what is now recorded as the climax already lies in all that John writes from v. 4 onward. The Logos could not have been the life and the light of men from the beginning if in the fulness of time he had not been "born of God" and "become flesh."

Now that the climacteric statement is made, the subject is once more named: ὁ λόγος; but this name is now illumined by all that John has said of him thus far, and, in turn, what he now writes lights up and makes clearer all that he has said of him thus far. We understand the way to the goal the better after having reached the goal. And this, indeed, is the goal, for it transcends the previous statements about the shining of the light and the coming into the world (speaking of it only as a coming). Here is the INCARNATION in so many words: the Word, who *was* in the beginning, the life and the true light from eternity, this Word *"became flesh."* The aorist states the historical fact. In an interesting comparison of several aorists in the prolog R. 829 calls this aorist ingressive, because it "accents the entrance of the Logos upon his life on earth." We should rather say that this aorist marks the momentary act which made the Logos flesh, to remain flesh in the sense of man forever after. From the start the thought must be rejected that ἐγένετο here means a transformation of the Logos into flesh. The Word did not cease to be what it was before; but it became what it was not before — *flesh.* "Without controversy great is the mystery of godliness: God was manifested in the flesh," I Tim. 3:16. The identity of the subject re-

mains. *The Word* became flesh and remains in every
sense *the Word* though now made flesh. This Word,
being God, could not possibly change into something
else, for then God would cease to be God.

The mystery of how the Logos, the Creator, (v. 3)
could assume our created nature will forever challenge our finite comprehension. The tremendous fact
itself is beyond question, and for us that is enough.
Thus we have only one care, that when we ourselves
restate what John records we may in no way deviate
from the fact. It will not do, for instance, to compare
ἐγένετο as here used with γεγενημένον in 2:9, "the water
that has become wine." Of the two, the water and
the wine, the water had ceased to be; but the Word
did not cease to be — he was not turned into flesh. We
need a caution here in regard to all the uses of γίνομαι
in ordinary speech, for in all the universe no analogy
occurs for the incarnation. Hence we can find no
analogous uses of the verb. Such uses as those in
2:9; Matt. 4:3; Rom. 2:25; I Cor. 3:18; John 9:39;
16:30, are of a totally different type. The uses in
John 5:6; 5:9; 5:14; 8:33; 12:36; I Cor. 13:11; Luke
23:12, also cannot be compared with our passage. The
incarnation is absolutely unique — nothing even faint-
ly like it has ever been known. The only being with
two natures is the Son of God.

Thus we decline to say "that the divine subject
entered into the human mode of being at the cost of
renouncing his divine mode of being"; or that "he exchanged the divine state for the human"; or that "the
purely spiritual existence, independent of bodily material, . . . was exchanged for the existence of a
bodily living man." For one thing, such expressions
confuse the incarnation with the humiliation, whereas
these two are entirely distinct, and John's ἐγένετο predicates only the former. In heaven the Logos still
has his flesh but at the cost of nothing, nor by any

exchange, nor with any dependence. Stressing the "bodily material" and "a bodily living man" as decisive for the incarnation is especially unfortunate. R. 394 calls ἐγένετο in our passage a copula, which is far nearer the truth, for all that this verb does is to *predicate* what the term "flesh" contains in the moment of the Incarnation of the Logos. Note the careful way in which the church has worded this miracle of the ages in the Nicene Creed: "who for us men, and for our salvation, came down from heaven, and was incarnate by the Holy Ghost of the Virgin Mary, and was made man." Likewise the Creed of Athanasius against the Arians: "God of the Substance of the Father, begotten before the worlds; and Man of the substance of his mother, born in the world; Perfect God and perfect Man, of a reasonable soul and human flesh subsisting. Equal to the Father as touching his Godhead, and inferior to the Father as touching his manhood; Who, although he be God and Man, yet he is not two, but one Christ; One, not by conversion of the Godhead into flesh, but by taking of the manhood into God; One altogether; not by confusion of Substance, but by unity of Person. For as the reasonable soul and flesh is one man, so God and Man is one Christ." *Concordia Triglotta*, 32 and 35. For precision and exactness these confessional statements have never been excelled.

"By *flesh* we understand the whole man, body and soul, according to the Scriptures which call man flesh." Luther, who adds, "This lofty humility, which no tongue is able to express, the evangelist wanted to indicate by the little word *flesh.*" Christ's flesh was real flesh, born of the Virgin Mary, not a mere appearance of flesh (Docetism). But while the Word became flesh, he did not become sinful flesh; for the word flesh itself, as describing our nature, does not include sin. When we are raised from the dead, no sin will be found in our flesh. Sometimes "flesh" is identified with "body," whereas "flesh" = body, soul, and spirit. Mary gave birth to a living son, whose soul afterward became sorrowful unto death, who groaned in the spirit and in death gave up the spirit (παρέδωκε τὸ πνεῦμα, John 19:30; ἐξέπνευσεν, Luke 23:46), commending his spirit into his Father's hands. The manhood of Christ was thus perfect in every respect.

On the one hand, nothing dare be subtracted from "flesh," the human nature, the perfect humanity; on the other hand, nothing dare be subtracted from the Word, the divine nature, the perfect divinity. These two, each being perfect, combine in the one Person. This person is the eternal, uncreated Logos (v. 1, 2), who in his divine nature was with God in eternity and was God. This person assumed "flesh," a human spirit, soul, and body; he did not join himself to some human being. The ego in the God-man is the ego of the Logos. This divine ego took the place occupied in all other men by a human ego. Hence the incarnate Son is able to declare that he and the Father are one. The human nature of the Logos is thus ἀνυπόστατος, without a human ego, and yet ἐνυπόστατος by possessing the divine ego, hence not imperfect but the more perfect. Whoever met Christ met God's Son not the person of some man. In him were not two egos, nor was there in him a double or a composite ego. The path between Nestorianism and Eutychianism is narrow but perfectly straight if only we follow John and stop rationalizing and speculating, which always end by losing either the Logos or the flesh. The marvel remains that this great mystery should be expressed by the evangelist in such few and simple words, a mystery on which the greatest minds have spent their most intense efforts. Here Inspiration again becomes so tangible that one wonders why all eyes do not recognize its presence. No uninspired pen could ever have set down the words, "And the Word became flesh."

The first effect of the incarnation is added by a simple "and" in John's fashion, "and tented among us," ἐσκήνωσεν. This recalls the Tabernacle of Israel in which God tented and dwelt among his people. The pillar of cloud and of fire filled and covered the Tabernacle, making visible the glorious presence of God, Exod. 40:34-38. Compare the final dwelling of God with his people in Rev. 21:3. This is the imagery back of John's figurative verb "he tented among us." The flesh of the Logos is the true Temple of God (2:21), the tent in which he dwelt; the Logos fills this flesh with his presence even as the Tabernacle was filled with the Shekinah of Jehovah. Yet the verb "tented," as well as its historical aorist tense, indicate a temporary sojourn. The Logos remained ἐν ἡμῖν only until his redemptive work was finished, then not to discard the tent of his flesh but to transfer his human nature into the Holy of Holies above by the miracle of his glorification and ascension. John writes "among us" without further specification since his readers know whom he means. Comparing v. 16 "we all" and I John 1:1, etc., this pronoun "we" signifies only the chosen ones who were called to be Christ's special witnesses in the time to come. Some wish to extend this pronoun to include all those who beheld Christ with the eyes of faith while he walked on earth. The fact of their so beholding him is true enough and may pass as such. But John is writing to a different generation which he addresses as ὑμεῖς, "you" in 19:35, whom also he places in clear contrast with "we" and "our" in the opening of his First Epistle. These notable persons who "declare" what they have seen, heard, and handled are Christ's chosen witnesses only. We should, however, not fail to note that this important "we" includes the Apostle John himself who thus also attests himself as the writer of this Gospel.

The second effect of the incarnation is added with another "and," "and we beheld his glory," but "we" is now in the inflectional ending of the verb. Here again the historical aorist, like the one preceding, reports what once took place and could never be repeated. R. 834 makes this aorist "effective" as marking the end of an action, as stating that finally this vision of Christ's glory was achieved. We decidedly prefer to regard this as a "constative" aorist, one which summarizes an entire course of action. For John himself reports that all along the Apostles beheld and were attracted by the glory of the God-man, beginning notably with the first miracle, 2:11, where also τὴν δόξαν αὐτοῦ recurs.

John refers to "the glory" of the Logos. This term δόξα is constantly used either to designate all the attributes of the Godhead as they shine forth in one or in another way before the eyes of men, or to indicate the manifestation of any one or of several of these attributes. Thus "his glory" may designate the radiance of the infinite love that dwelt in Christ, breaking forth again and again in word and in deed; the heavenliness of his grace, or his mercy, or his compassion; the divine depth and comprehension of his wisdom and knowledge, against which also all human cunning failed; the absoluteness of his power in all the miracles that spoke so plainly of his divinity. Any one or more of these manifestations constitute "the glory" which John and the other witnesses beheld. The verb itself, θεάομαι, is weighty and much more expressive than ὁράω, "to see." The eye and the mind rest upon the object, penetrate and absorb it; and since the verb fits only great and notable objects, it generally has the connotation of wonder and admiration. Thus John writes, "We beheld, we actually viewed, his glory." It is quite

in vain to make "we beheld" mean only a beholding
with the eyes of the mind, an inner experience of the
soul. For that might be experienced by one who was
not an eyewitness.

John repeats δόξαν, investing it with emphasis, as
if he would say, "glory indeed," "glory most wonderful." And now he describes this glory, "as of the
Only-begotten from the Father." The rendering in
the margin of the R. V. is highly unfortunate, "as
of an only-begotten from a father." These translators
certainly knew that the absence of the article with
nouns like μονογενής and πατήρ does not render them
indefinite: *an* only-begotten — *a* father. Nouns designating persons or objects only one of which exists
need no article; the English idiom requires the article.
We simply must translate: *the* Only-begotten — *the*
Father. Moreover, in the Greek anarthrous nouns
are qualitative, R. 794; by omitting the article we
are asked to fix our attention on just what the noun
conveys. The sense of the margin of the R. V. is
equally unfortunate. It assumes that every only-
begotten son has a special glory and then informs us
that God's Only-begotten Son also has such a glory.
But how about the only son of a slave, or of a beggar, or of a criminal? Even if the father is a notable
person and the only son a credit to his father, who
would call the fact that he has no brothers "his glory"?
And if such a predication should be made, who would
ever think of using this human feature as illustrating
the glory of God's only Son?

The term μονογενής = "Only-begotten," the Greek
adjective here being used as a noun. We fail to see
how the connection makes it self-evident that we supply
υἱός, for "Son" has not occurred in the previous verses.
Nor are we ready to reduce this weighty term to mean
no more than "only child" as when it is used with
reference to human parents who either have had but

one child or have only one left after the rest have
died. The term rises above all such conceptions when
we note the combination, *"glory* as of the Only-begotten." This "as" is not the common "like" of ordinary
comparisons between two — for who would be the
other? This "as" matches the reality with the idea
and thus proves and establishes. What John saw of
the glory of the Only-begotten corresponded with all
that he could possibly conceive as belonging to this
being. He also had the Old Testament to lift his
expectations exceedingly high. The glory he actually
beheld never fell short of the rightful expectation
thus formed, in fact, exceeded it in every way. We
may add that μονογενής is also far more than ἀγαπητός,
"beloved," which the LXX used as a translation for
jachid (single one, only one) in Gen. 22:2; Jer. 6:26;
etc. To be sure, the Only-begotten was the Beloved
of the Father, but the effort to make these two terms
either identical or synonymous when they are predicated of the Logos is misdirected. The one denotes
being as such, the other, ethical relation and attitude.

John alone uses μονογενής, which he coined like ὁ
λόγος, to express what in many statements Jesus said
of his relation to the Father. All but a few of the
interpreters of the last generation have taken "Only-
begotten" in the metaphysical sense and have understood it as referring to the relation of the Logos to
the Father apart from the incarnation. In other
words, μονογενής and ὁ λόγος extend back into all eternity
and belong to the Son ἄσαρκος (unincarnate) as well
as to the Son ἔνσαρκος (incarnate). The very nature
of the title "Only-begotten" involves the relation of
"Father" and of "Son," which is usually called the
aeterna filii Dei generatio. No attempt is made to
penetrate the mystery of this relation, i. e., to unveil
what lies in this *generatio.* But this, indeed, is held

as surely being revealed to us, that the First Person of the Godhead is the Father, that the Second Person is the Son, and that their relation is that the one begot and the other is begotten. Some, meaning well enough, have called this a "process," but no word of Scripture can be found to this effect. To speak of an inner-trinitarian process is either useless or tends to mislead. When accepting the revelation granted us, we must remember that these divine realities are couched in imperfect human terms, which only dimly reveal the ineffable realities. Therefore we will halt all speculation. With the church through the past centuries we will expend our efforts in guarding the revelation which we have against all the perversions that constantly enter men's minds. This, too, will aid us: God would never have revealed to us what he did concerning the Holy Trinity and the inner relation of the three Persons, because all this leaves our powers of comprehension so far behind, but for the necessity involved in his plan of salvation, the Father sending the Son, the Son executing his redemptive mission, and the Holy Spirit appropriating this redemption to us.

During the last generation efforts were made to interpret "Only-begotten" with reference to the exceptional human begetting and birth of Christ. "The Only-begotten" is said to be such only because of the peculiar relation of Christ's humanity or flesh to the Father. Others are "Children of God" by grace, by adoption, by a transfer from sin to pardon; Jesus is the Son by nature, by his very conception in the Virgin's womb, and in this sense "Only-begotten." And John first speaks of the incarnation, "The Word became flesh," and then in close connection with this statement uses what this new teaching calls the correlate concepts "Only-begotten" and "Father," whereas, in v. 1-12 nothing is said about a generation or begetting of the pre-existent Logos. But this structure cannot stand. If the terms "Father" and "Son" are due to the conception that took place in the Virgin's womb, then we have a "Father" who begot something that was only human, for in the Virgin's womb only Christ's human nature was begotten. Then we should have a "Son" who is a son only in his human nature, i. e., only a human son. Moreover, the church has never confessed, "who was conceived *by the Father,* born of the Virgin Mary"; but, "who was conceived *by the Holy Ghost,*" etc. To base the Fatherhood and the Sonship on the human birth from the Virgin's womb contradicts John's statement, "The Word became flesh," the Word that in eternity was with God and that himself was God. If the Sonship is human, and only human, "flesh," as John writes, then "the glory" which he so emphasizes likewise becomes only human and thus fades away. We dare not overlook the fact that the mighty terms Logos, Life, Light, which run through v. 1-14, are in the same class with the terms that fill v. 14, Logos, Glory, Only-begotten, Father, Grace and Truth, all of which reach back to eternity, and all of them are so interlocked that not one can be singled out and dated from some point in time. When the Logos became flesh, and John with the others came to see his glory, this was the glory of the Logos — "the flesh" had no glory, save such as it received from the Logos whose organ it became. The objection that John beheld only the glory of the Logos ἔνσαρκος not that of the Logos ἄσαρκος is specious. To be sure, John did not see the unincarnate Logos. Yet we know nothing about two different glories of the Logos, his glory is only one. John and the others beheld the *divine* glory of the Son as it shone forth in his *divine* attributes manifested through the veil of his human flesh and that flesh during the time that it was in the state of humiliation. In due time, in the day of exaltation, the absolute fulness of this one glory would illumine also the flesh of the Logos in heaven above.

The phrase παρὰ πατρός, "from the Father," literally, "from beside," cannot be construed with μονογενής because of the verbal idea contained in the term, since the Greek would use the genitive for this construction or the preposition ἐκ, never παρά. Some combine "Only-begotten from the Father" by inserting an idea to match the preposition, "the Only-begotten *coming* from beside the Father." Aside from the fact that prepositions contain no motion, this would be a superfluous idea, since the Only-begotten could come from no one else, and we have already been assured in v. 1, 2, that he was with God. The phrase "from the Father" is coordinate with "as of the Only-begotten," both equally modifying "glory." What these witnesses beheld was "glory from the Father," a glory so great, so truly divine, resulting from the eternal relation of the Logos to the Father and thus shining forth in the Incarnate Son. This was the *kabod Yaweh* revealed in the Old Testament in a variety of ways, because of which also the Son is called "the effulgence of his glory, and the very image (impress) of his substance," Heb. 1:3.

The addition "full of grace and truth" has caused some discussion because the apparent nominative πλήρης seemed to depend on ὁ λόγος, thus forcing us to assume the parenthesis indicated in the R. V., or compelling us to accept a violation of grammar by making this supposed nominative depend either on the accusative δόξαν or on the genitive αὐτοῦ. The entire difficulty is brushed away since the new grammars have demonstrated that πλήρης is indeclinable. R. 1204 remarks: "The papyri have taught us to be chary about charging John with being ungrammatical in πλήρης χάριτος (John 1:14). These matters simply show that the

New Testament writers used a live language and
were not automata." He adds: "It is doubtless true
that no other writer used repetition of word and
phrase as did the author of the Fourth Gospel, but no
one will deny that he did it with consummate skill and
marvelous vividness and dramatic power." We are
thus perfectly free to regard πλήρης as a genitive modifying αὐτοῦ, or as an accusative modifying δόξαν. The
former seems preferable as connecting this fulness of
grace and truth directly with the person. Thus also
"grace and truth" specify the attributes particularly
meant by "glory."

When John writes "full" he means that all that
was in him and shone forth from him was grace and
truth. Once God proclaimed himself to Moses, "The
Lord, the Lord God, merciful and gracious, longsuf-
fering, and abundant in goodness and truth," Exod.
34:6. Now that the Son appeared in the flesh, the
same fulness shone forth in him. There was no half
measure, no fraction, but perfect completeness in every
thought, word, and action. While grace and truth are
especially named, this does not mean that other attributes of the Logos are excluded. These two, however,
are central for our salvation. Like a stream they flow
out to us poor sinners so that we may have, possess,
and enjoy what they bring. "Grace" is undeserved
favor. The term connotes sin and guilt on our part
which this grace removes by pardon, justification, and
adoption to childhood. The heart of this grace is the
redemption in Christ Jesus. Grace bestows a free and
unmerited gift, first the central gift of pardon, v. 12,
and then all the abundance of gifts that follow pardon.
Some identify grace with these gifts, but it is better
to think of it as the attribute whence these gifts
flow. "Truth" is linked with "grace," since the two
are intertwined: grace in truth, and truth in grace.
Truth is the saving light which John has mentioned

repeatedly. The word ἀλήθεια means "reality," the reality itself as well as any statement of it in words. While the term is general, it is constantly used, as here joined with grace, to denote the saving realities in God and Christ Jesus. Thus the incarnate Logos is the full embodiment of saving truth, and his name thus is both Truth and Light. Again truth is the reality of God's will, his purpose and plan for our salvation, and every act of his in accord therewith. The threats and judgments of God and of Christ are also truth, and yet the term is most frequently used with reference to saving promises, every one of which is fulfilled to the uttermost. Both grace and truth intend to kindle, maintain, and increase faith and trust in our hearts. They shine forth, "that believing ye might have life through his name," 20:31. It is ungratefulness itself to be met with the fulness of grace and truth and to reply with unbelief.

15) For the great facts attested in v. 14, in corroboration of what John and his associates beheld in Christ, the testimony of the Baptist is now adduced in brief. For this reason John introduced the Baptist to his readers already in v. 6, 7, as one divinely sent to bear witness of the light. If some still thought too highly of the Baptist, they will certainly be impressed by the words which John quotes from his lips, words which he himself and his companions had heard the Baptist utter. So important is the Baptist's testimony that John presently presents it quite completely in its historical setting. Here only the pith of it is used as directly and pointedly substantiating the incarnation and the glory of the Only-begotten. Yet this brief introduction of the Baptist's testimony seems out of place to certain interpreters, who for this reason would either cancel v. 15 or transfer it to a different place, making v. 16 follow v. 14. But corroboration is always in place, as the writer may desire it to re-enforce

his own testimony, and doubly in place when this testimony deals with supernatural facts of the loftiest type. The texts are solidly for the genuineness of v. 15. **John bears witness concerning him and cries, saying, This was he of whom I said, He that comes after me is become before me, because he was first compared with me.**

The present tense $\mu\alpha\rho\tau\upsilon\rho\epsilon\hat{\iota}$ is forceful, whether we regard it as dramatizing the past act of bearing witness, or take it that the evangelist's testimony is still sounding forth. The tense reads as if the evangelist still hears the Baptist speaking. The form $\kappa\acute{\epsilon}\kappa\rho\alpha\gamma\epsilon\nu$ is the perfect; but this is one of a group of perfects which has lost the punctiliar part of the action and has retained only the notion of duration, hence must be translated with the present: "cries," or "goes on crying," R. 894, etc. The Baptist's testimony is public, delivered with a loud voice so that all may hear. Moreover, the Baptist himself states that he gave this testimony twice. The fact that he repeated it shows its great weight. Here the Baptist has $\mathring{\eta}\nu$, whereas in v. 30 he has $\dot{\epsilon}\sigma\tau\acute{\iota}\nu$. This is due to the attraction of thought exerted by $\epsilon\mathring{\iota}\pi\sigma\nu$, which takes the speaker's mind into the past and disregards the fact that what he says is also true of the present. Similar $\mathring{\eta}\nu$ appear in 3:23; 4:6; 10:41; 11:18. The circumstantial $\lambda\acute{\epsilon}\gamma\omega\nu$, "saying," "declaring," helps to mark the formal nature of the utterance now made. When the Baptist first made this utterance concerning Jesus we are unable to determine; some think it was said before Jesus' baptism and was solemnly repeated after the baptism, as is shown in v. 29-34.

The Baptist's testimony consists of three clauses: "He that comes after me — is become before me — because he was first compared with me." The first two clauses form the strongest kind of a paradox, they are like a riddle or an enigma. How can one who comes *behind* the Baptist have come *in front* of him? The adverbs of place ὀπίσω and ἔμπροσθεν are here used to indicate time. Hence: 'How can, one who comes *later* than the Baptist have come *earlier* than he? The third clause furnishes the solution: He was *first* compared with me. We begin with the solution: ὅτι πρῶτός μου ἦν. The enigma turns on two points of time, only one of which seems possible, and yet both are declared to be actual. The solution must, therefore, also deal with time. In other words, πρῶτός μου, with its genitive of comparison, cannot denote rank. This would be out of line entirely, failing to solve the enigma and clashing with half of it, since great personages are ushered in and preceded by those of lesser rank or by their servants, and not the reverse. While the superlative πρῶτος has crowded out the comparative πρότερος when only two are being compared, this does not affect the solution of the problem. More important is the verb ἦν, which reaches back indefinitely, like the four ἦν in v. 1, 2. The solution, then, lies in the pre-existence of the person to whom the Baptist points as being present before him and his hearers, namely Jesus. That this pre-existence also involves the highest superiority in rank goes without saying and is a self-evident deduction. Yet rank is not the key to the solution of the problem. This pre-existence, to which the Baptist testified so emphatically, perfectly corroborates the evangelist's statement that the Logos became flesh and that he possessed the divine glory of the Only-begotten.

The objection has been raised that the knowledge of the pre-existence of Christ was beyond the experience of the Baptist. The evangelist is charged with putting his own ideas into the mouth of the Baptist. The same is done with regard to many of the great utterances of Christ himself. The very strangeness of the Baptist's utterance is unique. It is couched in

a form that the Jews liked and because of its very
form is easily remembered. The stress which the
evangelist puts upon this testimony of the Baptist,
both here and in v. 29-33, shows that this remarkable
testimony is genuine. The Baptist uttered not only
this testimony but all his preaching by revelation as
one who was sent and commissioned by God. If this
testimony of his is manufactured and false, then all
else that is recorded of him is equally spurious, he
himself becomes a figment, and the sacred records
which have invented him are unreliable throughout.
Even the prophets knew what the Baptist embodied in
his striking saying, for they spoke and wrote by the
same revelation, Isa. 9:6; Micah 5:2; Mal. 3:1; Dan.
7:13; etc.

Christ's pre-existence makes plain how one and the
same person could come later than the Baptist and
yet have come earlier than he; could be both his successor and his predecessor. We must note that the
substantivized participle ὁ ἐρχόμενος is a standard
designation for the promised Messiah. While Jesus
was born about six months later than the Baptist, and
the paradox would be true if this point is considered,
the "coming" of which the Baptist speaks is that of
entering upon his appointed office as the Messiah.
Jesus assumed his office later than the Baptist, for
the latter ushered him into that office by baptizing him.
And yet this wonderful person also preceded the
Baptist; ἔμπροσθέν μου γέγονεν. This verb, when used
with an adverb of place, has the sense of "come,"
(hin)kommen, gehen, as in 6:25. As in v. 6, the verb
speaks of appearance, *hervortreten*, being in action.
The perfect tense is especially important, reaching
back, as it does, indefinitely into the past, whereas the
aorist ἐγένετο would indicate only a fixed period in the
past. For we must note that in the solution of the
paradox this γέγονεν merges into ἦν (*has been coming*

before me; for he *was* first compared with me). These
two tenses should not be restricted to the Old Testament era and to the presence and the operation of the
Logos during that time but should be understood in
the sense of Micah 5:2, "whose goings forth have
been from of old, from everlasting." The Baptist's
paradox deals with the mystery of the incarnation.
Like the evangelist and like all of the Scriptures he
shows us the eternal Son of God who became flesh,
dwelt among us, and manifested forth his glory. The
relation of this Son to the Father goes back to all
eternity; that of the evangelist, the apostles, the prophets, and all men of God begins in time. Those who
reject the *Zweinaturenlehre,* or by a kenosis empty
the Logos of his divine attributes, or who make Jesus
divine only morally thus reject the solution of the
Baptist's paradox instead of solving it.

16) The old church made v. 16 a part of the Baptist's statement, so that "we all" in the Baptist's word
would mean himself and the ancient prophets. But
this cannot be correct. The Baptist's paradox and
his solution stand out as something complete in itself.
Then also ἡμεῖς πάντες plainly refers back to v. 14: ἐν
ἡμῖν and ἐθεασάμεθα. **For of his fulness we all received,
and grace for grace,** takes up the thought of v. 14
and thus continues the evangelist's own testimony. V.
15 is inserted only as a most effective corroboration.
That, too, is why John uses ὅτι and not καί as the connective. The latter would coordinate with v. 15; but
v. 16 is not coordinate with v. 15, unless in v. 16 the
Baptist is still speaking. "Fulness" and "grace"
evidently take up the corresponding terms in v. 14,
and "we all received" evidently advances the thought
started by "we beheld" in v. 14. Thus ὅτι intends to
establish more completely what v. 14 contains and
what v. 15 has corroborated in an objective way. In
a way, the fact that the Word became flesh, that the

Baptist's successor, Jesus, was his predecessor in the indefinite past, needs no subjective proof. And yet it is bound to have also this kind of proof. There would be eyes to see the glory of this Person, glory as of the Only-begotten, glory as from the Father, showing him to be full of grace and truth. And this seeing and beholding would not be only an external view, it would be connected with an internal receiving, a personal and abiding enrichment.

"Of his fulness" or "from his fulness," ἐκ, takes up the adjective "full" ,in v. 14. No modifier is needed with "fulness," for we already know that this consists of "grace and truth." Col. 1:19, "For it pleased the Father that in him should all fulness dwell." This is the "riches" of the Lamb, Rev. 5:12; "the unsearchable riches of Christ" which Paul was counted worthy to preach to the Gentiles, Eph. 3:8; "the riches of his grace," Eph. 1:7. Luther pictures the inexhaustible nature of this fulness: "This spring is inexhaustible, it is full of grace and truth from God, it never loses anything, no matter how much we draw, but remains an infinite fountain of all grace and truth; the more you draw from it, the more abundantly it gives of the water that springs into eternal life. Just as the sun is not darkened by the whole world enjoying its light, and could, indeed, light up ten worlds; just as 100,000 lights might be lit from one light and not detract from it; just as a learned man is able to make a thousand others learned, and the more he gives, the more he has — so is Christ, our Lord, an infinite source of all grace, so that if the whole world would draw enough grace and truth from it to make the world all angels, yet it would not lose a drop; the fountain always runs over, full of grace."

The terseness of the phrase "out of his fulness" is matched by the terseness of "we all received." By adding no object for the verb the contrast between the fulness and the receiving is enhanced. "We" have nothing — Christ has the inexhaustible abundance. He is the Giver — we are the recipients, and that is all that we are or could be. It was so in the case of John and his fellow-witnesses who directly beheld the Savior and are the persons included in "we all"; and it is so still in our case who now behold the Savior in the inspired testimony of these original witnesses. The verb λαμβάνω has an active sense, "to take"; but it is used throughout, whenever our relation to Christ, to God, or to the Spirit of God is mentioned, without a hint of meritorious activity on our part. God's gift, offer, call, etc., always come first and not only make possible our receiving but induce, effect this receiving. So we take, as a poor, helpless patient takes the medicine put to his lips by the physician; as the blind mendicant takes the coin dropped into his hand by the charitable giver; as the eye takes in the sunbeam falling from on high, or the sound that strikes its membrane; yea, as the dead Lazarus takes the life conveyed to him by the word of him who is the resurrection and the life. This is especially true of our first taking or receiving from Christ. But even when the gift and the grace of Christ have filled us with faith, so that we ourselves come to him for replenishment and ourselves beg for his saving gifts, this very energy and activity of coming and seeking is a gift of his to us, namely the constant drawing which his fulness exerts upon us and any measure of faith that we may have. Thus in its fullest sense it is true: "What hast thou that thou didst not receive? Now if thou didst receive it, why dost thou glory, as if thou hadst not received it?" I Cor. 4:7. And the Baptist himself said, "A man can receive nothing, except it be given him from heaven," John 3:23.

The connective καί in "*and* grace for grace" marks "an explanatory addition," "epexegetic or explicative,"

R. 1181. The preposition ἀντί denotes exchange. "As
the days come and go a new supply takes the place of
the grace already bestowed, as wave follows wave
upon the shore. Grace answers to (ἀντί) grace," R. 574.
Hence "grace for grace" is not the grace of the New
Testament for that of the Old; not ordinary grace
followed by charismatic grace; not merely one individual gift of grace followed by another individual
gift — but grace ever new and greater. One measure
of it assures another. It is like a stream flowing constantly; every day, every hour its banks are full, ever
fresh volumes coming down from above, so that no
longing for grace in our hearts is left without immediate and complete supply. We may specify justification, peace with God, consolation, joy, enlightenment,
love, hope, etc., Rom. 5; Gal. 5:22; Eph. 5:9. Grace
for grace is according to the divine rule, "Whosoever
hath, to him shall be given, and he shall have more
abundance," Matt. 13:12. This doubling of the word
"grace" reveals what is meant by "his fulness" and
casts a wonderful light upon our receiving. "Are there
sinners here? Certainly, many. But here, too, is the
malefactor's grace for the sinner's heart, and it
cleanses and saves. Are there sorrowing and heavy
hearts here? Lay down your bundle of cares, take
instead grace for grace. Are there poor people here?
Here is he who by his poverty makes us rich. Nothing but his grace makes us rich amid all outward
poverty, consoles us amid all sadness, strengthens us
in all our weakness, gives us the power of life and the
fulness of life." Schoener who writes once more:
"Grace is a treasure to which none others can be compared. Carry together all the treasures of earth, and
all together they will not balance what lies in the one
word grace. Grace is the blood-red mark which can-
cels the handwriting against us; the star of hope
which sends its rays into this earth-life darkened by

sin; the ladder which leads us upward; the immovable pillar which shall stand, though hills and mountains pass away, and shall support the covenant of peace; the staff to which we can cling in our weakness; the guide who leads us safely through sorrow and death into the open portals of eternal blessedness."

The concept χάρις has already been defined in v. 14. We may add that "grace" is the effective manifestation of God's undeserved love toward sinful men, offering to all the salvation obtained by Christ, by this offer working faith to accept it, justifying us without any merit of our own, sanctifying and glorifying us. Grace is the chief characteristic of the entire gospel of Christ, of the entire Christian religion, the center of the mystery, unknown to the world, revealed in Jesus Christ. The fact that in emphasizing "grace" John has by no means forgotten "truth," which he added in v. 14, is shown by v. 17.

17) The ὅτι in v. 16 answers the question, why John could in v. 14 say, "we beheld." It is because "we actually received." The ὅτι in v. 17 goes deeper, from the subjective reception to the objective coming into being of what was received. Here the question is, why John could say both "we beheld" and "we received." It is because grace and truth came through Jesus Christ. To enhance the great historic fact thus offered as a reason a comparison is made between the two mediators (διά), the human and the divine, Moses and Jesus Christ. **For the law was given through Moses; grace and truth came through Jesus Christ.** A threefold antithesis is brought out in this double statement: 1) the law — grace and truth; 2) was given — came; 3) Moses — Jesus Christ. The three pairs are opposites but opposites that correspond. One likeness is included, namely the idea of mediation in διά, which is used with respect to both Moses and Jesus

Christ.   The form is that of the Hebrew *parallelismus membrorum.*

"The law," ὁ νόμος (with the article), is definite, the moral and the ceremonial law as Israel had it on the tables of stone and in its elaborate worship and in its civil and social regulations.   This law was no mean treasure; by possessing it Israel was greatly blessed. Yet it was not the actual "fulness" from which one could receive grace for grace.   The law was only preparatory.   It revealed the holy will of God and thus man's exceeding sinfulness and the depth of our lost condition.   At the same time we must add that the law was full of types and figures of deliverance from sin, and it even mediated a deliverance but one based on the great atonement that was to come.   Of course, the law itself thus indicated that everything depended on that future perfect atonement.   The law itself contained no availing atonement, it could only point forward, awaken the longing for it, picture and foreshadow it in advance, and, like a παιδαγωγός, lead to it. *Lex iram parans et umbram habens,* Bengel. The law was much, but more had to follow even to make the law what it was.

It "was given," ἐδόθη, is a historical aorist.   God gave it, and it came wholly as a gift, although remnants and traces of the holy will of God were still found in human hearts.   The Israelites esteemed the law as a divine gift even when they failed to see its relation to the gospel.   It "was given" expresses exactly the historical manner of its bestowal.   It was not a human development, an outgrowth of the religious genius of the people of Israel, or a product of its great leader or of a number of its leaders (Moses and the prophets.)   This speculative idea of modern students of history is contradicted by our evangelist. In spite of all evolutionary ideas the sober fact remains that no human wisdom, genius, or development

could possibly produce "the law" either in Israel or
in any other nation since Israel's time, this wonderful
system, every feature of which points beyond all
human calculation, into the far future, to the coming
Messiah, the Word made flesh and his redemptive work
for all the world.

The law was given "through Moses"; διά after the
passive verb plainly indicates that Moses was only
God's instrument. God could easily have used any
one of a number of similar instruments. We know
how God used Moses to receive the two tables of
stone, to construct the tabernacle and all it contained
after the pattern shown him on the mount, and to in-
augurate the entire worship under the law as directed
by God. Moses was not the law, as Christ is grace
and truth; he was only its minister and servant, as
much under it, subject to it, taught by it, blessed by
it as were the people to whom he ministered. With
Christ, as regards grace and truth, quite the reverse
is true.

"Grace and truth" are the same as in v. 14, each
marked as such by the article of previous reference,
each thus also marked as distinct from the other.
While they are distinct, the two are most intimately
joined, for grace is proclaimed by truth, and truth is
the revelation and the doctrine of grace. Both have
already been defined in v. 14. We may add that for
us both are objective, for of both John writes that
they "came," ἐγένετο. So also in v. 14 it is the incarnate
Logos who is full of grace and truth. Yet both are
intended for our subjective appropriation. That is
why the two "came." And when it is thus
appropriated, grace always forgives and gives, and
truth reveals and assures both the forgiveness and
the gifts.

The verb ἐγένετο is used like γέγονεν in v. 15, grace
and truth "came." Here again the choice of words

evidences the guidance of Inspiration. Grace and truth "came"; they were not "given" like the law. No Giver used a human instrument and made grace and truth a gift. These two are too great and high. They are in their root divine attributes. Thus they were embodied in Jesus Christ, they "came" in his incarnation and his mission. God did not merely tell us about grace and truth, so that he could have used another Moses or an array of prophets. Jesus himself was grace and truth. His own person and his work constitute the very substance of grace and truth. The Lord who passed before Moses, "abundant in goodness and truth," Exod. 34:6, whom the Psalmist praised, "The Lord is good; his mercy is everlasting, and his truth endureth to all generations," Ps. 100:5, he it is "who of God is made unto us wisdom, and righteousness, and sanctification, and redemption," I Cor. 1:30 in the incarnate Son, Christ Jesus. Yet grace and truth "came" thus not in an absolute sense as though now for the first time they sprang into existence but relatively as far as the actual work of redemption and its historical execution are concerned after existing for a long time in the thought of God and after being conveyed to men by promise.

Not until this place does John mention the historic name of the incarnate Logos, the name that is above every name: grace and truth came "through Jesus Christ." What a glory is shed over it in all that John has said before! It is like the sun rising in the east and lighting up all the earth with its diffused light while films of clouds still spread before it until suddenly it breaks through, and we see the great majestic light itself. "Jesus" is the name of the person, "Christ" or Messiah is a designation of the office. But here διά is not used with a passive verb, hence it does not introduce an instrument or a tool as a medium. This διά is as lofty as the verb of being which it

modifies. He who himself is grace and truth
mediates these attributes and all that they effect and
bestow.

18) The line of thought from v. 14 onward is
quite straight; the incarnate coming of the Word who
is the Only-begotten, attested as pre-existent by the
Baptist. Being full of grace and truth, we received
from him grace for grace, for, as compared with Moses,
grace and truth actually came by him, in fact, could
come by him alone, who being the Only-begotten in
the bosom of his Father alone could bring us the ultimate revelation. In particular, v. 18 expounds the
ἐγένετο of v. 17 and helps to show how the Logos "came."
V. 14 shows how he arrived, he was born in Bethlehem;
v. 18 shows whence he arrived and thus how he could
bring what he brought. In form v. 18 is an advanced
parallel to v. 17, each with a negative and with a positive part. The advance is from the gifts (law, grace,
and truth) to the source of these gifts (the law not
requiring the sight of God, grace and truth requiring
even more, that the bringer be even in the bosom of
the Father). Because v. 17 and 18 are such parallels,
therefore v. 18 is simply set beside v. 17 and has no
connective word. **No man hath seen God at any
time; God Only-begotten, who is in the bosom of
the Father, he did declare him.**

The emphasis is on "God," "*God* no one hath seen
at any time" no matter whom or what else he may
have seen. The absence of the article with Θεόν has
no special significance, the word itself means "God" in
his actual being as distinguished from the theophanies
when God assumed certain mediums for appearing
unto men. The verb ὁράω means simply "to see" with
the eye and thus denies even this much in regard to
God: no man ever *even saw* him, to speak of nothing
more. This, of course, is in contrast with the Logos
who not only saw God but was in the bosom of his

Father. John uses many perfect tenses, all of which are highly expressive. Here he has ἑώρακε, which with πώποτε, "hath seen at any time," is an extensive perfect, R. 893, but of broken continuity, R. 896, 906 : . . . > . . . ; meaning that in all the extent of the past no one ever at this or at that moment had a glimpse of God. The denial is general and absolute, including Moses as a matter of course: but also all others whoever they may be. In Exod. 33:11 the Lord, indeed, spoke to Moses "face to face." "Face to face" = "mouth to mouth," Num. 12:8, and thus does not imply that Moses *saw* the face of God. God communicated with Moses in the most direct way, and in the directness of this communication Moses excelled all others save Christ, though God never appeared even to Moses *in solida sua gloria* (Calov). Luther says, the Lord showed Moses his back and mantle; "thus Moses saw the mercy of God from behind as in the divine Word."

Against this strong background of negation is placed the still stronger affirmation that the Word made flesh has more than seen God. The question of the true reading is no longer in doubt. It is μονογενὴς Θεός and not ὁ μονογενὴς υἱός, nor ὁ μονογενής without a substantive. The article in the variant ὁ μονογενὴς Θεός would even be misleading as indicating that there are several Θεοί, one of whom is Only-begotten. The absence of the article bids us stress the qualitative force of the terms, and the adjective μονογενής is attributive, R. 856. We have already rejected the interpretation that "Only-begotten" refers to the human conception in the womb of the Virgin, and that only in this human sense the Logos became the Only-begotten. Here the addition Θεός makes this certain beyond question. *"God* Only-begotten" cannot date from a point in the course of time, for this would be a contradiction in the very terms, the one term "God" being timeless,

eternal, the other term "Only-begotten" being 1900
years old. "God Only-begotten" is such from all
eternity, and the adjective predicates the inner Trini-
tarian mystery of the *generatio aeterna,* describing
the eternal metaphysical relation of the Father and
the Son. The objections raised against this evident
sense are futile. The chief one is that John speaks
of the revealed Savior, hence he says nothing about the
relation of the divine persons. The simple truth is
that John is revealing to us who Jesus Christ really
was: the Logos, true God, begotten of the Father from
eternity. He reveals this much, though it exceeds our
finite powers of comprehension, because we must know
at least this much, i. e., the fact thus stated, in order
properly to understand and value what the Logos has
done. The objection based on the glory (v. 14) of the
Only-begotten, that this is only the glory of his personal revelation, dating only from the incarnation and
embodied in the incarnation, is answered by the simple
fact that this was no human glory, however great it
may be made, but the divine glory, the manifestation
of the divine nature of the Logos. Many of the German theologians who thus lower the term "Only-
begotten" still hold that Jesus was the pre-existent
Logos and thus in the true sense Θεός, but others have
gone much farther. The breach made by removing
eternity from "Only-begotten" is widened. By way of
the kenosis Jesus loses also all that lies in the concept
Θεός. He has now only "one nature," the *Zweinaturenlehre* is a relic of the past. We have only a divine
man, differing only in degree from other godly men,
a beautiful ethical example and no more. This ends
with the statement that we have lost nothing in regard
to Jesus, yea, have gained ever so much, for is not
Jesus hereby brought much nearer to us?

At this point John goes beyond "Only-begotten"
which he has here added to the Logos as being "God."

He pours out the fullest measure of revelation: God
Only-begotten "who is in the bosom of the Father."
The interpretation of this participial clause is misdirected when "Only-begotten" is made temporal
instead of eternal. The present participle ὤν is timeless as Luther already perceived: "is — ever and
ever is." It is thus more than if John had written
ὃς ἦν, "who was," for this would only reach backward;
also better than ὃς ἐστι, which would sound like a statement merely about the present when John was writing.
The participle expresses only durative being and thus
more easily becomes timeless. The article ὁ ὤν does
only one thing: it attaches the participle to "God Only-
begotten" after the manner of a relative clause and
describes this wonderful person for us. In no way
does the article change or limit the timeless force of
the participle. This would, indeed, be greatly changed
if "God Only-begotten" dates only from the Virgin
birth, for then any further modifier would be equally
limited. Without the article the participle, though it
is separated from the main verb by ἐκεῖνος, would tend
to become adverbial, either temporal, "when he was in
the bosom," or causal, "since he was in the bosom";
and thus instead of the timelessness we should have
the mere historical time indicated by the constative
(R. 829) aorist ἐξηγήσατο. These are the assured grammatical facts regarding ὁ ὤν, which we should not
yield when they are modified in the interest of a
wrong view of the person who is truly "God Only-
begotten."

The view of the ancient church was that ὁ ὤν extended back from the time when Christ appeared on
earth, back to all eternity. Since the present participle may stand also for the imperfect tense, this
view has some justification grammatically. So understood, this participle would resemble the repeated ἦν
in v. 1, 2. While thus the participle would predicate

nothing concerning Christ since the time of his earthly appearance, by an easy inference at least we should be able to conclude that Christ as "God Only-begotten" is also now and, indeed, is forever in the Father's bosom. So the ancient interpretation can hardly be called wrong. The objection that the being with God of the Logos in v. 1 and his being in the world in v. 10 are exclusive opposites is untenable; these two do not exclude each other, for the second is an addition to the other, even as the title "the Word" in v. 1 already points to the revelation to be made to the world in v. 10. A second view that Christ was in the bosom of the Father only during his earthly life is shut out by the very language and is usually understood to mean only an intimate communion of the man Jesus with his God, which negatives "God Only-begotten." The view that Christ is in the bosom of his Father only since his exaltation to heaven clashes with the very point at issue in v. 18, which is how and why Christ could perfectly declare God to us *before* his exaltation.

It is surprising that in spite of all the information available through the recently discovered mass of ostraca and papyri, presented in all the newer grammars, for instance, also by R. 535, 586, and 591, etc., at some length, any recent first-class exegete and linguist should still insist that with ὤν we must regard εἰς as distinct from ἐν, as denoting a movement toward the Father's bosom ending with rest in that bosom. This is the old explanation of the use of εἰς with static verbs and verbs of being and was made when the Koine was not understood on this and on many other points. Let the student read the entire story of the rise of εἰς after ἐν had the field alone; how εἰς first divided the field with ἐν by taking over all the verbs of motion; how εἰς then began its invasion of the territory of ἐν, namely by starting to be used with verbs of being and condition, just as we see this in the New

Testament, with a case right here in ὢν εἰς; and how
this use went on until in the modern Greek vernacular
ἐν is dead and εἰς rules. We must translate, "*in* the
bosom" just as if ἐν were used and not εἰς. The preposition denotes place, and since persons are referred
to, it denotes their union and communion, whereas
πρός in v. 1 and 3 denotes reciprocity   The term κόλπος
is figurative and brings out the idea of greatest possible intimacy. God Only-begotten and the Father
could not be in closer union. They do not only "see"
each other, "know" or "speak with each other"; they
are in each other's embrace. This is only one step removed from the word of Jesus himself when he says
that he and the Father are one.

Hitherto John has written "God" and "the Logos"
when distinguishing the two persons, though at once
he also called the latter "God." Here he writes "the
Father" and "God Only-begotten," by the former making fully clear in what sense "Only-begotten" is to be
understood. This thus is the first instance in which
the word "Father" is used distinctively with regard to
"the Son" to express a relation that is far superior to
that which we have in mind when we speak of the
Father and regard ourselves as "God's children," v. 12,
or as "God's sons," Gal. 3:26; 4:6, 7. Jesus never
unites himself with us by saying "our Father." When
he says "my Father" he distinguishes himself, the
essential Son, from all others who are only adopted
sons. This is made evident with greatest clearness
in 20:17, "I ascend unto *my* Father and *your* Father,
and *my* God and *your* God." It will not do, then, to
see in this distinctive term "Father" only the character
and the scope of what Christ revealed to us, that in
a sense God is truly *our* Father, or that he is Christ's
Father by virtue of the incarnation. "God Only-
begotten" and "the Father" are the correlatives of
the Son by virtue of their eternal relation through

the *generatio aeterna*. And this relation is immutable, grounded in the divine essence itself, unaffected by the incarnation, though our human reason is able to fathom neither the unincarnate nor the incarnate side of it.

The wonderful person thus described to us can, indeed, and did, indeed, bring us the ultimate revelation, "he did declare him." The demonstrative ἐκεῖνος is resumptive and emphatic, taking up "God Only-begotten" together with the appended relative clause, R. 707 and 708. The verb ἐξηγήσατο is choice and impressive and is not used otherwise by the evangelist. It goes far beyond what any man could do, assuming even that it were possible for him to see God and then to tell us what he had seen. The tense is the historical aorist, summing up all that Jesus "did declare" concerning God not only by his words and his deeds but also by his very coming and the presence of his person. The Logos is the supreme exegete, the absolute interpreter of God. The verb means more than *erzaehlen,* "to narrate or tell"; it means "to expound" or "set forth completely." The Greek is able to dispense with an object, but the English cannot imitate this brevity. So some supply "it," which is too weak and means too little; others, what he beheld while being with God, which is well enough in substance but too long in form; "him" is best of all. "Christ did not receive the revelation in time, like the Old Testament prophets, by means of the inspiration of the spirit of God, passing it on to others; he is himself the eternal Logos and the essential truth. He made known on earth what he beheld with the Father and heard from the Father as the Son of God before the foundation of the world, John 3:32; 6:46; 8:26, 38, 40; 12:50 (compare the analogous expression concerning the Holy Ghost, 16:13). And this which he received and obtained not merely in time but beheld and heard before his incarnation in eternity he sees and hears also continuously as man, since it is an eternal seeing and hearing and not subject to the change of time. For as we have already learned, he is the exegete of the Father, as the one who *is* in the bosom of the Father, and he knoweth the Father, as the Father knoweth him, John 8:55; 10:15. And as he knows the Father, so he knows also men, his brethren." Philippi, *Glaubenslehre*, IV, 1, 443. Thus also the last word ἐκεῖνος ἐξηγήσατο re-echoes and joins again the first word ὁ λόγος: The Word — *he* did declare. And this ushers in the historical account, setting down for us what "he did declare."

CHAPTER I — Continued

THE ATTESTATION OF JESUS CHRIST AS THE SON OF GOD IN HIS PUBLIC MINISTRY
1:19-12:50

I

The Opening Attestation as his Ministry Begins, 1:19-2:11

The sections here grouped together evidently constitute the first great chapter in the body of the book. The sections are all linked together with references to time: v. 29 — 35 — 43 — 2:1. This group of events marks those occurring on four successive days and another that happened three days later, thus coming to pass in one week of just seven days. Jesus emerges from the quiet life in Nazareth and now takes up his public ministry. We may divide into two parts: The Baptist's Attestation of Christ as the Son of God, 1:19-42; The First Testimony of Jesus Himself, 1:43-2:11.

The Attestation of the Baptist, 1:19-42. — All four evangelists begin their accounts of the Messianic ministry of Jesus with a reference to the appearance and the activity of John the Baptist as the promised herald who was to prepare the Messiah's way. John's Gospel, however, takes the general history of the Baptist for granted; his Christian readers have it in the earlier Gospels. John is satisfied to use only the specific testimony which the Baptist gave to Jesus as the Messiah and Son of God. The other details of the Baptist's preaching John passes by as not being pertinent to his theme. He selects the most notable testimony offered by the Baptist on three consecutive days: 1) before the commissions sent to him from Jerusalem; 2) before his own disciples; 3) before two of his disciples who then follow Jesus. The three episodes are exact, detailed, and circumstantial, recorded in a way which indicates the indelible impression made upon the heart of the writer, changing his entire life most completely. Here began the faith of the first believers in Jesus, and thus Christian faith, in the specific sense, in general.

19) **And this is the witness of John when the Jews from Jerusalem sent to him priests and Levites, in order to inquire of him, Who art thou? And he confessed and denied not; and he confessed, I am not the Christ.** To begin an entirely new section, in fact, the body of John's Gospel with καί is Hebraistic, entire books and many independent parts of books beginning with *vav,* "and." This eliminates the idea that "and" here intends to connect with v. 15 as though the summary testimony of the Baptist introduced in v. 15 is now to be furnished in detail. A close reading of the entire paragraph, v. 19-28, shows that this paragraph deals with a different time and a different occasion entirely. It is the next paragraph, v. 29-34, which tells the story of the testimony quoted in v. 15. If this introductory καί could connect with anything preceding, we should choose v. 7, where the Baptist is introduced as the witness, connected with which we would be told how he gave this witness. But this καί is merely formal and connects with nothing. As such it not only belongs to the entire sentence, including the ὅτε clause, but is even repeated at the head of v. 20. This repeated καί at the head of v. 20 is often ignored, yet it is just as prominent as its original at the head of v. 19. This second καί also bars out the suggestion that καὶ αὕτη ἐστὶν ἡ μαρτυρία τοῦ Ἰωάνου forms

a kind of heading for the three paragraphs which follow, "And this is the witness of John." A new sentence would then begin with ὅτε, "When the Jews
. . . , he confessed," etc. John, however, wrote, "*and* he confessed," etc.

Without further ceremony we are introduced to the Baptist at the very height of his ministry and his influence. Not a word is added describing the Baptist's person and his appearance, his mode of life in the desert, his message in general, and his Baptism. We are supposed to know in advance also how the excitement grew to huge proportions among the people until they flocked in thousands to the lonely desert region, and until even the central authorities of the nation at Jerusalem felt constrained by the volume and the character of the reports to send out an official committee to make a firsthand investigation. The evangelist at once places us at the dramatic moment when before the gathered multitudes out in the wilderness this official committee faced the Baptist and received his telling answers to their questions. The evangelist was there, saw and heard it all and has left to us the record of what occurred. We see that for him the Baptist's μαρτυρία is the essential thing. All else his readers may gather from the other evangelists; this "witness" indeed, is also recorded by them, yet our evangelist wishes to make full use of its great weight in this new Gospel which is to record the attestation that Jesus is the Son of God.

"The Jews," οἱ 'Ιουδαῖοι, first meant the members of the tribe of Judah. After the exile when Judah and Benjamin returned, the nation as such was called "the Jews," and the term "Israel" or "the Israelites" marked its religious character. John uses the term in this general sense, but as the narrative proceeds often with the note of hostility to Jesus. In certain contexts "the Jews" reads like "the enemies of Christ" although this is due to what must be reported concerning them. Just what persons are in each instance intended by the term the context makes plain. In this first mention "the Jews from Jerusalem" are evidently the Jewish authorities, namely the Sanhedrin, consisting of ἀρχιερεῖς, γραμματεῖς, and πρεσβύτεροι, high priests, scribes, and elders, who had their seat in the Holy City. It is perfectly in order to use "the Jews" when the Sanhedrin is referred to, for this ruling body was the highest legal representative of the nation; its findings and decisions counted for the nation as such. We, of course, must assume that the movement produced by the Baptist had stirred the Sanhedrin into action, in particular the surmises and reports that this man might be the long expected Messiah. To make an official firsthand investigation was not only within the province of the Sanhedrin, it was really obligatory for this authoritative body to investigate and then to take such action as the case might warrant. The matter of a false Messiah, inflaming the people to fanatical action, might prove a very serious thing. So the commission is sent. The phrase "from Jerusalem," as its position shows, is not to be construed with the verb, as the English versions have translated it, but with the noun, "the Jews from Jerusalem." We note two forms for "Jerusalem," the indeclinable feminine Ἰερουσαλήμ (LXX), which merely transliterates the Hebrew, and the neuter plural Ἱεροσόλυμα, which has more of a Greek dress.

The commission consisted of ἱερεῖς καὶ Λευῖται. The former were common priests not ἀρχιερεῖς, high priests, a term which includes the reigning high priest and those who had held the office before him or belonged to his family. John uses ἱερεῖς only in this one instance. The Levites, members of the tribe of Levi, performed the menial and the police work in the Temple and in the latter capacity were marshalled under the στρατηγὸς τοῦ ἱεροῦ, the Temple captain with his lieutenants. A detachment of Levites was sent along with the committee of priests first, on account of the dangers of the road from Jerusalem to the Jordan wilderness and, secondly, to lend a more official character to the committee of priests when it appeared among the great multitudes that were gathered about the Baptist. The verb ἐρωτάω used in the purpose clause refers to a formal and a dignified inquiry and hence reflects the importance which even the Sanhedrin accorded the Baptist, "in order to inquire of him"; the translation "to ask" in our versions is too light.

The narrative is compressed, for what this committee was to inquire and what it did inquire when it arrived on the scene is combined. The actual question: Σὺ τίς εἶ; is retained as the object of ἐρωτήσωσιν in the purpose clause. The question itself cannot be considered as hostile or even inquisitorial, although it is legally formal and betrays no trace of longing or desire either on the part of the Sanhedrin or on the part of its committee. The emphasis is on σύ, *"Thou, who art thou?"* The Baptist was proclaiming the coming of the Messianic kingdom and was baptizing great multitudes as a preparation for this kingdom. Now Deut. 18:21, etc., implies that Israel should examine and test any prophet who might thus appear. Naturally, the Sanhedrin would act as the executive of the nation in the matter.

20) The striking feature is the elaborate way in which John introduces the Baptist's reply, "And he confessed and denied not; and he confessed" — positive — negative — then again positive. Why this apparant redundancy? Not for one moment could we entertain the suggestion that this question contained a temptation for the Baptist to make himself more than he actually was, to play, at least in his mind, with the thought that he himself might be or might become

the Messiah. The entire character of the Baptist, every act and word of his, bars out the idea that either now or at any time he felt tempted in this direction. No; this elaborate preamble reflects not the Baptist's state of mind but that of the evangelist. It is as if John would say, "I myself heard him confess and not for one instant deny — and this is what he confessed." The Baptist answered readily enough, but the evangelist intends that we, like himself, shall feel the full weight of the testimony that this answer contained. This, too, is why he uses these verbs "to confess" and "to deny" instead of the ordinary "to reply," which is all that is needed to match "to inquire." The Baptist's reply was more than a reply, it was a full, complete, clear-cut confession; it withheld nothing, hence had no trace of denial. This solemn preamble thus introduces all that the Baptist said in the entire dialog that follows and not merely the first brief word, "I am not the Christ."

The evangelist retains the direct dramatic form of the original scene, indicating that he writes as an eye and ear witness. We shall meet this vivid directness again and again in our Gospel. Those who deny John's authorship ignore or minimize this strong feature or explain it away by making the supposed author play the part of a novelist-historian who invents his own scenes and paints in the details from his own imagination. The Baptist might have answered the question addressed to him in a positive form by stating his name, parentage, and divine commission. Instead of this he answers the implication that lies in the question and thus from the start meets it squarely and directly. In all his proclamation to the people he had said nothing about himself. He himself was only a minor figure, one who came to point to Another far greater than himself, which all who heard him could have no difficulty in perceiving. When he is now asked directly who he himself really is, he replies in the same way, pointing away from himself to this Greater One. That is what makes his reply a confession (v. 20) and a testimony (v. 19).

After the ὅτι recitativum, which is the equivalent of our quotation marks, the oldest texts read: Ἐγὼ οὐκ εἰμὶ ὁ Χριστός and place ἐγώ forward to match the emphatic forward σύ of the question; later texts read: Οὐκ εἰμὶ ἐγὼ ὁ Χριστός. *"Thou,* who art thou?" *"I,* I am not the Christ," since this is really what you wish to know. The emphatic ἐγώ is proper where there is a contrast with another person. Ὁ Χριστός with the article is appellative, "the Anointed One," whoever this may be. In v. 17 "Jesus Christ" names the specific person. This prompt and pointed denial when the question itself was not, *"Thou,* art thou the Christ?" indicates that the rumor was abroad crediting the Baptist with being the promised Messiah, the Christ. One thing is certain, the Baptist himself had given no occasion for such a rumor. It sprang from the general expectation that was abroad, from the intensification this expectation received through the Baptist's preaching and work, and from the imagination that went beyond the bounds of the Baptist's own words.

21) Sent by the supreme authorities to probe the matter to the bottom, the spokesman of the committee, speaking for all, makes further inquiry. **And they inquired of him, What then? Art thou Elijah? And he says, I am not. Art thou the prophet? And he replied, No.** The second question with οὖν builds on the Baptist's answer, "What then?" i. e., if thou art not the Christ, and is at once followed by a more specific question, "Art thou Elijah?" Whether σύ is placed at the head or at the end of this question makes little difference, as in either place it would carry emphasis. The question itself rests on Mal. 3:23 (in

the English and the German versions Mal. 4:5) as
understood by the rabbis regarding the return of
Elijah in person to prepare the Messianic kingdom.
Perhaps something in the stern preaching of repentance by the Baptist, aided by his austere dress and
mode of life, may have prompted the surmise that this
rabbinic expectation was fulfilled and that the Baptist
actually was Elijah returned to life. In this sense
the Baptist utters his denial: οὐκ εἰμί, "I am not,"
omitting any pointed ἐγώ, which would add the wrong
implication: *I* am not, but *another* is or will be. The
Baptist's denial, therefore, does not clash with what
was promised regarding him in Luke 1:17, and with
what Jesus afterward said of him in Matt. 11:14;
17:11, three statements which correctly interpret
Malachi.

Without connecting words, as in drama, the third
question follows with its briefest answer, "Art thou
the prophet?" and we must note the article in the
Greek: ὁ προφήτης, hence not "a prophet" (Luther)
but *"the"* specific prophet, the one mentioned in Deut.
18:15 and 18, 19, and conceived to be, as 7:40 shows,
a special prophet who would precede the Messiah.
When the article is thus used with the predicate, it
is both definite and treated as identical and interchangeable with the subject, R. 768. The apostles
afterward understood correctly that in Deuteronomy
the prophet like unto Moses is Christ himself, Acts
3:22; 7:37, which also is the understanding of the
Galileans in John 6:14, etc. The Baptist answers the
question in the sense in which it is put to him without stopping to correct the views of the questioners.
His "No" is categorical. Note the progressive blunt-
ness of the Baptist's denials, until οὐ comes out flatly
at the last, R. 1157. The assumption, attached to
Matt. 16:14, that the questioners here have in mind
Jeremiah who is supposed to return in person is

really only a legendary notion drawn from II Macc. 2:4, etc.

22) The results obtained thus far by the committee are negative, though they are valuable as far as they go. Various ideas concerning the Baptist have been eliminated, some of which the questioners had in mind when they began, "Thou, who art thou?" So they begin again with a more elaborate question: **They said, therefore, to him, Who art thou? that we may give an answer to them that sent us. What dost thou say concerning thyself?** If instead of εἶπον we read εἶπαν, this is only the Alexandrian form which a certain group of texts follows. The addition of οὖν after εἶπον indicates that what is now asked is the outcome of the previous questions. Hence also the very general form: Τίς εἶ; which merely asks for information about the Baptist without reference to someone who he might be.

A natural ellipsis occurs before the purpose clause, "in order that we may give an answer," etc., namely, "Tell us, in order that," etc. The questioners here urge the Baptist to consider their position as a committee. The mere negative reply that he is not the Christ will not suffice the Sanhedrin nor the mere denials of various suppositions held by the people. They must bring more or receive heavy censure for having left the main part of their task undone. The "answer" they thus request from the Baptist is one that is positive, "What dost thou say concerning thyself?" The question thus put naturally reveals no personal concern or interest in regard to the Baptist and his mission. These men think only of the answer they are expected to bring to the Sanhedrin. It may, indeed, be quite true that their personal thoughts and desires went no farther, that personally they were left quite cold by what they saw and heard out here in the wilderness. But all this is beside John's narrative.

He reports only what was said by these men and goes no farther.

23)   Thus approached, the Baptist complies. **He said, I am a voice shouting in the wilderness, Make straight the way of the Lord, as said Isaiah the prophet.** The Baptist uses Isa. 40:3, and himself mentions the prophet whose words he uses when characterizing himself. Compare the author's *The Eisenach Old Testament Selections*, 66, etc. The claim that the Baptist here merely appropriates Isaiah's words and does not mean to say that he and his work are the fulfillment of Isaiah's prophecy would certainly be remarkable if true. Matt. 3:3; Mark 1:3; Luke 3:4 interpret Isaiah's word as actually being fulfilled in the Baptist and in his work. Even without this decisive evidence no other conclusion can be drawn from the Baptist's answer to the committee of the Sanhedrin. He furnishes this committee with more than they had asked when they requested, "What dost thou say concerning thyself?" He supplies them with a divinely inspired statement from the greatest of their own prophets concerning his person and his work. Isaiah's words do not merely happen to fit the Baptist's thought, these words constitute the authority for his work.

The fact that the Baptist quotes in a free and an abbreviated way is entirely immaterial. This liberty is constantly used by those who quote. Isaiah writes, "Voice of a crier, In the wilderness prepare ye the way of the Lord, make straight in the desert a highway for our God!" The Baptist declares not that he is such a voice, not that this picture of a voice in some way fits him also; but that he himself is this voice. He even imitates the Hebrew when he says, literally, "I — voice of a crier." While the parallelism of the Hebrew lines induces us to connect the phrase "in the wilderness" with the verb prepare instead of with "the voice" (A. V.), this makes little difference. The Baptist evidently understands Isaiah to mean that both the voice and the highway are "in the desert," and, surely, the fact of the fulfillment shows that this is correct. The synoptists follow the LXX in the translation ἑτοιμάσατε, "prepare," "make ready," and εὐθείας ποιεῖτε (τὰς τρίβους); "make straight." The Baptist spoke Aramaic and may have used the Aramaic for the second of these two verbs, which the evangelist translates into Greek without following the LXX, using εὐθύνατε which only approaches the LXX. Here we have a plain case which shows that John was quite independent of the LXX. Whereas the prophet has two poetic lines in a synonymous parallelism, the Baptist uses only one. Such condensation and abbreviation are constantly employed when quoting.

In the Baptist's reply the entire stress is on his work and office, none on his person. He is merely a voice with a message. The absence of the article with φωνή and also with βοῶντος beautifully recalls the original Hebrew: *qol qore'*, "voice of a crier!" the two Hebrew words being like an exclamation. In the Greek this absence of the articles emphasizes the idea of each word: the Baptist — a voice — shouting. We need not picture God as the one who uses this voice and shouts. The voice is the speaker's own, and he does the shouting. Yet βοῶντος connotes a herald making a public proclamation, which is necessarily done with a loud voice in order to reach the multitudes. This, too, suffices to show that what the Baptist uttered was not his own but the message of one greater and higher than himself.

By thus incorporating the message itself into his reply to the committee the Baptist actually does his work also upon these men, whether he used a loud voice in so doing or not. He is actually calling upon them also to make straight the way of the Lord, Κύριος,

Jehovah of the old covenant. He came in Jesus Christ.
The figure in Isaiah's words is that of an oriental king
with his retinue for whom the roads are prepared
when they are making a royal passage in state. So
Christ, now assuming his office, comes. "Such preparation is spiritual. It consists in deep conviction and
confession that you are unfit, a sinner, poor, damned,
and miserable with all the works you are able to do."
Neither the prophet nor the Baptist are to be understood as intending that men should by their own
natural powers make straight the way of the Lord
into their hearts, for this would demand the impossible.
The power for this spiritual preparation the Baptist
himself offered in his preaching and his Baptism, i. e.,
in these means of grace.

24) With the textual question settled that John
wrote: καὶ ἀπεσταλμένοι ἦσαν ἐκ τῶν Φαρισαίων, various difficulties are removed. We must also note that ἐκ τῶν
Φαρισαίων is partitive (ἐκ and ἀπό are frequently so used)
and the phrase = "some Pharisees," which may be
either the subject or the predicate in a sentence. We
must, therefore, translate: **And some Pharisees had
been commissioned** and correct Luther, both of our
versions, and the margin of the R. V. "They *which*
were sent," etc., assumes οἱ before the participle, which
reading is that of a faulty text. "Had been commissioned from the Pharisees" or "from among the Pharisees" misconceives the final phrase. John deviates
from the genuine Greek idiom and writes in a Jewish
way, although what he says is entirely plain. The
reference thus is no longer to the committee of priests
and Levites sent by the Sanhedrin. It would be
strange, indeed, if after characterizing this committee
in v. 19, at this late point a new characterization should
be incidentally introduced. The leading men in the
Sanhedrin were Sadducees, and it would be remarkable for them to send out a committee composed of

Pharisees, especially on a mission relative to the Messiah concerning whom the Sadducees and the Pharisees held different views. The Pharisees were attached to the Rabbis, and we lack any intimation that the priest were Pharisees, on the contrary, being dependent on the high priest and the Sadducees, they very likely followed their lead.

The real situation, then, is that the committee of the Sanhedrin had ended its inquiry and stepped aside. In addition to this committee the Pharisaic party in Jerusalem had sent a representation of its own. These men had stood by while the committee from the Sanhedrin had made its inquiry. When these were through, the Pharisaic representatives speak. The explanation that the men who now speak are Pharisees is necessary for the understanding of the question which they put to the Baptist. They were of the party which laid utmost stress on the strictest outward observance of the law, around which they had also built up a forbidding hedge of traditions and human commandments. They were utterly self-righteous and cultivated a formalism that was ostentatious to a degree, especially in observing ceremonies, fastings, almsgiving, long prayers, tithes, etc. The Sadducees were freethinkers, skeptics, usually men of wealth and prominence, and given to loose and luxurious living. The people reverenced the Pharisees for their supposed holiness and for their zeal regarding the law; and even the Sadducees had to accomodate themselves to their demands in many ways.

25) The question now asked is one that would naturally occur to Pharisees. While the committee of Sadducees is silent and has nothing more to say, these Pharisees note what seems to them an unauthorized and thus illegal act on the part of the Baptist. **And they inquired of him and said to him, Why, then, baptizest thou if thou art not the Christ, neither Elijah,**

neither the prophet? The condition is one of reality and thus has οὐ as is usual in such conditions in the Koine, R. 1160. The Baptist himself had just acknowledged that he was none of the persons mentioned. Taking him at his word, how, then, dared he baptize? With οὖν, "then" or "therefore," the question is based on the admission all have heard. Incidentally the fact is here brought out that John was engaged in baptizing; the evangelist takes it as a matter of course that his readers know what is necessary to know on this point.

Passages like Ezek. 36:25; 37:23 led the Jews to expect a lustration and cleansing of the people. That this should be accomplished by way of a baptism would seem quite in order. But they expected that it would be the Messiah himself who would thus cleanse the people, and, if not he, then at least his forerunners as they imagined them. When John denied that he was one of these, they naturally asked how, then, he came to be baptizing. Their wrong preconceptions concerning the Messiah's forerunner blinded them to such an extent that, when they had the real forerunner before their very eyes, they failed to recognize him. In a way this scene with its question to the Baptist resembles the scene in the Temple with its similar question to Jesus 2:18; for in both cases the Jews ask, "On what authority art thou acting?"

26) John answers the Pharisees as readily and as succinctly as he had answered the Sadducees. **John answered them, saying, I baptize with water: in your midst stands one whom you yourselves do not know, even he that comes after me, the latchet of whose shoe I am not worthy to unloose.** This answer is straight and true. First, by pointing to what he was actually doing, namely baptizing with water, the Baptist clears up and clears away the misconceptions

in the minds of his questioners concerning the expected lustrations, which they looked for either from the Messiah or from their expected Elijah or special prophet. This confusion is cleared up if these Pharisees will only observe what the Baptist is actually doing, *"I* (emphatic) am engaged in baptizing with water."* This "I" is like the one in v. 20 and is set in opposition to another, namely Christ. To baptize with water simply says that John is using a means of grace. This both marks his person and defines his work. The Messiah will both be a far greater person and will do a far greater work. As the God-man he will redeem the world and will furnish a cleansing that is far beyond any cleansing that any mere man, be he Elijah, that prophet, or the Baptist himself, could provide. Christ's redemption is the basis of the means of grace. Without this redemption no means of grace would exist. Thus with the simplest kind of statement the Baptist conveys the thought that he is nothing but a man, and that his work consists in applying a means of grace that rests on a far mightier act.

This clears away the confusion that commentators have introduced into the Baptist's simple words. They are apt to overemphasize ἐν ὕδατι. Some stress the preposition in the interest of immersion and do not observe that, even if ἐν were εἰς, immersion would not follow and would not be the point stressed by the Baptist. Some stress "with water" as being opposed to "with the Spirit." The Baptist has no such contrast here. Where he does have it, as in Matt. 3:11; Mark 1:7; and Luke 3:16, the Baptism with the Spirit is also one with fire. In these passages the simple work of applying a means of grace is contrasted with the miracle of Pentecost, the only instance in which the Spirit and fire are associated. And this contrast means that all that a person like the Baptist could do in his office was to use a means of grace, to baptize

with water, while Christ who would work our redemption could and would crown that work by pouring out
the Spirit from on high in a Baptism rightly called
one of Spirit and of fire. Thus disappear all derogations of what has been called "water Baptism" with
the understanding that this could be only a water
ceremony, an empty sign, devoid of power and of grace.
These derogations have been applied especially to
John's Baptism, making it a mere ceremony devoid
of Spirit, although Mark so clearly says that John
preached "the baptism of repentance for the remission of sins," Mark 1:4; and Luke 3:3 repeats that
statement. Such a Baptism, connected with repentance and effecting remission of sins, cannot be conceived without the presence and the gracious operation
of the Spirit, John 3:5.

When the Baptist replies, "*I* baptize with water,"
he declares: *My* work is to apply this means of grace.
And this must be taken in connection with the following statement that the Messiah is right "in your
midst," already actually at hand and about to manifest himself. So the Baptist's first statement also
means: *I* who thus baptize am this Messiah's true
herald and forerunner. Thus all the uncertainty regarding what John meant when he said, "I baptize
with water," disappears, and the full pertinency of
his reply comes to view. The questioners referred
only to the Baptism not to John's preaching. Hence
the reply also restricts itself to this sacrament. In
reality, as the references to Mark 1:4 and Luke 3:3
show, the preaching and the sacrament go together.
The answer John gave to the priests and Levites when
he called himself a voice crying in the wilderness, a
herald going before his King, must not be forgotten
in the present connection. That answer is valid also
for the Pharisees. The Baptist preached in order
to bring the people to true repentance and to a baptism

for the remission of their sins, and he baptized those who were converted by his preaching.

The tense of the verb means, "I am engaged in baptizing." The preposition ἐν is instrumental and merely indicates the earthly element employed, "with water." The verb βαπτίζω has a wide range of meaning, denoting any application of water, and it cannot be restricted to immersion. It is traditionalism when the commentators continue to speak of the "plunges beneath the water," the *Vollbad,* etc., as being the mode of John's Baptism. The mode that John used is nowhere indicated, but no single indication points to the mode being that of immersion. The lustrations common in Jewish practice were not administered by complete immersion, many were mere dipping or sprinkling. The πολλὰ ὕδατα at Ænon, where John also baptized, were springs and rivulets of water. This place was chosen because it afforded good drinking water which is so necessary where many people are gathered together. The vast multitudes which John baptized during his short ministry could not have been immersed without his living an aquatic life. Clement F. Rogers, M. A., has made an exhaustive study of the original mode of Baptism in the pictorial representations, *Baptism and Christian Archæology,* Oxford, Clarendon Press, and has found not one that depicts immersion; even the ancient fonts were shallow, making an immersion impossible. While no one is in a position to say in just what way the Baptist proceeded, the nearest we can come is to say that he took a bunch of hyssop or a twig, dipped it into the water, and then sprinkled those who were to be baptized.

John's Baptism was the true and complete sacrament, of the same nature and efficacy as our present Baptism. Jesus took up and continued John's Baptism, 3:22; 4:1, 2, and after his resurrection instituted it for all nations. To consider John's Baptism as a mere symbol in the face of Mark 1:4 and Luke 3:3 is unwarranted. The remission connected with John's Baptism cannot denote a future remission but, as surely as the repentance led to the Baptism, a forgiveness then and there. When Jesus speaks to Nicodemus about Baptism, this must refer to John's Baptism, which makes plain that it had the Holy Spirit and the power of regeneration, for of these Jesus speaks to Nicodemus. None of Christ's Apostles received a baptism other than that of John, yet Peter who was thus baptized declares that Baptism "saves," I Pet. 3:21. The baptism referred to in Acts 19:1-7 was invalid because it had been administered not by the Baptist but by faulty disciples of his, who had declined to follow Jesus and had proceeded on their own account and were not even able to teach as much as the existence of the Holy Ghost. What they had received was not Baptism, hence Paul instructed and baptized them — just as we would do today in an analogous case. As far as differences can be indicated: John's Baptism rested on the preliminary revelation made to John, Christ's on his own full and complete revelation. John's made followers of the Christ to come, Christ's made followers of the Christ who had come. John's Baptism bestowed the forgiveness about to be bought, Christ's the forgiveness that had been bought. John's was thus for Israel alone, Christ's for all nations.

After clearing up the matter regarding his baptizing John clears up the matter regarding the Messiah and shows how he is connected with this Messiah. His reply may be divided into three statements: 1) Unknown, the Messiah is already in your midst; 2) He is already in the act of coming after me; 3) And he is infinitely great. Thus John more than answers the question put to him. His work is not only legal in the narrow Pharisaic sense, it is legal in a far higher sense and has the stamp of approval from the present Messiah himself.

In μέσος the Greek has an adjective which we are able to produce only by a phrase, "in your own midst," the pronoun being quite emphatic as it is again in the subject clause. The absence of a connective makes the two statements, the one regarding John himself (ἐγώ) and the one regarding the Messiah, stand out prominently. "Whom *you* (yourselves, for your part) do not know," i. e., people like you, is the subject of στήκει a later verb formed from the perfect ἕστηκα, of ἵστημι. "He stands in your very midst" although *you* do not see or know him as yet while *I* certainly do, means more than that the Messiah "is" already in their midst. "He stands" means: ready to begin his great Messianic work. These Pharisees, too, will presently "know" him after a fashion; the Pharisaic mind will never really know him.

27) The addition, "even he that comes after me," modifies the subject clause, "whom you do not know," but really helps to explain the verb "stands." This wonderful person stands ready to carry out his great work, and this person is to be John's great successor, to perform the Messianic task of which John's work was only the herald. With the Messiah thus on the very point of succeeding John, it is foolish to question his right to baptize, in fact, his right both to preach and to baptize. This close connection between John and the Messiah seals John's work as being divine. In this testimony of John to Jesus a note of joy and mighty satisfaction throbs. To usher in Jesus — what more blessed task could be assigned to any man! And does anyone question John's work? Jesus is its justification and seal. When John tells these Pharisees that *they* do not know though *he* does, and that Jesus is on the very point of taking up his great

work, he suggests to these men that they on their part should also desire to know him and should ask to have him pointed out to them. But this suggestion falls on deaf ears, after hearing John's reply they, too, step aside. Even the final statement about the supreme greatness of this wonderful person awakens no response in their hearts.

The participial clause is a duplicate of the one used in v. 15, and it occurs again with a finite verb in 30, showing that the Baptist more than once used it with reference to Jesus. Throughout the verb forms ἐρχόμενος and ἔρχεται are significantly Messianic and must have been so understood by those who heard John speak. This Coming One is vastly greater than John, which shows how seriously mistaken they were who thought John might be he, "the latchet of whose shoe I am not worthy to unloose." The sandal was fastened to the foot by a leather strap, ἱμάς, "latchet." When an honored guest or the master of the house himself entered, it was the task of the humblest slave in the house to unfasten the straps, remove the shoes, bathe the feet, and cleanse the shoes. With this imagery John compares himself and Jesus. Did many consider John wonderfully great? He himself says that he is nothing compared with Jesus. Picture Jesus, the Coming One, either as come unto his own (v. 11) as the Master of his own home, or as the most exalted Guest at the home of his nearest kin and friends, the Baptist is not great enough to perform the menial service indicated — John being only a sinful man — Jesus, the very Son of God (v. 34).

In v. 31, etc., John tells us that he himself at first did not know that Jesus was, indeed, the Messiah and Son of God. He had always known Jesus and he may well have had his convictions concerning him. But when he spoke as God's prophet he had to have more than these. He received more, the fullest revelation

through the Father and the Spirit, on the occasion
of the baptism of Jesus. This had come to him prior
to the arrival of the two delegations from Jerusalem.
Constructions like ἄξιος with the non-final ἵνα are quite
usual in the Koine, especially in our Gospel. About
half of the infinitives are thus crowded out; ἵνα λύσω =
λῦσαι.

28) The remark is sometimes made that the evangelist fails to finish and round out so many of his narratives, and the present incident is pointed to as a case
in point. Yet, what more should the evangelist have
added? He is concerned with the testimony which the
Baptist uttered concerning the person and the office of
Jesus. Most graphically and completely he has
recorded the testimony offered on this occasion. What
more was there for him to say? The two delegations
left, which is rather self-evident. The Baptist went
about his business — should that be told? Has anyone
this or that curious question he would like to ask?
None of the evangelists attempt to answer such questions. John's first historic incident is surely quite
complete.

As in 6:59 and in 8:20, the evangelist mentions
the place of the incident at the end of his narrative.
Shall we say that this was a way he had? This naming the place of the occurrence seems to be more than
an appended piece of information; it sounds as though
John recalls the exact locality because the importance
of what transpired there impressed him so deeply at
the time. **These things took place in Bethany
beyond the Jordan, where John was, engaged in
baptizing.** "In Bethany" is the assured reading but
the addition "beyond the Jordan" should not be overlooked. The latter phrase is written from the point
of view of Palestine proper, the country between the
river and the sea. Incidentally this marks the writer
of our Gospel as one who was a native of Palestine,

who thus thinks of the land east of the Jordan as being "beyond the Jordan." There is another Bethany near Jerusalem which has the Mount of Olives between it and the city; this was the home of Martha, Mary, and Lazarus. Origen found the variant reading "in Bethabara" and helped to pass it on; but it cannot be regarded as genuine. This little place cannot now be located, but it lay not in the hot gorge at the riverside but away from this, yet in such a way that from it the river could easily be reached.

It seems, too, that we should not picture the Baptist as camping out in the open in all sorts of weather and in all seasons, or as resorting to some cave beside the river while he was doing his work. The same is true regarding the multitudes. It is more preferable to think that he used a house, and that his disciples did likewise, and that from time to time all went to the river whenever anyone was to be baptized. In 1:38 Jesus who was then with the Baptist has a house as shelter, to which he invited the inquiring disciples of the Baptist. There is no apparent reason why ἦν βαπτίζων should be a circumscribed imperfect which would greatly stress the durative idea of continuous baptizing. It seems more natural to regard ἦν as the verb, "where John was," and to regard the participle as modifying "John," "engaged in baptizing."

29) The very next day after the appearance of the two delegations the Baptist made a double notable statement concerning Jesus: v. 29-31; 32-34. This was made before his disciples, as we must conclude from 3:26, where John's disciples refer to this testimony and regard it as something for which Jesus should be grateful. Many others must also have been present, especially people from the neighborhood, as we must conclude from 10:41; for, when a long time after this Jesus again came to this locality, the people there recalled the Baptist's testimony. Since the evangelist

is concerned only with the testimony itself, he adds very little, centering our entire attention upon the Baptist's words, which certainly also deserve all the attention we are able to bestow. **On the morrow he sees Jesus coming towards him and declares, Behold, the Lamb of God, which takes away the sin of the world.** Since this occurred on the very next day, the place must also be the same. We may picture the Baptist somewhere in the neighborhood of the village in the midst of his work. John's record is strictly historical. He uses two finite verbs: John "sees" and "declares," instead of reducing the first verb to a participle: he "seeing . . . declares." He would lay equal stress on the two actions. The two present tenses are the dramatic present, reckoned, however, as aorist in force since they intend to record only the fact of the actions, although in a realistic and vivid way, as if the reader were witnessing what transpires. These tenses are touches in the narrative which make us feel John's deep personal interest: as he writes "sees" and "declares" the entire action is before him although it lies decades in the past.

Only the fact of Jesus' approach is mentioned, for this much is needed for the Baptist's words, who could not well say, "Behold, the Lamb," etc., unless Jesus were near. The surmise that Jesus was coming to be baptized is incorrect, for the Baptist's testimony on the previous day rests on the revelation that immediately followed Jesus' baptism. Likewise the surmise that Jesus was coming to say farewell; for he remained the entire following day, v. 35. Most likely the purpose of his coming was to win disciples, for this is what he actually did as the following episode shows. The present participle pictures Jesus as he gradually comes toward the Baptist. While he is busy with his work the Baptist looks up and sees Jesus coming, βλέπει indicating a momentary glance with the impression it registers (not ὁρᾷ, indicating comprehension and activity of the mind). While Jesus is still a way off, these words fall from the Baptist's lips while, as we may suppose, his outstretched arm indicates the approaching figure. They are deathless words, after all those years that intervened before John places them in his Gospel still freighted with meaning infinitely richer than the mind of John grasped at the moment when these words first fell upon his ears and penetrated to his heart.

The imperatival interjection "Behold!" is dramatic, pointing out Jesus, riveting all eyes upon him, opening all ears for what the speaker will say of him. Here we have a sample of the perfect reproduction of the words originally spoken. After all the intervening year the evangelist might have reproduced the Baptist's words in a much cooler form. Indelibly impressed upon his heart, where the Spirit kept them unchanged, he records them exactly as they were spoken. "The Lamb of God," ὁ ἀμνὸς τοῦ Θεοῦ, with its significant article point out Jesus as the one particular Lamb of God, the Lamb in the most eminent sense of the word. Compare *"the* prophet" in v. 21 and similar uses of the Greek article. The genitive is a true possessive: the Lamb which belongs to God, *his* Lamb, i. e., which he ordained as a sacrifice for himself. This is far better than to make the genitive: the Lamb which comes from God (origin), or which God presents to the world. The word "Lamb" connotes sacrifice, the Lamb whose blood is to be shed. Thus also and especially in the full title, "Lamb of God," lies the idea of being without blemish, i. e., sinlessness, and joined with this the divine purpose and aim of substitution, expiation, and redemption. A truer and more expressive title could hardly have been found for the Savior; he was, indeed, "the Lamb of God." In his *Westminster Sermons* Trench has well said, the Baptist's title for Jesus should not be referred back to this or that particular "lamb" mentioned in the Old Testament rituals, but rather to all of them, since each could typify and illustrate prophetically only some part of the stupendous work God's own Lamb would perform.

The attributive participle describes this Lamb, "which takes away the sin of the world." The present tense ὁ αἴρων is frequently used to furnish a characterization of a person: this is the kind of a Lamb Jesus is. The verb itself may mean either "to take up and bear" or "to take away," "to remove." For the latter compare John 11:48; 15:2; 17:15; 19:31 and 38, passages which show that this meaning is beyond doubt. If the meaning "to take up," "to bear," is preferred, the force of the present tense would be peculiar: the Lamb in the act of taking up. Something would have to be supplied, namely, the very thought brought out by the other meaning. For this Lamb will not again lay down its burden, will not carry its burden indefinitely, but will take it completely away. So we correct Luther's version *traegt* and abide by our English versions, "taketh away." Nor is it necessary to make ὁ αἴρων a timeless present, one that indicates only the quality of the action irrespective of the time that may be involved. Cases occur in which the time feature practically disappears. But here Jesus at this very moment is engaged in removing the sin of the world. He had just assumed this burden by assuming the office of mediation at his baptism; and his baptism itself signifies that, though he is sinless himself, he ranges himself alongside of sinners to take on himself and bear away the load they never could bear.

The thing to be taken away is named "the sin of the world," τὴν ἁμαρτίαν τοῦ κόσμου (world of men). This is one of those great collective singulars, so easily

pronounced by the lips without proper comprehension
by the mind. The idea is that of a mass, all sins as
one great body are called "sin," *una pestis, quae
omnes corripuit,* Bengel. Like most of the terms for
sin, this term, too, is negative, "missing the mark,"
i. e., the one set by the divine law, missing it by
thought, word, or deed, yea, by our very condition
which is corrupt by nature. As many men as there
have been, are now, and will be in the world, each
with his daily life stained with many sins, so many
individual masses of sin are formed, and all these
masses are combined in one supermass, "the sin of
the world." Isa. 53: "He laid on him the iniquity
of us all" . . . "for the transgression of my people was he stricken" . . . "thou shalt make his
soul an offering for sin" . . . "he bare the sin
of many." We may unfold this collective by taking
the law and dwelling on all the many kinds, types,
forms, and effects of sin. Again we may set forth
the deadly, damning power of a single sin, and then
multiply this power a million fold and again a million
fold. Yet we should not make the rather specious —
merely abstract — distinction between the "sin" itself and the "guilt" of sin, for sin exists nowhere
apart from its guilt, and guilt nowhere apart from
its sin. The same is true with regard to "sin" and
its "consequences." As the guilt inheres in the sin,
so the consequences stick to the sin, closer than a
shadow. Neither the guilt nor the consequences are
taken away, really taken away, unless the sin itself
is taken away. With the sin also its guilt and consequences are cancelled. "World" means the universe
of men from Adam onward to the last babe born just
before the judgment breaks. "That taketh away the
sin of the world" includes the entire work of Christ,
especially and most directly his sacerdotal work, his
active and his passive obedience.

It is idle and nearly always misleading to ask regarding the Baptist or regarding his disciples, to what extent they comprehended the testimony here uttered. The Baptist spoke by revelation, he uttered thoughts which towered above his own mind. They still tower above ours although we now have the full New Testament light. And yet, as in the case of Simeon, Anna, and the long line of Old Testament prophets (Isa. 52:15; 42:6, 7; 49:6, 7), the Baptist uttered no empty sounds as far as his own mind and heart were concerned, no riddles or enigmas without key or solution, but glorious truth which his own mind beheld as truth, absorbed and penetrated more and more, in which his own heart trusted with ever-increasing joy. One thing is certain, that the Baptist understood his own words far more perfectly than many who are today regarded as great theological leaders and interpreters in the church. Nor should it be thought that the evangelist here puts his own later thoughts into the Baptist's mouth. The Baptist's word to his disciples is not treated as a thing unheard of, an impossible extravagance; it does not repel but attracts these men to follow Jesus as being, indeed, the Lamb of God.

The Baptist's word has passed into the confessions of the church, also into the catechisms for instruction, as one of the clearest proofs for the universality of the atonement and the redemption. It has likewise passed into all her devotional literature, especially also into her hymns for public worship: "O Christ, thou Lamb of God" (*Agnus Dei*) in the Communion service; "Lamb of God, O Jesus"; "Lamb of God, without blemish"; "A Lamb bears all the guilt away"; "Lamb of God, we fall before thee"; "Not all the blood of beasts"; endless other incidental references, often combined with the thoughts of Rev. 5:6; 13:8; 12:11; 22:1. Luther: "Sin has but two places where it may be; either it may be with you, so that it lies upon your neck, or upon Christ, the Lamb of God. If now it lies upon your neck, you are lost; if, however, it lies upon Christ, you are free and will be saved. Take now whichever you prefer."

30) **This is he of whom I said, After me cometh a man who is become before me, for he was first compared with me.** This paradoxical description with its solution is identical with v. 15 and is here recorded in its historical setting, whereas in v. 15 it is quoted merely for the sake of its thought. The verbal variations are only formal: ἐστίν for ἦν, for Jesus is now present in person; ἔρχεται ἀνήρ ὅς for the masculine ὁ ἐρχόμενος. Here is a beautiful example of what Verbal Inspiration really means. It is not a reproduction of so many letters, syllables, and *Woerter*, but a reproduction in which every word and expression are true to the intent and the thought of the divine Spirit. It is not mechanical but dynamic, living, and hence free in form; but never imperfect, inadequate, or faulty, but inerrant in every expression. The exposition of this verse is found under v. 15.

31) All that follows in v. 31-34 is really one piece which forms the full and complete answer to the question that would naturally arise in the minds of the Baptist's hearers as to how he could be so sure of the great things he was saying about Jesus. This certainty he did not have of himself, but being the chosen instrument through whom God purposed to make Jesus manifest to Israel, the great revelation was granted to him which establishes the certainty forever. And that, too, is why the evangelist recorded the Baptist's testimony regarding the revelation to him and regarding the resultant certainty for him. This record is more than a recital of the history of Jesus' baptism; it is the Baptist's own exposition of that history, showing what it meant for him. **And I knew him not, but**

**that he should be made manifest to Israel, for this
came I baptizing with water.** Twice the Baptist
freely admits, "I knew him not," which in its connection means, "him" in his divine greatness. The Baptist
had known Jesus personally since childhood and may
have had his own personal convictions regarding who
Jesus really was. All this is here brushed aside, for
a prophet's certainty must come from a higher source,
from one that is beyond all question. We may note
the three successive κἀγώ, "and I," here and in v. 33
and 34. For none of them we need "even I," since
ἐγώ is emphatic enough, and "even" would introduce
a comparison where none is intended. While ᾔδειν is
pluperfect in form, it is one of those forms in which
the durative idea alone is left and thus is used exactly
like the imperfect: all along in the past the Baptist
was without the knowledge that was eventually vouchsafed to him in such a wonderful manner.

But the Baptist could not be left in this ignorance
and uncertainty, for God had sent him as the Messiah's
forerunner in order to make the Messiah known
to Israel. The absolute certainty regarding who and
what the Messiah was thus had to be given to the
Baptist. Thus ἀλλά = "but" in the sense of *aber* (not
sondern, Luther), it is an ordinary adversative not one
in contrast with a preceding negative. The ἵνα clause
is placed forward for emphasis and is made doubly
emphatic by the summary of it in διὰ τοῦτο: for this
very reason that he should be made manifest did John
come baptizing. The aorist φανερωθῇ denotes a purpose
actually accomplished not one merely attempted. The
verb itself is defined by what the following verses
relate: the Baptist was granted the experience to see
and to know who Jesus really was, and through the
Baptist this knowledge and certainty was to be communicated "to Israel." This is the course followed
by God throughout: chosen witnesses are granted

undoubted revelations, and their testimony communicates these revelations to the world.   Our entire Gospel constitutes such a communication; it consists entirely of such testimony.   Note "we beheld" in v. 14; "John bears witness" in v. 15; "this is the witness of John" in v. 19; "and says" in v. 29. God's way is not to the liking of many: instead of answering the divinely offered testimony which makes Jesus manifest as he actually is by ready and joyous faith, they dictate some other way to God, treat his testimony accordingly, and end in a maze of false "certainties."   Behind the passive "should be made manifest" is the agent of the action, God.   The correlative of "to manifest" or "to make manifest" is "faith" on the part of those who receive the manifestation.

Though Jesus as the Lamb of God takes away the sin of the world, the Baptist's mission was restricted to Israel, and his task was to make Jesus manifest only to his own nation. But this in the sense that Israel was to be only the first to know him; God had his own way for making Jesus manifest to all nations both by other witnesses and by using the Baptist's witness through these others, even as it is here used for the wide world through the evangelist.   The verb "came," *trat auf*, is the same as in v. 7 and denotes coming on a mission, but here ἐγώ makes the subject emphatic like οὗτος in v. 7, "*I*," whom God chose for this great purpose.   The fact that the Baptist's mission is referred to is evident from the addition, "baptizing with water."   The way in which the participle is added to the verb "came": "came baptizing," parallels v. 28, "was John baptizing."   This addition, "baptizing with water," does nothing more than to describe the distinctive feature of the Baptist's mission as the one to prepare the way for Jesus, as has been shown at length in connection with v. 26, "I baptize with water." The repetition of this expression in our verse fortifies the interpretation given in v. 26. It is out of line in these connections to regard "with water" as being in contrast with "with the Spirit," or to think that "with water" means "with nothing but water." The Baptist was commissioned to use this mode of lustration as an actual and an efficacious cleansing necessary for all Israelites who would receive their Savior by true faith.

32) In one respect v. 29, 30 stand out as a testimony by itself. So also v. 32-34. But the two are linked together by v. 31, so that what is said in v. 29, 30 rests on what is attested in v. 32-34. All that is contained in v. 29-34 was spoken at one time. The reason the evangelist inserts a little preamble in v. 32 is merely to emphasize that what now follows is the testimony that comes from the Baptist's own lips and constitutes the ultimate basis of all that he attested concerning Jesus. That, too, is why the verb ἐμαρτύρησεν is placed emphatically before the subject, "He bore witness," this man John, "when he said" what follows. The ὅτι. is recitativum, the equivalent of our quotation marks. **And John bore witness, saying, I have beheld the Spirit descending as a dove out of heaven, and he remained upon him.** The verb τεθέαμαι, one of the extensive perfects loved by the evangelist and well explained by R. 893, pictures what the Baptist beheld some time ago, when he had baptized Jesus, as a vision that is still before his eyes. The act is past and could prosaically be recorded by the aorist, "I did behold"; but this act was so effective that a "continuance of the completed action" may be predicated of it; hence this highly vivid perfect; compare another in v. 41. The verb denotes here, as well as in v. 14, a beholding filled with wonder and astonishment.

It is surely remarkable with what clearness and definiteness τὸ Πνεῦμα, the Third Person of the Godhead, is thus early named by the Baptist before his disciples and before the people in general without the addition of an explanatory remark. They seem to know who is referred to. No one raises a question. The same is true regarding ὁ υἱὸς τοῦ Θεοῦ in v. 34. The account of the other evangelists adds the detail that the Father was speaking from heaven and calling Jesus his Son. Those who deny that the Old Testament revealed the Trinity to the Jews, or who claim that it revealed the Trinity only dimly and imperfectly, have no explanation for the way in which the Baptist names the persons of the Godhead as being fully known to his Jewish hearers. Whence had they such knowledge? Later on the Jews object only to the fact that the insignificant looking Jesus calls himself God's Son and never raise the issue that God is but one person and not three. The old Jews must have read their Testament with clear eyes. As for the Baptist, he even "has *beheld* the Spirit."

There is no need to speculate as to how fully the Baptist grasped the reality of the three divine persons, as though the measure of his personal perception in any way might limit what he uttered by revelation. We ourselves utter many mighty natural facts, the full inner nature of which is not known to us. To rate the Baptist's personal knowledge low is unfair to this man of God. Because of his very nature the Spirit is invisible, but God never had difficulty when he wished to appear to the fathers. So here we are told how the Baptist could behold the Spirit by the participial modifier, "descending as a dove out of heaven," for which Luke has, "in a bodily form as a dove." Both the form and the descent were visible to the Baptist's eyes. The verb, "I have beheld," like the same verb in v. 14, cannot mean merely an inner beholding with the mind or the soul, an ecstatic vision, or anything else that excludes perception by the natural sense of sight. We are not told that the Baptist saw "a dove"; what he saw was "*as* a dove," a bodily form, indeed, but one that was "as" a dove. How did the Baptist know that this descending form was the Spirit? This was not his own surmise but the miracle announced to him in advance by his divine Sender, who thus not only prepared the Baptist for the miracle but gave him in advance the full significance of the miracle, v. 33. This, by the way, is always God's method: any special revelation he is pleased to make to a chosen witness is by God himself put beyond all doubt for that witness.

The question is constantly raised, "Why this form for the Spirit?" Luther's answer is: "God the Holy Spirit comes in a friendly form, as an innocent dove, which of all birds is the most friendly and has no wrath and bitterness in it; as a sign that he would not be angry with us but desires to help us through Christ, that we may become godly and be saved." Others point to purity, innocence, and meekness as being symbolized by the dove. It is easy to run into all kinds of fancies by picking up cues here and there regarding the term "dove." Gen. 1:3 is the only place in which an expression somewhat analogous occurs concerning the Holy Ghost. We may content ourselves by saying that the dovelike form intended to convey the idea of the graciousness of God's Spirit. The present participle καταβαῖνον describes the act of coming down in its progress, and what occurred when the dovelike form reached Jesus is then added, "and he abode upon him." The phrase "from heaven," without the Greek article, is as definite as our English equivalent (R. 792), and John always has the singular "heaven" (408). The grammarians (R. 440; B.-D. 468, 3) note that in v. 33 two participles are used, "descending and abiding upon him," whereas in our verse we have, "descending, and he abode upon him."

This change from the participle to a finite verb is usually explained as a desire to make the narrative more lively, or to turn the second action into a statement uttered by the Baptist. But the two participles are as beautiful and vivid as they well can be, and all that is said is stated by the Baptist. The difference is that in v. 33 the two durative present participles, "descending and abiding," are brought to a point of rest by the clause, "this is he," etc., i. e., conviction for the Baptist of the identity of Jesus. While in our verse the durative "descending" comes to rest in the finite punctiliar aorist, "and he did remain upon him," which leaves the matter at an end. This is the grammatical solution. In both cases we have what the Baptist saw. How long the dovelike form remained upon Jesus, who can say, and why should we ask? To strain ἐπ' αὐτον because of the accusative is unwarranted, since this case occurs also with verbs of rest.

All figurative interpretations of the dove must be rejected. Likewise, the view that an ordinary dove happened to circle over Jesus' head and flew down toward him. Equally to be rejected are the ideas of two kinds of vision, one of the senses and one of the spirit, namely, that what Jesus and the Baptist beheld was seen in the spirit and was only symbolized for their eyes (and ears, viz., the Father's speaking from heaven). As the shepherds actually saw and heard the angels, so the Baptist and Jesus (no reference occurs to any others as being present) saw and heard what here occurred when the Spirit came down and the Father spoke from above.

33) God told the Baptist in advance what he was about to behold and in advance informed him regarding the full meaning of what he should thus behold. This, too, the Baptist states in his testimony. **And I knew him not; but he that sent me to baptize with**

water, he said to me, Upon whom thou shalt see the Spirit descending and remaining upon him, this is he that baptizes with the Holy Ghost. The Baptist's testimony deals only with his own official interest in the wonderful event he witnessed, because his great Sender made this interest vital for him. Hence he says nothing concerning what the Spirit's bestowal meant for Jesus and his work; it is enough that this bestowal points out Jesus to him as the Messiah, shows him the divine greatness of Jesus, and indicates to him the Messianic climax of Jesus' work.

So he again states that before this time he did not know "him," i. e., that Jesus actually was the Messiah (see the comment on v. 31). God himself removed this uncertainty: *I* did not know him, *God* did and made him known to me in a way that was beyond all doubt. If one should be bold enough to ask why God did not simply tell the Baptist, "Jesus is the one," since he spoke to the Baptist; the answer is evident: God desired to do more than merely to point out the person, for which a word would have sufficed; he desired to display to the Baptist the divine character, the divine qualification, and the final saving act of Jesus as the Messiah. God is described as "he that sent me to baptize with water," the substantivized aorist participle characterizing God by means of the one act of sending. But this designation connects what God now does with God's original act of commissioning the Baptist. Just as the Baptist once received his mission, so he now receives this vital communication during his mission. Just as he accepted that original mission and labored in it, so he now accepts this communication and uses it. "To baptize with water" means exactly what it does in v. 26 and v. 31: to use this means of grace in preparing Israel for the coming of the Savior. When it happened that God spoke to the Baptist is not intimated; we can-

not even conjecture how long the interval lasted between the divine communication and the event which
it foretold. How God spoke to the Baptist is also left
untold, although we know that God is never at a loss
to find ways of making known to his servants what he
desires; he has many ways.

John quotes his Sender's words verbatim, "Upon
whom thou shalt see," etc. As far as firsthand competent testimony is concerned, this as well as all else
that the Baptist states meets every test. The modal
ἄν may be absent in the Koine, and when it is used
with a relative it may also be ἐάν. The futuristic subjunctive implies that presently the Baptist shall see
even as he did. On the two participles "descending
and remaining" we have already said what is needed
in v. 32. Since the relative phrase "upon whom" cannot well be repeated with the second participle, the
pronoun is used instead, "and remaining upon him,"
R. 724. The resumptive and emphatic οὗτος (see v. 2)
picks up the full description of the subject, to which
the predicate is then added. Since this is a substantivized participle, it needs the article in the Greek:
This is "the one baptizing with the Holy Ghost."

Here baptizing with water and baptizing with the
Holy Spirit form a kind of contrast, although only
incidentally, as John states the features of his humbler
mission, and as God himself states the supreme mission of his Son Jesus. The Baptist is called to
administer that means of grace which employs water,
Jesus will eventually miraculously pour out the Holy
Spirit to carry on his saving work in all the world.
The Baptist can only begin the great work and do
only part of it, only assist to prepare men for the
great Savior and for receiving the benefit of his
supreme work. Jesus will perform the mighty
work, and when redemption has been won, he will
make this redemption accessible to all men by sending

the Spirit to make this redemption their own. The commentary on our passage is Acts 1:5, "For John truly baptized with water; but ye shall be baptized with the Holy Ghost, and not many days hence," namely on the day of Pentecost, Acts 2; and the extension of this in Acts 11:16, the case of Cornelius and his relatives. None but the Messiah could baptize in this manner, and this Baptism with the Holy Ghost, once accomplished, cannot be repeated. The crucifixion and the resurrection, and the Spirit's outpouring, because of their very nature cannot be repeated.

In John's statement the major emphasis should not be placed on the two phrases "with water" and "with the Holy Spirit," thus making John's Baptism devoid of the Spirit and changing Jesus' act into something that is not suggested by the words. Let us note that all the faith and the godliness found in the Old Testament was wrought by the Spirit. All that the Baptist did by his preaching and his Baptism when he brought men to μετάνοια εἰς ἄφεσιν ἁμαρτιῶν (Luke 3:3) was wrought by the Spirit, for no true repentance and no real remission is possible apart from him. But until the day of Pentecost this work of the Spirit was limited, and that in two ways: in extent, it did not yet apply to the whole world; hence also in its nature, it was waiting for and pointing forward to the promised redemption to be accomplished in the great work of the Savior. Finally the miraculous Baptism with the Holy Ghost and fire took place on Pentecost, and now all restrictions were removed, the Spirit would now work among all nations and in all languages, Acts 2:8, etc., and would now make known all the revelation Jesus had brought. Since Pentecost the Spirit, once poured out, flows on and on through the world in the blessed stream of the means of grace. He is present and works with all his power wherever the Word is truly preached, wherever the two Sacraments are administered according to Christ's institution. Through the Word and the Sacraments the Spirit is given, and through these means alone. Through these means we today receive the Baptism of the Spirit. There is no other "Baptism by the Spirit." It is utterly impossible for any soul to come into contact with the Spirit save through these means. By these means he works regeneration, conversion, justification, and sanctification. No sudden seizure by the Spirit without these means takes place; no total instantaneous "sanctification" is thus wrought; no "second blessing" is bestowed. These views and their products are pathological human autosuggestions that may seem spiritual but lack the Spirit. In v. 33 we have only "Spirit," but here the full title "Holy Spirit" is used.

34) The Baptist rounds out and completes his testimony by a final statement. **And I have seen and have witnessed that this is the Son of God.** As one who himself saw, the Baptist is a competent witness. He did not merely see, God enlightened him in advance in regard to what he came to see, which makes his witness competent in the highest degree, for he saw with eyes enlightened by God's own revelation. The two perfect tenses are again extensive perfects as in v. 32, "I have seen," and the vision is still before my eyes as though I were still seeing; "I have witnessed," and my testimony stands as though I kept giving it continuously. Again ἐγώ is emphatic, "*I*," whom God chose for this purpose. The verb is varied from that used in v. 32: θεάομαι, "to behold" with a long look of wonder and astonishment; but now ὁράω, "see" with understanding and comprehension.

This meaning of the verb is matched by the object in the ὅτι clause which, of course, belongs to both verbs. What the Baptist "beheld" he states in v. 32; what he "saw" in what he thus beheld and what accordingly he testified he now states, "that this is the Son of God." This, however, is not a deduction made by the Baptist, one which we should thus feel we must test for ourselves before we accept it. In this summary the Baptist repeats what the Father's voice declared from heaven, "This is my Son beloved, in whom I was well pleased," ὁ υἱός μου ὁ ἀγαπητός, Matt. 3:17. Here the Baptist corroborates the evangelist's "God Only-begotten," v. 18, and agrees with all the other evangelists who make the attestation in the same connection. All efforts to reduce the term "the Son of God" to something less than essential Sonship, something less than "very God of very God" (Nicene Creed), by the contention that this title is one of the outworn ancient "categories of thought" beyond which we moderns have progressed, are less than Arianism and its allied denials and are but the old rationalism garbed in a somewhat modern dress. Since the Baptist quotes God himself when calling Jesus "the Son of God," the plea that this is an outworn category of thought makes the charge that the Eternal is guilty of using such a category. The other alternative is that the Gospel records themselves are false, and that God never called Jesus "my Son." The further comments made in connection with v. 32 on "the Spirit," in regard to the Baptist's own understanding of his words and in regard to the Jews and their knowledge regarding the Three Persons of the Godhead from the Old Testament, apply here as well as in v. 32.

Be placing the name "the Son of God" last the evangelist brings this testimony of the Baptist to a grand climax. All along the evangelist presumes that his readers know the historical fact of the baptism of Jesus and of the outpouring of the Spirit upon Jesus, as well as Luke's account of the Pentecost miracle. Hence these histories are not retold, nor are any new features of these histories brought forward by the evangelist. The great thing he does in the present record is to bring to our attention in the testimony made once for all by the Baptist the essential reality that stands out for all time, unchanged and unchangeable, in what occurred at the river Jordan when Jesus came unto John.

35) **On the morrow again John was standing and two of his disciples.** The three datives of time "on the morrow," τῇ ἐπαύριον (ἡμέρᾳ), which head three consecutive paragraphs, are all alike, each refers to the day that immediately succeeds the one mentioned before. To insert one or more other days at any point between these "morrows" is without warrant. When John here adds "again" he means to say that in a manner what the Baptist said on this day is a repetition of what he said on the day before. Here was the Baptist "again" standing in a prominent place and "again" proclaiming Jesus as the Lamb of God. The pluperfect form ἱστήκει (also written εἱστήκει) is like the similar form in v. 31 (which see), an imperfect in meaning, and while here it is coordinated with the following λέγει, it is after all circumstantial, since the chief thing is not the standing but the testimony here once more uttered by the Baptist. The finite form "was standing" makes this action more prominent than a mere participle would do.

In a simple way the person of "John" is distinguished in the scene here sketched, namely by placing the verb first and by using the singular and by placing the Baptist's name immediately after it. Two other persons, not yet named, also "were standing," but they are secondary as compared with the Baptist, hence are merely added, "and two of his disciples," ἐκ in the partitive sense in place of the genitive. Not incidentally, say somewhere along the path over which these three had come, did the Baptist repeat his great testimony concerning Jesus; no, he waited until he reached the spot where he had made this proclamation on the day before. There he once more "stood" as the great herald of the Messiah. We must not miss the impressiveness of what the verb conveys. This, too, is a touch that marks the writer as an eyewitness. Other details, such as what the Baptist was doing at this time, are irrelevant.

36) Now comes the chief feature: the Baptist looks up, sees Jesus walking some little distance away, and at once solemnly repeats his testimony of the day before. **And he looked upon Jesus as he was walking and declares, Behold, the Lamb of God.** The aorist participle ἐμβλέψας merely records the fact, and the dative object is regular with this compound verb. The Savior is described as "walking." That is different from the scene of yesterday when Jesus came directly to the Baptist, v. 29. We have no intimation that the participle "as he was walking" is meant in a figurative sense: engaged in his calling. Jesus, indeed, had assumed his office and Savior work, yet the mere statement of his walking imparts nothing on that point. We are not even told whence he came or in what direction he was going. We may surmise from what follows that he was proceeding to the place where he lodged at this time. What had brought him close to the Baptist's preaching place we cannot say, except that the whole narrative shows, that he was ready to gather the first disciples about him — that at least is what he actually began to do on this memorable day. Thus the Baptist looked upon Jesus as he was walking and, seeing him, "declares." The tense is the present, λέγει, explained in connection with v. 29. The Baptist's words still sound in his ears although they were spoken decades ago.

The words themselves, "Behold, the Lamb of God," are identical with those of the day before and, although they stop short with this exclamation, evidently intend to recall the fuller statement of the previous day.

Still more must be said. The full testimony of the previous day was addressed to all those present, all of the Baptist's disciples (3:26) and the multitude (10:41); see v. 29. The situation is now different. Only two of the Baptist's disciples are present, and thus this renewed testimony is directly addressed to them. They have had time to meditate on what they heard yesterday. Perhaps they had begun to feel what lay in the words as far as they were personally concerned. If Jesus was the Messiah, if their own master, the Baptist, attested him as the Messiah and that by divine revelation, then they must follow that Messiah. Did not the call to do that lie in the very first announcement of their master? And now the word is repeated — in a brief, pointed, almost challenging manner, "Behold, the Lamb of God!" Now it did penetrate. Some think that others besides the two disciples were present, but the record has no trace of others. These two, personally addressed by their master, at once proceed to act. Their master had rendered them the very highest service: he had given them God's call to follow Jesus.

The exposition of the words, "Behold, the Lamb of God!" is found under v. 29.

37) **And the two disciples heard him speak and they followed Jesus.** Two simple aorists record the great facts. Here is an example of the Word rightly heard. And why speak or think of man's natural powers when the Word is present with its efficacious power of grace? When the Baptist uttered the same words on the previous day, these two disciples also heard and yet they did not act. It is idle to speculate; yet we may recall in our own case how we, too, often need a second or a third invitation. Verbs of hearing are followed by the genitive to indicate the person heard, while the thing heard is placed in the accusative.

Faith comes by hearing, Rom. 10:17. There is but one
right answer to the truth — faith.

"They followed Jesus" here, of course, means that
the two disciples left the Baptist where he was standing and started to walk after Jesus. This was exactly
what the Baptist desired, "He must increase, but I
must decrease," 3:30. Yet beneath this obvious outward meaning lies a hint of something more. We
know to what this following led in their case, and
how the very word was afterward used by Jesus himself when calling men to discipleship, v. 43. "They followed Jesus," thereafter never to turn from him.

38) They surely did not go very far until, in
John's simple way of telling it, Jesus turned and spoke
to them. **Now Jesus, having turned and having beheld them following, says to them, What are you
seeking? And they said to him, Rabbi (which is
to say, when interpreted, Teacher), where art thou
staying?** The minor actions of turning and of beholding are expressed by participles, and their aorist
tense indicates merely the fact and the thought that
it preceded the speaking. After θεασάμενος the accusative pronoun and its present participle: having beheld "them following," is altogether regular. How
aoristic λέγει is we see in the sequence: λέγει (present)
. . . εἶπον (aorist) . . . λέγει (again present).
We might well translate, "he said . . . they said
. . . he said." On this aoristic present see v. 29.

The Baptist urges these two men to go to Jesus,
and Jesus opens his arms to receive them. Jesus first
speaks to them who might have been too timid themselves to address him. Since their following him
shows that they seek him, Jesus does not inquire
whom they seek but, *"What* are you seeking?" This
first word spoken by Jesus is a master question. It
bids them look searchingly at their inmost longings

and desires. "We are accustomed to seek what we have lost, or what otherwise is beneficial or desirable for us. But what was there more desirable, more longed for during forty centuries past on the part of so many illustrious men, the patriarchs, judges, kings, prophets, and all the saints of the Old Testament, than this Lamb of God, which John's testimony on the heights between the Old and the New Testament declared to be present at last?" Calov. Many are seeking what they should not, and others are not seeking what they should. Let us, too, face this question of Jesus in order that we may cast out all self-seeking, all seeking of ease in Zion, all worldy ambition even in churchly things, all unworthy aims, and rise to the height of our calling both as believers and as the called servants of the Lord, and let us help to confront others with this same question that they, too, may find in Jesus what he came to bring. For a hidden promise lies in the question, "What are you seeking?" Jesus has the highest treasure any man can seek, longs to direct our seeking toward that treasure in order that he may bestow it for our everlasting enrichment. Note how this verb "seek" corresponds to the verb "we have found" in v. 41 and 45.

The answer of the disciples is a question, "Rabbi, where art thou staying?" They address Jesus with the usual respectful title given to Jewish teachers. The Hebrew *rab*, an adjective meaning "much, great, mighty," was made a title: *Oberster* or "Master," the Greek equivalent for the honoring title "Teacher" (margin, R. V.). By a parenthetical relative clause John himself interprets the Hebrew title for his Greek readers and retains the vocative, though it is the predicate: Διδάσκαλε, R. 416, 432, 465. With the Hebrew suffix for "my" we have *rabbi* or *rabbei*, although this possessive was hardly more than formal. Jesus accepts this title even to the last, as we see in 13:13,

although Κύριος, "Lord," soon came to be used more
frequently by his disciples. The two disciples of the
Baptist do not venture to use a title derived from
their own master's designation of Jesus as "the Lamb
of God" or "the Son of God," v. 34. These designations certainly had their illuminating effect upon them
and yet were not of a kind to lend themselves to personal address in conversation. In the question, "Where
art thou staying?" lies the desire to have a private,
undisturbed conversation with Jesus regarding the
high thoughts and hopes which had begun to stir their
hearts. One cannot say whether they expected to con-
fer with Jesus at once or meant merely to find out
where he lodged in order to meet him later. They
probably intended to leave that to Jesus.

39) They are invited at once. **He says to them,
Come, and ye shall see. They came, accordingly,
and saw where he stayed; and they stayed with him
that day. The hour was about the tenth.** Jesus
places himself and the humble place where he lodges
at their service without delay. This readiness is
generous on his part and kind and satisfying for
them. There never was a time when Jesus was not
eager to satisfy hearts that truly sought his blessings. His answer is, "Come, and you shall see." They
would have been happy if Jesus had said, "Come to-
morrow or the next day and see me." But he opens
the door to them on the instant just as if he had been
waiting for them. Kings and the great men of the
earth hedge themselves about with servants and ceremony, so that it is difficult to reach them and get
speech with them; one must arrange an interview in
advance to secure audience at all. Nothing is easier
than to get an audience from the King of kings at
once.

The words are exceedingly simple — just a kind
invitation, "Come!" and a promise attached, "And you

shall see." But what significance lies in these few words! "Come!" meant, of course, to the lodging of Jesus; yet who that knows Jesus fails to read in this gentle imperative something of the meaning of those other invitations by which Jesus bade those that labor and are heavy laden to come unto him — to come from sin, from the world, from darkness, misery, damnation — unto him, unto pardon, peace, rest, and salvation? The present imperative ἔρχεσθε is here linked with the volitive future ὄψεσθε, which not only has some imperative force (R. 875) but even more, the note of assurance. To be sure, if the disciples would come, they would see the little place where Jesus stayed. But their desire went far beyond seeing this place. The entire conversation deals with deeper things. "You shall see" means: the place where you can speak to me and learn from me and about me all that prompts your hearts to follow me. The promise is broad, but the sequel shows that it was fully redeemed. We have an echo of this invitation and promise of Jesus in Philip's word to Nathanael, "Come and see!" v. 46.

Two simple historical aorists report the next facts, "They came, accordingly, and saw where he stayed," μένει, literally, as the Greek idiom requires, "where he stays." This was, perhaps, a house in a nearby hamlet or in Bethany itself, v. 28; or a temporary booth of wattles, covered, perhaps, with the striped aba, the usual cloth worn in the east (Farrar, *The Life of Christ*). To come — to see — to abide with Jesus has well been called an epitome of the entire Christian life. Another aorist completes the story, "and they stayed with him that day," the accusative of the extent of time. The prolonged stay is eloquent regarding the impression made on the heart of John and of his companion when they sat together with the Savior for the first time. We at once feel that these words relate one of John's experiences. Let us remember that they came from close association with another great master, the Baptist, the last great prophet of God whose disciples they had been and with whom they would inevitably compare Jesus. They had now found a greater — him of whom the Baptist had prophesied. Who would not like to know all that was said in that long interview in the humble lodging of Jesus? We know only the immediate effect: they could hardly tear themselves away, they remained the rest of the day. Then must have begun what John records in v. 14, "We beheld his glory, glory as of the Only-begotten, from the Father."

"The hour was about the tenth" — an incidental remark but one that is significant regarding the importance John attached to this meeting with Jesus and evidence that he himself wrote this Gospel. That hour shone bright in his memory until his dying day. But what point of time does the evangelist mean by "the tenth" hour? To ask this question is easier than to answer it. The best students have wrestled with the question as to how John calculates his hours. See, besides our present passage, 4:6; 4:52; 11:9; 19:14.

The crux of the problem really lies in John 19:14, where we read that Pilate pronounced sentence on Jesus at the sixth hour. The crux results because we read in Mark 15:25 that Jesus was crucified at the third hour. If both follow the Jewish mode of counting the hours, beginning with the break of day and counting twelve hours until sunset, the two statements would be sadly contradictory. One would say that Pilate sentenced Jesus at noon, the other that Jesus was crucified at nine o'clock. Inherently the statement of Mark, who beyond question followed the Jewish mode, is correct. The trial was hastened, the Jewish leaders had their festive arrangements to make. It does not seem likely that it required the entire half of the day to reach the point where Pilate pronounced sentence. The crux remains if we assume that John followed the Roman method of counting the hours, beginning at midnight with twelve hours until noon, and twelve more until midnight. Moreover, the Romans counted the hours in this way only for the *civil* day, for ordinary purposes they, too, reckoned twelve hours from sunrise to sunset. Reckoning according to the civil day, Pilate would pronounce sentence at six in the morning, which is both quite too early for all that happened since daybreak, and again too early for the crucifixion at nine, since sentence, once pronounced, was executed without delay, not requiring a delay of three hours. This is a statement of the problem.

No satisfactory solution has yet been found. Two that are offered bear the stamp of desperate expedients on their face. One is that some ancient copyist made an error in copying John 19:14. But the reading is assured. If all difficulties could be removed by the little key, "an error in transcription," much fruitful research would never have been undertaken. The other solution is still worse: Mark 15:25 is wrong, John 19:14 intends to contradict and to correct Mark. Again, this is rather easy: call one statement wrong, and your problem is solved. No; the problem must leave both Mark and John as they stand, and the solution must show that both are correct. Until this is done, we must confess that we do not know how John counted his hours. One suggestion is that he followed more than one method; but this seems improbable. Counted in the Jewish fashion, the tenth hour would be four o'clock in the afternoon — somewhat late for the statement: καὶ παρ' αὐτῷ ἔμειναν τὴν ἡμέραν ἐκείνην, although this satisfies some. According to the Roman civil reckoning the tenth hour would be ten in the morning, and this would agree well with the statement that the two disciples remained through that day, but it creates the other difficulties already noted regarding 19:14 when this passage is read according to this reckoning.

40) Not until this point does John mention a name, and here he mentions only the one. It seems to be a habit with John to append data such as names of persons and of places at the end of his narratives. **Andrew, the brother of Simon Peter, was one of the two that heard John and followed him.** Involuntarily we ask: "Who was the other of the two? and why is he not also named here?" We know the answer: "The other is John, the Apostle, himself, who never mentions his own name in his Gospel nor the name of any of his relatives." A comparison of the data establishes this fact beyond a doubt. By mentioning only Andrew, John does not intimate which of the two, he or Andrew, was the first in making the move to follow Jesus. He merely combines the two, first in hearing the Baptist's testimony and then in following Jesus. That is all. Only of one thing we may be sure: if Andrew had made the first advance, John would have recorded it to Andrew's credit although he wrote this Gospel years after Andrew was dead. Either both acted at the same moment and from the same impulse, or — and this is quite possible — John was the first and in his modesty declines to take the credit in a Gospel written by himself.

When naming Andrew the evangelist at once calls him Simon Peter's brother whithout further explanation, thus assuming that his readers know both men from reading the other three Gospels which had been written years before. Andrew's brother, however, is not mentioned merely in order to help to identify Andrew by means of his greater brother but apparently because of what John is now about to add to his narrative. This brother, too, is at once called by his double name "Simon Peter" because in a moment we shall hear how Jesus himself gave Simon his second name. In the Greek ἐκ is partitive, and in the genitive τῶν δύο we see that the dual form has disappeared from the Greek of this period. The two participles are made attributive to δύο by the repetition of the article and are aorist because they state the past facts that occurred prior to the time indicated by ἦν; we might translate, "who had heard John and had followed him (Jesus)," construing παρά with the first participle, "had heard from John" when he spoke those notable words.

41) This verse is closely attached to the foregoing by means of οὗτος, "this one," which resumes all that has just been said regarding Andrew; the English "he" is not emphatic enough. **This one as the first finds his own brother Simon and tells him, We have found the Messiah, which is, when interpreted, Christ.** John reports this concerning Andrew and Simon after having drawn especial attention to the former in the previous verse. Nothing is said directly concerning himself and *his* brother James. And yet truth compelled John to intimate something concerning himself. The reading πρῶτον, which some prefer, should give way to πρῶτος. If we keep the adverb, an incongruity results, for Andrew is then said to "find first," as if he did something else next — yet nothing else is reported. If we use the adjective we learn that Andrew *as the first* of the two disciples mentioned finds his own brother, leading us to infer that John, as the second of the two, was a close *second* also in finding *his own* brother. And this is the actual story. Thus also the reading πρῶτος is generally preferred. It goes well with the additional touch that Andrew finds "his own" brother, τὸν ἴδιον, instead of a simple αὐτοῦ, "his." It is all quite plain if we understand that John, too, "finds his own brother James." Yet we must note that John gives credit here, where

he is personally concerned, to the other man, Andrew — he was the first in the matter of this finding. In ὁ ἴδιος we have a strong possessive which is quite emphatic and convertible with the reflexive ἑαυτοῦ, although at times the adjective was used in an "exhausted" sense; see the discussion in R. 691, etc.

"He findeth" and "tells" are the vivid present in historical narrative, the action being very present to John's mind as he writes — of course, not only Andrew's action but also his own. From the verb "finds" we cannot determine whether Andrew and also John sought his brother or only happened upon him after leaving Jesus. But the situation itself as here portrayed, especially the deep impression made by Jesus on the hearts of the two visitors, leads us to think that both forthwith sought and found their brothers. They could not refrain from imparting what they had found in Jesus. We may also remember that Simon and James were likewise disciples of the Baptist, and if he directed Andrew and John to Jesus, he certainly wanted their brothers to follow the same course, namely likewise to attach themselves to Jesus.

Mark the word "findeth." It keeps recurring in a significant manner, twice in v. 41, and again in v. 43 and 45. So the man in the field "finds" the treasure, and the merchantman "finds" the pearl of great price. At best our seeking is only like a blind groping which would be useless if God in his mercy did not lay the great treasure so near us, direct our groping hands and blind eyes to it until, touching it at last, lo, we find it! Andrew's finding his own brother, John's finding his, is an excellent example of home mission zeal. Also from the very start we see a communion of saints in the following of Jesus: first two, whose faith is so blended together in the moment of its origin that we cannot tell which was the first, that of John or that of Andrew. And at once the number doubles, and the two are increased to four with two more immediately to join the four. This is how the church has grown and still grows to the present day.

The word with which Andrew greeted his brother is remarkable: "We have found the Messiah," which John interprets for his Greek readers, translating the term with "Christ." In v. 38 the case is preserved, "Rabbi," Διδάσκαλε, both vocatives; here the accusative "Messiah" is rendered by the nominative "Christ." In both cases the neuter ὅ refers to the word only as a word, and the participle may be combined with the copula to form a circumscribed present, or, since we have no call for this here, may be read as a modifier, "when interpreted," which we prefer. Andrew has the plural verb, "we have found," not the singular with inflectional "I." The church loves to make joint confession. Of course, the agreement in this quiet "we" means to strengthen the assurance for Simon. If John had had doubts or had hesitated in seconding Andrew, Simon would have been far less impressed. Here again we have the extensive perfect εὑρήκαμεν, "we have found," see v. 32 for the explanation of the tense, R. 893, and compare v. 34 and 45. The act of finding lies in the past, but the effect and result continue to the present. This is Andrew's glad news. "We have found him whom all Israel has been looking for!" Let us not miss the tremendousness of the announcement. The verb states a fact not a supposition, not a surmise, not a deduction, but an unqualified fact. Andrew did not *think* he had found; he *had* found and he *knew* he had.

John retains Andrew's "the Messiah" in the Aramaic just as he keeps "Rabbi" in v. 38, and writes Cephas in v. 42, though in each case he translates for his Greek readers. He writes as an original witness;

and these distinctive terms have a value of their own which ought to be preserved. It was natural for Andrew to use the title so familiar to the Jews, "the Messiah" — he in whom all their hopes and aspirations centered. The Messianic hope had in the first place drawn these men to leave their fishing nets up in Galilee and to come down to the lower reaches of the Jordan where the Baptist, the great herald of the promised Messiah, was baptizing. They had not been disappointed in him although he was only the advance herald. Now, however, their highest hopes were coming to fulfillment: they have found the Messiah himself. The Baptist had called him "the Son of God," v. 34, and most emphatically "the Lamb of God." This Andrew now restates in his own way just as Philip does a little later in v. 45. The Hebrew *Mashiach,* Aramaic *Meshiha,* is the Greek *Christos,* a verbal adjective made a noun, signifying "the Anointed One." The Greek name is derived from the ceremonial verb χρίω, "to anoint," as contrasted with the common verb ἀλείφω, any smearing with oil. The term is appellative, is like a descriptive title and designates the high office of the Promised One, whoever he may be. When this person was known as Jesus, the title "Christ" was used directly to name him, yet it always retained the original reference to the office involved. So also Andrew declares that he and John have found the person who is the Messiah.

To determine the nature of this office we must combine all that the Old Testament promised concerning the coming Savior, his prophetic, high priestly, and regal work. For that combined work he would be anointed, and by the anointing he would be formally invested with that work. As high as was this mighty office, so high, we know, was the act of anointing — God himself sending the Holy Spirit (not merely a few of his gifts) upon his chosen Servant. Again

the question is raised as to how far the knowledge of
Andrew reached regarding the Messiahship of Jesus.
It is enough to know that Andrew was making the
right beginning — Jesus himself would develop this
unto the fullest fruition. Whether John, when he met
his brother James, used the same designation for Jesus
— who can say? Of one thing we can be sure, he did
not employ a term that said less; and James, too, at
once followed Jesus.

42) **He brought him unto Jesus** with its historical aorist simply states the fact, which was certainly weighty enough in itself. It must have occurred
that very evening, for John carefully marks the days
in this section of his Gospel and does not write "on
the morrow" until we come to v. 43. Thus John also
rendered the same service to James that very evening
right after Andrew had done so. Peter became the
third disciple of Jesus, James the fourth, all of them
becoming disciples on that day. When they were
"brought" to Jesus they naturally were introduced to
him. We learn how Jesus received Simon and conclude that in some equally effective way he received
also James. One might stop with the outward act
of ἤγαγεν, "brought," but surely here is a hint that
Simon (and then James) was also brought spiritually to Jesus, brought so as to believe in him and
to follow him. That is what the following narrative
implies.

**Having looked upon him, Jesus said, Thou art
Simon, the son of John: thou shalt be called Cephas,
which is interpreted Rock.** The absence of a connective makes this narration stand out as an independent incident. Jesus lets his eyes rest on Simon
for a little while. John paints the scene by means of
the circumstantial participle ἐμβλέψας, compare v. 36,
also 29. John remembered that look of Jesus. The
attractive interpretation is offered that before

Andrew, when bringing Simon to Jesus, could say
a word, Jesus after one good look at Simon miraculously told who this man being brought to him was
and what he would become, thus in a double way dis-
playing his omniscience. The verb forms and the
tenses make this interpretation unlikely. John would
have had to write in one connection: ἄγων . . .
ἐμβλέψας . . . εἶπε, "while bringing him to Jesus,
after Jesus had looked upon him, he said," etc. But
John writes ἤγαγεν, which is wholly disconnected from
the next two actions. He makes two sentences without even "and" to join them. He connects only
ἐμβλέψας with εἶπε, this participle modifying the finite
verb. "He brought," an aorist verb, is an action complete in itself: Andrew actually and completely
brought his brother Simon. Then Jesus looked at
Simon and spoke as he did. Moreover, just to name
a stranger after one good look, even if it is actually
done, is too much like the tricks of charlatans to be
accepted by sober men as evidence of supernatural
power, to say nothing of omniscience. Even when
the thing is done in order to mystify, we have the just
suspicion (as in the case of spiritistic mediums) that
the name was secured in some secret and perfectly
natural way. Whenever Jesus makes revelations he
bars out all such impossibilities. As far as Simon's
name is concerned, Andrew as well as John may have
in their long interview with Jesus mentioned the fact
to him that they and their respective brothers (naming them) had come from Galilee to attach themselves
to the Baptist as disciples. Then ἤγαγεν would mean
that Andrew presented Simon saying, "This is my
brother." Or, if Jesus had not been told about this
brother in the interview, Andrew now "brought" him
to Jesus by saying, "This is my brother Simon, the
son of John." In general, we are constrained to follow the rule of interpretation which finds miraculous

action only where the text plainly demands it; *Wundersucht* is a mistake even in the case of the many miracles of Jesus.

After Andrew has made his introduction, Jesus looked at Simon. The participle ἐμβλέψας is sometimes misconceived as indicating a look that penetrated into the real character of Simon, so that Jesus now reveals that character when he renames Simon by calling him "Rock." The fact is that Simon had an impetuous character, and his impetuosity often led him into wrong actions. Thus he often shows anything but a solid and rocklike character. When Jesus renamed him he prophetically foretold what he would make of Simon by his grace.

The two statements, "Thou art Simon, the son of John," and, "Thou shalt be called Cephas," are parallels and direct opposites, each marked by the emphatic σύ, "thou." The one says what the man now is; the other, what he shall become and thus be called at some future time. "Simon, the son of John," is only the ordinary ancient way of stating a man's name in full by adding that of his father. It is the pointed contrast with the other name that this man shall come to bear which makes "Simon, the son of John," here mean: this is all that you are by natural birth and parentage; presently you shall be far more, something far higher, by the new power that will work upon you — you shall be called "Rock." Here, and in 21:15, etc., the faulty reading "Jonah" has been introduced in some texts from Matt. 16:17, which the margin of the R. V. unfortunately still passes on. Then fancy plays with "Jonah" = "dove," combining this with "Rock": from the son of a dove Simon shall become the rock where the dove finds refuge. This fancy also violates Πέτρος, a single boulder not a rocky cliff, which would be πέτρα, a feminine.

When Jesus declares, "Thou shalt be called Cephas," the verb means that he shall be called what he then shall actually be. Jesus here speaks with full authority and not like the Baptist who first had to receive a revelation. Here, too, Jesus is attesting himself as he continues to do in the next paragraphs. Here, however, the effect is not immediate. Jesus is ready to wait until Peter shall, indeed, have become what he now so positively promises him. The Hebrew *keph*, Aramaic *kepha*, is here rendered Πέτρος, since a single person is to bear this name: a boulder of rock, a large stone, and not πέτρα, a cliff of rock. Hence also: ὃ ἑρμηνεύεται, "which is interpreted," i. e., not, "which is translated." In v. 38 and 41 John writes μεθερμηνευόμενον, "when translated," although in v. 38 "Teacher" is not a real translation of "Rabbi," and some texts offer ἑρμενευόμενον, "when interpreted." The best interpretation of the name "Peter" Jesus afterward gave in Matt. 16:18, "Thou art Peter (Πέτρος), and upon this rock (ἐπὶ ταύτῃ τῇ πέτρᾳ) I will build my church," i. e., the confession of Christ which Peter had just made. Hence, not his original character or one later developed in Peter led Jesus to name him "Rock," but what Peter should become for others, i. e., for the church, which is "built upon the foundation of the apostles and prophets, Christ Jesus himself being the chief cornerstone." In this foundation Peter with his confession of Christ would be one of the apostolic foundation stones. His name Cephas indicates his future historical place in the church not his future personal excellence. Even as late as Gal. 2:11 we see Paul solid as a rock and Peter wavering again to such an extent that Paul had to rebuke him.

This rounds out the Baptist's testimony, recording not only that he made it but also that it proved effectual for its purpose: four of the Baptist's disciples believed in Jesus and became Jesus' disciples.

The First Attestation of Jesus Himself, 1:43-2:11.—
The testimony of the Baptist and that of Jesus link
into each other as the previous section shows. But
there the word of the Baptist still dominates, "Behold, the Lamb of God!" In what now follows we, indeed, have further effects of the Baptist's words, but
he himself is no longer before us. We now see Jesus
himself in full action. For the first time we hear the
significant call, "Follow me!" It carries the tacit implication that the first four who had come to Jesus
were already following him, i. e., had permanently
attached themselves to Jesus as their Master. Thus a
little band of men had been gathered. A few days
later we find them in Cana of Galilee. And now the
testimony of Jesus appears in the form of the first
miracle, the account of which closes with the words,
"and his disciples believed on him."

43) For the third time John writes "on the morrow" at the head of a paragraph. We thus have four
consecutive days beginning with 1:19. In 2:1 "the
third day" makes the first break. Therefore, Andrew
and John brought their brothers to Jesus on the evening of the previous day. Whatever the details of the
movements might have been, we abide by the days as
John indicates them, whether our imagination is able
to fill in the details with readiness or not. The view
that Andrew and John stayed all night with Jesus and
brought their brothers the next morning contradicts
what John writes when he now says "on the morrow."
**On the morrow he decided to go forth into Galilee
and he finds Philip. And Jesus says to him, Follow
me.** The aorist ἠθέλησεν implies that the intention
was carried out, otherwise the imperfect would be
used. The aorist infinite ἐξελθεῖν summarizes the entire
journey from Bethany beyond Jordan to Galilee. It
seems that Jesus announced his decision to the four
disciples who had attached themselves to him. Much

of his Messianic activity was to take place in this land despised by the Judean Jews. Galilee was less given to bigotry and narrowness. Matthew applies to this going of Jesus into Galilee the prophecy: "The land of Zabulon, and the land of Nephthalim, by the way of the sea, beyond Jordan, Galilee of the Gentiles; the people which sat in darkness saw great light; and to them which sat in the region and shadow of death light is sprung up," Matt. 4:15, 16.

At this point Jesus "finds" Philip. Note how this verb keeps recurring. So Christ, the gospel, and the gospel messengers keep finding men. It often seems accidental but it is all in the gracious plans of God. Commentators think that Philip must have come into contact with Jesus prior to this apparently sudden call. Strictly speaking, this is not correct, for the whole previous story, as John tells it, leads to the conclusion that he and Andrew were the first who came into direct contact with Jesus. But the indications show that John and Andrew, who first visited Jesus, reported what they had found not only to Peter and to James but also to Philip. The five were associated with each other as disciples of the Baptist; they came from the same city; and Philip's reply to Nathanael, "Come and see!" recalls Jesus' invitation to John and to Andrew. Why Philip did not at once with Peter and James go to Jesus that first evening we do not know. Perhaps he did not hear the news until late that night, until the four finally came away from Jesus. The call, "Follow me!" is so much like the other calls of Jesus that we must class it with them as a call to nothing less than discipleship. Not as a mere attendant on the way back to Galilee but as a permanent follower of Jesus, Philip is to join the little band. The present imperative, 'Ακολούθει μοι is durative to express a continuous course of action. What Philip replied is not recorded, we know from what follows that he joyfully obeyed. Philip's call is mentioned only incidentally as an introduction to the story of Nathanael and to testimony Jesus uttered in connection with his call.

44) **Now Philip was from Bethsaida, out of the city of Andrew and Peter.** This is a parenthetical explanation, showing the close connection between the men named and, as usual, is introduced by δέ. The preposition ἀπό is like the German *von,* and ἐκ, *aus,* is usual with πόλις, a variant of ἀπό for designations of home localities. Bethsaida, "House of Fish," lies west of and close to the Lake of Galilee, near Capernaum and Chorazin, its site at present is lost. On a recent visit to the Holy Land no trace of the place could be pointed out to us. The evangelist names only Andrew and Peter although Bethsaida was also his own home. If Philip's Greek name was derived from the Tetrarch Philip, he would be less than thirty years old. In the lists of the Apostles he is placed fifth, joined with Bartholomew and Thomas. Tradition reports that he afterward labored in Scythia and Phrygia and died in Hieropolis as a very old man.

45) Before the start to Galilee is made **Philip finds Nathanael and says to him, Him of whom Moses wrote in the law, and the prophets, we have found, Jesus, son of Joseph, from Nazareth.** Twice we here meet the significant verb "find," once in John's narrative, again in Philip's discourse; compare v. 34 and 41. Andrew's and John's finding is here repeated. Philip finds Nathanael by himself and at once pours out to him what now fills his heart. Nathanael = Theodore = God-given and is taken to be identical with Bartholomew, which is merely a patronymic. His home was Cana in Galilee whither Jesus was now going. It is but natural to suppose that he, too, was one of the Baptist's pupils and thus closely associated with the five who had already found the Christ. The

legend that he served as the conductor of the bride at the wedding in Cana is a fancy. Philip puts the object both in front of the verb and back of it, the latter by means of an apposition. Thus the entire emphasis rests on the object as if Philip says, "Just think *whom* we have found." He uses a descriptive clause to designate Jesus, "Him of whom Moses wrote in the law, and the prophets" but means exactly what Andrew said with the one word "Messiah." Philip's description of the Messiah is exactly to the point. In the closing apposition he names the person whom he has in mind, "Jesus, son of Joseph, from Nazareth."

"Moses and the prophets" often designates the Old Testament as such; it is sometimes also briefly called ὁ νόμος, the law. Here Philip separates the two terms: of whom Moses wrote in the law, in the Torah or Pentateuch, and (of whom) the prophets (wrote in their books). Moses is here said to be the author of the Pentateuch, which fact Jesus corroborates in 5:45, 46 and Luke 24:27. In his writings Moses transmitted the promises to the patriarchs; he gave Israel the law which with all its symbols and types points so directly to Christ; and in passages like Deut. 18:15-18 renewed the divine promise concerning the great Mediator Prophet to come. The entire history of Israel contained in the Pentateuch is senseless and purposeless without the Messiah, so that all that Moses wrote in the law actually refers to Christ. The prophets were the expounders of the law whose special duty it was not only to drive home the requirements and the threats of the law in the hearts of the people but also to hold out to them the glorious and comforting hope of the Deliverer to come, of whom they at times spoke directly as in Isa. 53. The Baptist continued this work in the most effective way, and we here have men trained in the Baptist's school, who naturally reveal their training. Philip spoke truly

when he said that the picture of the Messiah was
found in Moses and in the prophets. It has always
been there though the nation of the Jews eventually
refused to "find" and to see it, and modernism denies
that Moses "wrote" his five books and treats the prophets and their writings with the same destructive
criticism.

When Philip designates the promised Messiah as
"Jesus, son of Joseph, from Nazareth," this should not
be pressed to mean that Jesus was born in Nazareth.
Having lived in this town so long, naturally when anyone wanted to say from what place Jesus came he
would say "from Nazareth," ἀπό as in v. 44. The fact
that Jesus' home was in Nazareth may have been mentioned to his first followers by Jesus himself. He still
called himself "Jesus of Nazareth" in Acts 22:8. As
far as the wondrous conception of Jesus is concerned
and the actual place of his birth, Jesus preferred that
his disciples should first discover for themselves his
divine origin and nature and then learn the mighty
fact that he was conceived by the Holy Spirit and born
of a virgin. This applies also to the designation "son
of Joseph." Joseph was undoubtedly dead at this
time, probably had been for some years, since we hear
nothing at all concerning him after that memorable
visit to Jerusalem when Jesus spoke so plainly of his
real Father and of that Father's business. Yet the
fact is that Jesus actually was a "son of Joseph,"
namely legally; otherwise how could Joseph's name
occur in the genealogy of Jesus, Luke 3:23; Matt. 1:16?
To be sure, there is much more to the story of Jesus,
much that none of these disciples could know thus
early. But to say with Calvin that Philip here uttered
an error, yea two, is unwarranted. Philip uttered
facts, actual facts. He did not as yet know all the
facts, but when at last all would be known to him,

the last facts would illumine the first and not overthrow them.

Philip uses "we have found" exactly as Andrew did in v. 41; the tense is explained in v. 32, compare v. 34 and 41. The plural "we" now includes five and will impress Nathanael more than if Philip had said, "I have found." This plural also denotes the communion and fellowship of faith combined with joint confession. To say that Philip should have turned matters around, saying instead of "we have found," "we have been found," is only substituting one form of expression for another, both of which are true, although only the former fits here. No trace of synergism, of credit for himself, is found in Philip's, "we have found."

46) **And Nathanael said to him, Can any good thing come out of Nazareth? Philip says to him, Come and see.** Nathanael is not greatly impressed by Philip's enthusiastic, "we have found." He voices his doubt. Here the aorist εἶπεν is used beside the present λέγει, showing that the two are about equal in force, the latter adding a more vivid touch. Nathanael's question has bothered the commentators a good deal. "Any good thing," τὶ ἀγαθόν, is general but thus of necessity includes the good thing that Philip declares he and the others have found, the greatest possible Good Thing, the Messiah himself. If nothing good is to be expected out of Nazareth, how can the greatest good originate there? Nathanael can hardly be thinking of the smallness of Nazareth. We know nothing of evil reports concerning the place, and simply to surmise them is gratuitous. The later unbelief of the inhabitants cannot be referred to here; moreover, this was of the same kind as that which Jesus met with even in the very capital — Jerusalem. The fact that Nazareth cannot be reckoned with because it was

a town of the "Galilee of the Gentiles," a country despised by the men of Judea on this account, would require a mention of Galilee and a reference to Gentiles. The best explanation of Nathanael's doubting remark is that he knew nothing of any mention of Nazareth with regard to the Messiah in the law of Moses and in the prophetic promises to which Philip had made such strong references. We need not bring in Matt. 2:23, "He shall be called a Nazarene," for this is a play on words not a prophecy regarding Nazareth as being the home of Jesus; see Fausset, *Bible Cyclopedia*, 496, 3; Smith, *Bible Dictionary*, III, 2070.

Philip gives the finest kind of an answer, one that recalls the word of Jesus himself to John and Andrew, "Come and see!" The present imperative ἔρχου is combined with the aorist imperative ἴδε, thus differing from v. 39. This is excellent Greek, the first tense moving the action along until the action of the second tense brings it to a proper stop. To regard these two imperatives as equivalent to a condition, "If you come, you shall see," is to change the thought and to weaken its expression in spite of R. 949. Bengel calls this reply: *optimum remedium contra opiniones praeconceptas*, the best remedy against preconceived opinions. The answer was probably far better than Philip himself realized, for the only way to learn aright who Jesus is, is not to argue about him, about Nazareth, or about any other point that doubt may try to raise, but *to come* directly to Jesus himself (now in his Word, where he stands ready to meet us) and thus *to see*. This is the way Jesus led all his disciples, and they came, they saw, they were satisfied to the uttermost.

47) "Come and see!" is a call and an invitation, and while it is extended through Philip, it comes from Jesus himself who uses us to call others. In spite of

his doubts about a person from Nazareth being the
Messiah Nathanael comes to see. **Jesus saw Nathanael coming to him and declares concerning him,
Behold, truly an Israelite, in whom is no guile!**
Accompanying Philip, Nathanael was approaching
Jesus who thus "saw" him coming; εἶδεν merely notes
his approach, thus differing from θεασάμενος, "having
beheld," in v. 38, and from ἐμβλέψας, "having regarded,"
in v. 36 and 42. Jesus speaks to the four disciples
about him, "concerning" Nathanael, not to Nathanael
himself, yet he does this in such a way that Nathanael
hears what Jesus says about him. Jesus expresses
his joy at Nathanael's coming. Other instances similar to this one we note in the case of the Canaanitish
woman who cried after him, in the case of the centurion's humble and implicit faith, in the case of the
sinful woman in Simon's house, in the case of Zac-
chaeus' confession, in the case of the malefactor's
repentance. "They are not all Israel, which are of
Israel," Rom. 9:6, but Nathanael was one of them.

The adverb ἀληθῶς, "truly," "in truth or verity,"
modifies the entire statement, "Behold, here is in truth
an Israelite, in whom is no guile." Some connect
the adverb with the noun, but then an adjective should
have been used, "Behold, a true Israelite." Then, too,
the relative clause would merely define the adjective:
true because without guile. This would connote that
other Israelites were not true because they were full
of guile, a contrast that is entirely out of place here
where such Israelites are not thought of. Still less
can we draw the adverb to the relative clause, "in
whom truly is no guile," which ignores the position of
the word and removes the strong emphasis on "an
Israelite." This word of Jesus concerning Nathanael
can be understood only in connection with the conversation of Philip with Nathanael. In his divine way
Jesus knew what the two had said and how Nathanael,

instead of stiffening himself in his doubt about Nazareth, yielded to his desire for the Messiah and came
along with Philip. It cost Nathanael some effort to
come to a man from Nazareth; Jesus knows what it
cost him, and this rejoices his heart. Thus we cannot reduce this word of Jesus to mean merely that
Jesus sees the character of the man Nathanael; we
must elevate it to mean the character and quality of
his being an Israelite, a man who is absolutely sincere
about Israel's hope and salvation, so sincere that he
does not allow the mention of Nazareth to turn him
away from Jesus. Jesus' word does not mean that in
some way Nathanael will prove himself an Israelite,
indeed, as Simon would eventually be a Rock, but that
right here and now Nathanael is truly what he is.

The relative clause, "in whom is no guile," elucidates the adverb ἀληθῶς, and δόλος is cunning or deception as when one uses bait to catch fish or some cunning means to secure personal advantage. Nathanael
was without duplicity, altogether sincere. David calls
such a man blessed, Ps. 32:1, 2. Most men lack this
complete sincerity. Professing love to Christ, they
still secretly love the world and the flesh; promising
faithfulness, the promise does not fully bind their
hearts. This δόλος kept the Jewish nation from Christ,
proved the curse of Judas, almost wrecked Peter.
Church men and entire church bodies, while making
loud profession *sonoro tono*, yet squint secretly at
popular opinion, human authorities, supposed advantages, and with fair sounding excuses deviate from the
Word. "Blessed are the pure in heart, for they shall
see God," Matt. 5:8.

48) The implication of the narrative is that
Nathanael had never met Jesus before, also that Philip
had no opportunity to tell Jesus about Nathanael. No
wonder that, when Jesus touched the very center of

the desires and hopes of Nathanael, and did this even before this unprepared meeting, this filled him with astonishment. The question admits that Jesus knows Nathanael. The verb γινώσκεις is the present tense, speaking of the knowledge Jesus has just displayed in his words. Moreover, this verb signifies the true knowledge of insight or of experience. The aorist would be, "Whence didst thou come to know me?" and it would be out of place here. This question, at once coming to the lips of Nathanael as a genuine response to the words of Jesus, itself proves the man's utter sincerity as an Israelite, the very fact Jesus had expressed. Strike a beautiful bell, and it gives forth its sound on the instant.

Jesus answered and said to him, Before Philip called thee, when thou wast under the fig tree, I saw thee. The importance of this brief reply is shown by the two finite verbs in the preamble, "answered and said," which is stronger even than, "answered saying." The aorist passive ἀπεκρίθη is used as a middle to express replies of all kinds, as these are required not only by actual questions but also by actions and by situations. The answer of Jesus goes far beyond what Nathanael asked and what he expected. Jesus does not say, ἔγνων σε, "I knew thee," but, εἶδόν σε, "I saw thee," I perceived, noticed, observed thee. By this seeing Jesus knew. Nathanael asked in regard to the present, "Whence knowest thou me?" Jesus reaches into the past, "Not only do I know thee at this moment, I knew thee ere this, yea, saw thee." Since the reply, "I *saw* thee," answers the question, "Whence *knowest* thou me?" this seeing at a distance with supernatural powers of sight is evidence for the power to look also into men's hearts. Here is a case like that of the woman at Jacob's well, "He told me all things that I ever did," 4:39. Another case is that of the paralytic let down through the roof whom Jesus first absolved before he healed him, seeing that his chief ailment was spiritual. "Lord, thou hast searched me and known me," Ps. 139:1. In his state of humiliation Jesus did not constantly use his divine attributes according to his human nature, but he used these attributes, in which his human nature shared, whenever he deemed it necessary for the purpose of his office and work. To place Jesus, in the present case, on the same level with the prophets, saying that Jesus "saw" as they "saw," is to deny the union of his two natures, i. e., to make of the Godman what he never was and never could be.

What lies in the meaning of the verb εἶδον and its tense is brought out more clearly still by the two modifiers, one of time and one of place, "before Philip called thee, when thou wast under the fig tree." The subordinate clause of antecedent time is neatly expressed by πρὸ τοῦ with the infinitive, which takes the place of πρίν with the infinitive, R. 621 and 766. This clause modifies εἶδον and states *when* Jesus saw Nathanael. The participial clause, "when thou wast under the fig tree," modifies the object of εἶδον, "I saw thee, when thou wast," etc., literally, "thee being under the fig tree," and states *where* Jesus saw him. The supposition that ὑπό with the accusative must refer to motion like taking refuge under must be dismissed as being due to ignorance of the Koine, R. 634-5.

Who would not wish that the evangelist had told us more fully what actually happened under the fig tree when Nathanael was there before he met Philip? Something apparently disproportionate lies in the connection of this simple statement of Jesus and the instantaneous, magnificent confession of Nathanael who but a moment ago was filled with serious doubt; but we know that the disproportion does not really exist. As far as the fig tree itself and Nathanael's being under it are concerned, this was nothing unusual,

since it was the custom of pious Jews — a custom
encouraged by the Talmud — to study their office of
daily prayer in some secluded place. Even here, away
from Cana, his home, while lodging in some temporary
place, Nathanael may well have had his place for quiet
retirement, in this instance the shade of a fig tree.
What Jesus refers to is not this custom merely but
something of a deep personal nature, known only to
Nathanael and to his God, that occurred say a day or
two before when he had again sought seclusion under
that tree. For the reference of Jesus literally strikes
home in Nathanael's heart. He sees that what
transpired in his inmost soul lies open to Jesus' eyes.
"Under the fig tree" unlocks all that ever stirred within him regarding Israel's hope and deliverance. Imagination seeks to supply something that would be great
enough to justify the great confession that rose to
Nathanael's lips, such as wrestling in prayer for fulfillment of God's promise; resolve to be baptized by
the Baptist; prayer victory over some temptation;
perhaps, a direct response from God like Simeon's,
Luke 2:26, promising him that he should see the Christ.
We leave the mystery as John left it to us.

49) Almost involuntary is the instantaneous response. **Nathanael answered him, Rabbi, thou art
the Son of God; thou art King of Israel.** So spoke
this true Israelite heart, and his words were even
truer than he himself knew. Jesus had attested himself to Nathanael, and Nathanael believed the attestation. The title "Rabbi" is the same as in v. 38. The
double unqualified designation ὁ υἱὸς τοῦ Θεοῦ and
βασιλεὺς τοῦ Ἰσραήλ comes as a surprise, especially
when we remember how the Jews hated all deifica-
tion of men. The second title, "King of Israel," furnishes the clue for the source from which Nathanael
drew both, namely Ps. 2, "Thou art my Son," and,
"Yet have I set my King upon my holy hill of Zion."

The entire Psalm speaks of the enthronement of the Messiah who is the Son of God. Another view would trace Nathanael's confession to the Baptist, v. 33; but the Baptist's testimony lacks the significant title "King of Israel," which then would be only Nathanael's own deduction from the other title, "the Son of God."

It is no mean proof of the divinity of Christ that men like Nathanael at once felt impelled to acknowledge him as "the Son of God," and having done so, remained true to him as such, and in all their later daily, familiar intercourse with him never changed their minds, telling themselves that they had been carried away in a moment of enthusiasm and now in the light of a more sober knowledge must revise their estimate. Later impressions made these men second Peter's great confession, "the Christ, the Son of the living God," Matt. 16:16; John 6:69; compare Matt. 14:33; Luke 9:20; John 11:27; 20:28. What this means in regard to the revelation of the Trinity in the Old Testament and in regard to the knowledge of the Jews concerning the Trinity is stated in connection with v. 32. Men like Nathanael understood Ps. 2 and Ps. 110 and other pertinent parts of the Old Testament quite well. "Son of God" seems too far-reaching an expression even for many who admit Christ's Sonship; hence they tone it down to mean "an exceptional relation between Jesus and God" and point to Nathanael's emotion when he made the declaration. But John never would or could have used Nathanael's word if it had amounted only to so little.

We need not deny that in afterdays clouds arose to dim the clear vision of Jesus which Nathanael had at the very beginning of his discipleship. Yet the fact also stands out that the light always conquered, and the clouds disappeared, and every doubt was swallowed up by greater light and faith; for the glory that shone forth from the Only-begotten never waned for a single moment. "Son of God" rightly stands first as expressing the true relation of Jesus to God; "King of Israel" rightly stands second as expressing the true relation of Jesus to Israel. Nathanael places the two on a parallel, but in Jesus both predicates are joined. To make "King of Israel" alone mean Messiah is verbal play, for the only Messiah is Jesus who is both "Son" and "King."

50) Jesus might have said nothing more and might have continued his journey. But where he meets faith like this he praises and rewards it. **Jesus answered and said unto him, Because I said to thee, I saw thee underneath the fig tree, thou believest. Something greater than this shalt thou see.** Again the two verbs "answered and said" as in the case of the previous speech of Jesus in v. 48. Can we follow our versions and others in regarding the first statement of Jesus as a question, "Because I said, etc., . . . dost thou believe?" A question seems to be stronger and livelier than a declaration, but it is liable to be taken in a wrong sense, thus, "Believest thou already on such little evidence?" or, "Believest thou already? — I hardly expected it"; or, "Believest thou — art thou sure thou believest?" No; Jesus declares with joy, "Thou believest!" The grounds are sufficient, indeed, "Because I said unto thee, I saw thee underneath the fig tree." When Jesus said that he intended it to be fully sufficient to produce faith — it did, and Jesus acknowledges this. So here he first *praises* and secondly rewards faith. The reward lies in the promise, "Something greater than this shalt thou see." The neuter plurals μείζω (contraction for μείζονα) and τούτων are not intended as plural occurrences, for the latter plainly refers only to the fig-tree incident, and the former is explained by v. 51. Such neuter plurals are mere idioms; we should use

the singular. There is a contrast between the terms, "I *said* to thee," and, "thou shalt *see*"; and again between, "*I saw* thee," and, "*thou shalt see.*" Nathanael accepts the word of Jesus — he shall receive even more — as Jesus saw wondrously, so shall he. The verb may be written ὄψῃ or ὄψει, according as the editors contract -εσαι into η or into ει.

51) What "greater thing" Jesus means by his promise to Nathanael he now states clearly and fully. **And he says to him, Amen, amen, I say to you, you shall see the heaven opened, and the angels of God ascending and descending upon the Son of man.** The interruption of the evangelist, "And he says to him," is like that in v. 32, and is intended to draw special attention to the words of Jesus that follow. "To him," Nathanael, and yet in what Jesus says he uses the plural as a reference to all six disciples present. This was necessary, for they all "shall see" what is here promised.

This promise is introduced by a formula of assurance which Jesus often used: a double "amen" as a seal of *verity* and, "I say to you," as the stamp of final *authority*. In "Amen" we have the transliterated Hebrew word for "truth" or "verity," an adverbial accusative in the sense of ἀληθῶς, "verily," and so rendered in our versions. In Hebrew it is placed at the end to confirm a statement or to seal an obligation, it is like our liturgical Amen. "All search in Jewish literature has not brought to light a real analogy for the idiomatic use of the single or the double ἀμήν on the part of Jesus." Zahn, *Das Evang. d. Matthaeus,* 361. This means the use at the head of the statement. The best one can say is that Jesus used the double "Amen" when he spoke Aramaic, just as John reports; and that the synoptists, when reporting this in the Greek, deemed the single ἀμήν sufficient for the readers. The supposition that John's double ἀμήν is intended to produce the sound of the Aramaic words for "I say" is unlikly and leaves unexplained why he still adds to the two amen: λέγω ὑμῖν. In our Gospel the double amen occurs 25 times and always introduces statements of the greatest weight.

The word "hereafter," ἀπάρτι, dropped in the R. V., does not change the sense of Jesus' words but accords well with them. The Greek texts which omit the word seem to do so because they interpret the promised vision of angels as a reference to the actual appearance of angels, which, of course, occurred much later and not "from now on." While the future tense ὄψεσθε might be punctiliar, "you shall see once," here the durative sense is indicated, "you shall see again and again." These disciples, in fact, had the first vision of this kind three days later in the miracle at Cana. The tense also furnishes positive assurance, a definite promise and glorious prophecy, "you shall see, indeed," it will come to pass. We must also note that "you shall see" corresponds to "thou shalt see" in v. 50, the verb being identical, and the promise in v. 51 an elaboration of the one in v. 50. In both cases the verb denotes actual seeing with the eyes, and this seeing is in contrast to what Jesus has just *said* to him regarding the fig tree. The latter indicated the supernatural *knowledge* of Jesus; to this shall be added visions of the supernatural *works* of Jesus, beginning with the miracle in Cana. These works the disciples shall actually *see* and behold in them the divine power of Jesus. This seeing, then, is like that of v. 14, "we beheld his glory," etc.

They shall see "the heaven opened, and the angels of God ascending and descending upon the Son of man." The perfect participle ἀνεῳγότα means that heaven, once opened, continues thus, and thus it differs from the opening of the heavens after the baptism of Jesus, for which Matt. 3:16 and Luke 3:21 have the

aorist, indicating one act, a momentary opening.
What the disciples shall see is heaven permanently
open over Jesus. In all his miraculous works they
shall see that no bar exists between Jesus and God,
between him and the heavenly world, as this is the
case with us all who are subject to sin. When Jesus
adds, "and the angels of God ascending and descending upon the Son of man," this vividly recalls the
dream of Jacob, Gen. 28:12, although no medium like
a ladder is mentioned. For the sinner Jacob such a
medium (Mediator, the ladder typifying Christ) was
needed; not for God's own Son. "The angels of God"
are just what the words say and not figures, types,
symbols of some kind or other, such as "the symbol
of living communion between God and the Messiah,"
"divine perfection," "personal forces of the divine
Spirit," etc. The order of the participles "ascending
and descending" is the same as in Genesis, but here
they are used in the sense of a constant going and
coming — while some go, others come. When R. 423
calls this order of the participles a hysteron proteron,
"a natural inversion from our point of view," we do
not share his view. Only to sinners angels must first
come down not to the Son. When they went up to
God from Jacob and then came down, this was due to
the fact that he was already in God's favor, the dream
assuring him of that fact.

To understand the import of these movements of
the angels we should not overlook the contrast implied
in the terms "the angels *of God*" and "the Son *of
man.*" When God's Son dwelt on earth as the Son of
man, heaven itself was here among men, the very
angels of God, like an army, waited upon his least beck
and call. Though he came as the Son of man, God's
own angels were at his command. Recall Matt. 26:53,
"Thinkest thou that I cannot now pray my Father,
and he shall presently give me more than twelve

legions of angels?" The centurion in Matt. 8:9 made
a true comparison when he remarked that he had but
to say "Go!" to one of his soldiers, or to say "Come!"
and he would instantly be obeyed. Thus all power in
heaven and in earth was given to this Son of man.
We thus dismiss the ancient interpretation which held
that these six disciples would see the actual appear-
ances of angels, for these were but few, and only at
the ascension of Jesus did two angels appear to the
disciples. We likewise decline to accept the interpretation that the angels bore Christ's prayers to the
Father and returned the Father's answer, for no such
angelic mediation is indicated anywhere, nor would
it fit the close communion of the Son with the Father.
As God uses the angels for his purposes, so did the
Son of man. His mighty works would make these disciples see that. As the angels are sent forth to minister unto those who are the heirs of salvation, so they
will minister to the will of him who is the author of
this salvation, the great original Heir. In a way far
higher than was possible in Jacob's case the ascending and descending angels would serve Jesus. The
final phrase with ἐπί does not mean "resting upon
Jesus," which is excluded by the very nature of what
is described; or bringing divine powers upon Jesus,
for the very Spirit of God had already been made
his for his work. This ἐπί is in relation to "heaven"
which stands open above Jesus, hence the descending of the angels at Christ's beck and call would
be ἐπί, "upon" him, a coming to his great person.

Here for the first time Jesus uses the designation
"the Son of man," found nine times in John's Gospel
and over fifty-five times in the four Gospels. This title
is used exclusively by Jesus himself, except in 12:34
where, after his using it, others ask its meaning; and
in Acts 7:56, which reflects Matt. 26:64. It is clear
that this title was coined by Jesus himself, was un-

known before he used it, was by the disciples restricted
to use with reference to Jesus, and did not come to
be used in the church until quite late. Jesus always
uses it as a subject or as an object, always in the third
person, never as a predicate; he speaks in the full
consciousness that he is "the Son of man" yet never
says, " I am the Son of man." The title is always
ὁ υἱὸς τοῦ ἀνθρώπου, with the two Greek articles, which
is quite distinct from "a son of man," i. e., a human
being. There is a mystery in the title which is still
felt as we read the record of its use by Jesus, which
is clearly evident also when in Matt. 16:13, etc., Jesus
first asks who the people say is "the Son of man" and
who the disciples say he is.

"Of man," never the plural "of men," is generic;
not descending from some man but having the nature
of man, a son of mankind. The fact that the human
nature of Christ is expressed in the title is beyond question. But "the Son" of man lifts out this one man
from all men as being one who has this human nature
in a way in which no other man has it, who while he
is true man, indeed, is more than man, who accepts
the designation ὁ υἱὸς τοῦ Θεοῦ τοῦ ζῶντος, "the Son of
the living God." This is very clear from the mighty
acts attributed to "the Son of man" which prove that,
while he is man, he is also infinitely greater than
man. Hence "the Son of man" is not merely "the
ideal man," *homo* κατ' ἐξοχήν, the flower of our race,
toward whom all creation tended; but "the Word made
flesh," the Son ἄσαρκος who became ἔνσαρκος, who to
his divine nature joined our human nature, the Son
of God who assumed our human flesh and blood. In
the use Jesus makes of this title two lines of thought
converge: the one is lowliness, suffering, etc.; the other
greatness, power, and exaltation beyond that of men.
Once the title is properly conceived, both lines of
thought are seen to be clearly involved in this designa-

tion. It will also be noted that this title fits Jesus in an eminent way while he sojourned on earth and was thus used by him as early as his meeting with Nathanael. To give it an exclusively eschatological sense because Jesus calls himself "the Son of man" also in connection with the consummation, is to generalize from a few facts instead of from all.

Nathanael has just called Jesus "the Son of God," and now, it seems as though to counterbalance that true title, Jesus adds this other one as also being true, "the Son of man." The two belong together. Nathanael has just called Jesus "King of Israel," which again is true in the fullest sense. Yet the theocratic relation to Israel which Jesus himself stresses, 4:22; Matt. 15:24, is not enough, for he takes away "the sin of the world," he is the Savior of all men, and in his title "the Son of man" this great universality is brought out. So the narrow and the broad titles belong together. Here we may also note that Jesus carefully avoids the use of any title that might be taken in a political sense. Nathanael calls him "King of Israel," but Jesus does not adopt this as the usual designation for himself. When questioned by Pilate, he carefully defines his kingship as being not of this world, and when Pilate in the superscription on the cross calls him "the King of the Jews," he does this only to taunt the Jews because of their charges not because of a title that Jesus had given himself. This pertains also to the title "Messiah," which the Jews understood in a national and political sense. To the Samaritan woman Jesus reveals that he is the Messiah (4:26), but he does not make this title common when denominating himself. We may say that by most frequently calling himself "the Son of man" he desired to do what he could to denationalize his Kingship and his Messiahship and to lift it to its true universal plane.

Whence does Jesus derive this title? The answer is: from Dan. 7:13, 14: "I saw in the night visions, and, behold, one like the Son of man came with the clouds of heaven, and came to the Ancient of days, and they brought him near before him. And there was given him dominion, and glory, and a kingdom, that all people, nations, and languages should serve him: his dominion is an everlasting dominion, which shall not pass away, and his kingdom that which shall not be destroyed." Efforts are made by von Hofmann, C.-K., Zahn, etc., to reduce "one like the Son of man" to a symbolic figure (like the "beast" in the previous verses), this figure symbolizing Israel. But the words of Daniel will not yield such a sense. The Hebrew *ki*, ὡς, "like," is taken to mean that this person only resembled a man but *was* not a man, overlooking Rev. 1:13; 14:14, where this "like" is carefully retained in using the Daniel passage. Again, in Matt. 24:30 and 26:64 the Son of man comes in the clouds, exactly as in Daniel's description. Only God uses the clouds as his vehicle, hence "one like the Son of man" is divine. Yet Daniel sees him "like the Son *of man*," which, although it does not directly call him "man," intimates clearly enough that the grand figure described was also a man. See the thorough exegesis of Keil in *Bibl. Com. ueber den Propheten Daniel*, 197, etc., and 228, etc. Too indefinite is the explanation that Jesus drew the title "the Son of man" from the general references of the Old Testament to the *bene adam*, or *ben adam*, Aramaic *bar enasch*, "children of men," "children of man," "child of man," and that only in this general sense are Dan. 7:13; Ps. 8:5 evidence. How from such general terms, which denote only men as men, a title could be drawn which denotes the one unique man who is the very Son of God, is difficult to see.

Dan. 7:13, 14 pictures the Messiah, yet the Jews had not drawn a title for the Messiah from it. This Jesus himself did. Hence when he kept using this title, it seemed strange, and the question could arise as in John 12:34, "Who is this Son of man?" Hence also no political ideas could attach themselves to this title. In Daniel, too, we observe the universality that inheres in the original description, which presents one who rules all people, nations, etc., in an everlasting kingdom and judges all the world. In Daniel the term is eschatological; Jesus uses it in the same way in Matthew 24:30 and 26:64, which is done also in the Revelation passages. But this Judge at the great consummation cannot be the judge only then, his work must reach back much farther, through the entire process of redemption, the consummation of which is the final judgment. Very properly, thus, Jesus expands the title and uses it with reference to his person in the days of his humiliation. Even when speaking to these first six disciples, however, he refers to the heavenly glory of his person and to the angels at his command who shall also function so prominently in the judgment. Matt. 25:31; Mark 8:38. What Aramaic expression Jesus used for "the Son of man" no one is able to say. To search in Jewish literature for this title is hopeless. The references in the book of Enoch, even if the sections concerned are genuine, lead to nothing. The surmise that, since Jesus also spoke Greek as for instance to Pilate, he may himself have employed the Greek ὁ υἱὸς τοῦ ἀνθρώπου, may be quite correct, although the Gospels, Revelation, and Acts are wholly sufficient.

Modern criticism attacks the historical character of John's account regarding the call of these first disciples by making them contradictory to Matt. 4:18, etc., and the parallels. But these two calls are essentially different. John describes the first attachment of these six men to Jesus when he gathers them as believers; Matthew describes a later event, the prerequisite of which John furnishes us. When these men left house, home, and their old calling in life, they already knew Jesus. John describes how they were first drawn to him.

CHAPTER II

The First Attestation of Jesus Himself, Continued,
2:1-11. — By the power of his personality and by his
divine knowledge and words Jesus had attested himself as truly being the Messiah of whom the Baptist
had testified, as the Son of God and the Son of man.
To the attestation through the word is now added
that of the deed, which was made evident in the first
miracle.

1) **And on the third day a wedding took place
in Cana of Galilee; and the mother of Jesus was
there. Now there was invited also Jesus and his
disciples to the wedding.** John counts from the day
(1:43) when Philip and Nathanael became his disciples. The third day after that day means that
two nights intervened. On this third day a wedding
ἐγένετο, "took place." While the verb does not mean
"began" and mentions only the occurrence of the wedding, which usually consumed seven days, yet to say,
"occurred on the third day," must refer to the start
of the wedding. This wedding must be thought of in
the Jewish fashion. In the betrothal bride and groom
were pledged to each other in a way that truly made
them man and wife, although the two did not at once
live together following this ceremony. An interval,
longer or shorter, followed, and then the γάμος or γάμοι
took place. The groom with his companions brought
the bride with her companions to the groom's home,
and there without any further pledge the celebration
began, starting toward evening with a feast as grand
as possible and continuing for a week, the couple now
living together.

John's words have been scanned most carefully for all possible minor points. The fact that he writes "Cana of Galilee" is to inform his first readers in Asia Minor, where his Gospel was published, that the little town was located in the province of Galilee and not in order to distinguish it from some other Cana located elsewhere. For the Cana near Sidon did not belong to the Jewish land at this time. Names of provinces were also frequently attached to names of towns in cases where the towns were well known and were the only ones with that name. Even so we are unable at present to identify with certainty just what place John. refers to with the name Cana, whether it is Khirbet Kana, also called Kanat el-Dschelil, five hours' walk from Nazareth, or Kephar Kenna, two hours away, or Ain Kana, a half hour away, a spring by this name near the village er-Reineh. The traditional site is the second place, to which the commentators incline, but too many traditional sites in Palestine are uncertain or openly spurious.

The fact that Jesus and his six companions could make the journey from Bethany beyond the Jordan to any one of the three places indicated as Cana in the time limit of three days is assured. Yet a number of questions are left open by the brevity of John's narrative. Does he mean to say that the company arrived for the opening of the wedding feast on the evening of that third day, or that they arrived later during the progress of the wedding? Did the miracle occur on the evening of that third day or on a later day of the celebration? How and when did Jesus receive his invitation to attend the wedding with his disciples? The only clue we have is the fact that in the preceding paragraphs, 1:29, 35, and 43, the designations of time "on the morrow" fix each of the occurrences described in these paragraphs as taking place on the day indicated. The natural supposition, then, is that what is now recorded also took place "on the third day," since this designation of time is placed at the head of this new paragraph exactly like the preceding datives "on the morrow." We, therefore, take it that the miracle occurred "on the third day."

John tells us that "the mother of Jesus was there" because the story turns on her action and also because this in a manner explains how Jesus came to be invited. John does not mention her name either here or elsewhere in his Gospel. He refrains from naming himself and all other relatives of his among whom we thus must include Mary, possibly the aunt of John, the sister of his mother Salome. On the question regarding this relationship compare the remarks on 19:25. The adverb "there" means at the wedding and not merely in the town, for we hear what Mary did at the wedding. The verb ἦν contrasts with ἐκλήθη used regarding Jesus and marks a difference, which is also borne out by what follows. Mary was not present, like her son, as an invited guest but as a friend of the groom or of the bride or of both in order to aid in the feast. Perhaps she was related to one of the bridal couple. This would explain how she knew about the lack of wine and why she took steps in the matter.

2) Jesus was formally invited. The connective δέ adds this statement to the one regarding Mary and at the same time indicates that this is a little different. We have no connective with this delicate force in English. The point of difference lies in the verbs: Mary "was" there as a matter of course; Jesus "was invited" in a formal way. The tenses add to this, as well as the forward positions of the verbs, the one durative, ἦν, the other aorist to designate the one act of giving the invitation, the aorist also indicating that the invitation was effective — Jesus accepted. The verb is singular and thus lifts Jesus into prominence

over his disciples: *he* was invited and they, too, but
not on an equality — they only on account of Jesus.
The word μαθητής, as correlative to διδάσκαλος, means
more than pupil or scholar, namely a follower and
adherent, i. e., one who accepts the instruction given
him and makes it his rule and norm. While used,
as here, with reference to beginners, in its full sense
μαθηταί are those who have truly imbibed the spirit
of their master. The term thus came to mean the
true believers. When these were invited, we are unable to say; the tense of the verb records nothing but
the fact. As regards what follows we may also bear
in mind that, while Jewish weddings usually were
celebrated for a week, some even for two weeks, we
cannot be sure that this wedding lasted that long.
The impression left by the entire narrative is that
the present wedding, perhaps because the couple was
poor, lasted only the one evening and was celebrated
only by one feast, made as fine as possible by the
means of the groom.

3) With the situation thus briefly sketched, the
real story begins with the simple connective "and."
As regards the variant readings, which leave the sense
unchanged, we abide by the one that shows the greater
textual authority. **And when the wine began to
fail, the mother of Jesus says to him, They have
no wine.** The aorist participle in the genitive absolute is best regarded as ingressive, "began to fail."
The decline of the wine would be discovered before
the last of it was used. The usual explanation is
that the sudden addition of seven guests caused this
giving out of the wine. Yet this assumes that the
invitation was given so late that additional provisions
could not be secured. And why should only the wine
fail and none of the food? Had the amount of wine
been calculated so closely that it would have just
reached if these seven guests had not appeared? When

explanations are too easy they are sometimes wrong. In Palestine a universal drink such as wine would be provided even by a poor groom in such abundance that, instead of running short, the supply would leave plenty over. John simply records the fact, the wine began to run short; let us stay with that. God's providence thus provided "the hour" for Jesus. If we must have explanation, let it be that somebody had blundered by not obtaining enough wine — not enough for the company to be served counting also Jesus and his disciples.

Since Mary takes the matter in hand she must have been one of those who helped with the serving, in fact, the one who oversaw and managed affairs as also her word to the helpers indicates. It is she who thus turns to Jesus. Now here again some follow a course of explanation that is a little too obvious and easy. They think that by coming to her son she followed only the ordinary impulse of the long previous years when in any difficulty in her home life in Nazareth she turned to him. We are told positively that Mary never dreamed of a miracle when she came to her Son and said, "They have no wine," i. e., they are running short of wine. But what *did* Mary expect? Having just come from afar, in a village new to him, where he appears only as an honored guest, whence and how could Jesus at a moment's notice supply more wine? The sensible thing for Mary would have been, since she had come early to help and to manage, that she should have used her own resources or should have called in the aid of other helpers who lived in Cana, some neighbor or some friend of the groom who had a supply of wine close by. No; she goes to her Son Jesus! The old commentators are right — here is more than an ordinary appeal for help.

Here are the items that count. Jesus had left his home to begin his career as the Messiah; he had been baptized by John and had returned with six disciples; the report of what had transpired right after his Baptism together with the testimonies of the Baptist, of the six disciples, and of Jesus himself, reached Mary's ears first of all. These things brought back to her mind the great facts connected with her Son's conception, birth, etc. We know this woman's character, the depth of her nature, the clarity of her knowledge and intuition. She knew her son was the Messiah of whom wondrous things were to be expected. Like Mary of Bethany, who foresaw Jesus' death by violence and grasped the moment at the feast made for him by his friends and anointed him for his burying, 12:1-8, so Jesus' mother turns to her son at this critical moment during the wedding feast. Just what she did expect of him — was it fully clear to her own mind? The answer: ordinary help, fails to meet the case entirely. The answer must be: extraordinary, wondrous help. This touch, too, is true regarding Mary — she asks nothing, not even, "Can or will you do something?" She simply states the difficulty and humbly leaves all else to Jesus. To offer the suggestion that, since Jesus brought six extra men and thus caused the shortage, he had best leave at once and thus induce others to leave also, resolves the predicament mentioned by Mary in a rather trivial manner.

4) The answer of Jesus to his mother creates surprise. **And Jesus says to her, What is that to me and thee, woman? Mine hour has not yet come.** The question: τί ἐμοὶ καὶ σοί; is idiomatic, compare Matt. 8:29; Luke 8:28; Mark 1:24; 5:7, a fixed formula, well rendered by Luther, *"Was habe ich mit dir zu schaffen?"* It is elliptical, indeed, but not in the sense, "What have we to do with that?" meaning colloquially, "Never mind!" (R. 539). The literal thought is, "What is there for me and thee?" i. e.,

in common for us in this matter. Yet not, "This is
not my concern but thine"; but the opposite, "This
is my affair not thine." Thus already in this question a hidden promise is included. The other thought
is that Jesus thrusts his mother away — gently but
firmly. She comes to him with the expectation that
in the present difficulty he will show his Messianic
powers by doing something very much out of the ordinary. This he does not refuse to do but he declares
that it is his own affair entirely, and that even his
own mother must leave it altogether to him. Having
entered on his great office, the old relation obtaining
at Nazareth when he obeyed all her wishes like any
ordinary dutiful son, is forever at an end. He has
assumed his higher position, and even his mother must
recognize that fact. "Although there is no higher
power on earth than father's and mother's power, even
this is at an end when God's word and work begin."
Luther. The address γύναι, "woman," sounds harsher
in translation than it is or was meant to be in the
original. It is of a piece with the question itself. To
see and to feel that it contains no trace of disrespect
recall 19:26, where Jesus uses the same word in com-
mitting his mother to John. He does not say "mother"
but "woman," for, while Mary will forever remain his
mother, in his calling Jesus knows no mother or earthly
relative, he is their Lord and Savior as well as of all
men. The common earthly relation is swallowed up in
the divine. Matt. 12:46-50.

What the question tells Mary the additional statement makes still clearer, "Mine hour has not yet
come." In ἡ ὥρα μου the possessive must not be overlooked. This expression is not a mere reference to
time, as though Jesus only bids Mary wait a little.
Nor is it only like καιρός, the time proper for something, the season for it. We often meet the expression
with reference to Christ, his death, his resurrection,

etc. His enemies cannot triumph over him as long as his hour has not yet come; not until then will be their hour and the power of darkness, Luke 22:53. Note the similar expression ἡ ἡμέρα τοῦ Κυρίου. Jesus' hour is the one appointed for him by the Father; it may be the hour for this or for that in his Messianic work. When it comes, he acts, and not until it comes. So Jesus never hurries, nor lets others hurry him, he waits for his hour and then meets it. He is never uneasy or full of fear, for nothing can harm him until his hour comes; and when it comes, he gives his life into death. Here the hour is the one arranged for the first miraculous manifestation of his glory. In performing this miracle he will not be importuned even by his mother. In "not yet come" lies the promise that his hour will, indeed, come. Mary also thought that οὔπω, "not yet," intimated that the hour was close at hand. Compare the author's *His Footsteps*, 100, etc.

5) If the coming of Mary to Jesus in the first place is extraordinary in its motivation and its purpose, and if the answer of Jesus is still more extraordinary in its signification and implication, both the coming and the answer are matched by the sequel: **His mother says to the servants, Whatever he shall tell you, do!** Mary's mind responds fully to that of her great son. What his question, his form of address, the word about his hour, mean flashes instantaneously through her mind and heart. We need not suppose that John abbreviates the dialog, and that Jesus really said more than is recorded. Other women may have required more, may have answered back with some querulous question or remark — not this woman. It sounds almost humorous when a commentator remarks about her "genuinely feminine quickness," with which she sizes up Jesus as following "a man's way" of rebuffing a suggestion coming from a woman. The

idiosyncracies of sex play no part with the mother of Jesus whose clear spiritual insight here comes to view. Of a piece with the suggestions noted is the surmise that Mary's direction to the servants means that she expects Jesus to order the servants to go out to get some wine from a place near by. Mary could have done that herself. How could Jesus do that as a guest? Whither would he send the servants in a place strange to him? And is this all that "his hour" means?

Mary speaks not to Jesus but to the διάκονοι. This means that she is wholly satisfied with her Son's reply, which also is evidenced by what she tells "the servants." These evidently had not heard her conversation with Jesus. The term διάκονοι is significant. They are not δοῦλοι, "slaves" or "servants" in the lowest sense of our English word, who just obey orders and no more. These are voluntary assistants, come in to help in a friendly way with the work at the wedding feast. They work for the help and the benefit their work brings to the young people and to their festive guests. They lay hand to what is needed of their own accord or at the request of those who manage affairs. Now Jesus was a guest and had no hand in managing affairs; hence to receive orders from him would sound strange to these διάκονοι. On the other hand, Mary's word to them shows her insight in expecting from Jesus an order that itself would sound extraordinary to persons bidden to carry it out. These voluntary assistants might thus hesitate and shake their wise heads, even smile and refuse to act. So as the one who manages the work and directs these assistants come to lend a helping hand Mary gives them positive directions.

These evidence her faith in her Son's implied promise and meet the situation regarding the servants so exactly that Jesus, too, accepted her order to them on his part and used those servants when working his miracle. "Whatever he tells you," is like the indefinite relative clause in 1:33, which see. The aorist imperative is peremptory, "Do at once! do without question!" However strange the act may seem to you, foolish even to your wise eyes, useless, trivial, whatever it proves to be — do it! If only more of us would obey Mary's word, "Whatever he tells you, do!"

6) Here John inserts a necessary parenthetical remark, hence δέ. **Now there were six waterpots of stone set there after the Jews' manner of purifying, containing two or three firkins apiece.** These were stoneware jars, amphoræ, such as are still used in Syria. We do not regard ἦσαν . . . κείμεναι either as a circumscribed imperfect or as "a past perfect in sense" (R. 906) ; B.-D. is right, in John the participle is nearly always independent, compare 1:9 and 28. This is especially true when the words are as widely separated as is the case here. John tells us that the waterpots "were there" and then adds how they came to be there, "having been set there in accord (κατά) with the Jews' manner of purification" (κεῖμαι is generally used as the perfect passive of τίθημι). Just where they stood no one can say, but it was certainly not where the feast was spread. From v. 9 we gather that they stood where the guests could not see them, and the entire action of filling up these pots was known at first only to Jesus himself and to the servants who did the work, probably also to watchful Mary and to a few others.

"In accord with the purification of the Jews" is added by John for the sake of his Greek readers. The old regulations for purification were greatly extended in unauthorized ways during the post-Babylonian period, so that also cups, pots, brazen vessels were

washed ("baptized") as a matter of ritual observance,
Mark 7:4, and some texts add couches, those on which
a person reclined when dining. The washing of hands,
especially before eating, Mark 7:3, was done only in
a formal way, merely by dipping the finger into water.
John adds that the number of pots was six and tells
us how much water each (ἀνά, distributive) could hold,
namely two or three "firkins." The Attic μετρητής is
estimated at over 8½ gallons (Josephus) and answers
in general to the Hebrew *bath*. The Rabbinists, however, make the *bath* equal to a little less than 4½
gallons. Which estimate John has in mind is hard
to decide, see Smith, *Bible Dictionary* for all the available data. The higher and more probable estimate
reaches at least 110 gallons, the lower and less probable
about 60 gallons. John is at pains in his brief narration to let us know about the great quantity of wine
which Jesus created, giving the number of the vessels
and what amount of water they held, χωροῦσαι, literally,
"giving place to," i. e., containing. But it has been
asked, "Was so much water necessary for purification
purposes on this occasion?" If we ourselves could
have attended the wedding, counted the number of the
guests, and watched just how the water was used, we
could answer this question in detail. As it is, we can
only say that, even if the young couple was poor, the
company of guests seems to have been a considerable
number. As far as the addition of seven more persons by the coming of Jesus and his disciples is concerned, this cut but a small figure in general and none
at all in explaining the shortage of wine. The wash-
ings, too, which the Jews practiced seem to have included much more than is usually assumed. The six
pots of wine which Jesus created correspond in a
striking way to the six disciples with whom he appeared at this wedding and recall the miracle of the

loaves when twelve baskets of fragments were left over, one for each of the twelve disciples with Jesus, Matt. 14:15-21.

7) Now Jesus acts. **Jesus says to them, Fill the waterpots with water. And they filled them to the brim.** Jesus' hour had come. The supposition that Jesus waited until the wine provided for the wedding was actually used up, until the moment when it would have to be announced to all the guests that no more wine could be served, may be in accord with the facts, since the ingressive aorist in v. 3: ὑστερήσαντος οἴνου, "wine having begun to give out," points to a total lack that would presently set in. Jesus might have ignored Mary's order to the helpers, but he uses it and thereby honors his mother. The gender of αὐτοῖς, "them," easily refers back to τοῖς διακονίοις in v. 5. The aorist imperative γεμίσατε is strong like ποιήσατε in v. 5, a straight, authoritative order. Verbs of filling take the genitive, here ὕδατος, "with water." If Jesus reclined at the feast with the other guests, we may assume that he quietly arose and went out to where the pots stoods and the helpers were busy. So Mary, too, when she first spoke to Jesus, may have beckoned him to come to her and then made known to him the impending lack of wine. Were the pots empty when Jesus gave his order? John skips such details. But we may well assume that nis order meant that the pots should be filled with entirely fresh water. The order is carried out by the helpers with alacrity, which implies that a well or spring was not far off. One wonders what the helpers thought while they were filling up those jars. John adds only the little touch ἕως ἄνω, "to the brim." Did managing Mary insist on their obeying orders promptly and strictly? Well, they would! Did the helpers smile at each other when they carried all that water to the pots and crack jokes with each other about this Rabbi who

would give the guests this precious water as a new
kind of wine?

8)   The job is done, the pots are full, the eye of
Jesus watching until the last one was filled.   Was
Mary in the background also looking on?   Now comes
the second order, as astonishing at the first.   **And
he says to them, Dip out now and go on bringing
to the steward of the feast.   And they brought.**   The
miracle had been wrought, the water was now wine.
Crashaw has the beautiful poetic line:

Lympha pudica Deum vidit et erubuit.

Note the tenses, first the aorist ἀντλήσατε, for a quantity
is to be dipped out into some fair-sized vessel; then the
durative present φέρετε, "go on bringing" as wine may
be needed at the tables for the guests.   R. 855 is correct when he says that in the midst of the aorists in
v. 5-8 this present tense stands out; but when he explains it as being "probably a polite conative offer
to the master of the feast," he regards this tense as
an aoristic present.   The durative sense is far more
natural in this connection.   What Jesus ordered the
helpers did.   The ἀρχιτρίκλινος was the manager of the
feast, whether he himself was one of the guests selected
for the office by the groom or one who did not dine
with the rest as a guest, is hard to say.   One of his
functions is incidentally mentioned, namely that of
tasting food and drink before these were offered to the
guests.   He is named from the *triclina,* couches for
three persons each, three of them usually placed on
three sides of a low table, for the guests to recline on
while dining.

9)   John reports in detail what happened.   **Now
when the steward of the feast tasted the water that
had become wine and knew not whence it was (but
the servants knew, who had dipped the water), the
steward of the feast calls the bridegroom and says**

**to him, Every man sets on first the good wine, and
when they have drunk freely, the worst; thou hast
kept the good wine until now.** The first δέ continues
the narrative, the second indicates the parenthesis.
We must read as one concept τὸ ὕδωρ οἶνον γεγενημένον,
"the water having become wine," οἶνον without the
article being marked as the predicate of the participle.
This perfect participle has its usual present implication: the water once turned into wine remained wine.
The addition, "and knew not whence it was" (ᾔδει,
see 1:31), explains the steward's subsequent action.
Busy with his duties, he had not observed what had
been going on elsewhere. We infer that if he, whose
business it was to watch all the proceedings, did not
know, then also none of the guests knew. But the
διάκονοι "knew," knew at firsthand, even also as John
now adds the attributive participle, "who had dipped
the water," οἱ ἠντληκότες, not an aorist to indicate the
one act, but the perfect tense, describing these servants as what they continued to be. It seems that at
the moment they said nothing but allowed the triclinarch to proceed. It also took them a while to
realize fully what had occurred under their very eyes
and hands. When they awoke to the situation they
surely talked volubly enough.

10) The moment the triclinarch tasted the wine,
it flashed into his mind that someone had made a
grand mistake in regard to the wine. He hastens to
call the bridegroom, and John reports this detail first
in order to indicate the actuality of the miracle:
water turned into wine; and secondly, to indicate the
quality of this wine. Note this: as Jesus made a
great quantity of wine, so he also made this of the
greatest excellence. The triclinarch points out the fact
that the bridgroom has made a serious mistake. He
has allowed the poor wine to be served first and kept
this excellent (καλόν) wine until the last; whereas

everybody, when he is compelled to use two such qualities of wine, does the reverse. The groom, of course, is even more astonished than his steward, for he knew of no such good wine. No doubt he, too, at once tasted it and thus saw the situation for himself.

In describing the usual custom the steward uses the clause: καὶ ὅταν μεθυσθῶσιν, aorist passive subjunctive to denote the definite future fact. Some are overanxious regarding the verb μεθύσκω, "to make drunk," and the passive used in the same sense as the middle, "to become drunk," as if this steward here implies that the wedding guests were really drunk, and this excellent wine was thus utterly wasted on them. The entire context and the entire situation obviate this anxiety. The context implies only that after some time of drinking the sense of taste is blunted and does not readily distinguish the exact quality of wine. The steward is stating a general rule followed at feasts; it would be wholly untrue for him to say, when stating this rule, that the participants at such feasts always became drunk and were then fooled by having cheap wine passed to them. The situation here, as far as any application of the steward's rule to the guests at this wedding is concerned, on its very face bars out all excess. The steward cannot mean that the guests are drunk, and therefore this excellent wine will be lost upon them. It is utterly impossible for us to imagine Jesus being present in a tipsy crowd, to say nothing of aiding such carousing by his first miracle. The very thought could be entertained only by those "eager to mar, if by any means they could, the image of a perfect Holiness, which offends and rebukes them," Trench.

The word of the steward has frequently been allegorized. The wine that is worse is made to mean all that the world offers us, or again all that the false

Judaism of the day offered; while the excellent wine which Jesus created is made to mean the gospel and its true riches and joys. The text itself contains no such thoughts. The word on which these thoughts are based is not even a word of Christ but of an ordinary Jew who voiced a common observation. Allegory, especially in preaching, easily misleads. It only superimposes our own thoughts on words of Holy Writ. If it is used at all, it should be used with great care and always in such a way that our own thoughts remain clearly distinguished from what the written words actually state.

John's account is criticized as being incomplete. Such incompleteness is charged against him in quite a number of cases. We are told that he only furnishes "sketches." But this is a misconception of the evangelist's chief purpose, which is never to tell all that is interesting and all that we might desire to know about this or that great event but simply to present the attestation which reveals the Savior as the God-man. Viewed from this point of the evangelist's own purpose, the account of this miracle is perfect and complete.

11) John himself corroborates this when he closes his account as follows. **This did Jesus as a beginning of the signs in Cana of Galilee and manifested his glory; and his disciples believed in him.** The account as written by John purposes to show this first miracle as a sign, i. e., as signaling or manifesting Jesus' glory. Hence no name of bride and groom and no details about the minor persons, and no record as to what they thought or did during or after the wedding. All centers on Jesus and this "sign" and is used in the account only as helping to direct our attention to that center. We must read ταύτην by itself, namely as τοῦτο, which is attracted to the gender of the following ἀρχήν, "this . . . as a beginning

of the signs," etc. Our versions translate as if the text were: ταύτην τὴν ἀρχήν (at best an inferior variant), "this beginning," etc. After telling us in v. 1 that this miracle was wrought in Cana of Galilee, it would be a lame repetition again to say this at the close of the account. What John in closing tells us is that this miracle which was the first of all the miracles was done in Cana of Galilee. John wants it impressed upon us — not in Judea but here in Galilee the signs began. This is again emphasized in 4:46 and 54.

To designate these deeds John uses σημεῖα (σημαίνω, to make known by a σῆμα), "signs," deeds that indicate something, that convey a great meaning to the mind and to the heart. The translation "miracles," deeds which produce wonder, is inadequate; for it loses the ethical force of "signs." These point beyond themselves to something which they accredit and attest, first of all to the person who works these signs and to his significance; by that, however, also, in the case of Jesus most directly, to the new era he is ushering in. The ethical side, then, is that signs always require faith in what is signified, coupled with obedience on the part of those who see the signs. Unbelief and disobedience thus become the great crime against the signs. The term as well as its sense were well known to the Jews from the Old Testament, were constantly used in the apostolic church, and, doubtless, were used by Jesus himself to designate his own works. John's Gospel naturally uses this term in the sense of the strongest and the most tangible testimony for Jesus' divinity, always counting those guilty who meet the signs with unbelief. A few days before the wedding Jesus had attested himself by his words to the men who then became his disciples; these attestations were the prelude to the sign now wrought, one of those deeds of which he himself afterward said that no other man before him had wrought such works, 15:24. We often find σημεῖα linked with τέρατα (τέρας), "wonders," startling, amazing portents; but the latter is never used alone but always in conjunction with other terms that bring out their difference from the pagan portents. Frequent, too, is δυνάμεις, indicative of the divine power in the deeds. Next ἔνδοξα (neuter plural) as revelations of the divine glory; παράδοξα, strange things, only Luke 5:26; θαυμάσια, provoking wonder, only Matt. 21:15, though we often have θαυμάζω as a result of miracles.

"And he manifested his glory," is John's own description of what Jesus really did in this sign at Cana. The δόξα is the sum of the divine attributes or any one of these, shining forth to the eyes and the hearts of men; compare 1:14.

To the inner significance John appends the effect, "and his disciples believed in him." On the verb compare 1:12. The aorist states the fact: they rested their confidence in him as the Messiah and did this in consequence of the sign here wrought. Following their original acceptance and faith, as recounted in the previous chapter, ἐπίστευσαν here implies an increase of faith. It was, indeed, faith in the true sense of the word and yet it was only initial, needing more revelation and strength for its full development. On the term μαθηταί see v. 2.

This pericope opens up the entire question of miracles in the sense of the Scriptures, to which rationalism and a certain so-called "science" have always objected and will always object. The effort to believe the sacred record and at the same time to explain the accounts of the miracles so that they become only natural occurrences, must in the nature of the case always fail. The alternatives are exclusive, and only self-deception of a strong kind is able to hide that fact.

Minor thoughts are that by his first sign Jesus honors marriage and the family relation. By the great quantity of excellent wine he actually makes a valuable wedding present to the couple at Cana. The prohibition movement looks askance at Jesus who not only himself drank wine but presented such a quantity at Cana. The plea that, if Jesus had lived in our time, he would never have wrought this sign, virtually attacks the moral character of the Savior and of God who made wine to gladden the heart of man. The fact remains, the Scriptures nowhere condemn wine and its right use but only any and all forms of its abuse.

II

The Public Attestation Throughout the Holy Land, 2:12-4:54

The attestation by the Baptist and that by Jesus himself, as recorded hitherto, are preliminary. Even the first sign is wrought in a family circle. The evangelist now shows us the public ministry of Jesus in its full swing, grouping together a number of most notable attestations to his divine Sonship. First, The Cleansing of the Temple with its Further Effect, 2:12-25; secondly, The Conversation with Nicodemus, 3:1-21; thirdly, Jesus in Judea and the Last Testimony of the Baptist, 3:22-36; fourthly, Jesus in Samaria, 4:1-42; fifthly, Jesus in Galilee, 4:43-54.

The Cleansing of the Temple with its Further Effects, 2:12-25. — Quite simply the events are connected: after the miracle at Cana Jesus moves his home to Capernaum and from there he attends the festival at Jerusalem. **After this there went down to Capernaum he himself and his mother and the brothers and his disciples; and they remained not many days.** In John's Gospel the singular μετὰ τοῦτο connects quite closely in point of time, while μετὰ ταῦτα bridges a longer interval. The verb is singular to match the first subject, which is, therefore, also expressed by αὐτός and is followed by the other subjects. The force is: "He went down to Capernaum, and when I say 'he' (Jesus), this means he with the family and with the disciples." So the family changed its residence from Nazareth to Capernaum. Since the fact is known to John's readers from the other Gospels, he does not need to say that after the wedding all went back to Nazareth, packed up, and moved. Whether "the brothers" were at the wedding is not indicated; if they were, John finds no occasion to mention this fact. Yet we see that the disciples remained with Jesus. There is no discrepancy with Matt. 4:13, for Matthew omits what lies between the temptation in the wilderness and Christ's return from Jerusalem to Capernaum, hence he reports only that Jesus made his home at Capernaum on his return from Jerusalem. John supplements this by stating just how early the transfer was made.

It remains an unsettled question as to who the ἀδελφοί were, whether they were sons of Joseph and Mary born to them after Jesus; or sons of Joseph by a former marriage; or only cousins of Jesus through Clopas, the brother of Joseph. Each supposition has some proof but also some undeniable disproof. This, of course, is true also regarding the sisters, who are not mentioned here, since in all probability they remained in Nazareth, being held there by their marital ties. Capernaum on the shores of the Sea of Galilee was a populous place, through which passed the caravan trade route from Damascus to the Mediterranean. Here John and James had their home with Zebedee and Salome, their parents; and Peter lived here with his mother-in-law, Mark 1:29, etc. Just why Jesus made the transfer is hard to say, except that it was possible for his disciples to be near him without all of them forsaking their homes, and for the future it offered a field that was better suited for Jesus' labors than the small and retired Nazareth in the hills. When John adds that "here they remained not many days," he includes all the persons mentioned and implies in the sequel that at the end of these days all of them went to attend the Passover at Jerusalem. In v. 13 John reports this regarding Jesus, but in v. 17 we see that the disciples were with him at the festival. It is entirely in order to think that Mary and the brothers were also there. During this first brief stay in Capernaum Jesus lived quietly in contact with his disciples, away from the excitement his miracle had caused in Cana. Even now Jesus knows how to wait.

13) **And the Passover of the Jews was near, and Jesus went up to Jerusalem.** The approach of the Passover marks not only the time but indicates also the motive for the journey. This is the first Passover since Jesus assumed his ministry. The festival lasted seven days. Its crowning glory was the eating of the roasted lamb by a party numerous enough to consume it together with the bitter herbs. Every man of the Jews from twelve years up was supposed to attend this festival at Jerusalem, which overflowed the city with pilgrims. The addition "of the Jews" shows that John is writing for general readers. On the use of this term by John see 1:19. Invariably the Jews "went up to Jerusalem," no matter how elevated the locality from which they started. The verb, often enough true physically, (the Lake of Galilee lies 600 feet below sea level), is really meant ethically and spiritually. The hour has come for Jesus to step forth publicly before his nation. His first great public act would take place in the capital, yea, in the Temple itself. The great Paschal Lamb, of whom the Baptist had testified to his disciples, attends the

great Paschal Feast and there foretells his own **death** and sacrifice.

14) Without a single further word the evangelist presents the account which he wants his readers to have. **And he found in the Temple those that were selling oxen and sheep and doves, and the money-changers sitting.** The verb merely states the fact, not — as has been said — an occasion God offered for his Son's work. The condition of the Temple at this time was the work of men; it was what they had made of the Temple that Jesus "found." The part of the Temple here referred to is the court of the Gentiles, the ἱερόν. About the sanctuary proper (ναός) were four courts, that of the priests surrounding the building, that of the men toward the east, that of the women likewise, beyond that of the men. Around these three was an extensive court, called that of the Gentiles, since Gentiles were permitted to enter it. The outer side consisted of magnificent colonnades. "There, in the actual court of the Gentiles steaming with heat in the burning April day, and filling the Temple with stench and filth, were penned whole flocks of sheep and oxen, while the drovers and pilgrims stood bartering and bargaining around them. There were the men with the wicker cages filled with doves, and under the shadows of the arcade, formed by quadruple rows of Corinthian columns, sat the money-changers, with their tables covered with piles of various small coins, while, as they reckoned and wrangled in the most dishonest of trades, their greedy eyes twinkled with the lust of gain. And this was the entrance-court of the Most High! The court which was a witness that that house should be a House of Prayer for all nations had been degraded into a place which for foulness was more like shambles and for bustling commerce more like a densely crowded bazaar; while the lowing of oxen, the bleating of sheep, the babel of many

languages, the huckstering and wrangling, the clinking of money and of balances (perhaps not always just) might be heard in the adjoining courts, disturbing the chant of the Levites and the prayers of the priests!" Farrar, *The Life of Christ*, 455, etc.

The cattle and the doves were a necessity for the prescribed sacrifices, but to make of the great court a stockyard was the height of abuse. The little banks were also necessary, for a tax was taken from every Israelite who was twenty years old, Exod. 30, 11-16. This tax was collected during the month preceding the Passover and was either sent in by those at a distance or paid in person by those attending, who then, however, had to have Jewish coin, compelling all who came from foreign parts to have their money changed. For this a small rate was charged. A κερματιστής (from κέρμα, that which is cut off, i. e., a small coin) is one who deals in coins; and καθημένους describes these bankers "sitting" crosslegged behind low stool-like τράπεζαι on which their stacks of coins were ranged — open for business.

15) Jesus makes short work of this abuse. **And having made a scourge of cords, he cast all out of the Temple, also the sheep and the oxen, and he scattered the coins of the money-changers and upset their tables; and to those selling doves he said, Take these things hence! Stop making my Father's house a house of merchandise.** The public ministry of Jesus begins with an act of holy wrath and indignation. The Son cleans his Father's house with the lash of the scourge. No halfway measures, no gradual and gentle correction will do in a matter as flagrant as this. Here at the very start is the stern and implacable Christ. The aorists of the narrative are impressive; they state what was done, done in short order, done decisively and completely, begun and finished then and there.

Without speaking a word Jesus picks up a few pieces of rope, such as were ready at hand where so many cattle were tied. The aorist participle ποιήσας marks this as the preparatory action. He twists these into a scourge. Tender souls have imagined that Jesus only menaced with the scourge, at least that he struck only the animals. They are answered by πάντας ἐξέβαλεν, and πάντας is masculine, its antecedent being τοὺς πωλοῦντας and τοὺς κερματιστάς the men who were selling and the money-changers. With fiery indignation Jesus applied the scourge right and left to these men. Then also to the sheep and the oxen. John never uses τε . . . καί in the sense of "both . . . and," so that here we might read: he drove out "all, *both* the sheep *and* the oxen." This is shut out also by John's reversing the order, now placing the neuter πρόβατα first, whereas in v. 14 he has this word second. We must translate: he drove out "all" (the men), "also the sheep and the oxen." The verb ἐξέβαλεν refers to the three objects alike, and the participle ποιήσας which is to be construed with this verb explains that he drove all these men and these beasts out by means of the scourge he had made. Ethically nothing is gained for Jesus by making him only threaten to strike either the men and the beasts or only the men; for ethically, to threaten is equal to carrying out the threat. The scourge was no mere sham.

The same summary proceeding drove out the money-changers. The κόλλυβος is the small coin paid for exchange, hence κολλυβιστής is the banker who makes the exchange. Jesus "poured out" or "scattered" their κέρματα or "coins," perhaps with a flip of the scourge. But he also upset their τράπεζαι, the low little tables behind which they squatted. This reads as if he kicked them over. Short work, thorough and complete, a general scatterment and stampede.

16) Fancy has stepped in to say that Jesus dealt more leniently with the doves and their sellers, either because the doves were gentler (forgetting the gentle lambs), or because the doves were the offering of the poor (forgetting that the poor paid also the half shekel Temple tax), or — more strangely still — because the dove is the symbol of the Holy Ghost (forgetting that the lamb certainly symbolized Christ himself). The doves were in closed crates. To get rid of these crates they had to be carried away; hence the peremptory aorist, "Take these things hence!" with the derogatory ταῦτα referring to the crates and their contents, which have no business to be here. It is invention to say that when Jesus came to the doves he suddenly regained his self-control. During the entire proceeding Jesus never lost his self-control; if he had, he would have sinned. The stern and holy Christ, the indignant, mighty Messiah, the Messenger of the Covenant of whom it is written: "He shall purify the sons of Levi, and purge them as gold and silver, that they may offer unto the Lord an offering of righteousness," is not agreeable to those who want only a soft and sweet Christ. But John's record here, and that of the second cleansing of the Temple (Matt. 21:12, etc., and the parallels), portray the fiery zeal of Jesus which came with such sudden and tremendous effectiveness that before this unknown man, who had no further authority than his own person and word, this crowd of traders and changers, who thought they were fully within their rights when conducting their business in the Temple court, fled pell-mell like a lot of naughty boys.

In peremptory fashion, without a connective, comes the second command, "Stop making my Father's house a house of merchandise!" The present imperative in negative commands often means that an action already begun is to stop; so here, R. 861, etc. While this follows the command to the sellers of doves, it is evidently intended for all the traffickers. This is not the voice of a zealot vindicating the holiness of the Temple, nor of a prophet speaking in the name or Israel's God; this is the voice of the Son of God himself to whom the Temple was "my Father's house." As God's Son, who has the Son's right in this house and the Son's power over this house, Jesus uses his right and his power. And the Father supports his Son by lending his act power to drive these Temple desecrators out through the Temple gates in wild flight. By this word, "my Father's house," Jesus attests both his Sonship and his Messiahship. "And the Lord, whom ye seek, shall suddenly come to his Temple, even the Messenger of the Covenant, whom ye delight in: behold, he shall come, saith the Lord of hosts," Mal. 3:1. Thus Jesus again attests himself, and this time publicly.

There is strong contrast between "my Father's house" and "a house of merchandise." This Father and any house of his have to do with prayer, worship, true religion. What a desecration to make his house deal with ἐμπορία, trading, gain-getting, which is so much mixed with unjust dealing and at best is only secular, even if it is here conducted on the plea of providing things that were necessary for worship. Have we not enough places for buying and selling — "emporiums" as our time loves to call them — without invading the place that should be sacred because it is dedicated to God?

But why did these men not resist since they were conscious of their vested rights, having paid the Temple authorities for their concessions? Why, if at first they were startled, did they not presently recover but actually allow themselves to be driven out? Jesus was lone handed, they were many. Not even a show of resistance was offered. The answer is not to be found in their moral cowardice, in the inherent weakness of a sinful course, and on Jesus' part in the conviction of the righteousness of his cause. Sin is not always cowardly but is often bold and presumptuous. When money is at stake, wrong is often arrogant. Besides, this case is wholly extraordinary, beyond the usual clash of sin and righteousness. One explanation alone is adequate to account for this: the Son of man wielded his *divine* authority. Another question is: "Of what good was this outward cleansing as long as the hearts were not cleansed? Of what good was it to shake off a few rotten fruits while the tree itself remained corrupt?" If the object of Jesus' zeal was only these merchants and these bankers, Jesus would sink to the level of our modern reformers who try to mend the leaking ship by repairing the rigging. This question, contrasting the inward with the outward, is not correctly stated. The Temple was the very heart of the Jewish people. Luther is right when he here sees Jesus doing a part of Moses' work. The law must be applied, especially in flagrant cases, on the basis of the light and the knowledge which people have at the time. This Jesus does with his word, "Stop making my Father's house a house of merchandise." On the score of the law alone he corrects the open abuse, so that the gospel with its loftier motive may follow.

17) We now learn, incidentally, that the disciples were with Jesus and witnessed his astounding act although themselves taking no part in it. **His disciples remembered that it had been written, The zeal of thine house shall eat me up.** The aorist "remembered" is like those that precede and those that follow and tells what happened at the time: they remembered this word of Scripture when they beheld what Jesus did. In v. 22 the temporal clause records that, when Christ had risen from the dead, they re-

membered his word about destroying and rebuilding the Temple. The Greek retains the present perfect "has been written" after the aorist "remembered," whereas the English would use the pluperfect "had been written," or the past tense "was written" (our versions) ; γεγραμμένον ἐστίν is the circumscribed perfect to designate the completed act that stands as such.

Ps. 69, repeatedly quoted as being typical of Christ, expresses what David was made to suffer in his zeal for the Lord. Thus in v. 9, "The zeal of thine house hath eaten me up," is explained by the next line, "And the reproaches of them that reproached thee are fallen upon me." His zeal netted him reproach, hatred, and persecution. The fear comes into the heart of Jesus' disciples that the same thing will happen to Jesus. They thus apply Ps. 69:9 to Jesus, the application appearing in the change of the tense of the verb. In the Hebrew, David has the perfect tense which is rightly rendered with the aorist by the LXX, for David spoke of his past experience. The disciples think of what the zeal of Jesus will lead to for him in the future, hence they use καταφάγεται, "will eat up." The very word of Jesus about "my Father's house" involuntarily recalled the Psalm passage to the disciples' mind. They did not think of an inward consuming that uses up one's strength and vitality, which is suggested neither by the Psalm nor by the act of Jesus, but of a consuming that is due to opposition and harm inflicted by others. Here appears the limitation of the faith of the disciples. Though they believed Jesus to be the Son of God, having beheld his glory (v. 11), and though they again heard the attestation of his Sonship in "my Father's house," they were yet afraid that Jesus might come to harm and his work to a stop through human opposition. That is why John puts into his record this remark, as if

he would say, "And we foolish disciples became
frightened for Jesus, remembering what once happened to David." We need not assume that they at
once thought of a violent death for Jesus; their
thoughts did not go that far. The fact that Jesus
had no illusions on this point, v. 19 reveals. The
genitive zeal "of thine house" is objective and thus
may be rendered "for thy house"; the object of the
zeal is God's house.

We need hardly say that we hold, with the best
commentators over against the critical schools, that
Christ cleansed the Temple twice, once at the beginning and once at the close of his public ministry. The
first has been termed an act of grace, the second an
act of judgment; but both are manifestations of grace,
judgment descending on the wicked nation and its
Temple at a far later time. Christ's act is often
viewed as being symbolic: as he here purified the outward Temple, so his mission was to purify it inwardly,
hence not to purify the Temple alone but also the hearts
of the nation. This is quite legitimate, and it opens up
a wide range of application for all time.

18) The commotion caused by Jesus and the quick
report of his unheard of procedure brought the authorities down upon him. John is not concerned with the
dramatic story as a story, hence he abbreviates this so
as to bring correctly only the great testimony elicited
from Jesus. **The Jews, accordingly, answered and
said unto him, What sign showest thou to us, since
thou doest these things?** The fact that ἀπεκρίθησαν is
used to "answer" situations as well as questions, and
that doubling the two finite verbs "answered and said"
(instead of making one a participle) is more formal
and adds more weight, has been shown in 1:48. John
conveys the thought that the demand of the Jews was
formal and serious. John likes the resumptive οὖν,
"accordingly," which, after the remark in v. 17, re-

verts to the situation as it was left in v. 16: "accordingly," after the sellers and the truck had been removed, these official interrogators appear.

John merely calls them "the Jews" as though he cared to give them no higher title; see 1:19, where the term is explained and where its first use by John already has an unpleasant sound. Here the hostile attitude is quite marked. We infer from their formality and from their words as also from the character of Jesus' reply that these were Sanhedrists who were accompanied by some of the Temple police. They speak as men who have full authority and demand that Jesus show his credentials *to them,* ἡμῖν emphatically at the end. The question put to Jesus is based on the assumption that he has no official authority to proceed as a public reformer of the established Jewish customs. An unknown layman and mere visitor cannot be allowed to take matters into his own hands. A second thought behind the question put to Jesus, one that may in some part also help us to understand why Jesus met no resistance from the traders and the money-changers, is the general Jewish expectation of a "reliable prophet" who, when he would come, would either confirm their cultus arrangements or appoint better ones. For this reason also many of the rabbis attached to their decisions the formula, "until Elias comes." The same thought lies behind 1:21. These authorities, therefore, are quite careful in their proceeding against Jesus. They demand his credentials and take it that these must consist in some "sign" of a nature to vindicate his right to interfere in the Temple arrangements. We may read "what sign" or "what as a sign"; and ὅτι, "since," may be called elliptical: this we ask since, etc. Also "these things" implies that Jesus may attempt to go farther and to upset more of the Temple arrangements. On σημεῖον see 2:11.

19) The simple, quiet Jesus who had spent his days in little Nazareth is not in the least flustered by this clash with the supreme authorities of the nation — he meets them as their superior. **Jesus answered and said unto them, Destroy this sanctuary, and in three days I will raise it up.** John retains "answered and said" when introducing the reply of Jesus, thus marking its great weight. This reply is a flat refusal to furnish the kind of a sign demanded by these Jews. The explanation that, instead of considering the inner justification for the act of Jesus, these Jews ask for outward credentials, is insufficient. The same is true regarding the observation that an unspiritual outward miracle is demanded for a deed that appealed inwardly to the conscience, and that such a course could keep on with its demands for a sign and would never be content. More must be said, much more.

This is unbelief that demands a sign. Whenever unbelief asks a sign to convince itself, it does so only in order to reject every sign that could be given it, save one. So whenever unbelief made its demand for a sign on Jesus, he did the only thing possible, he pointed to that one sign which even unbelief will have to accept: the sign of the judgment. Jesus did signs enough, signs of grace, but these leaders, even while they admitted their occurrence (11:47), accepted none of them. Only when at last the Temple would fall about their ears, and the wrath of God visibly descend upon their guilty heads, then, too late, they would have their convincing sign and would by *that* sign know that Jesus was the Messiah indeed. And this explains another point that all the commentators whom the author has examined overlook: why Jesus answered by a veiled reference to the judgment. The unbelief that rejects the proffered grace and its signs is bound to stay in the dark, God intends to leave it there. So, indeed, it is pointed to the sign that shall crush it at

214   *The Interpretation of John*

last but never as though that sign could or should change such unbelief into faith. When that sign comes, it will be too late for faith. Even the premonitions of the sign of final judgment, which faith is only too glad to heed, unbelief scorns as it does all the signs of present grace as not being sufficient to meet its exacting demands.

The reply of Jesus, therefore, fits the men who make the demand. They want a convincing sign, one that will convince *them*. Well, Jesus has one, of course, only one. They cannot have that now, but in due time they shall have it. What that sign is they are told in a way that piques their curiosity. If it were told outright, they would only resent the telling; but since it is told in the way in which Jesus tells it, his words will stick in their minds and secretly haunt them with their mysterious, threatening meaning. Jesus could the more easily do this since the Semitic mind loves mysteries and often uses enigmatical words which require either that the hearer have the secret key or go in search for it and find it. These Jews could have found the key to the enigma given them here if they had allowed the grace of Jesus to enlighten their hearts during their day of grace. The disciples found that key as v. 22 shows, but the Jews, because their unbelief grew only more intense, never found it (Matt. 26:61; 27:40; Mark 14:57; 15:29).

Like a flash of lightning the answer of Jesus illumined an awful abyss and cast a glare into regions which still lay in darkness for every mind except his own. The word about destroying the Temple reveals the inner character of the whole Jewish treatment of Jesus; and the following word about the raising up of that Temple unveils in all its greatness the work Jesus had now begun. The form of statement is the *mashal,* a Hebrew term that is similar to the German *Sinnspruch,* a veiled and pointed saying, which is sometimes equal to a *chidah* or riddle. The history which follows shows that this first word of Jesus to the Jews did its work, sticking to their minds to the last and plainly causing them no small discomfort despite all their violent unbelief. "Destroy this Sanctuary, and in three days I will raise it up" — that is the one sign *for them*. The aorist imperative to express the one decisive act is followed by the future indicative which is also punctiliar, the second action being contingent on the first. The word ναός refers to the Sanctuary proper, comprising the Holy Place and the Holy of Holies, as distinct from ἱερόν which included the entire Temple area with its various extensive courts and structures. What follows shows that *"this* Sanctuary" could not have been spoken by Jesus accompanied by a gesture pointing to his own body. Jesus speaks of the Sanctuary before the eyes of all, the material building with its white marble walls and its gilded roof and pinnacles sparkling in the sun.

20) **The Jews, accordingly, said, Forty and six years was this Sanctuary built, and wilt thou raise it up in three days? But he was speaking of the Sanctuary of his body.** The connective οὖν joins this reply with Jesus' word of mystery. The temporal dative "forty and six years" views the entire time as a unit, R. 527, which corresponds with the constative aorist "was built," the entire extended work being summarized as one past act, R. 833. In the phrase "in three days" the preposition lays stress on the length of the time, here, of course, by comparison so brief a length. The imperfect ἔλεγε in v. 21, "he was speaking," dwells on what Jesus was saying, as one turns over in his mind the meaning of what one is uttering, for the hearers to do the same thing.

The Jewish Temple was originally built by Solomon and was destroyed by Nebuchadnezzar. It was rebuilt on the ruined site by Nehemiah and Ezra. While it was not again destroyed, its inferior condition led to a gradual rebuilding from the foundations up, on a grander and more elaborate scale, under Herod (hence it was also called Herod's Temple). About 2 years, beginning 20 or 19 B. C., were spent in preparation, 1½ in building the Porch and the Sanctuary with its Holy of Holies (16 B. C.) ; 8 years later the court and the cloisters were finished (9 B. C.) ; other repairs followed until the time of the present visit of Jesus. The whole work was not considered as completed until A. D. 64. The 46 years = 20 until the Christian era (when Jesus was 4 years old), plus 27 until the beginning of Jesus' ministry, thus making 46 to 47 in all. The questions of chronology that are involved are more or less intricate. Compare Josephus, *Ant.* 15; 20, 9, 7, where we are told that in the final stages more than 18,000 workmen were employed.

The Jews, of course, did not grasp what Jesus meant, but their misunderstanding did not lie in applying his words to the Sanctuary, as though Jesus had not referred to that building. Their error lay in applying Jesus' words to this building exclusively. Their unbelief saw only this building and nothing of its true significance and higher connection. The unbelief of modern critical minds which rejects "the two nature theory" regarding Christ's person fares no better with regard to this word of Jesus than these Jews. Now the Sanctuary, the house in which God dwelt among Israel, was the type of the body of Jesus in which the Godhead dwelt and tented among men, 1:14. The Sanctuary and Jesus thus belong insolubly together, the one is the shadow of the other. This is what the key to the *mashal* conveys, "But he was speaking of the Sanctuary, of his body."

The command to destroy the Sanctuary sounded blasphemous to Jewish ears, for what Jew would think of such a thing, especially now, when so many years had already been spent in the rebuilding? Mark that Jesus does not say that *he* will destroy it, nor that he *wants* the Jews to do this terrible thing. His words imply the very opposite, namely that he is trying to restrain the Jews from doing this frightful thing but that for some reason and in some way they are bent on doing it in spite of him. He also implies that he knows what secret force impels them to the desperate act: their unbelief and their opposition to the true Messiah, the divine reality for which the Sanctuary stood, without whom it would be an empty, useless shell. Thus the command of Jesus signifies: "Go on in your evil course, since nothing will deter you, and you will have the sign for which you call, the sign that will really convince you!" The imperative is not merely concessive: *If* you destroy. It reckons with the unbelief of the Jews as a deplorable fact that cannot be changed, just as Jesus reckoned also with the treachery of Judas when he gave the command, "That thou doest, do quickly," 13:27. We have a third command of this kind, "Fill ye up the measure of your fathers," i. e., since you are determined to do so, Matt. 24:31. This monstrous deed of destroying their own Sanctuary the Jews will perform by rejecting and killing him who was the divine reality for which the Sanctuary stood, whom it was to serve with all its services.

21) By means of "his body" Jesus dwelt among men. Because of his human nature God's Son became one with us and our Savior. "His body" is thus the "Sanctuary" in and by which we have this Savior. That body of Jesus was prefigured by the material Sanctuary of the Jews. It was a kind of substitute for it until the fulness of time should come. It was a promise of the true and everlasting connection which our Savior-God would make with us sinners by means

The Interpretation of John

of a more sacred Sanctuary or dwelling place, namely our own human nature which was assumed even in a material body but in altogether sinless form when he became man for our sake. At this time when Jesus had cleansed the Temple and was confronted by the guardians of the Temple, there stood side by side the beautiful type and the heavenly antitype: the earthly Sanctuary and the Son of God in his human body. The promise had been replaced at last by the fulfillment. But instead of being impressed by the Savior whom their own Sanctuary had pictured to them for so long a time, they met him in the courts of that Sanctuary with an incipient hostility which would grow into violent rejection. Can they have the type when they reject the antitype? Can they keep the promise when they spurn the fulfillment? What is the use of a beautiful photograph of father or mother when the moment the person himself appears he is thrown out with abuse? By killing the body of Jesus the Jews would pull down their own Sanctuary. It was impossible for the Sanctuary to go on pointing to the human body of the divine Savior when that Savior had come and had been finally rejected. The rejection of the Savior involved judgment (Matt. 26:67) and thus also the taking away of the Sanctuary.

This also explains the promise, "and in three days I will raise it up." The manner of the rebuilding must match the manner of the destruction. If, then, the Sanctuary is destroyed by the killing of the person of the Messiah, it must also again be erected in the resurrection of the Messiah. As his body is killed, so his body will be raised up. And Jesus himself will effect this raising up. The Scriptures use both expressions when speaking of this *opus ad extra*. God raises him up; Jesus himself rises. Thus the sign

the Jews demanded will be theirs indeed: a sign of
infinite grace for all believers but a sign of final judgment for these enemies. All the Jewish efforts to
maintain their Sanctuary and Temple in opposition
to all for which it stood would be in vain. To this
day it has not been rebuilt. The Mohammedan Dome
of the Rock occupies the ancient site. The Temple of
the Jews served its last purpose with its destruction.
It is still the sign that answers unbelief once for all,
the type of the judgment to come. The resurrection
of Jesus wrought the new spiritual temple of God's
people with a new cultus in spirit and in truth (4:21-
24), it needed no more types and symbols since in
Christ we have the promised substance itself. Zech.
6:12, 13; Heb. 3:3.

22) The Jews not only did not understand what
the *mashal* of Jesus meant, they did not want to understand. They wholly ignored its first half and fastened
only on the second half, that Jesus would in three days
erect a building that it had taken forty-six years to
erect. Later, at the trial of Jesus, they boldly falsified
that troublesome first half, making Jesus say, "I am
able to destroy the Sanctuary of God" (Matt. 26:61),
or, "I will destroy this Sanctuary" (Mark 14:58).
From the start the Jews must thus have felt the sting
in that command, "Destroy it by your evil, vicious
practices!" So also the second half, the Jews could
tell themselves, did not mean and could not mean that
Jesus would erect this great complex of a stone structure "in three days." Though they clung to this even
at the trial of Jesus, Mark's rendering, "and in three
days I will build another *made without hands*," indicates that they had an inkling that the Sanctuary Jesus
intended to build was something other than another
structure of stone. The one point, however, that mystified the Jews completely and was intended by Jesus

to do so was the phrase "in three days." This reference to the resurrection of Jesus was absolutely beyond
the Jewish unbelief.

This phrase exceeded also the faith of Jesus' own
disciples. Whatever they made of the destruction and
of the raising up of the Sanctuary, the "three days"
were beyond them. They, to be sure, kept their
Master's saying inviolate and in their thoughts neither
ignored its first half nor falsified it as the Jews did.
But John tells us that they did not understand it until
Jesus was actually raised from the dead. **When,
therefore, he was raised from the dead, his disciples
remembered that he was saying this, and they believed the Scripture and the word which Jesus
spoke.** Not until that time did John discover the
key and realize that Jesus was speaking of his own
body, v. 21. Especially also the "three days" were
solved when Jesus died on Friday and arose on Sunday.
What kept Jesus' word dark for them was their un-
willingness to believe that Jesus would actually die
as he kept telling them he would, i. e., that by killing
him the Jews would wreck their Sanctuary. Thus they
also never caught what Jesus said of his resurrection
even when he added that this would occur on the third
day after his death. But they remembered at last when
the risen Savior stood before them. After the active
"I will raise up" John now has the passive "he was
raised up." Both are true and both are freely used,
one indicating Christ's agency, the other that of his
Father. The phrase ἐκ νεκρῶν denotes separation and
nothing more, R. 598. The absence of the article
points to the *quality* of being dead not to so many
dead individuals that are left behind; and the sense
of the phrase is, "from death." In the interest of
the doctrine of a double resurrection the effort has
been made to establish the meaning, "out from among
the dead." Linguistically and doctrinally this is un-

tenable. When it is applied to the unique resurrection of Jesus, this is at once apparent; the idea is not that he left the other dead behind but that he passed "from death" to a glorious life. No wonder ἐκ νεκρῶν is never used with reference to the ungodly. The phrase is used 35 times with reference to Christ, a few times with reference to other individuals in a figurative way, and twice with reference to the resurrection of many, Luke 20:35; Mark 12:25, where the phrase cannot have a meaning different from that which it has in the other passages.

John has the imperfect ἔλεγε, "he was saying this," as in v. 21, and here it is set in contrast with the aorist εἶπεν, "which Jesus did say," noting only the past fact as such. Then at last, when Jesus had risen from death, the disciples properly connected the word of Jesus that had stuck in their minds all this time with the Scripture, ἡ γραφή, namely with passages like Ps. 16:9-11; Isa. 53; the type Jonah; etc.; compare Luke 24:25, etc.; John 20:9; Acts 2:24-32; I Cor. 15:4. Thus at last with full understanding the disciples "did believe the Scripture and the word which Jesus (once) spoke." The thought is not that they had disbelieved or doubted either of the two before but that now their implicit faith became explicit faith. A statement like v. 22 which gives us a glimpse into the inner biography of John and of his fellow-disciples bears the stamp of historical reality in a manner so inimitable that only the strongest preconceptions can ignore its implications. No pseudo-John living in the second century could invent this ignorance of the apostle regarding a saying of Jesus that he himself had invented. The critics who make such a claim, as Godet well says, dash themselves against a sheer moral impossibility.

23) The brief glimpse of the effect of the first public activity of Jesus presented in v. 23-25 rounds

out the preceding account of the cleansing of the
Temple and forms a transition to the conversation with Nicodemus, furnishing us with the historical background and the general attitude of Jesus.
**Now while he was in Jerusalem at the Passover dur-
ing the feast many believed in his name, seeing his
signs which he was doing. Jesus on his part, however, was not entrusting himself to them on account
of knowing them all, also because he was not in
need that anyone should bear witness concerning this
or that man, since he was aware what was in the
man.**

We hear nothing more about the authorities who
challenged Jesus to produce his credentials. They had
received their answer, and as far as John is concerned
are thus dismissed. The two modifiers "at the Passover" and "during the festival" are not tautological,
for the Passover was observed on the fourteenth of
Nisan, and the festival lasted the whole week following. Jesus remained for the entire time. What he
did John records only incidentally, for his purpose
is to inform us that at this first public appearance of
his he gathered no close disciples as he did down at
Bethany beyond Jordan after his Baptism, and we also
learn the reason why. The fact that by his attendance Jesus meant to step out into public view and to
begin his public Messianic work right here in the
capital of Judaism and right at this greatest festival
of Judaism, should not be denied by making his cleansing of the Temple the sudden impulse of the moment,
and his further activity during the week only incidental
to his presence here at the time. The great hour for
his public labors had come.

While the authorities from the first met him with
unbelief and a show of hostility, this was not the case
with "many" of the pilgrims who had assembled for
the festival. They "believed in his name," i. e., re-

ceived the revelation he made of himself with faith and trust; compare the remarks on τὸ ὄνομα αὐτοῦ in **1:12.** John, however, prevents us from regarding this definite statement with its historical aorist as meaning that thus quickly Jesus gained many true disciples who were like the six that believed on him beyond the Jordan. He does this by describing the nature of their faith, "seeing his signs which he was doing." This was the only basis of their faith, not the attestation in the words of Jesus which had kindled the faith of those first six disciples and which was then confirmed by the first miracle of Jesus at Cana. Yet we must not regard this remark about the character of the faith of these many believers as implying that the signs Jesus wrought were not intended to produce faith, which would conflict with their character as "signs" and with passages like **5:36; 10:37, 38;** and **14:11.** Faith may well begin by first trusting in the signs. But the signs and the Word belong together like a document and the seals attached to it, as the passages just mentioned show. The seals alone eventually amount to nothing. Some advanced from the signs to the Word and thus, believing both, attained abiding faith. Others saw the signs just as clearly but refused the Word and remained in unbelief. When some today would take the Word and yet discard the signs, they invalidate the Word itself, a vital part of which the signs remain, and also fail in faith. The signs so establish the Word that all who began and who now begin with the Word and then accept the signs attain true and abiding faith. The "many" in Jerusalem still hung in the balance with such inadequate faith as they had.

While the incidental object "his signs" only intimates that during this week Jesus wrought such signs for the public, the added relative clause with its imperfect tense ἐποίει, "which he was doing" or "kept

doing," declares positively that Jesus wrought a goodly
number of such signs. Yet John relates none of them;
in his Gospel he records only certain select miracles,
such as most clearly and directly serve his purpose.
We have seen one of these, that at Cana. By telling
us that the "many" in Jerusalem rested their faith
only on the signs which Jesus kept doing John does
not need to add that during this week Jesus added to
the signs by also testifying by his teaching. This
the "many" passed by, giving it little, too little,
attention.

24) The addition of αὐτός to ὁ Ἰησοῦς intensifies
the subject; yet it does not mean "Jesus himself,"
which would wrongly contrast him with others, but
means "Jesus on his part," contrasting his *action* with
the other *action* just reported, with adversative δέ,
"however," pointing this out. The contrast lies between ἐπίστευσαν in v. 23 and οὐκ ἐπίστευεν αὐτόν (some
prefer αὐτόν, R. 688) : they "trusted," he "was not
entrusting himself." Πιστεύω with the accusative means
"to entrust," R. 476. This contrast extends to the
tenses: the first is an aorist to indicate the closed act,
"trusted," which trust, however, rested only on the
signs; the second is an imperfect, leaving the even-
tual outcome open, "was not entrusting himself," i. e.,
waiting to see what the faith of the "many" would
prove to be. To the six disciples Jesus fully entrusted
himself; from the many at the festival he held aloof,
formed no closer union with them as being people who
were really committed to him.

This was wholly an act on the part of Jesus and
in no way dependent on information he received about
these people from either his six disciples or from
other sources. In this connection John informs us
about the power of Jesus to read the very hearts of
men. We must know about it; Jesus had already used
it in the most astonishing way in the case of Peter

and of Nathanael (1:42 and 47, 48), and he constantly used it, notably also in his dealings with his
foes. These are never able to deceive him; all their
cunning schemes lie open before his eyes. Thus here,
too, Jesus holds aloof from the "many," whereas an
ordinary man would have been deceived by their first
flash of faith and would have wrecked himself by
injudiciously relying upon it. John has διά with the
articular infinitive (this infinitive is rare in John's
writings, R. 756), "on account of knowing (them) all."
Since πάντας refers specifically to πολλοί in v. 23, it
refers to all of these "many" not to "all men" in
the world. During his humiliation Jesus used his
supernatural knowledge when and where it served
the purpose of his saving work and not beyond that.
Note the present tense in τὸ γινώσκειν, not an aorist: he
was intimately acquainted with them all, and this continued in the case of not only the new additions as
the number grew from one day to another but also
in the case of each individual and of any change that
developed in his heart. This is a sad word — "all,"
for it means that among the "many" Jesus found not
one with whom it would have been safe to form closer
contact.

25) The διά phrase includes only the "many."
From this we ourselves might generalize, that as Jesus
knew these so he would know others also. John does
this for us, because he wants it kept in mind as we
read on, for instance immediately in the story of Nicodemus and that of the Samaritan woman. So John
coordinates (καί) the second reason, which also helps
to elucidate the first, "also because," etc. The durative imperfect εἶχεν says that this was always the case
with Jesus, "he was not in need (at any time) that
anyone should witness concerning this or that man,"
as we so often are when we do not know what to
make of a man and feel that we must ask for the judg-

ment of someone who knows him more intimately. Here ἵνα with the subjunctive crowds out the classical infinitive, a construction found frequently in John and in the Koine, and, as here, with impersonal expressions, B.-D. 393, 5. The article in the phrase περὶ τοῦ ἀνθρώπου is scarcely generic but rather specific, "this or that man," anyone who approaches Jesus with a confession of his name, with hostility, or in any other way.

The reason Jesus needed no testimony from others is added in order to make the information complete, "for he was aware what was in the man," i. e., the one in question, the article taking up the one found in the περί phrase. The imperfect ἐγίνωσκε states that Jesus always knew, in every single case. What he knew was "what was in the man," in his very heart and mind, better even than he himself knew. Here ἦν is accomodated to the tense of ἐγίνωσκε, which is sometimes done in the Koine after a secondary tense (always in English), although ἐστί would suffice, R. 1029, 1043. The glorified Christ sees to the bottom of every heart, detects every superficial confession, every trace of indifference or hostility.

CHAPTER III

The Conversation with Nicodemus, 3:1-21. — This conversation connects naturally with 2:23, 24, Nicodemus being one of the "many" there mentioned as believing because of the signs, to whom Jesus would not entrust himself. Yet the conversation with Jesus did not yet bring this man to faith. But the story of Nicodemus is not John's real concern. As far as that is concerned, the sequel appears in 7:15 and 19:39. Here John's interest is in the *teaching* of Jesus as the counterpart to the signs (2:23). Though it is conducted in private, this conversation was a part of Jesus' public ministry, just as was the conversation with the Samaritan woman. John records this conversation because it really constitutes a *summary* of Jesus' teaching, dealing, as it does, with the kingdom, regeneration, faith, the Son of man, God's love and the plan of salvation, judgment and unbelief. The observation is correct that, as in the forefront of Matthew's Gospel the Sermon on the Mount presents a grand summary of Christ's teaching on the law as related to the gospel, so here in the opening chapters of John's Gospel this conversation with Nicodemus presents a grand summary of the gospel itself.

This also explains the way in which John records the conversation. Only the first part is dialog (2-10), and the rest is a discourse of Jesus. What else Nicodemus may have asked or said is immaterial for John's purpose; hence he omits it. In this respect the record of the conversation with the Samaritan woman is different, wherefore also the form of dialog is continued to the end. In the second half of this chapter we have a record only of what Jesus said. We may take it that the conversation continued much longer than the few moments required to read John's report of it, and that thus toward the end John simply reports the chief and essential things which Jesus told Nicodemus. We have every reason to think that not only John but also the other five disciples (see 1:35-51) were present at the visit of Nicodemus, just as they were also silent witnesses in 2:17. The historical character of John's report is beyond question. And this is true not only for the first but also for the last half of his account; for all that Jesus said exactly fits the condition and situation of Nicodemus. The historical character of John's report should, therefore, not be questioned.

1) **Now there was a man of the Pharisees, named Nicodemus, a ruler of the Jews.** The report is introduced by the transitional δέ; R. 1185 has a different view. Nicodemus is described at length. His party connection, his actual name, his official position are stated. First we are told that he belonged to the Pharisees (with the partitive ἐκ), which fact is made emphatic by being placed ahead of his name. On the Pharisees compare 1:24. All that follows is governed by the Pharisaic character of Nicodemus; a conversation such as this would have been impossible with a Sadducee or a mere Herodian. John is somewhat chary about mentioning names. He records that of Nicodemus, it seems, because of the subsequent acts of this man; the Samaritan woman he leaves unnamed. The Greek has the parenthetical nominative, "Nicodemus name for him." The fact that Nicodemus was "a ruler of the Jews" must here, in Jerusalem, mean that he was a member of the Sanhedrin; as such he appears also in the session of this body in 7:50. Combined with his being a Pharisee, this means that Nicodemus was one of the "scribes," a rabbi learned in

the Old Testament Scriptures; for the γραμματεῖς that were in the Sanhedrin were Pharisees, the entire body of some seventy consisting of high priests, elders, and scribes. In v. 10 Jesus directly calls Nicodemus "the teacher of Israel." Incidentally we see how high the first public work of Jesus reached — into the very Sanhedrin itself, I Cor. 1:26 ("not many," but some).

2) **This man came to him at night and said to him, Rabbi, we know that from God thou art come as a teacher; for no one can do these signs that thou doest except God be with him.** With οὗτος, in the Greek fashion, all that is said in v. 1 is picked up: "this" is the man who did and said what is here told. Two points are implied: he had seen some of the signs, and he had heard some of the teaching. The impression made on him had been so strong that he risked this visit "at night," νυκτός, the genitive of time within which something takes place. Both this impression and the venturesome visit it produced are part of this man's attitude toward Jesus, an attitude produced *in toto* by Jesus himself, in fact, a vital part in the course of his conversion. Caiaphas, other Sanhedrists, kept aloof from Jesus, thrust every favorable impression aside — and were never converted. Their attitude was due wholly to themselves, it was an abnormal, wilful resistance, 1:11. The fact that Nicodemus came "at night" was, of course, due to fear lest he be seen, and thus his standing be compromised. Yet this is not cowardice but rather careful caution, for, although Jesus had made an impression on Nicodemus, the man was not sure about this young Rabbi from Galilee who might turn out a disappointment after all. So he cautiously investigates. The fact that Nicodemus "came to him," taking the risk involved, shows his seriousness, shows how deeply Jesus had gripped his heart. He did not ignore or

wipe out the impression made on him. He took a
step that was certainly decisive. In the study of
conversion Nicodemus, like the Samaritan woman, will
always stand out as an illuminating example.

He addresses Jesus with the respectful title
"Rabbi" as Andrew, John, and Nathanael had done,
see 1:38. The plural "we know" refers not to other
Sanhedrists but to the preceding πολλοί, "many," in
2:23. He, however, does not come as a representative
of these others but only for his own sake; yet the
fact that others were impressed like himself means
a good deal to him. Of what he and others are convinced is, "that from God thou art come as a teacher,"
the perfect ἐλήλυθας with its present implication meaning "hast come" and thus art now here. The phrase
"from God" is to be understood in the sense, "commissioned by him and thus sent forth from him." It
does not intend to express the divine nature of Jesus
but the conviction that Jesus has assumed his office
and work not on his own accord but by God's direction, like the prophets of old. The statement is true
as far as it goes. Yet behind this admission lurks the
question whether this man Jesus, who evidently has
come from God, may not prove to be the Messiah. This
is the real purpose of Nicodemus' coming, the thing
he would like to discover.

On what grounds Nicodemus rests the conviction
that Jesus is "a teacher come from God" he himself
states, "for no one can do these signs which thou
doest except God be with him." Nicodemus, too, saw
"the glory" (1:14) in these signs; what they indicated
to him he states. Both ποιεῖν and ποιεῖς are durative,
"can be doing" and "thou art doing," and thus include
the signs already done and any others Jesus might
still do. The noteworthy point, however, is that Nicodemus connects these signs with the teaching of Jesus.
On σημεῖον see 2:11. As a διδάσκαλος Jesus presents

these signs; they are his credentials. Nicodemus
regards these credentials as proving that this teacher
has surely come from God, for who could do such
signs "except God be with him?" μετ' αὐτοῦ, in covenant
or association with him; σύν would mean "with him"
to help him. We see just how far Nicodemus has
progressed. The signs loom up in his mind, the contents of the teaching is not mentioned and seems not
to have entered far into his mind, although he connects the two. This explains the course of Jesus' instruction: since Nicodemus accepts the signs, Jesus un-
folds to him the teaching which these signs accredit
and attest. And this teaching centers in Jesus' person
in such a way that Nicodemus at once has also the
answer to the question that troubles him — he learns
who Jesus really is.

3) **Jesus answered and said unto him, Amen,
amen, I say to thee, Except one be born anew,
he cannot see the kingdom of God.** On the use of
ἀπεκρίθη and the doubling of the verbs "answered and
said," see 1:48. Jesus saw what was in the man
(2:25) and thus told him what he needed; and the
two verbs show that this is highly important. When
Jesus "takes the word" (ἀπεκρίθη) he does not begin
with his own person although Nicodemus had put this
forward. In due time Jesus will cover that point.
Jesus begins with the kingdom of God and the entrance
into that kingdom. And we must note that this kingdom and the coming of the Messiah belong together,
for he is the King, and only where he is the kingdom
is. Nicodemus, too, understood this relation and, like
every serious Israelite, desired to see (ἰδεῖν) this Messianic kingdom, i. e., as a member entitled to a place
in it. This is the background of Jesus' statement. So
he begins with the solemn formula, explained in 1:51,
"Amen, amen (the assurance of verity), I say to thee"
(the assurance of authority) and follows with a state-

ment regarding what is essential in order to see the
kingdom as one of its members.

This word of Jesus, as also its elaboration in v. 5
and 11, goes back to what the Baptist had preached
when he declared the kingdom at hand and called on
men to enter it by the Baptism of repentance and
remission of sins, meaning the kingdom in its new form
with redemption actually accomplished by the Messiah,
the Lamb of God, i. e., the new covenant that would
supersede the old. This grand concept ἡ βασιλεία τοῦ Θεοῦ
must not be defined by generalizing from the kingdoms
of earth. These are only imperfect shadows of God's
kingdom. God makes his own kingdom, and where
he is with his power and his grace there his kingdom
is; whereas earthly kingdoms make their kings, often
also unmake them, and their kings are nothing apart
from what their kingdoms make them. So also we are
not really subjects in God's kingdom but partakers
of it, i. e., of God's rule and kingship; earthly kingdoms have only subjects. In God's kingdom we already
bear the title "kings unto God," and eventually the
kingdom, raised to the nth degree, shall consist of nothing but kings in glorious array, each with his crown,
and Christ thus being "the King of kings," a kingdom
that has no subjects at all.

This divine kingdom goes back to the beginning
and rules the world and shall so rule until the consummation of the kingdom at the end of time. All
that is in the world, even every hostile force, is sub-
servient to the plans of God. The children and sons
of God, as heirs of the kingdom in whom God's grace
is displayed, constitute the kingdom in its specific sense.
And this kingdom is divided by the coming of Christ,
the King, in the flesh to effect the redemption of grace
by which this specific kingdom is really established
among men. Hence we have the kingdom before

Christ, looking toward his coming, and the kingdom after Christ, looking back to his coming — the promise and the fulfillment to be followed by the consummation — the kingdom as it was in Israel, as it now is in the Christian Church, the *Una Sancta* in all the world, and as it will be at the end forever. It is called "God's" kingdom and "Christ's" kingdom (Eph. 5:5; II Tim. 4:1; II Pet. 1:11) because the power and the grace that produce this kingdom are theirs; also the kingdom "of heaven" or "of the heavens" because the power and the grace are wholly from heaven and not in any way of the earth. The Baptist preached the coming of this kingdom as it centers in the incarnate Son and his redemptive work.

Jesus tells Nicodemus the astonishing fact, "unless one is born anew" he cannot enter this kingdom. He makes the statement general, "one," τίς, not singling out Nicodemus as though making an exceptional requirement for him. Not until v. 7 do we hear "thou," although the application to Nicodemus personally lies on the surface throughout. The requirement of a new birth is universal. The form ἐάν with the subjunctive shows that Jesus counts on some entering the kingdom, i. e., that the new birth will be received by them. While ἄνωθεν may mean "from above" (place, local), here it must mean "anew" (time); for in v. 4 we have δεύτερον, "a second time," in the same sense. Nor is ἄνωθεν the same as ἐκ Θεοῦ (in John's First Epistle), for while God bestows this birth, the means by which he does so do not descend "from above" (Word and Sacrament), for which reason also what Jesus says of the new birth belongs to the ἐπίγεια, "earthly things" (v. 12). Not new and superior knowledge is essential; not new, superior, more difficult meritorious works; not a new national or ecclesiastical or religious.

party connection that is better than the Pharisaic party; but an entirely new birth, the beginning of a newly born life, i. e., the true spiritual life.

This rebirth is misconceived when the Baptist and Jesus are separated and it is thought that the former was unable to bestow the Spirit. On this subject compare the comments on 1:26. The Baptist's requirement is identical with that which Jesus makes. The Baptism of repentance and remission of sins bestows the new birth even as it is and can be mediated only by the Spirit. Jesus is not telling Nicodemus, "Go and be baptized by John and then wait until the Messiah gives thee the Spirit (how would he do that?), and thus thou wilt be reborn." True repentance, the Baptist's μετάνοια, consists of contrition and faith; and these two, wrought by the Spirit, constitute conversion which in substance is regeneration. All these focus in Baptism: every contrite and believing sinner whom the Baptist baptized was converted, was regenerated, had the Spirit, had forgiveness, was made a member of the kingdom, was ready for the King so close at hand to participate in full in all that the King would now bring. The Baptist stressed repentance and forgiveness in connection with his Baptism because these mediated the great change; in this first word to Nicodemus Jesus names only the great change itself and its necessity, "born anew." In a moment Jesus, too, will name the means.

Jesus' word regarding the new birth shatters once for all every supposed excellence of man's attainment, all merit of human deeds, all prerogatives of natural birth or station. Spiritual birth is something one undergoes not something he produces. As our efforts had nothing to do with our natural conception and birth, so, in an analogous way but on a far higher plane, regeneration is not a work of ours. What a blow for Nicodemus! His being a Jew gave him no part in the kingdom; his being a Pharisee, esteemed holier than other people, availed him nothing; his membership in the Sanhedrin and his fame as one of its scribes went for nought. This Rabbi from Galilee calmly tells him that he is not yet in the kingdom! All on which he had built his hopes throughout a long arduous life here sank into ruin and became a little worthless heap of ashes. Unless he attains this mysterious new birth, even he shall not "see" (ἰδεῖν) the kingdom, i. e., have an experience of it. This verb is chosen to indicate the first activity of one who has passed through the door of the kingdom.

4) **Nicodemus says to Him, How can a man be born when he is old? He certainly cannot enter a second time into his mother's womb and be born?** These questions of Nicodemus have sometimes been misunderstood. This is not mere unspiritual denseness that is unable to rise above the idea of physical birth; nor rabbinical skill in disputation that tries to make Jesus' requirement sound absurd, which Jesus would never have answered as he did; nor hostility to the requirement of Jesus. Nicodemus simply puts the requirement laid down by Jesus into words of his own; and by doing this in the form of questions he indicates where his difficulty lies. He thus actually asks Jesus for further explanation and enlightenment, and Jesus gives him this.

When Nicodemus says γέρων ὤν he is thinking of himself, although his question would apply to one of any age, even to a babe. This touch indicates both that the conversation is truly reported, and that one who saw the old man when he said "being old" remembered and wrote it down. The second question elucidates the first. We must note especially the interrogative μή, which indicates that in the speaker's own mind the answer can only be a no. This completely exonerates Nicodemus from the charge that he under-

stood Jesus' words only as a reference to physical
birth; or that he tried to turn those words so that
they referred only to such a birth. The fact is that
he does the very opposite as if he would say, "I know
you cannot and do not mean that!" or, "That much I
see." He clearly perceives that Jesus has in mind
some other, far higher kind of birth. But "how can
such a birth take place?" He might also have asked,
"*What* is this birth?" and the "what" would probably
have explained also the "how." He did the thing
the other way, he asked, *"How,"* etc., and the manner, too, involves the nature — "how" one is thus born
will cast light on "what" this being born really is. As
in the word of Jesus, Nicodemus also retains the
passive, here two infinitives, γεννηθῆναι, the second after
δύναται. The term κοιλία denotes the abdominal cavity
and thus is used for "womb."

Although Jesus' word must have struck Nicodemus
hard, being uttered, as it was, by a young man to one
grown old and gray as an established "teacher" (v. 10),
Nicodemus shows no trace of resentment. He neither
contradicts nor treats Jesus' statement as extravagant
and ridiculous. He takes no offense although he feels
the personal force of what Jesus says. He does not
rise and leave saying, "I have made a mistake in coming." He quietly submits to the Word. This attitude
and conduct, however, is due to the Word itself and to
its gracious saving power. Changes were gradually
going on in this man's heart, some of them unconscious-
ly; not he but a higher power was active in producing
these changes. He was not as yet reborn, nor do we
know when that moment came. Enough that Jesus
was leading him forward, and Nicodemus did not run
away.

5) **Jesus answered, Amen, amen, I say to thee,
Except one be born of water and the Spirit, he cannot enter into the kingdom of God.** In no way does

Jesus rebuke or fault Nicodemus — clear evidence that he who knew what is in a man (2:25) regards the questions of this man as being wholly sincere. Jesus explains his former word — again evidence that Nicodemus really has asked for an explanation. Jesus repeats his former word exactly, adding only one phrase and substituting "enter" for "see," a mere explanatory detail, for only they who "enter" "see" the kingdom. The preposition ἐκ denotes origin and source. The exegesis which separates ἐξ ὕδατος καὶ Πνεύματος, as though Jesus said ἐξ ὕδατος καὶ ἐκ Πνεύματος is not based on linguistic grounds; for the one preposition has as its one object the concept "water and Spirit," which describes Baptism, its earthly element and its divine agency. The absence of the Greek articles with the two nouns makes their unity more apparent. The making of two phrases out of the one is due to the preconception that the Baptist's Baptism consisted only of water and that figuratively the Messiah's bestowal of the Spirit can also be called a Baptism — yet leaving unsaid how and by what means the Messiah would bestow the Spirit. The fact that Jesus thus also postpones the very possibility of the new birth for Nicodemus (and for all men) into the indefinite future, when he and others may already have been overtaken by death, is also left unsaid.

In the Baptist's sacrament, as in that of Jesus afterward, water is joined with the Spirit, the former being the divinely chosen earthly medium (necessary on that account), the latter being the regenerating agent who uses that medium. When Jesus spoke to Nicodemus, the latter could understand only that the Baptist's sacrament was being referred to. This was entirely enough. For this sacrament admitted to the kingdom as completely as the later instituted sacrament of Jesus. Therefore Jesus also continued to require the Baptist's sacrament, 3:22 and 4:2, and after his resurrection extended it to all nations by means of his great commission. No need, then, to raise the question as to which Baptism Jesus here had in mind, or whether he also referred to his own future sacrament. It was but one sacrament which was first commanded by God for the use of the Baptist, then was used by Jesus, and finally instituted for all people. Tit. 3:5 thus applies to this sacrament in all its stages. Jesus tells Nicodemus just what he asks, namely the "how" of regeneration. How is it possible? By Baptism! But Jesus cuts off a second how: How by Baptism? by using the description of Baptism, "water and Spirit." Because not merely water but God's Spirit is effective in the sacrament, therefore it works the new birth.

Jesus here assumes that Nicodemus knows about the preaching as well as about the baptizing of John. In passing note that the Holy Spirit is here mentioned, and that Nicodemus accepts this mention and all that follows regarding the Spirit without the slightest hesitation, as though he knew this Third Person of the Godhead; compare 1:32. Thus this reference of Jesus to Baptism is not understood by Nicodemus as an *opus operatum*, a mere mechanical application of the earthly element with whatever formula God had given the Baptist to use, but as being in the Baptist's entire work vitally connected with μετάνοια or "repentance." Strictly speaking, this repentance (contrition and faith) itself constitutes the rebirth in all adults yet not apart from Baptism which as its seal must follow; for the rejection of Baptism vitiates repentance and regeneration, demonstrating that they are illusory.

6) Without a connective Jesus takes up the remark of Nicodemus regarding the impossibility of a physical rebirth and carries this to its ultimate limit

— even if it were possible, a rebirth in the flesh would reproduce only flesh. Jesus formulates this as a general principle which is self-evident and final in its clearness and then sets beside it the opposite, the Spirit birth, again as a principle with the same evident finality. And the parallelism of the two principles once more brings out the necessity Jesus has twice stated, that only by this latter birth a man can enter the kingdom. **That born of the flesh is flesh; and that born of the Spirit is spirit.** The Greek has the neuter τὸ γεγεννημένον, which states the thought abstractly, by this form emphasizing the fact that a principle is being established, and one without a single exception: anything whatever that is born thus, certainly also including man. In the elaboration Jesus has the masculine ὁ γεγεννημένος, "he that is born." The perfect participle has its usual force: once born and now so born.

Any birth from flesh produces only flesh. A stream never rises higher than its source. The fact is axiomatic. Its statement is its own proof. There is a contrast between σάρξ and πνεῦμα, and this determines that the former does not refer merely to the human body or to nature, or to this with its connotation of weakness and mortality, but to "the flesh" in its full opposition to "the spirit": our sinful human nature. Thus σάρξ includes also the human soul, the human ψυχή and the human πνεῦμα, for sin has its real seat in the immaterial part of our nature which uses the gross material part as its instrument. A hundred rebirths from sinful flesh, whether one be old or young, would produce nothing but the same sinful flesh and leave one as far as ever from the kingdom. This is not later Pauline theology, which the evangelist puts into Jesus' mouth and which is thus beyond the mind of Nicodemus. We meet this same thought already in Gen. 6:3; Ps. 51:5; Job 14:4. In fact, it is so simple that it is clear to any man who has the least idea of what flesh means.

In the second member Jesus does not say, "that born of the water and Spirit," but only, "that born of the Spirit," although he refers to Baptism. In this sacrament the regenerator is not the water but the Spirit who uses this medium. This also settles the question as to whether we must regard this second principle in a way that is wholly abstract, "that born *of the spirit* is *spirit*," or more concretely, "that born *of the Spirit* is spirit." The entire context decides for the latter, especially also the interpretative expression in v. 8, "one born of the Spirit" (not, "of the spirit"). In addition, the other translation would produce a false contrast, namely that of human flesh and that of the human spirit. Nor is there such a thing as a birth of the human spirit — in English we should say, soul — apart from and in contrast with the human flesh. Only God's Spirit produces a spiritual birth, a new nature and life, one that is $\pi\nu\epsilon\tilde{\nu}\mu\alpha$, the opposite of $\sigma\acute{\alpha}\rho\xi$. Underlying both axiomatic statements is the thought that "the flesh," our sinful human nature, cannot possibly enter the kingdom but that only the "spirit," the new life and new nature born of the Spirit, can do so. This, too, casts light on the kingdom itself, on its nature, and on the people who alone are partakers of it.

7) Perhaps astonishment was written on Nicodemus' face, or a movement and gesture betrayed his thought. It all sounded very strange to this old Pharisee who all his lifelong was set on works — works — works and was admired by the mass of the nation for this very fact, to hear from Jesus: birth — birth — birth by the Spirit, by Baptism, which would bring forth "spirit," an entirely new nature and creature. The objective tone of Jesus, therefore,

takes a subjective, pastoral turn. Jesus lights up the mystery of this birth by describing one who is actually reborn by means of an analogy. **Marvel not that I said to thee, You must be born anew. The wind blows where it will, and thou hearest its sound but knowest not whence it comes and whither it goes — thus is everyone that is born of the Spirit.** In prohibitions for the second person the Greek has the aorist subjunctive instead of the aorist imperative, hence μὴ θαυμάσῃς, "Do not marvel!" What Nicodemus marvelled at is this new birth on which Jesus insisted instead of urging something else. Jesus uses the plural, "You must be born anew," for the principle applies to all men alike, of course, including Nicodemus, holy as he, the Pharisee, deemed himself because of his close observance of the law. To be sure, in itself this new birth is marvelous enough, transcending even the wonder of our physical conception and birth. But merely to marvel at it may lead to unbelief and to denial of its possibility. A thing may be marvelous, mysterious, even incomprehensible and yet it may not only be possible but actual, an indisputable fact.

8) Jesus furnishes a striking and pertinent example which was apparently suggested by the two meanings of πνεῦμα, which are found also in the Hebrew *ruach* and the Aramaic *rucha*, namely "wind" and "spirit" ("Spirit"). Take the wind, Jesus says to Nicodemus, *the reality and fact* of it is beyond question, for you hear its sound, you know it is there as a fact; but whence it came, and whither it goes, how it starts, how it stops, these and many other facts "thou knowest not." With the verbs ἀκούεις and οἶδας Jesus addresses Nicodemus personally. Was there, perhaps, a sound of wind outside as Jesus was speaking? The two clauses "whence it comes" and "whither it goes" do not refer to the mere direction of the wind,

north or south, east or west, for this anyone can
know; but to the original origin and source of the
wind, this vast mass of moving and often rushing
air, and to its ultimate goal, where it piles up and
stops.   Despite all our wise modern meteriological
knowledge we still do not know this "whence" and
this "whither," how this vast volume of air leaves
one place and goes to another.   In both the LXX and
the New Testament ποί, "whither," is replaced by
ποῦ, "where," R. 548; which means that we must not
read the latter as though it also meant to indicate
where the wind comes to rest.

The application which Jesus makes of this illustration comes as a surprise.   He does not say, "thus also
is the Spirit of God."   This is one of the numerous
and interesting cases, occurring in the sayings of Jesus
as well as in the writings of the Apostles, where the
thought overleaps an intervening point and at once
presents the final point.   So here the intervening point
is *the fact and reality* of the working of God's Spirit.
This is taken for granted because it is involved in
the fact and reality of the result of this working,
namely every man who is actually reborn of the Spirit.
In the present case Jesus has to make the comparison
in this way.   The two features that are alike, one in
the wind, the other in the Spirit, must be such as
we ourselves can verify.   If the wind did not affect
our senses, we should never know its blowing; if
the Spirit did not produce reborn men, we should
never know his presence and his activity.   Thus the
fact and reality of the wind that *we hear* in its activity
and its effect illustrates the Spirit whom *we observe* in
his activity and his effect (the regenerated man).   Jesus
takes only this one effect of the wind, the sound of it
that we hear in the rustling breeze or the roaring
storm.   So also he matches it by only one effect of
the Spirit, the regenerate man who himself knows

the great transformation that has taken place within him, and whose transformation others likewise can observe and know. To be sure, the wind works also other effects, and the Spirit performs also other works. Jesus has no call here to enter on these points. The illustration as he uses it fully meets his purpose.

Sometimes this illustration has been misapplied by commentators because they fail to discover the point of comparison. They find three such points, whereas every true comparison has but one. This is also done by those who stress the clause, "wherever it will," and then speak of the free and unrestricted working of the Spirit. This misconception often becomes serious, for it easily leads to the false dogmatical idea that the Spirit regenerates this or that man at random, passing over the rest. It may also lead to the error that the Spirit works without means, suddenly seizing a man to convert and regenerate (or sanctify) him, whereas the Scriptures teach that the Spirit always and only works to save through his chosen means, the Word and the Sacraments, and through these means equally upon all men whenever and wherever these means reach men. The fact that all who are thus reached by the Spirit are not reborn is not due to a lack of saving will on the part of the Spirit, or to a lack and deficiency in the means the Spirit employs, but to the wicked and permanent resistance of those who remain unregenerate. Matt. 23:37; Acts 7:51-53; 13:46.

Little needs to be said regarding the interpretation that would take these words of Jesus to speak of the Spirit instead of the wind, "the Spirit breathes where he will," margin of the R. V. and a few expositors. This is done because the ordinary word for "wind" is ἄνεμος, because only here in the New Testament πνεῦμα would denote "wind," and also because the wind has no will. As to the latter, the expression "wherever

it will" predicates no intelligent will when it is used
with reference to the wind but conveys only the idea
that now it blows one way, now another without
apparent control. But this interpretation cannot be
carried through consistently. When it is read in this
manner, the entire sentence remains confused. Comparisons are intended to clarify. This comparison
greatly clarifies when it is thought of as referring
to the effect of the wind; it does the opposite when
it is regarded as a reference to the Spirit. In v. 6
πνεῦμα is rightly taken once in one sense, once in another. The fact that in v. 8 Jesus uses πνεῦμα, "wind,"
instead of the commoner word, is due to the entire
connection in which this word has repeatedly been
used. Finally οὕτως, "thus," makes a comparison; and
how the Spirit can be compared with a reborn man, or
how the action of the Spirit can be so compared, has
never been clearly shown.

9) **Nicodemus answered and said to him, How
can these things be?** Nicodemus has progressed —
a little. In v. 4 his "how" questions the possibility
itself, especially for an old man like himself. In v. 9
his "how" admits the possibility but questions the manner. "These things" admits that they exist — so much
Jesus has attained. And yet Nicodemus does not believe (v. 11 at the end). Why? Because, after Jesus
has so clearly pointed him away from the mystery
of the manner, especially by the illustration of the
"wind" and has told him that the essential point is
the fact and reality of the Spirit birth, Nicodemus
still harps on the manner with this second "how."
He is like a man who is told that he must eat yet holds
back from eating because he cannot see "how" the
food will be digested and assimilated. The fact that
the Spirit works the rebirth *somehow,* and that it is
enough for the Spirit to know *just how,* is not enough
for Nicodemus — he, too, must know and thus does

not come to faith. That explains the reply of Jesus which scores the man's unbelief.

10) **Jesus answered and said to him, Art thou the teacher of Israel and understandest not these things? Amen, amen, I say to thee, We are uttering what we know and are testifying what we have seen; and you receive not our testimony.** The two double verbs "answered and said" in v. 9 and 10 (see 1:48) indicate that both statements thus introduced are weighty — a kind of climax is reached. In v. 4 we have only "says." The question of Jesus is one of surprise. The article with "teacher" cannot mean that Nicodemus was *the* teacher, was superior to all others, which would have given an undue sting to the question; but the well-known and acknowledged teacher who even has a place in the Sanhedrin. Of a lesser man less might be expected; of a man who knows his Old Testament as such a teacher does certainly so much at least could be expected. Jesus says: the teacher "of Israel," using the honor name to designate the nation: the people of God to whom God had given his Word of revelation and his Spirit in and with that Word. Could "these things" still be hidden from Nicodemus, that the fact and reality of the Spirit's work in its results is the essential and not the manner in which he brings the results about? The verb γινώσκεις means more than intellectual comprehension, which, even if it were possible in a man like Nicodemus, would be valueless; it means inner apprehension, a knowing which embraces and appropriates in the heart. Knowing what Nicodemus did from his study of the Old Testament, plus what he knew of the teaching of the Baptist, plus what Jesus had just so emphatically and so clearly set before him, Nicodemus still did not understand in his heart. He still laid the stress on the how instead of on the fact; he still let the mystery of the how block his joyful appropriation

of the undeniable reality of the new birth. This question of surprise on the part of Jesus is to shake Nicodemus from his foolish how.

11) The surprise is followed by solemn assurance which directly names unbelief as the cause of Nicodemus' ignorance (7:17). Jesus uses the same formula as he did in v. 3. The plural "we" refers to Jesus and the Baptist. By thus combining himself with the Baptist Jesus acknowledges and honors him. Jesus never uses the majestic plural, and in v. 12, where he refers to himself alone, he uses the singular. The disciples had not yet testified publicly, and the prophets are too far removed from the context. The Baptist was still in full activity, and Nicodemus knew a great deal concerning him; so he at once understood this "we." The two great witnesses to Israel at this moment were Jesus and the Baptist.

The two statements, "we are uttering what we know," and, "we are testifying what we have seen," are the same in substance. The doubling is for the sake of emphasis. Yet to tell what one knows is augmented by the statement regarding testifying what one has seen. Each pair of verbs also corresponds, and those in one pair also correspond to those in the other pair. One naturally tells what he knows; but in order to testify he must have seen. To know is broader than to have seen and thus also more indefinite; hence the more specific having seen is added, concerning which one cannot only tell but actually testify. The tenses harmonize with this, "we know," second perfect always used as a present; "we have seen," regular perfect; "seen once and still have before our eyes." To tell is less than to testify. In both statements the singular ὅ should be noted, for it points not to a number of things told and testified but to the one thing noted in the context, the fact and reality of the new birth. The Baptist knew and had seen this even as he told and testified of it in preaching and in Baptism; Jesus likewise, even now telling and testifying to Nicodemus. Both knew and even had seen the Spirit who works the new birth. Both, too, were sent to tell and even to testify which includes, of course, that God who sent them intends that they who hear shall believe and thus receive the saving grace which is the content of this testimony.

But what is the result? It is added with καί although its substance is adverse, "and you receive not our testimony." The inflectional plural is unemphatic yet it includes all those who remain unbelieving. This plural is a gentle touch for Nicodemus, allowing him to include himself in this class if he is determined to do so. It almost sounds as though Jesus pleads that he shall not do this. Here, then, is where the trouble lies: clear, strong, divinely accredited testimony, and yet for one reason or another men decline to receive and to believe it although believing it would work in them the wondrous new birth. The full seriousness of unbelief in the face of such testimony Jesus brings out in v. 19.

12) It should have been easy for Nicodemus and the others to believe this testimony regarding the new birth wrought by the Spirit, for this belongs to the lesser parts of divine revelation, to the *abc* of the gospel. The greater is the guilt for not believing. Far greater and higher things are included in the gospel and must also be told and testified. If the lesser are met with unbelief, what will happen in the case of the greater? **If I told you earthly things, and you do not believe, how, if I shall tell you heavenly things, shall you believe?** Here Jesus confronts the "how" of Nicodemus with a "how" of his own. For that of Nicodemus the answer is always ready, for that of Jesus none exists. Now Jesus omits

reference to the Baptist and speaks of himself alone, hence we have the singular in the verb forms. This does not imply that we need to press the point so as to shut out the Baptist from knowing any of the heavenly things or anything at all about them. He had the measure of revelation which he needed regarding these things. Yet he could not testify of them as one who had directly seen them (v. 13 and 1:18)

We now have the plurals τὰ ἐπίγεια and τὰ ἐπουράνια, which, of course, are not general: any and all earthly and any and all heavenly things; but specific, those pertaining to the kingdom. Nor are the earthly and the heavenly opposites but are most intimately related, are actual correlatives. The kingdom has an earthly and a heavenly side; the earthly side has an exalted heavenly background. To the earthly belong contrition and faith (μετάνοια, "repentance"), Baptism and regeneration, and many things of like nature. If these are to be fully and properly understood and received, the heavenly must be added, those things which occurred in heaven in order to establish the kingdom on earth: the counsel of God's love for our salvation (v. 16), the sending of the Son and of the Spirit; and all this not merely for the consummation of the kingdom but equally for its establishment, progress, and continuance to the end.

The first is a condition of reality, "if I told you . . . , and you do not believe." It expresses what is a fact. The second is a condition of expectancy, "if I shall tell you . . . , how shall you believe?" Jesus expects and reckons with this future unbelief. Yet it would be a mistake to think that Jesus admits some justification for unbelief in the heavenly things; or, to put it in another way, that he would more readily excuse this unbelief. The "how" of Jesus is not measuring degrees of guilt, is not justifying or excusing unbelief, but is reckoning with the likelihood of faith with this or that content of the gospel from men who, like Nicodemus, meet already the earthly things of the gospel with their "how" of unbelief.

13) Now as regards both the verity of these heavenly things and any genuine testimony concerning them a word is in place, which Jesus simply adds with "and" (not, "and yet," R. 1183). **And no one has ascended into heaven except he that descended out of heaven, the Son of man, he who is in heaven.** If any ordinary man were to become a direct witness of heavenly things, this would necessitate that he first ascend to heaven and then come down again and thus testify what he had seen and heard while he was in heaven. But "no one has ascended into heaven." The perfect tense ἀναβέβηκεν includes the past act of ascending together with its resultant effect; the one past act of ascending would apply to that person indefinitely, i. e., he could always speak as one who actually has been in heaven. The universal denial in οὐδείς, "no man," has one grand and notable exception. We are not left without direct testimony regarding heavenly things; we are not dependent only on men like the prophets and such revelations as they may receive from heaven. This exception is Jesus; εἰ μή, as so often, introduces an exception, "except he that descended out of heaven." Any other person would first have to ascend to heaven, not so this person — he was in heaven to begin with. Hence all he needed to do was to come down from heaven. And this he did as ὁ ἐκ τοῦ οὐρανοῦ καταβάς asserts with its historical aorist participle, "he that did descend" when he became incarnate, which also explains the apposition that names this exceptional and wonderful person,

"the Son of man," man, indeed, and yet far more than man; see the exposition regarding this title in 1:51.

A second apposition is added, "he who is in heaven." For it would be a misconception to think of this person as a mere man who in some unaccountable way had originated in heaven instead of on earth like all other men and then had merely changed his abode from heaven to earth by coming down to us, thus being able to tell us about the things in heaven. Not so is ὁ καταβάς to be understood. This person is God, the Son, himself, whose coming down in the incarnation is not a mere change of residence. Though he came down and now speaks to Nicodemus as the Son of man, he remains ὁ ὢν ἐν τῷ οὐρανῷ, "he who is in heaven." He cannot change his divine nature, cannot lay it aside, cannot cancel even temporarily his divine Sonship, his unity of essence with the Father and the Spirit. This is unthinkable although men have tried to think it. To think such a thing is to make also "the Son of man" an illusion, to say nothing of undoing in thought the very Godhead itself and the Trinity of immutable Persons. This person who is first ὁ καταβάς and secondly ὁ υἱὸς τοῦ ἀνθρώπου is thirdly ὁ ὢν ἐν τῷ οὐρανῷ. The participle ὤν is substantivized exactly like καταβάς, the article in each case converting the participle into a noun. The first, an aorist, names the person according to one past act, "he that *came down*"; the second a durative, timeless present, like ὤν in 1:18, names the person according to his enduring condition or being, "he that *is*, ever and ever *is* in heaven." And this designation ὁ ὤν dare not be altered into something else such as mere communion with heaven and thus with God. It denotes being. We may have communion with God, and yet who would dare to express that by saying that we ὄντες, "are," in heaven.

Verse 13, therefore, says nothing about an ascension of Jesus into heaven, which will occur in the future after his resurrection, or has occurred in the past, least of all is it to be understood in the Socinian sense of a *raptus in coelum*. These words are not figurative, meaning only that Jesus has immediate heavenly knowledge or superior, direct communion with heaven through his mind or soul. All such interpretations, which offer a *quid pro quo*, fail to grasp and to accept the real sense and offer another in its stead.

The addition of ὁ ὤν, etc., has caused a good deal of perplexity. Hence the attempts simply to cancel this addition and thus to get rid of the perplexity at one stroke. But the textual evidence is so strong that today cancellation would be arbitrary. The substitution of ἐκ for ἐν, "he who is *out* of heaven," changes the sense. Next comes the translation, *qui in coelo erat*, in old Latin versions and in recent expositions. This is based on the grammatical fact that the present participle ὤν serves for both the present and the imperfect tense, the more since εἶναι really has no aorist. While the grammatical point is correct, ὤν means "was" only when it modifies an imperfect tense of the verb and from that verb, like other present participles (all of which serve also for the imperfect tense) derives the sense of the imperfect. In the statement of Jesus no imperfect tense of a verb appears to which ὤν could be attached.

Some interpreters regard ὁ ὤν ἐν τῷ οὐρανῷ as the equivalent of a relative clause, which is then sometimes attached to ὁ καταβάς as a mere modifier, more frequently to ὁ υἱὸς τοῦ ἀνθρώπου. The article in ὁ ὤν is thus explained as indicating that the participle is attributive. The fact that Jesus "was" in heaven lies fully and clearly already in the previous participle, "he who came down out of heaven"; for no one can come

out of a place unless prior to the coming he *was* in
that place. Others see that the participle must be
present, even though it be a timeless present; yet
they cling to the idea of a relative clause, a mere
modifier. This brings them to the thought that the
modifier describes only a quality of the Son of man:
having come down from heaven, he has a heavenly
nature and character, he *is and remains* (ὤν) an
ἐπουράνιος. This appears to be an escape from the imperfect tense, "who was in heaven," but it only appears
so. For the Son of man so described can have this
character only because prior to his incarnation he was
in heaven; that he *is* there now, even while speaking
to Nicodemus, is the one thing that, so many think,
must be eliminated.

And this brings us to the dogmatical bias back of
this interpretation of ὁ ὤν. What is so evident, namely
that Jesus here uses three coordinate titles for himself: he that came down — the Son of man — he that
is in heaven, is not seen. In other words, that "the
Son of man" is an apposition, and that "he that is
in heaven" is likewise an apposition. Again in still
other words: he that came down is now here as the
incarnate Son of man, and yet, having come down,
does not mean leaving heaven — he is both here and
is still in heaven. Impossible! is the reply. Why?
This would destroy the unity of Christ's person and
the unity of his self-consciousness! In simple language
this dogmatical objection declares: We do not see
and understand how one can be in heaven and on earth
at the same time, hence such a thing cannot be —
Jesus *must* mean something else; and then the search
begins for what he must mean. Thus the story of
Nicodemus is here repeated when in v. 9 he asked,
"How can these thinks be?" and was told that his
question meant nothing but plain, persistent unbelief.
Jesus *is* in heaven though as the Son of man he walks

on earth — that fact stands whether it staggers our reason and powers of comprehension or not. Preconceived dogmatical considerations have always been the bane of exegesis. They have vitiated the plainest grammatical and linguistic facts. The plea about the unity of person and consciousness transfers what would be true of an ordinary human being with only one nature to Christ, the unique divine Being who after his incarnation has two natures. The further plea that from John's prolog onward Christ's being on earth or in the world and his being with God (1:1, 2, and 1:10) form an exclusive contrast, reveals how far back this dogmatical preconception reaches and how it misunderstands the prolog. It will do the same with other statements in our Gospel, such as 10:30; 17:11 and 22. When the Spirit in the form of a dove came down out of heaven upon Jesus, he did not thereby remove his person and presence from heaven, nor did he do this when he was poured out upon the disciples on Pentecost. The same is true of Jehovah when he appeared to Abraham, to Moses in the fiery bush, and when he descended on Sinai, to mention only these.

The interpretation that "who is in heaven" is an insertion by the evangelist and means that now, as he writes, Jesus is again in heaven, destroys the entire historical character of John's Gospel.

Did Nicodemus understand what Jesus here tells him? The same question arises as the discourse moves on. The answer lies in v. 10. He understood and did not understand. But the end toward which Jesus is working with Nicodemus is furthered by the strong impression the words create as Nicodemus now hears and later on as he ponders these words. Jesus counts not on the passing moment alone but on the future when the little that Nicodemus now grasps will grow into fuller insight until faith arrives, and increasing faith learns to see more clearly still.

254   *The Interpretation of John*

14) From the great person who came from heaven and can testify to the heavenly things Jesus advances to the great salvation coming through this person. For he shall be far more than a witness, he is the Savior himself. Thus Jesus seeks to kindle faith in Nicodemus, faith in the divine salvation offered him. **And as Moses lifted up the serpent in the wilderness, thus lifted up must be the Son of man, in order that everyone believing may in him have life eternal.** When describing this salvation in and through the Son of man Jesus employs one of its Old Testament types, Num. 21:8, 9, placing beside it the great antitype, thus aiding Nicodemus both in understanding and in believing what is now told him. To chastise the people who murmured against God he sent fiery serpents among them, from the bite of which many died. When the people came to their senses and repented, God directed that a brazen serpent be put up on a pole and promised that all who would look upon it when bitten would be cured. The Book of Wisdom 16:6 calls this serpent σύμβολον σωτηρίας, and in church decotions it is constantly used to picture Jesus. Ideas such as that like cures like, or that the serpent was a symbol of blessing for the ancients (a notion that is wholly pagan), darken the miracle instead of casting light upon it. Jesus makes the reference to the type brief, not adding the statement that by merely looking every bitten person should live. Yet v. 15 implies that he includes this in his reference. Jesus here places the stamp of verity on the act of Moses and on the record that recounts that act. The miracle of the healing by a mere look on a brass serpent is so real for Jesus that it typifies a still greater reality.

The point of comparison lies in the verbs ὕψωσεν and ὑψωθῆναι, wherefore also the latter is placed before δεῖ, "lifted up must be," and not, "must be lifted

up." But these two upliftings are here not compared abstractly, merely as such, but in their saving
significance. This is not a second point in the comparison but the heart of the one point on which type
and antitype turn. Debate arises regarding what
Christ's being lifted up includes: the crucifixion? the
ascension to heaven? or both? If both are included,
the passive infinitive would have to refer to two
diverse agents: the wicked men who crucified Jesus
and God who lifted him to heaven, Acts 4:10. The
parallel with the act of Moses holds us to the one
act of raising Jesus up on the cross. In 12:32, 33
Jesus himself confines his being lifted up to "the
manner of death he should die"; compare 8:28. Both
acts, too, lift up physically, one on a pole, the other
on the wooden cross. The mystery of the sacrificial
nature of Jesus' elevation on the cross is not yet revealed to Nicodemus and to the disciples who stood
by listening. In 12:33 John appends the remark that
the crucifixion is referred to, much as he does in 2:22.
After the lifting up had actually occurred, many of
the words Jesus had spoken became fully clear to the
disciples. Then, too, Nicodemus fully understood.

The tendency to elaborate the type in allegorical
details should be resisted. Thus the brazen serpent
itself is made to picture Jesus, the former being without poison, the latter without sin. Luther: *Doch
ohne Gift und aller Dinge unschaedlich.* Also the dead
serpent and the dead Jesus are compared, although
the serpent never was alive, and Jesus was when he
was uplifted. Again, the serpent signifies "the old
serpent, which is the devil and Satan," Rev. 20:2,
dead and helpless like Satan whom Jesus conquered
on the cross. Suffice it to say that the brazen serpent
is thus allegorized nowhere in the Scriptures. We
must leave both type and antitype without allegorical
embellishments of our own. The type, the brazen ser-

pent on a pole, was held up to the eyes of the Israelites as the symbol of their own serpent plague, which had come on them through God's just wrath. It was thus held up so that by obediently looking up to it they might acknowledge their sin and God's just wrath in true repentance. Wise fellows among the Israelites may have argued, "How can looking at a brass serpent stuck up on a pole cure poisonous snakebites?" Reason, science, philosophy, ordinary human experience, all support this impenitent how; compare that of Nicodemus in v. 9. The antitype, Jesus hung on the cross, not in a symbol but as the Son of man and Lamb of God himself, holds up to the eyes of the whole world of sin the wrath of God for its sin in him who bleeds to death in order to atone for all this sin. And again, the antitype is held up thus for all men to look upon, that seeing what their sin did to Jesus, they may bow in repentance and faith and thus escape. No allegorical elaborations are needed where the facts themselves are so full of weight. All types of necessity are expressed by δεῖ with the infinitive, our English "must," or "it is necessary." The "must" here meant is that of v. 16, the compulsion of God's purpose of love.

15) This being lifted up and its divine purpose constitute a unit; neither could be possible without the other. When considering both type and antitype this must be retained, "lifted up, in order that." The universality that lies already in the title "the Son of man" (see 1:51) comes out with wonderful clearness in πᾶς ὁ πιστεύων, "everyone." This "whosoever" of our versions is like a check or a deed, signed by God himself, with the place for the beneficiary's name left blank, thus inviting each one of us (here Nicodemus) by the act of faith to write in his own name. Note the singular: faith, life, salvation are personal. "To believe" (see 1:12) is to have the true confidence of the

heart, kindled by the Word, even as this was seeking with its power of grace to win the heart of Nicodemus. The present tense ὁ πιστεύων describes the person by its durative action.

The reading ἐν αὐτῷ is textually assured. But since John always uses εἰς αὐτόν when he employs a phrase with πιστεύω, we should here not construe, "believing in him," but leave the participle absolute, "every believer." In the New Testament πιστεύω ἐν is infrequently used. On the other hand, ἔχειν ἐν appears in 5:39; 16:33; 20:31. So we read, "may have in him life eternal," i. e., in union or in connection with him. The objection is ill-advised that the Israelites did not have healing "in" the brazen serpent but in the kind will of God; for they, too, had it only in connection with that serpent — whoever failed to look at it died. The verb ἔχῃ matches the durative πιστεύων. The believer has life the moment he believes and as long as he believes; he is not compelled to wait until he enters heaven.

On ζωή compare 1:4. John has "life eternal" seventeen times. This is the life-principle itself which makes us alive spiritually. Its beginning is the new birth or regeneration of which Jesus spoke to Nicodemus. Nothing dead can give itself life, least of all that life which has its source in the Son of God himself. He bestows it, he alone, but he does this by kindling faith in us. Thus faith has life, and life is found where faith is. The faith that clasps the Christ uplifted on the cross makes us alive in and through him. A thousand evidences show the change from death to life, namely every motion of that life Godward, Christward, against sin, flesh, world. And this life is "eternal," it goes on endlessly unaffected by temporal death, except that then this life is transferred into the heavenly world. While its nature is "eternal" and deathless, it may be lost during our stay in this sin-

ful world, but only by a wilful and wicked cutting of
the bond "in him," a deliberate renunciation and
destruction of faith.

16)   Why a new paragraph should begin at this
verse is hard to see since the connection with γάρ both
here and in v. 17 is close. The fact that the dialog
stops, also all forms of personal address such as "thou"
to Nicodemus, is naturally due to the simple didactic
nature of what Jesus says and begins already at v. 13,
where, if for such a reason a paragraph is to be made,
it might be made. The idea that a new paragraph
starts with v. 16 because Jesus' words stop here and
John's own reflections are now added, is contradicted
by the two γάρ, by the close connection of the thought,
which runs through to v. 21, and by the absence of
even a remote analogy for a conversation or a discourse that goes over, without a word to indicate this,
into the writer's own reflection.

Jesus tells Nicodemus that the Son of man *must*
be lifted up for the purpose indicated. This δεῖ is
elucidated in v. 16, hence γάρ which so often offers
no proof but only further explanation. **For thus did
God love the world, that he gave his Son the Only-
begotten, in order that everyone believing in him
should not perish but have life eternal.** The "must,"
the compulsion, lies in the wonder of God's love and
purpose. By telling Nicodemus this in such lucid,
simple language Jesus sums up the entire gospel in
one lovely sentence, so rich in content that, if a man
had only these words and nothing of the rest of the
Bible, he could by truly apprehending them be saved.
They flow like milk and honey says Luther, "words
which are able to make the sad happy, the dead alive,
if only the heart believes them firmly." What a revelation for this old Pharisee Nicodemus who all his lifelong had relied on his own works! And this testimony
concerning what was in the heart of God comes from

him who came down from heaven, came down so that
he still is in heaven, from the Son of man and Son
of God himself, the only ἐπουράνιος, who alone can declare
the ἐπουράνια at firsthand, 1:18 and 3:12, who thus in
the very highest degree deserves faith.

The word οὕτως, "thus," denotes manner and degree,
"in this way" and "to such an astounding degree"
did God love the world. No human mind would have
thought it, could have conceived it — God had to
reveal it, the Son had to attest it. The verb ἠγάπησεν
is placed ahead of the subject and is thus made
emphatic, not: *God* loved the world; but: God *loved*
the world. The verb ἀγαπάω denotes the highest type
and form of loving, as distinct from φιλέω, the love of
mere affection, friendship, and ordinary human relation; compare the distinction made between the verbs
in 21:15, etc. In ἀγάπη lies full understanding and
true comprehension, coupled with a corresponding
blessed purpose. How could God *like* the sinful, foul,
stinking world? How could he embrace and kiss it?
He would have to turn from it in revulsion. But he
could and he did *love* it, comprehending all its sin
and foulness, purposing to cleanse it and, thus cleansed,
to take it to his bosom. We see this force of ἀγαπάω
whenever it is used, for instance in the command to
love our enemies. We cannot embrace and kiss an
enemy, for he would smite, revile, thrust us away, as
the Sanhedrists did with Jesus at last; but we can see
the baseness and wickedness of his action and by
the grace of God we can do all that is possible to
overcome this enmity. We may fail in this purpose,
as Jesus did in the case of the Sanhedrists, but to
have it and to adhere to it constitutes "love" in the
sense of ἀγάπη.

The attempt is made to deny this distinction between ἀγάπη and φιλία on the ground that Jesus spoke
Aramaic which has only one word for all types of

love. The answer is that we have only a limited
knowledge of Aramaic, and even if we knew all its
forms of speech and found there only the one word,
there would certainly be other ways of bringing out
a difference in the character of love. But in the
inspired Greek which God gave us this distinction is
so marked that in scores of cases the two words
ἀγαπᾶν and φιλεῖν could not be exchanged; especially
would it be impossible here to substitute the lower
form of love and say, "Thus did God *like* the world."
Jesus uses the aorist tense because the manifestation
of his love toward the world was an accomplished
fact. We may call this aorist constative; it reaches
back into eternity and culminates in Bethlehem.
"God," here the Father, as the mention of the Son
shows, like proper nouns in the Greek may or may
not have the article — here it has the article but not
in v. 21. There is no real difference but only a slight
grammatical variation in certain connections. In this
discourse of Jesus with Nicodemus the entire Trinity
is mentioned as a subject that is well known (the Spirit
from v. 5 onward, Father and Son now). On what
this means for the Old Testament and for the Jews at
this time see 1:32.

The universality already expressed in the title "the
Son of man" (1:51; 3:14) and in "everyone who believes" (v. 15), is brought out with the most vivid
clearness in the statement that God loved "the world,"
τὸν κόσμον, the world of men, all men, not one excepted.
To insert a limitation, either here or in similar passages, is to misinterpret. We know of nothing more
terrible than to shut out poor dying sinners from
God's love and redemption. But this is done by inserting a limiting word where Jesus and the Scriptures have no such word. Thus "world" is made to
mean only *omnes ex toto mundo electos*; and "all men"
in I Tim. 2:4, *omnis generis homines*; and again, *Nul-*

lum mundi vel populum, vel ordinem a salute excludi, quia omnibus sine exceptione (i. e., to all nations and orders and in this sense only "to all without exception") *Evangelium proponi Deus velit.* Thus "the world," "all men," is reduced to signify only that no nation, no class, as a nation or as a class, is excluded; God offers his love and the Savior only to *all kinds of men* — not actually to all men as such. The reason for this misinterpretation of the universal promises of God is that the divine *voluntas beneplaciti* is placed above the divine *voluntas signi* or *revelata,* and the latter is interpreted by the former. In other words, the real will of God is said to appear in his acts, in what we see him do, not in what he plainly says in his Word. So we see him damning some men. Hence we are told to conclude that he never loved these men, never gave his Son for them, never intended to save them. Hence we are told to limit all such expressions as "the world" and "all men" in the written will (*voluntas signi sive revelata*). But this view disregards the fact that we are able to see God's will only partly, dimly, imperfectly in his acts; we often only think we see it, for as we look at his acts, they are often full of mystery. But the will as revealed in the Word is always clear. Hence we dare never to interpret what God clearly says in his own Word by our conception of what he does. We must do the exactly opposite: interpret what we see him do or think we see in the light of the Word; and when the two do not seem to us to square, we must abide by the Word, never change it in one iota, and leave what is dark in the acts of God to the light of the future world. Always, always and only, *Scriptura ex Scriptura explicanda est* and not by anything *extra Scripturam.*

Even after carefully defining "love" no human intelligence can fathom how God could thus love the world. The revelation of this love distinguishes the Christian religion so radically from all others, that no bridge can possibly connect the two. The former is divine, the latter only human. And this love of God is the pinnacle of his glory, the crown of all his attributes. It makes God supremely attractive to every sinner needing this love, a most efficacious call to trust this love and thus to have all it gives.

"So . . . that" indicates correspondence: the love and the gift tally. And ὥστε with the indicative expresses the attained, actual result (R. 1000); with the infinitive it would be only the intended result, one toward which this love would tend. The gift was actually made; the aorist marks the past fact. God's own Son sat before Nicodemus at that very moment. Jesus does not again use "the Son of man" as in v. 13, 14. There it fits as describing what he who came out of heaven became here on earth. Here the divine act of love takes us into heaven and shows us the gift of that love as it was when the act of giving occurred. That gift was "his Son the Only-begotten." On the repetition of the article in the Greek see R. 762, 770. This repetition lays equal weight on both terms; it bids us consider "his Son," secondly, in the same way "the Only-begotten." The addition of the second lifts this "Son" above all others who in any sense may also be called "sons." On the meaning of the title "the Only-begotten" see 1:14 and 18.

Strange reasoning argues that because John uses this title in the prolog, therefore this section, v. 16-21, is John's composition not Jesus' discourse. This assumes that John himself coined the title "the Only-begotten." Even when this section is regarded as Jesus' discourse, its wording is often supposed to be so peculiarly John's language that he inserted, here and in v. 18, the designation "the Only-begotten," which Jesus himself never uttered. This strange reasoning must be reversed. This title is so strange, striking, unique, exalted, that it is easier to believe that Jesus coined it, and that John adopted it from Jesus, than to think that John himself coined it. This title is so distinctive and striking in every way that we must say: if Jesus did not use it in this discourse, if it originated in John's mind during John's later years, then the fact that John inserted it here as though Jesus used it is unbelievable. Whatever wording of John's own is found in this discourse must be minor and must leave intact the distinctive terms and expressions that Jesus actually used, quite a number of which may be noted: loved — world — believe — perish — life eternal, etc. Among the grandest, the most unusual is "the Only-begotten." If Jesus here used it, John had to preserve it, and he did; if Jesus never used it either here or elsewhere, John would not dare to insert it here, and that twice. All is normal if John here heard Jesus say, "the Only-begotten" and thus placed this title in his prolog; all is abnormal if Jesus never used the expression and John yet writes as he does.

What is said when expounding 1:14 and 18 in regard to the meaning of the title and the fact that it cannot refer to the exceptional human birth of Jesus but must express the eternal relation of the Son to the Father, the *generatio aeterna,* is made inevitable by the way in which Jesus himself here uses this title. God's gift of love must here name this gift as it existed in heaven before the time of the giving and at that time. There with the Father in heaven was "his Son the Only-begotten" who was such from all eternity, and as such God gave him to the world. So great, so tremendous was the gift, and so astounding the love that made this gift. Luther's word must stand, "true God, begotten of the Father from eternity," expressing, as it does, the conviction of the church of all past ages.

The aorist ἔδωκεν, "did give," denotes the one historical past act. Jesus speaks objectively throughout, using the third person when speaking of himself and general expressions like "world," "he that believes," etc., when speaking of other persons, and thus he here uses the aorist. This verb "gave" really refers to an act that took place in the other world, where any consideration of time would be inadequate, meaning only that we are in a poor human way speaking of things beyond us. Keeping this in mind, we may say that "gave" neither refers to the death on the cross nor to the incarnation alone but to these and to all else by which God bestowed his Savior as a gift. No indirect object follows "gave" — significant omission, for Jesus could hardly say that God gave his Son "to the world," because the world as such did not on its part receive the Son (1:10). Nevertheless, all is clear when we hear what purpose God had by giving his gift, "in order that everyone believing in him should not perish but have life eternal." This repeats the purpose clause of v. 15, which see for the explanation. The repetition links the verses so closely that no new paragraph is in place at v. 16. The gift is a unit act, but the purpose attached to it holds until the end of time. The repetition stresses this purpose clause, even as repetition constantly marks emphasis. Jesus virtually says: Note well once more this *fiducia* of believing, this personal singular, this universality, this possession, this wondrous life.

But as is the case in many such emphatic repetitions, the emphasis is enhanced by an addition. The object of faith is indicated by John's usual εἰς αὐτόν, "in him," where, however, εἰς is not to be stressed as including motion. In the Koine especially this would be a linguistic anachronism, for εἰς here follows verbs of rest and even verbs of being as an ordinary idiom; cf. R. 591, etc., on its static use. John does not need to repeat that the believer "should have ἐν αὐτῷ, in him, life eternal," for this is clearly implied in the other phrase. In εἰς αὐτόν, "him" includes all that has been said of the Son in v. 15, 16. This wonderful Person is the object of faith. The real amplification lies in the addition of the negative, "should not perish" to enhance the positive, "but have life eternal," using the strong adversative ἀλλά. "To perish" denotes total and eternal rejection by God, and it is so used especially in the middle voice by John and by Paul, C.-K. 788. The word never means to suffer annihilation. Here the aorist subjunctive μὴ ἀπόληται is in place to indicate the one final act of perishing in contrast with the present subjunctive ἔχῃ to indicate the present and enduring having of life eternal. Not to perish is to have; not to have is to perish. To perish is defined in what follows as the opposite of being saved (v. 17), as being judged (v. 18), and as being reproved or convicted (v. 20). In this negative "should not perish" Jesus touches the first great warning for Nicodemus: God does not want him to perish — does he himself mean to perish, nevertheless? He surely will if he becomes obdurate in unbelief.

17) With γάρ this verse links into v. 16. The giving of the Son is wholly an act of love not of justice and judgment, wholly in order that men should escape judgment and be saved. **For God sent not the Son into the world in order to judge the world but in order that the world should be saved through him.** The explanation introduced by γάρ extends to details. Thus the giving of the Son is now expressed by the aorist: God "did send"; he gave by sending. The gift is the mission. As being thus sent Jesus was before

Nicodemus at that very moment. The briefer designation "the Son" means the same as the fuller "his Son, the Only-begotten." With the new verb the addition "into the world" makes the action of God clearer, whereas with the verb "gave" such a modifier could not be added. The way in which God "gave" his Son was by "sending him into the world."

We may say that in order to judge the world God would not have needed to send (certainly not to give) his Son. He could have sent another flood, or fire, or some other cataclysm. The verb "to judge" is a *vox media*, it means simply to pass a decision. But since the world was lost in sin and unbelief, this could be only a condemnatory decision. Hence the interpretative translation of the A. V., "to condemn the world," is not really incorrect although Jesus used only the simple verb "to judge." Its aorist tense implies a final act of judging.

But God's purpose was not the judgment of the world, worthy of condemnation though it was, but the salvation of the world; hence he sent a Savior into the world. "Not . . . but," or "on the contrary," forms the strongest kind of an antithesis. The same is true regarding the two ἵνα and the verbs, "in order to judge," and, "in order to save," which are made stronger by placing the verbs forward. The effect of the whole is heightened by thrice repeating "the world."

The passive "should be saved" involves God as the agent; but "through him" shows that God will use a Mediator, namely his own Son, διά here and so often being used regarding mediation, the use of a personal or other medium. The verb itself, like the equivalent adjective and the nouns, carries with it the imagery of rescue from the terrible danger referred to in the previous term "perish." In fact, the passive "to be saved" is the opposite of "to perish." But the verb always has the strong connotation: to keep sound, uninjured; to preserve sound and safe. Thus "to be saved" = "to have life eternal," to enjoy eternal safety. The aorist matches that of "to judge." God's purpose was actual, complete salvation for the world. By combining the negative and the positive Jesus throws into bold relief the great purpose of God's love and at the same time intensifies the call to faith for Nicodemus.

18) With God's purpose of love thus clearly stated, the manner of its realization is again emphasized. But this is altogether personal, for each one as an individual, hence the singular is used in this sentence. While Jesus still speaks objectively, in the third person, he yet aims directly at Nicodemus who would involuntarily turn this third person into the second and regard it as being addressed to him personally. **He that believes on him is not judged; he that believes not on him has already been judged, because he has not believed in the name of the Only-begotten Son of God.** Though no connective is used, none being needed, what the previous verse states in general in regard to being judged and in regard to being saved is here made personal, and the decisive factor in this is faith. Hence these striking opposites, "he that believes on him"—"he that believes not on him" ($\mu\dot{\eta}$ being the regular negative with a participle). Both substantivized participles are durative as in v. 15 and 16; continuous believing marking the one man, continuous non-believing the other. The whole world is divided into these two.

Jesus might have used the positive verb "to be saved" in connection with v. 17 and might have said: The believer "is saved," the non-believer "is not saved." Instead he takes up the negative verb from v. 17 and says: The believer "is not judged," the non-believer "has already been judged." This verb has the stronger tone of warning. Nicodemus must know that escape is accomplished by faith alone, escape now at this very moment, for the tense is present, "is not judged." He must know that lack of faith is the destructive force, destructive from the very start, for the tense is the perfect, "has already been judged" and thus now stands as one already so judged. In a way this explains why God did not need to send his Son to judge the world. By sending his Son to save the world the judgment takes care of itself. The believers need no judgment. Being saved, they belong to God as his own. He will institute no trial for them as if he had to decide their case pro or con either now or at any time including the last day. This also is true with regard to the non-believers. Their refusal to believe already judges them; they already have their verdict which, as the perfect κέκριται shows, stands indefinitely.

That is why Jesus uses the indeterminate verb κρίνεσθαι, "to be judged," instead of the verb κατακρίνεσθαι, "to be condemned," which, by the way, is not found in John. Even such an act as judging is not at all needed. But will not a grand final judgment take place at the last day? Not in the strict sense of the word. Then all men will already have received their judgment even as Jesus tells Nicodemus at this moment. Immediately after they are raised from the dead they will be ranged either on the right or on the left of the Judge by the angels. That could not be done if they were not already judged. What follows is the public announcement of the verdict which was long before this determined by the Judge, and with the verdict the evidence on which it rests.

Since the believer is not judged, nothing more needs to be added concerning him. He is not judged — that is all. But since the non-believer has been judged, Jesus states the charge against him, using the actual form of a legal indictment. Unfortunately this is lost in our English translation because we have only one negative while the Greek has two, one objective, regarding the fact presented as such, one subjective, regarding the opinion of the speaker. Jesus uses the latter. If he had used οὐ, he would simply have stated the fact regarding the unbeliever: *quod non credidit,* nothing more. By using μή he states the charge against the man as God would make it: *quod non crediderit.* So stated, it includes what God or Christ think and hold against the man. In fact, we may call it more than a charge, for this charge becomes the verdict of God on the man, R. 963. That, too, is why this is stated in such a full and formal way. We need to add only one implied word: Guilty "because he has not believed in the name of the Only-begotten Son of God!" The crime is thus solemnly named. The perfect μή πεπίστευκεν matches the preceding perfect κέκριται, for they are concurrent as to time, setting in at the same instant and continuing on equally after that.

When stating the charge and the verdict, we again meet τὸ ὄνομα (compare 1:12) : he has not believed "on the name" of the Only-begotten Son of God. In all such connections "the name" denotes the revelation of the Son that is made to a person. Jesus was now making this revelation to Nicodemus. "The name" is thus the Word (v. 11). It tells all about this wonderful Savior and his grace and his work for us. "The name" is thus used in these connections because it contains the trust-producing power. Here all the greatness of this name and revelation is brought out by the genitive: the name "of the Only-begotten Son of God." Can there be a greater? Could God come to your soul with a more effective trust-producing power? Hence the outrageousness of the crime named in this indictment. It is not hard to imagine the impact of these words of Jesus on the soul of Nicodemus. Those who regard these words as mere objective reflections of John himself miss the personal urge that throbs in them. We also need not wonder that we have no more dialog, for we can well imagine the significant silence of Nicodemus as he sat there with such words gripping his soul. That, too, is why John placed this discourse into his Gospel: Jesus is making a wonderful revelation of himself, his attestation to his divine nature and his work could hardly be stronger.

19) The connection is close. Speaking of coming not to judge the world (v. 17), then of one man not judged and of another already judged (v. 18), the question is vital: "Just what is meant by this judgment?" Jesus gives a direct answer. **Now this is the judgment, that the light has come into the world, and men did love the darkness rather than the light; for their works were wicked.** This is the κρίσις or decision of which Jesus is speaking. If all men believed, no κρίσις like this would be necessary (v. 18a). Because men refuse to believe, this "judgment" sets in in the very nature of the case. But in defining this judgment as Jesus here does two revelations are made conjointly: the full inner justice of this judgment together with the inner moral wrong that makes this judgment just and thus inevitably brings it on the guilty man.

Since this description of the judgment is somewhat like a parenthetical statement, we have δέ, "now," R. 1184. Also the ὅτι clause is in apposition with αὕτη, "This . . . that," etc., R. 699; and is not causal as some have supposed, R. 964. "The light" with its significant article really means "the Spirit," the Son himself (1:4, 5) who as "the Truth" (14:6) brings the complete revelation of God (1:18; 3:11) and makes it shine into men's minds and hearts. In Jesus all the divine realities (this is the meaning of ἀλήθεια or "truth") concerning God, his grace and his love, his power to redeem and to save, lie open and bare so that men must see their shining. This Light "has come," and the perfect tense implies that it is now here and continues thus. In the person, signs (v. 3), and words of Jesus it was shining into Nicodemus' heart at this very moment. Normally, one would expect that by being made to see these realities men would be led to act accordingly. But no; deliberately they do the very contrary.

"And men loved the darkness rather than the light." This καί, like so many others in John, should not be taken to mean "and yet" as R. 426 would have it; it simply places side by side the unspeakably blessed fact of the coming of the Light into the world and the unspeakably tragical fact that men preferred the darkness to the Light. This coordination is finer than any disjunction would be. The verb ἠγάπησαν is placed first for emphasis. The aorist states the simple fact. Jesus could use this tense thus early in his work. We need not make it prophetic. It matches the subject "men," *die Menschen* (the generic article). Jesus speaks of his relation to men in a general way not merely specifically regarding what men had already done. This ἠγάπησαν is the answer of men to the ἠγάπησεν of God (v. 16). Note the identity of the verb. "They loved" with the love of intelligence and of purpose. "They loved," making a deliberate choice for a deliberate purpose. This purpose is stated in v. 20. Jesus says οἱ ἄνθρωποι although he does not refer to all men, for he has already spoken of those that believe, and his words cannot be misunderstood.

While it is true that with disjunctives ("rather . . . than") the nouns naturally have the article, R. 789, here they are needed also for another pur-

pose: "*the* Light" and "*the* darkness" are both decidedly definite. "The darkness" (compare the remarks
on 1:5) is not the mere absence of light but is
always conceived as a hostile power. It is the specific
power of sin and death that actively wars against
the Light. As the Light is the actual reality concerning God, his love, etc., so the darkness is the direct
opposite, all the unreality that men imagine and invent
in their folly regarding God, their souls, and eternity.
Not a bit of it is true, yet they stake their very souls
upon it and that in the face of all the light which
displays the real facts to them. This choosing of the
darkness instead of the light is the utterly unreason-
ing and unreasonable folly of men. Eventually, when
they are asked why they chose thus, they will remain
dumb. We must construe μᾶλλον . . . ἤ with the
nouns not with the verb, R. 663, because the nouns are
placed in contrast, "the darkness rather than the
Light." This, too, is a sad miosis, a soft way of saying
that they *hated* the Light.

Jesus exposes the inner motive for this choice.
This is not one which in any degree excuses the
choice but one which more fully reveals its utter baseness, "for their works were wicked." The order of
the words in the Greek rests the emphasis on both
"works" and "wicked." "Their works" are not scattered, individual deeds but those that make up and
display their real inner nature and will, the net sum
of their lives. And πονηρά is always meant in the
active sense: doing evil, putting it forth, set on wickedness. To get the force of the adjective we must not
think merely of gross immoralities but especially of all
forms of ungodliness, all self-righteousness, all religious perversions, carnal and material religious hopes,
with every action and practice that displays these
inclinations. The implication is not that men helplessly lie in the toils of wickedness but that, when

the saving power of the Light comes to them and battles to free them, they fight the Light, hug their wicked works, and continue to make them the sum and substance of their lives.

Jesus here reveals the terrible moral inwardness of all unbelief, laying bare the cold facts. Unbelief never means that a man "cannot see the Light." The Light cannot be charged with deficiency or weakness. God's grace is always *gratia sufficiens*. The trouble is not intellectual but moral. Paul learned this from Jesus. When he describes the heathen ungodliness he, too, goes back to the ἀδικία, "unrighteousness," the moral motive, Rom. 1:18. Every man who rejects the divine light of truth when it comes to him to draw him from evil unto God and instead determines to hold to the darkness of untruth and lies, does this at bottom for a moral reason, namely because he will not part from the evil that he loves and that thus marks his soul and his life.

20) In v. 19 γάρ establishes the reason why the evil choice is made. In v. 20 γάρ elucidates the reason stated in v. 19. This is quite necessary, for the case is not that when a man chooses the darkness in preference to the light he then leaves the light alone. The moral reason that prompts that choice, i. e., the evil work from which he will not separate himself, does not let him rest but makes him hate and war against the light. **For everyone that practices things worthless hates the light and comes not to the light lest his works should be convicted.** Here again, as in v. 18, Jesus individualizes and for the same reason. This moral baseness and the hatred it produces is personal, and the ensuing guilt is personal. The singular thus grips Nicodemus personally, who surely must think of himself as he hears these words.

A radical and far-reaching difference separates the two interpretations of v. 20, 21: the one that Jesus

here describes two men who have come into decisive
contact with the light that Jesus brings, the one accepting, the other rejecting that light; and the other interpretation that Jesus here adduces only a general rule,
namely that any man who does wrong likes to keep
it dark while any man who does right is not afraid
to come into the light. The words of Jesus can be
made to express the latter very ordinary thought only
by altering a number of the concepts which Jesus
uses in their distinctive sense. Thus "the light" is
not daylight or the public light but the light that is
Jesus and in Jesus, the light that has come into the
world. This is also true with regard to the other
expressions. This view leads to the false notion that,
to begin with, "the world" is composed of two classes
of men: the one inwardly false and hypocritical who
forever remain so and thus are not converted; and
the other a better class, better from the very start,
upright and honest, who before Jesus is brought to
them already follow the light and the truth that are
found in natural revelation and then embrace Jesus and
become converted. Rom. 2 and all that the Scriptures
teach concerning man's sinful condition contradict this
view. Jesus' own words in these two verses shut it out
most decidedly.

"Everyone that practices things worthless" refers
to all those who have spurned the light and have
definitely chosen the darkness instead. Verse 19 puts
this beyond question. Jesus characterizes this kind
of a man according to his works not according to his
act of preferring the darkness to the light, because
in v. 19 the inner motive of this preference has been
revealed, the determined love of wicked works. The
substantivized present participles ὁ πράσσων and, in
v. 21, ὁ ποιῶν are exactly like ὁ πιστεύων in v. 15, 16,
and 18. The continuous action indicated describes
the man referred to in each case. The variation be-

tween ὁ πράσσων in v. 20 and ὁ ποιῶν in v. 21 is slight, and yet the difference may be noted. The one verb has the idea of aim: *wer treibt, agit*; the other has the idea of effecting: *wer tut, facit*. Hence also the addition in v. 21: that his works "are wrought" in God, εἰργασμένα. In v. 19 the evil works are called πονηρά, "wicked" (actively so), now Jesus uses φαῦλα, "worthless." Trench, *Synonyms*, II, 169, etc.: "That which is morally evil may be contemplated on two sides, from two points of view; either on the side of its positive malignity, its will and power to work mischief, or else on its negative worthlessness, and, so to speak, its good-for-nothingness. Πονηρός contemplates evil from the former point of view, and φαῦλος from the latter." Thus the one term amplifies the other. The latter brings out the utter folly of him who chooses the darkness, for the deeds for which he wants this darkness are absolutely worthless and net him nothing for his life.

But having made his choice for the reason indicated and now practicing such worthless things, he "hates the light and comes not to the light." Jesus repeats "the light," which thus plainly, even emphatically, takes up v. 19, reaches back to 1:4, 5, and forms one of the cardinal terms in John's Gospel. This is the light of the divine truth which always displays everything as it really is. This light, once being definitely rejected for the darkness, this man is bound to "hate"; he cannot tolerate it, he "comes not to the light," will not let its truthful, revealing rays fall upon him. The light is there, and he knows it is there; it is there for him, and its rays go out to reach him. Deliberately he avoids it. Coming to it would mean that he is attracted by it and by what it does; not coming means that he recoils from it, dreading what it does.

Instead of stating the cause or reason for this hate and avoidance Jesus indicates the purpose, which also is negative, ἵνα μή, "lest" or "in order that . . . not." Rejecting the light is negative; the following worthless works are negative; hating and avoiding the light is negative; trying to run away from conviction is negative. "Lest his works should be convicted," ἐλεγχθῇ, not merely, "reproved," our versions, and still less "discovered," A. V. margin; but shown up as what they actually are, evil, worthless, fit only for "the darkness." And "his works" are here again not merely certain individual deeds but the works that sum up and characterize the man as what he really is. Here we see the inner, hidden self-contradiction and self-condemnation of all such doers of evil who in unbelief act contrary to Christ and the gospel. They choose the worthless but they do not want its worthlessness revealed. They want to be undisturbed in thinking the worthless valuable. This they can do only in "the darkness" where they themselves and others cannot see. Where religious error prevails, as in the delusion of Pharisaic work-righteousness, or in any other aberration, this self-deception literally becomes tragic. When speaking of the wicked and worthless works Jesus is certainly not excluding those that transgress the second table of the law, but just as certainly he has in mind especially those that transgress the first table. The supreme issue for him is and remains faith or unbelief and the works only as evidence and fruit either of the one or of the other. Moreover, the thought behind being convicted is not mere condemnation of the worthless works but a condemnation that produces contrition and repentance and thus turns the heart from these works unto faith and the works that flow from faith.

21) Strong in warning in the last statements, the discourse of Jesus ends with a note of blessedness

and joy. Over against the negative Jesus sets the positive. The matter must be made complete. Besides, each casts light on the other. Many may reject the light, but by no means all do so. God's Only-begotten cannot fail. **But he that does the truth comes to the light, that his works may be made manifest, that they have been wrought in God.** No need to repeat πᾶς which is understood without the repetition. The surprising feature is that in describing this man Jesus does not say, "he that does things good," but that he at once penetrates to the one and only source of all things really good in the sight of God: he that does "the truth." To do the truth is a pregnant expression and means that one puts the truth which he has received in his heart into his life and actions, so that thus the truth stamps him as "one that is of the truth," 19:37. Only a believer who has the truth in his heart can do the truth, i. e., live according to it in his life. In this doing the truth the first table of the law will have the first place, and the second will, of course, not come short.

"Truth" sounds very general, and many are thereby misled. On the lips of Jesus who called himself the Truth, being its very embodiment, the word here can mean only one thing: the saving truth of God's grace in Christ Jesus as it shines forth in both Testaments. Any wider sense, such as the truth in nature, is shut out by the entire context and by the statement that the works of the doer of the truth (note the article τὴν ἀλήθειαν) are such because they "are wrought in God," i. e., in union and communion with God. In no other way than through faith in the Messiah can even a single work be wrought in God. Here, then, is a man to whom "the light" came as to the other mentioned in v. 20. He, too, up to that time was doing things wicked and worthless like the other. But when the light began to shine into him and to draw him, he did

not wrest himself willfully away and cover himself up
completely in "the darkness." The light did its work
in him; it entered his will and began to control it —
he began to do the truth. The result was "works
wrought in God," works of the gospel, works of
faith. The first of these will always be contrition and
repentance for all past evil works, confession of faith,
and the continuance of these from day to day, to be
followed by the entire range of good works. A perfect and complete doing of the truth will not at once
be achieved; weaknesses, faults, sins enough will appear. But the doing has begun and by the help of the
truth will go on.

What of this man? He "comes to the light." Once
the light came to him, now he is able to come to it.
There is no need to specify that this man "loves" the
light, whereas the other "hates" it. His coming to the
light proves his love for the light. This man has no
reason whatever to fear this divine light of truth when
it shows up the inward realities of his heart and his
life. The idea is not that this light will find nothing to
convict in him. It will show up sins, weakness of faith,
and faults enough. But this man wants to be rid of
these and gladly submits to the healing power of the
light. Jesus passes this feature by, but we may well
add it to his brief words. The purpose which Jesus
names for this man's coming to the light is, "that his
works may be made manifest, that they have been
wrought in God." To translate ὅτι "because" gives a
wrong turn to the thought. The verb "manifest," applied to this man's works, requires that *what* is made
manifest be stated. This is "that (declarative ὅτι) they
have been wrought in God," ἐστιν εἰργασμένα, the perfect
tense saying that, once so wrought, they stand permanently as such. This is what the light of grace
already now does for all such works. It is a kind
of judgment of grace. It helps, encourages, confirms,

and strengthens us day by day as we fight the darkness that still assails us. What a glorious manifestation that will be when on the last day the unerring "light" seals this approval before the whole universe of angels and men!

Did Jesus say any more? We need not know. The attestation in the words which John reports is full and complete. What did Nicodemus say or think? John is not making this a story about this man but a report of the testimony of Jesus to himself. To say that John's account is incomplete is to misunderstand what the account really is. We may well say, however, that Jesus' words must have made an indelible impression upon the old Pharisee and must have shaken him profoundly. In due time he came to faith.

Jesus in Judea and the Last Testimony of the Baptist, 3:22-36. — The historical remarks which John inserts in v. 22-24 serve only to present the situation in which the dispute arose that furnished the occasion for the Baptist's final testimony regarding Jesus. This testimony is John's real subject; all else is incidental. **After these things came Jesus and his disciples into the Judean country, and he was tarrying there with them and was baptizing.** The plural pronoun in the phrase μετὰ ταῦτα includes all that Jesus had done in Jerusalem (2:12-3:21) although John has given only a slight hint in 2:23 as to what this included. Jesus now moves from the capital "into the Judean country." No specific locality is named as this is done in v. 23 in the case of the Baptist, probably because, while the latter had a fixed place where he worked, Jesus moved about from one place to another. The verb in the singular followed by "Jesus" as the subject, adding the disciples with "and," is like 2:2 and makes Jesus the important person. Why Jesus made this move John in no way indicates. The guess that he was discouraged by what is called his failure in the capital, the addition that he tried less radical measures than the cleansing of the Temple and thus descended to the level of the Baptist's work, is a good example of judging Jesus according to the standards of ordinary men. He had made no mistake in Jerusalem. There as well as here in the country district he did exactly what best furthered his great purpose. The imperfect tenses which state that in the country he "tarried" or spent some time in company with his disciples (μετ' αὐτῶν) and "baptized" are the usual duratives to indicate continued action. The fact of his baptizing would indicate that the locality was the neighborhood of the Jordan. On the subject of this baptism see the remarks on 1:26. Jesus did not baptize in person but did it through his disciples, 4:2.

23) The other evangelists say nothing about Jesus' baptizing. John's remark amplifies their account. Yet, lest someone should combine John's statement with those of the others in an incorrect manner and think that Jesus did not take up this baptizing until the Baptist's labors were ended, John adds the remark: **Now John also was baptizing in Ænon near Salim because much water was there; and they were coming and being baptized.** The δέ makes the statement parenthetical. The evangelist himself helps us to determine only two points about the location of Ænon (springs). The way in which the Baptist's disciples refer to the former testimony of their master as having been made "beyond Jordan," v. 26, shows that now they were on its hither or western side. Immediately after the evangelist tells us that Jesus went "into the Judean country" he names Ænon as the place where the Baptist labored, and by adding no name of a country he leaves our thoughts in Judea. On the disputes about the actual site consult the Bible

Dictionaries. The place was so named on account of its springs, for which reason also it was suitable for the Baptist's work. The plural πολλὰ ὕδατα denotes either the springs themselves or the rivulets that flowed from them and not a large body of water. In the long search for the site of Ænon only such places have been considered which show such springs, and neither ancient nor modern records speak of a place that had water enough to immerse numbers of people. Nor is the consideration here only water for the purpose of baptizing but also and very vitally, where multitudes camped for some time, water for drinking purposes. The imperfect tense of the verbs, the coming and the being baptized on the part of the people, as in the previous verse, means to state that the Baptist was here carrying on his work for some time.

24) **For John had not yet been cast into the prison,** elucidates the previous statement. Readers of Mark 1:14 and Matt. 4:12-17 might question our evangelist's account to the effect that the Baptist and Jesus thus baptized at the same time. So John states that this occurred prior to the Baptist's imprisonment. This is the reason for the statement and not the self-evident fact that the Baptist's work ceased when he was cast into prison. That also is why John has the article: had been cast "into *the* prison," referring his readers to this well-known prison and the Baptist's confinement there, of which they had knowledge from the other evangelists.

25) Now follows the episode which occasioned the Baptist's final testimony. **A dispute, accordingly, arose on the part of the disciples of John with a Jew about purifying.** With οὖν, "accordingly," John indicates that this dispute arose out of the situation sketched in v. 22-24, hence was not about purifying in general, i. e., the old Jewish ways and regulations,

but about the Baptism of Jesus as compared with that
of the Baptist. What the actual question of the
dispute was the evangelist does not say since his
concern is something more important. All we can
gather from the complaint of the Baptist's disciples
in v. 26 is that the Jew maintained the superiority of
Jesus' Baptism over that of the Baptist, which the
disciples of the latter refused to admit as it would
also involve that men should leave the Baptist and
go to Jesus. The dispute started with the disciples,
as ἐκ shows (R. 515, ablative)'. This preposition is
not used in the partitive sense, *"some* of John's disciples," when the construction calls for the genitive or
the dative. The suggestion that 'Ιουδαίος here means
a Judean not a Jew is strange, since the man's
nationality is of no moment. By calling him a Jew
the evangelist classes him with the opponents of Jesus,
whom he steadily calls "the Jews." The man's interest
in the dispute would thus be to cause perplexity and
discord.

26) **And they came to John and said to him,
Rabbi, he that was with thee beyond the Jordan,
to whom thou hast borne witness, behold, this one
is baptizing, and all men are coming unto him.**
These are the disciples alone, and they go to their
master who is near at hand. They lay before him not
the question of dispute but the situation from which it
arose, and this in the form of an aggrieved complaint. Hence they even avoid naming Jesus, they
only describe him, but in a way that brings out first,
their thought that Jesus is under great obligation to
the Baptist and, secondly, that Jesus is showing himself ungrateful to the Baptist. In their complaint
lies the question, "Is this right?" They refer to what
is recorded in 1:29-34. By saying that this occurred
"beyond the Jordan" they specify what testimony
they refer to and at the same time indicate that they

were now on the western side of the river. **They speak
as though the Baptist had done much for Jesus by
testifying of him as he did.** But, behold, οὗτος (see
1:7), "this man," is now competing with their beloved master, competing with him after having received so much from him! By adding the exaggeration
that "all men" are running after Jesus these disciples
betray their state of mind. In the perfect μεμαρτύρηκας
we note the effect of the testimony as continuing in
the present.

27) The reply of the Baptist which now follows
in extenso and is our evangelist's chief concern is so
thoroughly true, so illuminating and at the same time
so demonstrative of his perfect humility that it stands
as a monument to him forever. He begins with a
general truth, one to which every child of God must
at once assent, one that applies equally to himself and
to Jesus. **John answered and said, A man can receive nothing except it have been given to him from
heaven.** The great importance of the Baptist's
statement is indicated by the doubling: he "answered
and said," compare 1:48. When men arrogate something to themselves, rob others, snatch what does not
properly belong to them, they really do not have what
they have; for it shall be taken from them, and God's
judgment condemns them. What is really our portion,
including our position, work, success, especially in the
kingdom of God, is a gift allotted to us, which we
thus receive and truly have. "Given" and "receive"
correspond. The doubling of the negatives in the
Greek (οὐ . . . οὐδέν) is common, R. 1162. On the
periphrastic perfect subjunctive see R. 907: has been
and thus remains given, punctiliar-durative.

28) Now the application of the general principle.
**You yourselves bear me witness that I said, I am
not the Christ, but that (I said), I am one that
has been commissioned before him.** The Baptist

meant and still means what he said on the occasion when the delegation from the Sanhedrin questioned him, 1:19, etc. His entire conduct has borne that out, and his disciples must today give him this testimony. He here briefly states what has not been given to him and, over against that, what has. On that other occasion he did not use the wording, "I am one commissioned before him," but it certainly sums up what he said in 1:23 and 26, 27. He may even have spoken these words, either on that occasion or on another, our evangelist merely not recording them. We regard the perfect participle as the predicate of "I am"; ἐκεῖνος is often used with reference to a person that is absent, as in this case.

29) The Baptist really states only what heaven (God) has apportioned to him, yet he does it in such a manner that the disciples at once gather how much more God has apportioned to Jesus. This implication continues in v. 29, 30. The Baptist's statements through to v. 36 are without connectives, simply being ranged side by side, each standing powerfully by itself. The second has a beauty of its own in that it uses a figure hallowed by the Old Testament yet not as this is used in Isa. 54:5; Hos. 2:18, etc., with reference to Jehovah and Israel, where no room would be found for "the friend of the bridegroom," but as it is used in the Song of Solomon and was interpreted also by the Jews with reference to the Messiah. **He that has the bride is the bridegroom; yet the friend of the bridegroom, he that stands and hears him, rejoices greatly because of the voice of the bridegroom. This my joy, therefore, has been fulfilled.** The Baptist's meaning is transparent. Jesus is the bridegroom who has the bride. Thus the Baptist is the friend of the bridegroom. God arranged this relation, and for the Baptist it is blessing indeed. The

bride are all they who by faith truly belong to Jesus. If, indeed, "all men" are going to Jesus, v. 26, the Baptist cannot show the slightest touch of envy but can only rejoice in the fact.

No special task is here indicated for the friend of the bridegroom, who, as the article indicates, is the one formally functioning as such during the celebration. We should not transfer into the picture our present weddings with their wedding ceremony in which "the best man" has a function. The Jewish wedding was only a joyful feast at the groom's home, following the procession in which the groom brought the bride to his home. No special time in the progress of the wedding feast is in any way indicated, although commentators have tried to fix such a time, and some with gross indelicacy. The Baptist pictures only the relation and the proper attitude of the friend to the groom, for which alone also he uses this figure; for he intends to describe his own true relation and his attitude toward Jesus.

So he adds the apposition, "he that stands and hears him." The two participles are substantivized and united by the one Greek article and thus should not be made a relative clause. The friend's place is near the groom (ἑστηκώς is always used as a present not as a perfect). So he also hears the groom (αὐτοῦ, the genitive to indicate the person speaking) not his commands during the wedding but the voicing of his happiness and joy. With what feelings the Baptist (friend) does this he is happy to state: he "rejoices greatly because of the voice of the bridegroom." The article with the genitive points to the specific bridegroom referred to, namely Jesus, a point that is lost by translating, "the bridegroom's voice." The Hebrew infinitive absolute is imitated in χαρᾷ χαίρει by thus adding the cognate noun as the instrumental dative,

R. 94; B.-D. 196, 6; and the sense is that the action takes place in the highest degree, "rejoices greatly," literally, "with joy."

With one stroke the picture is transferred to the reality, "This my joy, therefore, has been fulfilled," or, "has been made full," R. V., American committee. The perfect tense means: and will remain thus. The Baptist's desires are satisfied to the uttermost. His joy, hitherto one in anticipation only, is now realized in actuality as he sees men flocking to Jesus. So far removed above all envy and rivalry or any other unworthy feeling is the Baptist's soul.

30) Hence also the direct reply to the wrong complaint of these foolish disciples: **He must increase, but I must decrease.** "Must," δεῖ, as the nature of the two persons and of their offices demands in the blessed will of God. The full development has not yet been reached, but much is already visible. "He must grow," refers both to the office of Jesus and to his success in winning men. His work had only begun (ἐκεῖνος as in v. 28). "I must become less" likewise refers both to the office and the followers of the Baptist. Presently his task will be entirely done. But it will stand as a great and blessed success.

31) The Baptist has thus far spoken of the relation between Jesus and himself, shutting off the foolish notions voiced in the complaint of his disciples. Now he turns to the other side, the relation of Jesus to men, which includes in particular also his relation to these complaining disciples. The Baptist wants them to follow Jesus as Andrew, John, and the others did. Their whole view of Jesus must be changed accordingly. Thus we receive the supreme part of the Baptist's final testimony to the Sonship of Jesus. **He that comes from above is above all men, he that is of the earth is of the earth and of the earth he speaks; he that comes from heaven is above all**

men. The heavenly origin of Jesus makes him
supreme over all men, who are wholly of earthly origin.
Both substantivized present participles ὁ ἐρχόμενος and
ὁ ὤν are here used without reference to time, and ἐκ is
used to express origin or source. Yet we should note
that the former is a standing designation for the expected Messiah. Even now since he has come he is
in the eminent sense "the Coming One." Since the
entire contrast from v. 27 onward deals with persons,
"above all" must mean not "above all things" but "above
all men." Of him who is "of the earth" nothing can
be said except that "he *is* of the earth," on a level
with all others who are like him and above nobody.
Hence also all his speaking, whatever utterance he
makes (λαλεῖ), is of the same nature, "of the earth."
On the other hand, "he that comes from heaven" (now
using this elucidating phrase) "is above all men" not
merely in his speaking but in everything. The two
πάντων show that the contrast is here not between
Jesus and the Baptist only but between Jesus and
all men in general. This mighty contrast these disciples must know and keep in mind.

32) With this clear, the Baptist proceeds to the
speaking of Jesus, save that λαλεῖν is too ordinary a
verb to apply to him. **What he has seen and did
hear, of that he bears witness; and no man receives
his witness.** That this is, like his origin, testimony of
things seen and heard in heaven goes without saying
(1:18). Grammarians have difficulty with the two
verbs, one a perfect, the other an aorist, "has seen,"
"did hear." They ask whether the perfect is aoristic,
or the aorist is used in the sense of the perfect. They
certainly can be understood most easily just as they
stand. The perfect is extensive: what Jesus has seen
in heaven all along; the aorist is punctiliar noting the
past fact (historical). Jesus "has seen" all there is
to be seen in heaven and can testify accordingly. The

aorist "did hear" is not added as a duplicate of all that
Jesus also heard in heaven, all the lovely music and
the heavenly language in the conversations with God.
This aorist is specific and refers to the punctiliar word
or commission which sent the Son forth into the
world. It indicates the counsel of God for our salvation, the loving commands of the Father, 7:16;
8:28; 12:49, 50; etc. Of these things Jesus came
to testify.

The καί coordinates two contrary acts: this superlative testimony and its rejection. Not by mere revelation does Jesus speak as did the prophets of old, but
from actual presence in heaven he "bears witness" at
firsthand, absolutely directly. Nothing truer and more
trustworthy can ever reach men. And the things he
testifies thus are the very ones men need most
of all, the facts and realities about God in heaven,
his will, purpose, and plans concerning men. "And
his testimony — this wondrous testimony — no one
receives." The very coordination of the statements
lets us feel the enormity of the guilt implied, as in
1:10, 11. To receive testimony = to believe it; not
to receive it = to disbelieve it, refuse to trust it, treat
it as a lie. The fact that the negation is not meant
to be absolute the very next words show.

33) **He that did receive his witness did seal
that God is true.** At this point and through the
next verse commentators present views with which
we cannot agree. Who is this that received Jesus'
witness and sealed that God is true? The Baptist
here does what he has done in his previous statements,
he allows us to infer to whom he is referring. Both
the aorist participle and the aorist main verb are
definite, each denoting a past act. The Baptist refers
to *himself*. There were, indeed, a few others besides
the Baptist who also did receive Jesus' witness. In a
manner the words apply also to these. But in their

full sense they apply only to the Baptist himself. As far as the receiving is concerned, he stands first and foremost and helped the first of his own disciples also to receive Jesus' witness. At this very moment he is trying to make his remaining disciples do the same. The actual situation is sometimes lost sight of, and the comment of some expositors reads as though the Baptist here utters abstract, general statements, like a man who is writing a book not like one who is talking face to face with a few men in order to move them to a definite act. The Baptist here virtually tells his disciples, "*I* did receive his witness, *I* did seal," etc. To let this aorist ὁ λαβών refer also to such as in the future will receive Jesus' witness, is to extend its force too far. Such a thought is an inference not the meaning of the word itself.

When the Baptist speaks of sealing that God is true, veracious, *verax*, he, of course, does not mean that God's being true would not be sufficiently certified without such a seal. The declarative ὅτι (R. 1034) states what the seal attests. God is true even if all men called him a liar. A seal is not intended for the person issuing a document but for the one to whom it is issued, to assure him. So God himself adds seals to his truth not for his own sake or for the truth's sake but for our sakes. What does the Baptist mean by saying, "He that did receive his witness did seal that God is true"? Here again some generalize: the seal is faith or the saving effect of Jesus' testimony. This, they say, acts like a seal or proof, helping to assure the believer and others that God is true in his revelation of Jesus. Thus again sight is lost of the actual situation: the Baptist trying to assure his disciples who were finding fault with Jesus. And how about faith and trust in error and deception? Does it, too, "seal" and make error truth? The Baptist is speaking of *himself* and by no means of himself

as an ordinary believer. He is divinely commissioned
(1:6), to him special direct divine revelation was given
(1:31, etc.). He had far more than his own personal
faith to append as a seal, he had *his word and testimony as a prophet of God, the word of the revelation
he had received.* For his disciples this seal ought to
have great weight. There were to be others like this,
namely the apostles (1:14). Their personal faith is
an entirely minor matter. The seal they present is
far higher.

34) The commentators who misunderstand v. 33
are also not clear with regard to v. 34. **For he
whom God did commission speaks the words of God;
for the Spirit gives not from** (insufficient) **measure.**
What does γάρ prove or explain? The fact that faith
acts as a seal? Impossible. The thought of v. 34
runs in an entirely different line. Only properly
related statements can be joined by "for." Therefore
v. 34 does not refer to Jesus himself but to the Baptist.
The simple story is this: John tells his disciples, in
order to convince and assure them, that he himself
puts the seal of his authority and his person on God's
truth that Jesus is the Messiah; and then, in order to
establish the weight of this statement more fully, he
explains (γάρ) that he, sent by God, utters nothing
less than the words of God, and this he can do because the Spirit gives such utterance to him in adequate
measure.

"He whom God did commission" is the Baptist and
not Jesus. The claim that only one "from heaven"
(v. 31b) can be "commissioned" is contradicted by
1:6 and 1:33, where the Baptist is the one "commissioned." In v. 31, 32 Jesus is ὁ ἐρχόμενος, "the One
Coming." Now it is true that Jesus, too, is "sent"
or "commissioned," and that he afterward tells the
Jews much about his "Sender." But here the fact
that Jesus is sent is out of line both with what pre-

cedes and with what follows. The aorist ἀπέστειλεν indicates the past act when God sent the Baptist on his great mission. Thus sent — let his disciples note it well — "he speaks the words of God," literally, "he utters the utterances of God." For λαλεῖν is the opposite of being silent; and ῥήματα are merely utterances, whereas λόγοι are the thoughts put into statements. Of Jesus the Baptist has just said far more in v. 32, namely that he "testifies" the actual things he has seen and did hear in heaven. Why should he now reduce this exalted statement? But of the Baptist this is, indeed, the highest that can be said: God places his words on his prophet's lips. He is in the same class with the prophets who were sent before his day.

Another γάρ explains how the Baptist can utter God's words, "for the Spirit gives not from (insufficient) measure." It is hard to decide from the Greek whether God is the subject of the sentence, as our versions take it, or whether it is "the Spirit." The sense, fortunately, is quite the same, for the point to be explained is the Baptist's ability to convey God's utterances. He can do this if *God* gives him the Spirit in proper measure; or if *the Spirit* gives him the utterances in proper measure. Yet this γάρ clause convinces so many that Jesus is here meant and they do not think that it could be the Baptist. The present tense of the verb, δίδωσι, which means "continues to give," should give them pause. If Jesus were referred to, this would have to be the aorist ἔδωκε, "did give," i. e., when the Spirit descended upon him "as a dove." This continuous bestowal is vouchsafed to the Baptist, as it was to the prophets before him, day by day for his work.

Finally, οὐκ ἐκ μέτρου is taken to mean "unmeasured," "without measure," "not by measure," a litotes for "in complete fulness." This misconception has led many to refer the entire verse to Jesus. The phrase means: not in narrow or insufficient measure, as though the ordinary limits could not be exceeded. The English has no corresponding idiom; ἐκ is not our English "by." The Spirit (or if we prefer the other subject: God) gives as he wills, in richest measure, by revelation and by inspiration, the words he wants his messengers to utter. This, indeed, establishes the fact that the Baptist, as God's messenger, can and does speak God's own words when he points his disciples to Jesus. The Spirit sees to it that he is properly equipped. The disciples have every reason to believe and to obey his words as being "the utterances of God" himself.

35) After this efficient preparation the Baptist, as one sent of God and fitted out by the Spirit in adequate measure, speaks to his disciples this weighty word of God as the climax of all that he has previously said. **The Father loves the Son and has given all things into his hand. He that believes in the Son has life eternal; but he that obeys not the Son shall not see life, on the contrary, the wrath of God remains upon him.** Let the disciples note well what the Father thinks of the Son (Jesus) as the Baptist here tells them by the Spirit. In the Baptist's own hearing God had declared, "This is my beloved Son!" Matt. 3:17. The Baptist only echoes that word just as he did that about "the Son of God" in 1:34 (compare the comment made there). The fact that here again the Baptist refers to Jesus by "the Son" is wholly evident. On the verb ἀγαπᾶν here used compare v. 16 — the highest form of love, made even infinitely high by being predicated of the Father with regard to the Son.

As this love is the basis and the adequate reason for giving all things into the Son's hands, so this supreme gift is the evidence and the proof of that

love. The extensive perfect δέδωκεν marks the gift as
once being bestowed and then becoming permanent
forever. Not in the divinity of the Son but in his
humanity must this gift be placed as we think of
Jesus. Omnipotence belongs to all three Persons of
the Godhead alike and thus cannot be given by one
Person to the other. But in and according to his
human nature Jesus could and did receive also this
gift. The evidence for his possession of this gift
lies in the miracles which Jesus wrought during the
ministry of his humiliation when he used this gift
only at times and in furtherance of his work. After
his exaltation he used it according to his human nature
without such restriction. "All things" cannot be restricted to those pertaining only to the kingdom, for
even when only the kingdom of grace is thought of,
"all things" would extend far beyond its bounds, Eph.
1:10 and 22. The things of the kingdom are the
greatest by all odds; why then should the lesser be
withheld? Compare also Matt. 11:27; 28:18; John
13:3, where also no restriction appears. "Into his
hand" means for Jesus, God's Son in human flesh, to
rule and to command at will. Did the Baptist's disciples think that their master had merely done Jesus
a favor by testifying of him as he did and had thus
placed Jesus under obligation to him? Their ideas
need a radical modification. And this also for their
own sakes.

36) These are not abstract or theoretical propositions that the Father loves the Son and has given all
things into his hands. They apply most directly to
these disciples — and to us. Since all things are in
Jesus' hands, "life eternal" is included. It is the
highest gift dispensed by the Messiah. Therefore
everything depends on each man's personal relation
to Jesus. In fact, the Baptist is here doing over again
what he did in 1:35, etc., he is urging his own disciples

to follow Jesus. So he places before them the two great alternatives: "he that believes in the Son," and "he that disobeys the Son" (the dative is the direct object, R. 540). The matter is personal, hence these singulars. Twice again "the Son" is used and not a mere pronoun; and "the" Son, this Jesus who is the Son in the supreme sense. In this thrice repeated "the Son" the climax of the Baptist's testimony is reached, and for this reason John here records the entire incident, v. 22-36.

The great personal "either — or" is made plain in the two substantivized participles, "he that believes," and "he that disobeys." For the second, the Baptist might have used, "he that does not believe." But ἀπειθέω, "not to be persuaded by the Son," involves unbelief and is a designation for it; hence "obedience of faith" in Rom. 1:5 is a description of faith. He who trusts the Son, by that very trust obeys the Son; he who will not trust the Son, by that very act of refusal disobeys him. The divine greatness of the Son makes trust and the obedience of trust our only normal and right response to him, and refusal of trust the most desperate challenge of the very character of the Son and of his words and his signs. This disobedience of unbelief is the crime of crimes.

That is why the other two contrasts are bound up in this one of believing and of disobeying. To trust the Son means not only abstractly to rely on him as being trustworthy but to rely on his word and promise concerning life eternal, i. e., to accept this gift by our trust. Hence, the moment we trust the Son we have the gift, ἔχῃ, and continue to have it even as we continue to trust. The glory and the full blessedness of this life does not at once appear, I John 3:2, but we do have this life, and in due time its glory will appear. On the terms used here compare the remarks on v. 15. Thus it means the world and all to the Baptist's disciples that they should stop their blind hostility to Jesus and should trust him with all their heart in a way far beyond any trust they have in the Baptist. Yea, unless they want to distrust the latter, they must give their very souls to Jesus, the Son, in the trust that obtains life eternal.

If anything is yet needed to eradicate the hostility of these disciples to Jesus and to open the way to trust in him, the consequence of disobeying the Son should do this. He who disobeys the Son incurs the worst possible guilt a mortal, sinful being can incur. This at once, by separating him from the Son, cuts him off from life eternal, "he shall not see life" ("see" as in v. 3), shall not "have" it and thus in any way experience what it is, now and in the next world. This is infinite loss. This negative result of the disobedience of unbelief involves the corresponding positive result, "on the contrary (ἀλλά), the wrath of God remains upon him." His sinful state of life made him subject to the wrath of God in the first place (Eph. 2:3), his disobedience now fixes that wrath upon him forever (unless he should repent). A certain type of exegesis and all types of rationalism have assailed "the wrath of God" as being an impossibility — which it is, indeed, if the unholy conception of it which these men harbor were reality. Their pictures of a God angry with the passion of a man, cruel, bloodthirsty, etc., are inventions of their own. God's wrath is the inevitable reaction of his righteousness and holiness against all sin and guilt. While the term "wrath," like other terms used in the Scriptures with reference to God, is anthropopathic, it clearly expresses the terrible reality that, when God is challenged by human sin and unbelief, God in accord with his very being must cast far from him those who persist in this desperate challenge. A holy and righteous God must come to a final issue with all those who reject him and his saving grace in the Son. They who will not have life by that very fact remain in death.

The Baptist's last testimony is ended. What did these disciples do? Just as little as John told us the full story of Nicodemus, so little he tells that of these disciples. The unanswered question about them leaves us with the same question concerning ourselves: "What are we doing under the impression of the divine testimony here offered also to us?"

CHAPTER IV

Jesus in Samaria, 4:1-42. — **When, therefore, the Lord knew that the Pharisees had heard that Jesus was making and was baptizing more disciples than John (although Jesus himself was not baptizing, but his disciples), he left Judea and departed again into Galilee.** The evangelist's interest in this brief preamble is to inform us how Jesus came to Samaria and thus how the great testimony culminating in v. 26, in the following paragraph, and in v. 42, came to be uttered.

"Therefore," οὖν, connects with 3:22, and brings the result. The two imperfect tenses in 3:22 come to the end of their action in the aorists in 4:3. How Jesus "knew" about these Pharisees is not indicated. We have no call to insert miraculous knowledge; someone brought him the information. On the Pharisees here involved see 1:24. They would be the leaders who were in the Sanhedrin, plus their followers in the capital. What they heard was not only what had become of Jesus when he left the capital, or merely what Jesus was doing since he left, but a more significant report, "that Jesus was making and was baptizing more disciples than John." The Greek retains the original present tenses in the indirect discourse, for the messengers said, "Jesus is making and is baptizing," etc. By stating that the report heard by the Pharisees included this comparison with the Baptist the evangelist implies that the Pharisees used it to cast reproach upon this entire movement. Perhaps they said that it was breaking up in competition, adding, somewhat in the manner of the Baptist's disciples in 3:26, that the very man of whom the Baptist testified in such a grandiose way was disrupting the Baptist's own work. On the term μαθηταί see 2:11.

2) For the benefit of his readers the evangelist adds in a parenthesis that Jesus was not baptizing in person but only through his disciples as his agents. This remark is, of course, not intended to mean that the disciples of the Baptist in 3:26, and now the Pharisees were wrong in their assumption of a competition between Jesus and the Baptist on the ground that Jesus himself really baptized nobody; for this ground would not hold. What one's agents do is the same as one's own act. In this final reference to this work of Jesus the evangelist merely wants his readers not to form the wrong impression that, like the Baptist, Jesus baptized with his own hands. Why he bade his disciples to act for him has been variously answered. It seems best to infer: In order that later on no one might claim that he had received a baptism superior to that of the Baptist. The claim that a baptism by Jesus' own hands would be one including the Spirit, whereas the Baptist's baptism and that of Jesus' disciples remained only "a water-baptism," is wholly specious. See the explanations of 1:26.

3) So Jesus left Judea and went back to Galilee. This means that he ceased baptizing not that he transferred the baptizing to Galilee. To think that Jesus now just changed his mind, or that he finally felt that he had made a mistake by beginning to baptize, is to make God's Son an ordinary mortal. The Baptist's work was fast coming to a close (3:30). Jesus aided it as it was approaching its end. He stopped when the hostile Pharisees turned this aid against the Baptist's work. God himself changes his actions because of men's evil acts, and we shall see that Jesus does the same as occasion requires.

4) **Now he had to pass through Samaria.** Any kind of necessity may be expressed by δεῖ, here the

imperfect ἔδει. One could, of course, go around Samaria and thus pass from Judea to Galilee, but the nearer
and more natural way necessitated crossing Samaria.
On the tense see R. 887, who also makes this verb
personal, "he must," 393, which is questionable. This
open tense is closed by the following historical present
ἔρχεται.

5) **He comes, then, to a city of Samaria, called
Sychar, near to the parcel of ground which Jacob
gave to Joseph, his son. Now Jacob's spring was
there.** The historical present "he comes," like those
in the following narration, adds vividness. The preposition εἰς invaded the territory of ἐπί and πρός, R. 596,
so that here it is used when Jesus comes only "to the
city." That this cannot be the old Shechem, now
Nablus, a mile and a half from Jacob's well, as some
have thought, is plain, because the woman could not
go that far for water, nor is the well visible from
Nablus, nor would John introduce the name of the
place by writing, "*called* Sychar," which indicates an
otherwise unknown place. In all probability Sychar
is the present village Askar, from which the well is
reached by a moderate walk, with Joseph's tomb
about a third of a mile from the well. John alone
employs πλησίον as a preposition, R. 547, 646. The
remark about the burial of Joseph is made by the
evangelist not so much to fix more closely the locality
as to enrich the references to past history in the following narrative. Compare Gen. 13:18, etc.; 48:22;
Josh. 24:32. The ground, bought by Jacob, tradition reports he gave to Joseph whose body, brought
along from Egypt by the Israelites, was then buried
there.

6) The word πηγή means "spring" and is to be
distinguished from φρέαρ, "a shaft or well," v. 11, 12.
The word refers to the water at the bottom of the
well or shaft. The author visited the place, one of the

few really assured sites in the Holy Land, in 1925. A Russian orthodox church covers the well. Through a small wooden door, down neat stone steps one comes to the well in a little chapel; there is a hole in the vaulting above to let the light shine down. The well itself is a rock-faced shaft 105 feet deep, a rectangular stone is placed at a convenient height over the well, with a hole about two feet wide in the center of the stone. A neat windlass lowers a kettle, by which the water is drawn up, and the visitor may drink from a chained cup. Candles on a tray were let down by the windlass and lit up the well down to the water, which seems, indeed, to well up like a spring. Formerly the well was partly filled with debris, it is now perfectly clean, and the water is most excellent. While one might prefer a restoration of the well to the condition that prevailed in Jesus' time under the open sky with a few ancient jars as were then (and still are) used, the well is now at least clean and neatly kept. The village, now a few houses, supposed to be Sychar, was pointed out on the hillside. Standing outside of the chapel, it was easy to conceive the scene, with Jesus resting at the well, and "this mountain" (v. 20), Gerizim, rising high not far away.

Jesus, therefore, having been wearied from his journey, was sitting thus at the spring. Jesus is introduced to us at this point of his journey. The perfect participle "having been wearied," i. e., and now in this condition, draws a vivid picture. So also does the durative imperfect "he was sitting," which bids us linger with the sitting figure. The adverb "thus" cannot intend to repeat the participle "having been wearied," for which repetition no reason appears, which also would require that οὕτως be placed before not after the verb. "Thus" = as he was, without any further preparation. Just as he came, so he sat down. The entire sketch, also this adverb, shows that the writer was an eyewitness. Here, as elsewhere in John's Gospel, the true human nature of Jesus is brought to our attention just as vividly and just as forcibly as in other places his true divine nature is emphasized. It is a mistake to think that John writes only of the latter. This man, tired, dusty, hot from his long walk as the sun rose higher and higher, and thirsty, this is God's own Son, the Only-begotten, from whom in such humility his divine glory shone forth. The evangelist even names the hour: **It was about the sixth hour,** near noon according to Jewish reckoning; see the question at issue in John's reference to the hours of the day, 1:39. By naming the hour the evangelist indicates how deeply his soul was impressed by what began here in Samaria at this notable hour.

7) The lone figure by the well is joined by another. A brief sentence tells all we need to know: **There comes a women of Samaria to' draw water,** and ἐκ Σαμαρίας must be the same as Σαμαρεῖτις in v. 9, designating her as being from "Samaria," the country, not from the city by this name (called Sebaste). How came this woman to draw water at this hour? While we are not told and cannot make a positive statement, a conjecture such as, having worked in the fields and passing near the well, she desired to refresh herself, is a mere guess. We must not forget that she brought a waterpot, which indicates that she came from her home to obtain water. John's mention of the hour of the day seems to refer particularly to this woman's coming at such an hour. She also comes alone, no other women are with her, whereas oriental women like to go in companies to draw water for their homes. Piecing these observations together and joining them to what is revealed of this woman's character, we may take it that she was a social outcast. The other women would not

tolerate this woman who now lived in open adultery after a checkered career with five husbands. The more must we marvel at the condescension of Jesus who stoops to ask a favor of such a woman, and this with a love that longs to save even her miserable soul.

She would never have spoken to this Jewish stranger. **Jesus says to her, Give me to drink.** Here the Fountain asks for water, and he who bids all that thirst to come to him himself asks to have his thirst quenched. The two aorists in the request indicate two simple acts. There is no need to allegorize, "Give me *spiritual* refreshment through thy conversion." Whatever was in Jesus' heart, his words mean just what they say: he asks this woman for a drink.

8) The evangelist is even at pains to show how a kind of necessity moved Jesus to asks this *woman* for a drink. **For his disciples had gone away into the city in order to buy food.** No one was there to serve Jesus, he was alone. In later times the traditions of the Jews forbade the buying and the eating of Samaritan food; this rule evidently was not in force at this time. The supposition that only some of the disciples had gone for food, that all were not needed for this, that at least John had remained behind who then heard and afterward related the ensuing conversation, cannot be entertained, for then Jesus would have asked a drink not only for himself, nor would John have written "the disciples," without a qualifying word.

9) **The Samaritan woman says to him, How dost thou, being a Jew, ask of me to drink, being a Samaritan woman? For Jews have no dealings with Samaritans.** Thus was the simple request of Jesus denied; nor do we read in the entire narrative that his thirst was quenched. We may assume that Jesus made his request after the woman had drawn

the water not before. The aorist ἀντλῆσαι ὕδωρ in v. 7, however, does not imply this, stating only the single act of drawing water. The situation itself makes it probable that she drew up the water, that then the strange conversation followed, and that finally, when the woman hastened away, in her excitement she forgot to take the filled vessel along. The woman probably recognized the Jew in Jesus by his speech, no other mark being apparent, such as peculiar Jewish dress. The woman neither shows "a smart feminine caprice of national feeling," nor are her words "intended to tantalize." They are quite simple and self-explanatory. She puts them in the form of a question simply because she is surprised. The request is altogether unexpected, and the reason why it is unexpected lies in the relation between Samaritan and Jew. She does not say that the Samaritan is against the Jew, which, of course, would also be true; but that the Jew is against the Samaritan — this because Jesus, the Jew, asks a favor of her, the Samaritan.

With his Gentile readers in mind, the evangelist inserts the remark that the Jews "have no dealings" with the Samaritans, οὐ συνχρῶνται, no ordinary social intercourse. Some codices omit this clause, the verb of which is, indeed, unusual in the New Testament. Yet it states a fact, and, aside from textual authority, this explanatory remark is exactly like others interspersed in John's Gospel. After the return from the captivity in Babylon the Jews rightly denied any participation in the rebuilding of the Temple and in the public worship to the Samaritans, who were a mixture of former Israelites and of Gentiles, II Kings 17:24-41, and also had a mixed religion. Even after renouncing idolatry they acknowledged only the five books of Moses as the Word of God, Ezra 4:1, etc. Thus a bitter enmity existed between the Samaritans and the Jews, which continues to the present day. The hand-

ful of Samaritans that exists today at Nablus, the old
Shechem, about 175 persons, neither eat, drink, nor
intermarry with the Jews, nor have anything to do
with them except in the way of trade. The author
met their high priest Isaac Ben Omrom and visited
their little synagogue in 1925. They have a dearth
of girls and are thus dying out. Since others refuse
brides to the Samaritans, their own girls are betrothed
shortly after birth; but they are gradually dying
out. Suspicion of each other divides them, so that
it required three men to unlock their synagogue with
three separate keys to allow our party to enter and
to inspect their scrolls of the Pentateuch, to which they
ascribe a fantastic antiquity, one of which is said to
be 3579 years old, written by a great-grandson of
Aaron, a second of which is said to come from the era
of the Maccabees, and a third is said to be 1000
years old.

10) **Jesus answered and said to her** (on the
combination of the two verbs see 1:48), **If thou
knewest the gift of God and who it is that says to
thee, Give me to drink, thou wouldest have asked
of him, and he would have given thee living water.**
The absolute mastery of the reply is at once apparent.
In the most effective manner Jesus uses the very
refusal of this woman to make her the offer of the
drink she so greatly needs. This offer contains a
kindly rebuke for her ungracious refusal to extend so
small a favor, coupled with the assurance of a far
greater gift if she would ask of him. Modestly Jesus
speaks of himself in the third person. His object is
to reach this woman's soul. Tired and thirsty as
he is, his wants may wait if only he is able to supply
hers.

"If thou knewest" — sad, deadly ignorance! Yet
this is the voice of heavenly pity. So he spoke with
tears concerning Jerusalem: "If thou hadst known,

even thou, at least in this thy day, the things which
belong unto thy peace! but now they are hid from
thy eyes," Luke 19:41, etc. The two cases, however,
are not parallel, for Jerusalem rejected the knowledge
so long and so lovingly offered to her, while this
woman was now for the first time receiving the offer
of this knowledge. "The gift of God," τὴν δωρεὰν τοῦ
Θεοῦ = "living water." The genitive reveals the great‑
ness and the blessedness of the gift: it flows from
God. Yet Jesus connects it with himself as the agent
and the channel through which this gift is bestowed,
"and who it is that says to thee, Give me to drink."
This can be no ordinary person, such as the woman
had known before, not even some holy priest or
teacher in Samaria or in Jerusalem. For he who is
so significantly designated, "he would have given thee
living water," i. e., this very gift of God. Jesus does
not directly say who he is; he only indicates that he
may be the one by the reference to his request for a
drink. The woman could conclude, as she also did,
that Jesus was a great prophet, a man sent by God
to be a human mediator in the bestowal of this gift
of God. But the words of Jesus, purposely left in‑
definite at this stage of the conversation, may also
imply — and actually did imply — that Jesus himself
is the author and giver of this gift of living water, i. e.,
that he himself is God. The light is veiled; the woman
is led gradually to see it.

The conditional sentence is of the mixed type. The
protasis εἰ ἤδεις, "if thou knewest," is present unreality,
while the apodosis σὺ ἂν ἤτησας καὶ ἔδωκεν ἄν, "thou wouldst
have asked and he would have given," is past unreality.
"If thou knewest" — but thou dost not know! "Thou
wouldst have asked" — thou didst not ask. "He would
have given" — but, alas, he could not give. And yet
Jesus continues the offer. "Living water," ὕδωρ ζῶν, is
an allegorical expression, a large number of which

occur in the Scriptures. The illustration (here "water") and the reality (here "life" in the word "living") are combined, but always in such a way that the expression is self-interpretative. See Trench, *Parables,* 9, where this type of Biblical allegory is well elucidated. Unless we understand the little secret of this much-used form of figure, we shall go astray, as many have gone when interpreting "living water," saying that it means "grace and truth," "faith," *gratia renovationis,* "the Word," *"the Spirit* of the new life," or "the Holy Ghost," whereas "living water" means no more than "life," spiritual life, the life regarding which Jesus told Nicodemus that it comes by the new birth. The figure of water, which connotes drinking, intends to show that this life is a vital necessity for us and yet that it may be received so easily. But even as Jesus, physically thirsty and in need of water, remained so although Jacob's well had plenty of water, as long as no one drew and gave him of that water: so this woman, dead in sin and in need of life, would remain so although Jesus, the very fountain of life, sat there before her, as long as she would not desire, ask, and accept this life when Jesus, unlike herself with regard to the common water, unasked offered this heavenly lifewater to her.

11) **The woman says to him: Sir, thou both hast not a drawing vessel, and the well is deep. Whence, then, hast thou the living water? Art thou greater than our father Jacob, who gave us the well and himself drank of it and his sons and his cattle?** Involuntarily the respectful address κύριε, "lord," "sir," comes to the woman's lips. Those who think that her words have an ironical tinge are no doubt mistaken. This woman's question is like that asked by Nicodemus in 3:4. Told that he must be born anew, by his question about again entering his mother's womb, he really says to Jesus, "I know you cannot

mean that." This woman, told that she should have
and ask for living water, by her reference to Jesus'
lack of a vessel, the depth of the well, and the appended
question, really means to say, "I know you cannot
mean this water." The woman is sensible, her words
are true. Neither Nicodemus nor this woman are so
dense that they do not perceive that Jesus is speaking
of something that is above the physical. And Jesus
is not so bungling in his language that neither Nicodemus nor this woman are unable to see that he is
speaking of something that is higher than the natural.
Both state that they understand this, he with his
"how" question, she with her "whence" question. Both
questions are like a premise with an evident conclusion: "Thou canst not mean the natural, the merely
physical; ergo, thou must mean something higher."
And both are right — that *is* what Jesus means. But
here: What kind of water can this be that Jesus
means? and whence can he obtain this strange water?
In the woman's question the emphasis is not only
on "whence" but equally on the final participle τὸ ὕδωρ
τὸ ζῶν (R. 777), for this reason it is added with a
second Greek article, "*Whence* . . . the water that
is *living?*" In οὔτε (οὐ + τέ, the negative plus the
copulative conjunction, R. 1189), followed by καί, we
simply have τέ . . . καί, "both . . . and,"
with the first member negated, R. 1179. Also ἄντλημα,
"a drawing vessel," corresponds to ἀντλῆσαι, "to draw,"
in v. 7.

12) At once the quick mind of this woman leaps
to a second conclusion, and again a correct one,
although the mere suggestion fills her with surprise
and even incredulity. If Jesus means other water
than this in Jacob's well, better water than this, why,
that is really saying that he is greater than Jacob
who dug this well and left it for his descendants,
yea, was himself satisfied with the water of this well.

The surprise and the incredulity come out in the interrogative particle μή, which in the woman's thought involves a negative answer, "Certainly thou canst not mean to say that thou art greater than Jacob?" Hence also she dwells on what Jacob did, calling him "our father" who gave us the well and who with his sons and his cattle never sought other, better water (ἔπιεν, the aorist to express the undeniable fact).

Through Joseph the Samaritans claimed descent from Jacob. Hence John's note in v. 5 on the tomb of Joseph near by and the woman's proud "our father Jacob." The point has been disputed, but compare II Kings 17:24 with II Chron. 34:6 and 9 — in Josiah's time not a few Israelites remained in devastated Samaria, so that the Samaritans became a mixed race, Israelitish and heathen elements being mingled, so that they were able in a way at least to point to Jacob as "our father." Josephus *Ant.* 11, 8, 7, reports that the Jewish element was increased by renegade Jews, who, on violating the laws and traditions of their own land, fled to Samaria. As the woman's eyes rested on the tired, thirsty, dusty traveller, it seemed incredible to her that he should be greater than the ancient patriarch.

The reasoning of this woman is typical and therefore very interesting. Her conclusions are altogether sound and yet they remain false. The good feature about them is that she, like Nicodemus, puts them into an interrogative form, thus holding her mind open and even asking for more instruction. This effect is produced entirely by Jesus. Both the woman's conclusions and her questioning are her reactions to Jesus' own words. Both also are intended by Jesus. The woman did not laugh at Jesus and call his words absurd, did not turn away and walk off with her waterpot. She thought, considered, drew conclusions, asked in surprise. Step by step Jesus enlightened her. Her conclusions were still false, because she still knew too little. Her spiritual darkness rapidly disappeared as Jesus spoke.

13) **Jesus answered and said to her** (compare on 1:48), **Everyone that drinks of this water shall thirst again; but whoever shall drink of the water that I myself shall give him shall in no way thirst forever; on the contrary, the water that I myself shall give him, shall become in him a spring of water welling up unto life eternal.** This reply of Jesus answers both questions in the mind of the woman and answers them squarely, adequately, first regarding *the kind of water* he has in mind, secondly regarding *the person* he is. This water is spiritual not material; heavenly not earthly; permanent not transient. And thus it helps to reveal who this ἐγώ, this great Giver of such water, really is.

The proposition is self-evident, "Everyone that drinks of this water shall thirst again." No material water exists that allays thirst forever. While Jesus' word refers only to the material water in Jacob's well, the inference lies close at hand that nothing material is able to quench the thirst of the soul permanently, and this is implied by the contrast which deals with the spiritual water that Jesus gives. Some, indeed, succeed in stilling their thirst but they do it in a lamentable way. In the parable of the Prodigal a citizen of that far country had gathered himself a herd of swine — significant wealth! — and was satisfied. In the parable of the Rich Fool a man was satisfied with his grain fields. These men satisfied their thirst by stifling it. Germany's greatest poet Goethe, a favorite of fortune, confesses that he was seldom happy. Augustine is right, the soul, created for God, will not rest until it rests in God.

14) The corresponding opposite is just as true and self-evident, "But whosoever shall drink of the

water that I myself shall give him shall in no way
thirst forever." Jesus accepts the challenge of every
man, no matter who he may be and what he may have
to offer. And the test shall be only this: the true and
permanent quenching of the thirst of the heart. But
not in theory, not in argument; on the contrary, in
actuality, in actual experience, "whosoever shall
drink" — actually "shall drink," "shall in no way
thirst forever" — actually never thirst. The indefinite
relative clause: ὃς ἂν πίῃ is like a condition of expectancy and is thus followed (regularly) by the future
indicative: οὐ μὴ διψήσει. The implication is that some
will so drink and will then never thirst again. The
aorist subjunctive πίῃ expresses one act of drinking,
which is never repeated. Note οὐ μὴ as the strongest
negation with the future indicative (also with the subjunctive).

Jesus retains the figure throughout. As the water
is *life,* so the drinking is *faith,* i. e., its inception. The
interpretation that the drinking is the *continued* use
of the Word and the Sacraments goes beyond the
words of Jesus when he says that *one act* of drinking
removes the thirst forever. To bring in prayer and
intercourse with God's children is irrelevant. No
prayer of ours and no association with Christians
have life in them to bestow on us. Christ alone has
and bestows that life. The thought must here be
ruled out, that, once we have life, we must feed,
nourish, replenish it by Word and Sacrament. While
this is true, Jesus here speaks only of the bestowal of
life, which, the moment we obtain it, becomes a permanent possession. He does bring the dead to life
day after day. Once made alive, we live on. Once
born anew (Nicodemus), we need not be born again.
Twice, for emphasis, Jesus says, "which I myself shall
give him." The pronoun ἐγώ is strongly emphatic,
which we attempt to convey by translating, "I my-

self." He, and he alone, gives this wonderful water. In the first clause the relative οὗ is attracted from the accusative to the case of its antecedent ὕδατος. The use of ἐκ is partitive, R. 599, with a verb that requires the partitive idea, R. 519: drink "of," i. e., "some of" the water.

The wonder of this water's quenching thirst εἰς τὸν αἰῶνα, "for the eon," the Greek idiom "forever," is explained in a simple fashion, but the wonder is thereby only increased, "on the contrary, the water that I myself shall give him, shall become in him a spring of water," etc. This repetition, "that I myself shall give him," involuntarily raises the question, "And who art thou to give such water?" It is *the* question Jesus wants to raise, *the* question that must be rightly answered, or we shall after all thirst forever. Whoever heard of a gift of a drink which, on being drunk, forms a living spring within the person, so that he never needs to drink again! It is wholly obvious that Jesus is not speaking of physical but of spiritual realities. All the terms he has used are lucid: "living," "gift of God," "water that I shall give," "drink," "never thirst." Even natural life, once started, lives on; more so spiritual life, which is to have no termination whatever. The fact that it may be lost by unbelief is not mentioned here, where the first fundamentals alone are in place.

Jesus uses πηγή, "a spring"; φρέαρ, a shaft or cistern that merely holds water and may also be empty and without water, would be the wrong word, see v. 12. Of this "spring" Jesus says, "a spring of water welling up unto life eternal." We must leave the words in their natural order and combination and not make "unto life eternal" a modifier of "shall become" or even of "spring" or of "water"; it modifies "welling up," ἀλλομένου, a middle participle, whose voice puzzles R. 812 but it surely means "bubbling up of itself." But "unto life eternal" does not refer to time — continuing that long or that far. Nor should we bring in the idea of a little stream, which starts from the spring, flows on, and finally empties into life eternal. Jesus uses no such figurative expansion when he says "welling up of itself unto life eternal." This wonderful spring here differs from the figure employed in 7:37, etc. Here it denotes life, in the other connection the drink denotes the Holy Spirit. The spring or life remains within the person; the gift of the Spirit does more, it also flows out from the person. Thus "welling up of itself unto life eternal" = keeping the person spiritually alive for the eternal life of heaven. Thus also in the final concept "life eternal" all that Jesus says about this "living" water is fully clarified.

15) **The woman says to him, Sir, give me this water, that I may not thirst nor come all the way hither to draw.** John writes πρὸς αὐτόν, whereas after the verbs of saying he has had only the dative because of the reciprocal idea in πρός. The woman is responding to what she felt was an offer and invitation on Jesus' part, she is reciprocating by accepting. She thus shows that she understands Jesus far better than those commentators, who regard the future tense δώσω in the two relative clauses in v. 14 as not to be fulfilled until Jesus gets ready to baptize with the Spirit. This woman rightly understands that Jesus means "I will give" with reference to a giving at any time where he finds acceptance. As far as the Spirit is concerned, Jesus has not mentioned him in the conversation with this woman as he did in that with Nicodemus. Yet no sinner receives life, no sinner obtains faith except through the Spirit. The Spirit was bestowed through Jesus now. This woman and many in her village came to faith and confessed their

Savior, v. 42, and no one can do either except by the
Holy Spirit, I Cor. 12:3.

The entire conversation on Jesus' part is misunderstood when it is not observed that up to this point
Jesus is using the gospel and that from now on he
employs the law. This means that Jesus knew that
the woman could not yet believe and he did not expect her to believe so soon. The law must first crush
the heart in contrition, then faith can enter in, and
not till then. So both law and gospel must be
preached, and Jesus preaches both; the two appear
here most plainly marked. Either may be offered
first, or both may be intertwined, though each always
remains distinct, likewise the proper effects of each.
Here Jesus uses the gospel first. It is a mistake to
imagine that in doing this he failed and then tried
something else. Not one word of the gospel was lost
upon this woman; its effect presently comes with a
rush when the law begins to take hold upon her heart
and to show her her sins and her tremendous need of
the gospel.

The misconceptions indicated prevent a right
understanding also of the woman's replies to Jesus,
both up to this point and in the remainder of the conversation. The comment is wrong that Jesus has
been offering her "theoretical considerations," which
the woman "evaded by trifling replies." Jesus gave
her pure gospel, to which the woman replied with
surprise, indeed, but respectfully, seriously, with real
effort to understand. That, too, was all that Jesus
wanted and expected. She was not yet competent to
grasp and to appropriate. When the woman now
actually asks Jesus for "this water," this request of
hers is the response to Jesus' offer. When after all
she still clings to the thought of some wonderful
natural water, which stops natural thirst permanently

and obviates coming all the way (διέρχωμαι) from her home to this well for a supply, she only shows what is inevitable in all who are strangers to the life of God, namely her inability to rise from the natural to the spiritual. Jesus does not rebuke her. Nicodemus he had to rebuke (3:10) when he began to cling to unbelief; this woman with her response of readiness is in advance of the learned "teacher of Israel."

16) In the case of this woman Jesus has gone as far as he could with the gospel. He has laid the foundation and has laid it well. He now suddenly turns to the law. **Jesus says to her, Go call thy husband and come hither.** The imperative ὕπαγε is used with a second imperative without adding καί, much as we say: "go call," etc. This thrust of Jesus' is direct and goes home. Jesus bids this woman to do what he knows she cannot do. Such biddings are like the Ten Commandments; like the command to the lawyer, "This do and thou shalt live!" Luke 10:28; and like that to the rich young ruler, "Sell all!" Luke 18:22. Biddings and commands like these are intended to reveal to the person concerned this very inability and the sin and guilt connected therewith. The divine law demands perfect love and by that very demand shows us, who lack this love, that we are full of sin. The lawyer, ordered to do the commands he recites, by that order is to discover that he cannot do them and must seek a different way to heaven. The rich young ruler, bidden to sell all and to give it away, finds that here lay his guilt in an outwardly moral life — he loved his possessions with an unholy love. This woman, who cannot go and call and bring her husband to Jesus, by that very fact is to see just what kind of a woman she is, what a wretched, sordid, immoral life she had led.

Yet some have thought that Jesus actually regarded this woman as one that was properly married and that he desired the presence of her husband. The fact that in the next breath Jesus reveals the woman's whole past life is explained by supposing that suddenly between v. 16 and v. 17 God revealed these facts to Jesus. Thus in v. 16 Jesus speaks in ignorance and in v. 17, 18 with knowledge. But 1:42 and 48, etc., plus 2: 24, 25, declare that Jesus himself saw, himself knew what was in men. He is not made dependent on special revelations for this knowledge as were the prophets. To say that, unless Jesus thought the woman had a husband and could call him, he would be uttering "fiction" in his command; and that when the woman was thus bidden to go, she would have taken this chance to disappear and never to return, is to misjudge both the woman and Jesus. The fear that precipitates this judgment is the fact that certain critics charge that John's Gospel makes Jesus walk like a God on earth equipped with omniscience. But to get rid of one exaggeration we must not employ another. The Gospels and the entire Bible make Jesus God incarnate, possessing also in his human nature the divine attributes but using them only at proper times and in properly executing his office. What is Matt. 25, etc., but omniscience? yet in his human nature the Son of man does not know the time of the end, Matt. 24:36; Acts 1:7. The ancient allegorizing of the five husbands of this woman and of the man she now lived with, and the attempt to revive these fancies, needs no refutation.

17) **The woman answered and said unto him,** the doubling of the verbs marking the great importance of her reply, **I have no husband.** Jesus' bidding her to call her husband is really a call to confess her sins, to confess them voluntarily. For in saying "go call" Jesus, indeed, gives her the opportunity to pretend that she has a husband and that she now goes to call him, thus avoiding confession, and

thus also getting away from Jesus altogether. When the bidding of Jesus to this woman is contemplated from this viewpoint, the perfect mastery of it comes to view. The woman makes no move to go — she is not trying to get away. She does not lie by pretending that she has a husband, since Jesus mentions "husband." She stands there before this strange Jew and confesses her shame, "I have no husband." Those few words cost the woman something. Cold comment says that she is half lying and does not understand what it takes for a woman to reveal, even partly, her disgrace. Why fault the woman for confessing only so much? Her quick mind surely tells her that Jesus may probe farther, but this does not seal her lips, does not make her evade, does not rouse her temper, does not make her say, "What business are my private matters to thee?" No, she confesses. The fact that she does this before this stranger is the effect of what he has been saying to her. The gospel aids the law, as the gospel is also aided by the law. It helps the sinner by making him ready to confess. To Jesus, whose lips are filled with the gospel, the sinner finds he can confess.

Jesus says to her: Well didst thou say, A husband I have not. For five husbands thou didst have and whom thou now hast is not thy husband. This, a true thing, thou hast said. Jesus accepts, Jesus commends, Jesus completes her confession. We now see why by doubling the verbs of saying when giving the woman's reply John marks it as being of great importance. The commendation lies in καλῶς and in ἀληθές. "A husband" I have not, places the object forward with emphasis, bringing out the full contrast that the man whom she now has is not her husband; on ἔχειν τινά to express illegal relations compare I Cor. 5:1. Instead of wringing the rest of the confession from the woman, Jesus makes it for her. It is a touch of his gentleness with the sinner. So the father of the prodigal stops him in the middle of his confession — the same gentleness in a different way. How the woman came to have that many husbands we are not told and need not be told. These five were at least legal husbands, for only so can the words be understood. The lax divorce laws may help to explain, Matt. 5:31; 19:7; compare Deut. 24:1 and 3, which the Jews greatly extended, and very likely the Samaritans also. Those five were bad enough, but now she is living with a man who is not even in loose legality her husband.

It is wrong to imagine the woman as brazen and shameless in her confession. The sin had touched her conscience more than once, but she had hushed the disturbing inner voice. Now Jesus was making it speak again. The notion that Jesus at this moment received a revelation from God regarding this woman's life has already been answered. To read irony into Jesus' words when he says, "Well didst thou say," and, "This, as a true thing, hast thou said," makes Jesus receive a poor sinner's confession with irony — a thing impossible for Jesus. We must not overlook the fact that by her silence or non-denial the woman acquiesces in the confession that Jesus makes for her. Plainly Jesus is succeeding and succeeding rapidly.

19) **The woman says to him, I see thou art a prophet.** By that statement she admits that Jesus has spoken the truth about her life. Thus she really completes her confession. Nor does she qualify, excuse, or minimize. But involuntarily she also makes a confession regarding Jesus. She admits that only in a supernatural way could he know her past life; compare v. 29. The fact that she calls him only "a prophet" is natural at this stage. It never, however, entered her head that in some ordinary way this

strange Jew had discovered the things he said. This
was done by men of a later age, who eliminate from
this Gospel every divine trait in Jesus.

What now follows has again been misunderstood.
In fact, the previous wrong conceptions culminate at
this point and create confusion. Thus it is said that
a gap occurs at this point, and that John skipped
what lies between. Again, that the woman with quick
wit here turns the conversation away from these delicate and painful personal matters to a question that
Jews and Samaritans argued; that she makes a tricky
dialectical evasion. But then Jesus would never have
answered as he did, carefully and to the point, the
very question the woman raises. He would have rebuked her and have driven in more deeply the hook
of the law she would thus be evading. **Our fathers
worshipped in this mountain; and you say that in
Jerusalem is the place where they must worship.**
The woman really asks Jesus, who are right, her
ancestors or the Jews (emphatic ὑμεῖς). This she does
in connection with her unqualified admission of sin
and guilt. The matter is of the gravest personal concern to her for this reason and for this alone. She
admits that she needs cleansing. Where is she to
obtain it? Where her people say, "in this mountain,"
Gerizim, looming up not far from the well; or where
the Jews say, in the Temple at Jerusalem? Will not
Jesus send her to the latter place, to bring her sin
offering and to obtain the absolution? Zerubbabel had
refused the Samaritans permission to join in building
the Temple at Jerusalem, and Nehemiah had driven
out a son of Joiada who had married a daughter of
Sanballat (a Moabite of Horonaim and a constant
opponent of Nehemiah), Neh. 13:28. This man with
others instituted the worship on Gerizim in Samaria,
built a temple there, and established the high priest-
hood. This temple was destroyed 129 B. C. and was

not rebuilt, yet the worship continued and still does at
the Passover when seven lambs are offered for the congregation, at Pentecost or the Feast of Weeks, and at
the Feast of Tabernacles.

21) Jesus answers at length. **Believe me,
woman, that the hour is coming when neither in this
mountain nor in Jerusalem you shall worship the
Father.** She had just called Jesus a prophet. "Believe me, woman," links into that confession, for a
prophet's words surely require belief. This call to
believe him also ushers in another astounding statement, that at first might seem incredible, namely that
a time (ὥρα in the wider sense) is not far away when
the Samaritans shall worship neither in Gerizim nor
in Jerusalem. This prophecy, in the sense of fore-
telling the future, is thus another evidence of divine
omniscience used for Jesus' saving purpose. The fact
that this Jewish prophet should declare that the
Temple worship in Jerusalem was to be temporary,
was even soon to cease, must have astonished this
Samaritan woman greatly; that he should say as much
regarding Gerizim naturally surprised her less. "You
shall worship" must refer to the Samaritans and
should not be generalized to refer to anybody or to
men in general. The point in Jesus' words is that the
specific *place* of the worship is a secondary question,
whereas the true *worship* itself is the essential. Only
for the time being the place still has importance,
then it will disappear. And it did. Yet strangely
enough, Gerizim is still sacred to the handful of
Samaritans in existence today, who still worship
there; while all these centuries the site of the Temple
in Jerusalem has been in pagan and in Mohammedan
possession, and the Jews have been completely de-
barred from worshipping there. The Mohammedan
"Dome of the Rock" has long occupied the site of the
old Jewish Temple. Again, the Samaritans soon

dwindled to a tiny number, the Jews multiplied and spread over the world. Such are the ways of God.

A sweet gospel touch lies in the expression, "you shall worship the Father." It opens the door also to the Samaritans so that they may become the children of this Father by faith in the Son. The word "Father" here means so much more, also to this woman, than the word "God" could mean. Jesus keeps the verb προσκυνεῖν, literally "to touch with kisses," but used regarding the oriental prostration in worship and adoration of God.

22) Yet while both Gerizim and Jerusalem shall pass away as places for worship, they are not on an equal basis. **You are worshipping what you do not know, we are worshipping what we do know; because the salvation is from the Jews;** ἐκ to indicate origin or derivation. The personal pronouns "you" and "we" intensify the contrast that lies in "do not know" and "do know." With προσκυνεῖν we may have the dative of the personal object of the worship or the accusative of the impersonal as in the present instance. Jesus says, *"what* you do not know," and, *"what* we do know," for no revelation was given to Gerizim, all revelation was limited to the Jews and to Jerusalem. The facts always count, the facts alone, and not what men think or think they know. R. 713 makes the neuter ὅ refer to God, a grammatical impossibility.

And this difference between Gerizim and Jerusalem is not a mere theological dispute, it is a vital soul issue; for God's revelation contains ἡ σωτηρία, compare on the term 3:17. Though in the Greek abstract nouns may have the article as a matter of course, here "the salvation" denotes the specific and only salvation contemplated in God's promises and to be realized in his incarnate Son. This salvation is in no way promised to the Samaritans, so that it

would emanate from their midst, but to the Jews alone.
The Messiah could not be a Samaritan, he had to be
a Jew. While the Pentateuch might have made the
Samaritans "know" this, they, by rejecting all the
other books of the Old Testament containing so much
more of the Messianic revelation and by thus running
into a blind opposition to the Jews, lost this most
precious knowledge. What Jesus thus tells this woman
answers the question about the place, and in the most
effective way, namely by explaining and by holding
up to view what is essential.

23) Yet, significantly, Jesus neither says nor implies, "Thou must go to Jerusalem." He does not
even say, "The salvation is of Jerusalem." Yet we
should misread his words if we should take him to
mean, "Gerizim and Jerusalem make no difference —
just so you worship God aright." For since "the salvation is of the Jews" not "of the Samaritans," Gerizim
is plainly ruled out. The fact that the alternative,
however, for this woman is not "Jerusalem" is now
made plain by further elucidation. **Yea, the hour
is coming and now is, when the genuine worshippers shall worship the Father in spirit and
truth; for the Father also seeks such as worship him.**
Here ἀλλά is not contradictory ("but") ; it is copulative
and climacteric ("yea"), R. 1186. It reaches across
the parenthetic thought in v. 22 to the chief thought
in v. 21. This appears also in the repetition of "the
hour is coming." Both times this present tense "is
coming" states that the approach is still in progress
and not yet complete. And yet Jesus can add, "and
now is," without contradicting himself. His redemptive work is not done but is only definitely undertaken
("the hour is coming") ; but he himself is here, the
Redeemer and Savior ("and now is"). Thus all that
the Temple and the ceremonial cultus at Jerusalem
had served so long was passing away, was in a sense

already gone — would forever be done with on Easter
morning. We must note that Jesus treated the Temple
and its cultus accordingly. He brings no sacrifices
like an ordinary Jew, we do not hear that he joins
in the prayer ritual. He uses the Temple, the festivals,
the worshippers congregating there, for his own high
purpose. As the Son he uses "my Father's house"
for the last use it should serve. The rent veil in the
Temple was "the sign" that both the Father and the
Son were done with the Temple.

Thus Jesus does not compel this woman to go to
Jerusalem. Instead he explains to her the true worship which abides when the Jewish ritualism presently
disappears altogether because it is no longer needed.
The "genuine" worshippers, ἀληθινοί, are those who
alone really deserve the name in distinction from all
who observe only the Jewish ritual practices. They
worship "the Father" as his genuine children in a
way that corresponds to their character. Here again
Jesus uses the significant designation "the Father,"
which connotes, first of all, that Jesus is this Father's
Son, sent to work out the promised salvation, and,
secondly, connotes that all genuine worshippers are
the children of this Father by faith in his Son, by
accepting the salvation wrought and brought by this
Son.

They shall worship the Father "in spirit and
truth." One preposition joins the two nouns and thus
makes of the two one idea. But not in the superficial
sense that genuine worshippers shall worship in a
genuine way; for they would not be such if they
used a different way. Jesus here describes what the
genuine way is. It centers in the worshipper's own
"spirit" and spirit nature (Rom. 1:9), moved, of
course, by God's Spirit (Rom. 8:14, 16, 26). We
should say, all true worship is one of the soul. But
this is not enough, for many put their very souls into

their worship and yet are only false, self-deceived worshippers. Hence the addition: in spirit "and truth." The fact that this means more than "truly," i. e., sincerely, with subjective truth, should be obvious at a glance. The essential subjective feature of genuine worship is fully covered by "in spirit." To this the objective counterpart must be added, which evidently is ἀλήθεια, "truth," in the sense of reality. So many labor over this term. They fear that if "truth" is here regarded as God's revealed truth, the reality embodied in the Word, the single phrase would become two: "in spirit" and "in truth"; i. e., that then the preposition ought to be repeated. So "truth" is made to mean: "in genuine contact with God"; or "so that the worship tallies with its object, corresponds with the essence and the attributes of God, and does not contradict them." Fortunately, Jesus is speaking to a plain woman, and "truth" to her means truth. Moreover, if a genuine contact is to be made with the Father, if the genuine object of the worship is to be reached, does this not mean that these two: the worshipper's own "spirit" and God's own revealed "truth" joined together (καί) must form the sphere (ἐν) in which this worship takes place? All that forsakes this sphere is spurious worship. Omit the spirit, and though you have the truth, the worship becomes formalism, mere ritual observance. Omit the truth, and though the whole soul is thrown into the worship, it becomes an abomination. Thus "spirit and truth" form a unit, two halves that belong together in every act of worship.

This was the case in the Old Testament Judaism, where by God's own institution ceremonies had to be observed. From Moses onward prophets and psalmists insisted, though the people often failed to heed, that the worship must be "in spirit and truth." Jesus does not here condemn this old worship on account

of its connection with ceremonies. What he does is
to foretell that these ceremonies are on the verge of
ceasing altogether. Likewise our present worship.
We assemble in churches, and the service follows a
certain outward order, now a hymn, now a prayer,
now the sermon, etc., though we ourselves now
arrange all this. This Jesus does not here condemn.
What he does is to state that not in any outward
forms but "in spirit and truth" the real worship is
rendered. For the woman this means that she need
not wait, need not go to the Temple, need not offer
a sacrifice, but can right here and now perform
the very highest act of worship, namely accept the
Father's pardon for her sins and return to him her
spirit's gratitude.

To assure the woman fully Jesus adds, "for the
Father also seeks such as worship him." "For" explains that "of such a kind" are the worshippers that
God desires. He seeks them, not as though they have
already become such by efforts of their own, but as
longing to make them such by his Word and his
Spirit. He was now doing this with this sinful woman.
The seeking is the outcome of his love. The position of καί connects it with the subject: "the Father
also," not with the verb: "also seeks." The participle is made attributive by the article: "such
as worship," i. e., such worshippers; and προσκυνεῖν
here has first a dative then an accusative personal
object.

24) Why God seeks only such worshippers is
answered by pointing to his nature: **For God is
spirit; and they that worship him must worship in
spirit and truth.** The predicate "spirit" is placed
forward for emphasis. While one might translate
"A spirit is God," this makes the predicate sound too
much like a classification of God who is "spirit" from
all eternity and uncreated, while all other, namely

created spirits, have a beginning. "Spirit" does not here classify; it only states God's nature. Jesus makes no new revelation concerning God; he only recalls to the woman what she has long known regarding God. And he does this only to show her what accordingly all genuine worship of God must be, namely worship "in spirit and truth." This deduction is not new. For δεῖ, "must," is not meant regarding a new precept, a new commandment, or worship. This "must" expresses far more, namely a necessity that is due to God's own nature and that has always held and always will hold true.

While the fact that God is spirit is not stated in so many words in the Old Testament, all that the Old Testament reveals regarding God is to this effect. Neither Jew nor Samaritan would controvert the statement for one moment. The prohibitions to make images of God, the comparisons of God with idols (for instance Isa. 40:13-26), Solomon's reminder that he whom "the heaven and heaven of heavens cannot contain" does not dwell in a house, and many other statements show how fully God's nature was understood. Even the naive anthropomorphic and anthropopathic utterances are made and can be made with such naivete only on the absolute certainty of God's infinite spirit nature. To urge these human expressions against this certainty is to hurl a pebble at a mountain, thinking thereby to knock it over. Accordingly, also the Old Testament is full of genuine worship, of its descriptions, and of injunctions so to worship and so alone. Consider the Psalms, the prayers, Daniel for instance, the many warnings that sacrifices, gifts, lip-prayers, observing festival days, etc., without a broken, contrite, believing heart are in vain. Thus the genuine worship was known well enough. The new feature which Jesus presents is that from now on this worship is enough, i. e., that the ceremonies, restrictions of time and of place, are even now to fall away. In this sense the worship will, indeed, be new.

25) The impression Jesus makes upon the woman is that she automatically thinks of the Messiah. We are reminded of Nathanael in 1:49, save that this woman does not go that far. Yet Messiah-ward her thoughts turn like the flower to the sun. **The woman says to him, I know that Messiah is coming (who is called Christ); when that one shall come, he will announce to us all things.** It is no doubt wrong to think that by this response the woman seeks to end the conversation. Then Jesus would not have replied as he did. What ideas the Samaritans held concerning the Messiah has been investigated at great pains but with small results. Their name for him was Taheb, probably meaning "the Restorer." He was to be both a great prophet and a wonderful king, although the strong political feature of the Jews seems to be absent from the Samaritan conception. In many respects the Samaritan ideas of the Messiah coincide with those of the Jews. The woman uses the Jewish name "Messiah" not the Samaritan "Taheb." Was it because she was speaking to a Jew? That the Samaritans used also the Jewish title has not yet been established. We know why John preserves the title the woman actually used, himself in a parenthesis translating it for his Gentile readers, as in 1:41: It is because Jesus testifies to this woman that he is the Messiah.

The thought that perhaps Jesus is the Messiah has not struck the woman, although she is not far from it. Perhaps she expected Jesus to state how all that he had said about God, salvation, and true worship was related to the hope of the Messiah. When she says that Messiah (without the article, as if it were a proper name) "shall announce to us all things," she voices one of the great expectations concerning the Messiah but she does more; for this thought comes to her because of the great things she has just heard from Jesus' lips. We see how Jesus' person and his words had affected this very ordinary woman who was not even a Jewess. The learned, self-righteous, exceedingly prominent Pharisee Nicodemus in the capital and this unlearned, sin-laden, ordinary unnamed woman in the country district of despised Samaria are companions. Opposites in all respects, yet both are drawn mightily by Jesus. The woman gained the goal far more quickly than did the man.

26) **Jesus says to her, I am he, (I) who is speaking to thee.** As Jesus helped the woman with her confession of sin in v. 17, 18, so he now helps her with her confession of faith (compare v. 29). To this obscure woman Jesus reveals point-blank what he had revealed to no one else. One surprise has followed another for this woman, but the climax is now reached. Nor has Jesus misjudged the woman. She does not, indeed, sink down in worship at his feet but she is ready to believe. Ἐγώ εἰμι is the good Greek idiom for, "I am he," the English requiring that the place of the predicate be filled. The substantivized participle ὁ λαλῶν σοι, "the man speaking to thee," is in apposition to ἐγώ, R. 778 and is not the equivalent of a relative clause, "I that speak unto thee" (our versions). Jesus adds the apposition because of what the woman has just said that the Messiah would do, namely announce all things. This, Jesus intimates to the woman, is just what he is doing for her right now — announcing to her the very things she needs. The person and the words are vitally joined together. They always are. And as we treat the one, so we treat the other.

Here then John has given us another great attestation of Jesus.

27) The record might close at this point just as that of Nicodemus does at 3:21; but Jesus both attests himself still further on this occasion (27-38) and also receives most notable attestation from the Samaritans (39-42). So the account continues. **And upon this came his disciples. And they were marvelling that he was speaking with a woman; yet no one said, What seekest thou? or, Why speakest thou with her?** The disciples returned from buying food (v. 8) and were not a little astonished to see their Master engaged in talking (ἐλάλει, durative, imperfect) with (μετά, with the idea of association) a woman. Jewish custom forbade that a rabbi should speak in public with a woman and most especially on matters of the law. But the reverence of the disciples for Jesus is so great that they only keep wondering (ἐθαύμαζον also imperfect and thus durative), and no one brings that wonder to an end by actually inquiring. On μέντοι see R. 1188. The first question that John thinks of is specific, τί ζητεῖς; namely, "What desirest thou of her?" which also was close to the truth, for Jesus had asked the woman for a drink and thus had started the conversation. Or, John suggests, the disciples might have asked in general why he was speaking with the woman. This, too, would have hit the truth, for it would have brought to light Jesus' saving motive.

28) **Accordingly the woman left her waterpot and went away into the city and says to the people, Come, see a man who told me all things that I (ever) did. Can it be that this is the Christ?** The connective οὖν indicates that the woman quickly left at the approach of the disciples. She would have been bold, indeed, to face all these additional strangers. And yet God in his providence had so timed her arrival at the well that her conversation with Jesus could reach the supreme point before the arrival of the

disciples. Quick-witted as she showed herself in her answers to Jesus, she now strangely forgets to take her filled waterpot along and in spite of her great reverence for Jesus forgets too all about his original request for a drink. These are exquisite psychological touches in John's narrative, indicating how deeply the words of Jesus had gripped her heart, making her forget all else for the moment.

This historical present λέγει beside the two matter-of-fact aorists lends a vivid touch to the narrative. She hurries back and without hesitation stops and addresses the people (τοῖς ἀνθρώποις), men and women whom she meets and who begin to congregate about her. The interjectional adverb δεῦτε, always with the plural, "hither," in the sense of "come hither," is sometimes joined to an imperative as here, or to a subjunctive, or is used independently. The woman is wise — these people are to come and to see for themselves, which recalls 1:39 and 46. She characterizes Jesus as "a man who told me all things that I (ever) did" with supernatural insight into her past life. "All things" is not an exaggeration when we note that these things cover her entire past life since her first marriage. With the aorist εἶπε she states the fact. No doubt, she had to repeat just what Jesus "did tell" her in his exact words. And the people at once saw that this was astounding because coming from a Jewish stranger; the facts about the woman these people, her neighbors, knew only too well.

As wise as the woman is in calling on the people to come and to see for themselves, so wise, too, is she in indicating what they will find. She puts this into a question but with μήτι not with οὐ. The English has no such delicate distinctions, hence we must circumscribe, which is always bunglesome, "Can this perhaps be?" "Οὐ would have challenged the opposition of the neighbors by taking sides on the question whether Jesus was the Messiah. The woman does not mean to imply flatly, that Jesus is not the Messiah by using μήτι, but she raises the question and throws a cloud of uncertainty and curiosity over it with a woman's keen instinct. In a word, μή is just the negative to use when one does not wish to be too positive. Μή leaves the question open for further remark or entreaty. Οὐ closes the door abruptly." R. 1167. More briefly: οὐ heading a question = I think so, and you, too, must say so; μή = I do not think so, and you will agree; and then modified: I can hardly think so — yet it might be (so here μήτι).

30) The wrought-up condition of the woman and her astounding report had their effect. **They went out of the city and were coming to him.** The imperfect ἤρχοντο pictures them on the way and holds the outcome in abeyance. This is due to the fact that something transpires while they are on their way and must be told before their arrival is stated in v. 40, which then closes the open "were coming."

31) So we learn: **In the meanwhile the disciples were requesting him, saying, Rabbi, eat!** Strange, indeed — Jesus asks for a drink and is refused (7-9); now he is asked to eat and he himself refuses. The verb ἠρώτων denotes a most respectful request and is thus the proper word; and its imperfect tense implies repeated urging on the part of the disciples and also that Jesus did not comply. The aorist φάγε, "eat," is not "be eating," which would require the present but, "eat and finish." On "Rabbi" see 1:38. The request is full of respect and without familiarity. The disciples never addressed Jesus as "Brother," though Jesus on notable occasions called them "my brethren," Matt. 28:10; John 20:17; see also Rom. 8:29; Heb. 2:11.

32) **But Jesus said to them, I have meat to eat that you do not know.** Here we catch a remark-

able glimpse of how Jesus put his very soul into his work. Instead of doing it mechanically, in a business-like sort of way, with professional ease, he did it with all his heart. It so occupied him that all else for the time being was excluded. The exaltation of it prevented him from at once descending to lesser and lower things. It filled him with such joy and satisfaction that it acted like food and drink to his body, weariness, thirst, and hunger being forgotten. Not having been present when Jesus saved the woman's soul, the disciples could not know the βρῶσις Jesus had enjoyed.

33) **The disciples, therefore, were saying to each other, Surely, no one brought him (aught) to eat?** The imperfect ἔλεγον indicates that the disciples said this repeatedly; they could think of no other solution. The aorists ἤνεγκεν and φαγεῖν speak of actual bringing and eating. The μή in μήτις (compare μήτι in v. 29) indicates that for the disciples the only answer must be "no." Some have chided the disciples for their lack of spirituality and deeper understanding. They would be more severe than Jesus himself who did no chiding, who admitted that the disciples did not know what food he had had, who quietly went on to explain. The disciples had left Jesus thirsty and hungry and now found him refreshed and declining to eat. Someone had been there in their absence and had just left. How could they help but ask whether this person had perhaps brought Jesus something to eat? Yet they do not ask him, they question quietly among themselves. They are respectfully reticent as in v. 28 not bold to pry and to quiz.

34) **Jesus says to them, My food is that I do the will of him that did send me and that I finish his work.** Both βρῶσις in v. 32 and βρῶμα here are derivations from βιβρώσκω, the former denoting more the act of eating combined with the food, like the

German *das Essen*, the latter the food only, *Speise*.
The plural τροφάς in v. 8 = different kinds of food.
The disciples had bought and brought different eat-
ables, but one βρῶμα was all that Jesus' heart desired.
Jesus himself explains the figure, "that I do the
will of him that did send me and that I finish his
work." The double ἵνα clause is subfinal (R. 992, etc.),
exactly like a ὅτι clause, here used as a predicate
nominative: "my meat is that," etc. John uses this
ἵνα extensively. Here, for the first time, Jesus speaks
of his great Sender whom he will mention again and
again, always using the substantivized aorist participle, which names this Sender according to the one
past act of sending, ὁ πέμψας με. As such he has
a will, θέλημα, namely regarding a specific work, even
called "his work," αὐτοῦ τὸ ἔργον, the possessive being
emphatically forward. The sending or mission of
Jesus is "to do" this will, "to finish" this work, and
the aorists state actual doing and finishing. Doubling
the statement thus makes it decidedly strong. Compare 17:4, "I have finished the work which thou gavest
me to do," where the same verb is used. Also 19:28
and 30, "Jesus, knowing that all things are now
finished," etc. . . . . he said, "It is finished,"
τετέλεσται The double clause is thus a description of
Jesus' entire Messianic work. This "will" of his great
Sender is his good and gracious will regarding the sinful world, the will of his comprehending and purpose-
ful love, ἀγάπη; this "work" is our redemption from
sin and all that belongs to it. The will and the work
were done, finished completely, when Jesus died on
the cross.

So completely are the mind and the heart, the will
and the life of Jesus taken up with this will and this
work of his Sender that they actually are his "food."
This metaphor, however, conveys not only the thought
that Jesus is devoted to this task with his whole soul

but that doing this task, accomplishing it, is a necessity for him, something he must have, as we must have food. Not only was there no other work possible for him here, but if this work would not have been given him to do, his very being here would not have been possible, i. e., the Son would not be here incarnate in human flesh (1:14). What Jesus says lies far above the thought that human talent and genius devote themselves to some special task with signal energy. It also lies above a Christian's devotion to the work of his spiritual calling. God, indeed, gives us spiritual life and powers in order to serve him; but we and our service of God — at best imperfect — are not bound together so essentially as Jesus and his work; for we could separate ourselves from our work, leave it undone, do a contrary work, but Jesus never. Thus only in a clearly modified sense could we appropriate these words of Jesus and say that our meat, too, is to do our Father's will and his work.

35) A part of this work Jesus had just been doing, and another part of it was soon to be done by him, namely the work of a prophet (Luke 4:17-21), dispensing "living water" to famishing souls. So Jesus continues. **Say you not, Yet it is four months, and the harvest comes? Behold, I say to you, Lift up your eyes and view the fields, that they are white already for harvest.** Jesus changes the metaphor of food to one closely allied, that of the harvest. Between Jacob's well and Sychar the fields had been planted in wheat or in barley. In Palestine the harvest comes in the middle of Nisan, our April. So Jesus was at the well in our month of December. The grain had been sown in November and now covered the fields with a thrifty growth of green. Jesus does not mean that his disciples are talking about the coming harvest, saying how long it will be until harvest time. He asks

an implied question, to which he takes for granted (οὐχ expects an affirmative answer) that the disciples on their part (ὑμεῖς) will say, "Yes, about four months yet until harvest" (a τετράμηνος, sc. χρόνος). Jesus says, that is what *you* would say. But I say to *you*, the harvest is already here, the grain ready to be reaped. Note the contrast: ὑμεῖς λέγετε, "*you* are saying," and: λέγω ὑμῖν, "I am saying to *you*." The contrast is thus not between the persons: you — I; for we have no ἐγώ to balance ὑμεῖς. It is between the two statements, which is indicated by the emphatic pronouns: *you* say, ὑμεῖς — I say *to you*, ὑμῖν. One statement *you* make, the other is made *to you*. And the two statements seem contradictory: "yet four months," and "already." These temporal modifiers are in the emphatic positions, the first at the head of its statement, the second at the end. This point of contrast demands that ἤδη be drawn to what precedes and not to what follows, as the R. V. margin proposes, "Already he that reapeth," etc.

Now both statements are true, that the harvest is still four months off, and that the fields are right now white for harvest, ready to be cut. It is all clear the moment the disciples do what Jesus bids them do, "Lift up your eyes and view the fields." There on the path through the young grain the Samaritans were coming, impelled by the report from the woman. We now see why John has the picturesque imperfect ἤρχοντο in v. 30 — there they were, still coming. They were the grain Jesus saw, white for harvest, ready to be gathered into the granary of the kingdom. Thus the contrast of the two kinds of "food" (v. 31 and 33) is carried over into the two kinds of "harvest." The disciples and we with them are ever inclined to see only the material and must have our attention drawn especially ("behold!") to the spiritual. It often seems less real to us than the material, yet if anything it is more so. At least it is infinitely more important and vital. We go into a large city and see great buildings, a vast amount of commerce, etc., but we often fail to see the millions of poor sinners for whom Christ died, the "much people in this city" who may be gathered into Christ's kingdom. Acts 18:10. We see a man's wealth, social position, learning, power, etc., but we often overlook the immortal soul he has to be saved. On the other hand, we see a poor wretch, criminal, outcast, loathsome, but again we do not see that he, too, is a soul bought by Christ's blood and desired by him for Paradise (Luke 23:43). To the eyes of Christ all this is different. Our meat may be only the earthly, his meat is the spiritual; our view may be only concerning grain, his is concerning souls to be gathered into his garner.

36) From the harvest the thought of Jesus extends to the reapers and backward also to the sowers and then turns (v. 38) to the disciples personally. See the comprehensive grasp it thus reveals and the grip it puts on the souls of the disciples. **He that reaps receives wages and gathers fruit unto life eternal, in order that he that sows and he that reaps may rejoice together.** This is not a general proposition applicable to both material and spiritual harvesting. Jesus speaks only of the latter. The "and" is explicative, it explains that the wages received are the fruit gathered unto life eternal (καρπός, fruit of trees or of fields, here the latter). The wages of the spiritual reaper are the souls gathered for life eternal — here not necessarily only heaven but eternal life also as a present possession reaching unto heaven. On "life" and on "life eternal" compare 1:4 and 3:15. How these souls can be called "wages" appears in what follows.

God's purpose (ἵνα) in thus rewarding the reaper is that the reaper and the sower "may rejoice together." Here it becomes plain why the gathered fruit is called wages: it is because of the χαίρειν, the rejoicing. This appears partially now already: our true reward we feel and know are the souls saved through us, the holy joy we have in their salvation. It will appear perfectly in heaven, where the vanity of all other rewards fully appears, and where the joy is perfect and supreme. But this rejoicing is intended for both the sower and the reaper. Here we see that in spite of the present tenses of the participles and the verb the statement is not general with reference to the material and the spiritual but general only with reference to the latter. Materially a man may sow a field of wheat and never live to have the joy of reaping it; his laughing heir has that joy. Spiritually this cannot happen. The harvest never escapes the sower. It belongs to him as well as to the reaper.

37) **For herein the saying is genuine, One is the sower, another is the reaper.** Here ὁ λόγος = τὸ λεγόμενον, a saying commonly used. But the sense is not that in this exceptional case (ἐν τούτῳ, "herein") this common saying fits. For Jesus is not speaking of an exception but of an invariable rule in the kingdom. Nor would this common saying fit, for its common sense is that many a man is cheated out of his reward: he does the hard sowing, and another steps in for the glad reaping. That, too, is why Jesus does not say, this saying is here ἀληθής, i. e., states a true fact. This would be ambiguous. In its ordinary sense it states a fact only in the sorry experience with earthly affairs; in its ordinary sense it states no fact at all in the blessed experience of the kingdom. Jesus says, here this saying is ἀληθινός, i. e., it has genuine reality. For God never meant that any man, even in material things, should ever be cheated out of his proper reward. So even now I Cor. 9:7-10 is the

ruling thought of men. The fact that in spite of
this so many are cheated that men even formed this
saying about one sowing and another reaping, one
losing what another then gains, is due to the perverse
effects of sin. But in the kingdom the genuine divine
order prevails fully and surely. Here, Jesus declares,
the very saying which men use to express a bad
reality in their common affairs of life becomes a
"genuine" saying for the blessed reality in the pur-
poseful divine arrangement of the kingdom, where
the sower and the reaper are never in opposition but
always joined in unity of reward and of joy. The
ordinary sense of the saying is superseded by a divine
sense.

38) But who is meant by ὁ σπείρων and by ὁ θερίζων,
"the sower" and "the reaper"? The terms are entirely
general. Jesus, indeed, has pointed to the people on
the way from Sychar, but then he uses these general
terms, which imply that he is thinking far beyond
these Samaritans, namely of all the sowing and of all
the reaping unto life eternal. More important than
ever is, therefore, the question, of whom Jesus is thus
speaking. He himself furnishes the answer. **I myself did commission you to reap that whereon you
yourselves have not labored. Others have labored,
and you have entered into their labor.** The general
statements are here made definite and concrete. The
general statements are here also made strongly personal. But neither of these is done by a special reference to the coming Samaritans. Jesus speaks of the
entire mission and work of his disciples. Here the
tenses cause dispute, the aorist ἀπέστειλα, "I did commission," and the following perfects. The "critical"
solution that John wrote these tenses from the standpoint of his old age when he penned his Gospel without noticing the incongruity that the disciples had not
yet been commissioned when Jesus spoke here at

Jacob's well, destroys all faith in John's veracity and imputes to him an error that not even a tyro would make. Others regard these tenses as prophetic past tenses, i. e., tenses which state future acts as if they were already lying in the past. But Jesus is here not uttering prophecy. But had he already commissioned these disciples, and had they already entered into other men's labor? The answer is found in 4:2. Also in 1:42 with its implication. Jesus uses only the general term, "I did commission," not "I did commission you to the world" (17:28; Matt. 18:19), which might seem strange here. The purpose in attaching the disciples so closely to the person of Jesus must from the first have been made clear to them by Jesus, and on this fact rest the later more formal commissionings.

The disciples were sent to reap. But they never could reap if others had not labored before them, κεκοπιάκατε, grown weary with arduous exertion, i. e., in doing the preparatory sowing. This plural ἄλλοι cannot be a mere plural of category and thus refer to Jesus alone. In almost the same sentence Jesus cannot possibly use ἐγώ, the strong pronoun "I" with reference to self and in the same breath the plural ἄλλοι, "others," in the same sense. The old interpretation is correct, these "others" are Jesus and those back of him, the Baptist, the prophets, Moses, etc. But it is going too far to include the priests, teachers, moralists, etc., of pagan nations among the sowers after whom the disciples could reap. By placing his own work alongside of that of God's other agents Jesus by no means cheapens it or makes it less fundamental than it is. He is the Sower of sowers without whose sowing all other sowers would be naught, whose sowing alone made that of others what it was. Yet others also sowed, and Jesus is never averse to giving credit where it belongs, Jesus thought even of the labor (κόπος, strain, effort) preparatory to his own labor. The Baptist prepared the way for him, and in a certain manner every prophet and minister of the law does the same. Jesus is adding his own work to theirs. And the apostles are as reapers entering into all this labor of others, are simply appropriating and using it, having done nothing of it themselves.

In a supreme sense Jesus is *the* Sower, for there is no reaping except after his sowing; in fact, before Jesus came, those who reaped did so on the strength of the sowing he was to do. Jesus did some reaping. He had gathered the disciples and other believers and would gather in these Samaritans. But Jesus chiefly did the sowing; he did not leave a field that was reaped bare to his disciples but a field thoroughly seeded, fast maturing unto harvest. When we compare the 500 brethren, who gathered in Galilee to meet Jesus by appointment after his resurrection, with the 3,000, the 5,000, and the ever-increasing multitude of believers in the next few years, we see, indeed, that Jesus was the Sower, the disciples the reapers. Yet, looking at the work of those who preceded and who followed Jesus, we see that one set of men always enters into the labors of another set. The apostles reaped but they also sowed, from which their pupils again reaped, and so on down the ages. So we today have entered into other men's labors. Recount their long line, their blessed names, their great exertions! But let the reaper ever be humble and remember the Sower and the sowers and not attribute the success to himself. On the other hand, if called to sow, complain not; this hard work is just as necessary, just as blessed as the reaping. Both sower and reaper shall rejoice together. When the sheaves are brought in at last, when the reapers raise the great song of praise, the sowers who began the work that proved so successful shall lead the procession, and so even they shall enter into other men's labor, even that of the reapers who harvested what these sowers sowed. But among them all we shall see not one who does not altogether enter into the labor of Christ.

39) John might at once have gone on from v. 31 to v. 39, but he records Jesus' great testimony concerning his work as an episode. **Now from that city many of the Samaritans believed on him for the sake of the word of the woman, testifying, He told me all things that I did.** The aorist ἐπίστευσαν, "they believed," may be ingressive: "they began to believe," but even so it states the fact. This occurred at once after the woman had testified, and while the Samaritans walked out to meet Jesus, for it precedes ὡς οὖν ἦλθον, "when, accordingly, they came to Jesus," in v. 40. The decisive part of her testimony is carefully mentioned, "He told me," etc. How slowly did Nicodemus come to faith, how rapidly these Samaritans! Both cases have been frequently repeated.

40) **When, accordingly, the Samaritans came to him they kept requesting him to remain with them; and he remained there two days.** The resumptive οὖν, "accordingly," connects with v. 30, as also the aorist ἦλθον marks the end of the imperfect ἤρχοντο in v. 30: they "were coming" — finally they "did arrive." The imperfect ἠρώτων indicates repeated urging and this ended with Jesus' staying at Sychar for two days, the accusative δύο ἡμέρας denoting the extent of time. The citizens of Jerusalem never asked Jesus to stay; afterward he passed through Jericho, and not a soul asked him to stay. Matt. 10:5 in no way conflicts with John 4 and Jesus' stay in Samaria, since that order to the disciples was temporary, and Jesus also stopped at Sychar only in passing and did not go from one place in Samaria to another. Matt. 28:19, etc., and Acts 1:8 cancel the temporary order of Matt. 10:5.

41)   Those were two blessed days for Sychar. **And many more believed for the sake of his word, and they were saying to the woman, No longer because of thy speaking are we believing; for we ourselves have heard and know that this is in truth the Savior of the world.** The aorist ἐπίστευσαν is the same as in v. 39. Coming after the statement that Jesus "did remain" for two days, it summarizes the entire effect of his stay: many more "came to faith" (ingressive), or simply: "did believe" (historical). These came to faith "because of his word," spoken to them during these two days. We read of no signs that Jesus wrought at Sychar, only of this pointed reference to "his word," though it was sign enough in the woman's case (v. 17, 18).

42)   The καί at the head of v. 41 and the τέ in v. 42 are not coordinate; the former merely introduces the sentence, and the latter joins something "in intimate relation with the preceding" (the regular function of τέ), R. 1179. The imperfect ἔλεγον describes how these believers told the woman repeatedly that now they believed on account of what they themselves had heard. This, of course, only substantiated and corroborated the woman's word. Two kinds of faith are here distinguished: one, based on the true testimony of others; the other, based on one's own personal experience and firsthand acquaintance with the Word. The former is that of many beginners, especially also of children taught by parents and by others. It is true faith and has saving power but stands below the other and is more easy to destroy. This kind of faith should grow into the second kind, which believes without human mediators, by direct contact with Christ and his Word, and is thus far stronger than the other type of faith. In v. 39 the woman's testimony is called her λόγος by John, for the *contents* of her speaking are meant; so also the λόγος of Jesus, v. 41. The Samari-

tans speak of the woman's λαλιά, the mere *fact* of her speaking and not keeping silence, i. e., that she told it and did not hide it. And they say, "we are believing," using the present tense with reference to their continuing faith.

This faith they thus joyfully confess, πιστεύομεν, "we believe"; and this with no empty credulity but for solid reasons, "for we ourselves have heard and know." This is genuine confession, from the heart, *ex animo*, not merely formal, by the lips. It springs from a corresponding faith. "We ourselves have heard" means: we, just as the woman, directly from Jesus in person. Jesus stands before us today in person in his Word, and we can hear him directly and personally in that Word as if we had sat among the listeners at Sychar. We can do this every day; they had him only two days. They had to hold what he said in their memories; we can examine the inspired written Word as it is fixed for all time. And thus these believers confess, "we know." Their faith is explicit, not ignorance, the great mark of unbelief, but sound, genuine knowledge, the knowledge that one attains by himself drinking the living water, eating the bread of life, actually being reborn of the Spirit. Argument, science, philosophical reasoning cannot affect such faith; the true believer simply smiles and says, "I know." Only contact with Jesus can work this knowledge of faith, Acts 4:13, 14. All false faith merely imitates this knowledge of true faith, it thinks it knows and yet does not know, 9:24, compare with 9:31-33.

The assertion is advanced that here the evangelist puts his own words into the mouth of the Samaritans when he makes them say that Jesus is "the Savior of the world." This charge casts reflection on John's veracity and the truth of all that he has written. The entire narrative depicts people who are not bigoted, not hypocritical, nor proud. Faith found a steady entrance into their hearts. The very fact that they were Samaritans not Jews, that Jesus lodged with them and taught them, that he did not bind them to Jerusalem and the Temple, all implies that he taught the universality of God's grace and salvation. In other words, by accepting Jesus as the Messiah these Samaritans had to accept him as "in truth the Savior of the world." If Jesus accepted the Samaritans, whom the Jews ranked as heathen, whom could he reject? The fact is that John records this entire episode for one reason only, because Jesus attested himself and his work (v. 26; 35, etc.) so clearly and received an equal attestation from these Samaritans (v. 42).

Jesus in Galilee, 4:43-54. — The fact that Jesus left Sychar after "the two days" already mentioned in v. 40 is again brought to our attention — so long only in spite of his success did he linger here. Then he proceeded without further stop to Galilee, for which 4:3 shows that he started. If Jesus had prolonged his stay and his work in Samaria he would have turned all the Jews against him; and his real work was to be done with Israel.

44) **For Jesus himself did testify that a prophet has no honor in his own country.** The statement is simple enough, it is a kind of proverbial saying which Jesus corroborates from his own experience; hence, "he did testify." People show regard to a man who comes from afar more readily than to one who is merely a native like themselves. But this remark has puzzled the commentators to such an extent that one of them calls "the history of the exegesis of this passage a sad chapter."

The first question is: Did Jesus say this in connection with his second return to Galilee, or is it a word spoken by Jesus at another time and only

brought in here by the evangelist? We know that
Jesus used this saying later on in Nazareth when
his own townspeople turned against him, Matt. 13:57;
Mark 6:4; Luke 4:24. Yet it may well be possible
that in Nazareth Jesus only repeated the saying he
first uttered on his second return to Galilee. The fact
that John uses only indirect discourse without mentioning just when, where, and to whom Jesus first
spoke this word, is sufficiently explained by the connection: John uses this word only in reporting the
return of Jesus to his homeland Galilee. He thus
supplements the synoptists by incidentally inform-
ing us that Jesus made this utterance before he
came to Nazareth and that he applied it not only to his
home town but also to his homeland.

As regards "his own country," πατρίς, his father-
land, we need not hesitate long. This cannot mean
the town Nazareth, nor Capernaum, for in the entire
narrative of Jesus' return only countries are mentioned: Judea in 4:3; Samaria in 4:4; and Galilee in
4:3 and in v. 43 and 45. The mention of Sychar is
only incidental. This homeland is either Judea, where
Jesus was born, or Galilee, where he had spent his
life from childhood to manhood. The fact that Judea
is out of the question should be apparent from the
use Jesus made of this identical saying in Nazareth,
where it simply cannot mean Judea. Nor can we
assume that once when using this saying Jesus had
in mind Judea, and the next time he had in mind
Nazareth and Galilee. In comparison with the few
days of his babyhood spent in Judea the almost thirty
years spent in Galilee are decisive when Jesus now
speaks of his homeland.

But the chief difficulty is in the connective γάρ,
"for," followed in v. 45 by οὖν, "accordingly." If a
prophet is not esteemed in his homeland, how can
that be a reason or serve as an explanation for Jesus'

present return to his homeland? Would it not rather
serve as a reason or an explanation why he should
leave his homeland? This point is urged by those who
would regard Judea as his homeland, and they add that
Jesus thus far had had little success in Jerusalem and
in Judea. This is the reason, they say, why Jesus,
after vainly trying out Judea, now transfers his work
to Galilee, where he expects greater success. Others
turn the point around. Jesus is returning to Galilee
just because a prophet is not esteemed in his homeland, meaning Galilee. Some say, that he now determines to win this esteem in spite of this handicap, at
the cost of whatever hard effort. Some say, that Jesus
intends to return to Galilee, where he will not be
esteemed, because here he can in a manner retire and
live quietly. But these suppositions leave out the
greater facts and thus show that they labor only
in some way to solve the strange "for" and "accordingly."

The facts are that after the assumption of his office
Jesus had returned to Galilee only for a brief time and
had wrought only the miracle at Cana. Beyond that
nothing had been done in Galilee. Jesus proceeded to
Jerusalem (2:12) and there began his public work.
He spent from April until December (v. 35) in Judea
with the result that now he was famous also in Galilee,
for v. 45 reports that the Galileans received him gladly
because they were impressed by the miracles they had
seen him work while they, too, attended the previous
Passover in Jerusalem. So now Jesus does not need to
win his way in Galilee with hard effort. Also, he now
comes, not for retirement, but to proceed energetically
with his ministry in Galilee. Also, he has not failed
in Judea but has created a mighty impression, reaching back even into and throughout Galilee. "For" explains that Jesus *now* starts his real work in Galilee;
and "accordingly" corroborates this "for." Since a

prophet is not esteemed in his own land, Jesus now,
after winning his esteem in another land, comes back
to his own land and finds that esteem awaiting him.
As far as a prophet's having "honor" is concerned, it
is wrong to press the expression and to point to 5:41;
7:18; 8:50. Every prophet seeks and needs esteem
(τιμή), in order that his message may reach open ears
and, if possible, open hearts. The honor and the glory
mentioned in the other passages are of an entirely different type, namely such as men love; and Jesus
spurned all mere human glorification but never the
esteem which brought men to listen to him.

In a simple way John thus again supplements the
synoptists. They skip the eight to nine months of
Jesus' work in Judea, taking us at once from the baptism and the temptation of Jesus into his Galilean
work (Matt. 4:12; Mark 1:14; Luke 4:14). John
reports that all these important months, spent in
Judea, intervened. Yet John's plan is not to write
a chronicle of all that Jesus did during those months
in Judea just as he does not write a full account of
the following Galilean ministry. His plan takes in
only the great attestations of Jesus, and thus he selects
his material. The other Gospel writers followed other
plans.

45) **When, accordingly, he came into Galilee,
the Galileans received him, having seen all the
things he did in Jerusalem at the feast; for they also
went to the feast.** Among the many who had believed in Jesus in Jerusalem (2:23) were these pilgrims to the feast from Galilee. John, however, again
adds that they were impressed chiefly by the miracles
of Jesus; the particle is causal, "since they had
seen," etc., R. 1128. We must, therefore, remember
also 2:24, 25 with its bearing on Jesus' return to these
people. Add to this Jesus' complaint in 4:48; and
again in 6:26. This shows how we must under-

stand, "the Galileans received him," i. e., only as their countryman now made famous by his miraculous deeds.

46) **He came, therefore, again unto Cana of Galilee, where he made the water wine.** He took up the work where he had left it. The second miracle in Galilee was wrought at the same place where the first had been done. The first had prepared the ground, the second builds on that. **And there was a certain royal official, whose son was sick at Capernaum.** The report of Jesus' arrival spread rapidly also to the larger city of Capernaum. The term βασιλικός denotes one who in some way is connected with the king, here Herod Agrippa, who, although being only a tetrarch, ruling only the fourth part of the country, was commonly given the title of king by the Jews. Just what functions this official performed either in the king's court or in his household we have no means of knowing; the title βασιλικός is not used to designate a military officer. Identifications such as Chuza, Luke 8:3, or Manaen, Acts 13:1, are rather useless. Because the son was sick "in Capernaum," we see that the official's home was there, hence also ἀπῆλθε in v. 47; he hastened from Capernaum to Cana.

47) **He, having heard that Jesus was come out of Judea into Galilee, went away unto him and requested him to come down and to heal his son; for he was about to die.** All that v. 46 contains is summarized in οὗτος: this important official who is so distressed about his son's life. He heard the news: Jesus is come! The Greek retains the present tense ἥκει, "is come," whereas we after "having heard" change it to "was come," or to "had come." Although he is a royal official with servants at his command, he goes in person to beg help of Jesus. Yet only his desperate need drives him, his own free heart's desire

does not draw him. If it were not for his sick son,
he would not have troubled much about Jesus. God's
providence often uses our need thus to drive us to find
even more than just what we think we need. The
aorist ἀπῆλθε merely states the fact that the man
"went away" to Cana, while the imperfect ἠρώτα, "he
was requesting," holds us in suspense as to the success
of his request. It pictures the man to us as torn between fear and hope. This suspense continues until
the decisive word which heals the son is spoken.

The man's request is stated by the ἵνα clause, which
in the Koine is a substitute for the infinitive. The
request is made urgent by the additional, "for he is
on the point to die," ἤμελλε followed by the infinitive.
The case is nothing less than desperate. The father
fully acknowledges that all human help has been exhausted, that only a miracle can save his child's life.
Modern "healers" are careful not to touch such cases;
when they do they fail. The fact that this royal
official runs to Jesus with this case shows his faith —
Jesus can save his child from imminent death, Jesus
alone. The fact that he himself comes with his request
shows the humility of his faith. Yet he thinks and
clings to the thought (v. 49) that Jesus must come to
his son's bedside to heal him and that, if the coming
is not hastened, death may win the race and may
make any help from Jesus impossible. This reveals
the imperfection and the limitation of the father's
faith.

48) **Jesus, accordingly, said to him, Unless you
see signs and wonders you will in no way believe.**
"Accordingly" refers to more than the mere fact of
the request; it takes in all that Jesus sees involved in
this request. And this extends far beyond the man
who here makes his request. He is only one of the
"many" we have met in 2:23 (compare 4:45), who

believed only because of the signs they saw, whose faith stopped with the signs and did not advance to Jesus' word as such, with whose faith Jesus, therefore, could not be satisfied. Jesus thus, indeed, speaks to this official (πρὸς αὐτόν) but he uses the plural, "unless you see," etc., and not, "unless thou seest," etc. This also softens the rebuke. The implication, too, is that this official (since Jesus includes him in the class indicated) is a Jew. Nor is it impossible to believe that the man was among the pilgrims who at the last Passover had been in Jerusalem and had seen Jesus work one or more miracles, little thinking that in a few months he would run to Jesus for miraculous aid for himself.

We should not emphasize the verb, "unless you *see*, actually with your own eyes *see*, signs and wonders," for the object "signs and wonders" has the emphasis. The point of Jesus' complaint is not the fact that he is asked to come down to Capernaum and to do the miracle where the man could see it done, but the fact that the kind of faith represented by this man can be kept alive only by means of miracles. The man never thought of Jesus as healing at a distance. Asking Jesus "to come down" is only incidental to the real request, which is to heal his child. So also when Jesus speaks of "seeing" miracles, this is not in opposition to hearing of them, for the effect would be quite the same. The complaint of Jesus is that so many would cease to believe in any manner, or would never believe even as they did unless he furnished them miracles on which to rest this faith of theirs. They would not advance from the miracles to faith in Jesus' person and his Word. Thus Jesus here does, indeed, refuse to hurry to Capernaum and to work the miracle under this condition. By this refusal, however, Jesus calls for and seeks to waken a better faith in the heart of this royal official. In the refusal lies a covert promise to help if only the man will rise to a truer and a better faith. Compare 11:40.

The complaint is that these people have to see "signs and wonders" (the terms are explained in 2:11). The second term is explicative of the first: "signs" in so far as they are "wonders" or portents and arouse excited astonishment. These people do not read the "signs" and see their true significance, that Jesus is the Messiah and Son of God, and that these "signs" seal him as such; they only want to marvel at the wonder of them. Thus they avoid the true purpose of the signs. The strong denial in οὐ μή with the futuristic aorist subjunctive πιστεύσητε, R. 938, etc., for which also the future indicative could here be used, is to the same effect, "you will not believe at all," or "in no way," i. e., not even in the faulty way in which you now believe. Jesus does not deny the poor faith which this official had but declares that this is not enough. His thus calling for a better faith, one that is real, must, however, not lead us to the hasty generalization that Jesus wrought signs only in answer to real faith and never where faith is absent. A study of the miracles reveals that they were used in both ways. Jesus often calls for faith and seals faith by a miracle, and then again he simply works the miracle in order that faith may follow. Thus miracles, indeed, always aim at producing faith, but as signs, not as mere wonders, once in the one way, and again in the other.

49) The man is not rebuffed by the rebuke in Jesus' words. He does not turn away in sad disappointment. He does just what the Canaanitish woman does, Matt. 15:25 — he just throws himself upon the mercy of Jesus. **The royal official says to him, Sir, come down ere my little child die!** We should not stress the fact that the man again begs Jesus "to come down"

and implies that unless Jesus arrives in time even Jesus can do nothing. For in v. 48 Jesus makes no attempt to correct these limitations of the man's faith. Jesus takes only one step at a time, the true pedagogical way. He first attempts to turn this man's faith in a higher direction, namely upon Jesus' own person and his heart. And Jesus succeeds. With pleading reverence the man lays all his distress upon Jesus' heart. If we could have seen the expression on Jesus' face and could have heard his tone of voice, we could better understand his meaning and the man's response. "Unless you see signs and wonders," etc., really means, "Oh, that you would think less about the wonders and more about me!" This brings the address Κύριε, which looks up to Jesus; the renewed pleading, in the strong aorist κατάβηθι, "come down!" and the tender appeal in τὸ παιδίον μου, "my little child." On πρίν with the infinitive after a positive verb see R. 977, 1091. So much Jesus' word has produced, the first tiny advance to real faith in Jesus.

50) And Jesus says to him, Be going on thy way; thy son lives. The man believed the word which Jesus said to him and went his way. The plea that casts itself upon Jesus' heart is heard and in a way that is utterly surprising, far beyond the man's expectation. The two statements of Jesus are not, however, in opposition, as if the first intends to dash down, in order that the second may then raise up the more. The first does not intend to say, "No; leave me, I will not go down!" but, "Be assured and go home — thy son lives!" In other words: "It is not at all necessary for me to go to Capernaum to save thy child's life, not necessary that I should thus prolong thy suspense and anxiety — right here and now I grant thy prayer and give thee thy little son's life." Thus Jesus now corrects the man's poor notion about hurrying to the child's side and he does it with

one stroke. The power to heal lies in the person of
Jesus — where else could it lie? It is a matter of
his will and his word, not one of inches or miles. Jesus
gives the man only his word and even that in the
tersest form, "Thy son lives" — not a syllable more.
On him who speaks this little word, and on the little
word this person speaks, the man is thus bidden to
rest his faith. On paper, and as we read it from the
printed page, it does seem little — too little; yet as
there spoken by Jesus it was mighty, it bore all the
power of Jesus' will, a divine pledge, an unconditional
assurance, an absolute promise. As such it struck
upon the man's heart full of faith-kindling power.

The mild present imperative $\pi o \rho \epsilon \acute{v} o v$ = "just be going on thy way." Then follows the intensive present
tense $\zeta \tilde{\eta}$, the direct opposite of the man's fear about
his child's dying, thy son "goes on living indefinitely."
With this one pregnant word Jesus changes death into
life: the death about to close in, into life that goes
happily on. It is unwarranted to intimate or to assert
that in some way, if by no other than by clairvoyance
or telepathy, Jesus merely knew that the child's fever
was breaking just at this time, and that thus in a perfectly natural way the child would after all escape
death. These attempts of rationalism to "explain
away" the actuality of Jesus' miracles and to leave
only the appearance of miracles, turn Jesus into a
charlatan, from whom every sincere and honest man
should turn away. The fact that Jesus wrought this
miracle, as he did every other deed of his, in conformity with his calling and office and in harmony
with his Father's will, needs no saying. But to add
that in each case Jesus had and had to have a decision
or an intimation from his Father to do the deed is
devoid of Scripture support. To think that every
miracle came only as an answer to a prayer from
Jesus reduces him to the level of the ordinary pro-

phets and is contradicted by all the cases where Jesus
reveals that he acts by his own will and power. So
here, "Thy son lives" = I grant thee his life. Compare Luke 7:11, "I say unto thee, Arise!" On John
11:41, 42 see below. It is fancy to bring in the angels
here or elsewhere in connection with the miracles on
the strength of 1:50; where angels are employed they
are mentioned.

The man believed the word of Jesus, the dative ᾧ
being attracted to the case of its antecedent (some
read ὅν). The aorist states the fact. The man had
only this "word," but now resting on that, asking no
more, he came away with a better, truer trust than the
one that first made him come. His faith was becoming
more like that of the Samaritans in v. 41. This faith
was kindled in the man's heart by Jesus and by his
mighty word, "he lives." "He believed" without
visible or tangible evidence. Yet the man had the
very highest and best evidence — Jesus' word, 20:29b.
In due time the corroborative evidence of sight follows
the decisive assurance of the Word. The inadequate
faith in so many of whom Jesus complained is such
because it clings only to the lower evidence and will
not move to the true ground on which saving faith
alone can and does rest. The imperfect ἐπορεύετο pictures the man as he was on his way and matches the
present imperative πορεύου. It also intimates that we
shall presently learn what the man found. We see
him going back hugging to his heart Jesus' word "he
lives," by that overcoming all doubts and misgivings
that very likely kept assailing his mind.

51) He did not have to wait until he actually
reached home. **Now already while going down his
servants met him, saying to him that his boy lives.
He, accordingly, inquired of them the hour in which
he became better. They, accordingly, told him,
Yesterday at the seventh hour the fever left him.**

The anxiety of the family for the boy's life is indicated by this sending of servants to report to the father the sudden change and the recovery at the earliest possible moment. John puts the glad news into indirect discourse, so that we cannot be entirely sure that the servants almost exactly repeated the word of Jesus, especially the significant verb ζῇ, "lives." It may well be that they used just that word and in the sense of Jesus: all danger of death is gone.

The father's inquiry in regard to the hour of the change sounded only natural to the servants, but the answer to that inquiry was freighted with the greatest significance to the father. Why B.-D. 328 should call the aorist ἐπύθετο "incorrect" and demand the imperfect instead, is strange, since either could be used, the aorist merely stating the fact that the father so inquired. The expression κομψότερον ἔχειν is idiomatic. The Greek likes the adverb with this verb; we use a different verb with an adjective. "One must be willing for the Greek to have his standpoint," R. 546. We say "better," the Greek prefers the comparative of κόμψος, "handsome." The aorist ἔσχε = "got better," R. 834; "better than before the word of Christ was spoken," R. 665. The servants use neither the endearing term παιδίον, which fits the father's lips, nor the weighty υἱός, which fits the lips of Jesus, but simply παῖς, "thy boy," which fits the general family relation. The father learns that the fever left the boy "yesterday at the seventh hour." Instead of the accusative ὥραν we should expect the dative to designate a point of time, or the genitive to indicate time within; but B.-D. 161 finds this accusative in the classics, and R. 470 tries to explain it: "Either the action was regarded as going over the hour, or the hour was looked at as an adverbial accusative like τὸ λοιπόν," of which, if we need an explanation at all, the latter is decidedly preferable. Note the aorists, ἔσχε in the question, ἀφῆκεν in the answer. We meet the latter in Mark 1:31, in a parallel case, when Jesus healed Simon's wife's mother: ἀφῆκεν ὁ πυρετός, "the fever left her," and so completely that she was instantly entirely recovered and rose from her bed and "ministered unto them." These, then, are not ingressive aorists, so that we should translate, "began to amend" (our versions), and the fever "began to leave." The recovery did not merely start at the seventh hour. If that had been all, the boy might have suffered a relapse, and it would have been foolish to dispatch servants to the father. An anxious wait of hours, of a day or two, would have followed with fear lest the fever set in again. The boy was completely restored, so completely that the servants were at once hurried off to the father. From the word "the fever" we are unable to determine the exact nature of the disease, since some fevers are themselves diseases, while others are only symptoms of diseases.

53) **The father, accordingly, knew that it was at the hour in which Jesus said to him, Thy son lives; and he himself believed and his whole house.** Thus the miracle was revealed, one that was even greater and more astonishing than the man had hoped for. He "himself" believed with a new measure of faith (compare 2:11). His entire household (οἰκία) joined him in that faith. The mention of the entire household may well indicate that in the days to come this family, certainly an important one, being connected as it was with the king's court, took a prominent part among the members of the church. This leads some to think that the official may have been Chuza, but even then we have nothing but surmise.

Here we again meet the perplexing question of the "hours" in John; see 1:39. If the seventh hour is one o'clock (according to Jewish reckoning), the man could easily have reached home that evening, the

distance being less than six hours' travel. If the
servants started not long after one o'clock, he and
they would surely have met at least late that same
afternoon. Yet when they meet they say, "*Yesterday*
at the seventh hour." Invention steps in and in some
way manufactures a delay long enough to extend to
the next day. The man travelled leisurely, his mind
being perfectly at ease; the servants did not start until
the next morning — both suppositions are wholly unnatural, for both would hurry. Even when father
and servants are thought to have met hours after
sundown and thus, since sundown begins a new Jewish
day, on the day after the miracle, we have too much
time with both the father and the servants hurrying
toward each other. A goodly delay has to be worked
in the account also on this supposition if John counts
the hours in the Jewish way. According to the Roman
reckoning the miracle was wrought at seven in the
evening. Then, indeed, father and servants could
meet only on the next day, and all would be clear
without inventing delays. But did John use this
Roman reckoning? Nobody knows. Our quandary
remains.

54) **This again as a second sign Jesus wrought**
after having come from Judea into Galilee. "This"
is the subject, to which is added predicatively, hence
without the article, "as a second sign"; and "again"
modifies the verb, "again he wrought." The whole is
made clear by the participial addition, "after having
come," etc. The first time Jesus came back to Galilee
he turned the water into wine (v. 46); now, having
returned a second time, he again signals his return
by a miracle, a second one to place beside the first.
During the eight or nine months spent in Judea many
other miracles had been wrought, 2:23; 4:45. Because
John does not tell us about other miracles that Jesus
wrought here in Galilee after his second return, the

conclusion is by no means warranted that Jesus remained in retirement for a considerable time. He proceeds with his public work in Galilee as all the synoptists report.

Matthew 8:5-13 and Luke 7:1-10 relate a miracle which in one point, and only in one (healing at a distance), is similar to this one. In all other points, outward as well as inward, a radical difference prevails. Nevertheless, critics identify the two, but thereby they show to what lengths they are ready to go to find their hypotheses in the sacred record.

CHAPTER V

III

The Attestation Arousing Unbelief
Chapters 5 and 6

Five and six are evidently companion chapters.
The former shows how the antagonism against Jesus
arose in Jerusalem among the rulers of the nation
when he manifested and declared himself to be the
Son of God. The latter shows a similar opposition in
Galilee, where the people at first were favorable to
Jesus. Both hostile movements finally resulted in the
complete rejection of Jesus as the Messiah and Son of
God on the part of the Jewish nation.

THE RISE OF OPEN OPPOSITION IN JERUSALEM
CHAPTER 5

1) *The Healing on the Sabbath Day, 5:1-18.* —
**After these things there was a feast of the Jews;
and Jesus went to Jerusalem.** "After these things"
bridges the entire gap between the second return of
Jesus, distinguished by the miracle upon the royal
officer's son, and his return to Jerusalem as now
reported. "These things" include all that Jesus said
and did during this period, of which "things" the
miracle is a sample.

Commentators, from the ancient fathers onward,
are hopelessly divided as to what festival of the Jews
John here refers to. The codices are about equally
divided between the reading "a festival of the Jews"
(without the Greek article) and "the festival of the

(358)

Jews" (with the article), although inner reasons would speak for the former reading. Jesus had left Judea in December (4:35) for the reason stated in 4:1-3. First there came the feast of Purim in March; next the Passover in April; fifty days later the Jewish Pentecost; in October the feast of Tabernacles. Purim we may dismiss in short order, since this festival had no connection with the Temple nor with any service there. The book of Esther was read only in the local synagogues, no work was done, and the time was spent in eating and in drinking, often to excess. Having left Judea as indicated, Jesus would not return there so soon, and surely not for the observance of a festival that compelled nobody to go to Jerusalem. So much is certain: the feast we seek to determine must be sought between the Passover of 2:12, when Jesus cleansed the Temple, and the Passover of 6:4, during which Jesus remained in Galilee. With Purim out of consideration, the choice narrows down to one of the three pilgrim feasts, Passover, Pentecost, or Tabernacles. This means that whichever of these three we choose, we must allow two years between 2:13 and 6:4. In other words, the Passover mentioned in 2:13 is followed by another, and this by the one in 6:4. It is certain that the one mentioned in 6:4 cannot be the next in order after that of 2:13. For the time from April (2:13) to December Jesus spent in Judea; late in December he came to Galilee. Then if the next April is the festival mentioned in 6:4, the feast referred to in 5:1 must be Purim, which with Jesus' return to Galilee leaves only three weeks at best till the Passover of 6:4. But in 6:4 we find Jesus in fullest activity and at the height of his work in Galilee. It is impossible to assume that his work in Galilee reached that height in so short a time, i. e., from the end of December to the beginning of April, with time taken out in March for the pilgrimage to Jerusalem for the observance of Purim. Thus 6:4 simply must be placed one year later; it is the second Passover after 2:13.

With this established, it really makes little difference which feast we assume for 5:1, the first Passover after 2:13, or the following Pentecost seven weeks later, or Tabernacles in October. The chronology remains fixed: one Passover (2:13) at which the Temple was cleansed; two Passovers following, the second of which is that of 6:4; then the next at which Jesus died — three years in all, plus the weeks or the months that precede 2:13 (Jesus' Baptism, first return to Galilee, first appearance in Jerusalem). With the choice for the festival of 5:1 thus reduced, we may eliminate the Passover (the one following the return to Galilee in December). If John had meant this Passover in 5:1, we have every reason to assume that he would have used its name instead of writing merely "a (or: the) feast of the Jews." He writes thus indefinitely because what follows did not occur at the feast, or in the Temple, nor was it connected with the feast. It took place on a Sabbath following the feast, at the pool called Bethesda. Most likely, then, the feast of 5:1 is either Pentecost or Tabernacles. The latter, by all odds, is the preferable choice. Having left Judea because of the evil agitation of the Pharisees (4:1-3) in December, Jesus would hardly return to Jerusalem in three months (April, Passover), or a few weeks later (Pentecost), but would delay till Tabernacles in October. This assumption at least meets most adequately all the data available, and, as we shall see, even the character of the miracle related in 5:2, etc. We note that Jesus then attended only two Passovers at Jerusalem during his ministry, the first and the last; and remained away for the two that intervene. Why he did not attend that of 6:4 John tells us in 7:1.

2) **Now there is in Jerusalem by the sheep gate a pool, which is called in Hebrew Bethesda, having five porches.** "Is" = is still, after the destruction of Jerusalem, when John wrote; it is not the "is" of vivid narrative, since the narration goes on with ordinary tenses. With ἐπὶ τῇ προβατικῇ supply πύλῃ, as is usual with such substantivized adjectives: "by the sheep *gate.*" Besides having other names, this swimming pool had the Hebrew (i. e. Aramaic, R. 104) name "Bethesda," House of Mercy, which was most likely bestowed upon it because of the erection of the five porches for the charitable accomodation of the sick, or because of the mercy of God manifested in the supposed periodic healing. The exact location of this pool the archaeologists must determine, but we refuse to accept as the probable site the excavation seventy-five feet deep near the gate now called St. Stephen's, because it would be impossible for sick people to plunge into it except to drown. The exact location is immaterial for the narrative. John mentions the Aramaic name of the place because in this language the name bears a significant relation to the miracle here wrought by Jesus.

3) **In these was lying a multitude of sick, blind, lame, withered.** The five porches or covered colonnades were like a hospital, filled with a crowd of sufferers, four classes being mentioned, this number often being used for indicating completeness. The first group, the "sick," takes in all that are not included in the other groups. The absence of the articles draws attention to the qualities indicated by the nouns. When so many sufferers are brought together they impress us much more than when we see them singly; we then see more adequately all the wretchedness, the misery, the broken lives that form the result of sin among men.

Verse 4: "for an angel of the Lord went down at certain seasons into the pool and troubled the waters:

whosoever then first after the troubling of the water
stepped in was made whole with whatsover disease
he was holden," is a spurious addition. The final
words in v. 3, "waiting for the moving of the water,"
may, indeed, state what was true, and may rest on
v. 7, but are textually so doubtful that they must
be cancelled. Since the details of these findings really
belong not to commentaries but to works on technical
text criticism, we here pass these details by. Tertullian used this spurious passage for his favorite conception of "the baptismal angel"; somewhat later
Ambrose saw in it a prophecy of the descent of the
Holy Spirit, consecrating the water of baptism to a
mystical washing away of sin; and Chrysostom had
the same conception. The spurious passage reflects
only a popular notion of the time. The fresh water,
bubbling up periodically, may have had some medicinal qualities. These were exaggerated as being curative for all kinds of ailments. Popular superstition
did the rest. Thus shrines and fountains still attract
multitudes of sick people; and since certain nervous
troubles yield to strong suggestion, some sufferers
find relief or cure at places of this kind and in a perfectly natural way. Catholic shrines, Christian
Science, faith healers, etc., operate in this manner. In
John's account Jesus completely disregards the pool,
the cure the sick man hoped to find there and thought
that others found.

5) **And a certain man was there, having been
thirty-eight years in his infirmity.** Longer than an
average term of life this man had suffered; how long
he had been at Bethesda we are not told, though the
implication is that he had been there for some time.
His ailment rendered him helpless and may have been
a form of paralysis, which was possibly due to youth-
ful excesses (v. 14). With adverbs and adverbial
expressions $\check{\epsilon}\chi\omega$ = to be; here, "having been," the

present participle getting its time from the main verb ἦν.

6) **Him, when Jesus saw lying and knew that he had been thus already a long time, he says to him, Dost thou want to become well?** Jesus selects what was probably the worst case then present at Bethesda. The two aorist participles ἰδών and γνούς merely state the facts that Jesus saw this man, just described in v. 5, and that he knew about the long time he had been sick. Here ἔχει is again used with an adverbial modifier as in v. 5. Its present tense "gathers up past and present into one phrase" (Moulton in R. 879), for which we use the perfect, "has been," which after a past tense we change to the past perfect: knew that he "had been." We need assume no miraculous seeing and knowing in this case. This exceptional case would be generally known, perhaps even be paraded before visitors. It is true, the disciples are not mentioned in this entire chapter, and from this silence the conclusion has been drawn that Jesus visited Jerusalem alone at this time. But the latter is altogether unlikely. The disciples are not mentioned because John finds no occasion for referring to them. They may have drawn Jesus' attention to this man, having had their attention drawn to him by others.

The question of Jesus, "Dost thou want to become well?" could not awaken and was not intended by Jesus to awaken faith in the man. Here is a plain instance where the miracle precedes the faith, where the faith even follows some time later. Jesus merely attracts the sick man's attention (Acts 3:3) and makes him think of his sad condition and how desirable it would be to change that for complete health. Note the punctiliar aorist γενέσθαι: "be well," or "become well" at one stroke; not: gradually be getting well.

7) The man's reply is discouraging enough; it is only the whine and complaint of many a man who has been sick a long while. He does not rouse up enough even to answer with a decided, "Yes!" or, "Yes, I do!" All he answers is the hopeless plaint he had often repeated before. **The sick man answered him: Sir, I have no man, when the water is troubled, to put me into the pool; but while I am coming, another goes down before me.** The address Κύριε is most likely due to the dignity in the appearance and the manner of Jesus. "I have no man" voices the disappointed wish of past days, "Oh, if only I had some man to help me!" Did the look of interest on Jesus' face, the tone of power in his voice, perhaps lead him for a second to think that this man would help him finally to reach the water in time, or obtain some other man to do so? In the clause, "whenever the water is troubled," the aorist indicates the brief moment of the disturbance. We may accept this periodic welling-up of the water in a certain part of the pool as being true; but the angel is the invention of the author of v. 4. The man also believed in the curative power of this freshly bubbling water and imagined it would cure him, too, if only he could reach it in time. What virtue the water really had it is not in the interest of John to report. After ἔχω the ἵνα clause takes the place of the infinitive, B.-D. 379; although R. 960, 1011 makes it usurp the function of a relative clause, which, however, would be a different conception, one about the man instead of about the action. "To throw," βάλῃ, is summary, standing on no ceremony, losing not a second because of gentle handling.

Always he gets there too late. While he is still coming, another goes down before him, pre-empts the precious spot where the water churns for a little while, and in the rush to get there with others he is hopelessly left behind. The Greek heightens the effect by the abutting of ἐγώ and ἄλλος.

8) Three mighty words from the lips of Jesus do more than this man's years of effort. **And Jesus says to him, Arise, take up thy bed, and walk.** The punctiliar aorist imperative ἆρον expresses the momentary lifting of the κράββατος or pad on which the man lay; and the durative present imperative the indefinitely extended action of walking. The two tenses are good illustrations of their use. We must regard ἔγειρε as merely being attached to ἆρον, hence no comma or καί is necessary; hence also, like other such attached imperatives, we have the usual present tense without independent tense force, and here it is aoristic because it is attached to ἆρον, R. 855; not, however, ἔγειραι, another reading, see the verb in R. 1215.

9) The effect of the three verbs is instantaneous. **And straightway the man became well and did take up his bed and was walking.** The evidence for cancelling εὐθέως is too meager. But apart from this adverb the verbs and their tenses express an immediate effect. The man was sound and well on the instant, all traces of the ailment of thirty-eight years had vanished and were gone. Strength surged through his body: he did pick up his bed (again aorist) and he was walking away (the durative imperfect). Some interpreters think that faith was necessary for the miraculous healing. Some claim that Jesus saw this faith before he spoke the words; others, that faith instantly followed the words. If not faith in the ordinary sense, then at least the faith of the man in his own ability to do as Jesus said. Thus, we are told: "The man believed that word to be accompanied with power; made proof, and found that it was so." Or, "the command of Jesus brings the courage of faith to his soul, and power into his limbs, to obey the command." On the con-

trary, the man suddenly was sound and well, and this apart from faith in any sense of the word. He no more needed to believe either in Jesus' word to arise, etc., or in his own health and strength, than any hale and hearty man does. He had the soundness, that was all. He had more; for when a man has not walked for a long time he must learn again, and this man needed not to learn. His muscles were firm and responded to his will as if they were perfectly trained and practiced. Why should not the man pick up his bed and walk away?

But did not Jesus go too far when he told the man to carry away his bed? Would it not, in view of the faultfinding it would surely arouse on the part of the Sanhedrists, have been wiser to let the man abandon his bed and go on without it? As regards the second question, it is plainly Jesus' intention to oppose, openly and positively, both the human traditions and the false spirit of the Jewish leaders. One must study their barren, legalistic, and casuistic methods of building up a hedge of human traditions or regulations around the law of God, in order to see how utterly impossible it was for Jesus to avoid clashing with the exponents of these traditions. They found thirty kinds of labor forbidden on the Sabbath and they insisted on these prohibitions, deduced by their own wisdom, in such a way as to lose sight of the law's chief requirements and true spiritual intention. Jesus could have lived in peace with these men only by submitting to their spirit and their methods, and this was an utter impossibility. So he even invites the conflict.

As regards the first question Moses had, indeed, said, Exod. 20:10, "In it thou shalt not do any work"; and Jeremiah 17:19-27 especially forbids burden-bearing. But this latter passage speaks clearly of that desecration of the Sabbath to which the Jews were ever prone, of doing business on the Sabbath and of working at common labor for gain. The prophet meant marketing and trading. Nehemiah (13:15, etc.) had difficulty with "the merchants and sellers of all kinds of ware," treading wine presses on the Sabbath, bringing in sheaves, and lading asses; as also wine, grapes, figs, and all manner of burdens. The men of Tyre brought figs and all manner of ware and sold them on the Sabbath to the children of Judah in Jerusalem. A glance is enough to show the difference between this sort of burden-bearing and that of the healed man carrying his bed. The former dishonored God, the latter glorified God and his mercy. That was done for private gain, not being satisfied with six workdays, this was done for the Master's praise. That was clearly forbidden, this Jesus himself, in perfect harmony with the law of Moses, commanded. For the miracle wrought at Bethesda was not intended only for the man upon whom it was wrought but for as many as should see this man. It was a *sign* to the Jews. As such it was intended, while in no way transgressing God's law, to run counter to the false Jewish traditions and thus to turn men's hearts — if they would be turned at all — to the true authority of Jesus, who, while upholding God's law, brought to view the mercy which both heals the sufferer's body and sets free his soul from spiritual bondage. Such was the significance of the sign set before the eyes of the men in Jerusalem: a man marvelously healed carrying his bed before men's eyes through the streets to his home, on the Sabbath!

10) The clash comes. **Now it was the Sabbath on that day. The Jews, accordingly, were saying to the man who had been healed, It is the Sabbath, and it is not lawful for thee to carry the bed.** Jesus purposely chose the Sabbath for performing this sign. As on his first visit he cleansed the Temple of traffikers, so on this second visit he seeks to cleanse the

people of their false traditions. John records this miracle for the very purpose of showing how the first preliminary clash is now followed by one that is more violent. Here we get the full hostile sense which John puts into the designation "the Jews." These were not ordinary people whom the man met on the streets as he walked along, but, as the sequel shows, men of authority (v. 16), Pharisees, some of them perhaps Sanhedrists. Their chief concern was whether a thing was "lawful," ἔξεστιν, permitted or not, *they* being the sole judges in their casuistic fashion. The verb αἴρω may mean either "to take up" or "to bear," "to carry," according to the connection; see 1:29.

The imperfect ἔλεγον describes how these authorities urged the point upon the man. John calls him, with the perfect participle, "he who has been healed," i. e., is such now. Not one word "were they saying" to the man about his wonderful healing. Significant silence!

11) The healed man knows a different authority. **But he answered them, He that made me well, that one said to me, Take up thy bed and walk.** We must read ἐκεῖνος not only as resumptive but at the same time as strongly emphatic, "that one," or "that man," *he* who did this wonderful deed, ὁ ποιήσας, the aorist to indicate the one deed. This is the man's authority for doing what he does, and this authority not only permitted but commanded the act. We are not informed whether the man put down his bed in deference to the Jews, or not; it seems that he did not do so. Pointedly he describes Jesus as "he that did make me well."

12) But this is lost upon the Jews — and yet not lost; for on his first visit to Jerusalem Jesus had wrought a goodly number of such signs and had impressed many, 3:23. These Jews had no use for such

signs; they deliberately refuse to ask this man about the great deed of healing. **They inquired of him, Who is the man that said to thee, Take up and walk?** Their minds are fixed only on the supposed transgression, on this violation of their all-important traditions. For these Jews Jesus is not the man who healed this great sufferer, who bestowed on him divine mercy, but a man who broke their traditions, who had to be punished. When they here inquire who it is that issued this unlawful command, we must not suppose that they did not from the start know that it was Jesus. They know only too well. They ask in order to secure legal testimony against Jesus. They want the man's direct testimony, in order then to take legal action against Jesus. That, too, is why they quote only the verbs "take up and walk," for these mark the crime in their eyes. The sign was before them, placed there by the master hand of Jesus, but these Jews neither read its meaning nor think of obeying its admonition.

13) **But he that was healed knew not who it was; for Jesus slipped aside, a crowd being in the place.** The very presence of the crowd made Jesus postpone the completion of his work upon the man; he would finish the task at a more opportune time. So he slipped away from the man through the crowd, ἐκινεύω, "to lean sideways," thus "to evade" or slip away; the aorist simply states the past fact, for which the English prefers the pluperfect as bringing out the time relation (see R. 840, etc.). Why such a crowd visited the place on this Sabbath is not explained. But those are evidently wrong who suppose that Jesus did not consider that the day was the Sabbath, and who say that Jesus meant to do a kindly deed in a sort of private way. An ordinary man might not think about the Sabbath in such a way, though a sincere Jew would scarcely do so. Moreover, the crowd was

evidently present because it was the Sabbath, when many visitors were free from occupation and could go to visit sick friends. But the idea that Jesus forgot about the Sabbath would make this decisive miracle of his with its consequences so vital for him a kind of accident — which we simply cannot believe. Then, with this crowd present, how could Jesus tell the man to carry his bed without at once attracting public attention? The man did not go far through that crowd before the Jews, those with some authority, stopped him. No; it was Jesus who deliberately set this sign of his before these people. Not a few must have stood around when the man was catechized.

The aorist ὁ ἰαθείς simply states the past fact that the man was healed, while the perfect in v. 10 adds to the past fact the present implication of his now being one thus healed. There is something noteworthy about Jesus' sending of this weak beginner in the faith against such powerful antagonists as "the Jews," and in his putting these antagonists to silence by the man's very weakness and ignorance. For all the man could reply to the probing of the Jews was that the man who had healed him had given him the order to carry his bed. In other words, all he could do was to reiterate the miracle (the credential and authority of Jesus) and the command that went with it (resting on that credential and authority). Because the man himself was compelled to tell about the miracle and the command he was fortified in his young faith.

14) After these things Jesus finds him in the Temple and said to him, Behold, thou art become well. Sin no more, lest something worse come to thee. This finding may have occurred on the same day or on the following day. On Jesus' part it is intentional, for he now means to complete what he began with the unexpected miracle. It was a good sign that Jesus found the man in the Temple, where the man evidently had gone in order to thank God for the great mercy he had found in the House of Mercy and to render due sacrifice.

The word Jesus addresses to the man is remarkable. First a vivid reminder of the priceless benefit, "Behold, thou art become well!" the perfect tense implying that he stands here as a well man this very moment. This is the lever whose motive power is to lift the man to a higher plane. For Jesus adds, "Sin no more!" and like a flash lays bare the man's distant past (4:18), extending over more than thirty-eight years. He had sinned, sinned in a way which his conscience would at once painfully recall, sinned so as to wreck his life in consequence. The objection that Jesus here has in mind sinfulness in general, because in Luke 13:1-5 he will not let his disciples infer a special guilt from a special calamity, cannot hold, for certain sins do entail painful and dreadful results. And if Jesus here enjoins perfect sinlessness upon the healed man, how could he ever hope to escape the worse thing? No; the man had great sins on his conscience. The bodily suffering these sins had caused him Jesus had removed. Here lay the grace of pardon — by far the best thing in the miracle for the man personally. This Jesus now impresses upon the man's soul. "Sin no more" involves that Jesus pardons the man's past sins; for if the great sins of the past still stand against this man, what would abstinence from future open sins avail?

But, alas, even after thirty-eight years of suffering the root of the old evil remains, which may now shoot up again and spread its poisonous branches. Let every man who has by divine grace conquered some sinful propensity, some special "weakness," some dangerous habit, remember that "Sin no more!" must ever ring in his ears in warning. "Watch and pray,

that ye enter not into temptation: the spirit indeed
is willing, but the flesh is weak," Matt. 26:41. But
now that Jesus has freed this man, the admonition to
sin no more comes with an effectiveness, bestowing
strength and help, such as the man had never experienced before. So it is in every case. Not by our
own unaided strength are we to fight our foe and sin
no more but in the strength which Jesus gives and is
ready to renew and to increase daily.

"Lest something worse come to thee," χεῖρόν τι
(neuter comparative of κακός), by its very indefinite-
ness heightens the warning — something worse than
thirty-eight years of suffering. We need not think
only of the damnation of hell, although this, too, is
meant. "Let no man, however miserable, count that
he has exhausted the power of God's wrath. The
arrows that have pierced him may have been keen;
but there are keener yet, if only he provoke them, in
the quiver from which these were drawn." Trench.
On the one hand Jesus sets the benefit received, on
the other hand the grace of warning, and between
these two the admonition to sin no more. Thus, held
by a double cord, the man will surely be found true in
the end. It is a double healing which we witness, and
the latter is the greater of the two.

15) **The man went away and told the Jews
that it was Jesus that had made him well.** This
action of the man has been misconceived as being a
malicious reporting of Jesus to the authorities. Such
a treacherous person Jesus would neither have healed
nor have treated with pastoral care after the healing. Others seek for the man's motive by supposing
that the man wanted to bring the Jews to faith, or
wanted to challenge the Jews with an authority that
was superior to theirs, or wanted to discharge his duty
to the authorities, or wanted to cover himself against
blame by thrusting it upon Jesus. We must not for-

get that Jesus set this great sign publicly before the
Jewish authorities, and that he purposely did it on
the Sabbath. The man also reports to the Jews, not
that it was Jesus who told him to carry his bed, but
that it was Jesus who made him well. The Greek indirect discourse retains the original tenses of the
direct; the man actually said, "It *is* Jesus who *did
make* me well," which the English indirect discourse
changes, "that it *was* Jesus who *hade made* him well."
Jesus wants his person and his name attached to the
sign which he himself had publicly advertised by the
bed carried on the Sabbath. Through the man Jesus
furnishes the Jews exactly what they want: direct
legal evidence that he is the man back of everything.
The man's motive is only a tool in Jesus' hands; the
motive of Jesus dominates. John reports briefly. Did
the man not tell Jesus how the Jews had stopped and
quizzed him? Perhaps Jesus actually directed the
man now to go and to tell these Jews what they
demand to know.

16) **And on this account the Jews were persecuting Jesus, because he was doing these things
on the Sabbath.** We see that by "the Jews" the
authorities are meant. The imperfect ἐδίωκον, "were
persecuting," means continuously persecuting. The
second imperfect ἐποίει, "he was doing," instead of
the aorist ἐποίησε, "he did," contains the inference
of the Jews; for from the one act of healing and ordering the man to carry his bed on the Sabbath they
rightly conclude that further acts such as this performed on the Sabbath will be regarded by Jesus as
being perfectly in order. Whether Jesus thus performed more deeds of this kind on the following
Sabbaths or not is immaterial. The Jews held Jesus
liable not merely for once breaking the Sabbath by
the one act (which would require the aorist) but for
his general attitude regarding their traditional Sab-

bath observance. This also explains ταῦτα, "these
things," a plural not because of the miracle plus the
order about the bed, but a plural to include all that
Jesus deemed proper to do on the Sabbath in contradiction to the Jewish traditions. The fact that the
persecution involved the determination to make away
with Jesus is seen from μᾶλλον in v. 18. To these fanatical Jews their own hatred, persecution, and murderous intentions were virtues, and the mercy, the
miracles of Jesus, and his showing them as signs
and seals of his divine Sonship, mortal crimes. They
broke the law in the most glaring way by their pseudo-
vindication of the law against him who never broke it
and could not break it. "And sought to slay him" (A.
V.) seems to be an interpolation from v. 18 and should
be cancelled.

17) Part of the persecution venting itself upon
Jesus consisted in charging him with violating the
Sabbath. John is not concerned with the details of
time, place, and other circumstances when these attacks
occurred, but only with Jesus' replies, filled as they
are with the weightiest attestations concerning himself. As short and striking as is the first reply, so
full and elaborate is the second (v. 19, etc.). **But
Jesus answered them, My father works till now.
Also I myself work.** That is all — not another
word. But this brief word is like a shot into the center
of the target, such as Jesus alone is able to deliver. It
absolutely and completely refutes the Jewish authorities. This time Jesus uses no *mashal*, as in 2:19, with
a hidden meaning that requires a key to unlock it,
but a word that is as clear as crystal. He does not
say *"our* Father" and thus place himself on a level
with the Jews or with men generally but pointedly
"my Father" (see 20:17). And the Jews at once
grasp the meaning that Jesus declares God to be his
Father in a sense in which no other man can call God

Father, i. e., that in his person as the Son he is equal
(ἴσον) with the Father. Hence also the emphatic ἐγώ
which parallels ὁ πατήρ μου. Hence also the two identical verbs: "he works — I work." The entire reply
of Jesus centers in this equality of his as the Son with
the Father.

The sense of this reply is so plain that the Jews
could not and did not miss it. Do these Jews mean to
accuse the Father, the very author and giver of the
law, who, as every child knows, keeps on working
(durative present tense) till this very day, stopping
for no Sabbaths? Are they making God a lawbreaker? Well, Jesus says, this is my Father, I am
his Son, we are equal. I work exactly as he does
(again durative present). The point is that it is unthinkable that the Father and the Son or either of
them, the very givers of the law, should ever break the
law. When thus the Jews, as they do, charge Jesus
with breaking the law, something must be radically
wrong with their charge.

18) **On this account, therefore, the Jews were
seeking the more to kill him, because he not only
was breaking the Sabbath but was also calling God
his own Father, making himself equal with God.**
This verse is built exactly like v. 16, "On this
account . . . because," etc. But v. 18 is a strong
advance upon v. 16. The cause is greater, also the
resultant effect. Jesus' word of defense and justification made matters much worse. In v. 16 the Jews
charge only that Jesus was doing certain wrong things
on the Sabbath; now they charge that he is breaking
the Sabbath, ἔλυε, dissolving and annulling it, the imperfect meaning that he is making this his business,
R. 884, not only by what he is doing on the Sabbath
but by his entire claim. And not only is he busy
destroying the Sabbath but on top of that he is calling (ἔλεγε, the same iterative imperfect) God his own

Father, which these Jews define as "making himself equal with God." This definition of what the Jews understood Jesus to mean by pointedly calling God "my Father" removes all doubt on the subject. All who claim that Jesus never called himself the Son of God, equal with the Father, must reject this entire Gospel as a piece of falsification. If Jesus did not mean what the Jews here understood him to say and to mean, Jesus should and could and would have said, "But this is not what I mean." Instead Jesus accepts this as being in reality his meaning. He does this not once but again and again until his final trial and even on his cross. And that is the very reason why John records this altercation with the Jews. It embodies another clear and decisive attestation of Jesus regarding who he really is.

As it is with the cause, so it is with the result. While v. 16 has the more indefinite ἐδίωκον, "they were persecuting him," we now have μᾶλλον ἐζήτουν ἀποκτεῖναι, "they were the more seeking to kill him." What is only implied in v. 16 now comes out boldly; for μᾶλλον = *magis* not *potius*. The Jews are not seeking to kill *rather than* to persecute; but are seeking to kill *even more* than they sought this before. So early the fatal issue was drawn.

In this first summary reply to the Jews Father and Son are simply placed side by side as Father and as Son. Both work, yet neither breaks the Sabbath law by so doing. When Jesus adds in regard to the Father that he works "till now" this is to make plain that the Father's work since the creation is referred to, including all the Sabbaths even to the present day; of course, no such explanatory modifier is needed when Jesus speaks of his own working. In both instances Jesus uses the unmodified verb: the Father "works" — "I work." The statement is unrestricted:

take any and every work of either Father or Son, none break the Sabbath. We have no right to limit the Father's working to his work of grace only and to justify that limitation by pointing to Jesus whose office was this work of grace. Jesus does not say: the Father and I in this work of grace do not transgress the Sabbath. The Sabbath law was, indeed, temporary (Col. 2:16, 17), but we should misunderstand Jesus if we supposed that he already abrogated, at least for himself, the divine regulations of the Sabbath law as God had given them to Israel. He does not mean that the Father and the Son are superior to this old Sabbath law, since both are God, or that he (Jesus) is free to disregard its regulations. The fact is the contrary. As the Messiah Jesus was put under the law and in his entire life and during his entire office fulfilled every jot and tittle of the law, including all the divine Sabbath regulations. Only confusion results when we bring in the Christian Sunday and when we make Jesus live according to this instead of according to the Jewish Sabbath. The entire contention of Jesus was intended to uphold the divine Sabbath law in its full integrity against the Pharisaic traditions with their vain and empty regulations which smothered even the spirit and utterly defeated the very purpose of God's Sabbath law. As the Son of God Jesus could and would not bow to these traditions or to any others the Pharisees had foisted upon the law. These "commandments of men" would make the Son, who worked only in harmony with the Father, being one with him, a slave (δοῦλος) of arrogant, blinded, perverted men. His Sonship, his Messiahship, his entire office by their very nature made Jesus challenge this attempt to make him bow as a slave to these wretched commandments. As the Father repudiated them, so did Jesus, the Father's Son.

*The Attestation Regarding the Person and the
Work of Jesus before the Hostile Jews in Jerusalem,
5:19-47.* — The contention that Jesus appeared at this
feast in Jerusalem only in the capacity of a private
pilgrim cannot be correct, for no private pilgrim
would work such a miracle and order the man upon
whom it was wrought to carry his bed home in the
most public manner on the Sabbath day. This also
disposes of the contention that on this visit Jesus
appeared without his disciples. They are not mentioned in chapter five, because John has no occasion
to mention them. Neither in 2:13 nor in 7:10 are the
disciples mentioned, yet in 2:17 we incidentally learn
that they were present. Neither in chapter seven nor
in chapter eight do the disciples play a part, and hence
again John makes no mention of them. John writes
of the miracle in our chapter as though he were
an eyewitness, and he with the other disciples heard
the words of Jesus' defense with their own ears.

Was the discourse of v. 19-47 uttered in one stretch,
without interruption, or is it pieced together and
made one by John? The more one reads this discourse, the more the impression deepens that it was
spoken as it stands. The thought is closely knit together, and the force of the discourse depends on this
continuity and this close coherence. The brief reply
in v. 17 reads like a thesis, of which v. 19-47 are the
elaboration. This creates the impression that the
discourse followed the thesis, perhaps after only a
very brief interval. Just as in v. 17 time, place, and
other circumstances are omitted as being wholly immaterial, so here in v. 19. All we know and need to
know is that **Jesus, therefore, answered and said
unto them,** the hostile Jews, what now follows. The
two verbs (see 1:48) mark the gravity of what follows, but here the first is the aorist middle instead

of the more frequent aorist passive, the sense being
the same, R. 818.

The thesis of v. 17 contains two points, and the
discourse elaborates these: 1) regarding *the person
and the work* of Jesus, v. 19-29; 2) regarding *the
testimony* he bore concerning himself, v. 30-47.

19) **Amen, amen, I say unto you** (see 3:3) **the
Son can do nothing of himself, except what he sees
the Father doing; for what things that One does,
these also the Son does in like manner.** The double
seal of verity, "Amen, amen," is combined with the
voice of authority, "I say to you." Compare 1:51. It
is absolutely impossible that Jesus should ever break
the law, including that of the Sabbath. It is absolutely
impossible just because he is the Son, from eternity
one with the Father and now the incarnate Son, come
to earth to carry out absolutely nothing but the
Father's will. If the Son, then, be charged by the
Jews with breaking the Sabbath law, the charge
would strike the Father himself. He is, indeed, "the
Son," this Jesus who stands before the Jews in human
flesh. The Jews were perfectly right when in v. 18
they understood that Jesus made himself "equal with
God." This very relation of the Son to the Father
makes it simply impossible (οὐ δύναται) that Jesus
should do (ποιεῖν, now or ever) anything "of himself," ἀφ' ἑαυτοῦ, so that the thing would emanate from
him alone and be done by him alone, separate and
apart from the Father and thus deviating from and
contradictory to the Father's will — even as the Jews
charged that Jesus was breaking God's Sabbath law.
Such a thing is possible for men; even Moses thus
did a thing "of himself" (Num. 20:11, 12) : but in
the case of the Son, since he is the Son, this is absolutely excluded.

Over against this negative Jesus sets the opposite affirmative, "except what he sees (or: shall see) the Father doing," the participle ποιοῦντα after the verb of seeing. The sense is not that the Son merely *can* do this, as though he might still omit his doing. For the γάρ clause at once shuts that thought out, "for what things that One does, these also the Son does in like manner." In ἄν we merely have ἐάν, R. 190, 1018, John alone using the shorter form. The demonstrative ἐκεῖνος is strongly emphatic, "that One," i. e., the Father, R. 708. Moreover, καί is to be construed with ταῦτα, "these also," in the sense of "precisely these," R. 1181; not, "the Son also" (R. V.). Jesus even adds "in like manner": *the things* both do are identical and *the manner* of the doing by both is identical. These tenses are present throughout; they state principles inherent in this relation of the Father and the Son, enduring and without exception. Since these two are Father and Son they also continue in intimate communion: the Son constantly "sees" the Father and what the Father "is doing." This is predicated of the Son, not for the reason that he is inferior to the Father as the Son, but because it was he who assumed the redemptive mission, because it was he who was executing that mission in the incarnate state. As the Son in human flesh thus engaged in his mission his eyes were ever upon his Father, and no man will ever fathom the real inwardness of this seeing on the Son's part. Thus, however, Jesus asserts not only that he as the Son does what the Father does, all that and only that, but also that all he thus does, he does as if the Father himself does it, for it is all and in every way the Father's will and work.

In spite of the perfect simplicity and lucidity of Jesus' words their sense is often darkened or misunderstood. Jesus asserts an impossibility (οὐ δύναται, the negative even being re-enforced in οὐδέν), one

based on the very nature of this Father and this
Son. Yet some interpreters tell us that the Son might
have done something "of himself," but his love and
his obedience held him in check. We, however, believe
what Jesus says. Also, the word of Jesus is misunderstood when it is refered to the divine *concursus* of
providence, the dependence of the man Jesus as a
creature on his Creator and Preserver. Thus, we are
told, the Jews were wrong, Jesus never meant to make
himself "equal with God" and corrects this view in
v. 19 as a serious misunderstanding. The fact that
he twice calls himself "the Son" and twice refers to
"the Father" (once with the emphatic ἐκεῖνος) is
brushed aside. For the perfect union and communion
of the Father and the Son because of their equal divine
nature the creature dependence of Jesus is substituted,
the inferiority of his nature as compared with that of
his Father. Thus, we are told, Jesus only imitates
the Father, copies a superior model, moved only by his
love and obedience. We, however, still believe just
what Jesus says.

20) Jesus draws the curtain aside still farther.
**For the Father has affection for the Son and shows
him all things that he does.** One in essence, Father
and Son are naturally bound together also in affection, and this explains still further what Jesus has
said (γάρ). Here Jesus uses φιλεῖν, the love of affection,
whereas in 3:35 he uses ἀγαπᾶν, the love of full comprehension and purpose. This does not imply that the
former here denies the latter, which it does not do,
but that the former harmonizes better with the relation of the two equal persons and their consequent
affectionate intercourse. In v. 19, "what he may (or
shall) do," might refer only to some things the Father
does; here we learn that the Father shows the Son
"all things that he does," πάντα, without restriction,
which, as a matter of course, includes all that per-

tains to our redemption. The verb "shows" corresponds with the verb "sees" in v. 19. The communication between these divine Persons is perfect and
complete in every way. "Shows" and "sees," because
the Son is incarnate and in his humiliation on his
redemptive mission. In the last clause αὐτός merely
marks the fact that the Father is intended as the subject, otherwise it might be regarded as the Son. Note
the undetermined present tenses: "has affection" —
"does" — "shows," always, ever. The very action of
Jesus in saying these things to the Jews is a reflex
of the Father's will and act.

The general statement is made more specific:
**and greater works than these will he show him, in
order that you may marvel.** We must not miss the
implication regarding the works Jesus has already
done, including the healing on the Sabbath and the
healed man's carrying his bed, that these were done
by Jesus not "of himself" and apart from the Father
but altogether in union with the Father. These were
certainly great works, at which the Jews might well
marvel. But these Jews are to know that for the
Father and the Son, namely Jesus, these great works
are only a beginning. Prophets, too, have wrought
miracles and yet were only men. Jesus is infinitely
greater — he is the Son. Hence in the days to come
(δείξει, future) the Father will show him "greater
works," which shall, indeed, reveal Jesus as the Son.
"Will show" means far more than "let him see," for
Jesus knows and thus already sees these works; he
even enumerates them to the Jews. "Will show" implies that when the time comes, the Father will execute
these works through Jesus, his Son. These greater
works are the raising of the spiritually dead, the final
raising of the bodily dead, and the last judgment.
They are "greater" because they are fuller and loftier
manifestations of the same power that displayed itself

in the incidental miracles. The future tense "will show" must not be pressed as though no spiritual vivification had as yet taken place, for some had already been reborn; the tense refers to the mass of believers yet to follow before the day of resurrection and judgment. On and after the day of Pentecost, before the very eyes of these Jews, literally thousands obtained the new life.

"That you may marvel" is the intention of the Father and of Jesus. Note the emphatic ὑμεῖς, which means: people like *you*, unbelievers. These greater works are marvelous also to the disciples, but in their case the marveling is filled with faith, and in their case this faith is mentioned as the essential thing. This is true already with reference to the miracles, 2:11 for instance, and 20:31. In the case of the Jews and in the case of all unbelievers it will be empty marveling alone. They will not know what to make of these works, they will be astonished and finally overwhelmed by their progress and their power. The final exhibition of this marveling Paul describes when he tells us that at the name of Jesus every knee shall at last bow, Phil. 2:9 and 11.

21) With γάρ Jesus exemplifies and begins to describe the greater works, the μείζονα ἔργα which are parts of the one great ἔργον of Jesus as our Redeemer. They furnish the details for the refutation of the Jewish charges. So mighty is each detail that the accusers should have become terrified because they had called Jesus a lawbreaker and should have fled in consternation. But the doom of unbelief is the wicked and presumptuous blindness which leads men to war against a gracious and an almighty God to the last. **For just as the Father raises the dead and quickens them, thus also the Son quickens whom he wills.** Verses 21-25 describe the raising and the quickening of the spiritually dead. Here Jesus does

not include the raising of the bodily dead, Lazarus and others, and all the dead of the last day; and still less does Jesus here speak only of the bodily resurrection at the last day. The raising of the three dead persons were miracles and thus belong only to the great not to the greater works. The final raising of all the dead at the last day is described in v. 28 in connection with the final judgment.

Note how v. 21 parallels the Father's and the Son's work just as v. 17 had done, save that in v. 21 "just as . . . thus also" formally emphasizes the parallel actions. The equality of the work evidences the equality of the Persons. The raising and the quickening are two sides of *one* work, the one negative, the other positive; for where death is removed, life is assuredly bestowed. It is impossible to regard these as two works: first, bodily raising; secondly, spiritual quickening. For both verbs have the identical object "the dead," which cannot be divided so as once to refer to the bodily dead and then to the spiritually dead. All the present tenses used in this verse have the same meaning; they refer to these acts as being in continuous progress. We cannot refer one or the other of these equal tenses to a peculiar time. In other words, all the spiritual raising and quickening that has ever taken place (from the beginning onward), takes place now, or ever will take place, is equally the work of the Father and the Son; and we may add from the following: because they are wrought by the Father through the Son.

Only the one verb "quickens" is used in the clause with reference to the Son, to avoid a pedantic repetition of the two in the first clause. The addition "whom he wills" does not intend to mark a difference between the Father and the Son, for the Father certainly raises and quickens also only those whom he wills; and the will of Father and of Son is identical. This is the gracious and saving will, revealed in a large number of passages of Scripture, among which 3:16 stands out prominently, look also at 5:24. Neither here nor anywhere in the Scriptures are we told of a secret, mysterious, absolute will, which governs the bestowal of life and salvation. "Whom he will" cannot imply that in some case the Son might will contrary to the Father; their very relation excludes that idea. The clause is added to bring out the supreme greatness of the Son. That, too, is why Jesus here calls himself simply "the Son," for the act here predicated of him is not restricted to the time since his incarnation. Yet all the quickening both by the Father and the Son is possible only because it is made so by the redemptive work of the incarnate Son.

22) This second γάρ exemplifies still further; it parallels the other in v. 21. Here is a second greater work. Yet it naturally goes together with the first; it is the outcome of the other. Since the Son quickens whom he will, how about those unquickened? They, too, are committed to the Son. Both quickening and judging are in his hands. How the latter is involved in the former Jesus explains in 3:17, etc. Jesus could have said, "Just as the Father judges, thus also the Son judges"; even as he could have said, "The Father quickens no one but has given all quickening to the Son." Jesus first simply parallels Father and Son, as if to say: Mark that they are of equal dignity; and then, secondly, he unites Father and Son as if to say: Mark how they work together, the Father through the Son. **For neither does the Father judge anyone but has given all judgment to the Son.** The Greek doubles and strengthens the negative, as in v. 19. The fact that the Father judges no one does not mean that, while the Father quickens, he does not judge, or that the Son alone without the Father and apart from him does the judging. This would

contradict the statement that the Son does nothing of himself, v. 19. The Father's giving the judgment to the Son shows that it is, indeed, the Father's. But he exercises it by giving it to the Son, "all judgment," the preliminary judgments in time and the final judgment at the end of time.

In order to understand the work of judging we must first understand the work of quickening. Both involve the incarnation and the work of redemption by the incarnate Son. In v. 21, where the Father and the Son are only set side by side as both quickening, no reference to the incarnation appears. In v. 22 a veiled reference is added, namely in the verb δέδωκε, "has given." The fact that this giving applies to the human nature of the incarnate Son is fully brought out in v. 27. All the greater works here mentioned by Jesus belong equally to the three equal divine Persons and in that sense are not given or received by one Person. And yet the Son alone became incarnate and performed the redemptive mission. It is thus that the Son takes from the Father the works that go with his mission. Thus the perfect tense δέδωκε reaches back into eternity but rests on the incarnation and the mission of the Son and, of course, carries with it the implication for the present: the one act constantly stands as such. As in 3:17-19, Jesus uses the *vox media,* κρίνειν, likewise κρίσις, which does not intimate whether the verdict is acquittal or condemnation. This the context decides. Because, as in the present case, the spiritually dead are referred to, "to judge" and "the judgment" refer to condemnation. The quickened do not come into this judgment.

23) First, the equality of the Persons, secondly, the equality of the works, and now, thirdly, the equality of the honor and this expressed strongly with a positive and a negative statement. **In order that all**

may honor the Son even as they honor the Father. He that honors not the Son honors not the Father that sent him. Why this is and must ever be the Father's purpose lies on the surface: the Father would deny himself if he had a lesser purpose regarding the Son. His very truth demands that where the Persons and the work are equal, the honor must be likewise. But note that this is the Father's gracious purpose, desiring that men by thus honoring the Son receive that Son's salvation. Hence Jesus does not here say, "that all *must* honor the Son." So little did the Jews misunderstand Jesus in regard to his claim to be equal with God (v. 18), so little does Jesus disavow claiming this equality (v. 19), that here in the clause, "even as they honor the Father," he asserts that equality in the clearest possible manner. Recall Isa. 42:8: "I am the Lord: that is my name: and my glory will I not give to another (a creature), neither my praise to graven images." This honor is constantly due to the Son, hence the durative present τιμῶσι, was due even then as the Son stood before those Jews in the flesh of his human nature.

Now the mighty warning in the negative statement, more forceful because it is without a connective, "He that honors not the Son honors not the Father that sent him." The negative μή with the participle needs no explanation, R. 1137, it is the regular usage. Jesus does not say, "he that *dishonors* the Son," but, "he that *honors not*," which is stronger. What is meant v. 24 shows: refusal to hear and to believe the Son. Merely to disregard or to ignore the Son is fatal. What, then, does it involve, like these Jews, to accuse the Son, to persecute, to seek to kill him? This word applies to all the followers of those Jews down to the present day. They thought that they were honoring God by contending for God's Sabbath law against God's Son and were thereby robbing God of all honor. So men today talk of "God," "the Father," "the Great Architect of the Universe," or whatever other name they use, and set aside the Son and thus rob God of all true honor. Every religious profession and practice, whether by individuals or by organizations, that does not honor the Son, our Redeemer and our Judge, has its sentence of condemnation here recorded. The attributive participle modifier: the Father "that sent him," brings out the vital point with which God is concerned and with which all men ought to be equally concerned: the saving mission and work of the Son incarnate. See 3:17 and note how often in the following utterances of Jesus he refers to "my Sender." Others, too, are sent both by the Father and by the Son but none is like the Son (1:18), very God himself, the actual fountain of salvation, through whom alone we can come to the Father (14:6), in whom alone we see and have the Father (14:9-11).

24) With the same assurance of verity and authority with which Jesus began in v. 19 he now explains what he means by saying that "he quickens whom he wills." For the figure of quickening he now uses literal terms, and the mystery of "whom he wills" is made plain by describing the persons: "he that hears and believes." **Amen, amen, I say to you, He that hears my word and believes him that sent me has life eternal and comes not into judgment but has passed out of the death into the life.** Jesus "quickens whom he wills" means that he gives life eternal to everyone that hears and believes his Word. This Word he utters and sends out, and it comes to men as the bearer of life, Rom. 1:16. The Word itself causes the hearing — men's ears perceive its invitation, offer, gift, and blessing. The more they hear, the more they perceive. As the Word impels men to hear, so it impels them to trust ($\pi\iota\sigma\tau\epsilon\acute{\upsilon}\epsilon\iota\nu$) as

its message is made more and more clear. The very nature of what the Word offers induces trust to appropriate that offer. The normal and natural effect of the hearing is to trust. The Word is not only itself absolutely trustworthy, it is full of efficacious power to implant truth in the heart. That trust, when wrought, is always the product of the Word not of any goodness or ability in the hearer. Yet it never works irresistibly. Man can exert his depraved will in such an abnormal way as to prevent the faith-producing power from accomplishing its purpose. Those who do this are not quickened.

The hearing and the believing go together. They are always correlatives of the Word, i. e., the latter is intended for the very purpose of being heard and believed. And these are personal acts, hence the singular, so personal that Jesus combines person and act: ὁ ἀκούων καὶ πιστεύων, "the one hearing and be-lieving." Jesus does not say: the one believing "my Word," but: believing "him that sent me." This really states the contents of the Word, which is all about the Father sending the Son for our redemption. To trust that Sender is to trust the Word that reveals and brings him to our hearts. Jesus here uses this sum-mary of the Word because of the accusations of the Jews which he is refuting, and by this summary he again points to his relation to the Father, which the Jews refused to admit. The key word is ὁ πέμψας με. To this day Jesus proclaims that the Father sent him; and on this Word, on the Father so having sent the Son, and on the Son so sent by the Father our faith rests.

He that hears and believes "has life eternal" (see 3:15), ζωὴ αἰώνιος, the very life itself that flows from God, is grounded in God, joins to God, leads to God (10:28). The moment one has this life he is quickened, or made alive, or reborn (3:5). Temporal death only leads him into a fuller measure of this life. The present tenses ἔχει and οὐκ ἔρχεται may be considered gnomic or prophetic, R. 897-8, being used regarding constant truths, irrespective of time; as such, however, they include the immediate blessed possession of this true, spiritual, heavenly life that goes on endlessly into eternity. The obverse is that the believer, who has this life, "comes not into judgment" (elucidated in 3:18). Since ζωοποιεῖν and κρίνειν, both committed to the Son Jesus, are opposites, where the one is effected, the other is shut out. As one of God's children, how can the believer be judged now or at any time? No adverse sentence can ever be passed upon him.

This is made more vivid by the statement, "but has passed from the death into the life," the perfect tense meaning that once having gone from the one to the other he remains where he is, I John 3:14. Whereas Jesus speaks of "the dead" in v. 21 he now speaks of "the death," and the article points to the specific death here meant, namely spiritual death that ends in eternal death, the opposite of "the life," again the article and again the specific life here referred to, namely spiritual life that ends in eternal blessedness.

In saying these things Jesus utters the most effective call to faith in the ears of the hostile Jews. In every word the gift of life was knocking at the hearts of his hearers, trying to break the bonds of their death; but they held to death and wilfully rejected the gracious gift of life.

25) Once more and with cumulative effect the voice of verity and authority rings out: **Amen, amen, I say to you, The hour is coming and is now when the dead shall hear the voice of the Son of God; and those that did hear shall live.** In v. 21 everything is compressed into the brief term that the

Son "quickens." In v. 24 this is expanded by adding the fact that life is received by means of "my Word" heard and believed. In v. 25 this is expanded still farther by stating that the hour for this coming to spiritual life "is now" already. That is why the words, "The hour is coming and now is," are emphatically forward; compare for the same expression and in the same sense 4:23. The time referred to is that of the New Testament era ($\omega\rho\alpha$ in the broad sense), which, as Jesus speaks, still "is coming," since the work of redemption is not yet complete and which yet "now is," since Jesus is here and his saving Word at this very moment rings in men's ears. It is thus impossible to refer these words to the last day and to interpret them with reference to the resurrection at that day. The Jews to whom Jesus is speaking need not wait till a later time, the hour to escape from death is now right here.

— Again Jesus describes the quickening. In v. 21 it is the fact that the Son "makes alive," $\zeta\omega\omega\pi\omega\iota\epsilon\hat{\iota}$, he *bestows life* on the dead. In v. 24 it is the fact that the believer *has life*, $\check{\epsilon}\chi\epsilon\iota\ \zeta\omega\grave{\eta}\nu\ \alpha\iota\acute{\omega}\nu\iota\omega\nu$. Now it is the fact that the believers *shall live*, namely on and on to eternity. But now the figure is intensified into a spiritual resurrection. The preparation for this is the reference to "the death" in v. 24; to go "out of the death into the life" means a resurrection and no less. Thus $\omega\grave{\iota}\ \nu\epsilon\kappa\rho\omega\acute{\iota}$ (plural of the category), the spiritually dead, lie lifeless. Then there sounds "the voice of the Son of God," identical with "my Word" in v. 24. Note the correspondence in the terms: "my" (subjective, personal) "Word" (objective); "the voice" (subjective, personal) of the Son of God (objective, because in the third person). In the objective "Word" speaks the personal "voice" as one stands before another and speaks to him. "My" Word, i. e., that of Jesus in his humiliation, whom

the Jews had before their eyes; but this is no less a
person than "the Son of God." Note the weight of the
article τοῦ υἱοῦ, R. 781. A resurrection is to take place,
and this only *the* Son of God, who as *the* Son is equal
with the Father, can effect. In this entire discourse
Jesus again and again calls himself "the Son" and now
he calls himself "the Son of God." The modernistic
claim that he never so called himself is maintained
only by eliminating this and all other testimony of
Jesus and of the Scriptures in general to the identity
of his Person.

Twice Jesus mentions the hearing of his voice in
his Word, using first the middle then the active of
ἀκούειν, however with no difference of meaning in the
forms, R. 356. Jesus means effective hearing, such as
actually reaches the heart. In v. 24 this is expressed
by two participles: "he that hears and believes."
The fact that some close their hearts and refuse the
hearing of faith is omitted, enough having been intimated regarding these in v. 22, 23. The future "shall
hear" refers to the coming hour, although it includes
also all the hearing from the present moment onward
("and now is"). The instant of the hearing is the
instant of the awakening of the sleeping dead. Hearing, they awake; awaking, they hear. "Shall hear"
and "they that did hear" do not denote two kinds of
hearing, the one hearing only outwardly with the ears,
the other inwardly with the heart. Both denote the
identical act of hearing: first, this act as it follows
the Son's voice (future tense), then, this act as it
is followed by their living (aorist participle). The
voice produces the hearing, the hearing produces
the life.

The article in οἱ ἀκούσαντες is vital, "the ones that
did hear," for this changes the subject, which is vital
to the sense of what Jesus here says. "The dead shall
hear" — "they that did hear shall live." This change

of subjects focuses everything on the hearing, even on the first instant of hearing. If the article is omitted, Jesus would say, "The dead shall hear" — "after hearing they (the dead) shall live." This separates the hearing from the living and nobody would know by how long an interval: first the dead would hear, then at some time after the hearing they would live. No; the dead, the very instant they shall hear, in that instant become οἱ ἀκούσαντες, "they that did hear," and from that instant onward "they shall live." Thus the Son "makes them live" (v. 21), and each of them "has life eternal" (v. 24). The verb ζῆν cannot here mean merely *aufleben*, "come to life," but must mean "to live," i. e., ἔχειν τὴν ζωὴν αἰώνιον, v. 24. The figure of death, however, must not be pressed by bringing in omnipotence for the Son's voice, for this would result in an omnipotent and irresistible grace, which is contrary to all Scripture teaching. We must abide by the *tertium comparationis:* the dead cannot bring themselves to life, the Son alone can and does give them life; and this he does by his Word and the voice of gospel grace. The spiritually dead may resist that grace; many do. We know of no omnipotence that man is able to resist.

26) From the work Jesus reverts to the Worker. Everything depends on who he really is. "For" gives the reason why Jesus is able to do this work. This is not the evidential reason; for that would be the accomplished work itself, proving by his having done the work that he could indeed do it. This is the causal reason: Jesus, being what he is, can do what he says. **For as the Father has life in himself, thus also he gave to the Son to have life in himself.** The one fountain of life thus flows in one stream from the Father and the Son. We must remember that this is not a truth uttered in general but a refutation of the charge of the Jews that Jesus made himself equal

with God. The Jews certainly agreed that God the
Father "has life in himself," i. e., not derived from
or dependent on, another. They would equally agree
that God the Son "has life in himself" in the same
way. To explain to these Jews the relation of God
the Father and God the Son in the matter of both alike
having life, each in himself, would thus be utterly
pointless. This already shuts out the interpretation
that ἔδωκε, "he did give," refers to the eternal generation of the Son and a gift involved in that generation. This idea is again shut out by the same aorist
ἔδωκε in v. 28. Both times "he did give" is the historical aorist. Both verbs refer to the incarnate Son,
to a giving for his mission and work. When Jesus
says that this gift was made "to the Son," he once
more uses "the Son" to assert to the Jews that he,
Jesus, is actually "the Son of God." After explaining
at length his work of making the spiritually dead alive
with a life that is eternal, of doing this by "my
Word," the very Word the Jews were now hearing
from his human lips, Jesus now adds the explanatory
reason (γάρ) why this Word thus sounding in the ears
of the Jews does, indeed, bestow life as he says. It is
because of the Father's gift, made when he sent his
own Son on this mission to redeem and to quicken.
"He did give" thus refers to the Son in his human
nature, joined as it was to the divine. The great mission of the Son was carried out through that Son's
human nature. In itself this nature never "has life
in itself"; in Jesus it received this gift from the
Father, the Sender of Jesus. Thus Jesus sets before
the Jews the answer to the question how he,
being man, does, indeed, not only as the Son but
equally as man, not only by one nature but by
both indissolubly united in his Person, bestow life
eternal.

27) And now again Jesus reverts to the other side (as in v. 22), for some reject this life. **And he gave him authority to execute the judgment, because he is man's son.** Those who obdurately remain in spiritual death the Father has not reserved for himself, he has placed them, too, in the hands of Jesus, the incarnate Son (v. 22). The two ἔδωκε go together. The second is only the negative side of the first. It is the same throughout: to believe — not to believe; to honor the Son — to dishonor him; to receive life — to reject life. Thus the Son has life in himself to bestow of himself on all who hear and believe — and authority to judge all who remain in their death.

We must note that the antecedent of αὐτῷ is "the Son" in v. 26; so that we may read, "He did give *to the Son power* to execute the judgment," literally, "*Power* did he give," etc., with the emphasis on "power." The present tense ποιεῖν refers to all judgment throughout time and on the last day; if the latter only were meant, we should have the aorist infinitive. And now Jesus adds what he left unsaid in v. 26 but what applies equally there, the statement that this act of giving on the Father's part refers to the human nature of the Son, "because he (the Son) is man's son." In υἱὸς ἀνθρώπου neither noun has the article. This designation is not equivalent to ὁ υἱὸς τοῦ ἀνθρώπου, "the Son of man," which Jesus constantly used as a title when referring to himself. Compare on this title the remarks on 1:51. The Son was born man (1:14), the son of a human being, ἀνθρώπου (not denoting sex) not ἀνδρός (which denotes a male). True, the Virgin birth is here not specifically predicated, because ἄνθρωπος may refer to either sex; and yet it is predicated, because Jesus speaks this word only with reference to his mother. What he tells the Jews is that only in one way, by a gift from the

Father, could he as man receive the ἐξουσία, the right and the power, to act as the judge. And this only he, the Son, could receive for *his* human nature, joined as it was to the divine in personal union. No other "man's son" could possibly be made the recipient of such a gift as the power to judge. So great is this gift that any mere man would be crushed by it.

Among the untenable interpretations are the following: "man's son" = "the Son of man"; the hidden God cannot judge, hence he had to select a man (a gnostic idea; the Jews always knew God as the judge); judging came as a reward to Jesus for his redemptive work; ἐξουσία = only the *right* not also the *power*.

28) Jesus now states how he will exercise the right to judge. Thus he names and describes another of the greater works. **Stop marvelling at this; for the hour is coming, in which all in their tombs shall hear his voice and shall come out, they that did do the good things unto resurrection of life, but they that did practice the worthless things unto resurrection of judgment.** The present imperative with μή forbids what one is alreay doing, hence we translate, "Stop marvelling!" R. 890, i. e., at what Jesus has just said (τοῦτο refers to v. 24-27). In 3:7 the aorist forbids Nicodemus to begin marvelling. People such as the unbelieving Jews are indeed to marvel; it is God's intention. When Jesus here tells the Jews to stop this marvelling, this, like all that he says to them, is his call to cease their unbelief, to grasp and to believe the truth of what he says. Hence also Jesus states the great reason why these Jews should stop marvelling and begin believing: lest at the judgment they be found among those that practiced the worthless things.

As v. 25, 26 repeat and amplify v. 24 regarding the subject of life, so v. 28, 29 repeat and amplify v. 27 regarding the subject of judgment. Verse 25 and v. 28 are parallels also because both have the statement regarding the time, "the hour is coming." Yet the difference is marked, for in v. 28 Jesus cannot add, "and now is." Spiritual quickening starts now and will spread over the world when redemption is once wrought, but the universal judgment comes at the end of time. Yet "is coming" means that now, with Jesus here and redemption at hand, nothing else intervenes between this present and the final judgment day. The word ὥρα is again used in the broad sense. In what Jesus tells the Jews about this hour he states only what they themselves believed about the resurrection and the judgment (Dan. 12:2, and back to Abraham, Heb. 11:19). The only point he adds is that he connects all this with himself, the Son of God and man's son. That these Jews are most assuredly to know, they who now have the very judge before them and are seeking to destroy him.

Note the important and decisive πάντες, "all," and the attributive phrase, beyond question made such by the article, "all in their tombs," i. e., all the bodily dead. With intentional similarity to v. 25 Jesus says that these too "shall hear his voice," Jesus' voice, that of God's Son and man's son. Now the voice of grace sounds forth in Jesus' Word; spiritually dead hear it and are made spiritually alive. Then the voice of omnipotence will sound in the last trump, and all the bodily dead shall hear it, for that voice comes with resistless power, "and shall come out" of their graves, raised, all of them, from bodily death, their bodies once more being joined to their souls. This statement of Jesus' is the foundation for *one* resurrection, and that occurring at the last day. In Rev. 20:6 "the first resurrection" uses "resurrection" symbolically with reference to "soul" (v. 4). The transfer of these "souls" into heaven is called "the first resurrection." Nothing is said in Rev. 20 about "the second resurrection," but the implication is that the final transfer of the bodies of these blessed "souls" into heaven constitutes "the second resurrection." So little can Rev. 20 refer to *two bodily* resurrections that it does not even refer to one; for Rev. 20 does not imply that bodies come from graves but that bodies are transferred to heavenly glory, as their souls were previously transferred to that glory. In John 5:28 only preconception can split into two parts the one word, "All in their tombs shall hear his voice and come out," i, e., on the instant when that voice sounds.

29) But "all," thus coming out in one moment, shall appear as two classes: "they that did the good things" — "they that did practice the worthless things," the substantivized participles exactly as in 3:20 and 21, save that now they are plurals. On the difference between οἱ ποιήσαντες with reference to the believers and οἱ πράξαντες with reference to the unbelievers see 3:20, 21; also for the distinctive meaning of τὰ φαῦλα, "the worthless things," which are here set overagainst τὰ ἀγαθά, "the good things" in the sense of excellent and thus valuable. The aorist tenses of the participles sum up the entire life of each class. For the one class it is, "they did do the excellent things"; for the other, "they did practice the worthless things." The one class is marked by the good works that spring from faith; the other by the worthless works that spring from unbelief. Each class of works is specific, hence the articles τὰ ἀγαθά and τὰ φαῦλα, i. e., the well-known works that God regards as excellent and prizes as valuable in us; the well-known works that God regards as worthless. Some

of the latter men prize highly, as the Pharisees do
their formal outward observances, as men's work-
righteous, humanitarian, philanthropic works today;
see Matt. 7:22, 23. The connection of the two classes
of works, the one with faith, the other with unbelief,
is furnished by the preceding statements on hearing,
believing, having life, and the opposites of these. We
may add that ποιεῖν, so distinctively used with reference to the believer's works, accords with the idea
of obedience to God, even as we always have this verb
with reference to the obedience of Jesus to his Father's
will; while πράσσειν lacks this connotation in these connections and accompanies actions that are self-chosen,
was einer selber treibt.

The actual judgment is here compressed into two
mighty phrases: "unto resurrection of life" — "unto
resurrection of judgment," keeping the two cardinal
terms in the two genitives. Both classes "come out
unto resurrection," their bodies being made alive by
being joined to their souls. In neither case has εἰς
ἀνάστασιν the article, though our versions add it. Its
absence stresses the quality of the noun: both classes
come out to what is truly and rightly called ἀνάστασις,
"resurrection." How R. 500 can call the two added
genitives objective is a puzzle. No transitive verbal
idea lies in the noun "resurrection"; even if it could
be inserted, neither "life" nor "judgment" could possibly be the object of the transitive action. These
genitives are qualitative; each describes and characterizes. The mark of the one resurrection is "life,"
of the other "judgment." Before they arise, the classes
are already so marked; in their earthly existence the
one obtained life through faith, the other remained
under judgment because of unbelief (3:18). What
Jesus here compresses into phrases he describes at
length in Matt. 25:31-46.

So little can Jesus be charged with breaking God's Sabbath law that he does all his work as God's Son in divine intimacy with his Father. This is the first part of his answer to the Jews.

They also assailed his testimony concerning himself, saying that he lied when he made himself equal with God. Thus the second part of the discourse deals with the testimony concerning Jesus. No less than nine times does Jesus in the first part of his answer repeat his own testimony that he is, indeed, the Son. This testimony is so true that it only re-echoes God's own double testimony, that of the works he gave Jesus to do, and that of the Scripture he gave to the Jews themselves.

Does the second part of the answer begin with v. 30 or with v. 31? It is attractive to think that Jesus closes the first part as he began it by saying, "I can do nothing of myself," compare v. 19. But it is equally attractive to have him begin the second part in the way in which he began the first. What seems to mislead some is the fact that in v. 31 Jesus still speaks of his judgment; hence they conclude that this still belongs to v. 27-29, where Jesus speaks of the final judgment. They overlook the force of the present tense, "I judge," and of the statement, "My judgment is righteous." They likewise overlook the fact that Jesus says, "As I hear," I judge. He speaks of his judgment concerning himself, i. e., of his testimony that he is, indeed, God's Son.

30) **I can do nothing of myself. As I hear, I judge; and my own judgment is right, because I seek not my own will but the will of him that did send me.** The pronoun ἐγώ is emphatic, for which v. 19 has "the Son." Compare the explanation of v. 19. Both the nature of Jesus as the Son and his mission as the incarnate Son absolutely shut out even the possibility that he should ever do (ποιεῖν, durative

present) anything "of myself," apart from and conflicting with the Father. But this fundamental statement is now applied to all the testimony of Jesus,
whereas in v. 19, etc., it was applied to all his deeds
and works. Hence, while in v. 19 Jesus speaks of
seeing what the Father shows him for his great mission in the line of works, he now speaks of *hearing*,
· "As I hear, I judge." The present tenses mean now
or at any time. This, of course, includes also the
final judgment. But the clause, "as I hear," now
speaks of the judging of Jesus, not as a work, but as
a pronouncement, as a verdict of his lips. Not a
single word that Jesus utters in stating a judgment,
whether it be on men, believers or unbelievers, or on
matters or subjects of any kind, or on his own person
and work, ever deviates from, or clashes with, the word
of his Father. On the contrary, it only restates the
Father's word and judgment. And "as I hear" implies
that the Son Jesus is in constant and most intimate
communion with his Father. As little as Jesus could
deny his Sonship, as little as he could repudiate his
mission as the incarnate Son, so little could he utter
one word that might be in disharmony with his
Father's word and verdicts.

Jesus merely coordinates, "and my own judgment
is right," although the relation of thought is that this
being right is the consequence of Jesus' judging as
he hears. Jesus uses the emphatic pronoun: ἡ κρίσις
ἡ ἐμή, "this judgment of mine," whatever may be the
judgment of others, in particular the false judgment
of these Jews. "Right," δικαία = in perfect harmony
with the Father's norm of right (δίκη). The word is
chosen to match κρίσις and κρίνω; in a moment, when
the judgment is defined as testimony, we have the corresponding adjective "true."

Why the judgments of Jesus are always right is
now established ethically: "because I seek not my

402   *The Interpretation of John*

own will but the will of him that did send me." In every word and judgment Jesus utters he has only one purpose: to carry out the great mission on which his Sender sent him. "The will of him that did send me" means, not the faculty of willing, but the content of the Father's will, *what* he wills. Exactly *that* Jesus wills. "My own will," the pronoun being emphatic, would be *something else,* determined by Jesus himself in contravention of what his Sender determined. Such a "will" does not exist. When the Son entered on his mission, all that that mission should include and effect was determined. When the Son became man, his human consciousness and will entered perfectly into all that had thus been determined. Jesus and his Sender were in constant communion: "as I hear." No possibility existed that Jesus should ever will anything of a different nature. "I seek," is a pregnant expression for "I seek successfully," or "I seek and carry out."

31) After the general statement that every judgment of Jesus accords with the will and the word of his Sender, Jesus turns in particular to the word which the Jews claimed to be false (v. 18), making himself equal with God. **If I bear witness regarding myself, my witness is not true.** According to R. 1018 this means, "If perchance I bear witness," and looks at the matter either as a present reality or as a future possibility (we prefer: as something Jesus expects to do). In 8:13 the Jews say the same thing: when a man bears witness regarding himself, his witness is not true. In 8:14 Jesus contradicts this and says that if he bears witness concerning himself, such witness is, indeed, true. The contradiction is only apparent. Legally a man's unsupported testimony regarding himself or his own case cannot stand and be accepted as true. Yet in fact, as 8:14 shows, Jesus' witness concerning himself is true, for he knows

about himself, the Jews do not. The contrasts in
the two passages are different. In 5:31, etc., it is
Jesus, the Baptist, and the Father — their witness
agrees. In 8:13, etc., it is Jesus and the Jews — their
witness clashes. In the one case the appeal is to two
witnesses that are competent and must be accepted.
In the other case the appeal is from the incompetent
witnesses, who do not know, and whose attempt nevertheless to witness must be rejected. So here Jesus
accepts the common rule concerning testimony in a
man's own behalf. He says in substance, "I do not
ask you to take *my* word alone concerning who I
really am."

32) Hence also the sharp contrast: **It is another that bears witness concerning me; and I know
that the witness is true which he witnesses concerning me.** The emphasis is on ἄλλος and on ἀληθής.
Not for one moment does Jesus ask the Jews to accept
his own lone testimony in his own behalf. Then,
indeed, they might appeal to the common legal rule
stated. On the contrary, Jesus has the greatest and
most competent witness imaginable. When he adds,
"and I know that the witness is true," etc., the word
"true" must be taken in the same sense as in v. 31:
"true" legally, so as beyond question to stand as true
in any court of law. What Jesus says is that he is
offering the Jews a witness of whom *he knows* that
he is legally and in every other way competent. What
the Jews will say to this witness and his mighty testimony, whether they, too, will accept it as legally competent Jesus does not here intimate. If they do, well
and good; if they do not, they condemn themselves.
The reading "you know," οἴδατε, instead of "I know,"
οἶδα, is due to the misconception regarding the word
"true," which is so often taken to mean "true in
fact." This sense of the word would make Jesus by
his testimony establish the truth of this "other" wit-

ness to whom he appeals. By that implication Jesus would himself admit that the testimony of this "other" is after all insufficient. In fact, he would thus fall back on his own testimony. This, of course, is not and cannot be Jesus' meaning. To evade it the reading was changed. The explanations of the correct reading "I know," when these are combined with the wrong sense of the word "true" as meaning "true in fact," are labored and unsatisfactory.

33) Jesus speaks of "another" as his all-competent and legally irreproachable witness but does not at once name him or state his testimony. When introducing this "other" he declares that he is not the Baptist, valid and valuable as the Baptist's testimony is. **You yourselves** (emphatic ὑμεῖς) **have sent** (a delegation, this the sense of the verb) **to John, and he has testified to the truth,** openly and without reservation. Jesus' hearers know what that "truth" is, for some of them had helped to send that delegation, and all of them knew what report that delegation brought back, 1:19-23, namely, that the Baptist declared that he was not the Messiah, but that another was, namely, one so great that the Baptist, mighty prophet that he was, was not worthy to untie his sandal latchets. That, indeed, was "the truth." The two perfect tenses "you have sent" and "he has testified" are the dramatic historical kind, presenting a vivid and realistic view of past acts, R. 897, as in effect still standing for the present moment.

34) Jesus might, indeed, appeal to this witness of the Baptist and in a way he does — not in his own personal interest but in the interest of these Jews, whom Jesus would yet, if possible, save. **But I on my part not from a man do I take the testimony; but I say this, in order that you on your part may be saved.** As ὑμεῖς in v. 33, so now both ἐγώ and ὑμεῖς are emphatic; and "I on my part" and "you on

your part" are in contrast. The Jews even dispatched
a delegation to the Baptist to get his testimony. Jesus
can afford to dispense with the Baptist's testimony,
great though it is, because he has "the testimony"
that is far greater than his. Grimm regards λαμβάνω
as here being equal to *capto*, "to snatch at"; Ebeling
as "seek to secure." Jesus, of course, "receives" or
"accepts" the Baptist's testimony. When he here says
that he does not "take" it, the verb means: take in
order to use it against his opponents. In other words,
Jesus, as the defendant facing these Jews as his
accusers, does not call on the Baptist to bring in the
decisive testimony (τὴν μαρτυρίαν, note the article).
Jesus' great witness is God himself.

But why, then, does he mention the Baptist at all?
"But I say this, in order that you on your part may
be saved." Though the Baptist was only "a man,"
though Jesus thus very properly excels the Baptist
by at once taking his greatest witness, namely the
Father, the Baptist's testimony should greatly impress
the Jews, for among them generally the Baptist was
deemed a great prophet who spoke by revelation from
God. Among the hostile hearers of Jesus some might
be found who, remembering what the Baptist said
regarding Jesus, might be aided by his true testimony to believe what he testified and thus to "be
saved" (on the verb see 3:17). Thus as ever when
Jesus deals with his enemies, he holds out salvation
to them.

35) How highly Jesus thought of the Baptist is
made plain in the testimony.Jesus now gives him and
in the way in which he scores the Jews for the treatment they accorded him. **That one was the lamp
burning and shining; and you on your part willed
to exult for an hour in his light.** A λύχνος is a port-
able lamp, which, when lit, burns and *shines*. The
article means that the Baptist was "*the* lamp" intended

by God specifically for that generation. The two participles, added attributively by one article, denote only one action: "burning and thus shining." The entire figure describes the Baptist as showing the Jews the way to salvation in the Messiah who now was come. The Baptist was, indeed, *"the* lamp," not *"the* light," (1:9). Both tenses here used, he "was" and you "willed" or "did will," imply that the Baptist was now imprisoned. If the tragic news of this event had just become known, this reference to what the Baptist was to his generation would come with greater effect upon the authorities Jesus was facing. That burning and shining lamp had now been quenched forever.

So great was the Baptist in his short career, and how wretchedly had the Jews treated him! Again ὑμεῖς is emphatic, "you on your part," in contrast with ἐκεῖνος, "that one" and all that *he* was. Your will went only so far as "to exult" in his light, ἀγαλλιασθῆναι, the passive form in the middle sense (R. 334), i. e., to disport yourselves in his light for the time being πρὸς ὥραν (by position unemphatic), πρός with the accusative indicating extent of time. Instead of repenting and believing you only ran out to see and to hear the Baptist, delighted to have again after so long an interval the spectacle of a prophet in your midst. The aorist "you did will" implies that now it was all over and done with for the Jews. When Herod laid hands on the Baptist, no popular uprising took place, no violent indignation because of this outrage upon a prophet of God was voiced, no concerted effort was made to effect the Baptist's release. The Jews let Herod do with him as he pleased, and now their interest in the Baptist was gone.

36) Jesus now proceeds to present the witness on whose testimony he relies. **But I have the testimony that is greater than John's: for the works which the**

**Father has given me, in order to complete them, the
very works which I do, they testify concerning me
that the Father has sent me.** As in v. 34, the article
τὴν μαρτυρίαν designates the decisive testimony, decisive
legally and in every other way. When Jesus says
"I have" this testimony, he means that he has it to
bring it forward in any court and thus by presenting
it to establish that, when he himself says he is God's
Son, his statement is the truth. The addition of μείζω
without the article is predicative and equal to a
relative clause, R. 789; B.-D. 270, 1: the testimony
"that is greater"; and the unmodified genitive τοῦ
'Ιωάννου is a common case of breviloquence, as R. 1203
states, for: greater "than that of John"; and we
should not say, with B.-D. 185, 1; R. 516, that it is
not clear whether we should understand: greater "than
as John had it," or: greater "than that given by John."
The difference between μείζων and μείζω is only that
in the former contraction of μείζονα the irrational ν
is used, R. 220. This disposes of the contention that
the former is masculine, the latter feminine (with
τὴν μαρτυρίαν) ; and that we should read the former:
"I . . . as one greater than John." This would
also clash with the entire context in which the Father
(not Jesus) is contrasted with the Baptist, and thus
the Father's testimony with that of the Baptist.

This greater testimony is that of Jesus' works,
meaning all his Messianic works, his miracles, his
making spiritually alive, his final judgment. Some
would exclude the latter, because these Jews cannot
now see the work of judgment and because Jesus says
ἃ ποιῶ, "which I am engaged in doing." But the latter
is quite general, and we should not slip in a "now":
"engaged in doing now." For Jesus also says: ἵνα
τελειώσω αὐτά, "in order that I complete them," the aorist
signifying: actually bring them to an end. This
reaches even to the final judgment. Let us recall

2:19, etc. (compare the exposition), where the judgment forms the final and convincing sign for all obdurate unbelievers. These works, Jesus says, the Father "has given to me," and by this perfect tense he refers to the giving in his mission as the Messiah, a giving which stands indefinitely. This is not a constantly repeated giving, as some think, each miracle, as it were, a new gift. The giving was complete from the start, and, once made, stands thus. Compare "he gave" in v. 26 and again in v. 27, especially also the reference in this repeated verb to the human nature of the incarnate Son. How much the gift includes in the line of works the ἵνα clause states, which we may regard as an ordinary purpose clause, or, if we prefer, as a substitute for the infinitive, but then the infinitive of purpose; hence they are practically the same. And ἃ ποιῶ states that Jesus is now in the midst of these works. Here Jesus uses the plural "the works," spreading them out, as it were, in their great number, while in 4:34 (where also the same verb is used) "his work" compresses them into one great unit.

With strong emphasis Jesus says, "the very works that I do testify concerning me," each one and all together now as they are being done and ever after. They stand up as witnesses in any court that may be called and testify. And their united, unvarying testimony is "that the Father has sent me," the perfect tense stating that, once sent thus, Jesus is now on this his mission. By saying that he can do nothing of himself (v. 30), by adding that all his works are the Father's gift to him, the testimony of all these works is presented as the testimony of the Father himself. A silent implication underlies what is thus said of the works and of their testimony, namely that they are such as admittedly no man could do of himself, in fact, no man at all, not even by way of a gift;

for no man is great enough to receive and to administer a gift that is so tremendous. "That the Father has sent me" means: "has sent me on the Messianic mission." The Baptist, too, was sent (1:6), and all the prophets were sent, but the sending of Jesus went far beyond the sending of all these. The sending of all others rested on that of the Son, while the sending of Jesus rested on no other sending.

37) Yet Jesus here mentions this great testimony of the Father's only in a secondary way, for it is still in progress. Moreover, this testimony is mediate: the Father utters it through the works, although, of course, all the works are directly connected with Jesus, since he in his own person does them. Jesus brings to court a testimony that is all complete and one made immediately and most directly by the Father. **And the Father that did send me, he has given testimony concerning me. Neither his voice have you ever heard, nor his form have you seen.** Purposely Jesus reveals this all-decisive testimony only little by little, keeping the attention of the Jews on the alert to the utmost. Here he names the ἄλλος, left unnamed in v. 32 and named indirectly as regards the works in v. 36. Now the name comes with full emphasis: "the Father that did send me, he," or "that one," ἐκεῖνος, the demonstrative making the name prominent. This is the person whom Jesus brings in as his witness. To call him "the Father" is not enough in this connection. For not merely as such is he this witness. But as "the Father that did send me," for as the Son's great Sender this Father appears as Jesus' witness. In other words, all his testimony is occasioned by the act and the fact of thus sending his own Son as the Messiah, deals with his sending, prepares for it, explains it, and thus accredits that sending. By thus designating his great witness Jesus gives an intimation regarding the character of the testi-

mony of this witness, or, we may say, what the sum
and substance of his testimony is. When Jesus calls
the Father to the witness stand, that Father appears
and testifies as the Sender of his Son.

The next feature is expressed by the perfect tense
of the verb, "he has given testimony concerning me."
This is in contrast with the present tense used in
v. 36: the works "give testimony," i. e., now and right
along as they occur and will occur. This other testimony stands complete. It was offered long ago, and,
thus offered, now stands for all time. Not yet does
Jesus say that this complete and enduring testimony
consists of the Father's own Word, although we can
almost guess that this is what Jesus means. Long
ago the Father gave his testimony regarding Jesus
and the sending that followed; long ago, then, this
testimony was known. Why, then, did the Jews know
nothing about it? Why must Jesus now at this late
date tell these Jews about this ancient testimony?

Because they do not even know this great witness!
"Neither his voice have you ever heard," although his
testimony has sounded out all along; "nor his form
have you seen," although in his testimony he has stood
before your very eyes all along. Both "voice" and
"form" are anthropomorphic and, of course, are not
to be understood literally. Both expressions: hearing
the voice and seeing the form, refer to the witness,
whom one both hears and sees when he gives his
testimony. Thus Jesus tells these Jews that they
have never met this witness, they have never been
near enough to him either to hear or to see him. In
other words, they know nothing at all about his testimony, in fact, do not know that he ever thus testified.
"Voice and form," like hear and see, are only companion terms. Both are plainly meant in a spiritual
not in a literal sense, i. e., to hear and to see with

the heart. On this sense of seeing the Father compare 14:9; 12:45.

This disposes of the labored explanation caused especially by the saying that these Jews never saw God's εἶδος or "form." The prophets and the Baptist are usually brought in, who literally heard God's voice and saw him in some visible form in a vision (Isa. 6 for instance). But what these prophets heard and saw they only told the people who themselves, even the most godly among them, never heard and saw in this way. The point of Jesus' words is lost when we are told that the blame does not begin until v. 38; for then the words of Jesus about these Jews never having heard and seen the Father become pointless. Nor is this pointlessness removed by making Jesus mean, "I know you have never been granted a direct voice and vision of God like the prophets." No ordinary Jew and no Christian today expects such a thing. Equally inadequate is the idea that Jesus here alludes to certain apocryphal expressions (Baruch 3:14-37; Ecclesiasticus 24:8-14), and that these indicate that Jesus here has in mind the Jewish institutions for teaching and for guiding the people, as a kind of embodiment of the divine authority and presence, in which they could have heard and seen God. Why take these institutions, and that on apocryphal evidence, when in the entire Old Testament the Father as the Son's Sender stood for ages as the supreme Witness for all the hearts of his people to hear and to see? The perfect tenses "have heard" and "have seen" match the perfect "he has testified," i. e., you have not in the past nor do you now.

38) With plain literalness Jesus continues: **And his Word you have not remaining in you; because whom that one did send, him you do not believe.** We must note that οὔτε . . . οὔτε . . . καί

οὐ, "neither . . . nor . . . and not," go together and form one statement, R. 1179, 1189. Three
negations are thus linked together, for οὔτε is not dis-
junctive but only a negative copulative conjunction,
"and not." While the third negation is thus added to
the previous two, in substance it states what results
from those two: they who have never heard the
Father's voice and have not seen his form naturally
have not his Word abiding in them, τὸν λόγον αὐτοῦ, the
substance of truth which constitutes his Word as distinguished from the sounds by which it is uttered. The
emphasis is on ἐν ὑμῖν μένοντα, which must not be divided,
making only the phrase "in you" emphatic and not
the participle also. Then we should have the phrase
placed after the participle, and even so the two would
go together. This third negation shows in what sense
hearing the Father's voice and seeing his form is
meant, namely, an inward hearing and seeing in the
heart by faith and true understanding. For only thus
by the heart and by faith does the Word remain in
us. If these Jews had heard what the Father's voice
speaks (but they have no ear for his voice), and if
they had seen therein God's presentation of himself
(but they had no eyes for his form), then through such
spiritual seeing and hearing the substance of God's
Word would become an abiding power in their lives.
Meyer.

The ὅτι clause furnishes the undeniable evidential
proof: "because whom that one (the Father) did send,
him (the Son Jesus) you do not believe." The Greek
is highly effective in placing side by side the three
emphatic words: ἐκεῖνος — τούτῳ — ὑμεῖς: *he* (no less a
person than the Father) sent him; *him* (no less a
person than the Son he sent) ; *you* (just think what
wretches you are!) do not believe. Can they who
reject the ambassador when he arrives and presents
his credentials (Jesus and his works) claim to honor

the announcements which tell them of that ambassador's arrival? The dative with πιστεύω means to believe the person, i. e., that what he says is true; this is said because in v. 18 the Jews refuse to accept as true the word of Jesus that God is his Father.

39) So the testimony of this supreme Witness is the Father's Word, i. e., the Old Testament Scriptures, in which God long ago and all along stood as a Witness and uttered his testimony regarding the Son whom he would send and did then send in Jesus. Though he stood there as concretely as possible and spoke as clearly as possible, these Jews never saw or heard him, and his Word and its meaning (ὁ λόγος αὐτοῦ) never entered and found lodgment in their hearts. What these Jews had hitherto failed to attain Jesus bids them attain now at last. **Search the Scriptures, for you think in them you have life eternal; and these are they that testify of me; and you are not willing to come to me that you may have life.** All the old exegetes with the single exception of Cyril read ἐρευνᾶτε as the imperative, likewise a host of others. More recently a number regard this form as the indicative: "You are searching" (also the R. V.). The question is purely one of context, since no other evidence is available. When R. 329 concludes: "probably indicative," he does so on grammatical grounds.

The imperative fits the entire situation, the indicative requires modifications, which we have no right to make. The situation is that Jesus introduces the Father together with the Scriptures as his all-decisive witness (v. 37). Really, this great Witness is a stranger to the Jews, and thus, of course, they have never known his testimony (v. 38) although it was given long ago (v. 37). Jesus tells the Jews: Here is my Witness — examine him! This testimony he gave long ago — "search it!" He could not say to

these Jews: You are already searching it. If Jesus
should want to say that, he would have to add, "You
are, indeed, searching it, but in the wrong way." And
then he would have to indicate what is wrong and
what the right way is. He does nothing of the kind.
Yet this the pleaders for the indicative have Jesus
say: "You Jews are searching only outwardly, only
the bare letter of the Old Testament, only in your
sterile rabbinical fashion." Not one word of this is
found in what Jesus says. And, of course, also not one
word of what Jesus then certainly ought to add, namely how these Jews should correct their false way of
searching.

Again, take the situation. After Jesus introduces
his great Witness with his decisive testimony, telling
the Jews to search it, he adds the reason in full why
they themselves should want to proceed to do so. We
must note, however, that this reason extends through
the three following clauses: ὅτι . . . καί . . . καί
(v. 40), which, therefore, must not be divided, or
joined only in loose fashion. Some find the reason only
in the ὅτι clause, a few advance upon this and add the
first καί clause, but the second καί clause (v. 40) is read
as a statement by itself.

The first part of the reason why these Jews should
certainly want to examine the Scriptures again is
the statement of Jesus, "because *you think* (ὑμεῖς,
emphatic) you have in them eternal life." With "you
think" Jesus plainly tells them they are mistaken.
He, indeed, does not add, "*I* think otherwise," merely
pitting his thought against theirs, which would make
no impression on these Jews. He does what is bound
to carry more weight with them. He adds a second
part of his reason. Over against the emphatic ὑμεῖς
he sets the equally emphatic ἐκεῖναι (R. 707), "*you*
think" — but just search the Scriptures, "*these*," the
very ones in which you think you have life eternal,

they are "*the* ones that testify (αἱ μαρτυροῦσαι) concerning me." And περὶ ἐμοῦ means far more than that the Scriptures only say this or that about Jesus; "concerning me" means that all their testimony centers in Jesus, centers in him so that only *by and through him* men are declared to have life eternal. Thus Jesus adds the second point to his reason why the Jews should certainly want to examine the Scriptures. And this demands that Jesus state also the third point, which is already involved in the other two.

40) For when these Jews are so sure that they have life eternal in the Scriptures, they think that they have it *without Jesus*. Therefore Jesus says, "and you have no will to come *to me* (emphatic by position) in order to have life." You think that life can be had without me. And again, when Jesus tells these Jews what they have never realized before that the Scriptures testify *of him*, i. e., of life only through him, he adds for this too, "and you have no will to come *to me* in order to have life." The threefold reason which Jesus gives these Jews as to why they most certainly should want to search the Scriptures really forms a syllogism, one that refutes the false and shallow conclusion of these Jews. They conclude: We have life because we own and accept the Scriptures. Jesus answers: You merely think you have. Major premise: To have life you must, indeed, have the Scriptures, but that means *me*, of whom they testify, *me* the fountain of life in the Scriptures. Minor premise: You do not come to *me* for life, in fact, you do not even know that the Scriptures thus testify of *me*. Ergo: You have not life; you only think so; you are sadly mistaken. This forceful reason and reasoning must stir even these Jews. They are challenged with the very Scriptures in which they proudly trust. They must meet this challenge; to refuse is to let the contention of Jesus stand. And

there is only one way to meet it: just what Jesus says: "Search the Scriptures!" The surer these Jews are that they are right and that Jesus is wrong, the more eager they will be to do just that, "search the Scriptures." Thus, only when ἐρευνᾶτε is the imperative does it fit the situation; an indicative would not meet the situation adequately. It is the same situation over again that occurs in the case of Isaiah and his opponents, Isa. 8:20.

Formally these Jews were right when they thought that life eternal is to be had in the Scriptures; and this Jesus not only admits but himself asserts with his command to search the Scriptures. Concretely, however, these Jews were wrong, for they failed to find the one fountain of life in the Scriptures, the Father's Son, whom he sent as the Messiah to bring them life. What made them wrong was not that they merely clung to the Book as a book, or merely studied it outwardly, its shell or letter, or merely went at this study with rabbinical refinement. Paul presents the matter more clearly in Rom. 10:3 and elsewhere. The Jews found the law in the Scriptures, the law alone. When they were so sure of having life eternal "in them," they based their assurance only on this law and on their diligence in its observance. They even added to this law a lot of regulations of their own, intended to support this law, among them the Sabbath rules which Jesus spurned, thereby bringing on the present conflict. They trusted in their works. They established a righteousness of their own. It was thus that they remained blind to the gospel, the very heart of the Scriptures, "ignorant of God's righteousness," the very righteousness revealed in the gospel (Rom. 1:17), the righteousness of faith in God's Son and their Savior. Hence also the one cure for the Jews was the one Jesus here applies: "Search the Scriptures!" — "they are they that testify of me."

41) The call, "Search the Scriptures!" still dominates what Jesus now adds, first on the real moral or spiritual reason for the unbelief of these Jews (v. 41-44), and secondly on the fearful consequences of this unbelief (v. 45-47). When men truly search the Scriptures to find what they say concerning his Son and their Savior, they begin to assume the right attitude toward God, the opposite of which these Jews now manifest, v. 42-44; then, too, they will escape the consequences of unbelief, into which they are now bound to run, v. 45-47.

Jesus has said: these Jews would not believe in *him* (v. 38), the Scriptures testify of *him*, the Jews will not come to *him*. Jesus reads their hearts and sees how they may think that he is motivated just as they are, that he is piqued because they do not honor and glorify him. This he cuts off at once. **Glory from men I do not take,** compare 8:50. The object is placed forward for emphasis: "glory," honor, praise, distinction "from men," in distinction from "the glory that comes from the only God" (v. 44). Even when men offered it to him (6:15) he spurned it and did not catch at it, λαμβάνω in the sense of *capto,* R. 110. Jesus took only the glory which God gave him, God directly, and God through the faith of believing men. Let not these Jews imagine that Jesus is miffed because *they* do not honor him, that this is why he is scoring them so severely.

42) The unworthy motive is not in Jesus but in the Jews, the very motive back of their rejection of Jesus, back of their misjudging Jesus, back of their misreading of the Scriptures, back also of the consequences which therefore shall come upon them. This *their* motive makes Jesus charge them as he does.

On the contrary (ἀλλά after a negative statement), **I have known you, that the love of God is not in yourselves.** Let these Jews not screen themselves behind Jesus when something is radically wrong with themselves. The perfect tense involves the present: "have known" all along and so know now. Compare on this knowing 2:24, 25. Why R. 499 and 500 wavers regarding the genitive τὴν ἀγάπην τοῦ Θεοῦ is strange. This is without question the objective genitive, the Jews' love for God, not the subjective, God's love for the Jews. This is shown by οὐ ζητεῖτε in v. 44, they cared nothing for God's opinion of them but only for the opinion of men. Behind the negative, not loving God, lies the positive, loving men instead. To be sure, they may profess love to God with their lips, even think they honor God by rejecting Jesus, but ἐν ἑαυτοῖς, in their hearts, a far different motive prevails. No wonder God's testimony counted so little with them. It is so to this day. All lovers of God accept his testimony, by it quickly recognize and accept his Son Jesus, care nothing for and are influenced in no way by the opinions of men who spurn Jesus. When men do otherwise and claim to love God nevertheless, their claim is refuted by the evidence of their act of rejecting Jesus.

43) To this undeniable evidence Jesus points the Jews. **I have come in the name of my Father, and you do not receive me; if another shall come in his own name, him you will receive.** That is how much they really love God. Note the strong contrasts, each strengthening the other: I — another; have come — shall come; in the name of my Father — in his own name; you do not receive me — him you will receive. In Matt. 23:36, etc., Jesus shows this utter lack of love on the part of the Jews from the treatment they bestowed upon all the prophets, crowning this with their treatment of his Son; here he speaks only of

the latter. To come "in the name of my Father" does not mean: by his authority or as his representative. See on τὸ ὄνομα in 1:12. "The name" here means the revelation of the Father, in other words, the testimony of the Scripture. By this Jesus is recognized as indeed coming from the Father, and by this those Jews should and could have recognized him. Having no love for God, his "name" or revelation made no impression on them, and when Jesus came, with his coming all in connection with that revelation, "the name," counted for nothing with them: "and you receive me not" (1:11). The very people to whom "the name" was given, that by it they might know him who was to come in that name, refused that name and did not receive him who came in that name. The tenses correspond: "I have come," perfect, and now am here; and: "you do not receive," present. "Not to receive," a litotes, = to reject. While the negatiye is milder than the positive, it really is stronger. The mere omission already constitutes the crime. As in 1:12 "to receive" = to accept in faith; hence "not to receive" = to reject in unbelief.

Jesus, so perfectly accredited by "the name," the Scriptures, their testimony, and this by the Father himself, these Jews do not receive. When "another" shall come, any other, for ἐὰν ἔλθῃ is general, "in his own name," in connection with a revelation concocted and made up by himself, hence accredited by himself alone and not like Jesus by God — though it seems astounding and incredible when looked at sensibly: "him you will receive." And yet it is not so astounding after all. Such an impostor is of the type and the character of these Jews, out for glory from men, caring not for glory from God.

The words of Jesus are a prophecy concerning all the false Messiahs and other false religious leaders that would come in the future. To generalize and to refer to any man who is out only for his own interest is to loose the contrast between ἐγώ and ἄλλος, between the acts of coming, and between the two ὀνόματι. While the statement is not that broad, neither is it so narrow as to refer only to *one* person, say to the anti-Christ (older exegetes), or to Simon Barkochba, whom Rabbi Akiba termed "the star of Jacob" (Num. 24:17), and who was acclaimed by the leaders of the Jews in the years 132-135, many giving up their lives for him. This would require the direct statement: ἄλλος ἐλεύσομαι, "another shall come," not the conditional: "if another shall come." Bengel notes that up to his time sixty-four such messiahs had come, including, of course, the notable Barkochba. Since then more religious deceivers have been added, and the end is not yet. II Thes. 2:11, 12. It is truly astonishing how one coming in his own name (not long ago even a woman!), seeking in the boldest, rankest way his own glory, advantage, power, money, by making people his dupes and victims, is received by thousands with open arms. They who count the Son of God too small to give their hearts to him, the name, Word, and revelation of God too unreliable to trust their souls to him of whom God thus testifies, yield their hearts, their happiness, their property, their all, to any fool who condescends to impose upon their credulity and to use them as his tools. The generation of the Jews never dies out.

44) This calls forth the dramatic indignant question: **How can you come to believe, since you receive glory from each other and the real glory from the only God you seek not?** Jesus combines non-belief in himself and belief in any deceiver. Both rest on this seeking for glory not from God but from men. "How is it possible with such people as you (ὑμεῖς) to come to faith (πιστεῦσαι, ingressive aorist, R. 857)? It is altogether out of the question." But the impos-

sibility is due not to God but to themselves. The participle is not equal to a relative clause, "who receive" (our versions), which would require articulation; it is causal, R. 1128, "since you receive." Jesus might also have continued with a second participle, "and since you seek not," etc. Instead he uses the stronger indicative, "and you seek not." Note also δόξαν without the article and then τὴν δόξαν with the article; the former "any glory" in the line of poor, passing honor from men, the other, "the real glory," the specific praise and commendation of God which he bestows when he calls a man his own child and heir. The former these Jews actually "receive," the latter they do not even "seek," to say nothing of "receiving" it.

The emptiness of the one over against the value of the other is brought out still more by the two opposite παρά phrases. The one is glory only "from each other," who are all on the same poor and wretched level, none of whom can give more than any other. The other is glory "from the only God," or as some texts read, "from the Only One." (Entirely wrong, "from God alone"). He, infinitely exalted above men, bestows glory indeed, here that specific glory which lifts us up as his own. In τοῦ μόνου we have an allusion to Deut. 6:4, etc., "Hear, O Israel, the Lord our God is *one* Lord." Jesus had this in mind already in v. 42, where he speaks of "the love of God"; for Deut. 6:5 continues, "And thou shalt love the Lord thy God with all thine heart," etc. These words each devout Jew prayed twice daily in the prayer called *Shema*.

Jesus scores the vanity of the Jews, by which they boasted to each other of being Jews, instead of letting God bestow on them the true glory of Israel in his Son Jesus. Jew still boasts to Jew of their mutual prerogatives and is pleased when Gentiles praise Jews and Judaism. This self-exaltation proved their abasement, Luke 18:14. A special sting lies in the designation "the *only* God," which is not in contrast with the Jews as being many but a designation for monotheism as against polytheism. The special boast of the Jews to each other was that they adhered to monotheism, and is used by them now in opposition to the Christian doctrine of the Trinity, although the Jews in the Old Testament and in the time of Jesus knew "the only God" as Triune: compare 1:32. Examples of the general Jewish greediness for honor are found in Matt. 23:5-7; John 12:43. Paul describes a real Jew as one "whose praise is not of men but of God." Rom. 2:29. So our skeptic scientists, our "critic" theologians, our gaudily bedizened lodge brothers, and others like them, still shower honors, titles, laudations, offices, and emoluments upon each other, boosting their own pride in themselves and in each other while "the real glory from the only God" they do not even seek.

Luther writes: "It is an exceedingly proud and glorious honor, when a man can boast of God, that he is God's servant, child, people, over against which all the honor of the world is as altogether nothing. But the world regards not such honor, seeks honor from men. The false apostles teach what pleases men, and this in order to have peace and the favor and applause of the mob. And, indeed, they get what they seek; for such fellows get the prize and have the thanks of everyone, Matt. 6:2 and 5. . . . If you want honor, give all honor to God alone, and for yourself keep nothing but shame. Despise yourself and let all your doing be nothing and thus you will sanctify God's name and give honor to God alone. See, as soon as you do this, you are already full of honor, which is greater than the honor of all kings and abides forever; for God adorns you and honors you with his name, so that you are called God's servant,

God's child, God's people, and the like. What now could God do more for you, who gives you so much temporal and eternal good and in addition the highest, even his own name, and the eternal honor? It seems to me, this is, indeed, worthy of our thanking him from the heart and praising him. Who is able for one of these things constantly to praise and thank God sufficiently?''

45) Now Jesus presents to these Jews the consequences of their rejecting the Father's testimony in his Word. **Think not that I will accuse you to the Father; there is he that accuses you, Moses, on whom you have set your hope.** We must not forget that Jesus faces the Jews with the consequences of their unbelief in a final effort to shatter that unbelief and turn it into faith. These last three verses are full of terrific force; either this will crush the hearts in contrition or be met with desperate obduracy, blindly set on its own destruction. We feel the force of Jesus' words when we understand how the Jews clung to their Moses, boasted in him, gloried in him, felt themselves absolutely safe in him — not, of course, the real Moses but the figure they had made of him in their own minds. With one sweep Jesus not only takes their Moses away but hurls the real Moses against them, as the one who already condemns them. The mastery with which Jesus does this must ever captivate our hearts.

"Do not think" implies that the Jews had been thinking this very thing, R. 853. We need not press the future "that I shall accuse you to the Father" as referring to the future judgment and urge that then Jesus will appear only as the judge; for this tense is in correlation with the substantivized present participle "there is he that accuses you, Moses," etc. What Jesus tells these Jews is that he does not need to accuse them, that Moses already attends to that. Why should

Jesus accuse those who are already under the strongest kind of an accusation? Moreover, the contrast is between ἐγώ and this accuser ὁ κατηγορῶν ὑμῶν (objective genitive: "he that accuses you"), whom Jesus not only names but also characterizes, "on whom you have set your hope." Any accusation Jesus might bring forward these Jews would treat lightly, thinking him only a man who makes great unwarranted claims for himself (v. 18). But Moses is their own great and acknowledged authority. More than that, they "have set their hope on him," that Moses will acknowledge them as his disciples and as faithful adherents and defenders of his law, and that thus through the mediation of Moses God will undoubtedly pronounce a favorable verdict upon them in the judgment. On the perfect ἠλπίκατε see R. 895. Proudly they say in John 9:28, 29: "We are Moses' disciples; we know that God spoke unto Moses: as for this fellow (Jesus), we know not whence he is." But by thus setting their hope on Moses and on his law they made of both something that neither was, much as the teachers of work-righteousness and of salvation by morality do today, who do not, like the Jews, stop with Moses but reduce even Jesus to the same level. When Jesus now says that this their Moses, on whom all their hopes rest, is their accuser, to whose accusation Jesus needs to add not a thing, he delivers a blow to their proud self-assurance which strikes home. They may recoil in outraged feeling, but they are bound to feel the shock. Placed first, ἔστιν has the regular accent and means "there exists."

46) **For if you believed Moses you would believe me; for concerning me he did write.** This statement cannot intend to prove at this late point why Moses accuses the Jews. The reason has already been furnished in v. 41-44, which also is full and complete. With γάρ Jesus elucidates why any accusation

of his would be superfluous when Moses already attends to this. If these Jews would treat Moses right, so that he would have no accusations against them, they would treat aright also Jesus, of whom Moses wrote, and thus, of course, he, too, would have no accusations against them. Jesus uses "believe Moses" and "believe me," two datives: accept Moses' and my words as true. The condition is one of present unreality and in regular form: εἰ with the imperfect followed by the imperfect with ἄν. This implies that the Jews are not believing what Moses said and thus are also not believing what Jesus says. The former is enough and more than sufficient for accusation; so Jesus leaves that work to Moses.

But Moses and Jesus are not merely paralleled, nor is the Jewish unbelief against Jesus treated merely as a case similar to the Jewish unbelief against Moses. The two cases of unbelief are made one by the second explanatory γάρ: "for concerning me he did write." What Moses wrote and what Jesus has been testifying concerning himself is identical. Thus to believe the one is to believe the other; to disbelieve the one is to disbelieve the other. Moses with his writing came first, Jesus now follows. Since the unbelief is one, whether of Moses or of Jesus, the one accusation, that of Moses, covers the case.

"He wrote" — *Moses!* Let the critics who repudiate the Mosaic authorship of the Pentateuch face this authoritative declaration of Jesus. It is worth more than all the so-called "research" that has ever been put forth and it stands overagainst these critics as Moses overagainst these Jews, as ὁ κατηγορῶν ὑμῶν, as "he that accuses them." Nor did Moses write of Jesus only in a few detached places, as some suppose. Bengel: *Nusquam non — nowhere* did Moses *not* write of Jesus. Nor did Moses *also* write of Jesus; for the whole center and substance of what he wrote is Jesus. The entire twenty-five centuries with which he deals he views in relation to the Messiah. Ever and always faith in the Coming One decides the fate of man. Great things he touches slightly, and little things, dry genealogies, small occurrences in the lives of the patriarchs, he describes at length, because these have a bearing on the Messiah. From the story of creation onward, through all the following history, ceremony, prophecy, and promise, he is ever in the mind of Moses. Moses in person and in office is even himself a type of the Mediator to come. All this the Jews of Jesus' day did not believe, nor do the Jews believe it today. And this Jewish unbelief has been adopted by thousands of others who with the Jews count it the very height of Bible knowledge.

On "if you believed Moses." Stier writes: "The Jews believed not Moses in his account of the creation and in his testimony on the fall of man; for if they had accepted this as truth, they as sinful men would have had to seek with all earnestness the living God, as did Enoch and Noah. They did not believe him in the account concerning the fathers and their faith, else they would have followed in the footsteps of Abraham. They did not believe in the sacred earnestness of the law he delivered, judging the hearts, else their Pharisaic work-righteousness would have fallen to the ground. Finally, they did not believe him when his entire order of priests and sacrifices constantly renewed the memory of their sins and pointed in shadowy outline to a future real fulfillment, else they would have become through Moses already what the Baptist finally tried to make them, a people ready and prepared for the Lord, embracing his salvation with joy like Simeon."

47) The condition of unreality is now expressed in a condition of reality. **But if his writings you do not believe, how shall you believe my words?** The

structure of the statement is chiastic and thus places the two objects into the emphatic positions. Not only does Jesus say, "Moses wrote"; he now adds, "Moses' writings," placing a double seal of authorship and truth on the Pentateuch. The contrast is between "his" and "my," not between "writings" and "words." Of course, the Jews had only the *writings* of Moses whereas they had the *words*, ῥήματα, the living audible speech of Jesus. Though we now have the utterances of Jesus in writing, the relation between Moses and Jesus is still the same. In conditions of reality the Koine uses εἰ with οὐ as the negative.

With a sad question, the implied answer to which is negative, Jesus breaks off and says no more. His task was done. Deep into the callous conscience of these Jews he had pressed the sting of the law. They pretended mighty zeal for the law, raging against Jesus for breaking the Sabbath law. But what Moses really wrote, what God through Moses really testified they did not believe. So Jesus leaves them with this gripping question. John is right in adding no remarks of his own at the end of this discourse. Its testimony is most effective just as it stands.

CHAPTER VI

The Preliminary Events, 6:1-21. — As chapter 5 relates the rise of opposition in Jerusalem, so chapter 6 relates the rise of opposition in Galilee. Hence only the pertinent events and discourses are selected, and these are presented only with such details as serve to bring clearly to view the attestation of Jesus and to show how it caused such opposition. **After these things Jesus went away beyond the Sea of Galilee, the Tiberian.** With the simple phrase μετὰ ταῦτα (compare 5:1) John passes over the months between the festival at which Jesus healed the impotent man (5:1, etc.) and the Passover now approaching, the third Passover during Jesus' ministry. When John says that Jesus "went away beyond the Sea," the implication is that for some time Jesus had been working in Galilee, whence he had come from Jerusalem, and that now for the events to be narrated Jesus crossed the Sea of Galilee to its northeastern side. John adds "the Tiberian" for the sake of the general reader, to make sure that he thinks of the right sea, not of the Mediterranean.

2) Without telling us in so many words, John presents Jesus at the height of his Galilean ministry. **And there was following him a great multitude, because they were beholding the signs he was doing upon those that were sick.** The three imperfect tenses picture Jesus in the full exercise of his activity at this period, including, of course, the present crossing of the Sea. The statement that the crowds were attracted by "beholding the signs he was doing"

is intended to parallel 2:23 and to show that in general the situation here in Galilee was a duplication of the previous one which occurred in Jerusalem. Not the teaching but merely the signs were the great attraction. This John wants us to bear in mind for the sake of what follows.

3) **And Jesus went up into the mountain and was sitting there with his disciples.** Jesus crossed the Sea in order to find a respite from the crowds that followed him, for the news had just come to him that the Baptist had been killed (Matt. 14:13), and because Jesus also had other business with his disciples (Mark 6:31, etc.). The view that Jesus failed to find this respite because the crowds followed him, is refuted by the imperfect ἐκάθητο, "was sitting," and it is also evident that the crowds, who had had to walk along the shoreline, arrived at the place to which Jesus had crossed by boat some hours later. Without telling us, John assumes that we know that "the disciples" are now twelve in number.

4) The connective δέ (note that it is not γάρ) is parenthetical. **Now the Passover, the feast of the Jews, was near.** The article "*the* feast" is not stressed, for in 7:2 another feast is also so designated. The apposition is intended for the general reader who is not particularly versed in Jewish matters. Of course, the mention of the Passover marks the date of this narrative, which also must be John's intention. But it does more. It does not, however, explain the flocking of the multitude to Jesus. This has already been most adequately explained in v. 2, and this applies not only to this one day but to this period in general. Moreover, the pilgrim caravans going to the Passover would not follow a route around the Sea to its northeast side, but routes leading southward. Nor is this mention of the Passover to give a setting for the final discourse on the Bread of Life. The two events

are too far apart. In the entire discourse not even a slight reference is made to the Passover. The idea that Jesus would dispense the Bread of Life as a better substitute for the Jewish Paschal feast, a better feast also as typifying the Lord's Supper, is not only without support in Jesus' own discourse but contrary to Jesus' own action when a year later he celebrated his last Passover with the disciples in Jerusalem. Not until after that event was the Jewish Passover abrogated, because not until then was it completely fulfilled. We must not carry thoughts, attractive to ourselves, into the Scripture and then persuade ourselves that we have found them there. The reference to the Passover at this point in John's narrative is intended to explain the action of the multitude when after the miracle of the loaves they conceived the plan of forcing Jesus to go with them to Jerusalem, there to be made a king. Perhaps we may add that the approach of the Passover and the news of the Baptist's death foreshadowed to Jesus his own approaching death at the Passover a year hence.

5) John assumes that his readers know the fuller narrative found in Matt. 14:13-21 and in Mark 6:35, etc., together with the briefer account in Luke 9:12, etc. Thus John briefly sketches the situation and adds from the conversation with the disciples what serves his purpose in showing their helplessness to meet the problem that was facing them. After the parenthetical remark οὖν merely resumes the narrative. **Accordingly, having lifted up his eyes and having seen that a great multitude was coming to him, he says to Philip. Whence shall we buy bread, in order that these may eat?** John is not worried in the least whether his account of what preceded and led up to the miracle will harmonize with the accounts of the other evangelists, for he knows that it does

harmonize with them. John alone tells the incident about Philip, and this he does to amplify the other accounts on two points. If we had only these other accounts we might conclude that the disciples took the initiative when toward evening they asked Jesus to dismiss the multitude; from John's account we learn that Jesus thought about the needs of the multitude when the crowd first appeared, and that already then he asked Philip whence bread might be obtained for them. We thus see that the request of the disciples to send the multitude away was made after the situation had become acute, namely toward evening, when everybody was hungry. The disciples saw only one thing to be done, namely that Jesus send the multitude away at once. They act as though Jesus had forgotten to think of their needs and, therefore, also add that it is high time to act if all these people are to reach the neighboring villages and are there to buy bread. The answer of Jesus, that the people need not depart (Matt. 14:16), that the disciples should give them to eat, shows that Jesus all along had in mind that he and his disciples should feed these people. That is why he had taught and healed all this time, unworried about the eating. He had not forgotten by any means but had purposely waited until this time, when at last something had to be done. And he had purposely waited until the disciples could keep still no longer, until they felt that they must take the initiative. But now that they do so, none of them musters faith enough to think that perhaps Jesus himself intended to feed these people and that for this reason he had taught and healed until so late an hour.

The other point is the explanation of Mark 6:37, where the disciples ask, "Shall we go and buy two hundred pennyworth of bread," etc.? Why did they think of this sum and of asking this question? John tells us: because when Jesus first saw the crowds as they were coming (ἔρχεται), he had first raised the question of getting bread for so many, asking Philip, "Whence shall we buy bread," etc.? Philip had told the others about this question and about the answer he gave. The other evangelists omit this detail in their accounts, John adds it. The subjunctive ἀγοράσωμεν (always in the first person) is used in a question of deliberation when one asks himself or himself and others what to do. The aorist indicates the single act of buying.

6) **Now this he was saying as testing him; for he himself knew what he was about to do.** As δέ shows, this remark is parenthetical. We should not wonder why Philip was selected for this testing (πειράζω, "to try out," thus also in an evil sense "to tempt") and then try to find a reason in the disposition and the character of Philip. Jesus selects Philip merely as being one of the entire number of the Twelve. If the others stood by and listened or if presently Philip told them about the question and of his answer, the test was intended for all of them. The fact that they passed this test no better than Philip we see from Mark 6:37, where they ask whether they shall go and buy bread, putting Philip's answer to Jesus into the form of a question. None of them rose higher than Philip's low level.

Now Jesus asked Philip when the multitude was first gathering. Philip and the Twelve thus had hours of time in which to think over what Jesus might have intended with his question. Yet towards evening, as we learn from Mark, they still think that Jesus had actually contemplated only buying bread for all these people. Note, too, how by this question Jesus raised the problem of food from the very start and bade the disciples solve it. When then he proceeded entirely unconcerned, as though the problem did not exist, until evening was approaching and everybody, the Twelve included, grew real hungry, the disciples could have guessed that Jesus, who saw the problem long before the disciples did, must have had in mind an adequate solution. Yet none of them thought of the wine furnished in Cana, nor of the "hour" for which Jesus there waited. The fact that Jesus knew all along (ἤδει, used as an imperfect) what he was about to do, John reports as something that he discovered later. Only afterward he saw why Jesus spoke to Philip so early and yet continued until evening, until the Twelve could stand it no longer and felt that they must tell Jesus what to do. The imperfect ἔμελλε is due to indirect discourse, R. 1043, 1029; and the present infinitive following it indicates the course of action in Jesus' mind.

7) Philip answered him, Two hundred pennyworth of bread is not sufficient for them, for each to take a little something. Philip thinks only of buying and answers only regarding that. He mentions the lowest possible amount, one that would give only "a little something" to each person, not by any means enough to satisfy the appetite. Contrast with this v. 12, "they were filled," and v. 11, "as much as they would." To provide only "a little something" would cost two hundred δηνάρια (at 17 cents this would amount to $34), a sum far beyond the balance in the joint treasury of Jesus and the disciples. The genitive is one of price. Jesus, of course, wants to bring out the hopelessness of buying food for all these people. Philip stops at the prohibitive price; he might have added that no place to buy such a quantity of food was at hand. One impossibility is enough. The idea that the realization of this impossibility should turn Philip's thoughts into an entirely different direction, and that by means of his question Jesus tried to turn them thus, never occurred to Philip.

8) Evening is coming on, no food is in sight, the case is reaching the acute stage. The disciples tell Jesus to send the multitude away. Jesus replies that they need not depart (Matt. 14:16). He tells the disciples to give them to eat. Even this does not awaken in their minds an inkling of what Jesus has in mind. All they know is to ask whether Jesus at this late hour wants them to go and to scour the country to buy the least amount for these many mouths (Mark 6:37). To this Jesus replies by telling them to go and to see how many loaves they have. They do this, and a report is quickly made (Mark 6:38). Here John adds more detail. **One of his disciples, Andrew, Simon Peter's brother, says to him, There is a lad here who has five barley loaves and two fishes; but what are these for so many?** Whereas the other evangelists mention only the disciples, John says that their spokesman was Andrew, whom we met in 1:45, whose relation to his brother Simon Peter is again noted. This was perhaps done because Andrew was one of the first two who became disciples of Jesus. The deduction that Andrew was a practical man and that thus he made this investigation, falls by the board, for Jesus told the disciples to go and to see how much bread was there.

John also adds Andrew's hopeless expression, which has often been repeated since, "What are these for so many?" As was the case with the first question to Philip, so also with regard to this order to the disciples, these men think only that Jesus has in mind by means of purchase or by means of gathering up the supplies still available, to feed this vast crowd. So both times Jesus is told that his suggestions are hopeless. The παιδάριον or "lad" seems to have been a boy who tried to make a little money by selling to the crowd such supplies as he could carry. Barley bread was much used by the poorer classes. In the present instance ὀψάρια, the diminutive plural of ὄψον or "cooked food," are fish, since this was a great fish country, and prepared fish was eaten with the thin, flat cakes of bread. The singular ἄρτος means "bread," bread as such or a sheet of bread, which nobody thought of cutting since it was so easily broken for the purpose of eating. The Greek has the plural ἄρτοι, "breads," which the English lacks, so that we substitute "loaves," but should think of flat, round sheets. On ταῦτα τί as also being classical see R. 736.

10) According to Matthew, Jesus orders the bread and the fishes to be brought to him, which means that they are to be bought from the lad. Did the disciples think that Jesus intended to secure this food for himself, so that he and a least some of his disciples should not go hungry? At the same time **Jesus said, Make the people sit down. Now there was much grass in the place. Accordingly, the men sat down as to number about five thousand.** Note the peremptory aorist in the command and the aorist which states that the command was carried out. What did the Twelve now think — all these people sitting down as if to dine, and only this bit of food in sight? In the command οἱ ἄνθρωποι includes the women and the children in the count, οἱ ἄνδρες counts only the men, compare Matt. 14:21, "besides women and children." Mark 6:40 lets us see how the count was made: "they sat down in ranks, by hundreds, and by fifties." Matthew, too, mentions the grass, but John states that the place was covered with grass, both writing as eyewitnesses in distinction from Mark and Luke who were not present. All are seated in orderly fashion with lanes between the groups to enable proper serving. The impressiveness of the miracle is thus also brought out, for over five thousand at one meal is quite a host;

τὸν ἀριθμόν is the adverbial accusative, R. 486, and ὡς, "about," states that absolute exactness was not intended.

11) The miracle itself is described in the simplest manner by mentioning only the actions of Jesus. In points such as this the control of inspiration is tangible, for an ordinary writer would certainly elaborate on this great climax of the account. **Accordingly, Jesus took the loaves and, having given thanks, distributed to those sitting down; likewise of the fishes, as much as they would.** Not even a single exclamation! Not one word beyond the bare facts that John saw and heard! We are not even told that a miracle was taking place; not even that the food kept multiplying as it was being handed out, or how many each sheet of bread and each fish served. Our familiarity with this account should not blind us to all these features.

"Jesus took the loaves" probably as they were together with the fishes in the lad's basket. Then he "gave thanks" or said grace by using a customary table prayer or perhaps a new form for this occasion. If the prayer was unusual, one of the evangelists would have intimated this fact; none does so. Matthew adds κλάσας, "having broken," which John covers by διά in the verb, "he distributed"; the bread was about an inch and a half in thickness, baked thus for the purpose of breaking. The other evangelists state that the pieces were taken by the disciples, probably in baskets, collected from people who had carried something in them. Thus loaded down, the disciples functioned as the waiters on this grand occasion. Jesus gave and gave and gave, and as he gave, there was always more to give. He did not stint, as Philip and the others thought to do by purchasing only two hundred pennyworth of bread, omitting anything to go with the bread. The fact that Jesus did not stint is mentioned in connection with the fishes; each person could have as much as he wanted, to go with his bread. The imperfect ἤθελον is used because of the repetition.

12) **And when they were filled, he says to his disciples, Collect the superfluous broken pieces, in order that nothing may be lost.** Only incidentally, as it were, in a subordinate temporal clause, the great fact (aorist) comes out that all these people "were filled," each having eaten all he could eat. But now, after all this prodigality, Jesus becomes exceedingly saving. A comparatively few had taken more than they could actually eat. Jesus will not have these left-over pieces wasted and thrown away — certainly a lesson for us. Yet here is more. The great sign has been wrought, its significance is plain to all who will read. It does *not* mean that Jesus will thus keep on feeding the people with exhaustless supplies of earthly food; he has come on no such mission. We should misunderstand this sign, if we thought that Jesus merely stepped in to meet an unexpected, great bodily need. Verse 6 eliminates that thought. Jesus purposely let the need develop until toward evening it became acute, because from the beginning he intended to work this sign. He could easily have obviated the need. Any man could foresee that presently all these people would be hungry and, using his common sense, could have sent them away betimes to places where they might find food. But Jesus deliberately detains them, "for he himself knew what he would do."

13) **Accordingly, they made the collection and filled twelve baskets with broken pieces from the five barley loaves which were left over to those having eaten.** A κόφινος is a small basket used by travelers for provisions, etc. More was left over than Jesus began with, as John intimates by mentioning side by

side "twelve baskets" and "the five barley loaves."
Each of the Twelve came with a basketful. It seems
that Jesus did not forget that his disciples, too, must
be hungry. How about himself? Why not one more
basketful, one for him? May we say that Jesus
expected the Twelve to share their abundance with
him? He still pours his abundance out to us and
expects us to remember him in the poor and needy and
in the support of the church.

14) John amplifies the account of the synoptists,
Matt. 14:22, etc.; Mark 6:45, etc., but in accord with
his purpose. They report only that Jesus sent his disciples away to sail back across the Sea, while he dismissed the multitude and retired into the mountain to
pray. John reveals the cause for this action in accord
with his purpose to show how also in Galilee the opposition to Jesus now developed. **The people, therefore, having seen the signs which he did, were saying, This one is truly the prophet that is coming into
the world.** The reading varies between the plural
"signs" and the singular "sign"; in any case the last
sign just narrated is the decisive one, which precipitated what follows; σημεῖον is explained in 2:11. In
the relative clause ἃ ἐποίησε σημεῖα the antecedent is
drawn into the relative clause, R. 718. The imperfect tense, "they were saying," describes how this
word circulated and was repeated and at the same
time intimates that something follows in consequence.
"The prophet" these people have in mind is the one
promised by Moses in Deut. 18:15, whom some conceived as the great forerunner of the Messiah
(1:21), and others as the Messiah himself. Note
the Messianic designation in ὁ ἐρχόμενος, "he that is
coming."

15) **Jesus, therefore, having realized that they
were about to come and kidnap him in order to
make him king, withdrew again into the mountain**

himself alone. The acclaim of the multitude was about to eventuate in action. We need not spend time explaining γνούς, for the purpose of the multitude was obvious, and the powers of perception on Jesus' part were beyond question (2:24, 25). Their plan was "to come and kidnap" or "snatch him away," whether he would consent or not, "in order to make him king," βασιλέα, predicate accusative with αὐτόν. They would carry him to Jerusalem at the coming Passover (v. 4) in a grand, royal procession, gathering increasing adherents on the way, sweeping the capital off its feet in universal enthusiasm. This scheme Jesus frustrates by withdrawing again into the mountain from which he "went forth" in the first place (Matt. 14:14) to meet the multitude. But this time he slips away "alone," thus it will be harder to find him in the approaching darkness.

16) John writes for readers who have Matt. 14:22-34 and Mark 6:45-51 before them, who thus know to what he refers (v. 17) and are able to combine the new features he offers with the accounts they already know so well. **Now when evening came, his disciples went down to the Sea.** They lingered until evening (ὀψία, supply ὥρα), not the so-called first evening, from 3 to 6, but the second, from 6 until dark, for we hear that darkness soon set in. "They went down" means from the place where the 5,000 had been fed, where Jesus left them with strict orders ("constrained," Matt. 14:22) as to what to do, namely to sail for Capernaum without him a little before dusk.

17) **And having embarked in a boat, they were proceeding beyond the Sea to Capernaum. And darkness had already come, and Jesus had not yet come to them.** The boat was the one in which they had come (v. 1), the only one on that shore (v. 22). The descriptive imperfect ἤρχοντο pictures the disciples

sailing away, withholding for the moment the information as to how their voyage turned out. "Beyond the Sea" states their general and "to Capernaum" their specific destination. We catch the intention of their Master in this way to remove them from the foolish multitude and its plans to make him an earthly king. In a little while he would show them and also let the multitude infer what kind of a king he really was. In the meanwhile we see the little vessel in its progress toward the setting sun. All is calm and beautiful. The experienced sailors in the boat anticipate no difficulty in reaching their destination not long after dark.

When, after thus picturing the disciples as proceeding on their journey, John remarks that darkness "had already come" and furthermore that "Jesus had not yet come to them," he refers in advance to what his readers know from the accounts of Matthew and of Mark. The two pluperfect tenses are well explained by R. 904: "The verb in the sentence before is ἤρχοντο (descriptive), and the verb following is διηγείρετο (inchoative, the sea was beginning to rise). The time of these imperfects is, of course, past. But the two intervening past perfects indicate stages in the going (ἤρχοντο) before they reached the shore. Both ἤδη and οὔπω help to accent the interval between the first darkness and the final appearance of Jesus which is soon expressed by the vivid historical present θεωροῦσιν (v. 19). Here we have a past behind a past beyond a doubt from the standpoint of the writer, and that is the very reason why John used the past perfects here." R. is right when he adds that these tenses "form a very interesting study," that John often uses them to take us "behind the scenes."

The gathering storm very likely hastened the darkness. John writes from a very vivid recollection. The puzzling of the commentators about the statement that

"Jesus had not yet come to the disciples" is solved, likewise their proposed solutions, such as that the disciples had some kind of an expectation that Jesus would come to them either before they sailed or while they were sailing, or that Jesus had made them such a promise. Nor can the supposed puzzle be solved by charging John with contradicting the synoptists. With "not yet" John merely refers to the coming of Jesus which his readers know from Matthew and from Mark; as Robertson puts it, John's reference is "beyond a doubt from the standpoint of the writer." The disciples were sailing on Jesus' orders. What he intended to do he had kept to himself. Darkness and storm were upon them — and they were alone. John and his readers know that Jesus came to them, but John says: here they were in this position — Jesus had not yet come.

18) **And the sea, a great wind blowing, was beginning to rise.** On τέ see R. 1179. The inchoative imperfect means that the sea was rising more and more. The genitive absolute, "a great wind blowing," states the reason. Matthew writes that the boat was distressed by the waves, the wind being against them. Mark says the disciples were distressed with the rowing. At the start they had used their sail, since the boat was large enough to hold so many passengers and was fitted with a sail. But the contrary wind, as well as its violence, with the darkness complicating the situation, soon made them resort to their oars, thus trying to keep the boat head on against the raging waves — a distressing task, indeed.

19) **Having rowed, therefore, about twenty-five or thirty stadia, they behold Jesus walking on the sea and drawing nigh unto the boat; and they were affrighted.** The other evangelists mention the time when Jesus came to the boat, about the fourth watch of the night, i. e., toward morning, between 3 and 6,

showing that the disciples had fought against the storm all night long. John adds to this information the short distance they had covered by all this work of rowing against the storm, 3⅛ to 3¾ miles, a stadium being ⅛ of a Roman or English mile. As to their location with reference to Capernaum or to any part of the shore we have no intimation, and it is safe to assume that, rowing as they did in the dark and in the open lake, the disciples themselves did not know. Only one thing is certain, they were still far from their destination.

John reports the miracle itself only in a summary way, "they behold Jesus walking on the sea and drawing nigh to the boat." The only touches are the dramatic present tense "they behold" and the descriptive participles "walking and drawing nigh." John writes "Jesus," but at first they could have seen only the indistinct figure on the water moving toward them. Mark adds this point, together with the superstitious thought of the disciples that they were seeing a "phantasm" or ghost. The darkness, the hour of night, the storm and the danger still in full force, the exhausting battle with the oars, all combined to make the disciples give way to the superstitions still lurking in their minds. What would some who now smile at superstition have felt and said if they had held an oar in that boat? Mark adds that Jesus was about to walk past the boat; John reports only his drawing nigh. Jesus was giving the disciples time to recover from their fright, also time to ask him to enter the boat. When trying to imagine Jesus walking on the sea, we must not overlook the storm and the raging waves. These howled and dashed about him, but they did not affect him in the least. He was not tossed up and down; his clothes and his body were not wet with spray. Before him as he moved his feet a smooth, apparently solid path lay, on which he

walked as on ordinary ground. He did not move as
a specter is supposed to move; no unearthly light
played around him, as painters often imagine. It was
simply Jesus as they had left him the evening before — only now he was walking on the storm-tossed
sea. One might inquire whether he had walked all
the way from the shore to the boat or had suddenly
transported himself to the spot where the disciples
first saw him. Curious questions, for which no sign of
an answer exists, should not be raised. The aorist
"they were affrighted" states the mere fact, and the
verb includes all of the Twelve.

20) **But he says to them, It is I — stop being
afraid!** This was done to calm the disciples' superstitious fear. "It is I" = and no specter. "It is I" =
your Lord and Master whom you know so well. The
other evangelists report that Jesus' first word was,
"Be of good cheer!" assuring them that all their
troubles were ended. And Mark 6:52 adds that despite
the wonderful feeding of the 5,000 the disciples failed
to understand with their hardened hearts. These
obdurate hearts Jesus now tries again to penetrate
with faith. The present imperative often forbids what
one is already doing; so here μὴ φοβεῖσθε = "stop being
afraid!" John makes no reference to the incident regarding Peter but tells us about the landing.

21) **They were willing, therefore, to take him
into the boat; and immediately the boat was at the
land to which they were going.** Overagainst the
dreadful fear that they were seeing a ghost, a portent
presaging that they were all doomed to destruction,
John sets the durative imperfect ἤθελον, "they were
willing" to take him into the boat, which describes
the new feeling and desire: instead of paralyzing
fright, this desire and this willingness. If John had
written the aorist, he would have expressed the will
only as a single act; he chose the imperfect in order

to describe a new state of will. True enough, this imperfect does not itself indicate that the will to take Jesus into the boat was carried into effect. That, however, lies in the following aorist ἐγένετο, "immediately the boat *was* at the land." For no reader for a moment would think that Jesus was left out on the sea while the boat with only the disciples in it was at that instant at the land. Besides, John counts on his readers knowing what the other evangelists had recorded long ago, how Jesus did enter the boat and also lifted Peter into it. Thus all the worry about the tense of ἤθελον is brushed away. John neither "differs from" the other evangelists nor "contradicts" them. On the other hand, we need not insist on making the imperfect tense of this verb exceptional, as including the execution of the wish. Least of all will we resort to the supposition that Jesus walked past the boat after calling to the disciples, then suddenly disappeared, and finally came to the disciples after they had landed.

John now mentions something that the other narrators omit. They report only that Jesus entered the boat, and that the storm then instantly ceased, due, of course, to the will and the power of Jesus. John adds the detail that "immediately" the boat "was at the land to which they were going." In other words, the exhausted disciples were not compelled to begin their rowing again in order to cover the considerable distance to the shore. We now see why John notes the distance covered during the stormy night voyage, some 25 to 30 stadia. He means to say that the boat was still far from shore when Jesus came to it. That distance melted away the moment Jesus stepped into the boat.

By "the land to which they were going" the reader will understand Capernaum, even as v. 17 indicates. This is made certain by the following references, that "on the morrow" the multitude crossed by boats to Capernaum and there found Jesus teaching in the synagogue (v. 59). Besides this the situation requires that the discourse on the Bread of Life be spoken immediately on the day after the feeding of the 5,000, for it is addressed to those who were thus fed and who certainly would not have remained together for a couple of days waiting in Capernaum for Jesus, but, coming as they did "from all the cities" (Mark 6:33), would have scattered again to their homes in those cities. John's account is too compact and too closely knit for us to insert at this point Matt. 14:34-36, and Mark 6:53-56, letting Jesus and the disciples land on the plain of Gennesaret on the morning after the storm, spending one or more days among the people of this region, and then finally going to Capernaum. The two aorist participles in Matthew and in Mark, "having crossed over," are quite general and do not compel us, like the close reference in John, to connect the visit to the region of Gennesaret with the journey by boat through the stormy night. This visit must be set at a later time. The assumption that 6:59 occurred on the Sabbath, because Jesus was teaching in a synagogue at Capernaum, coupled with the observation that the multitude would hardly have taken so long a journey by boat on the Sabbath in trying to find Jesus, overlooks the action of Jesus and of his disciples. For if the day after the feeding of the 5,000 was a Sabbath, that Sabbath began the very evening when Jesus himself ordered the disciples to sail the identical distance to Capernaum and would include the night of the storm during which the disciples labored to exhaustion. Assemblies, however, were held in the synagogues not only on Saturday but also on Monday and on Thursday. We are not compelled to think of a Sabbath every time we find Jesus in a synagogue. The statement in 6:4 that the

Passover was near is too indefinite to justify a dating
of the day of the miracle. It is useless to figure the
day of the Passover of this year as being Monday,
April 18, in the year 29; and then to set the date of
the miracle on the day before, and thus to fix the date
of the discourse in the synagogue on the Monday of
this Passover.

John narrates the two miracles, that of the feeding of the 5,000 and that of Jesus' walking on the sea
not merely in order to inform us that these great
miracles occurred but for a much higher purpose.
They constitute the divine prelude and preparation for
the attestation of Jesus in the discourses on himself
as the Bread of Life. By placing these miracles into
this vital connection John gives us far more than the
other evangelists, who say nothing of the teaching on
the Bread of Life and content themselves with the
miracles as such. In John's Gospel they are introduced as aids given in advance to faith in order that
all concerned might believe that Jesus is the Bread
of Life and thus might have what is far greater than
earthly help.

*The Decisive Discourse on the Bread of Life, 6:22-
59.* — Its three parts are not coordinated in the ordinary fashion, but the second advances beyond the first,
and the third beyond the second. The structure is like
that of an inverted pyramid: 1) Jesus gives to him
that believes the Bread of Life; 2) Jesus gives to him
that believes himself as the Bread of Life; 3) Jesus
gives to him that believes his flesh as the Bread of
Life.

Jesus Gives the Bread of Life, 22-40

22) **On the morrow the multitude which was
standing beyond the Sea saw that no other boat
was there except one and that Jesus did not enter
with his disciples into the boat, but his disciples**

alone went away. Instead of combining the thoughts
of v. 22-24 in one balanced period in the Hellenistic
style of writing, John strings them together in the
Hebraistic fashion, which results in less smoothness.
The perfect participle ἑστηκώς is always used as a
present: the multitude "which stands." It is the situation described in the two ὅτι clauses, the situation
produced already the evening before, that John tells
us the multitude "on the morrow saw." We thus need
not change εἶδον into the participle ἰδών (a far inferior
reading), to throw the seeing back to the previous
evening; nor need we put a pluperfect sense into
the simple aorist. It was not until the next morning that the multitude really "saw" the situation:
first, that yesterday (hence ἦν and not ἐστί, R. 887)
no other small boat (πλοιάριον) was there except one,
i. e., the one in which Jesus and the disciples had
crossed; and secondly, that Jesus yesterday did not
go into that boat with his disciples (hence the article
εἰς τὸ πλοιάριον), but the disciples yesterday went away
alone. How much of this the multitude had seen
yesterday does not matter to John, but that "on the
morrow they saw" this is the point for him, for not
until now does the multitude begin to put two and
two together. When we understand John thus we
need not, by resorting to ἰδών, regard v. 22-24 as an
awkward anacoluthon or broken sentence, just because
we think that the multitude should have seen all this
already during the evening.

23) The next statement is parenthetical, explaining how boats arrived in the morning on which the
multitude could also cross to Capernaum. **But there
came boats from Tiberias near to the place where
they ate the bread after the Lord had given thanks.**
None came from Capernaum, for in the morning Jesus
was found there together with his disciples. John does
not state for what purpose these boats from Tiberias

crossed the lake. It is a fair guess to say, because the boatmen knew that the multitude could not long stay on this lonely shore, and many would want to ride back instead of once more going the long road around the upper end of the Sea. These boats, it seems, brought no passengers, for they are now ready to take on passengers and to carry them just where these want to go. If the boats had come from Tiberias loaded, they could not have helped the multitude to cross and would, of course, have taken only their original passengers back to Tiberias.

Tiberias had been built on the southwest shore of the lake by Herod Antipas, the murderer of the Baptist, and was named in honor of the emperor Tiberius. We have no record that Jesus ever visited that city, for its character was· strongly pagan. Outside of the two designations of the sea as being that of Tiberias (6:1; 21:1) the city is mentioned only here and that quite incidentally. Until the fourth century it was the seat of the rabbinical school which produced the *Mishna* or Jerusalem Talmud and the *Masora*. In 1925 the author found it a small town, with two ancient towers at the water's edge, while practically no assured trace can be found of even the location of Capernaum, Bethsaida, and Chorazin (Matt. 11:20, etc.; Luke 10:13, etc.). Note that here for the first time in his Gospel John himself calls Jesus "the Lord."

24) **Accordingly, when the multitude saw that Jesus was not there nor his disciples, they themselves entered the boats and came to Capernaum, seeking Jesus.** They evidently first made a thorough search. The Greek preserves the tense of their present finding ἐστί: "Jesus *is* not here"; compare ἦν to express the absence of any other boat on the previous day, v. 22. They also made sure that the disciples whom they had seen sail away in the evening had

not returned during the night. The singular εἶδεν treats "the multitude" as a collective, while εἶδον in v. 22 and the two plurals in v. 24 refer to the individuals. As a body they "saw" that Jesus and the disciples were not there, but they embarked and went away as so many individuals. They were still a large number, but hardly any longer 5,000; many, we must suppose, had left the evening before, and others in the morning. Those that secured passage in the boats go to Capernaum, either following a guess that this was the most likely place to find Jesus, or because someone of their number had heard Jesus tell the disciples to sail to Capernaum.

25) It was not long before they found him. **And having found him beyond the Sea, they said to him, Rabbi** (see 1:38), **when hast thou come hither?** It is grace on Jesus' part that he allows these people to find him; he is still willing to work upon their souls. Their question is full of curiosity and yet entirely natural, surmising something miraculous, as John's elaborate explanations in v. 22, 23 show. They ask "when," since the time was so short and the way around the shore so long. This "when," therefore, also includes a "how." The perfect tense "hast thou come" = and thus art here, R. 896. Let us note that this question could never have been asked a day or two later, for then Jesus would have had more than enough time to get back to Capernaum in the ordinary way. This again shuts out the view that Jesus and the disciples landed south of Capernaum in Gennesaret and remained there a day or more.

26) While the question hints at a new miracle, it comes from hearts that are eager only to see miracles and not to understand them aright. Hence Jesus does not tell these people when or how he came across so mysteriously but in his answer rebukes their wrong spirit. Many answers of Jesus are on this order. He

replies to men's hearts not merely to their words.
He would give what men need not merely what they
would like to have. **Jesus answered them and said**
(see 1:48), **Amen, amen, I say to you** (see 1:51),
**you are seeking me, not because you saw signs, but
because you ate of the loaves and were filled.** The
two verbs in the preamble mark the reply as being
weighty, likewise the two "amen," which stamp the
reply with verity, and "I say to you," which stamps
it with authority. They ask about *him*, he answers
about *them*. What he tells them is the plain truth..
People do not like to hear what their real spiritual
condition is. Shams are so popular, but verity alone
saves, even though it is bitter.

"Not because you saw signs" means that these
people only saw *wonders* and never saw *signs* at all,
i. e., signs full of great meaning. We need not make
the plural "signs" one of category in order to make
it cover only the feeding of the 5,000; for v. 2 reports
that Jesus healed many sick at the place where presently he also fed the multitude, and these healings, too,
were "signs" full of significance. On the term "signs"
see 2:11. These people failed to see what was so gloriously pictured to them, the divinity of Jesus, his
ability to feed their souls as he had fed their bodies,
his Savior qualities as the Messiah sent of God. They
had held the wonder bread in their hands, had eaten it
with their mouths, but had never understood its true
meaning with their hearts.

Overagainst the negative Jesus puts the positive,
"but because you ate of the loaves and were filled."
Jesus drives this home by using the coarse word
χορτάζω, from χόρτος, fodder or hay; they were satisfied like the ox when his belly is full of fodder. That
is all these people obtained ἐκ τῶν ἄρτων (note the
article), "out of the bread" that meant to give them
so much more. It is easy to see how coarse and low

were the desires of these people; but thousands today have no higher desires.

27) As stern as is the rebuke, so strong is the renewed call of grace. **Work not for the eating which perishes but for the eating which remains unto life eternal, which the Son of man shall give you; for him the Father did seal, even God.** The pivotal word is the imperative, "Work for," which was selected so as to fit the two kinds of "eating," βρῶσις, that which perishes and that which remains. On the distinction between βρῶμα and βρῶσις compare 4:32 and 34; the latter signifies both the food and its eating. We are to exert ourselves so that we may have not merely earthly food to eat but spiritual and heavenly food to eat. But "work for" excludes every Pelagian and synergistic sense. Even earthly food for bodily eating we do not produce by any "working" of ours, it is God's creature and gift; witness every earthly harvest, also the miracle of the feeding of the 5,000. In a far higher sense the spiritual food for our eating is that "which the Son of man shall give you." The entire subject is perfectly elucidated in *Concordia Triglotta*, 901, 48, etc. Here the question is answered, "How we should conduct ourselves towards these means (Word and Sacraments) and use them" (48). In brief: 1) *"go to church and hear"* (53); 2) "be certain that when the Word of God is preached purely and truly, according to the command and will of God, and men *listen attentively and earnestly and mediate upon it,* God is certainly present with his grace and grants, as has been said, what otherwise man can neither accept nor give from his own powers" (55). When Jesus bids the people at Capernaum to "work" thus, he implies that they have not as yet done so. They, indeed, had come and had heard, but altogether superficially, with their ears not with their hearts. They had clung to the tem-

poral and transient, and every effort of Jesus to give them the eternal they had passed over coldly and indifferently.

Note the utter folly of working for τὴν βρῶσιν τὴν ἀπολλυμένην, a food and eating the very nature of which is that it perishes. Here is a true description of all earthly food and bodily possession and satisfaction — it "perishes." True, this food, etc., is also one of God's blessings — did not Jesus himself feed the 5,000? For it, too, we may work; for the command, "Work not!" is meant relatively, i. e., do not make earthly food, etc., your life's chief concern. But ever we must know that because of its very nature all we thus obtain "perishes." When life is done, what is left of it all for us? Nothing, absolutely nothing.

In striking contrast with this perishable food Jesus places "the eating which remains unto life eternal." This is the food and eating which truly satisfies the heart and soul, the very nature of which is that it does not perish or come to nothing but remains forever with its blessed effect. The phrase "unto life eternal" should not be construed merely with the participle, as though this food endures to a future period called life eternal, but with the entire expression. For the εἰς phrase denotes purpose with the idea of result, R. 897. This abiding food and eating is "unto life eternal," it produces life and salvation here and hereafter. How few are those who seek this eating, knowing what it brings forth! This wonderful βρῶσις has been defined as the Word of God; as grace and truth; as a treasure which Jesus bears in himself and gives, namely eternal life; or simply as Jesus himself. But in v. 32 Jesus interprets βρῶσις as "the true bread out of heaven"; in v. 35 and 48, "I am the Bread of life"; in verse 51; and in verse 55, "my flesh is meat indeed, and my blood is drink indeed." Summing up these statements, we have as the βρῶσις: Christ who is sacrificed for us. But the term implies also that by faith we eat this βρῶσις and thus have and enjoy "life eternal," see 3:15.

In the relative clause, "which the Son of man shall give you," the verb "shall give" removes every synergistic notion from the command, "work for." For this food and its eating is entirely a gracious gift of Jesus as "the Son of man," the divine incarnate Messiah (on this title see 1:51). The reading "shall give" has more authority than the present "gives," although the sense is quite the same. The future "shall give" is relative to the present tense "work for," in the sense that the moment we are moved to want this gift Jesus bestows it by his blessed grace.

The explanatory clause, "for him did the Father seal, even God," shows how this Son of man is able to do this wonderful giving. This time Jesus does not say merely that the Father sent him, but that the Father "sealed him," i. e., sent him and confirmed or attested him as one so sent to give this enduring food unto life eternal. The addition "even God" is placed emphatically at the end. The Father as "God" is the highest possible authority, beyond which no man can go. His seal should at once be recognized and accepted without question. The seal he affixed to Jesus these people had seen on the previous day in the miracles he wrought, especially in that of the bread. This seal should at once produce faith, and Jesus now refers to it in order to call forth faith from these people now. Luther writes: "It is a Hebrew way of speaking to say that our Lord God has a ring, a signet and seal on his thumb, with which he stamps when he writes and sends out a letter. Such a seal Christ is to be, and no one else; he thereby rejects and condemns all other seals. This is a strong word, which reaches exceedingly far, that whoever would live forever must have this meat which the Son gives and must be found in the Son who is sealed; otherwise, if he has him not, he will miss eternal life, for here is the seal and testimony attached. See now what you have in this text; there you find clearly: the Father has given his seal to the Son. With this word he snatches away from all other teachers, who would nourish me eternally, their honor and merit, and admonishes us to remain with Christ alone. Therefore go and see whether God the Father has sealed what is preached to you and you are asked to believe; if not, tear the seal away."

28) **They, accordingly, said to him, What shall we do in order to work the works of God?** Jesus secures a response, but what a response! Remember the response of blind Nicodemus and that of the Samaritan woman. Yet note the deliberative subjunctive in the question, which suggests doubt on the whole subject, or a wish to do something, not being certain what that ought to be; this is quite different from the present indicative, R. 923, etc. The subjunctive would take Jesus' answer under advisement; the indicative would ask for Jesus' orders. The tenses, too, must be noted, "what are we to be doing, in order to be working," etc.? The worst part of the answer, however, lies in the use of the plural: in order that we may be working "the works of God," those commanded by God. These people imagine that there is an entire scale of such works, a multiplicity of meritorious deeds to be done by them. Moreover, they imply that if they knew just what these works are, they may with powers and efforts of their own decide to do them. They think that the "giving" of which Jesus speaks is like the bestowal of wages for such works. Thus these people completely lose sight of the meaning of the miracle of the past day when Jesus gave them a free gift, which was to signify a still greater free gift to be received by them through

faith. Jesus speaks of grace; they think only of work-righteousness.

29) The answer of Jesus is a masterpiece. **Jesus answered and said to them** (the two verbs mark the weightiness of the reply), **This is the work of God, that you believe on whom he did send.** He keeps the term "work," the verb for which he used in v. 27, and by one stroke corrects the wrong idea put into it by these people. He turns their wrong plural, "the works of God," into the correct singular, "this is the work of God." He makes the genitive "of God" mean, not "commanded by God," but "wrought by God." And then in the ἵνα clause, which is in apposition to "this," R. 400, he plainly defines just what work God works in us. Faith is here called a "work" in a peculiar sense, differentiating it entirely from "works" as righteous acts of ours. We, indeed, must do the believing, but our believing is the work of *God*. *We* trust, but *God* kindles that trust in us. Compare v. 37, "All that the Father giveth me shall come unto me"; v. 44, "No man can come to me, except the Father which sent me draw him." Faith is "of the operation of God," Col. 2:12. Hence faith is not "the fundamental virtue" from which the other works flow. Faith is the opposite of all other works. For faith receives from God; the other works make return to God. All law works (works of unregenerate men) are the very opposition of faith, for by such works men would climb to heaven on their own merit, without a Savior and without faith. All Christian good works do, indeed, spring from faith, like fruit from a good tree, but always and only from a faith which already has Christ, salvation, life eternal, and needs no good works to merit these treasures which never can be merited.

The present subjunctive "that you believe" means continuous believing; compare the verb in 1:12:

trust or *fiducia*, relying for salvation wholly on Christ. No man can trust anyone of himself; the person whom he trusts by his character, words, acts, etc., always instills the trust. This Jesus ever sought to do by his person, words, deeds, and by his Father's mighty attestation. Thus *we trust*, but at the same time this *trust is wrought in us.* Only to him who trusts Jesus can he give salvation; all who refuse to trust him would not accept the gift from him but think they can obtain it elsewhere. Thus also Jesus at once designates himself as the one who is absolutely trustworthy: believe "on whom he did send." This summarizes his Messianic mission and at the same time points to his exalted person. Only then dare any man refuse to trust Jesus if Jesus is not the person he says he is, and if he is not sent by God as he says, and if God's attestations of Jesus are false. The relative "on whom" has the antecedent drawn into itself: "on him whom," etc.; and ἐκεῖνος is emphatic: *he,* the Father, God! Note how faith recurs in this discourse: v. 35, 40, 47, and figuratively: v. 50, 51, 53, 54, 56, 58. Also in the confession of Peter, "We have believed," v. 69.

30) **They, therefore, said to him, What, then, art thou doing as a sign that we may see and may believe thee? What art thou working?** Both John's οὖν and that in the question itself bring out the idea that this question is intended to be a legitimate deduction from what Jesus has just said. Asking so much of *us,* they say, what art *thou* doing to justify that? Note the emphatic σύ placed after the verb. They keep both of the verbs they used in v. 28 and thus emphatically give Jesus back his own demand: "what art thou *doing?* what art thou *working?*" i. e., now or at any time. What they mean comes out in the predicate accusative: what art thou doing "as a sign"? They thus cast the blame back on Jesus him-

self. If *he* would do more, *they* would respond with
more. When Jesus fed them miraculously the day
before, had they not wanted to make him king? If
Jesus wants them to do more, he himself will have
to do more in the way of a sign. They fail entirely
to see that they had not understood the meaning of
the miracle they had witnessed. If Jesus had given
them a list of works to do, they would have been
ready to attempt them; but this insistence of his on
faith only makes them balk. Not grasping what
Jesus means by this faith, they catch only that he
means more than they have done and so ask for more
from him.

The two aorists in the ἵνα clause are not ingressive,
"come to see and come to believe," as R. 850 states;
their force is, "that we may actually see and actually
believe." The latter verb is construed only with the
dative, "believe thee," i. e., what thou sayest.

31) To re-enforce their counterdemand that Jesus
do more if he demands so much, these people point
to what Moses had done. **Our fathers did eat the
manna in the wilderness, as has been written, Bread
out of heaven he did give them to eat.** The periphrastic perfect "has been written" implies: and is
now on record. In Ps. 78:24 the LXX has "bread
of heaven," but these Jews revert to the Hebrew
"bread out of heaven." Exod. 16:4 reads, "I will rain
bread from (out of) heaven for you," the prepositional
phrase modifying the verb. In the quotation the
emphasis is on the character of the bread not on the
manner of giving, hence the wonderful gift is termed
"bread out of heaven." That, these people mean to
say, was a sign far greater than what they had witnessed yesterday. Jesus only multiplied some bread
he already had, but Moses gave the fathers bread
right out of heaven. What had Jesus to compare with
that? A shrewd kind of reasoning is thus offered which

is apparently sound yet is false in its very premises. As they put it, Moses is far greater than Jesus — why, then, does Jesus claim to be so exceedingly great? If he is, let him bring on a sign that is greater than this one of Moses'.

32) This demand Jesus ignores because it is met the moment these people are shown what "the true Bread out of heaven" really is. **Jesus, therefore, said to them, Amen, amen, I say to you, Moses did not give you the bread out of heaven, but my Father is giving you the genuine bread out of heaven. For the bread of God is that which comes down out of heaven and gives life to the world.** Only in a superficial sense could the manna in the wilderness (as is done in the Psalm) be called *dagan shamajim*, "heaven-bread," for after all it was only like other earthly bread, satisfying only the body from day to day. So again with the seal of verity and authority (see 1:51) Jesus corrects these people. The point of the correction lies in the twice used term "bread out of heaven," which is then defined at length as "the bread of God," actually "coming down out of heaven (origin) and giving life to the world" (exceeding great effect). Note the constrasts: Moses — my Father; did not give — is giving; bread out of heaven, as these people understand it — bread out of heaven, as Jesus understands it; out of heaven, not applicable to the manna, which never was in heaven — out of heaven, applicable to the genuine bread, which actually was in heaven and actually comes down out of heaven. This genuine (ἀληθινόν) bread Moses could not give, nor even God through Moses. Since Jesus speaks of this bread he says nothing about the fathers but uses the pronoun "you" in both clauses.

33) The γάρ clause makes Jesus' meaning plain by stating just what "the bread out of heaven" is.

It is "the bread of God" — "*bread*," indeed, always "bread," because we are to receive and to eat it and thus to obtain what it conveys. But actually bread "*of God*," derived directly from God himself, *das wesenhafte Brot Gottes.* What lies in this weighty genitive is expressed in the predicate, the two present participles being combined under one article and thus made a unit. These participles describe the character and the quality of this bread of God, hence are really timeless. Like no other bread that ever existed, not even the manna, this bread is such as actually "comes down out of heaven" from God himself in heaven and thus is such also as "gives life to the world." This ζωή (1:4; 3:15) is the life principle itself. It does not only keep the life that one already has alive by nourishing it, it actually brings and gives life, the true and eternal life, to those who are dead and have no life. In this sense it is "the bread of God," and a bread that does this is not a mere creature of God like other bread and like the manna, it descends from God's own being out of heaven where God is. And being such bread, its effect is for no limited number but actually for "the world," for the universe of men. The manna fed only "the fathers," only for a few years, and only their bodies which perished in the wilderness. Think, then, by comparison, what this "bread of God" is. The sentence reads naturally with "bread" as the subject and the articulated participles as the predicate. Some would invert this and would make the articulated participles the subject, regarding them as substantivized, "he that comes down and gives is the bread of God," i. e., proving by coming down and giving (the effect) that he is the bread of God (the cause). But this inversion is unnatural, and no reader would make it of his own accord. The fact that this bread is a person descended from God in heaven on a mission to bestow life on the world, is still not revealed but will be most clearly stated in a moment.

34) So captivating is this description of the bread of God that it draws even from these unspiritual people the request that Jesus give them this bread. **They said, therefore, to him, Sir, evermore give us this bread.** This case is identical with that of the Samaritan woman in 4:15. The respectful address "sir" or "lord" shows that no irony is intended as though these people mean, "We do not believe there is such bread, but since you claim there is, give us some of it!" They do really want this bread; they are impressed by its great desirability. But the emphatic adverb "evermore" betrays the fact that they still think only of bodily bread that will obviate their baking and their buying from time to time, that they can eat constantly without effort whenever they grow hungry.

35) Right through this unspiritual denseness flashes the reply of Jesus, destroying once for all every notion of bodily bread and bodily eating. **Jesus said to them, I am the Bread of Life. He that comes to me shall in no way hunger, and he that believes in me shall in no way thirst ever.** Here is one of the great *I AM* statements of Jesus, shining like the noonday sun. Jesus is this bread. Who now can any longer think of mere bodily bread? He it is who came from God out of heaven and gives life eternal — he, sent of God on this mission for the world. To him men must come, in him they must trust, and thus men eat and drink him with the result that they shall never again hunger or thirst. No reply, in words so few, could be more to the point once for all to set these people right.

"The Bread of Life," like "the water of life" in chapter 4, is Biblical allegory which unites the figure

"Bread" with the reality "Life" and thus always interprets itself; compare "living water" in 4:10. In 14:6 the allegory is dropped and only the reality is predicated, "I am the Life." Compare Gen. 3:22; Rev. 22:2 and 17. The figure "Bread" connotes eating, which in the reality "Life" means coming to Jesus and trusting in him. It is especially necessary to note that the predicate has the article. Jesus does not say, "I am Bread of Life," which would mean that others, too, are such Bread; but, "I am *the* Bread of Life." Subject and predicate are indentical and thus interchangeable (R. 768, read at length), so that Jesus could also say, "The Bread of Life is I." He and he alone is "the Bread of Life"; apart from him no such Bread exists. Other "I am" statements of Jesus are of the same type, such as, "I am the Light of the world"; "I am the vine"; etc.

As clear as is the brief word on the Bread, so clear also is that on the eating. This statement resembles the parallelism of Hebrew poetry:

"He that comes to me shall not hunger,
And he that believes in me shall in no way thirst ever."

The present participles are substantivized by the articles, with the present tense indicating only quality; and the second elucidates the first, for only he comes to Jesus for this Bread who trusts him. "Coming" is often used for believing, but here, in order to obtain the greatest clearness, both are placed side by side. In the two phrases with the participles the textual authority is in favor of πρὸς ἐμέ and εἰς ἐμέ, the emphatic pronouns instead of the enclitic forms of these pronouns; which also harmonizes with the emphatic ἐγώ: "*I* am . . . comes to *me* . . . believes in *me*." A striking point for correcting the notion of mere bodily eating is that Jesus without a word of explanation adds the idea of drink to that of bread. Faith is both eating and drinking, so that either may be used or both; compare 4:10, etc. Thus to eat and to drink, Jesus says, abolishes hunger and thirst forever, 4:14, which corrects the request, "Evermore give us this bread." Life, once given, lives on and on, even natural life, although this has a terminus, while spiritual life (unless it is destroyed by unbelief) has none. In both statements note the strongest form of negation in οὐ μή, first with the aorist subjunctive, "shall in no way hunger," and secondly with the future indicative, "shall in no way thirst," to which is added the adverb "ever."

36) To the Jews at Jerusalem Jesus had to say, "You will not come to me, that you may have life," 5:40. To these Jews in Galilee Jesus must now say the same, **But I said to you that you have both seen me and do not believe.** With "I said to you" Jesus refers to v. 26, where he told these people of their guilty unbelief; and here, where his self-revelation is so vivid and clear, this unbelief still persists. These Galileans now know both the Bread and the eating; but *this* Bread does not attract them, *this* eating they refuse. "Both . . . and," καί . . . καί here connect opposites: instead of "you have both seen and do believe," Jesus is compelled to say, "you have both seen and do *not* believe." The perfect "have seen" implies that what they saw is still before their eyes, i. e., the miracles of the past day together with all that Jesus reveals to them. The present tense, "and do not believe," matches this perfect; they still go on without trusting Jesus. Here the guilt of unbelief becomes evident. When the blessed reality of life and salvation in Christ is placed before the eyes and the hearts of men, so that they are made to see them, and when they then refuse to believe and to accept these gifts, their guilt is on their

own heads. But Jesus points these people to this
their guilt, not in order to cast them off forever (although they deserve that), but in order to
drive fear into their conscience.

37) The Jews of Jerusalem had turned against
Jesus, and now these Galileans were doing the same.
But Jesus is not a mere man, operating alone as best
he can with his human wisdom and his strength. He
tells these Galileans plainly who is behind him, and
how, therefore, his work will reach its glorious goal
without the least question. But by saying this to these
people and by telling them how he will carry out the
Father's gracious will in all who believe by giving
them eternal life and by raising them up on the last
day, Jesus raises the question for them: how about
themselves? Do they mean to turn against the
Father, contradict his saving will, and thus, as far
as they are concerned, by their own folly shut themselves out from life now and hereafter? Thus once
more Jesus grips their hearts, drawing them from
unbelief to faith. The absence of a connective need
not indicate a pause on the part of Jesus; it is sufficiently explained by the turn of the thought. The
Galileans are not believing; from them Jesus turns
to the great host that will believe. **All that the
Father gives to me shall get to me; and him that
comes to me I will in no wise cast out.** First the
mass: "all that," etc.; then each individual: "him
that," etc. The neuter singular is used as an abstract
expression and as such sums up the whole mass of
believers of all ages and speaks of them as a unit
(R. 409) ; it is even stronger than if Jesus had used
a masculine plural. Yet beside this unit mass Jesus
places each believer as an individual, for all faith is
highly personal.

When Jesus says of this unit mass that the Father
"gives" it to him, he describes the gift as being in

progress, as more and more of this mass is being made Jesus' own. In v. 39 Jesus uses the perfect tense: all that the Father "has given to me," which describes the gift as having been made once for all and as now being permanent as such a gift. The difference between the tenses lies only in the point of view, which is brought out in the respective predicates. For all that the Father "gives to me," Jesus says, "shall get to me." He sees the gift flowing to him in a great stream through the coming ages; and although the gift is so great, running through so long a period, all of it shall reach him, not even the slightest part of it shall fail to come into his possession. That is the case, of course, because the Father's gift cannot possibly fail. To match the neuter πᾶν Jesus uses ἥξει, "shall get to me"; not ἐλεύσεται, "shall come to me." The former does not suggest a voluntary action on the part of the mass, because πᾶν indicates mass only as such. When it comes to the individual, we see that each is described as ὁ ἐρχόμενος, "he that comes to me." In v. 39 the perfect tense, "all that he has given to me," pictures the gift from the viewpoint of the last day when Jesus will appear and will not have lost any part of this gift and will then put it beyond all possibility of loss by raising the entire mass of believers from their graves.

But in these expressions, "all that the Father gives," and, "all that he has given," Jesus speaks of all believers of all ages as already being present to the eyes of God, he also thus is giving them to Jesus. This Jesus does repeatedly: v. 65; 10:16 and 29; 17:2 and 9 and 24. There, however, is not a fixed number, in some mysterious way chosen by an absolute decree of God to be such a gift to Jesus. Such an exegesis is wholly dogmatic and carries into what Jesus says a thought that is not contained in his words. On the other hand, equally dogmatic is the view that those who constitute God's gift to Jesus are those who in the first place are morally better than the rest, or who at least act better than the rest when the gospel is brought to them. These words of Jesus are without a trace of either predestinarianism or synergism. God's grace is universal. He would give all men to Jesus. The only reason he does not do so is because so many men obdurately refuse to be part of that gift. On the other hand, God's grace is alone efficacious. Every man who believes does so only and wholly by virtue of this grace. Thus the words of Jesus concerning the Father's gift to him and its getting to him raises the question for these Galileans, "Do they want to be a part of this gift, or do they mean to exclude themselves?" "Shall get to me" implies that Jesus accepts the gift.

"Him that comes to me" makes the matter individual, personal, and a voluntary act. The Father's drawing (v. 44) is one of grace alone, thus it is efficacious, wholly sufficient, able to change the unwilling into the willing, but not by coercion, not irresistibly. Man can obdurately refuse to come. Yet when he comes he does so only through the blessed power of grace. Him that comes thus (the present participle only describing the person as such) Jesus "shall in no wise cast out," a strong litotes for "shall most certainly receive." The Son could not possibly contravene the will of his Father. Back of the individual's coming to Jesus lies the Father's giving (and having given, v. 39) that individual to Jesus. And in the same way getting to Jesus means complete reception by Jesus. And this reception is made so strong, not because Jesus would refuse no one coming to him, but because Jesus could not possibly deviate from his Father's will.

Observe how subject and predicate are reversed, so that each becomes emphatic: *gives* to me *the*

Father. Likewise, "all that," etc., is emphasized as being the object by being placed in front. And again, "to me *shall get,*" places the stress on the verb. These points are unfortunately lost in translation. The strong negative οὐ μή, "in no wise," is the same as that used in the previous sentence in v. 35. Also, ἐκ in the verb is strengthened by the appended adverb ἔξω. "To throw out outside" means out of the blessed circle of those who belong to the Son: "outside," into outer darkness.

38) The perfect agreement of Jesus as the Son with the Father he now states in the most direct way. Then in v. 39, 40 he adds the sum and substance of the Father's will which alone is normative for Jesus as the Son. By thus putting himself back of the Father, Jesus makes plain to these Galileans that their unbelief is really opposition to the Father and to that Father's gracious will which Jesus is carrying out in his work with them; and that faith in Jesus alone makes them true to the Father. The stress is on the unity of the Father and Jesus as his Son. **For I have come down from heaven not in order to be doing my own will but the will of him that did send me.** While the stress is on the purpose clause, which, therefore, also is expressed both negatively and positively, we must not overlook the main clause, in which Jesus says in so many words: "I (the Father's Son) have come down (perfect tense: and thus am now here) from heaven (ἀπό, elucidating ἐκ, 'out of' in the previous verses)." And "I have come down from heaven" states in most literal fashion what in v. 33 Jesus says of himself as "the Bread of God," that this "comes out of heaven." Standing there in human form before his hearers, Jesus tells them whence he came: "from heaven" to earth. He himself thus enunciates the Incarnation in the simplest and most matter-of-fact way. The fact that these people

understand Jesus to say just this their own questioning in v. 41, 42 shows beyond a doubt. Here in Galilee the same issue regarding the identity of Jesus as the Son of God is raised as was controverted in Jerusalem, 5:19-47. And here in Galilee unbelief again turns on this supreme issue. It has always done so, and it always will.

But the Person is wholly tied up with the purpose of his coming from heaven. This is not and never could be the doing of his own will, i. e., one different from that of the Father, a will with volitions conflicting with those of the Father. "My own" is the possessive adjective, added by a second article in the Greek, thus has as much emphasis as the noun "the will" to which it is attached. This negation is made so strong because it constitutes the real basis of all unbelief. Only then is unbelief in Jesus justified when it is able to prove that Jesus is doing only his own will and not the Father's will. In fact, all who still claim to believe in God and yet reject Jesus thereby assert that he was false to God. The other way out is for unbelief to alter and to falsify God's will and then to say that Jesus performs this altered will (to be nothing more than an example for men to copy), which, however, is nothing but rejection of God and his Son by one and the same perversive act. And this thought, too, Jesus meets in the next two verses.

After a negative ἀλλά brings in the contrary: "on the contrary, I have come down from heaven in order to be doing the will of him that did send me," and we might translate the substantivized aorist participle: the will "of my Sender." Having come for this purpose and for this alone as the Son from the Father, how could this Son possibly be untrue to his Father? He would have to repudiate his mission, repudiate his Father, whose mission he came to carry out, repudiate his own Sonship. Do these people mean to say that Jesus is guilty of such an act? Only then would their unbelief in him be justified. It rests on an utter and a monstrous impossibility. Jesus convicts the unbelief of his hearers and once more presses them to believe in him.

39) Jesus says "the will of my Sender," and this must be defined, for everything depends on what this will is. Thus Jesus twice over defines this will. **Now this is the will of him that did send me, that all that he has given me I shall not lose any of it but shall resurrect it at the last day.** Once more (v. 37) the neuter πᾶν, "all," is used as a designation for the whole mass of believers. But now, since Jesus is thinking of the consummation at the last day, he uses the perfect tense "has given to me." This tense reaches back to the point where the Father "did send" his Son on his saving mission "from heaven." Then the gift was first made, and it stands as such since then. It was made by virtue of the infallible foreknowledge of God, to which all who would ever be brought to faith were present before they came into existence. In the mind of God, the giver, and of his Son, the receiver, no uncertainty ever existed about those who in all ages are made his own by grace through the gospel and by faith.

The subfinal ἵνα clause is in apposition to "the will of him that did send me" (R. 992) and states the contents of that will. This will, however, has two parts, one that pertains to acts of Jesus (v. 39), and another which pertains to the blessing of believers (v. 40). The construction is anacoluthic, B.-D. 466, 3, and R. 718. We may regard πᾶν, etc., as either a nominative or an accusative absolute that, after the two verbs, is resumed first by the phrase ἐξ αὐτοῦ, secondly by αὐτό. The Father's will is (negatively) that Jesus shall lose no part of this great gift to him but shall bring the whole of it to the consummation of the resurrection at the last day. Regard ἐξ αὐτοῦ as partitive: not lose "out of it" any part; and αὐτό as the opposite: resurrect "it," all of it. The verb ἀπόλλυμι occasionally means "to lose," and the aorist tense (here, of course, the subjunctive) is constative: in all that Jesus does from the beginning to the final consummation of his mission he is not to lose any part of all that the Father has given him. This blessed and gracious will Jesus will most certainly carry into effect. Let none of these Galileans for a moment suppose that in his dealings with them he is making a single mistake and losing a single soul that otherwise could be won. All who are lost are lost altogether through their own perverse and unnatural unbelief.

Not to lose = to keep, and that forever. This includes the final act of Jesus' mission: "on the contrary," the Father's will is "that I shall resurrect it (all of it) at the last day." After ἵνα the Koine permits the future indicative, especially when a second verb is used. Even the bodies of those given to Jesus shall not be lost through the power of death. Jesus says, "I shall resurrect *it*," i. e., *"all* that he has given to me"; and again in v. 40, "I shall resurrect *him*." The verb ἀναστήσω (from which we have ἀνάστασις, "resurrection") is too definite to think of anything save the bodies of believers. *We* are resurrected when our bodies are called out of the grave and are united with our souls and are glorified as are they. Souls cannot be resurrected. As the very body of Jesus was raised from the tomb, so our very bodies shall be raised from their dust and decay. As an act of omnipotence, like the creation, the resurrection of our bodies is utterly beyond human conception.

This resurrection of believers, of all of them, shall take place "at the last day." Then time shall be no

more. This surely is a specific date and is in perfect
harmony with 5:29. Those who speak of a double
resurrection, one at the opening of the millennium
and one at its close, place the resurrection of the
godly first, that of the rest last. Here Jesus says
nothing about the latter, but he says most clearly
that "*all* that he (his Sender) has given him" he
shall resurrect "at the last day." No other day shall
follow. No further resurrection shall follow. The
godly shall not be divided into two or more groups.
All of them shall rise "at the last day," all of them
at the same time. The dream of a millennium is thus
shut out.

40) What the Father's will is regarding the acts
of his Son cannot be fully understood unless we further
know what his will is regarding those who believe
in Jesus. Thus v. 40 is added to v. 39 by an explanatory γάρ. **For this is the will of my Father,
that everyone that beholds the Son and believes on
him shall have life eternal; and I myself will
resurrect him at the last day.** In v. 39 we have the
Father's will concerning Jesus and his mission, hence
the designation: the will "of him that did send me."
We have no such mission, hence now: the will "of
my Father." In v. 39 we have the mass as an un-
divided whole: "all that he has given me," just as
in the first part of v. 37. Now we have each and
every individual composing this mass: "everyone that
beholdeth," etc. But note that not one is left out.
So in v. 37, too, the mass was individualized. But
there the description was only general: "him that
comes to me"; now this coming is fully described by
two characterizing or qualitative present participles:
"everyone that beholdeth the Son and believeth on
him." To come to Jesus is to behold the Son and to
believe on him. The two participles really refer to
one act, involving the intellect which by beholding

aright recognizes truly, and the heart or will which
in that moment of true recognition gives its trust or
confidence. In order to behold, someone or something
must be brought to our vision; and in order to believe or trust, someone or something must come to
us that is able to awaken and arouse such trust. Here
it is "the Son," purposely thus named, the Son of the
Father, more trustworthy than whom no one can be
named. Our beholding and our trusting are the normal effect of the Father's showing us his Son and
bringing us into contact with him. It would be the
height of abnormality, of flagrant perversity, of senseless unreason to have the Son thus brought to us and
for us to turn from him in distrust.

Jesus does not say that it is the Father's will for
us to behold the Son and to trust in him. Instead
he passes by these subjective means and at once names
the goal, which is that every believer "shall have life
eternal," touching the intervening means only lightly.
Yet he who desires the end must necessarily desire
also the means. Hence we may say that the Father's
will is that we behold the Son and believe in him.
But only to this end: that we "shall have life eternal,"
ζωή, the principle or very substance that constitutes
life. Beholding and trusting in the Son puts us into
true inward contact with him, and since he is the
Bread of Life, or literally Life itself, this inner contact with him fills also us with life. His life enters
our souls, and so we "have life." The present subjunctive (3:15, 16) ἔχῃ = "shall be having" from the
instant of beholding and believing on and on forever.
This spiritual life, like our physical life, is itself invisible but is strongly manifested by its activities.
The believer does a thousand things that unbelievers
cannot possibly do. To say that the believer "has
life eternal" is to say that the unbeliever lacks this
life, in other words, is spiritually dead, far from the

source of all the light, joy, and blessedness that goes with life. Shall this blessed will of the Father be done in these Galileans, or do they mean by guilty unbelief to frustrate that will?

This life of the believer is not merely to pass unharmed through temporal death and to last forever as the believer's possession, it is to fill also his body as well as his soul. Thus the Father's will is that our bodies should be raised from the grave and be at last made full partakers together with our souls of this life in all its final glory. Thus Jesus adds, not now as an expression of his Father's will, not in a second clause after ἵνα (as in v. 39), but in a coordinate separate statement of his own, "and I myself will resurrect him at the last day." That he shall do this as the consummation of his mission is his Sender's will. That he will do this is his own personal promise to every believer. Hence he now says ἐγώ, using the emphatic pronoun, "I myself," which is absent in v. 39. We may imitate the Greek emphasis, primary on the verb, secondary on the pronoun: "and UPRAISE him will *I Myself.*" All that this means for the believer's body, for the date of this act, etc., has already been shown in v. 39 and should again be considered here.

Jesus Gives Himself as the Bread of Life, 41-51

41) The offense in Jesus' words is practically the the same as that in his words spoken to the Jews at Jerusalem, 5:18. **The Jews, therefore, were murmuring concerning him, because he said, I am the Bread which did come down out of heaven. And they were saying, Is not this Jesus, the son of Joseph, of whom we ourselves know the father and the mother? How now is he declaring, Out of heaven have I come down?** Here John calls these Galileans "the Jews," a term which he uses so con-

stantly in combination with the hostility to Jesus. The two imperfects describe their grumbling and their talking to each other after Jesus had stopped speaking. They fastened their objection on the statement of Jesus that he is the Bread "which did come down out of heaven." For in v. 33 they substitute the aorist participle which refers to the single act of thus coming down out of heaven. In this they were right, for only this past act lends this quality to Jesus.

42) Over against this declaration of Jesus these Jews place what they themselves (emphatic ἡμεῖς) know about him. They are acquainted with his parentage: "Is not this Jesus," etc.? "It most certainly is!" With οὗτος they use a contemptuous tone, R. 697. Only Galileans from the neighborhood where Jesus lived so long could thus speak of his father Joseph and of his mother. The mention of Joseph is no evidence that he was still alive at this time. The final question specifies the point of the objection, how the son of parents they knew so well can stand before them and expect them to believe his declaration, "Out of heaven have I come down." That, indeed, is the vital point in all that Jesus said to them. It has ever been the stumblingblock and rock of offense for unbelief.

43) Although nothing was said directly to Jesus, he interrupts their grumbling, understanding it completely (3:23, 24). **Jesus answered and said to them** (1:48), **Stop your murmuring.** The present imperative refers to the preceding imperfect and thus bids the action that was going on to stop, R. 851.

Only in one way can the question raised by these Jews be effectually answered. Not by the way of the mere intellect, but by the way of actual experience. The former is hopeless in man's sinful state. Tell the intellect that this man Jesus is the incarnate Son and gives eternal life; forthwith the intellect with its theoretical reasoning and argument will deny the one, or the other, or both statements. That is why the gospel is not an argument, a piece of pure reasoning, a set of logical propositions and religious theory or hypothesis like those of science, or anything else addressed only to the intellect. It is *"the power of God* unto salvation," Rom. 1:16, "that your faith should not stand in the wisdom of men, but in *the power of God,"* I Cor. 2:5. Like any power, this divine power is not merely *known* theoretically or intellectually but is *realized in the actuality of experience* in a man's own life. He alone knows that power who has undergone its operation in himself. See the case of the Samaritan woman in 4:29 and of her townspeople in 4:41, 42. A fine example is the blind man in 9:30-33. Hence Jesus does not here commit the folly of explaining his Incarnation to these grumbling Galileans, for that would be the surest way of confirming them in their unbelief. Here, as always, Jesus follows the other way. He keeps applying the power that saves the sinner by changing his spiritual death into spiritual life eternal. Once this power actually enters a soul, that soul is taught of God and has learned of God by the actuality of its own experience. Its intellect is more than satisfied, because the soul itself is satisfied. It knows that Jesus did, indeed, come down out of heaven, even as he says, because it has as a most blessed gift the very life he brought us out of heaven, the life that shall live in heaven forever.

44) This is why Jesus continues his reply as he does. **No one can come to me unless the Father who did send me shall draw him; and I will resurrect him at the last day.** Luther has put these words into classical form: "I believe that I cannot

by my own reason or strength believe in Jesus Christ, my Lord, or come to him; but the Holy Ghost has called me by the gospel, . . . and will at the last day raise up me and all the dead, and give unto me and all believers in Christ eternal life. This is most certainly true." Here Jesus explains the Father's "giving" mentioned in v. 37 and 39: he gives men to Jesus by drawing them to him. This drawing (ἐλκύειν) is accomplished by a specific power, one especially designed for the purpose, one that takes hold of the sinner's soul and moves it away from darkness, sin, and death, to Jesus, light, and life. No man can possibly thus draw himself to Jesus. The Father, God himself, must come with his divine power and must do this drawing; else it will never be effected.

But significantly the Father is here again called the one "who did send me." Only as the Sender of Jesus does he draw and as such he draws to Jesus. His drawing power is exerted altogether through the mediation of Jesus, whom he sent for this purpose. The drawing is here predicated of the Father; in 12:32 it is predicated of Jesus, "And I will draw all men unto myself." Like all the *opera ad extra*, this, too, belongs equally to all three Persons. The Sender of Jesus is here mentioned because of the unbelieving Galileans; they are to understand that it is God himself who is now dealing with them through Jesus whom he has sent. The power by which these Jews are at this very moment being drawn is the power of divine grace, operative in and through the Word these Jews now hear from the lips of Jesus. While it is power (Rom. 1:16), efficacious to save, it is never irresistible (Matt. 23:37, "and ye would not"). Nor is this power extended only to a select few, for in 12:32 Jesus says, "I will draw all men."

The power of the gospel is for the world, and no
sinner has fallen so low but what this power is able
to reach him effectually.

The promise in v. 40 is renewed with only the
shift of ἐγώ from one emphatic position to another
that is equally emphatic. By this emphatic pronoun
the Sender and the Sent are again placed on the
same level. In v. 40 Jesus summarizes what he says
in v. 37-40, inserting only the elucidation concerning
the Father's power which does the drawing. This is
why the promise concerning the final consummation in
the blessed resurrection is added to the work of drawing. The beginning of the work in the Father's drawing is coupled with the crowning of this work in the
Son's resurrecting those drawn.

45) Whereas Jesus first uses διδόναι, "to give," in
v. 37 and 39, he adds ἑλκύειν, "to draw," in v. 44. He
now takes the next step and makes fully clear how
this giving and drawing to Jesus is effected by the
Father. **It has been written in the prophets, And
they shall all be people taught of God. Everyone
that did hear from the Father and did learn comes
to me.** "It has been written" (periphrastic perfect)
and is thus still on record, "in the prophets," in that
portion of the Old Testament which the Jews commonly designated "the prophets." Isa. 54:13 (compare Jer. 31:33, 34; Joel 2:28; etc.) describes the
blessed condition of Jerusalem's children after accepting the sacrificed and glorified Messiah (Isa. 53) in
repentance and faith. Among these blessings is this:
all will be people taught of God, and great the peace
of thy children. The emphasis is on the genitive "of
God," which is subjective, naming God as the teacher;
R. 516 makes it ablative "by God." All that they
hold and believe is God's own teaching, none of it
comes from themselves or merely from men. Thus
we see what it means to be drawn by the Sender of

Jesus, namely to be "people taught of God." The verbal διδακτοί is used as a noun, the predicate of "shall be." This plural Jesus resolves into its component individuals: "everyone that did hear from the Father and did learn," he, and he alone, belongs to these people taught of God. The two aorist participles are really timeless (R. 859), but as qualitative aorists they describe actuality, actual hearing and learning. They also belong together as a unit idea, effective hearing resulting in actual learning; for the two participles have but one article. The fact that some, like these Galileans, hear with deaf hearts and ears and refuse to learn is here not considered by Jesus. This hearing and learning from God denotes reception from God who gives by means of teaching his Word; we receive when that Word makes us hear and learn. By attaching the phrase "from God" to the first participle this phrase has the emphasis; then by adding the unmodified second participle this participle receives emphasis. What we receive is *from God* by way of *actual learning*.

The result of this teaching and this learning is not by any means merely intellectual. We have already heard that God thus *draws* us by teaching us. Hence everyone so taught "comes to me." The participles "everyone that did hear and learn" are without an object, yet the great teacher is the Sender of Jesus, and the effect of his teaching is that everyone so taught comes to Jesus. This teaching and this learning thus deal with the coming to Jesus as to the Son sent by the Father to give life. To come thus means to believe and to receive life.

46) The quotation from the prophets, "people taught of God," and the interpretation, "everyone that did hear from the Father," παρὰ τοῦ πατρός, need further elucidation. How does God as a teacher meet his pupils? How do we get to his side (which is the

thought in παρά), so as then to hear "from this Father" as his children? Not in an immediate way but mediately through his Son. **Not that anyone has seen the Father, save he that is from God, he indeed (οὗτος, emphatic) has seen the Father.** The Old Testament is very plain regarding the impossibility of mortal, sinful man while remaining in this state seeing God. So that notion is shut out completely. When the prophet spoke of that most blessed future period, saying that then Israel should be a "people taught of God," he referred to the coming of God's Son in human flesh. In this Son the Father would actually come to his people and would so teach them that they would actually hear him speak, as one person speaks to another. The Son is, of course, the one exception (εἰ μή). He is, therefore, characterized as ὁ ὢν παρὰ τοῦ Θεοῦ, "he who is from God," he who has this characteristic mark. Note how the παρά phrase "from the side of God" explains the previous ἐκ phrases: "out of heaven." The demonstrative οὗτος takes up the previous characterization: he who is from God, "he indeed" has seen the Father. Both times we have the extensive perfect "has seen," so that the effect of that seeing is still present to him.

The entire statement has one purpose: if no one ever saw God, and Jesus alone has seen him because he comes from him, it is Jesus who makes us "people taught of God," for through him we hear and learn from the Father. This explains completely how the Father draws to the Son, and how by his drawing he gives to the Son. The question for these Galileans was: "Has this been done in us? are we people thus taught?"

47) After all this has been made plain, Jesus again turns to the main thought, the call to faith. He is even now executing the drawing of the Father,

and none who hear him can ever say, when they
refuse to come to him, that they have not been drawn.
**Amen, amen, I say to you, He that believes has
life eternal.** Once more Jesus uses the double seal
of verity and with it that of his final authority. The
Father's giving (v. 37 and 39), drawing (v. 44), and
teaching (v. 45), making us "hear and learn," is
accomplished as to its purpose and its effect when
faith is kindled in the heart. Hence the subject of the
emphatic statement is ὁ πιστεύων, "he that believes,"
the qualitative present participle describing the person
as one animated by confidence and trust. By adding
nothing further to the substantivized participle the
weight of thought rests on the believing as such. Of
course, just as in the drawing, teaching, hearing and
learning, so also in the believing, a corresponding object is implied, yet here the thought turns on the
participle, i. e., on the person who is described as
one marked by faith. He, and he alone, "has life
eternal," as already explained in v. 40. The participle
also has the force that this person has life eternal
from the first instant of his believing onward and as
long as he believes. The moment he would cease to
believe, that moment he would cease to have life. It
is believing or trusting that joins him to Jesus and
thus to life eternal. Faith *has* life and, we may also
say, *is* life. It *has* life because it is the constant
reception of that divine grace and gift which frees
us from death and makes us one with God. It *is* life
because faith is the divine spark or flame which
animates the soul and distinguishes us from the
spiritually dead (5:24-26).

48) With this statement Jesus has returned to
his central theme: **I am the Bread of Life,** i. e., the
Mediator of that life, v. 35. The repetition is, of
course, emphatic, but here it also introduces a fuller
elaboration. We also see that the human figure of

bread is strained in order to convey the greatness and
the fulness of the thought for which it is employed.
This is often the case with the figurative language
used in the Scriptures, for all human illustrations
are weak when it comes to portraying spiritual realities completely. Ordinary bread only *sustains* physical life, but Jesus as the Bread of Life not only
sustains spiritual life but even *gives* us this life. Hence
also he is not merely "bread" or "bread of life" but
actually "living Bread" (v. 51), i. e., Bread full of
life, the reception of which gives and sustains life.

49)   This is made exceedingly clear by reverting
to the manna mentioned in v. 31-33. When the Galilean Jews pointed Jesus to the manna which Moses
gave them, Jesus replied on the point of origin: the
manna never was in heaven and never came down out
of heaven whereas Jesus both was in heaven and came
down out of heaven. Now to the point of origin that
of the effect is added. **Your fathers did eat the
manna in the wilderness, and they died. This is
the Bread that comes down out of heaven, in order
that one may eat of it and not die.** The comparison
is striking indeed. Pointedly Jesus says "your"
fathers and does not include himself among these Jews
by saying "our" fathers. In the same pointed way
he speaks of "my" father in v. 32; compare the
elucidation of that verse. The two aorists are historical and state the undeniable facts: "they did eat"
and "they died." So after all, though it was miraculously given, the manna was not superior to other
earthly food. It only sustained the bodily life temporarily; it could never be called "the Bread of Life" in
the full sense of the word. "And they died" means only
that they were at last overtaken by temporal death,
including Moses himself. We have no right to make
the verb mean eternal death. It is true enough that
the Israelites perished in their sins (Acts 7:42 and 51;

Heb. 3:16-19, R. V.), but ἀπέθανον does not include that fact. What Jesus says is that the manna was only like other earthly bread, including the bread with which the 5,000 had been fed on the previous day. Those who get no better bread eventually die. They will have lived only the common earthly life with no higher life in them, and so their dying is a sad end, indeed. The only life they have they then lose, for the only bread they have eaten is one that thus lets them die at last.

50) But look at "the Bread of Life." Its very character is different, for it "is the Bread that cometh out of heaven." The present participle does not refer to a constant descent out of heaven but describes the quality of this Bread as being something constant. By having descended out of heaven, by having become incarnate, and by assuming his saving mission, Jesus is the Bread that has this wonderful quality of being derived from heaven. All that can be predicated of the manna lies on the plane of the natural life; all that can be predicated of the Bread of Life lies on the plane of the spiritual life. Hence the purpose clause governed by ἵνα, which modifies the entire statement: "in order that one may eat of it and not die." God's intention is that we shall eat of this Bread, and the intended result of this eating is that we shall escape death. As the food, so the eating and its effect both in the case of the manna and in the case of the Bread of Life. Those who eat only the earthly bread prolong only their earthly life and finally die in temporal death and never attain more. Those who eat of the Bread of Life obtain the spiritual and heavenly life, which passes unharmed through temporal death and enters into eternal blessedness. "He that believeth on me, though he die, yet shall he live; and whosoever liveth and believeth on me shall never die," John 11:25,

26. "And not die" refers to spiritual and eternal death. This death we who eat of the Bread of Life escape; this death they who spurn the Bread of Life fail to escape. Note the strong contrast in the two verses 49 and 50: "and they died" — "and (shall) not die."

51) The facts stressed in v. 48-50 are now restated with modifications and additions, so as to make them clear beyond all question. **I am the living Bread that did come down out of heaven. If one shall eat of this Bread he shall live forever; and the Bread, moreover, which I will give is my flesh, in behalf of the life of the world.** First, a restatement of v. 48, again focusing everything upon Jesus with the emphatic pronoun ἐγώ, "I," "I myself, and no other." And now "the Bread of Life" is explained by "the living Bread," or "the Bread that lives," for the participle is made as emphatic as the noun itself by having the article repeated: ὁ ἄρτος ὁ ζῶν. "The Bread of Life" = the Bread which belongs to the true Life; "the Bread that lives" = the Bread that is full of the life it is intended to impart; the Bread, the very quality and character of which is that it lives and makes him alive who partakes of it. In literal language, Jesus is full of Life and the Giver of Life. A second attributive participle is added by another article: "that did come down out of heaven." This time the participle is the aorist, declaring the historical fact of thus coming down. On this fact rests the quality of this Bread expressed in v. 50, as in v. 33, by the descriptive or qualitative present participle "coming down." Thus once more in the clearest and simplest way we are shown just what Jesus is for us.

The figure in "Bread" always connotes eating; and thus Jesus once more speaks of the eating. To eat = to believe in Jesus, v. 47. In v. 50 we are told that it is God's purpose that we eat this Bread, or literally that we believe in his Son (v. 40). This purpose will, of course, be carried into effect, and thus Jesus now adds, "if one shall eat of this Bread." He uses the condition of expectancy: there shall be those who eat. Some will refuse to eat, but many will be moved to eat. In v. 50 the negative effect of this eating is stated: he that eats "shall not die"; now the positive effect is placed beside the negative: "he shall live forever." The one, of course, always implies the other: not to die = to live forever. The aorist φάγῃ means "come to eat." One act of eating bestows life (4:14; 6:35). The phrase εἰς τὸν αἰῶνα, literally "for the eon," views eternity in human fashion as a vast extent of time and is the Greek way of saying "forever"; compare the corresponding adjective αἰώνιος, "eternal." See also on 14:16. We must place side by side the Bread of Life, τῆς ζωῆς; the Bread that lives, ὁ ζῶν; he that believes has life eternal, ζωὴν αἰώνιον; and shall live forever, ζήσεται εἰς τὸν αἰῶνα — each expression illuminating the other.

Thus the entire thought is rounded out and made complete, the wonderful circle of salvation is closed. Jesus, the Life, is the center. All who are made one with him by faith are joined to him and are made full partakers of his life, not only of something which he has, or of something which he does (we following his example), but of what he himself is.

But in this figure of the Bread lies a still deeper meaning, one which shows us completely just *how* Jesus is, indeed, the Bread of Life and also just *how* we eat of this Bread by faith. And so, with one circle of thought complete and closed, at once another, reaching out still farther, is started. The first centers in the origin of Jesus, in his being Life itself descended out of heaven from the Father on his sav-

ing mission into this world of sin and death. The
second centers in this mission, or rather in its vital
and central act, namely in his sacrificial death. The
new distinctive terms are thus "my flesh," or more
fully "the flesh of the Son of man and his blood (v.
53), and corresponding with these expressions our
"eating" his flesh and "drinking" his blood by faith.
This second circle of thought is joined to the first
when Jesus now adds, "and the Bread, moreover,
which I will give is my flesh, in behalf of the life of
the world."

The reading with the two connectives καί . . .
δέ is assured, not, however, in the sense of "but also,"
which in no way fits the thought, but in the sense of
"and . . . moreover"; for καί tells of an addition
that is made, and δέ presents this addition as something that is new and different from what precedes.
The new feature is "my flesh." Before the ὑπέρ
phrase some important texts add the relative clause
ἣν ἐγὼ δώσω, "which (flesh) I will give for the life
of the world," A. V. While the weight of textual
evidence is against this clause, its thought is in harmony with what Jesus here says. In the turn which
the thought here takes too little attention has been
paid to the emphatic ἐγώ: "and the Bread which *I*
shall give is my flesh." In what Jesus now states
the contrast is not between the Bread which he *is*
and the Bread which he *gives* but between the gift
the Father gives and the gift which *Jesus himself*
shall presently give. The former is the Bread of
Life coming down out of heaven, i. e., the incarnate
Son in his entire saving mission. As regards this
gift the Father is the Giver, yet so that the Son, too,
is called the Giver (v. 27 and 32, 33). When the
gift is viewed as coming down out of heaven, the
givers are the Father and the Son. But in this mission of the Son an act of giving is involved which

belongs in a peculiar way to Jesus alone as the incarnate Son. This gift Jesus had not yet made, hence the future tense, "which I shall give." It is the gift of his flesh and his blood in the sacrifice upon the cross. This gift Jesus himself will make. "The Son of God gave *himself* for me," Gal. 2:20. "Christ hath given *himself* for us," Eph. 5:2. "I lay down *my life*," John 10:17. "The Son of man came to give *his life* a ransom for many," Matt. 20:28. In this sense Jesus says, "the Bread which I shall give is *my flesh.*" This specific gift lies within the comprehensive gift. And this specific act of giving on Jesus' part is the vital part of the comprehensive gift, namely that act which truly makes him for us the Bread of Life, enabling us to eat and to drink by faith.

Since both subject (ὁ ἄρτος) and predicate (ἡ σάρξ μου) have the article, the two are identical and convertible, R. 767, etc. Thus the contention that we must here reverse the order and read, "my flesh (subject) is the Bread (predicate)" is untenable. The proposition is true either way. Yet the argument, that because the Bread has been mentioned before, therefore it must be the predicate, is specious; for the reverse holds good: since Jesus has repeatedly spoken of the Bread, he now tells us what it is, namely "my flesh." More important by far is the question, whether the word "flesh" here, and "flesh and blood" in v. 53, connote and imply the sacrificial death of Jesus on the cross. This has been emphatically denied. It seems that for this reason, too, the addition "my flesh *which I will give* for the life of the world" is repudiated. We dare drop these words for no such reason. The Scriptures know of no gift of Christ's "flesh," or, as these objectors put it, Christ's humanity or *Menschlichkeit* in behalf of the world apart from and without his sacrificial death on the cross. Take away the death, and the flesh of Christ ceases to be the Bread of Life for us. With the cancellation of the sacrificial death any participation in the flesh and the blood, any eating of his flesh or drinking of his blood, becomes an impossibility. The future tense δώσω demands the death, for this gift is yet to be made on Calvary. If "my flesh" refers to Jesus' humanity without or irrespective of his death, the tense would have to be an aorist, or at least the present, for then the gift of the flesh must refer to the Incarnation, a gift already made. Yet such a gift would be no gift, for the Incarnation without the sacrificial death would not bring life eternal to the world. Ideas such as that the flesh of Jesus, when it is imparted to us, becomes in us "a tincture of immortality," at last vivifying our flesh in the resurrection, or that by means of Jesus' flesh a germ is planted into our bodies and is kept alive and fed by means of the Lord's Supper to grow forth from our dead bodies in the resurrection, are completely shut out when the flesh of Jesus is rightly viewed as the Bread of Life in connection with the sacrificial death upon the cross.

If we adopt the text: my flesh "which I will give for the life of the world," the construction as well as the sense are plain. But we must drop the relative clause for textual reasons and must read: "the Bread which I will give is my flesh, in behalf of the life of the world." In this reading the ὑπέρ phrase cannot be construed as a modifier of "my flesh," for the copula ἐστίν intervenes. The article would have to be repeated before the phrase in order to make it a modifier of "my flesh," or the phrase would have to be converted into a participial or a relative clause. The construction, then, must be that the final phrase is an adverbial modifier of the predicate, and since the subject and the predicate are interchangeable, this adverbial modifier belongs to the entire sentence. In other words, when Jesus shall give as the Bread his flesh in the sacrificial death, this "is in the interest of the life of the world." While the phrase is brief and compact it is entirely clear: the Bread, the flesh, the future act of giving, all together have one purpose or object, they intend that the world may have the true heavenly life. It is mere quibbling to pit the one expression, "giving into death," against the other, "giving for us to eat," and to stress this difference as excluding the death in this statement of Jesus and in the others that follow. True enough, the two acts may be distinguished: it is one thing for Jesus to give himself into death, and it is another to give himself to us as the Bread of Life. Yet the two are indissolubly joined together: by giving himself into death Jesus gives himself to us as the Bread of Life. In v. 53 the blood is placed beside the flesh to indicate the more that Jesus is speaking of his death. Now this blood, once shed on Calvary when Jesus gave himself into death, is ever after the fountain of life for the world. By being given in the one atoning act on the cross it was given as the source of life for all sinners, I John 1:7; Heb. 9:14; Rev. 7:14; and I Pet. 2:24, where "stripes" are used for flesh and blood in conformity with Isa. 53:5. In v. 33 Jesus says, "The Bread of God . . . gives life to the world." This universality is now again emphasized: "in behalf of the life of the world." This living Bread, the flesh of Jesus sacrificed on the cross, is so full of life and salvation that all the world may take and eat and live forever.

Jesus Gives to Him That Believes His Flesh as the Bread of Life, 52-59

52) **The Jews, therefore, were contending with each other, saying, How is this one able to give us**

his flesh to eat! The moment Jesus mentioned his
flesh contention arose among his auditors, whom John
again designates as "the Jews," a term used by him
to indicate their hostile temper. The imperfect
ἐμάχοντο describes the passionate exchange of words
among themselves, no longer spoken in undertones
like the previous murmuring mentioned in v. 41, but
in open exclamations. The verb shows that they were
divided; yet this does not mean that some supported
Jesus while others contradicted them, but that some
raised one objection while others clashed with them
in raising a different objection. Thus there was a
battle among them. The objection of all of them is
summarized in what is rather an unbelieving exclamation than a question, "How is this one able to give
us his flesh to eat!" The derogatory οὗτος has a touch
of scorn: this man, the son of Joseph, whose father
and whose mother they knew, v. 42. In spite of his
miracles they persist in regarding him as a mere
man; and thus it appears wholly preposterous to
them that he should be able to give them his
flesh to eat.

The article τὴν σάρκα has the force of the possessive
pronoun "his flesh." These Jews understand Jesus
correctly when they exclaim regarding his giving them
his flesh "to eat," for this is exactly what Jesus means
(v. 53). If the Bread he will give is his flesh, then
the connotation of eating that lies in "Bread" extends
also to "my flesh." On the assumption that Jesus is
a mere man the eating of his flesh would be nothing
but a horrible cannibalism — an outrageous idea.
They say only, give "us" to eat, whereas Jesus said,
in behalf of the life "of the world." The fact that
Jesus himself has thus shut out their preposterous
notion of masticating his physical flesh with their
teeth and digesting it in their stomachs, their blindness fails to note. What these Jews voice here in

Capernaum has come to be called "the Capernaitic mode" of eating. For the old Jewish unbelief still persists, justifying itself by holding to the idea that the flesh of Jesus could be eaten only in the gross physical way, thus rejecting not only what Jesus says in this discourse on the Bread of Life, but also what he says when instituting the Lord's Supper, telling us to take and to eat his body and to drink his blood.

Both the spiritual eating by faith here meant by Jesus and the sacramental eating of Christ's body and blood in the Lord's Supper are *toto coelo* removed from all Capernaitic eating, which rests on a false conception of the person of Jesus and on the denial of the personal union of his two natures, the human and the divine. Luther lays his finger on the little word *my* flesh: "With great, mighty letters we ought to engrave what Christ says: MY, MY flesh. But they will not look at this *my*. The fanatics cannot grasp this word *my*. But with the word *my* he distinguishes and separates himself from all other flesh whatever it may be called. For here *my* flesh is as much as, I am God and God's Son, *my* flesh is filled with divinity (*durchgoettert*) and is a divine flesh. His flesh alone will do it. To this God would have us attached and bound fast. Apart from the person who is born of Mary and truly has flesh and blood and has been crucified we are not to seek nor find God. For we are to grasp and find God alone by faith in the flesh and blood of Christ and are to know that *this* flesh and blood is not fleshy and bloody, but both are full of divinity." On the different modes of the presence of Christ's body see *Concordia Triglotta*, 1005, etc.

53) **Jesus, therefore, said to them, Amen, amen, I say to you, Unless you eat the flesh of the Son of man and drink his blood, you have not life in your-**

selves. Instead of softening his words regarding the eating of his flesh Jesus, we may say, hardens them. On "Amen," etc., see 1:51. Yet this hardening is only a fuller and more explicit statement. It is impossible for him to retract a single word, for that would put falsehood in place of truth. Jesus had abundantly prepared these Jews and now reveals the truth in its fulness. He can do nothing else. If the truth, fully and clearly presented, does not produce faith, nothing else will.

The Jews exclaim, *"How* can this one give us his flesh to eat!" Some commentators think that this question is altogether wrong, having in mind not merely its Jewish or unbelieving feature but all inquiry as to the how. Likewise, the reply of Jesus is regarded as a simple declaration of *the necessity* of eating his flesh and as a refusal to explain *how* this eating can be accomplished. But this is a misconception. If we are to eat Jesus' flesh in order to have life we must surely know how this is to be done. If he gives us his flesh as the living Bread, we must know how this Bread is to be eaten, in order that we may receive it. Jesus answers this question but does so in his own way by combining the manner with the necessity. Of course, he does not satisfy either unbelief or curiosity, but he does open the way to faith. The speculation which would unravel all mystery will not be satisfied, but the soul that hungers and thirsts for life and salvation will know both how he gives us his flesh to eat and thus also how we may eat it and live. The case is somewhat like that of Nicodemus who also asked about the how in regard to regeneration (3:4). There as well as here Jesus uses the solemn assurance of verity and authority, "Amen, amen, I say to you," in order to overcome unbelief and doubt and to emphasize the importance of his words. There as well as here he repeats his former statement but with the necessity he combines the explanation needed for faith.

He begins with the negative side, as in v. 50; but at once (in v. 54) adds the positive side, as in v. 51. "Unless you eat the flesh of the Son of man" is a protasis of expectancy, ἐάν with the subjunctive, for Jesus expects that some will eat. Yet οὐκ ἔχετε, "you have not life in yourselves," is an apodosis of reality, as if Jesus reckons also with unbelief and its loss of life. Jesus adds his own Messianic title "the Son of man," he who is man, indeed, and thus has flesh and blood but who at the same time is far more than man, namely God's Son in human flesh sent for our redemption. On this title see the exposition in 1:51. The addition of this title is of the utmost importance. By thus naming himself, Jesus declares that if he were, indeed, a mere man, he could not give his flesh to men to eat; but since he is "the Son of man," the God-man, sent as the Messiah from heaven itself, therefore he can so give his flesh. The premise of unbelief is false, and that fact annuls its logical conclusion. Here the how of these Jews receives its first decisive answer.

The second lies in the significant addition "and drink his blood." The spirit of Jesus is misconceived when we are told that he made this addition "in order to increase the offense." Jesus never sets out to give offense. When men take offense they do so wholly without cause. Unbelief always takes offense at the truth, but always does so without reason. The more truth unbelief meets, the more it takes offense, revealing its true nature, its folly of unreason, and its inexcusable guilt. Yet truth alone can turn unbelief into faith, and the greater the measure of truth, the greater its power to convert offended unbelief into satisfied faith. To say that the addition about drinking the blood of the Son of man is without special significance, that it only helps to describe the humanity of Jesus, is to cancel from this final and fullest declaration of Jesus the very feature which is distinctive and most explanatory. For to parallel the eating of the flesh with the drinking of the blood of the Son of man, as Jesus parallels them here, is to point in the clearest way to his own sacrificial death. This parallel explains what eating and drinking really mean, namely participation in the sacrifice. By the death of the Son of man his blood is shed in sacrifice. It is folly, then, to think for one moment of drinking that blood in a physical (Capernaitic) manner. To drink the blood thus shed is a spiritual act *in toto*, an acceptance by the soul of the efficacy of that blood once shed and of the atonement and expiation wrought by its being shed. "Flesh and blood" is here not a unit as in Matt. 16:17 and Heb. 2:14, but "flesh" is separated from "blood," and "blood" is separated from "flesh" by means of the sacrificial death. On having life see 3:15. The present tense is noteworthy, since the negation refers to present possession and to its continuance. In the protasis the two verbs "eat" and "drink" are properly aorists, because only one act of reception secures life. The addition of the phrase "in yourselves" emphasizes the idea of permanent possession in the verb, "have not in yourselves."

54) The tremendous importance of eating the flesh and drinking the blood of Jesus is pressed upon these Jews by the addition of the positive statement to the negative: **He that eats my flesh and drinks my blood has life eternal; and I will resurrect him at the last day.** The English is unable to render the peculiar force of ὁ τρώγων, which is more realistic than the verb ἐσθίω, "to eat," the aorist of which is used in v. 53 (φάγητε). It is the German *knabbern*, audible eating, *manducare* or *mandere*. The two present

participles are qualitative and merely characterize the person, one article combining the two. We may read ὁ τρώγων καὶ πίνων like ὁ πιστεύων with regard to a quality conveyed by continuous action: eating and drinking and going on in these actions; or like ὁ καταβαίνων in v. 33 and 50 with regard to a quality impressed by the single act of eating and drinking once only, this one act producing a permanent character (compare with v. 33 and 50; the aorist for the same act in v. 41 and 51; and the perfect in v. 38 and 42.)

It is in vain to argue against what is so evident, that the present statement is only another form of v. 47 (compare v. 40), "He that believes has life eternal." The gospel knows of no way except believing by which I may "have life eternal." Some recent commentators are led astray by a misconception of faith, which they conceive as an act of man's own free will, something that God requires of us, "a moral obligation," "an ethical deed." This leads them to conclude that eating the flesh and drinking the blood of Jesus cannot denote faith, for so to eat and to drink is to receive something not to render something ourselves. But the essence of faith is exactly this, that we receive from Jesus, that we abandon all else and let him give himself to us, his blood-bought merits, his flesh and his blood sacrificed for us. The ancient saying is true: *manducatio est credere*. No truer and richer definition of faith can be given than this: faith = to eat Christ's flesh and to drink Christ's blood. It is idle to charge that "no sensible man would entertain the thought" that believing can be an eating and a drinking. Like this discourse on the Bread of Life is the word of Jesus in Matt. 5:6, "Blessed are they which do hunger and thirst after righteousness; for they shall be filled"; also John 7:37, 38, "If any man thirst, let him come unto me

and drink. He that *believeth* on me," etc.; also John
4:10, etc. If the point of comparison is asked for,
it is simply that eating and drinking, like believing,
is a receiving of the most intimate and vital kind.
As eating and drinking receive food to be assimilated
in the body, so believing receives Christ with the
atonement made through his sacrificial flesh and blood.
But the figure is less than the reality, for bodily eating
only sustains life already present while spiritual eating or believing expels death, bestows life, and sustains that life forever.

For the second time Jesus pointedly parallels his
flesh and his blood as sacrificial gifts and even continues this parallel in the next two verses. How his
death is connoted by the term "flesh" or σάρξ appears
in I Pet. 3:18, "being put to death in the flesh";
in Eph. 2:15, "having abolished in his flesh the
enmity"; in Col. 1:22, "in the body of his flesh through
death"; and in Heb. 10:20, "through the veil, that is
to say, his flesh." To these add the following concerning the blood, which point even more directly to
the death, and this a sacrificial one: Lev. 17:11, "For
the life of the flesh is in the blood: and I have given
it to you upon the altar to make an atonement
for your souls: for it is the blood that maketh an
atonement for the soul."   Heb. 9:22, "Almost all
things are by the law purged with blood; and without shedding of blood is no remission." I Pet. 1:18,
Ye were redeemed "with the precious blood of Christ,
as of a Lamb without blemish and without spot."
Acts 20:28, "the church of God, which he hath pur-
chased with his own blood." Add Heb. 9:14;
Eph. 1:7; Rev. 5:9. This more than answers the
claim that flesh and blood are here used only
for the *Leiblichkeit* of Jesus as in Matt. 16:17;
Gal. 1:16; I Cor. 15:50, without reference to Jesus'
death.

In order to make fully clear what kind of "life" this "eating and drinking" convey and what it means "to have life eternal," Jesus repeats his promise from v. 40, "and I (emphatic ἐγώ, I myself) will resurrect him at the last day"; compare the explanation in v. 39 and 40. This "life" or ζωή not only passes unharmed through temporal death, it also assures the body that is stricken by this death of a blessed resurrection at the last day of time. "To have life eternal" means the restoration even of the body at the last day in the resurrection of the blessed. This resurrection was a well-known article of the Jewish faith, 11:24. What the Jews did not know is that the life which comes to us by faith in Christ's death alone guarantees the blessed resurrection to us. In order to be raised up in glory at the last day we must eat the flesh and drink the blood of Jesus, i. e., partake of the Bread of Life, believe. Note especially the ἐγώ in this mighty promise. It is the answer to the derogatory οὗτος in v. 52. He indeed, who is able to say, "I myself will resurrect him," is able also to give us his flesh to eat so that we may have life even as he declares. Will not these Jews finally see with whom they are dealing?

55) With γάρ Jesus explains why the eating of his flesh and the drinking of his blood bestow life eternal and include the resurrection of the blessed. **For my flesh is real food, and my blood is real drink.** Both are ἀληθής, deserving that epithet in the fullest sense of the word, a βρῶσις or food that is eaten and will then do exactly what Jesus says, a πόσις or drink that is drunk and will then do exactly what he declares. Other meat and drink was offered in Old Testament times (for instance that mentioned in I Cor. 10:3, 4), and men have always had earthly food and drink. None of these deserves the predicate "real." The

sacred meat and drink of the old covenant could only typify and promise the "real" food that was to come, and all other meat and drink is but for a day and has in it no abiding vitality (v. 26, 27). The flesh and the blood of Jesus alone are able to bestow "life eternal" and the resurrection unto glory.

The word ἀληθής, "real" or "true," cannot be used to support the view that Jesus is here speaking of the Lord's Supper (some versions have the adverb ἀληθῶς, "really," "truly," which changes the thought only slightly). For here Jesus answers the Jewish objection that his flesh cannot possibly be the Bread of Life or be given to us to eat. To men of this mind Jesus asserts that his flesh and his blood are real food and drink which will do what he says; not an imaginary, or worse, a false and deceptive food and drink.

56)   The previous explanations answer the question as to how Jesus can give his flesh to us to eat by pointing to himself as the Son of man, by placing his blood beside his flesh, and by emphasizing that these are real food and drink. The answer thus far deals with the gift itself. When we understand the gift properly we shall no longer doubt or deny that it can be given. But the gift is to be received. The Jewish unbelief denied not only that Jesus could give his flesh but also that they, the Jews, could receive or eat his flesh. "How can this one give *us his flesh to eat!*" So complete is Jesus' reply that he fully covers also this vital point. **He that eats my flesh and drinks my blood remains in me, and I in him.** Compare the allegory of the Vine and the Branches, 15:1, etc.   To eat and to drink means to be spiritually joined to Jesus, the Son of man. Our souls embrace him and his sacrificial death in faith and trust, and he embraces us as now drawn to him (v. 44) and given to him (v. 37 and 39). That is why Jesus

once more speaks of "my flesh" and "my blood," his
sacrificial death, and of our eating and drinking,
which denote the reception of this death and sacrifice
by faith. By this gift from him and its reception in
us he and we are joined inwardly: ἐν ἐμοί . . . ἐν
αὐτῷ. As long as we remain apart from Jesus and inwardly separated from him we are in spiritual death;
the moment we are inwardly joined to him we are
freed from this death and have life eternal.

This effect of faith is usually termed the *unio
mystica*, or mystical union of the believer with Christ.
It is pictured as an indwelling (μένει) by means of the
figures of a house, a household, a temple, the marriage
relation, a body and its members, a garment, etc., in a
great variety of passages, the fundamental form of
which is Jesus in us, we in him. Both expressions
"in us" and "in him" designate our benefit and ours
alone; both denote our salvation. When it is said that
he abides in us, he is our life, light, joy, pearl of great
price, peace, crown. "He in me, and I in him" =
1) Jesus the life element in which we life and move
and have our being spiritually; 2) Jesus the life
center, preserving, molding the spiritual life within
us. A false mutuality and reciprocity are introduced
when Jesus is made the beneficiary with us, when it
is assumed that he cannot exist as the head without
us as the members, or that, when he makes us his
body, we in turn make him the head. For this entire
discourse a caution is in place, namely to curb the
imagination lest it run into a spurious and an over-
done spirituality and seek unknown depths which
prove mazes of error.

57) Eating and drinking (believing) join to Jesus
and thus give us life. Just how this effect is brought
about is also clearly explained, and in this part of
the explanation the climax of the entire discourse is
reached. **Even as the living Father did send me,**

I myself also live because of the Father; and he that eats me, he also shall live because of me.
While this explains all the previous statements on the believer's having live eternal even as the pivotal terms are "living," "live," and "shall live," this declaration summarizes all that precedes. Once more it reveals who Jesus really is, how we can thus be joined to him, and how as a result we can have life forever.

The life we receive through faith is traced back to this ultimate source, "the living Father," who as such has life in the absolute sense, as an essential attribute, whose life is not derived from another, from whom all other life is derived. When Jesus says that the living Father "did send me," by that weighty participle "living" he describes his mission as being one that is intended to convey life to us who had lost it through Adam's sin. As the one thus sent to bestow life Jesus is "the Bread of Life."

The second point in this explanation is: "I myself also live because of the Father." The emphatic ἐγώ = "I," who was thus sent to be the Mediator of life to men, Jesus, as he stood there in human flesh before his hearers; compare "the Son of man" in v. 53. "Even as . . . also" combines the living Father and Jesus who "lives" in a special manner. For καθώς is to be construed with the first καί (κἀγώ) not with the second (καὶ ὁ τρώγων). Our versions and many commentators translate the second καί "so," which is not correct and would require οὕτως. The thought expressed by this translation is also incorrect; for the similarity expressed by καθώς is one that exists only between the Father and Jesus, not one that obtains between the Father and us. We can never "live" καθώς, in the same manner as the Father. This is true only of Jesus, as 5:26 has made plain with ὥσπερ . . . οὕτως.

Here Jesus is speaking as the Son of man (v. 53), with reference to his human nature. He is meeting the objection of the Jews who see in him a mere man (v. 42), who, therefore, could neither give them his flesh to eat, nor impart to them life eternal. To these objectors he declares that as the one sent by the living Father, standing thus before them incarnate in his human nature, he "too lives," even as the living Father sent him to convey life to us. In 5:26 he says that the Father, who has life in himself, "did give" him to have life in himself also, i. e., in his human nature, that nature which he uses as the medium for bestowing life upon us ("my flesh," "my blood," "to eat and to drink"). The same thought is here expressed by the phrase διὰ τὸν πατέρα, "because of the Father," his Sender. This phrase states the reason or the ground for his having life even as his Sender has life. If only his divine nature and not his human nature had this life, he could not convey life to us by means of his sacrificial flesh and his sacrificial blood, which belong to his human nature. To make his flesh and his blood the means for bestowing life on us, life had to be in them, just as life is in the divine nature of Jesus and in the living Father who sent him. In the divine nature of the Father and the Son life dwells as an essential and absolute attribute irrespective of us; in the human nature of Jesus this same life dwells as a gift (5:26) by reason of the Father who sent Jesus (διὰ τὸν πατέρα) with respect to us, in order that through his flesh and his blood and his sacrifice on the cross life eternal might be imparted to us.

"And he that eats me," me, who lives because of the Father, me, whom the Father made the source of life for men by sending me on the mission that culminates in the sacrifice on the cross ("my flesh," "my blood"), "he, too, shall live because of me." It is true that Jesus abbreviates when he says "he that eats *me*"; for to eat *him* means to eat his flesh and to drink his blood by accepting his sacrifice in faith. This pronoun "me," however, includes much more than the flesh and the blood of Jesus. In the first place it reverts to the pronoun "me" in the previous statement: "the living Father did send *me*," and to the two pronouns in v. 56: "he remains in *me*, and *I* in him." Thus "me" denotes the entire person of Jesus with both of his natures. We are joined by faith to the entire person of our Mediator Jesus. Yet this union with him takes place only through his human nature or the reception of his flesh and of his blood. These are the one door by which he in his entire person comes to us, and we to him.

The emphatic repetition of the subject in κἀκεῖνος, "*he* also," has the force of "he alone and no other" shall "also live." The future tense "shall live" is not in contradiction to the present tenses "has, have life eternal, remains in me" (v. 47, 53, 54, 56), but like the future tense in v. 51, relative to the moment of eating; "shall live" the moment he eats. The final phrase, shall live "because of me" receives special force since it parallels the phrase "because of the Father." The former, like the latter, states the ground or reason for our living. This is not the mere act of our eating; it is the person to whom we are joined by this eating. The living Father's life reaches down to us through his Son, but through his Son as fitted out with flesh and with blood, by these and by these alone being enabled to make contact with us dead sinners. When this contact is made, the entire Son with his life is ours, "in us," and so we live "because of him," by reason of having no less than him. While the two διά phrases are parallel, this parallel must not be pressed. This is done by those who translate the second καί "so"; for they make us live because of

Jesus, just as Jesus lives because of the Father. Jesus
shuts this out by emphatically stating, "he that eats
me he also (he alone) shall live." Our living is conditional on our receiving Jesus; the moment the condition ceases in that moment our life is gone. No
such condition exists for Jesus. He lives as the
Mediator of life for us by virtue of the living Father's
mission. The every essence of the divine life of the
Father is the human nature of Jesus. We live because of him in a different way, not by also receiving
the essential divine attribute of life, but by having
that attribute touch our souls and by this touch
kindling spiritual life in us. His is the divine essence
of life itself, ours is the product, a creation, of that
life, II Cor. 5:17; Gal. 6:5; Eph. 2:10.

58) The concluding statement merely rounds out
the entire discourse by once more contrasting the
transitory effect of the earthly manna and the permanent effect of the Bread that came down out of heaven.
**This is the Bread that did come down out of heaven,
not as the fathers did eat and did die. He that eats
this bread shall live forever.** Jesus means to say:
I have now told you fully about this Bread that actually came down out of heaven (καταβάς as in v. 41 and
51; compare the other tenses in v. 33 and 50, and in
v. 38 and 42) and how it differs from the manna which
left the fathers to die (v. 49). The final thought which
Jesus impresses upon his hearers is the blessed effect
of eating this Bread: it makes him who eats it live forever (the εἰς phrase as in v. 51 and in 14:16). The
discourse thus closes with an implied invitation. Do
these Jews want to live forever? Let them come and
eat of the Bread of Life!

59) **These things he said by way of teaching
in a synagogue in Capernaum.** This remark intends
to separate what follows from the discourse just completed. We must combine "teaching in a synagogue,"

and not "he said in a synagogue." Note that "synagogue" is without the article. John means to tell us that this discourse was spoken by way of public synagogue teaching before all who had gathered there. What follows was spoken elsewhere and thus somewhat later and only to those who had begun to be Jesus' disciples. On the point that this teaching of Jesus in a synagogue does not imply that the day was necessarily a Sabbath see v. 21. The final phrase "in Capernaum" does not intend to repeat what we gather already from v. 24, for this would be quite unnecessary. Placed at the end, the phrase is made emphatic. John means to convey to us that Capernaum repeats what Jerusalem (5:1, 2) began, namely unbelief and opposition to Jesus. Chapter six is the counterpart to chapter five.

We must now answer the question whether this discourse deals only with the spiritual eating of faith or with the oral sacramental eating in the Lord's Supper. We reply, only with the former. The eating of which Jesus speaks throughout (note for instance v. 53) is absolutely necessary for salvation. Yet all the saints of the old covenant were saved without the Lord's Supper, so was the malefactor on the cross, so are all babes and children in the new covenant. This fact alone is decisive. It has never been answered by those who maintain the contrary concerning John 6. The old principle holds true: only the *contemptus,* never the *defectus* of the Supper condemns. — Secondly, the eating of which Jesus here speaks is always and without exception salutary (see for instance v. 54). It is impossible to affirm this of the oral eating in the Sacrament. — Finally, it is inconceivable that Jesus should urge upon these unbelieving (v. 36) Galileans a sacrament not yet instituted and urge upon them the sacramental eating of which no one could know until the institution had taken place.

It is in vain to point to Nicodemus upon whom Jesus urged baptism; for the Baptist baptized thousands, Nicodemus knew of this sacrament, and Jesus explains its effects to him.

Recognizing the force of these facts, some seek a compromise, admitting that primarily this discourse does not deal with the Lord's Supper, yet maintaining that secondarily or indirectly it does. They claim that Jesus so expressed himself that his words find their ultimate and most complete fulness in the Lord's Supper. These are divided among themselves as to the way in which they suppose that Jesus here refers to the Sacrament. Some hold that the words of Jesus constitute only a preparatory prophecy of the Supper; others, that the idea of the Supper is included, the feeding of the 5,000 being "a significant prefigurement" of the Supper; still others, that the Supper is included by way of inference. All these generally make much of the fact that John's Gospel reports neither the institution of Baptism after the resurrection of Jesus nor the institution of the Supper; and they assume that John reported the conversation with Nicodemus in lieu of the former, and the discourse on the Bread of Life in lieu of the latter. The general answer to these views is the old hermeneutical rule of Hilary: the true reader of the Scriptures is he who expects the passages of Holy Writ themselves to furnish their meaning, who carries nothing into them, who takes out only what they bring, and is careful not to make the Scriptures say what he thinks they ought to say. The specific answer to these views is, that they confuse the spiritual eating by faith, which is to take place equally with regard to the three means of grace (Baptism, the Word read, taught, and preached, and the Lord's Supper) with the oral eating peculiar to the Supper, which invariably takes place, All ought to eat and to drink by faith when they are baptized, when they hear and read the Word, when they receive the Lord's Supper; but all do not so eat and drink by faith, many use these means of grace so as not to receive life eternal through them. But no one ever partook of the Lord's Supper who did not eat and drink orally, with his mouth, the consecrated bread and wine, and in, with, and under this bread and wine the body and the blood of Christ conveyed to him by the earthly elements. To eat and to drink by faith is an inward spiritual act that is always salutary; to eat and to drink the elements of the Supper orally is an outward act which sometimes is not salutary but unto judgment, I Cor. 11:28, 29.

The Result of the Discourse on the Bread of Life, 6:60-71. — Jesus left the synagogue, and most of "the Jews" scattered. Only those who counted themselves among his "disciples" remained with him as he walked away. We now learn what occurred in the case of these. **Many, therefore, of his disciples after hearing (this) said, Stiff is this statement. Who is able to listen to him?** The "disciples" were Galileans who had begun to follow Jesus, and their number was considerable. A severe sifting now takes place among them. Many of them spoke as here indicated, yet not all. Comparing v. 66, we see that a number remained true, which explains how eventually five hundred brethren assembled to meet the risen Savior in Galilee, I Cor. 15:6. The aorist particle ἀκούσαντες, "having heard," or "after hearing," means to say that after the services in the synagogue were over, the more these disciples thought of what they had heard Jesus say, the more their objection grew. The verb εἶπον means that they voiced their thoughts to themselves.

These disciples find what Jesus says σκληρός, "stiff," dried out and hard, like a twig that has become brittle.

The word does not here mean dark and difficult to understand but objectionable, offensive, impossible to accept and to believe. By οὗτος ὁ λόγος we must understand the entire discourse on the Bread of Life, even also as it is a closely knit unit. The objection that began in v. 30, 31, that came out in the murmuring in v. 41 and in the open contention in v. 52, here continues. Some think that it refers especially to the idea of the bloody death in the way in which Jesus spoke of his flesh and his blood; others, denying that Jesus had such a death in mind, think of the carnal hopes and expectations of these disciples, which find no support in the words of Jesus; still others suppose that these disciples think only of a gross and carnal eating of the flesh of Jesus and of a similar drinking of his blood. Those, finally, who think that Jesus spoke only of his *Leiblichkeit* or *Menschlichkeit* in general imagine that the objection lies in the idea of eating and drinking the human nature of one whom these disciples saw standing before their eyes like any other man. These attempts reflect the various interpretations which the different commentators have applied to the cardinal points in the discourse itself, some of them being decidedly wide of the mark. These disciples objected to the entire discourse: that Jesus should call himself the Bread of Life, descended out of heaven, whose flesh they must eat and whose blood they must drink as the real food, full of life, and thus giving them life eternal and the resurrection of blessedness. The whole of it these disciples find σκληρός, intolerable. Hence they exclaim, "Who is able to listen to him?" If αὐτοῦ is to refer to λόγος, we should expect the accusative αὐτόν. Yet the old rule: the genitive to indicate the person heard and the accusative the thing heard, is not strictly observed. These disciples, however, turn away from

Jesus (v. 66) and refuse to hear him any longer,
so we translate, "Who can hear him?" and not,
"hear it?"

61)   Jesus does not need to be told what is passing
through the minds of these disciples. To some extent
the way in which Jesus saw them acting and talking
together betrayed to him what was wrong. But by
his higher powers Jesus perceives all that is in the
hearts of these disciples (3:24, 25). Like his omnipotence in the miracles, so he uses his omniscience
again and again in dealing with men to the extent
that this was necessary in his mission. **Now when
Jesus knew in himself that his disciples were murmuring concerning this, he said to them, Does this
entrap you?** The phrase ἐν αὐτῷ means: in his own
mind, R. 587. And "concerning this" refers to the
matter about which these disciples were complaining,
it is thus identical with "this" in the second question.
What is meant does not need to be specified, since
those concerned know. The verb σκανδαλίζειν means
to serve as a σκάνδαλον, the crooked stick to which the
bait is fixed in a trap and by which the trap is sprung;
thus, literally, "Does this entrap you?" The idea
is: "Does this prove fatal to you?" A trap that is
sprung kills its victim. This point is lost in the translations of our versions, "cause you to stumble" (R.
V.), "offend you" (A. V.), neither of which need be
fatal. On stumbling, even on falling, one may arise
again; so also one may be offended and get over it.
But a dead-fall trap kills.

62)   With a second question Jesus points these
murmuring disciples to the great key which unlocks
the difficulty that was entrapping and holding them
in unbelief. It is the same key he had offered his
hearers from the start when in v. 27 and then again
in v. 53 he had called himself "the Son of man," as
now also he again does, adding in v. 40 "the Son";

and when he said of the Bread that it comes down
out of heaven (v. 33 and 50), that it came down
out of heaven (v. 51 and 41), and that he himself
who is this Bread "has come down from heaven"
(v. 38), which the Jews repeat, changing only the
preposition. **If, then, you shall behold the Son of
man going up where he was before** — ? The
protasis stands alone, naturally with a rising inflection like a second question, leaving the apodosis to
be supplied by the hearers, "what then? say it yourselves!" This is a case of aposiopesis, which differs
from ellipsis or mere abbreviations by the passion or
feeling put into the words. "One can almost see
the gesture and the flash of the eye in aposiopesis,"
R. 1203.

By calling himself "the Son of man" for the third
time and by now adding his ascent to heaven to the
descent out of heaven, which he has mentioned
repeatedly, he once more in the plainest way tells these
disciples who he actually is. The key to the entire
discourse on the Bread of Life is Jesus, the Father's
Son (v. 40), sent out of heaven on his saving mission and thus now incarnate, the Son of man (see
1:51), standing as man before these disciples. The
mention of his ascent only completes the picture of
himself which he wants these disciples to have; for he
descended out of heaven only on his mission, and thus
evidently will again ascend when that mission is performed. The participle ἀναβαίνων is only the counterpart to καταβαίνων (v. 33 and 50) and καταβάς (v. 41
and 51). They are even connected by the clause,
"where he was before," which Jesus uses instead of
"to heaven." To the very place from which he
descended he will again ascend. Jesus thus tells these
disciples: "You are right, indeed, if I were only a
man like other men, no matter how great a man, I
could not be the Bread of Life out of heaven, could

not give you my flesh nor my blood, nor could you eat
that flesh and drink that blood, and, of course, you
could not thus have life eternal, nor could I resurrect
you at the last day; but I am the God-man, and thus
all that I say is true."

We thus see that Jesus is not increasing the offense
for his hearers but making the fullest effort to remove
the offense they had taken. Nor is he raising a new
point, which may cause new offense, but is stating the
key point over again and more clearly. The implication is the same as it was in the entire discourse:
How can unbelief find justifiable room when men are
shown who Jesus really is? "When you shall see the
Son of man ascending where he was before — ?" what
then? how then can you maintain unbelief? We need
not enter the debate regarding what "ascending" here
means. It certainly refers to the Ascension not merely the visible rising of Jesus' human form from the
earth until a cloud withdrew it from sight (which is
only the first part) but, as the addition "where he was
before" shows, combined with the visible also the
invisible part when beyond the cloud the earthly form
of Jesus was transferred in a timeless instant to the
glory of heaven. It is useless to make this ascending
refer to the "dying," or to bring in the general offense
always connected with the cross. Likewise, instead
of the ascent hindering faith in that it removes the
body of Jesus to heaven, it constituted a strong help
to faith by that very removal; for, like all the previous
references to Jesus as the God-man, this ascension of
his body to heaven leaves us most decidedly with the
one sacrificial act which makes his flesh "real food"
and his blood "real drink" (v. 55) such as can be
received spiritually by faith alone and thus shuts out
every carnal mode of reception.

The condition ἐάν with the subjunctive is one of
expectancy; hence we should translate, "if you shall

see" (A. V.) and not "if you should see" (R. V.). The
point to be observed in all conditional statements is
that they present to us only the speaker's or the writer's thought about the matter, how he wants us to look
at it, and not the actuality as it is or as it will be (if
it is future). So here. Jesus knows that he will, indeed, ascend. He might say so directly. But that
would be like a challenge to these already unbelieving
disciples, provoking their outright denial. By using
the condition of expectancy Jesus obviates such a
clash. He secures their consideration of his ascension
as a solution of their difficulty, as again revealing the
divine nature of his person. We need not disturb ourselves about the verb "shall see" addressed to these
disciples. Even the Eleven saw only Jesus' departure
from the earth and not his entrance into heaven. This
entrance the Eleven and all believers "see" in the same
way, by faith in the Word and by his rule at the right
hand of his Father in his church and over all the earth.
The verb θεωρέω includes the seeing with the mind and
the soul not only that with the physical eye.

63) As the statement on the ascension of Jesus
is formulated so as to call out faith, so also are the
next two statements: **The spirit is that which
makes alive; the flesh profits nothing at all. The
utterances which I have spoken to you, spirit
they are, and life they are.** Verse 62 deals with
the source, the divine person of Jesus; v. 63 deals with
the effect, the life bestowed by this divine person.
These two, the person as the source, the life as the
effect, form the framework of the entire discourse.
This is true even of the concentrated statement, "I
(person, *source*) am the Bread of Life (life eternal,
effect)." The discourse answers the question as to
how we dead sinners may obtain life eternal (the
effect). It answers: through the God-man alone via
his flesh and his blood (the source). Hence, like the

The Interpretation of John

discourse itself, any added explanations seek solely
to make plain these two: the source and the effect.
Thus the way to faith is opened, and all real cause for
doubt and unbelief is removed.

When this object of v. 62 and 63 is clear, we see
that the latter removes all false conception regarding
the life (the effect) as wrought by the person (the
source) through the medium of his flesh (including,
of course, his blood, here left unnamed only for the
sake of brevity). The proposition Jesus presents is
general, an axiom that needs no proof: the spirit not
the flesh makes alive. Leave out the spirit, and all
the flesh in the world, including that of Jesus, could
not kindle a single spark of life; the spirit alone
quickens and makes alive. This holds true even for
physical life (Gen. 2:7) and certainly also for spiritual and eternal life (Eph. 2:5). A flood of light
thus illumines the discourse. When Jesus spoke so
pointedly about his flesh and his blood bestowing life
eternal on all who eat and drink, how could anyone
dream that he meant flesh only as flesh and blood only
as blood? Did not Jesus constantly say *"my* flesh,"
"my blood," and add, "he that eats *me*," and name
himself as "the Son" (v. 40), and "the Son of man"
(v. 27 and 53, God's Son sent by the Father and
thus in human flesh)? Did he not tell these disciples
that his flesh is "the *living* Bread" (v. 51) and thus
"the *real* food" (v. 55), and that eating his flesh and
drinking his blood make us abide in *him,* and *him*
in us (v. 56)? Let the other Jews miss all this, of
these Jews who counted themselves disciples of Jesus
he certainly had a right to expect that they would
understand what he said so clearly, that *his* flesh and
his blood, sacrificed for us, unite us with *him* and the
divine spirit of life that dwells in him — thus and
thus alone giving us life eternal.

This abolishes the old error that when Jesus says, "the flesh profits nothing at all," he includes also his own flesh. Doing this, Jesus would deny every statement concerning his flesh made in his previous discourse and would assert that when he says "flesh" he means the very opposite, namely "spirit," thus turning his entire discourse into nonsense. The flesh of Jesus, given into death for us and lying in the tomb until the third day, was quickened again (I Pet. 3:18) and became the means by which Jesus himself with his spirit enters our souls and quickens us to spiritual life. The notion that "spirit" here means the true spiritual sense of the words of Jesus, and that "flesh" here means the carnal or Capernaitic sense held by the Jews, introduces figures of speech where no figures are indicated. As to the word "spirit" we must say that, as the opposite of "flesh," it cannot denote the Holy Spirit. When the general principle here enunciated by Jesus is applied to him, "spirit" means Jesus' own spirit and is identical with his person and his being. Those who press the figure of the Bread in the discourse to refer only to food for nourishment to sustain life already present overagainst the bestowal of life, are answered by τὸ ζωοποιοῦν, "that which quickens," which makes alive (see the remarks on v. 48).

When Jesus adds, "The utterances which I have spoken to you, spirit they are, and life they are," he continues his tone of rebuke to those disciples. Just as they should long have known that the flesh by itself never quickens, so they should have known the nature of every utterance that falls from Jesus' lips. The pronoun ἐγώ is emphatic: because *I* make these utterances they are what I say. The better reading is the perfect, I "have spoken," although the present, I "speak," does not alter the sense, for Jesus refers to all his utterances which include his recent discourse on the Bread of Life.

Both τὰ ῥήματα and the corresponding verb λελάληκα denote the vehicles which Jesus employs for communicating with his disciples, namely the terms and expressions he chooses for the speech that falls from his lips; λόγος and λέγω would refer more to the thought. Jesus thus refers to such terms as "bread," "flesh," "blood," "to eat his flesh," "to drink his blood," and, in fact, to every form of expression employed in the recent discourse and at other times. His disciples should surely by this time know that not one of these expressions coming from *his* lips is hasty, ill-considered, extravagant, or faulty in any way. On the contrary, the vehicles Jesus employs are perfect, and that in the highest possible sense: "spirit they are, and life they are." Note how the two predicates are kept apart, so that each stands out by itself. The sense is made trivial by those who interpret: My words are of a spiritual kind and the expression of my spiritual life. We must connect "spirit" and "life" with the preceding statement, "The spirit is that which makes alive." Thus every term and expression that falls from Jesus' lips is full of his own divine spirit and, therefore, full also of his own divine life and thus reaches out to us in order to enter our souls. This, however, cannot mean that now suddenly Jesus is substituting these ῥήματα for his flesh and his blood as conveyors of life to us, which would simply cancel his entire previous discourse. Nor can he place his "utterances" beside his flesh and his blood as a second means for bestowing life on us, which would again contradict that discourse (see its summary in v. 53). Cast aside all such dual notions. The ῥήματα and the realities are one; we have neither without the other; the identical spirit and life are in both. Take the ῥῆμα or vocable "the Son" in v. 40 — it is vacuous without the actual Son. Take the actual Son — he remains nothing to us until this word comes to us and tells us that he is "the Son."

64) What Jesus says about his ῥήματα being spirit and being life connects not only with the fact that the spirit is the quickening power but also with the other and very sad fact: **But there are some of you that do not believe,** which John elucidates (γάρ) by adding: **For Jesus knew from the beginning who they were that did not believe and who he was that would betray him.** The fault does not lie with the expressions which Jesus uses, every one of which is so filled with spirit and with life that it can be said to be spirit and to be life. No mind can suggest more adequate expressions for transmitting the spirit and the life to the hearers of Jesus. The fault lies with some of these disciples and hearers, who, indeed, hear these expressions but refuse to accept what they are and contain, namely the blessed realities, the spirit and the life. They understand Jesus well enough; they see what his ῥήματα bring; but this is what they do not want and will not have. They seek earth, and when heaven is urged upon them, they turn away in disappointment; in fact, the more they are made to see heaven in Jesus, the more they determine not to have it.

When Jesus here charges these disciples with unbelief, John feels compelled, because of what Jesus presently adds concerning Judas in v. 70, to inform us that Jesus became aware of this unbelief, not by the evidence it furnished of its presence by murmuring and raising objections, but that he knew of it "from the beginning"; and in this knowledge of Jesus John includes also the future traitorous act of Judas. The phrase ἐξ ἀρχῆς is definite as such, without the article, R. 792; but what point of time is referred to? John's statement is general and not restricted to the unbe-

514 The Interpretation of John

lief of these Galilean disciples alone. The Greek, unlike the English, does not change the tenses after
the main verb "Jesus knew" but retains the tenses
that indicate the moment when this knowledge first
began: "who they *are* that *do* not believe, and who
he *is* that *shall betray* him" (English: "who they *were*
that *did* not believe, and who he *was* that *would be-*
tray him"). We see that this is the same supernatural
knowledge, used by Jesus as needed in his mission, as
that with which John acquaints us in 1:42, etc., and
in 2:24, 25. We are thus led to say that Jesus knew
what course any man's heart would take from the first
moment when Jesus came into contact with that man.
The effort to make "from the beginning" mean only
from the moment when unbelief actually begins in
one attached to Jesus, is due to the desire to escape
what some consider a grave moral difficulty. They
usually exemplify by a reference to Judas: If Jesus
knew when he first met Judas that Judas would be
his betrayer, how could Jesus, having that knowledge,
nevertheless choose him as one of the apostles? A
moment's thought, however, shows that we fail to
escape this question with its difficulty when we
assume that Jesus did not know at the time he chose
Judas that Judas would betray him but discovered
the secret unbelief at a later time, i. e., not until that
unbelief actually arose in Judas' heart. For then
the question would be cast into a new form: Knowing the unbelief of Judas and to what it would
lead, how could Jesus retain Judas as one of the
apostles?

In the first place, the future participle ὁ παραδώσων
αὐτόν blocks any escape by dating the knowledge of
Jesus only from the moment when unbelief actually
enters. For ὁ παραδώσων αὐτόν refers to a future
definite act: Judas is he who shall betray Jesus. The

articulated future participle is futuristic not volitive,
R. 878, note also B.-D. 356. It states what shall take
place, not what one wills to do. In other words, Jesus
knew that Judas would turn traitor long before Judas
exercised his traitorous volition. How far in advance
Jesus knew this, therefore, makes no difference. Moreover, this exemplification by means of Judas must not
be allowed to mislead us. For the question here raised
is far older than Judas. It begins with Adam and includes a large number of others. How could God
create Adam when God knew that Adam would fall?
or create those of whom he knew that they would be
damned? or receive into the church those of whom he
knew that they would turn out hypocrites and rene-
gades? In fact, how could God create Satan knowing
what Satan would become? As regards Judas: Jesus
chose him *not for the purpose* of betrayal but only
with the knowledge of that betrayal. No act of God's
or of Jesus' shut the door of grace for Judas, their
foreknowledge did certainly not do so. This foreknowledge rested on the act of Judas, not the act of
Judas on the foreknowledge. If the act had been the
reverse, the foreknowledge would have accorded with
the reversal. The human mind cannot penetrate the
profundity of the divine mind in these questions. All
we can say is that Jesus bowed to the Father's will
and did this perfectly also in the grace he vouchsafed
to Judas to the very last. Furthermore, even if Judas
had never existed, the deadly wickedness of sin in
man would have turned in murderous opposition to
Jesus when the holy Son of man came to draw them
to heaven, and a tragedy like that of Calvary would
have been the result. One thing more must be added:
when the wickedness of any man becomes unchange-
ably fixed, God takes it in hand and in his providence
uses it for his own purposes. In the face of Mark

14:21 the intimation that the moment Judas felt the enormity of his crime, this may yet have become his salvation, must be rejected.

65) **And he was saying, On this account I have said to you, that no one is able to come to me except it have been given to him of the Father.** Jesus made no pause or break in his words; "and he was saying," with the descriptive imperfect ἔλεγε, merely informs us that Jesus went on speaking, the tense asking us to dwell on what he says. In v. 44 Jesus had said, "No man can come unto me except the Father which sent me *draw* him"; and in v. 37, "All that the Father *gives* to me shall get to me." To these two statements Jesus again refers, only changing the active form into the passive, "have been given to him." To come to Jesus is to believe in Jesus; and the ability to come is never without the coming. In our abstract thinking we must never separate the two and imagine that the Father grants the ability and that we then may decide whether we will use this ability or leave it unused.

The best commentary on this giving and this drawing is furnished in *Concordia Triglotta* 1087, etc.: "The Father will not do this without means, but has ordained for this purpose his Word and Sacraments as ordinary means and instruments; and it is the will neither of the Father nor of the Son that a man should not hear or should despise the preaching of his Word and wait for the drawing of the Father without the Word and Sacraments. For the Father draws, indeed, by the power of his Holy Ghost, according to his usual order, by the hearing of his holy, divine Word, as with a net, by which the elect are plucked from the jaws of the devil. Every poor sinner should therefore repair thereto, hear it attentively, and not doubt the drawing of the Father. For the Holy Ghost will be with his Word in his power and work by it; and that is the drawing of the Father. — But the reason why not all who hear it believe, and some are therefore condemned the more deeply, is not because God had begrudged them their salvation; but it is their own fault, as they have heard the Word in such a manner as not to learn (v. 45) but only to despise, blaspheme, and disgrace it, and have resisted the Holy Ghost, who through the Word wished to work in them."

Where the ability to come and the coming are not given, this is not due to the will or the effort of the Giver but to the contrary, hostile will and obdurate, resisting effort of him who should be the recipient, Matt. 23:37, "ye would not." "On this account," διὰ τοῦτο, refers back to the statement, "But there are some of you that do not believe." Faith and coming to Jesus is not theirs and is not given to them because in their persistent preference of unbelief they are determined not to receive it. Their lack of faith is not excused by any inactivity on the Father's part, for this does not exist; their non-faith is blamed onto them because they nullify the Father's activity of giving and drawing. "Judas would have liked nothing better than for Jesus to have allowed himself actually to be made a king by the Jews; that would have been a Messiah for his avarice, for his earthly-mindedness." Besser.

66) **In consequence many of his disciples went back and were no longer walking with him.** The phrase ἐκ τούτου is not temporal, although some think it is; for τούτου has no antecedent of time. Likewise, we cannot accept the view that "this" refers only to the hard statement of the discourse in the synagogue and not to the words spoken in v. 61-65. These disciples did not leave Jesus as they were departing from the synagogue, they left after Jesus once more spoke with them. The view that only the discourse in the

synagogue furnished them their reason for leaving, and that what Jesus said afterward furnished no such reason, misconceives the latter statements of Jesus. By charging these disciples with not believing (v. 64) and not receiving the Father's gift ·Jesus intimates that he does not consider them his disciples. "This" caused the break. "Due to this" they dropped Jesus. Jesus labors faithfully, patiently, and long, but · eventually calls for a decision. This withdrawal from Jesus should have included Judas, but, covering his inward defection with hypocrisy, he remained one of the Twelve.

The aorist "they went away" merely states the fact in a summary way. Inward separation ends in outward separation. But these are not losses, because, as John indicates in his remark in v. 64, Jesus never counted the presence of such disciples as gains. We need not assume that all of the "many" left in a body but rather that they dropped away in successive groups. When John says, "they were no longer walking with him," he intimates that hitherto they had done this, all of them following Jesus about from place to place, always returning to him, when for a little while it had been necessary for them to leave. This apparently promising custom now ceased. The phrase εἰς τὰ ὀπίσω, literally "to the things behind," means that they went away from the things Jesus was offering them, back to the things that had occupied them before, their common everyday affairs. These transient, empty affairs still seem to be the real values of life to many.

67) When these withdrawals had thinned the ranks of Jesus' followers and were about complete, which must have taken place some days after the discourse in Capernaum, Jesus spoke also to the Twelve. John assumes that his readers know how Jesus had chosen them in order to train them as his special mes-

sengers or apostles. **Jesus, therefore, said to the Twelve, You, too, surely will not also be quietly leaving?** The connective οὖν marks this question as the outcome of the withdrawal of so many others. The interrogative particle μή implies that Jesus expects a negative answer. This he actually received. Yet we must note that the shades of expectation suggested by μή vary greatly according to the emotion involved: protest, indignation, scorn, excitement, sympathy, etc., R. 917 and 1175. Here the feeling of assurance prevails. We may note that θέλετε is used as an auxiliary and, for one thing, gives the question a polite form. To what extent this verb refers to the will and volition of the Twelve may be questioned as it is used also for indicating only the future. Thus the question may be, "Are you, too, about to leave," or, "Do you, too, intend to leave?" To be sure, remaining with Jesus is without compulsion, entirely voluntary. Note, however, the difference between ἀπῆλθον and ὑπάγειν, the former denoting open withdrawal ἀπό or from Jesus, the aorist stating the past fact, the latter denoting secret or quiet slipping away, ὑπό, under cover, perhaps of some excuse, the present tense describing the proceeding. Jesus does not ask this question on his own account as though seeking comfort for the loss of the many in the faithfulness of the Twelve; but for the sake of the Twelve themselves, whom the defection of so many is to help to establish the more in faith and in the true and intelligent convictions of faith. Since this is the purpose of the question, we must drop ideas such as that Jesus here "sets the door wide open" and says, "if you will, you may depart."

68) **Simon Peter answered him, Lord, to whom shall we go? Utterances of life eternal thou hast; and we on our part have believed and have realized that thou on thy part art the Holy One of God.**

John agrees with the synoptists in picturing Peter as the leader and on notable occasions the spokesman of the Twelve. The critical view that throughout John's Gospel another disciple, one who remains unnamed in the Gospel, (meaning John himself) is put into greatest prominence ahead of Peter, is deprived of its support both in 1:40, etc., where Peter is first introduced, and here where John reports Peter's grand confession for the Twelve as a body. Undoubtedly, John called him only Simon in daily intercourse with him, but when late in life he writes this record for the church, he here adds the name the Lord bestowed upon Simon and writes "Simon Peter"; he does so also in 6:8 and elsewhere where "Simon" alone would suffice.

The question of Jesus, which betrays emotion, evokes deep feeling on Peter's part, which is at once revealed when he has his reply begin with a counter-question, "Lord, to whom shall we go?" Unjustified thoughts are read into this emotional question when the addition is made, "now or ever," for Peter's response refers to the question of Jesus and a definite going away such as that which the Twelve had witnessed in the unbelieving disciples. Peter's question is misunderstood when it is taken to mean that he and others had left the Baptist and had substituted Jesus for him, and that Peter's question contemplates the possibility of again substituting another master in place of Jesus. Peter had *not* left the Baptist in any vital sense but was following the Baptist's own instruction and direction by following Jesus (see 1:35, 36). Those disciples who had forsaken Jesus did not choose another master whom they preferred to follow instead of Jesus, they only disowned Jesus. Thus Peter also continues by stating why he and the Twelve cannot possibly follow a like course and also disown Jesus. Those others preferred to shift for themselves, and this, as Peter declares, the Twelve cannot do.

In the succinct statement of the reason why the Twelve cannot leave Jesus as others had left him, "Utterances of life eternal thou hast," there is no σύ as a contrast with πρὸς τίνα. Thus there is not a contrast between Jesus and some other possible master to whom the Twelve would go if they could find such a better master. The emphasis is on the object "utterances of life" which is placed in front of the verb. Since Jesus has *these*, they cannot leave him. Because Jesus has these utterances, the Baptist bade his own disciples to follow Jesus; he himself also followed Jesus as all his attestations show, although by God's arrangement he had his own office and was not to become one of the apostles. When Peter uses ῥήματα he borrows this term from the words of Jesus in v. 63 and uses it in the same sense (see the elucidation above). Of the two predicates: "spirit they are, and life they are" (v. 63), Peter chooses the second, but by no means. as though he were avoiding the first, for the second includes the first; for Jesus himself binds them together when he says that the spirit (agent, cause, source) makes alive (effect). The "utterances" of Jesus are the vital vehicles of language for the divine realities (Bread of Life, my flesh, my blood, etc.) by which "life eternal" is brought to us, that hearing these "utterances" we may appropriate the realities they name and thus have what they convey, namely "life eternal." When Peter says thou "hast" he means that these "utterances" form the treasure which Jesus dispenses to all who come into contact with him and hear him speak.

69) The counterpart is the next statement, "and we on our part have believed and have known that thou on thy part art the Holy One of God." The utter-

ances of Jesus were spurned by those who left Jesus
as being a stiff and objectionable λόγος (combining the
utterances with the realities they express) but they
won the hearts of the Twelve. The emphatic pronoun
ἡμεῖς balances only the equally emphatic following
pronoun σύ: "we on our part" have believed, etc., that
"thou on thy part" art, etc. Of course, what Jesus
has (and bestows) is balanced also by the reception
wrought in the Twelve, but this balance lies in the
thought as such not in any pairing of terms. Yet
"utterances" are fittingly followed by the verbs "believe" and "realize," for they are intended to be received in confidence and trust, with full reliance of
the heart, and in true understanding of just what
they mean, with full realization of the heart as to
what they bestow ("life eternal," v. 68). The perfect tenses reach back into the past, to the moment
when this faith and this realization first began, and
at the same time they reach to the present, in which
both actions continue. Thus Peter confesses that the
Twelve have long believed, etc., (in fact, from 1:42
onward), and all that Jesus has said has only confirmed their faith.

R. 423 is right when he says that the order of the
verbs is just as true here as the opposite order in
17:8. A certain kind and amount of knowledge precedes actual faith and trust and is usually also considered an integral part of it; for no one can possibly
trust a person or a truth of which he does not know.
On the other hand, a certain kind of knowledge always
follows faith and confidence, a knowledge that is possible only as a result of this confidence. This is the
knowledge of actual experience, here the experience
which the Twelve had with Jesus during the two years
and more of their contact with him. This knowledge
is impossible for those who refuse to trust Jesus. The

verb γινώσκειν invariably means "to know," but when it is used regarding spiritual knowledge, its meaning is intensified, and its sense is expressed by "to realize" with a knowledge that truly illuminates and grasps what it has learned.

The assured reading is: "that thou on thy part art the Holy One of God." This designation of Jesus is so exceptional that it is not surprising to find a commoner title in place of it in many texts, and this substitution has some variations; this is especially to be expected since Matt. 16:16; Mark 8:29; and Luke 9:20 (which describe another occasion when Peter confessed for the Twelve) contain more ordinary terms. Thus in the A. V. "that Christ, the Son of the living God" is derived from Matt. 16:16. We need not collect the Old and the New Testament passages in which ἅγιος is applied to other servants of God, for in Peter's confession it is used regarding Jesus in the supreme and the Messianic sense, in which no one save Jesus can be called "the Holy One of God." Jesus himself helps us to interpret this title when in 10:36 he designates himself as the One "whom the Father sanctified and sent into the world." He is "the Holy One of God" as the God-man sent on his saving mission into the world. As such he is ἅγιος, separate unto God. This includes the two thoughts, that Jesus is wholly separate from the world, which is unholy because of sin, yet that he comes from God to rid the world of its unholiness and sin and to separate men in true holiness unto God. The fact that Jesus in his person and his life is also himself sinless and "holy" in this sense is a self-evident but entirely minor thought. The genitive Holy One "of God" is possessive. A study of the adjective ἅγιος in C.-K. 34, etc., yields highly valuable results for all passages

in which this term or any of its derivatives are
employed.

70) Great joy fills the heart of Jesus on hearing
this adequate and earnest confession on the part of
Peter. But this joy is combined with deep pain, for
Jesus knows what Peter could not know, namely that
not all of the Twelve believed in their hearts as he
had confessed. **Jesus answered them,** since Peter
had spoken for all of them, and all had given silent
assent to Peter's words, **Did not I elect you the
Twelve for myself? and of you one is a devil.** The
question with its implied affirmation is rhetorical and
expresses the feeling of Jesus. Both pronouns are
emphatic and are made more so in the Greek by being
abutted: "I you" did elect. The middle voice "did
elect for myself" conveys the thought with sufficient
clearness, namely to be my followers in a special
sense, to be trained as my apostles for your great
future work. The apposition "the Twelve" is without
emphasis and yet has its significance. John felt it
deeply when in v. 71 he repeats: "one of the Twelve."
This number is symbolical, dating from the twelve
patriarchs and the twelve tribes of Israel, so often
used with reference to the apostles, and with the constant tragic meaning that Judas was "one of the
Twelve," finally in Rev. 7:4, twelve times twelve
thousand (144,000), 12:1, twelve stars, and 21:12-
22:2, six times in the description of the new Jerusalem.

By his own act (ἐγώ) and for himself (middle
voice) Jesus made this election of "the Twelve." John
is certain that his readers know the account of this
act from the other Gospels. With a simple "and" the
terrible adversative fact is added: "and of you (partitive use of ἐκ) one is a devil." All efforts to modify
διάβολος so that it means only a slanderer, adversary,
enemy, or traitor, break down before the analogy of

Scripture wherever this word is used as a noun. It is stronger and intended to be stronger than "devilish," or "son and child of the devil" (8:44; I John 3:10) ; it is as strong as the term "Satan," which Jesus once applies even to Peter, Matt. 16:23. "Devil" designates the real moral nature of Judas and the mind that had finally developed in him. Those other disciples who did not believe in Jesus left him, and nowhere are such men called devils; but Judas remains, remains even as one of the Twelve, remains and consents to Peter's confession, not with ordinary hypocrisy, but with lying deceit such as Jesus predicates of the very devil himself in 8:44.

So early Judas had completely broken with Jesus. *"Is* a devil" means now, at this time when Jesus says so, not that he already *was* a devil when Jesus chose him. When Judas lost his faith we are not told. Now that he has lost much more, we are told of it. This should suffice as the explanation as to why Jesus here makes this revelation. Usually it is assumed that Jesus means to utter only a pastoral warning to the Twelve not to think themselves safe just because he had elected them as apostles; but this is superficial and cannot be established by αὐτοῖς, namely that Jesus here speaks to all of them. He tells them about this "one" at this early time, so that a year from now they may remember how their Master foreknew all that Judas would do. Secondly, Jesus intends his revelation for Judas personally. This man is to know that Jesus knows him absolutely as just what he is, "a devil." He deceives his fellow-apostles but not the Son. With all his might Jesus strikes a blow at the conscience of Judas by this word "devil." In his dealings with this human devil Jesus omits nothing that may frighten him from his course and turn his heart from Satan to his Savior. So great is grace that it goes on with its blessed efforts even where

The Interpretation of John

foreknowledge infallibly makes certain that it shall fail. This, too, the Eleven are to remember after Jesus has died and has arisen and they go out on their mission.

71) The fact that Jesus secured this effect of his revelation John shows in his closing statement. **Now he was speaking of Judas, the Son of Simon Iscariot; for this one would betray him — one of the Twelve.** John gives us the full name of the traitor: "Judas, (son) of Simon Ish-Kerioth" (man of Kerioth, a town in Judea, Josh. 15:25). Some texts have an accusative instead of the last genitive: "Judas Iscariot, (son) of Simon." The traitor is thus distinguished both from the other Judas among the Twelve and also from the other eleven all of whom were from Galilee. The reflection that he hailed from Judea not from Galilee and thus became the traitor, is rather meaningless. The demonstrative οὗτος fixes our attention upon him in the explanatory remark that he was to become the traitor. The imperfect ἤμελλε with the present infinitive circumscribes the future tense but is able by means of the imperfect tense of the auxiliary to place this future back to the time when Jesus spoke as he did; the delivering Jesus into the hands of his enemies (παραδιδόναι) was future at that time. John usually reports without a show of feeling on his part. This makes the feeling, here expressed in the final apposition "one of the Twelve," the more effective. With this tragic apposition John closes the two chapters (five and six) in which he describes the rise of the Jewish opposition to Jesus, first in Judea, then in Galilee, and points in advance to the fatal deed which precipitated the final tragedy. This unspeakable deed was the act of "one of the Twelve."

CHAPTER VII

IV

Jesus' Attestation in Open Conflict with the Jews, Chapters 7-10

The entire fourth part of John's Gospel deals with the ministry in Jerusalem and includes two Jewish festivals, the Feast of Tabernacles and the Feast of Dedication. Comparing 6:4 and 7:2, we see that the interval between chapters six and seven is a little more than six months, from early April to the second half of October, thus about six months before the final Passover. We may divide this part into ten sections.

I. Jesus Goes to the Feast of Tabernacles, 7:1-13.

II. Jesus' Testimony Stirs the Authorities to Order his Arrest, 7:14-36.

III. Jesus' Testimony Impresses the Officers Sent for his Arrest, 7:37-52.

IV. Jesus Proves his Testimony True and Warns his Opponents, 8:12-30.

V. Jesus' Testimony Culminates in an Effort to Stone him, 8:31-59.

VI. Jesus Attests Himself by Healing a Blind Beggar, 9:1-12.

VII. Jesus' Attestation through the Blind Beggar Nonpluses his Opponents, 9:13-34.

VIII. Jesus' Testimony Concerning Spiritual Sight and Blindness, 9:35-41.

(527)

IX. Jesus' Testimony Concerning his Flock, 10:1-21.

X. Jesus' Attestation as the Messiah at the Feast of Dedication, 10:22-42.

I. *Jesus Goes to the Feast of Tabernacles, 7:1-13*

1) **And after these things Jesus was walking in Galilee; for he was not willing to walk in Judea, because the Jews were seeking to kill him.** The three imperfect tenses point to continuous situations. Instead of remaining in the populous Lake region in Galilee Jesus went to the more distant parts of the country, as far as the Phoenician border in the northwest, down into the region of the Ten Cities (Decapolis) in the southwest, and up to the extreme north; Matt. 15 and Mark 7:1-8:10. Thus Jesus prudently avoids the opposition that developed in Capernaum and in the populous Lake region. The murderous temper of the authorities in Jerusalem (5:18) is mentioned as the reason why Jesus avoided Judea also. This had developed a year ago, at the preceding Feast of Tabernacles (see 5:1), when Jesus had last been in Jerusalem. Jesus knows that the determination to kill him has not changed in the capital; when he returns thither he knows the danger he will expose himself to. When we now see him, nevertheless, visiting Jerusalem on two festival occasions, this means that his attestation at the capital has not yet been completed and that in spite of the danger he intends to finish also this task. But he is prudent enough to choose two festival occasions when the crowds of pilgrims from all over the land fill the city and afford a measure of protection for him; for large numbers of these visitors were at least favorably inclined toward Jesus, and the authorities at Jerusalem hesitated to outrage them by laying violent hands on him.

2) **Now the feast of the Jews was near, the Feast of Tabernacles.** John had no special reason for naming this festival in 5:1, but now he adds the name, because in the words of Jesus which he intends to report reference is made to certain customs connected with this particular festival (7:37, etc.; 8:12; 9:7). "Tabernacles," ἡ σκηνοπηγία (σκηνή, "tent," plus πήγνυμι, "to join or build"), was celebrated from the 15th to the 22nd of Tisri, our October, in commemoration of Israel's passage through the desert, and was made a festival of thanksgiving for the season's harvest of grain, fruit, and wine. The men were required to attend it at Jerusalem. Booths and tents, thousands of them outside of the walls, were occupied for a week; and in postexilic times many symbolic features were added, to some of which Jesus refers.

3) **His brethren, therefore, said to him, Depart hence and go into Judea, in order that thy disciples also may view thy works which thou art doing. For no one does anything in secret and seeks himself to stand out in public. If thou doest these things, manifest thyself to the world.** On these "brethren" compare 2:12. These relatives of Jesus urge him as they do in view of the approaching festival. Evidently they had learned from Jesus that he was making no preparation to attend this festival in the capital. They think that Jesus is largely wasting his efforts in these remote parts of Galilee, his place is on the grand stage in the heart of the nation. They say "Judea" and not at once Jerusalem, because they have in mind that Jesus should be in the midst of the great crowds of pilgrims proceeding from Galilee to Judea. This, of course, includes the grand entry into the capital city. For the Jew the great world-stage was Jerusalem. When these brethren add, "in order that thy disciples also may view thy works which

thou art doing," they do not mean that the number of
Jesus' disciples in Galilee has dwindled down to negligible proportions and that he was not winning disciples of any consequence by working in the borders of
Galilee. "Thy disciples" is general. Practically all of
them would flock to Jerusalem for the coming festival,
now more than ever drawn by the expectation of seeing and of hearing Jesus there. The implication in
the ἵνα clause is that if all these disciples gathered in
one mass they could really do something for Jesus in
forcing through his Messianic claims, whereas nothing
of consequence could be accomplished by traveling
around in the borders of Galilee. Moreover, we must
not miss the other implication, that the brethren of
Jesus would like to see their great relative in a
grand triumph at the capital with the nation bowing
at his feet. They suggest that the works he is now
doing are of such a kind that, if they are done on
this lofty stage, will certainly bring this triumph to
pass.

4) Their argument, too, is sound: "For no one
does anything in secret and seeks himself to stand
out in public." They see Jesus scattering his efforts
among small groups of people in these remote parts
and describe this as working ἐν κρυπτῷ, "in secret,"
in a kind of private way. This they feel is not the
proper method for one whose aim is αὐτὸς ἐν παρρησίᾳ
εἶναι, "himself to stand out in public." While παρρησία
often means unrestrained freedom of speech; with
εἶναι ἐν it means the public eye. These brethren were
right: Jesus claimed to be the Messiah of the nation
and had himself repeatedly said that he was sent "to
the world." Then, evidently, his place and the scene
of action were not in the distant parts of Galilee but in
Jerusalem at this coming festival.

"If thou doest these things" is a condition of
reality. Like the previous reference to "thy works

which thou art doing" in v. 3 this conditional clause asserts on the part of these brethren that the works of Jesus are sufficiently great. No fault is found with them, other supposedly greater works are not demanded, for all that these brethren suggest is a grander stage, one on which these works can be displayed as they deserve to be. Hence these brethren urge Jesus, "Manifest thyself to the world!" "To the world" is the complete opposite of "in secret." Perhaps they had heard the term κόσμος from Jesus himself; for Jesus indeed intended to do nothing less: he would manifest himself to "the world" and not merely, as these relatives of his most likely understood it, to the world of Judaism but to the world of all nations and all times.

Generally this proposal of the brethren of Jesus is viewed as a repetition of the temptation offered to him by the 5,000 who wanted to carry him to the capital as king, 6:15. But the propositions are quite different. The 5,000 think of making Jesus a king by their action; these brethren say nothing about a king and urge Jesus to an action of his own. So also the response of Jesus to his brethren differs entirely from the action with which he replied to the 5,000. The fact is, these brethren, with their imperfect insight into the real mission of Jesus, are in their way not far from the plan which only six months later Jesus actually carried out in his own superior way when he made his royal entry into the capital on Palm Sunday.

5) Before giving us the reply of Jesus John explains: **For even his brethren were not believing in him.** The force of οὐδέ, "not even," R. 1185, is that, although these men were related to Jesus, they could not as yet be counted among the true believers. The imperfect tense "they were not believing" refers to more than the duration of their non-belief; the

tense is open and points to an outcome which in their case eventuated in true faith. The way in which these brethren are impressed by *the works* that Jesus is doing places them in the general class indicated in 2:25; 4:45; and 6:2. In his confession Peter emphasized *the words* of Jesus (6:68), and in this the brethren could not yet join. But they remained with Jesus, were present with him now, and had not left like the many in 6:66. On the one hand, they themselves do not count themselves among "thy disciples" (v. 3), and they venture to criticize Jesus for working "in secret"; but on the other hand, they propose plans by which they think Jesus will succeed.

The names of these brethren are James, Joses, Jude, and Simon, Matt. 12:46; Mark 6:3. The complete openness with which John reports their unbelief as continuing as late as six months before Jesus' death is noteworthy in various ways. John tells the true facts; a fabricator would omit at least a fact like this if he knew of it, or would alter it in some way. In the face of the fact that these relatives of Jesus were not among the believers, the assumption, which is still advocated, that two of the four had been chosen by Jesus when he selected the Twelve, namely James and Jude, becomes untenable. Even the inferior reading ἐπίστευσαν instead of ἐπίστευον cannot alter this conclusion; for so certainly did none of the brethren belong to the Twelve that they are not counted even among the "disciples" in the wider sense. All the rest of the evidence is to the same effect, Zahn, *Introduction to the New Testament*, I, 105; II, 240, etc. What is true is the fact that all these brethren came to faith, apparently after the resurrection of Jesus, and that James became the first bishop of the Jerusalem church and the writer of one of the New Testament Epistles, and his brother Jude the writer of another.

6) **Jesus, therefore, says to them, My right time
is not yet at hand; but your right time is always
ready.** We must note that Jesus does not reject
the suggestion of his relatives as such, namely that
at one of the festivals he enter Jerusalem as the
Messiah, manifesting himself in the most public manner possible. All he does is to point out that the
proper time (καιρός) has not yet come. In a manner
he even excuses his brethren for urging him to proceed with this manifestation at the approaching
festival. They are judging Jesus according to their
own standard. Their καιρός or proper time is always
ready. It makes little or no difference what time they
select. They have no set mission to carry out. The
case of Jesus is altogether different. The term καιρός
is relative, the right time for a certain thing; the
close contrast "*my* right time" and "*your* right time"
also requires a parallel in the things for which these
times are the right ones. This parallel cannot be the
right time for going to the present festival, the fact,
that the brethren were free to go at any time, but
that Jesus had to wait and to go later. This restricts
everything to the point of time, which is minor, and
loses the main point, which is that for which the time
is to be used. Likewise, the mere going to the festival
cannot be meant, for this, too, is a minor action. If
Jesus were going to the festival like the rest of the
pilgrims, he certainly might go with them. This,
however, is not what his brethren urge upon him
but something decidedly greater, namely that now
is the right time to make himself manifest to the
world. On this point Jesus tells his brethren that
for him the right time to do this has not yet arrived;
but as far as they are concerned, who still belong
to the world, it makes no difference when the world
sees who they are.

7)   That this is the thought of Jesus we see when
he adds: **The world cannot hate you, but me it
hates, because I bear testimony concerning it, that
its works are wicked.** This is the vital difference
between Jesus and his brethren, decisive also for "the
right time" in regard to him and them, in v. 6. Their
relation to the world (ὁ κόσμος, ungodly men as a
great body or unit) is different. While the term
"world" here refers specifically to its present hier-
archical representatives in Jerusalem, it, nevertheless,
embraces all men who are spiritually like them.
In the very nature of the case it would be a
psychological impossibility for the world to hate these
brethren of Jesus, for they themselves were still part
of the world. That does not necessarily mean that
they, too, were filled with murderous hate against
Jesus; but it does mean that in their hearts an opposition to Jesus lurked which was capable of being
inflamed into violent action.   Let us apply Matt. 5:12,
etc. Even the authorities in Jerusalem at first showed
only a hostile attitude (2:18) and not until Jesus'
second visit advanced to violent plans (5:18).   Thus,
although "the world" embraces all forms of opposition
to Jesus, from the silent "no" in the heart to the voci-
ferous "Crucify!" of the mob, all these forms are
essentially agreed and thus support and acknowledge
each other.   When, therefore, Jesus tells these
brethren that the world cannot hate them, this should
shock them — it so plainly implies that they still belong to the world and not to God and to his Son.

The case of Jesus is quite the opposite (adversative δέ) : "but me it hates." Yet not merely because
he does not and never did belong to the world, which
fact also would serve as an explanation; but because of
the mission of Jesus to change and thus to save the
world. Jesus might have said, "yet me it cannot but
hate"; he is content to state the fact only, "me it

hates." And then he points to that feature in his mission which invariably arouses hatred when men determine to turn against him, namely his testimony regarding the wicked works of the world. This testimony is the application of the divine law to the sinner (3:19, 20; 4, 16-18), which intends to crush the heart in contrition, that it may bow to the pardon of grace. Where this testimony is spurned, the ἔργα πονηρά remain, to be used against the world as the decisive evidence that damns. And at the top of these wicked works is the most wicked of all, the hate of the Savior and all the manifestations of that hate.

When the brethren of Jesus say, "Manifest thyself to the world!" they little think what "the world" implies for Jesus. Yes, the right time for thus manifesting himself is coming, but it means that then the hate will rise to its highest pitch and that due to it Jesus will die. The assumption that at this time Jesus is still unaware of this final result is obviated by 2:19-22; and the view that the details of the tragedy are still hidden from him is answered by all the advance announcements that Jesus made of his passion.

8) Thus Jesus says to his brethren: **Do you go up to the feast; I do not go up to this feast, because my right time has not yet been fulfilled. And having said this to them, he remained in Galilee.** Jesus tells his brethren to go to he feast, and they no doubt went. As regards himself he states that he is not going "to the feast." Yet v. 10 informs us that he went after all, not publicly but in secret, and, as v. 14 shows, so as to arrive in the midst of the celebration. For Jesus to say that he is not going, and then for him to go after all, impresses many as being a contradiction, which they then attempt to remove. They forget the connection in which Jesus says that he is not going. The interchange with his brethren

deals not with an ordinary attendance of Jesus at the approaching festival but with an attendance which would make this festival the right time for Jesus to manifest himself to the world. The latter Jesus declines. He tells his brethren, "You go up to the feast!" namely in your customary way. Of himself he says, "I do not go up to *this* feast," namely to make *"this* feast" what you suggest. Whether he will go at all or not is another matter. He may stay away altogether; but if he goes, it will not be to make of *this* feast what his brethren propose. The pointed demonstrative *"this* feast" is in contrast with another feast, namely the coming Passover, which will, indeed, be the right time for Jesus to manifest himself to the world.

That this is the meaning of his words appears in the reason why Jesus declines to go to *this* feast: "because my right time has not yet been fulfilled." Six additional months will fill up that measure; then, and not until then, will Jesus carry out what at *this* feast would be untimely. We need only to understand what Jesus really declines to do, then even the appearance of a contradiction between his words and his subsequent act disappears.

Then, too, the proposed solutions for the supposed contradiction are unnecessary. One of the most ancient is a slight change in the reading, οὔπω in place of οὐκ; as if Jesus means to say, "You go on up *now,* I am *not yet* going but will follow *later on."* But this change in the reading is valueless unless we suppose a contradiction and make this change in the reading the means for its removal. The moment we understand Jesus aright, "not yet" would refer to the right time for the manifestation to the world — this right time is not the present festival but another that is not far off. Other solutions for the supposed difficulty are less convincing. One is that Jesus

changes his mind, first deciding not to go at all,
then deciding to go at least for the latter part of
the feast. Another is, that the Father changes the
mind of Jesus for him, ordering him to go after he
himself has resolved not to go and after he had told
his brethren that he would not go. But such a Christ
and such a Father the Gospels do not know: a Christ
who changes no to yes; but note ἐγώ — *this* festival is
not the right time for him to go up as they were pro-
posing. What Jesus declines is not an attendance at
the coming feast but to make *this* feast the time for
what his brethren suggest. Note that the demonstrative "this" appears only when Jesus speaks of
himself.

With this correct view of the declination agrees
not only the previous context but also the subsequent,
the quiet way Jesus chose for going, his late arrival,
and the continuance of the clash with the authorities
without decisive issue. We have no reason whatever to assume that Jesus changed his mind, first
deciding not to go at all, then deciding to go at least
for the latter part of the feast. Or that his Father
changed his mind for him, ordering him to go after
he himself had resolved not to go. Since no problem
exists, we need no solution.

9) Jesus, accordingly, remained behind in Galilee, the aorist merely noting the fact.

10) **Now when his brethren were gone up to
the feast, then he, too, went up, not publicly, but
as it were in secret.** His brethren wanted him to go
as publicly as possible. This Jesus refused to do. His
plan was to go as quietly as possible. So he delays
until his brethren have gone with the crowds of pilgrims, until the roads are deserted, and then he goes
with only the Twelve to accompany him. The
emphasis is on the way in which Jesus goes up, and
οἱ φανερῶς is in direct contrast to φανέρωσον σεαυτὸν τῷ

κόσμῳ in v. 4. This is even enhanced by adding the positive: "as it were (ὡς) in secret." After everyone had gone who intended to go, this was easy.

11) The situation in Jerusalem is now described. **The Jews, therefore, were seeking him at the feast and were saying, Where is that one?** These are the authorities, the members of the Sanhedrin (v. 48), as distinguished from the citizens of Jerusalem (v. 25), and also from the ὄχλος (v. 12; 20; 31, 32; 49). In what follows we must keep these three parties in mind. The rulers were nonplused by the absence of Jesus. They were well informed regarding his activities in Galilee during the past year since he had last been in Jerusalem (5:1) and had incurred their deadly hatred by ordering a man to carry his bed on the Sabbath and by making himself equal with God (5:18). They fully expected him at this festival and even instituted search for him. Note the durative imperfects "were seeking," "were saying," which at the same time indicate that the outcome will presently be stated.

12) **And murmuring concerning him was much among the multitudes. Some were saying, He is a good man; while others were saying, No; on the contrary, he is deceiving the multitude.** Perhaps John uses the plural "multitudes" because he at once speaks of two parties. The ὄχλος or ὄχλοι are the hosts of pilgrims who had come for the festival from near and far. John himself explains the extensive "murmuring" that was going on among these visitors concerning Jesus. He was the general subject of discussion, and two opinions were widespread. Those who favored Jesus called him ἀγαθός, the masculine adjective meaning "a good man," one who is excellent, in the sense that he brings benefit. This fits the type of miracles which distinguish Jesus, conferring healing, deliverance, and help. This estimate was weak

and poor enough; too weak to form the basis of faith. The fact that a large portion of the pilgrims should hold a contrary opinion comes as a surprise. These contradict the others with a flat "no" and mark their judgment as the direct opposite by ἀλλά, which after a negative has the force of "on the contrary." And, indeed, they assert that he "deceives the multitude," is intent on misleading it. They must refer to his teaching and imply that this is false and that his miracles are used only to cover up the falseness. Neither side could convince the other, and the two imperfects ἔλεγον allow the dispute to remain unsettled.

13) The fact that this talk about Jesus never rose beyond a subdued "murmur" John explains. **No one, however, was speaking with openness concerning him because of the fear of the Jews,** the rulers in the capital. This evidently refers to both parties alike. The authorities had not yet rendered an official opinion or verdict. Hence no one felt sure of himself. Here παρρησία has its more usual meaning: freedom to say anything. The genitive "of the Jews" is objective, R. 500. John's remark casts a light on the spiritual slavery in which the Sanhedrin and other Jewish authorities kept the nation. Compare v. 49 and 9:34. Woe to those who did not yield to this domination!

II. *Jesus' Testimony Stirs the Authorities to Order his Arrest, 14-36*

14) In a quiet way, without any demonstration whatever, Jesus arrives in the city. **Now when the feast was already half over, Jesus went up into the Temple and began teaching.** The genitive absolute τῆς ἑορτῆς μεσούσης (from μεσόω, to be in the middle), together with ἤδη, "the feast being already in its middle," i. e., half over with, shows at how late a time

Jesus appeared in the courts of the Temple. On the other two occasions when he had appeared in Jerusalem he at once made his presence felt by deeds that acted like a public challenge, cleansing the court of the Temple (2:13, etc.), and sending a healed man through the streets with his couch on his shoulder on the Sabbath (5:9, etc.). On neither occasion had he assumed the quiet role of a teaching rabbi. But this is what he now does. The imperfect is here ingressive: "he began to teach." What followed we are told presently. He found some convenient place, where he sat on the pavement under some porch or balcony, the Twelve and a group of hearers sat cross-legged in a circle about him, and he quietly began his instruction. On what subject he spoke John does not state.

Among those present, perhaps standing on the fringe of the seated group, were a few of the ruling class. Here was the man they were seeking. But they found him using only the ordinary privilege of a rabbi, teaching a group of interested hearers. We may take it that this group grew rapidly, for presently the ὄχλος utters an exclamation, v. 20.

15) After listening awhile to the teaching of Jesus the Jews start their interference. **The Jews, therefore, wondered, saying, How does this fellow know letters, not having learned?** These Jews had never before heard Jesus teach as a rabbi. But this wondering of theirs is not surprise because of the ability of Jesus to teach the Scriptures although, as they knew, he had never studied in any of the rabbinical schools. If they had felt such surprise they would have hidden it and would never have credited Jesus with ability along this line before a crowd of pilgrims assembled about Jesus. Moreover, οὗτος is highly derogatory and means "this fellow." By γράμματα they mean *litteras* in the Jewish sense, the rabbinical study of the Old Testament writings. We need not

change the sense of θαυμάζειν into offended wondering. What surprises them, they say, is that a man who has had no proper education should presume to teach in public and palm himself off as one who is versed in Scriptural learning. Their question is a general exclamation addressed not to Jesus but to the multitude. It charges Jesus with incompetency, with utter lack of proper qualifications for being a great religious teacher. The purpose of the rulers is to discredit Jesus before his audience. The force of their question is: "This fellow does not know what he is talking about because he has never studied in any of our Jewish schools."

We meet the same charge today when any man dares to contradict the "scientific" critics of Christ and the gospel. At once he is branded by them as an ignoramus, incompetent to speak on these subjects because he is not one of their guild, who has pre-empted "scientific" learning and does not bear the stamp of their approval. The object is to impress the crowd, and the secret object is to maintain their own authority by crying down the man who challenges it. Those commentators are mistaken who think that the marvelling of these Jews is genuine and that they are really surprised at Jesus as being *"ein schriftkundiger Volkslehrer," "ein wirksamer Haggadist," "ein genialer Autodidakt."* Instead of being a self-taught genius, they make him out the very opposite: *dass er als unbefugter Pfuscher an Stelle der alleinberechtigten Gelehrtenweisheit nur eigene Einfaelle vorbringe und fuer Weisheitslehre ausgebe.* The proceeding of these Jews is the height of cunning. They seek to shift the question: How true and genuine is the teaching of Jesus? to: What great and accredited schools has Jesus attended? They also count on the fact that the teaching of Jesus differs completely from that which the people have been accustomed to receive from the rabbis, both in contents and in form. To tell the people that Jesus has never attended a school of any standing for training rabbies, that he has no degree or certificate from such an accredited school, would certainly have its effect upon the ignorant.

16) *The Divine Origin of Jesus' Doctrine, 16-24.* — Without the slightest hesitation Jesus meets the wicked charge of the rulers. And he, too, does not direct his words to these rulers in particular but to all who are gathered before him and have heard the charge. These wise Jews, Jesus intimates in his answer, have certainly heard aright: the entire doctrine of Jesus is totally different from the arid refinements and empty distinctions of the rabbis, and it is plain to any man who has ears to hear, that Jesus has never "learned" from such teachers. Nobody needs to tell the people this. **Jesus, therefore, answered them and said** (see 1:48), **My doctrine is not mine, but his that did send me.** He has in mind the substance of what he is teaching; διδαχή corresponds to ἐδίδασκε. The adjective in ἡ ἐμὴ διδαχή is stronger than the possessive pronoun would be. The wonderful feature about the doctrine Jesus taught is that it is not his own at all, in the sense that he, like some human philosopher, had himself invented, had produced it by his own human brain. On the contrary (ἀλλά after a negative), it is "his that did send me," it belongs wholly to his great Sender. Jesus is only the mouthpiece, the spokesman, of that Sender. By rejecting and trying to discredit this teaching of Jesus these Jews are by no means dealing with Jesus alone but with the Sender of Jesus, with God himself. It is no wonder that God's great doctrine is wholly different from the speculations of the rabbis. If that is any discredit to the doctrine of Jesus, he accepts the discredit; but woe unto those who offer this

discredit! See what they betray concerning themselves.
They have never "learned" (v. 15; also 6:45) in God's
school at the feet of the great teachers and prophets
whom God sent them in the Old Testament. If they
had, they would at once recognize the doctrine of Jesus
as being that of God; but now they blindly slander it
and try to turn others from it.

17) As far as recognizing the fact that this doctrine is of God is concerned, no difficulty whatever
is encountered. Simply apply the right touchstone.
It is useless merely to reason and to argue about it
intellectually, if for no other reason than that man
by nature is spiritually blind and cannot even know
the things of God, since they are spiritually discerned.
Jesus is far from submitting his doctrine to the decision of blind human reason, which, indeed, constantly
endeavors to usurp the authority of a judge in spiritual
things. No; the right touchstone is a living experience
with the doctrine of Jesus. Such an experience at
once makes plain and convinces us inwardly that this
doctrine is of God. **If anyone shall will to do his
will, he shall know concerning the doctrine whether
it is of God or whether I am talking from myself.**
The condition of expectancy has the regular form, ἐάν
with the subjunctive (protasis) followed by the
future indicative (apodosis). Whenever a case like
this occurs, that a man wills to do God's will, the
result follows, he realizes that the doctrine is of
God (the article to indicate the doctrine here in question, R. 757). The present subjunctive θέλῃ indicates
more than a single volition; it denotes a durative
and lasting course. The Greek abuts θέλῃ τὸ θέλημα,
"shall will the will," and the present infinitive ποιεῖν
means "to carry out" God's will in a consistent course.
"His will" is objective, *what* God wills; "shall will"
is subjective, *accepting* by our will what God wants
carried out by us.

544 *The Interpretation of John*

This will of God is faith on our part. "This is the work of God, that ye *believe* on him whom he did send," John 6:29; compare 6:40. Before the coming of Jesus this faith was to believe the promises concerning Jesus, after his coming this faith is to believe the fulfillment of these promises in Jesus. God's will is that we believe, our willing to carry out his will is our actual believing by his grace. The entire thought of Jesus would be perverted if we should take it that God's will here refers to the law and our doing of the law; and correspondingly that our willing to do his will is our setting out to meet the requirements of that law. The doctrine of Jesus centers not in the law but in the gospel, in God's will of pardoning and saving grace. Again, it would be a perversion of the thought of Jesus if we conceived his meaning to be that we are to do God's gracious will by means of our own natural ability. Nothing is farther from his mind than that God commands us to believe and that we then obey by believing. Man's will as it is by nature cannot possibly itself resolve to do this will of God, i. e., to believe. So far is God from expecting this that ever in the very revelation of his gracious will his own divine will comes with efficacious power to set our will free and to move it to accept his will, i. e., to believe. The efficacy of his will our will may resist obdurately and persistently but always without excuse, and thus only with the most damnable guilt. When Jesus speaks of our willing to do God's will, he means that willing which God by his grace works in us through his Word and his Spirit.

This willing (believing) is the touchstone: "he shall know concerning the doctrine whether it is of God or whether I am talking from myself." "Know" means "realize," not by means of mere intellectual processes, not by reasonings and arguments but by the actual

experience of letting God's will move his will. When
God's will sets the human will free and fills it with
new power, then, and then alone, a man knows God's
will, what it really is, by having experienced in his
own will what God's will does. In no other manner
can this knowledge be attained. If your will is moved
by God's will as this will graciously reaches out and
changes your will; if your will is moved from sin
toward Christ and the salvation he brings; if, thus
moved, it finds the curse and the shackles of sin gone,
a new, heavenly power filling it and working in it:
then you will realize, indeed, that the doctrine which
brought this heavenly will to you is "of God" (ἐκ,
derived from him) and that in uttering it Jesus is
not talking (λαλῶ) "from himself" (ἀπό, from notions
he has invented).

18) But as far as the person of Jesus and his
doctrine are concerned, a more general criterion is at
hand. **He that talks from himself seeks his own
glory; but he that seeks the glory of him that did
send him, this one is true, and no unrighteousness
is in him.** To the Jews it was axiomatic that all
genuine religious teaching emanated from God, and
that therefore every genuine religious teacher must
teach as commissioned, authorized, and sent by God.
Whoever, therefore, as a religious teacher presented
anything emanating from himself instead of from
God could do so only by arrogating to himself the
glory and the honor that belong to God; he would
"be seeking his own glory." Thus Jesus says: "he
who seeks (not his own glory by offering his own supposed wisdom but) the glory of him that did send
him (as a teacher, by teaching only what he is commissioned to teach — this being God) this one
(οὗτος, only he and no other) is true (ἀληθής, *verax*,
namely, as a teacher, not false, lying), and no

unrighteousnes is in him" (he can be charged
with no wrong or unfaithfulness in his office as a
teacher).

The application of this axiom is easy. First, as
regards Jesus. He sought only the glory of God,
5:19; 7:16. Sincere people could have no difficulty
on that point. To insinuate that because he had not
been educated in the rabbinical schools he is a spurious teacher is base slander. Its worst feature is the
substitution of a false test for religious teachers.
This slander puts the authority and the praise of the
rabbis in place of God and his glory. Jesus insists on
the true criterion. The moment this is applied the
divinity of his teaching is established beyond question. But this axiom holds good also for the opposite. How about these Jewish rulers and their religious teaching as it is now being urged in opposition to
Jesus? They are notorious seekers after their own
glory and honor. They oppose Jesus for the very
reason that they fear to lose their position of honor
and of power among their people. Even Pilate, six
months later, knew that "for envy" they had delivered
him, Matt. 27:18. It is evident that as teachers they
are not "true" and not void of "unrighteousness."
This is the inner reason for their hostility to Jesus,
the cause of their blindness to the divinity of his
doctrine. Here again we touch the will as being the
real domain in which the battle is fought, and in what
follows we see how Jesus continues his attack upon this
central citadel.

19) In verses 17 and 18 Jesus lays down axiomatic principles. The first is regarding *the doctrine*:
anyone may test the doctrine and by his own experience with it convince himself that it is of God.
The second is regarding *the teacher*: anyone may test
the teacher. If he seeks God's glory alone (by teaching
the true faith which gives all honor and praise to God

alone) he is a true teacher with no unrighteousness
to discredit him as a teacher; but if he is after his
own glory and his personal advantage he is a false
teacher and stands revealed as such. Defense and
offense are combined in the enunciation of these principles. But now, with a sudden turn, Jesus takes the
offensive. Like a bolt of lightning he drops the charge
of the grossest kind of ἀδικία or unrighteousness upon
the heads of the Jewish rulers. **Did not Moses give
you the law?** That sounds innocent but is ominous.
Of course, Moses gave them the law, all of it as comprised in the five books of Moses (the *Torah* or "Instruction") and specifically its moral regulations in
the Ten Commandments. And the great boast of
these Jewish rulers was that they sat in Moses' seat
(Matt. 23:2) as teachers and guardians of the law
and as "disciples of Moses" (9:28). This reference
of Jesus to Moses and the law is a masked battery.
Two annihilating volleys will roar out from it: these
Jews, boastful exponents of the law, breaking the law
in the most horrible manner; these Jews, supreme
teachers of the law, circumcise on the Sabbath in
order not to violate the law and yet charge Jesus
with violation when on the Sabbath he extends a blessing far greater than circumcision.

And none of you does the law by no means
asserts only that these rulers, like all men, are sinners
in a general way. For if that disqualifies them as
guardians of the law, no man could ever be a true
teacher of the law. Like the previous question about
receiving the law from Moses, this assertion about
their not living up to the law still has a harmless
look. For Moses himself, through whom the law was
given, was a sinner in the general sense of the word,
and so were all the great prophets who taught the
law. The question and the assertion have a specific
bearing.

Why are you seeking to kill me? The briefest, simplest kind of a question but devastating in its effect. Its implication is that these rulers are even at this very time plotting and scheming to murder Jesus. The question is stronger than an assertion would be. This "why" is addressed to these Jewish rulers as the exponents, guardians, and teachers of the law, into whose keeping Moses gave the law. This unanswerable "why" reveals what these enforcers of the law were doing with that law in planning the murder of Jesus, sent to them of God with the doctrine of God. Compare 5:18. Consternation sealed the lips of the Jews; silence reigned. We may imagine how the eyes of all the pilgrims turned toward and for a moment searched the faces of their rulers. This was the ἀδικία that branded them as the type of teachers they were and as the kind of teaching they offered. Is murder of God? is murder the teaching of God's law? Murder is of the devil; and murder and lying are twins, 8:44. These Jews expected to have an easy victory over Jesus by pointing out that he had no professional training. In their attack they felt secure behind the plausibility of their insistence on proper qualifications for public teachers, behind the secrecy which hid their real motive for attacking Jesus. In a flash they now stand exposed as criminal lawbreakers.

20) The citizens of Jerusalem, at least those in touch with the rulers, know of the plot against Jesus, v. 25. But the pilgrims that came from all parts of the country are entirely innocent. When Jesus suddenly and publicly casts into the face of the rulers their scheme to kill him, these pilgrims are astounded and horrified. **The multitude answered, Thou hast a devil! Who is seeking to kill thee?** The adjective δαιμόνιον, here used as a noun, means some kind of evil spirit. The exclamation does not voice ill will

but impatient surprise that a man like Jesus, whom
so many of the ὄχλος admired, should utter a charge
involving what seemed to them a moral impossibility.
Surely, some evil spirit must be clouding his mind
with the mental aberration and fixed idea that he is
being persecuted. The added question shows how unthinkable it seems to the pilgrims that their rulers
should be seeking to kill Jesus. But — the rulers stand
there silently, with the eyes of the crowd searching
their faces. That silence speaks loudly.

21) In v. 19 Jesus addresses only the rulers; now
he ignores them — he is done with them. **Jesus
answered and said unto them,** αὐτοῖς, plural because
of the collective antecedent ὁ ὄχλος. On the use of the
two verbs see 1:48; also note that ἀπεκρίθη = *er nahm
das Wort.* This does not imply that Jesus makes a
direct reply to the question of the multitude. In no
way does Jesus qualify or alter the charge that the
rulers are seeking to kill him; on the contrary, he
involves also the multitude to a certain degree, because they, too, were angry with Jesus because of
the miracle wrought on the Sabbath. That miracle,
wrought a year ago (5:2, etc.), which first caused the
rulers to plot his death (6:18), Jesus now discusses.
**One work I wrought, and you all wonder because of
it.** Jesus means "one" especially that still causes
wonderment; many other miracles of his produced no
such effect. It is not the greatness of the deed that
causes this wondering as compared with other
miracles of Jesus. We must construe: "you all wonder *because* of it," διά. We need not here bring in
the constructions of θαυμάζειν with ἐπί or περί, because
these prepositions place the surprise or wonder on
the thing itself that is wrought. In this instance it
is not the fact that Jesus healed a man impotent for
thirty-eight years that causes the marvelling. It
is not in any sense the miracle itself but something

connected with the miracle, hence the preposition διὰ, "because" Jesus performed this deed on the Sabbath, and "because" he made the man carry his bed on the Sabbath. The thought is not complete, not even correct, without the phrase διὰ τοῦτο, "because of this."

The moment this is understood we shall not connect this phrase with the next sentence, as is done by a number of codices, by the ancients, by some of the moderns, by our versions, and by others. The claim that the phrase is superfluous when it is attached to v. 21 arises from the fact that its sense is not understood; for "you all are marvelling" is not what Jesus wants to say but "you all are marvelling *because of this*," i. e., the feature that you fail to understand and that upsets you, that I should do such a work on the Sabbath.

22) **Moses has given you the circumcision (not that it originates with Moses but with the fathers), and you circumcise a man on the Sabbath.** The emphasis is on Moses, on this great authority to whom all Israelites bowed. Jesus holds up Moses to the pilgrim crowd, as a moment ago he pointed their rulers to this same Moses (v. 19). If, however, we draw the phrase διὰ τοῦτο to v. 22, the emphasis would be transferred to this phrase. Instead of saying: *"Moses* (no less an authority) has given you the circumcision, . . . and you circumcise a man on the Sabbath," Jesus would say: *"For this reason* has Moses given you circumcision, not because it originates with Moses, but with the fathers; and you circumcise," etc. But if this were the sense intended, the sentence should read: *"Not* for this reason has Moses given you circumcision, *that* it originates with him *but that* it originates with the fathers," etc., οὐ διὰ τοῦτο . . . ὅτι . . . ἀλλὰ ὅτι, and the second ὅτι could

not be omitted. Such a statement, however, would not be true. The Jews did not circumcise on the Sabbath because this rite *originated* with the fathers and not with Moses. The historical origin of circumcision (ἐκ) is a side issue; i. e., the fact that the rite is older than Moses. Nor did Moses embody circumcision in the law because the patriarchs already had the rite but because God wanted him to command it in the law. If the point of origin and age were urged by Jesus, he would have said that the Sabbath goes back much farther than circumcision, to God himself and to the very week of creation. What Jesus does point out is that *Moses* gave the Israelites circumcision, *Moses* as the agent of God, and that thus — very properly — they circumcise on the Sabbath whenever the eighth day after birth happens to occur on a Sabbath.

The statement, however, that no less an authority than *Moses* gave circumcision, requires an explanation lest it be misunderstood. Jesus is not speaking historically but from the legal standpoint. Historically the fathers, i. e., the patriarchs, already had circumcision prior to Moses. Its origin dates back thus far. But legally the Israelites were held to this rite since the time of Moses, the great lawgiver of Israel. Hence the statement, "not that it is of Moses but of the fathers," is parenthetical, in the nature of an elucidation. This shows that in the main clause the emphasis on "Moses" dare not be shifted as it would be by placing the phrase before "Moses." But we also should not find other thoughts in the parenthetical statement, either that circumcision has more weight than the law because it antedates the law and because it is derived from the fathers; or that it has less weight than the law because it consists only of a tradition from the fathers. Such notions confuse the plain sense of what Jesus desires to convey.

The examples adduced for the use of διὰ τοῦτο at the head of a statement, such as 5:16 and 18; 6:65; 8:47; 10:17; etc., have no bearing on the present case because they all have ὅτι following: "for this reason . . . that," etc. Really analogous examples are those that illustrate οὐχ ὅτι . . . ἀλλά, such as 6:46; 12: 6; II Cor. 1:24; 3:5; 7:9; Phil.4:11 and 17; II Thess. 3:9. All these are parenthetical in their very nature. On the formula οὐχ ὅτι see R. 1429. To regard the parenthesis as superfluous is an indication that its purpose is not fully understood. It makes clear that circumcision is binding only as a legal requirement irrespective of its origin. The effort to explain διὰ τοῦτο as an ellipsis is unfeasible: "For this reason *I say to you,* Moses has given," etc.; or: "For this reason *hear,* or *know,* Moses," etc. Jesus is here not making an authoritative announcement but is only repeating admitted facts, that Moses has given the circumcision (the article pointing to the rite as one that is well known), and that circumcision is performed on the Sabbath.

23) Now just as these facts are beyond dispute, so should be their application to the deed of Jesus. **If a man receives circumcision on the Sabbath, in order that the law of Moses may not be broken, are you angry with me because I made a man completely well on the Sabbath?** Jesus puts the application in the form of a question, in order the more effectively to appeal to the judgment of his hearers. This question brings out the true point which ought to be decisive for the judgment of his hearers. It appears already in v. 22 when Jesus says that Moses "has given" you the circumcision. This rite was a good gift from God through Moses, not a burden, not an infliction, not a work done for God. So Jesus now continues and asks, if a man "receives" the circumcision on the Sabbath, receives this gift or

blessing. Jesus does not ask, "if you circumcise a man on the Sabbath," for this is not a question of so much labor in administering the rite. He also adds the purpose clause, "in order that the law of Moses may not be broken," for it is the law itself which requires that the gift be bestowed even if the day be the Sabbath, Lev. 12:3. In other words, to withhold the gift because the day happens to be the Sabbath would be a violation (λυθῇ, a dissolution) of this law. The emphasis is again on "Moses" and it shows that in v. 22 "Moses" is the emphatic word. "If" (εἰ with the indicative) is a condition of reality; for Jesus takes it that the rite is thus received as a blessing, and his hearers certainly agree with him.

Now the path is clear for the application to the healing of the impotent man on the Sabbath. The emphasis on the genitive "of Moses" is matched by the emphasis on the dative "with me," and for this reason the two are abutted in the Greek. What is an inviolable law in the case of *Moses,* can that be a cause for anger with *me?* In v. 21 Jesus uses only the verb "wonder," here he now employs the stronger term "to be angry." These people wonder that Jesus should heal a man on the Sabbath and are gravely displeased with him as a result. Yet Jesus had done a deed that was essentially identical with what Moses had commanded and the Jews practiced as a matter of course; for just as the circumcision of the bodily member is a blessing received by the child, so the healing of the entire body was a blessing received by the impotent man. The identity, however, lies not in the sanitary features of the two blessings, the one concerned with a single member of the body, the other with the entire body. The Scriptures show no trace of hygienic or sanitary valuation of circumcision. As part of the ceremonial law this rite effects the religious purification of the organ of procreation, and

thus Jesus pairs it with the restoration of the entire
body of the impotent man. The identity here stressed
lies in the fact that both are blessings, the one affecting
a single member, the other the entire body. By ὅλον
ἄνθρωπον, "an entire man," Jesus does not refer to both
body and soul but to the body alone. What Jesus did
for the impotent man's soul by warning him not to
fall into sin again was unknown to the Jews and may
not have been done on the Sabbath at all, nor would
such a warning have transgressed their conception of
the sanctity of the Sabbath.

The argument is thus quite simple: on the one
hand, a beneficial act involving one member; on the
other hand, a beneficial act involving the entire body.
The force of the argument, however, is increased in
two ways. Whereas Moses *commands* circumcision
also on the Sabbath, these Jews will not so much as
permit a healing on the Sabbath. The conferring of
a benefit means *so much* to Moses that he will not let
even the Sabbath stand in the way; the conferring
of a benefit means *so little* to the Jews that they misuse the Sabbath and force it to stand in the way.
This point in the argument operates *a majori ad
minus.* On the other hand, the benefit for the
bestowal of which Moses commands that it be conferred even on the Sabbath is *small* (one bodily member), whereas the benefit for the bestowal of which
these Jews forbid its being conferred on the Sabbath
is by comparison *great* (the entire body). This point
in the argument operates *a minori ad majus.* The
combination of the two points in the presentation
of the argument is unusual and utterly convincing. It goes to the very root of the matter and
does not, after the fashion of the rabbis, deal merely
with the superficial wording of the law. If the multitude would only use Moses it would not abuse
Jesus.

24) Therefore the closing admonition: **Do not
keep judging according to appearance but render
the right judgment.** This is not a general injunc-
tion against forming superficial judgments but a
demand to render the right judgment in the present
case. Hence the article τὴν κρίσιν. We may also translate the present imperative, "Stop judging superficially!" for it forbids what these people were already
doing. The preposition κατά indicates the norm,
namely the mere appearance of the act Jesus had performed. Looked at only from the outside, this act
might seem to be in contravention of the law. But
mere appearance is never to be the norm for directing
our verdicts. The very law itself, which these people
cited against Jesus, should teach them to follow a different course.

In the second clause the correct reading is the
aorist κρίνατε, which also matches the article τὴν δικαίαν
κρίσιν (an accusative of inner content, or cognate
accusative, R. 478): "judge the right judgment" in
this case, the one governed by the norm of right (δίκη).
This aorist plus the article restricts the command to
the case in hand. The reading κρίνετε is due, it seems,
to the use of the same present tense in the first clause
and to the idea that Jesus here voices a general rule for
deciding any and all cases. Righteous judgment will
see in the man carrying his bed no violation of the
Sabbath law but a publication of the astounding
blessing he had received on the Sabbath through the
grace of God.

The answer of Jesus is misconceived when circumcision and the miracle of Jesus are considered
exceptions to the sabbatical law. The law itself
demanded circumcision also on the Sabbath and not by
way of exception. Circumcision on the Sabbath was as
much a law as the observance of Sabbath rest. And the
miracle is placed on a par with the former. Like-

wise, Jesus does not abrogate the Sabbath by his
miracle. Jesus keeps the Sabbath law as given by
Moses, but he refuses to be bound by the rabbinical
regulations which had been added to the Mosaic law.
These were unwarranted human additions, to which
Jesus could never bow.

Moses upholds Jesus, and Jesus Moses. Both are
here shown to be true teachers of God, teaching nothing of their own but only what he who commissioned
them gave them to teach; and thereby they honored
him in the highest degree. But "the Jews" (rulers),
who opposed Jesus and only imagined that they were
supporting Moses, who even planned to murder Jesus in
flagrant violation of Moses; and in lesser degree
"the multitude" (pilgrims), who were displeased with
Jesus — are shown to be gravely in the wrong.

25) *The Divine Origin of Jesus' Person, 25-30.* —
After dealing with the rulers and then with a crowd
of pilgrims Jesus answers also a number of the
citizens of Jerusalem, who raise the question regarding his person and tell themselves that he cannot
be the Christ. **Some of the citizens of Jerusalem
accordingly were saying, Is not this he whom they
are seeking to kill?** These "Jerusalemites," as John
calls them, live in the city. "Accordingly" connects
what these citizens say with what they are witnessing
at the moment. They are a part of the crowd that
confront Jesus. No interval occurs between v. 24 and
v. 25. The imperfect ἔλεγον is descriptive; they were
most likely a little group and were speaking quietly
to each other, certainly not so that either the pilgrims
or the rulers heard their remarks.

These citizens are better posted than the pilgrims
who live elsewhere and visit the city only on great
occasions. So they are well informed about the intention of the rulers to kill Jesus, while the pilgrims are
shocked to hear of this intention (v. 19). But the

situation these citizens are witnessing puzzles them. "Is not this he whom they are seeking to kill?" They feel sure that this is, indeed, the man (οὗ at the head of the question).

26) **And behold, with openness he speaks, and nothing to him do they say. Can it be that the rulers have, indeed, realized that this is the Christ?** First the astonishing fact, then an explanation that would, indeed, explain the fact but that is presented as certainly being out of the question. Here to the astonishment of these citizens is Jesus speaking in public (παρρησίᾳ), and here are some of the rulers (οἱ ἄρχοντες), and they do not say a thing (οὐδέν) to him, namely to apprehend him and to carry out their determination to kill him. The rulers had, indeed, said something (v. 15), but Jesus had promptly closed their mouths, and they had kept them closed. "Nothing to him do they say?" means nothing to prevent him from speaking with freedom, nothing like declaring him under arrest, nothing like a criminal charge to justify arrest.

The possibility flashes into the minds of these citizens that their rulers have changed their minds about Jesus. The very clash, however, which they have just witnessed (v. 15-19) settles any such possibility. The very question in which they utter it carries in it their own denial, for μή implies a negative answer in their own minds: "Can it be ever (μήποτε)?" No, it cannot be. The Greek has the aorist ἔγνωσαν, "did come to realize," whereas the English idiom prefers the perfect tense; see the excellent discussion in R. 843, etc. This is due to the fact that in the Greek the perfect does not like the English perfect indicate an action just *recently* completed. The sense of ἀληθῶς is "indeed," or "really"; but the second ἀληθῶς in the *textus receptus* (A. V.) must be cancelled: "that this is the *very* Christ" ("is *truly* the Christ"),

the promised Messiah.   All the evidence is to the contrary — the rulers have not changed their minds about
Jesus.

27)   Moreover, these citizens agree on this point
with the rulers.   **On the contrary, him we know,
whence he is; but the Christ, when he comes, no
one will know whence he is.**   The negation in the
minds of the citizens (μήποτε in v. 26) is matched by
the adversative (ἀλλά) at the head of v. 27: No, the
rulers have not realized, etc.; "on the contrary," they
could not, for even these citizens know that Jesus
cannot possibly be the Christ.   Why not?   The mighty
evidence of his miracles, all the power of his
teaching, and the impact of his personality inevitably
felt in both, count for nothing with these men of the
metropolis, who refuse to be impressed as were the
pilgrim crowds, especially those from Galilee.   They
have their own little criterion for rejecting Jesus'
claims.   "Him we know, whence he is; but the Christ,
when he comes, no one will know whence he is."
This Jewish notion about the expected Messiah, with
which in the minds of these wiseacres Jesus does not
accord, they imagine keeps them from being deceived
by Jesus.   We have no evidence that the rulers use
the same line of argument.   On the contrary, like some
of the multitude (v. 41, 42), the rulers apply a different criterion, namely, that Jesus hails from Galilee
whereas the Scriptures say that the Messiah will be
born in Bethlehem, of the seed of David, in Judea
(v. 52).

The efforts to trace the notion of the citizens in
Jewish literature have produced no satisfactory results.   In the middle of the second century Justin puts
into the mouth of the Jew Tryphon the opinion: "But
the Messiah, even when he is born and exists somewhere, is unknown and does not even know himself,
and has no power until Elijah anoints him and makes

him know to all." Jewish literature, however, nowhere makes Elijah anoint the Messiah. Justin's version of Tryphon's opinion makes no reference to the
origin of the Messiah, "whence he is," but states only
that neither the Messiah nor anyone else will know
him as the Messiah until Elijah anoints him. The
assumption that the notion of the citizens is derived
from the low state of the house of David at the time,
supported possibly also by Scripture statements like
Isa. 53:2 and 8; Mal. 3:1, "shall suddenly come
to his Temple," is too farfetched to merit consideration.

The citizens think that they are fully informed
"whence" Jesus is. They have found out all about his
long residence in Nazareth, his family connection
(1:45; 6:42), especially also his career in Galilee
during the past year since his last visit to Jerusalem.
Thus they feel that they know all about him. No
reason appears for restricting "whence" to the family
of Jesus exclusive of his home and his residence, for
the two always go together. But this very information is proof to them that he cannot be the Messiah.
For their picture of the Messiah — however they may
have obtained it — is that "when he comes, no one
will know whence he is," i. e., from what town and
province and from what family. Not that his origin
will forever be shrouded in mystery, but that it will
be unknown "when he comes," or at the time of his
public appearance. This type of reasoning has often
been followed by men who imagine themselves to be
superior to others. They pick some flaw and fasten on
that and refuse to consider the real and decisive facts,
however great and convincing these may be.

28) The cool and self-satisfied way in which these
citizens dispose of Jesus arouses him to make the most
energetic reply. **Jesus, accordingly, cried out,
teaching in the Temple and saying, Both me you**

**know and know whence I am?! And (yet) I have
not come of myself, but one that is real is he that
did send me, whom you do not know.** With a loud
voice, showing how deeply he was affected, Jesus
cried out. What moves him is not the argument
of these citizens but the superficiality and shallow-
ness which satisfies them for disposing of his person
and his office. The position of the subject, ὁ Ἰησοῦς,
between the two participles διδάσκων καὶ λέγων shows
that the phrase "in the Temple" is not to be drawn
to the main verb: "he cried out in the Temple," but
that it must be drawn to the two participles: "teaching in the Temple and saying." The participles, however, cannot indicate the time: while still teaching
and speaking in the Temple; or: before he left the
Temple court. For v. 14 has already given us this
information, and no reason appears for repeating it
here. These are modal participles, describing the loud
crying of Jesus. "He cried out" draws attention to
the fact that he was deeply moved thus to raise
his voice; the participles add that he did this as
teaching and making a declaration (λέγων) here in the
Temple, the central place designed for this very purpose. In this loud cry we are still to hear the teacher
and speaker engaged in his Temple work. John writes
this preamble to Jesus' words as a witness who was
present, who heard and saw what took place.

The fact that Jesus cried out as he did should
dispose of the idea that Jesus merely acknowledges
what the citizens claim to know, namely, whence he
is, which naturally involves also who he is: "You
know both me and know whence I am." Why should
Jesus lift up his voice in order to make such an
admission? His ordinary tone of voice would have
sufficed for that. The emotion indicated on the part
of Jesus makes it quite certain that his first words
are an exclamatory question. In fact, Jesus cannot

admit that these citizens really know him, for their own little argument shows that they do not, and Jesus tells them in no uncertain way that they do not. Note the emphasis brought out by the two καί: "Both *me* you know and *know* whence I am?!" This matches exactly the words of these citizens. Not that Jesus actually heard what they said to each other; he understood of his own accord exactly what they said. They claimed to know "him, whence he is," *him*, that he cannot possibly be the Christ, that he must be an imposter, deceiving the people (v. 12), not sent of God, but foisting himself upon the people; and this because *they know* his home town and his family and are sure because of this knowledge of theirs. The force of Jesus' cry is: "So you think you know *me* since you are sure you *know* my home and family!" The question is debated as to whether these words contain a tinge of irony or not. The blanket denial that Jesus never employs irony is untenable. Equally unwarranted is the claim that irony is incompatible with a loud tone of voice, for many an exclamation is even sarcastic. In the present case the irony is sufficiently marked by the fact that these wise citizens treat as supremely significant something that has no significance at all.

The fact that Jesus grew up in Nazareth in the home of Joseph and Mary reveals nothing about his true origin and mission, and the assumption of the citizens that it reveals everything only demonstrates their foolish ignorance. With a third καί, used adversatively, Jesus himself testifies "whence he is": "and I have not come of myself, but one that is real is he that did send me, whom you do not know." The emphasis is on the positive clause, which the negative clause only aids in stressing. And in this positive clause the point is the reality of the great Sender of Jesus: "he is *real* that did send me." The predicate ἀληθινός opposes the idea which these citizens hold, that Jesus has come on his own initiative, that at best he only imagines that he is sent. His Sender, he testifies, is not a phantasy of his mind, a being whom he has invented, but One who is actual and real. This evident contrast, furnished by the negative clause, dare not be altered. Jesus is not comparing two senders, one who is such in the highest degree and one in an inferior degree; or one who has genuine authority to send and another whose authority may be called in question. Likewise ἀληθινός does not mean ἀληθινὸς Θεός: he that did send me is "the true God." While Jesus refers to God, the predicate "real" states only that as a Sender the person of whom Jesus is speaking is "real," One who actually exists.

The full impact of this testimony lies in the relative clause, "whom you do not know." We must note the emphatic pronoun ὑμεῖς, "you," such as *you* are. These citizens boast of their knowledge: "him we know whence he is." This supposed knowledge Jesus first calls in question: *"Me* you know?! and *you know* whence I am?!"* meaning: You do not know *me*, nor do *you know* whence I am! Then Jesus denies this supposed knowledge: this Sender, who is real, "whom *you* (being what you are) *do not know."* In spite of the Scriptures which these citizens had they do not know God (5:38), proof of which is the fact that, when God sent them his own Son, they failed to recognize that Son and the fact that God had sent him. They know a couple of minor and external things about Jesus, his home town and his family; with this shallow knowledge they could never know either his person or his mission. To know these they would have to know God, as God actually had revealed himself — and him they do not know.

29) These citizens are blind regarding the vital point; not so Jesus. **I know him because I am from**

him; and he did commission me. The reading with
δέ has insufficient support: "Yet I know him." This
means that ἐγώ is not meant to be in contrast with the
preceding ὑμεῖς, but in contrast with the following
ἐκεῖνος: "*I* know him, . . . and *he* did send me."
It is true that Jesus places his knowledge overagainst
the ignorance of these citizens. But we must add that
the knowledge Jesus has is of an entirely different
kind from that which these citizens might have had
and failed to have. They could and should have
known God from his Word, but Jesus was not
dependent upon this source for his knowledge of God.
He knows God in an immediate manner: "because
I am from him." In παρ' αὐτοῦ lies an original παρ'
αὐτῷ. He who is "from God" was originally "with
God." Compare 1:18; 3:13; 6:33, 38, 46, 50, and 58.
Before his incarnation Jesus was with God in heaven
and thus he now says of himself, "I am from God."
The knowledge he has of God is that which he brought
with him from heaven (1:18).

Certain texts have: ὅτι παρ' αὐτῷ εἰμι, "because I am
with him." The textual evidence has not established
this as the true reading. The claim that παρ' αὐτῷ
was changed into παρ' αὐτοῦ because the former conveys an "inconvenient" meaning is unwarranted; for
Jesus utters the same thought in 3:13 (the last clause:
"he who is in heaven"; see the explanation of these
words), and, of course, might use it again. The
"inconvenience" of this thought is rather in the
minds of the moderns, who do not admit that Jesus
can at the same time be present both on earth and
with God in heaven. For this reason they eliminate this thought from 3:13, and the παρ' αὐτῷ in
the present passage they refer to the communion of
Jesus with God, supporting their view by a reference
to 8:29, μετ' ἐμοῦ, God's communion with Jesus —
although the prepositions as well as the contexts

differ. In order to clear up the matter we must
note that the primary question at issue is πόθεν ἐστίν,
"whence Jesus is." In v. 27 this indirect question is
twice repeated by the citizens, and in v. 28 Jesus takes
it from their lips. When answering this question
Jesus brings in the point of knowledge; because the
citizens do not know God, therefore they know neither
Jesus nor whence he is; Jesus, however, knows God
because he is "from him," παρ' αὐτοῦ, even as also God
sent him. We thus see that it is not enough for Jesus
to say that he is "with God," for, while this would
show that he knows God, it would not state "whence
he is." Therefore Jesus says that he is "from God,"
which does both, namely, proves his origin from
heaven and thus his direct knowledge of God.

When Jesus testifies that he is "from him" he
already declares his mission, namely, that he is sent
as the Messiah. But he states this directly, "and he
did commission me." This is an independent statement which is no longer governed by ὅτι. It forms
part of the answer to the question "whence" Jesus
is. Note how ἐγώ and ἐκεῖνος are emphatically balanced:
"*I* am from him; *he* did commission me." In other
words, this God, whom these citizens do not know,
Jesus knows so well, for Jesus came from him, and
that God did himself send and commission Jesus. In
the completest way the question, whence Jesus is, is
thus answered. And at the same time these citizens
are shown why they know nothing of Jesus' origin
although they think they know everything, and why
Jesus knows what is hidden from them. The issue
is squarely drawn: on the one side utter ignorance
and empty boast of knowledge, on the other complete
and self-evident knowledge; on the one side a spurious
deduction, on the other firsthand testimony to the
fact; on the one side vain and empty denial that Jesus
is the Christ, on the other the assured reality that he

is, indeed, the Christ. While it is brief, this testimony
of Jesus is most direct and to the point and at the
same time highly dramatic.

30) It intensifies the hostility of the citizens.
**Therefore they were seeking to arrest him; and no
one laid his hand upon him because his hour had
not yet come.** No change of subject is indicated.
The irritated citizens of Jerusalem (v. 25), passively
averse to Jesus up to this point, are now filled with
the desire to aid the authorities in apprehending
the man who had contradicted them. The imperfect
ἐζήτουν leaves the outcome of this desire open; the
following aorist οὐδεὶς ἐπέβαλον reports that the desire
proved abortive. No one had the courage actually to
lay his hand on Jesus. The scene is overdrawn when
these citizens are made to press in on Jesus "in wild
rage" in order to drag him to prison. We are told
only what was in their hearts. When it came to
action, they hesitated. So also we read nothing about
"an invisible wall of protection surrounding Jesus"
so that he "remained untouched in the midst of his
raging enemies." But instead of reporting the secondary reason why no one laid his hand upon Jesus, John
at once points to the primary reason why these citizens
were restrained from carrying out their desire. "His
hour had not yet come," the time set by the Father
for Jesus to be delivered into the hands of his enemies.
On this occasion the invisible hand of God restrained
his foes by opening no way for them to carry out
their design. We may take it that the citizens were
afraid of the pilgrim multitudes who thronged the
Temple courts during the festival. It was God's
hand that protected Jesus, but that hand used natural
means.

31) *Jesus Warns the Jews regarding his Departure, 31-36.* — The encounter sketched in v. 14-24
took place on the day in the midst of the feast when

Jesus first appeared in the Temple. The clash with the citizens seems to have followed almost immediately on the same day. Verse 37 takes us to the last day of the feast. The intervening paragraph, v. 31-36, evidently reports an incident that occurred on one of the days between these two events. For the Sanhedrin has had time to call a meeting and to issue an order to the Temple police to take Jesus into custody. We must begin a new paragraph with v. 31. This verse states what moved the Pharisees to stir the Sanhedrin into action with the result that Jesus publicly warns all concerned that he will soon return to his Sender, at which announcement the rulers scoff.

But of the multitude many believed on him; and they were saying, The Christ, when he shall come, certainly will do no greater signs than this man has done? Not all, but a goodly number of the pilgrims gathered for the feast, believed in Jesus. The connective δέ contrasts these with the citizens of Jerusalem who had advanced to decided hostility. But we cannot conclude from the fact that Jesus only taught on this visit to Jerusalem and wrought no miracles that the faith of these pilgrims was the result of his words. We are compelled to connect the character of the faith of these people with the confession they make, and this shows that their faith as yet rested only on the signs and had not yet embraced the teaching of Jesus. It resembled the faith of those mentioned in 2:23; and again in 4:45; and was inferior to the faith of those mentioned in 4:41. The imperfect ἔλεγον describes how they question one with another. Note how ὁ Χριστός is placed emphatically forward. The question is really abstract; it supposes the coming of the Christ and then asks whether he could do greater signs than Jesus had already done. We must regard πλείονα, not as a reference to mere number: "more signs," but to a *plus qualitate*, as S. Goebel states: "greater signs." For this use of the term compare Matt. 6:25; 12:41; also Matt. 21:36; Heb. 3:3; 11:4; Rev. 2:19. The question with μή indicates that in the minds of these pilgrims the supposition must be denied. They cannot imagine that the Messiah, whoever he may be, would work signs that exceeded those Jesus "did work," the historical aorist to express the past fact. Among those present there must have been many who had seen some of these signs, and, no doubt, they told of them and exchanged reports. In ὧν the antecedent is drawn into the relative, and the case of the antecedent is retained: τούτων ἅ, R. 720.

32) For fear of the rulers no open demonstration was made in favor of Jesus, proclaiming him as "the Christ"; the pilgrims contented themselves with quiet talk. **The Pharisees heard the multitude murmuring these things concerning him; and the chief priests and the Pharisees sent officers in order to arrest him.** The Pharisees (see 1:24) were the great guardians of the law. Some of these moved among the pilgrims and heard this quiet talk. The genitive indicates the persons heard and is here modified by a predicative participle: τοῦ ὄχλου γογγύζοντος. These Pharisees at once reported to the rulers and stirred them to action. The term "Pharisees" denotes a numerous party among the Jews (see 1:24), but "the chief priests and the Pharisees" is John's designation for the Sanhedrin, the highest court of the nation, 7:45; 11:47, and 57; 18:3. Some of Pharisees who brought the report concerning the talk among the pilgrims may also have been members of the Sanhedrin. John sketches only sufficient of the situation to permit his readers to understand the following words of Jesus and the reaction which they caused. So he reports only that the Sanhedrin sent its police officers to arrest Jesus. Whether the Sanhedrin just happened to be

in session, or whether a special meeting was called, and what the deliberations were that ended in the order of arrest, is omitted. This legal and official order, issued by the proper court of jurisdiction to its lawful police force, marks a definite stage in the proceedings of the authorities against Jesus. In 5:18; 7:1 and 20 we learn only that the Jewish leaders "were seeking to kill" Jesus, i. e., that this was their desire and design. Now they take the first official and legal steps toward that end. As the sequel shows, this order of arrest is not peremptory, to bring Jesus in forthwith. The officers are to watch for their opportunity; for the Sanhedrin fears to enrage the pilgrims who are favorable to Jesus. This might prove dangerous. The Sanhedrin generally reckoned with the consequences.

33) The order is issued. The connective οὖν shows that in some way Jesus is fully aware of the serious move. Before him are the ὄχλος, as usual, some of the Ἰουδαῖοι or members of the Sanhedrin (v. 35), and the ὑπηρέται or police watching their chance. **Jesus, therefore, said, Yet a little while I am with you and I am going away to him that did send me.** We must cancel αὐτοῖς: he said "to them" (A. V.). While "the Jews," namely the Sanhedrists present, make a response (v. 35), this is not addressed to Jesus but to each other, it is a kind of scoffing uttered only so that Jesus, too, shall hear and be wounded the more. We may then say that the words of Jesus are intended for all present, in particular for "the Jews." With perfect calmness and assurance Jesus delivers his answer to the move that has been made against him, but a sorrowful tone of deep pity vibrates through his words.

Jesus speaks as one whose course is fully planned and will be completed in due order. He will yet remain with these people for a short time; then his task will be finished, and he will go back to his great Sender. The underlying thought is that nothing which these Jews, his enemies, may do will change that program in the least. In a short time he will complete his mission and return to his Sender to make his report. The emphasis is first on "little" (actually only six months remain) and next on "I am going away." Jesus says that he himself will stay yet awhile and then will leave. As far as the Jews are concerned, their actions do not count. There is something majestic in the words. When he again mentions "him that did send me" he speaks as the Messiah engaged in his Messianic mission, back of which is God himself. The other thought is that the Jewish authorities want to be rid of Jesus, at once if possible, and that their wish will, indeed, be fulfilled by Jesus himself, though not at once. But his leaving will not be as they desire. It will not be a mere killing him as a man and thus an ending of his career. Jesus will complete his mission and then, after everything has been finished for which he came to earth, he will return to his Father in heaven.

34) But this leaving has another side, one pertaining to the enemies of Jesus, one dreadful to contemplate. **You shall seek me and shall not find me; and where I am you cannot come.** Luther writes, "These are terrible words, I do not like to read them." Back of them lies the rejection of Jesus, God's Messiah, by the Jewish nation. "You shall seek me" cannot refer to a *hostile* seeking, for Jesus will be exalted at his Father's right hand. It cannot refer to a seeking *for help* to alleviate the calamities that will descend upon the nation, for Jesus nowhere intimates that he is a political or a military deliverer. A *repentant* seeking is also excluded, for Jesus adds, "and you shall not find me," and elucidates this in 8:21, "You shall seek me and shall die in your sins."

570   *The Interpretation of John*

This is the seeking of *despair* which always comes
too late. Amos 8:11, etc., describes it: "Behold, the
days come, saith the Lord God, that I will send a
famine in the land, not a famine of bread, nor a thirst
for water, but of hearing the words of the Lord. And
they shall wander from sea to sea, and from the north
even to the east, they shall run to and fro to seek
the word of the Lord, *and shall not find it.*" Again
Prov. 1:24, etc.: "Because I have called, and ye
refused; I have stretched out my hand, and no man
regarded; but ye have set at naught all my counsel,
and would none of my reproof: I will also laugh at
your calamity; I will mock when your fear cometh;
when your fear cometh as desolation, and your destruction cometh as a whirlwind; when distress and anguish
cometh upon you. Then shall they call upon me, but
I will not answer; *they shall seek me early, but they
shall not find me:* for that they hated knowledge, and
did not choose the fear of the Lord: they would none
of my counsel, they despised all my reproof. Therefore they shall eat of the fruit of their own way, and
be filled with their own devices." This terrible seeking comes when the day of grace is past. "Today if
ye will hear his voice, harden not your hearts as in the
provocation," Heb. 3:15. Note the juxtaposition of
ἐγώ and ὑμεῖς — in heaven and blessedness, *I, you* amid
death and damnation.

35) While Jesus addresses those present in the
most direct way, no direct reply is made to him. Only
the rulers speak, but to each other not to him. They
had not fared very well in their last attempt (v. 15)
when Jesus had promptly silenced them (v. 16-19).
**The Jews, therefore, said to themselves, Where is
this fellow about to go that we shall not find him?
He certainly is not about to go to the Dispersion
among the Greeks and to teach the Greeks? What
is this word which he said, You shall seek me and**

shall not find me, and where I am you cannot come? The phrase πρὸς ἑαυτούς, "to themselves," means "to each other"; πρὸς is reciprocal. These Jews want the crowd to understand that they do not deem Jesus worthy a reply. What they remark to each other is intended as insulting mockery. They act as though they did not hear the words, "to him that did send me," with all that these words implied. They heard well enough and understood fully. But in order to mock Jesus and to ridicule the prophetic threat in his words, they pretend to be mystified. So he is going to run off somewhere and hide where they will not find him? On ποῦ for "whither" see R. 299 (b); ὅτι is made causal, B.-D. 456, 2; R. 1205 "probably"; consecutive is much better, R. 1001. Well, about the only place that could be would be the Diaspora among the heathen Greeks, some distant country where scattered Jews live among the heathen Greek population. Smaller and larger groups of Jews were scattered far and' wide over all the Roman Empire; see the list in Acts 2:9-11. The genitive "of the Greeks" is called objective of place, R. 495, 500, etc., and is translated "among the Greeks." These genitives look like simple possessives: the Diaspora which the Greeks have. The form of the question implies a negative answer. Yet this does not mean that the Jews suggest "no" as the answer. Their question is intended as a sneer, and its negative turn with μή intends to make the sneer more cutting.

This is brought out by the addition, "and to teach the Greeks," τοὺς Ἕλληνας, pagan Greeks, not Hellenized Jews, which would be Ἑλληνισταί. The thought in the negative question is that Jesus, rejected by the acknowledged Jewish authorities at the capital, might turn to the Jews scattered in other lands, and, finding himself rejected also by these, would have left only pagan Greeks among whom to play the Messiah. Thus

for the statement of Jesus that he will soon go away
to his Sender the Jews would substitute the wild notion
that, if he does go away, the only choice he would
have is to go to the pagan world. This sneer intends
to reduce the Messiahship of Jesus to a bald absurdity.
We, therefore, do not need the explanation that the
Jews did not understand Jesus when he spoke about
his Sender; or that these Jews were other individuals
who had not faced Jesus before. Nor is the claim
warranted that Jesus never uttered the phrase "to
him that did send me," but that John added it of his
own accord. It is correct, however, that John records
this sneer of the Jews because the gospel afterward
took exactly the course sneeringly suggested by these
Jews. Paul carried it to the Dispersion and to
the Gentiles, and John himself labored in Ephesus
and wrote his Gospel in the very language of the
Greeks.

36) When the Jews inquire of each other, "What
is this word which he said?" etc., they merely continue
their pretense of being mystified, and this is the reason
why Jesus pays no further attention to them. The
police officers stood by but received no hint to step
in and to take Jesus into custody. Whether this
inaction was due to the effect of the calm and deliberate attitude of Jesus and to the force of his words
or merely to the outward situation, the presence of too
many friends of Jesus in the multitude, who will say?

III. *Jesus' Testimony Impresses the Police Sent for
His Arrest, 37-52.*

37) **Now on the last day, the great day of the
feast, Jesus was standing, and he cried, saying, If
anyone thirsts, let him come to me and let him
drink.** The question whether this last and great
day of the feast is the seventh or the eighth day is of

minor importance. John specifies the day, not merely because he vividly remembers it but evidently because the significance of the day and of the ritual connected with it are reflected in the words of Jesus. We join the majority in deciding for the eighth day, although the question is still being debated. The details of the argument deal chiefly with Lev. 23:36; Neh. 8:18; Josephus, *Ant.* 3, 10; and the Mishna treatise entitled *Succa.* The fact that the festival commonly comprised eight days ought no longer to be contested. The chief point, as all acknowledge, is the greatness of the day in question. Those who contend for the seventh must show that this exceeded the eighth. Yet it lacked the convocation which distinguishes the eighth day. The greatest number of sacrifices were offered on the first day, and this number decreased day by day, so that on the seventh day very few were offered. The eighth day had the special distinction that it was the last festival day in the entire Jewish church year and was called "the last good day" (*Succa* IV, 8), "the sacred close of the year" (Josephus), ἐξόδιον (LXX), a free translation of 'Atzerch, "Festive Convocation" (Lev. 23:36; Num. 29:35; Neh. 8:18). At least since the time of the Maccabees (II Macc. 10:6) the eighth day accords best with John's designation, "on the last day, the great day of the feast."

The action of Jesus accords with the greatness of the day. "He was standing and he cried" (compare v. 28). He now performed the role of a public herald, no longer that of a teacher, who usually was seated. The pluperfect εἱστήκει is imperfect in sense and describes the action of standing, while the aorist ἔκραξε notes the fact that Jesus shouted. Both are finite verbs and thus make both actions equally important. The crowds surging in the Temple court made it necessary for Jesus to seek some prominent place where he could stand above the people and be generally seen and to lift up his voice so that as many as possible might hear him. Oriental orators still sit while they are speaking. In the great mosque at Damascus and again in the mosque of the dancing dervishes in Constantinople the author heard the Koran expounded by speakers who were seated cross-legged on a small elevated platform, the audience being seated cross-legged on the floor around them.

Jesus shouts into the ears of the great crowd, "If anyone shall thirst," etc., (present subjunctive, "shall be thirsting"). The condition of expectancy implies that some will, indeed, thirst, yet the indefinite singular sounds as though Jesus does not expect that many will thirst. He refers to *spiritual* thirsting (4:14; 6:53-56), which, however, does not emanate from ourselves but, like the coming and the drinking, is the effect of the presence of Jesus, of his call and offer of living water (grace and salvation). He awakens the desire for spiritual satisfaction, even as he also satisfies this desire.

Each morning during the seven days of the feast, at the time of the sacrifice, a priest proceeded to the fountain of Siloah with a golden pitcher, filled it with water, and, accompanied by a solemn procession, bore it to the altar of burnt sacrifice, pouring the water, together with the contents of a pitcher of wine from the drink offering, into two perforated flat bowls. The trumpets sounded, and the people sang Isa. 12:3, "Therefore with joy shall ye draw water out of the wells of salvation." Compare the author's *Eisenach Old Testament Selections,* 701, etc. Late Jewish authorities report that this was done also on the eighth day. In the debate as to whether Jesus has this ceremony in mind when uttering his cry we need not be in doubt. It commemorated the water that gushed out of the rock at Meribah and that was intended to quench the *thirst* of the multitude in the desert, although the symbolic ceremony in the Temple repeated only the pouring out. Symbols seldom re-enact every feature. Water is not directly mentioned but is certainly implied in thirsting and in drinking. This water is usually identified as the Word. But 4:10 (which see) shows that the water which Jesus has in mind is life, and thus his Word is the means for bestowing it. Coming and drinking are merely two sides of one action, namely, believing in Jesus. This call to come and to drink is full of efficacious drawing power. Whoever does come and drink is moved thereto by the Word and the gift held out to him. The two present imperatives ἐρχέσθω and πινέτω are aoristic presents not durative or linear actions; see R. 864, etc., especially the three examples of imperatives in Luke 7:8, at the bottom of 865, under "specific presents." We are to come and to drink once only — then we shall never thirst again. Life, once received, lives on and on; we need not receive it over and over again. The figure of birth (3:3-5) is more adequate in this respect, as natural birth is without repetition. In the case of eating and drinking the explanation must be added that repetition is not necessary (4:14; 6:35) because in nature hunger and thirst recur, and we are compelled to eat and to drink daily.

38) The lack of a connective between v. 37 and v. 38 is sufficient ground for assuming that the two verses are independent statements, not uttered consecutively but taken from separate parts of a longer discourse. That Jesus said more on this last day when he stood in a prominent position and cried out may well be assumed, compare "these words" in v. 40. Verses 37 and 38, however, are too closely related in thought to be separated from each other. If anything at all intervened, it only expanded v. 37 and retained

the inner connection with v. 38. He who comes to
Jesus not only finds his own soul satisfied but also becomes a medium for conveying the same spiritual
satisfaction to others — this, of course, when the work
of Jesus shall be finished and the Holy Spirit given to
believers after Pentecost, v. 39.

**He that believes in me — even as the Scripture
has said, out of his belly rivers of living water shall
flow.** The sense will not allow us to draw "he that
believes in me" to v. 37, for Jesus bids the thirsty to
come and to drink and not him who already believes
and has his thirst quenched. It is equally impossible
to refer αὐτοῦ, out of "his" belly, to the pronoun "me"
in v. 37 and thus to have Jesus say that out of "his"
belly these rivers shall flow. The anacoluthon is
quite simple and fairly frequent, beginning the sentence with a nominative (a suspended subject, R. 437;
a *nominativus pendens*, R. 459, 1130) and continuing
with another subject while a genitive takes up the
first. "He that believes in me" is literal and thus
makes clear what the figurative coming to Jesus and
drinking mean, namely to become a believer. The
present substantivized participle ὁ πιστεύων characterizes the person as one who continues trusting in
Jesus. To the person thus described an astounding
promise is held out, one mentioned in the Old Testament Scriptures and now restated by Jesus.

"Even as the Scripture did say" (the English requires "has said") is not the formula for introducing
a direct quotation from the Old Testament but one
that reproduces Scripture thought. We may consider
Isa. 58:11: "And the Lord shall . . . satisfy thy
soul in drought, . . . and thou shalt be like a
watered garden, and like a spring of water, where
waters fail not"; Zech. 14:8: "And it shall be in that
day, that living waters shall go out from Jerusalem,"
this plural being individualized by Jesus; and other

passages verbally close. A point that is often over-looked is the question why Jesus fortifies what he here promises the believers by anchoring this promise in the Old Testament Scripture. He does the same in 5:39; 5:46, 47; and 7:22. His entire mission and work, together with all the blessings he has come to bestow, are the fulfillment of God's ancient promises, which fact proves beyond question the genuineness of his Messiahship. This reference to the Scripture is another direct answer to the rulers who scoff at his claims. The fact that through Jesus every believer actually attains what God promised ages ago by the mouth of his holy prophets is the subjective evidence for the truth of Christianity. In the present case, however, the festival with its rites renews the old promises of God to the people, and what Jesus shouts to the multitude interprets and shows the fulfillment of these promises. This is the real bearing of the reference to the Scripture.

The emphasis is on ποταμοί (placed forward) and on ὕδατος ζῶντος (placed at the end), which the English cannot imitate. Actual "rivers" not mere trickles shall flow forth; and these shall consist of "living water" (4:10). It is commonplace to remark that "living" means "flowing" as opposed to stagnant, for rivers always flow. "Living water" is one of the allegorical expressions frequently used in the Scriptures, in which the figurative term is at once expounded by the non-figurative (see 4:10). We may analyze as follows: the fountain = Jesus ("let him come unto me"); thirsting, coming, and drinking, taken together = believing; the κοιλία receiving the water = the inner man; the water = true life; the flowing rivers = life-giving influence on others. The abundance of the latter is indicated by the plural "rivers," saving influences in various directions and of different kinds. The ancients felt no impropriety in using κοιλία, which denotes the abdominal cavity and its contents, in a figurative way. The American Committee of the R. V. translates "from within him" instead of "out of his belly"; but for the modern imagination the gain is small. "Belly" merely continues the figure already used in thirsting and in drinking (v. 38) and extended to "water." All four expressions are to be understood spiritually.

In the figurative language of Jesus we must note certain features that are sometimes misunderstood due to the greatness and the strangeness of the realities that are pictured. At times the figure falls short, its imagery will not cover the reality; hence it is frankly abandoned and the reality itself is finally also stated, as in Matt. 25:30, "the outer darkness," "the weeping and gnashing of teeth." Again, the figure is utterly improbable, as in Matt. 21:37; no man would send his son under circumstances such as are narrated. Finally, a second figure is used to help out the first, as in Matt. 21:42-44, that of the stone (note the astonishing use in v. 44) completing that of the husbandmen. On this order is 4:14, one drink and a ceaselessly flowing inner spring — the entire realm of nature has no phenomenon like that. Similarly here, one drink to quench spiritual thirst; then rivers of water full of spiritual life flowing out in different directions. Whoever heard of one mouthful of water producing even one river? and whoever heard of one source sending out a number of rivers? This breath-taking boldness in using imagery, with a single turn going from a drink to a number of rivers, subordinates the figures to the reality and at the same time impresses that reality in an unforgettable way. The idea of water is thus used in the fullest manner, being based on that drawn from Siloah and poured out at the altar.

In 4:14 the figure of the "spring" pictures only the fact that the believer will never thirst again; here the "rivers" picture the fact that the believer will resemble Jesus himself in that he will help to quench the thirst of many others. The story of the Acts has been scanned to find the fulfillment of the promise here made by Jesus. "What is the apostolic Word itself through which we believe (John 17:20) ; what are the confessions of the church, in harmony with which we believe; what are her hymns, her prayers, her sermons, all the testimonies of the faith and love in saving word and sacred conversation — what are they but rivers of living water flowing from the body of the church?" Besser.

39) John adds an explanation for the instruction of his readers. **Now this he said concerning the Spirit whom they that believed in him were about to receive; for the Spirit was not yet present because Jesus was not yet glorified.** The connective δέ indicates that this is a parenthetical remark. Πνεῦμα is used with and without the article after the manner of proper names. John is not elucidating the figurative language of Jesus; the rivers of living water are not identical with the Spirit, nor is the water of life that quenches spiritual thirst. Nor dare we suppose that those who at this time believed in Jesus, like the apostles, did so without the Spirit. The translation for οὔπω ἦν Πνεῦμα, "not yet did the Spirit exist," is entirely too strong. The Spirit wrought throughout Old Testament times, in the work of the Baptist, and in the work of Jesus. And yet the believers "were about to receive" the Spirit; he "was not yet present," as presently he would be, i. e., was not yet present thus. The reason is that "Jesus was not yet glorified." That glorification would give them the Spirit.

The redemptive work of Jesus must first be completed, he must return to his Sender (v. 33), rise from the tomb, and ascend to heaven. Then, after all this work of Jesus was completed, he could at Pentecost send the Spirit upon his believers. And that Spirit would make rivers of living water flow from the believers throughout the New Testament era. Acts 1:8, "But ye shall receive power, when the Holy Ghost is come upon you; and ye shall be my witnesses," etc. No believer was ready or able to function as Jesus wanted him to function as long as he did not understand the sacrificial death of Jesus and his glorification. Prior to that completion of Jesus' work all faith was like that of the Old Testament saints, a trust in the promise. Jesus' glorification would fulfill that promise. Then, too, he would send down the Spirit; things were not ready so that he could send him before that time. From that great day onward, even as the Acts report at length, salvation would flow out in great streams to the ends of the earth. The reading should be the aorist οἱ πιστεύσαντες not the present participle; and the observation of R. 859 is valuable: this constative aorist is timeless, designating not merely those who up to this time, when Jesus spoke in the Temple, had believed, but also those who in future ages would believe in him.

40) John has finished his account of the testimony which Jesus delivered at the Feast of Tabernacles; he now records the effect in detail. **Some of the multitude, therefore, who had heard these words were saying, This is of a truth the prophet.** Here ἐκ is partitive for "some," these constituting one class or one side. We see that an advance from v. 31 has been made, where the signs convince many in regard to Jesus; now the deciding factor is the words of Jesus, and nothing is said about the signs. "These words," here the genitive (which is infrequent to indi-

cate what is heard), are usually taken to mean the ones recorded in v. 38, 39, and, because they are so brief, it is assumed that John has greatly abbreviated the address of Jesus. Even then, since this chapter reports other words of Jesus, also uttered before the multitude (v. 16, etc.; 28, etc.; 33, etc.), these others should be included. The reaction of the multitude is thus indicated in v. 20; in v. 31; and now as final in v. 40-43. In distinction from the pilgrim multitude the citizens of Jerusalem totally reject Jesus, v. 25-27; certain ones in the multitude show the same vicious temper, v. 44 (compare v. 30).

The verdict of this first class is expressed with great earnestness, ἀληθῶς, "truly." But when they call Jesus "the prophet," this cannot mean "the Christ," since another part of the multitude sets up this claim in contradiction to those first mentioned. Here, as in 1:21, "the prophet" is conceived to be a forerunner of the Christ. The Old Testament basis for the expectation of such a prophet is Deut. 18:15 and 18, 19. In John 6:14; Acts 3:22; 7:37, this prophet is identified with the Christ. By thus rating Jesus as "the prophet" this part of the multitude is at least deeply impressed and decidedly favorable to Jesus, although it is still far from the truth.

41) **Others were saying, This is the Christ**, the promised Messiah himself. The statement is positive and without qualification. These are believers, of course, with faith of varying degrees and quality. We see their helplessness when an objection is raised, which they seem unable to meet.

Some were saying, Why, out of Galilee the Christ certainly does not come? Did not the Scripture declare that the Christ comes out of the seed of David and from Bethlehem, the village where David was? The first group (ἐκ τοῦ ὄχλου) and the second (ἄλλοι) are placed side by side since their convictions merely vary. The third group (οἱ δέ) is placed in opposition to the second as though this had been designated by οἱ μέν. They offer an argument for their conviction that Jesus cannot be the Christ which is couched in two questions, the first with μή implying a negative answer, the second with οὐ implying a positive answer. The insertion of γάρ (R. 1190), translated "why," points to the proof that "out of Galilee" the Christ does not come, as all will admit. Over against this negative they place the positive, the assurance derived from Micah 5:2; Isa. 11:1; Jer. 23:5, and from their synagogue instruction, that the birthplace of the Messiah must be Bethlehem. "The Scripture" is a comprehensive singular designation for the Old Testament canon, the final authority beyond which no Jew could go. The Davidic descent of the Christ is added in natural connection with Bethlehem which was also David's birthplace.

Because of the long residence of Jesus in Nazareth he was commonly supposed to have been born there. Closer inquiry was not made. By recording without comment the appeal to the Scripture which these men make in regard to Bethlehem John intimates that their idea is correct. If their interpretation of the Scripture were incorrect, John would have pointed that out. He, too, accepts both the Davidic descent and Bethlehem as the birthplace of Jesus, but he knows that both are facts in regard to Jesus, of which these objectors, however, are not aware. "Where David was" refers to his stay in his father's home in Bethlehem before he left that place in later years.

43) The three descriptive imperfects ἔλεγον in v. 40, 41 show us the discussion as it went on, each of the three parties making its claim. The aorist that now follows states the outcome. **Accordingly there came to be a division in the multitude because of him.** Neither party convinced the others; they were

hopelessly divided. "In the multitude," however, shows that the three parties consisted entirely of pilgrim visitors. The argument of the third party in regard to Bethlehem thus differs from that of the citizens of Jerusalem in v. 27, where the claim is made that the Messiah's place of origin will not be known at all.

44) **Certain ones of them, however, would have arrested him, but no one laid his hands on him.** This fourth class must have been quite small (τινές), yet they were also pilgrims, possibly adherents of the Pharisees who had instigated the move to take Jesus into custody. The imperfect ἤθελον points to a will that was not carried into effect, as also the following aorist states. These violent opponents would like to have arrested Jesus and handed him over to the authorities, but, like the citizens in v. 30, they failed to act. Why, John does not say, but evidently for the same reason as that mentioned in v. 30. John varies his expressions slightly: in v. 30, "his hand," now "his hands." This closes the account of the effect of the testimony of Jesus on the pilgrim crowds who attended the feast. Note the extremes: some believe, others are ready to aid in killing Jesus.

45) At this point John reports how the order of the Sanhedrin to the Temple police to arrest Jesus broke down completely, so that the order was quietly dropped, and Jesus could remain in Jerusalem for some time after the feast was over. **The officers, therefore, came to the chief priests and Pharisees; and these said to them, Why did you not bring him?** The connective οὖν reverts to the inability of others besides the officers to lay hands on Jesus, though they are prompted by their own strong desire to do so. The officers were prompted only by the orders they had received. They now return to make their report.

We may suppose that this occurred in the late afternoon of the eighth festival day. By the next day the pilgrims would be on their homeward journey. The authorities thought that the arrest would have to be effected before the festival closed, assuming that otherwise Jesus, too, would leave together with the crowds. Thus we find the Sanhedrin in session, expecting that finally Jesus would now be brought in. The time for effecting the arrest having expired, the officers feel constrained to come and to make a report. They appear without Jesus and are at once faced with the peremptory question as to why they have not carried out their orders. In this verse one Greek article combines "*the* chief priests and Pharisees" as one class or one body, while in v. 32 two articles are used, "*the* chief priests and *the* Pharisees," since the Pharisees were the ones that instigated the order for the arrest (v. 31) and thus appear as a distinct group of the Sanhedrin.

46) **The officers replied, Never did a man so speak as this man.** Some texts abbreviate this reply, "Never did a man speak thus." The longer form seems the more likely in the mouth of men like these officers. Their reply is truly remarkable. They could truthfully have stated that they had failed because of the danger they would have incurred from the friendly part of the multitude always clustering about Jesus. The Sanhedrin itself feared these pilgrims, and, on receiving such a reply from their subordinates, could hardly have administered more than a mild rebuke. But whatever was the truth as regards the multitude, these officers had been restrained by something else, something that had made so deep an impression upon them that they openly avow it before the whole Sanhedrin, although they know in advance that they will be severely reprimanded and very likely even punished for admitting what they feel they must

admit. We must note these two points: the impression which lamed the hands of these officers, and then the impulse not to hide but openly to confess this impression. Both are due to Jesus.

The emphasis is on οὕτως, the manner in which Jesus spoke, and the verb ἐλάλησεν omits any reference to the substance of the thought that Jesus uttered. The authority, majesty, and power of the speaker restrained these officers, contrary to explicit orders; compare Matt. 7:28. They acknowledge that the manner of Jesus is superior to anything ever found in any other man. They are only one step from saying that this manner is superhuman, yea divine. Much as these officers felt constrained to obey their orders, a stronger influence had come over them — they simply could not and would not lay hands on a man who spoke as this man did. Thus another strange thing appears: the very tools through which the rulers planned to bring Jesus to prison and to death, by making this honest confession, disrupt the unity of the Sanhedrin and thus cause their own plan to be dropped. The means defeat the end. God often plays with his enemies and makes their schemes ridiculous.

47) The rage of the Pharisees in the Sanhedrin now breaks loose. **The Pharisees, therefore, answered them, Certainly you, too, have not been deceived?** The emotion displayed in these μή questions is indicated by the context: protest, indignation, as here, scorn, excitement, sympathy, etc., R. 1175. While in the mind of the questioner the form with μή implies a negative reply, this very form often conveys the fear or the suspicion that the real reply will be the very opposite. Hence here we have the perfect tense "have been deceived" and thus are even now in this condition. Note also the emphatic καὶ ὑμεῖς, "even *you — our own officers*, who ought to stick to

us and listen to us and not to the wily tones of another, one whom we despise. In this manner these Pharisees twist the reply of the officers, who say that never did a man speak *so*, οὔτως, by insinuatingly implying "so wily, with such cunning deceit."

48) This they follow up. **What, did anyone of the rulers believe in him or of the Pharisees? But this multitude, which knows not the law, — accursed are they!** This time μή takes the negative answer˙ as actually being granted. Observe the superior tone of these rulers over against their petty subordinates. What business have these dependents to follow impressions and thoughts of their own? The aorist of the verb marks the past fact: not for one moment did any of these superior men put confidence in Jesus. So old is the argument, which still is current, that in religious matters men of power, authority, and learning cannot err, and that all humbler people ought to be guided by them without question. It was the argument which the lone monk of Wittenberg had to face. Could he alone be right when the pope, the emperor, and all the prelates and the princes held the contrary view? Could he alone be right, and they all be wrong?

49) This argumentative question is followed by a fierce invective: "But this multitude," etc. The strong adversative ἀλλά is often equivalent to our No! We may translate with Zahn, "No; only this rabble," etc. Likewise, in this connection where it is contrasted with the rulers, ὄχλος seems to be the equivalent of the Hebrew *'am haaretz, die breite Schicht der Landbevoelkerung* (Koenig, *Hebraeisches und aramaeisches Woerterbuch*), the country rabble, a scornful designation for the ordinary people, here the pilgrims from outlying parts. What are they over against the high and holy Pharisees, especially those in the great Sanhedrin?

"Which know not the law" = is so ignorant as not even to know the law much less carefully to observe it. But the holy Pharisees make this their absolute specialty. They are the authoritative custodians of the law; they *know*. And here these fools of officers were following that miserable, ignorant rabble instead of these high representatives and guardians of the law!

But the heat of the enraged Pharisees almost makes them blurt out what they certainly do not wish to admit. Their invective starts as though they would say, "But this multitude, which knows not the law, *it believes in him*." A sudden shift avoids this damaging admission: " — accursed are they!" But by this veering even the sense is wrecked; for mere ignorance of the law on the part of common people who do not enjoy the advantages of the Pharisees cannot make them accursed. The real reason for cursing the multitude is not their ignorance but their listening to Jesus and their believing in him. Thus the Pharisees after all betray themselves. No measures were as yet taken against people who believed in Jesus, but note 9:22. The Pharisees soon tried to make good their curse. We hear no more about the officers. They seem to have escaped with the rebuke they had received.

50) But now the Sanhedrin hears another voice. **Nicodemus says to them (he that came to him aforetime, being one of them), Surely our law does not judge the man unless it first has heard from him and has come to know what he does?** If the avowal of the officers causes surprise, the objection of a member of the Sanhedrin itself must cause consternation. John's λέγει, too, is vivid. The parenthesis makes us recall 3:1. A textual question is raised in regard to the words: "he that came to him aforetime," especially also since the codices present different readings. Yet

the interference of Nicodemus cannot be understood
unless we recall his former meeting with Jesus. Merely to identify Nicodemus as "being one of them," i. e.,
a ruler and a Pharisee ("of them" = the Pharisees,
v. 47), would leave unexplained why he spoke out at
this critical moment. It was not because he was one
of them, for as one of them he would have remained
silent; it was because he had been with Jesus.

51) Immediately after the Pharisees asserted so
confidently that not one of their own exalted number
believes in Jesus, Nicodemus, one of their number,
speaks in defense of Jesus. Immediately after they
boasted about themselves as being the great guardians
of the law, one of their own number points out that
they are violating that law. These clashes are highly
dramatic. As a judge Nicodemus had both the right
and the duty to remind his fellow-judges of the requirements of the law when they were forgetting
them. He avoided every discourtesy, every appearance of arrogating to himself a judgment of his
fellow-judges, by merely raising the question, thus
allowing all to join in the answer. Yet it evinces
courage for him to do even so much. Some have
called him timid, but this is a mistake; timidity would
have closed his lips. By employing a question instead
of making an assertion Nicodemus shows wisdom.
Some questions answer themselves, and this is one
of that kind. By using μή Nicodemus indicates what
he on his part thinks the answer must be, but only
so that he intimates that all the rest will agree with
him. Actually they could not disagree. He, indeed,
had to betray his friendliness toward Jesus by asking
even this question that suggested so self-evident an
answer. Whatever odium may result to him from his
colleagues he is ready to bear. He is a noble figure
at this turn of affairs. By overplaying their hand
the Pharisees in a manner force Nicodemus to the

front. He probably would have preferred to say nothing, but his contact with Jesus had opened his eyes sufficiently to see the real character of what was now being enacted, and that gave him courage to speak. By speaking he was brought one step nearer to faith.

It is a mistake to think that Nicodemus uses "the law" as a pretext behind which he may hide. Quite the contrary; the Pharisees had mentioned "the law" and had cursed the people for not knowing it. For this reason Nicodemus refers to "the law." The legal provisions in question are Exod. 23:1 and Deut. 1:16, etc. Moreover, these legal requirements are broader than "the law" as it was laid down for the Jews by God, they are part of the commonest human justice, which is followed even in pagan courts. Here we may remark that fanatical religious zeal on the part of men who claim great holiness for themselves often blindly violates the commonest ordinary justice when dealing with religious opponents. The scene occurring in the Sanhedrin this day has often been repeated since, and often without a Nicodemus to call a halt.

No, the law does not render a verdict on a man, κρίνει, until that man (the one in question, τὸν ἄνθρωπον) is first heard in person by the court, and the court thus itself knows what he does. The verb κρίνει is indeterminate — according to the finding (γνῷ) the verdict may result either in acquital or in a fitting sentence of punishment. There must first be a proper trial. The man charged must first be heard, i. e., given an opportunity to make his defense. Only after all the evidence is in, including that of the man himself, after the court knows and has been able to make a just finding in the case, is the verdict rendered. The aorists ἀκούσῃ and γνῷ indicate actuality. Both are legal terms, as is also κρίνει. "What he does," τί ποιεῖ, = what the

real character of the man's deed is, the court rendering a verdict accordingly. All this, Nicodemus implies, still holds for the Sanhedrin, whether the ὄχλος
or Jesus be brought before its bar. The question
arises whether Nicodemus was present when the order
for the arrest of Jesus was issued, v. 32. We must
assume that he was absent. Since so many judges
made up the court, it no doubt frequently occurred
that one or more were not in their places when a
meeting was held. Some suppose that in spite of
the full title "the chief priests and the Pharisees" in
v. 32 only the executive managers had issued the order.
This is possible but doubtful.

52) The answer which Nicodemus receives is as
passionate as that given to the officers. **They answered and said unto him** (see 1:48), **Surely thou,
too, art not of Galilee? Search and see that no
prophet arises out of Galilee.** Of course they
know that he is not a Galilean, but by their question introduced with μή they insinuate that only on
this supposition could they possibly understand his
appeal to their legal obligations. Jesus hailed from
Galilee, there, too, he had risen to great fame, and the
Galilean pilgrims were the ones who especially acclaimed him at the festival. So the Pharisees, having no possible defense for their illegal procedure,
substitute an insulting attack upon the motive of their
monitor, namely, that he talks as though he, too, were
from Galilee. To this usual interpretation we must
add, that since all the Galileans at the feast are members of "the multitude," the Pharisees imply that
Nicodemus must be no better and stand no higher
in trying to defend the legal rights of the multitude
and of Jesus. Does he want them to think that he
is as ignorant as the multitude? Does he want to
share the curse they had pronounced upon this ignorant rabble?

That is why they add the admonition that Nicodemus search and see for himself that no prophet arises out of Galilee, to say nothing of the Messiah himself. This reference to the gross ignorance of Nicodemus must be coupled with the charge of ignorance against the multitude, among which so many were friendly to Jesus. At the same time this is their return slap at Nicodemus, calling him desperately ignorant for having intimated ignorance of the law on their part, while they thus vindicate their own pretense to knowledge. The aorist imperative "search" enjoins a search that will go to the bottom of things and obtain the actual facts. They do not say whether Nicodemus is to search the Scriptures or only history in general. "See" means: "convince yourself!" The emphasis is on the phrase "out of Galilee." The present tense ἐγείρεται, "arises," reads like the general proposition that at no time Galilee can furnish a prophet. Some texts have the perfect ἐγήγερται, "has arisen," which restricts the claim to the past and says nothing about future possibilities. "Arise," whether the present or the perfect was used, is wider than to be born. It seems almost incredible that these Pharisees did not know that Jonah hailed from Galilee, II Kings 14:25, and that most likely also Nahum and Hosea came from that country. If the present tense is taken in a restricted sense as excluding the past and the three prophets named, Isa. 9:1 (compare Matt. 4:15, 16) is in the way. As so often, blind passion made these men set up false and unwarranted claims which contradicted their own better knowledge. Whether Nicodemus further discussed the point we do not learn. The upshot of the proceedings was that at this time the Sanhedrin took no further action, so that Jesus, who remained in Jerusalem after the feast, continued his work.

CHAPTER VIII

IV. *Jesus Proves his Testimony True and Warns his Opponents, 8:12-30*

7:53-8:11 is not an integral part of John's Gospel but part of the early oral tradition (antedating the year 70) ; it was very early put into written form, and one of its two versions was eventually inserted into John's Gospel. These findings of the text critics must be accepted as facts. Between 7:52 and 8:12 nothing intervenes. The spurious section is foreign to John's Gospel, fits nowhere into the plan of this Gospel, and is easily recognized as an interpolation in the place which it occupies. The language differs decidedly from that of John's own writing. Yet this spurious section reports quite correctly an actual occurrence in the life of Jesus. Every feature of it bears the stamp of probability, although we are unable to say at what point in the story of Jesus it should be inserted. Since John did not write this section, we give no exposition of it.

12) The Feast of Tabernacles is ended. We hear nothing more about the ὄχλος, all the pilgrims have departed. **Again, therefore, Jesus spoke to them saying, I am the light of the world. He that follows me shall in no way walk in the darkness but shall have the light of life.** The movement to arrest Jesus had proved abortive, "accordingly," οὖν, he goes on delivering his testimony. When John writes, "again, therefore, Jesus spoke to them saying," πάλιν refers back to 7:35, where he stood and cried out to the multitude. He now again speaks after a brief interval. The verb ἐλάλησεν (λαλεῖν, the opposite of be-

ing silent) conveys the thought that Jesus simply continued with his public utterances as he had done before, and αὐτοῖς, "them," has as its antecedent the Pharisees (7:47), who also in v. 13 are named as making a reply. That others, too, are present it self-evident, compare "many" in v. 30, all of whom certainly were not Pharisees. The Temple was the most public place in Jerusalem, where crowds constantly gathered. The Pharisees, those that were members of the Sanhedrin, and others of their numerous party kept close watch on Jesus to note anything he might say or do.

This is the situation when Jesus now again speaks and declares (λέγων), "I am the light of the world." The emphatic ἐγώ means I and I alone, I and no other. When the predicate has the article as it does here: τὸ φῶς, it is convertible with the subject; in other words, the predicate is identical with the subject, R. 768. The question is asked as to how Jesus comes to use the figure of light just at this time. Because the context furnishes no hint, some say that no special reason or occasion suggests the figure; that Old Testament references such as Isa. 9:1; 42:6; 49:6; 60:3; etc., are basis enough for its use on this occasion. Others find a connection with a notable ceremony that was observed during the festival that has just ended. Grand candelabra with four vessels of oil were placed in the inner court. Young priests climbed ladders and lighted the wicks, and a grand torch dance was staged by the people, even men like Hillel priding themselves on their skill in taking part. We are told that the bright light shone all over the city. Maimonides states that this ceremony took place every evening during the feast, others are sure that it occurred only on the first evening. The main difficulty in connecting the word of Jesus with this ceremony is that it leaves out an essential part of the figure. Those candelabra were stationary, and men danced in the courts, while Jesus speaks of a movable light: "he that *follows* me." We may say more. In 7:37, when Jesus calls those that "thirst" and bids them come to him and "drink," he does not stop with the ceremony of drawing water from Siloah and pouring it out at the altar, in which no quenching of thirst by drinking is pictured; he reaches back to the original blessing received at Meribah where the thirsty actually received water to drink. He does the same here. One of the great blessings during the desert sojourn of Israel was the pillar of cloud and of fire, evidence of the presence of Jehovah with his people. As the entire feast, with Israel for a week dwelling in booths, commemorated the sojourn in the desert, so the shining candelabra pictured the pillar of fire that dispelled the darkness of night during the desert journey. Israel followed that pillar and camped in its light every night. What that pillar was for Israel in days gone by Jesus is for the whole world. That pillar was Jehovah, Jesus is God's own Son.

Following this word of Jesus that he is the light of the world, John in his prolog, 1:4-9, described the Logos as "the light." When speaking to Nicodemus on faith and unbelief (3:18), Jesus said that "the light is come into the world," and that the believer comes to this light while the unbeliever shuns it (3:19-21). Here we now have the basic word, "I am the light of the world." The idea in "light" is that of an active power which conquers the opposing power called "darkness." Each constitutes a power, each stands opposed to the other, and the light triumps, over the darkness. Note the article τῇ σκοτίᾳ, *the* darkness," not merely "darkness" in general. The best analysis of both is that of S. Goebel: divine truth, clear as light, over against human falsehood and ignorance; divine holiness, pure as light, over against human sin and impurity; divine blessedness and glory, radiant as light, over against the night of human woe, to which we would add death. In the various connections in which the term light is used one or the other of these features may be more prominent. Here where Jesus speaks unconditionally all three are combined. "I am the light of the world" means to say: "In the human person of Jesus, as in a focus of radiant light, the shining image of divine truth, holiness, and blessedness has appeared in the human world, by its victorious radiance to penetrate the darkness of the word and to deliver it from the night of falsehood, sin, and woe."

Like the pillar in the desert, Jesus as the light of the world must be followed: "he that follows me." While actual outward attachment is meant, even as many at that time followed Jesus about and kept in his company as much as possible, following Jesus here as elsewhere in the Gospels means permanent spiritual attachment (see 1:43). Of its own accord this gracious gift of God, this light, shines into the world's night. Its glorious, saving radiance attracts all whom it meets and draws them to remain with this light. Everyone who yields to this drawing power "shall not walk in the darkness," shall escape from its deadly power, shall no longer be lost, eventually to perish in the world's desert. This negation, however, and its individual formulation intimate that some whom the light reaches and begins to draw to itself will turn from it and prefer the darkness, 3:20. This is the tragedy that is connected with the coming of the light. Yet the positive "he that follows me" intimates also that some will truly follow Jesus, and the effect shall be that each of these "shall *have* the light of life." As so often in the words of Jesus, the positive is not made the mere counterpart of the negative. Jesus says more than that "he shall *walk* in the light." To be sure, he shall do this too, but he shall do it because this light shall actually penetrate him and shall become his personal possession. This is another case where the figure used is really inadequate to express the spiritual reality, it only approximates that reality. Natural light never becomes part of our inner being, it only shines outwardly round about us. Jesus, the light of the world, shall do far more.

"He shall have the light *of life*" states more than this inner penetration and personal possession; it adds the inner and permanent effect of the possession, which is life, ζωή, the spiritual life, abiding union with God who is the essence of life. Here we have the same combination of life and light as in 1:4. As the two go together in nature, so also in the world of the spirit. By implication the opposite is suggested: darkness and death likewise go together. The absolute mastery of expression used by Jesus must not escape us. Words so few, so simple in themselves, in such lucid combination, to express realities so profound, so exalted, so heavenly, that our minds stagger in the effort to apprehend them. God, who is life and light, sent his Son Jesus as the source of light and life to all the world, to fill each individual soul with truth, holiness, and blessedness, and thus to give it life eternal. Note the universality in "the light of the world," combined with the personal individuality in the singular "he that follows me." Both reach out to the universe of men, far beyond the bounds of national Judaism. When we visualize the lowly Jesus in the Temple court uttering these words, astonishment overcomes us. But two thousand years of Christianity have verified these words in millions of individuals in all the "world."

To follow Jesus as the light keeps to the figure and yet indicates all of the reality by one simple verb form. The light does all the drawing to itself, not we;

it makes us follow. Only wilful resistance, the most
unreasonable and unaccountable perversion, breaks
away from that drawing and chooses the deadly darkness instead of the light which brings life, yet not "to
follow" darkness but to remain in it. To follow Jesus
is to believe and trust him. How can anyone trust
the darkness? He must mistrust and flee from it when
the light shines over him. How can anyone mistrust
and flee from the light when it shines over him? We
are made for this light and its life, our whole being
responds to it. How can it help but draw, hold, and
fill us? While to follow means to believe and to trust,
it means this in its fulness, even as the verb "to have"
indicates. To follow is to believe and to obey, i. e.,
to walk in the path of this life. To follow means to
unite inwardly with Jesus — he in us and we in him,
"to have" in the *unio mystica*. The genitive "the light
of life" is not appositional, so that "the life" is identical with "the light." Nor is it the genitive of origin,
so that "the light" proceeds from "the life" (Jesus).
This is the simple possessive genitive, "the light"
which belongs to "the life" and is invariably connected
with it. Thus light and life are distinct concepts. The
former is here identified with Jesus, the latter is elsewhere also identified with him. By making the second
a genitive the two clasp hands in this case: Jesus is
the light, and this light is always linked with life.
Shall we ever be able to penetrate the depth of these
simple words?

13)   As soon as Jesus has uttered this great I AM,
the Pharisees, some of whom are present among the
auditors, object. **The Pharisees, therefore, said to
him, Thou art testifying concerning thine own self;
thy testimony is not true.** They pay no attention to
what Jesus says of himself and to his promises to his
followers. Their ears are deaf to anything of that
kind. They are completely satisfied with themselves

and care nothing for who he is and what he bestows. They are bent only on catching at any reason for rejecting him and for discrediting him, no matter how flimsy it may be. So now they fasten on "I am" and raise the formal objection that Jesus is testifying in his own behalf, and that such testimony "is not true," i. e., cannot be accepted as true before a judgment bar. Jesus had met this objection a year ago when in 5:31 he acknowledged the formal principle and made his own testimony legally competent by adducing his Father as a second witness, who had given the Jews his testimony in his Word, 5:37, etc. Here he does the same, v. 18.

14) But before he adduces his supporting witness he qualifies himself as a competent witness. **Jesus answered and said unto them** (1:48), **And if I do testify concerning myself, my testimony is true, because I know whence I came and where I am going; but you do not know whence I come or where I am going.** We cannot admit that Jesus here contradicts what he says in 5:31, although it be only formally. For in verse 17 Jesus himself enunciates the old principle of the law, which requires at least two witnesses, the very principle he admitted in 5:31 and met in 5:37, just as here he again complies with it in verse 18. Why the notion of at least an apparent contradiction persists, is hard to understand. To be sure, a second witness is necessary, and Jesus has that second witness. For that very reason the self-witness of Jesus must be accepted as being legally perfectly competent. While, if offered alone, it would amount to nothing before a court of law, corroborated by a second witness, it stands. So Jesus qualifies as a witness in his own case. "And if I myself (ἐγώ) do testify concerning myself, my testimony is true." Why? "Because I know whence I did come and where (ποῦ for "whither," R. 298, d) I am going." He is con-

versant with the facts, namely those concerning his coming into the world from heaven for his saving mission, and his return to heaven, whence he came, after completing his mission. Knowing these facts, though they concern himself, he is competent to testify concerning them.

It is, therefore, a misconception to say that "the ordinary rule of law does not apply to Jesus"; the contrary is true. Nor does Jesus here appeal to his divinity or to his holiness as a guarantee of his truthfulness. He says not one word about either of these. He declares his testimony to be true for the simple reason that it states the true facts regarding himself. That this testimony of his must be accepted as being legally competent is due to the fact that it is corroborated by a second unimpeachable witness, namely the Father, v. 18. Jesus claims no exemption of any kind for himself; on the contrary, he gladly and completely submits to every legal requirement regarding the admission of testimony. How could he hope to have his testimony accepted by anybody if he proceeded to set aside the very law concerning testimony? It tends to confusion to talk about "the consciousness of Jesus" in connection with the verb οἶδα, "I know." How far this confusion may lead appears in the assertion, that "Christianity is entirely based upon Christ's consciousness of himself," and in the admonition about "the heroism of faith" on our part in resting on that consciousness. Like any witness, Jesus tells what "he knows," knows by firsthand, direct, personal knowledge, not what he has heard from others at second hand, not what he merely thinks or imagines. "I know" — that marks the genuine witness. "Whence I did come" is a fact which he most certainly does know. Why would he be ignorant of it? "And where I am going" is a second fact of the same kind. Who can bring evidence that Jesus does not know either or

600 The Interpretation of John

both of these facts? He is not a witness who is not
in a position to know and thus to testify in regard to
these facts. Here Jesus does not specify the place
that is referred to. He has already done that, more
than once, and his hearers have heard it a long time
ago. All that he now needs to do and all that he
does, is to insist that he is doing the true part of a
genuine witness: telling what he actually knows. That
is all that anyone can ask of a witness. And when a
witness tells this, all men who are true and honest will
believe his testimony — provided, of course, that it is
duly corroborated (v. 18).

We do not believe that κἄν (καὶ ἐάν) is concessive
in this case in the sense of "although" I testify, or
"if also," or "if perchance" (R. 1018); for Jesus does
actually testify that he is the light of the world. In
fact, he keeps testifying so often that one of his titles
is "the faithful witness," or "the faithful and true
witness," Rev. 1:4; 3:14. His bearing witness is
not an incidental function but one of the chief functions of his office. R. 1010, 1018, and B.-D. 372, 1
(a) think that κἄν μαρτυρῶ (as in 5:31) may be the
indicative and not the subjunctive; and B.-D. offers
the explanation that ἐάν is used for εἰ, calling the construction a vulgarism. Whatever the real explanation of ἐάν with the indicative may be, an indicative
would here indicate actuality, and a present indicative
iterative actuality: "and if I do keep on testifying,"
wenn immer (B.-D.); but certainly not: "if I perchance testify" (R.). The subjunctive would indicate
future iterative testifying: "if I shall keep on testifying, as I expect to do."

By repudiating the testimony of Jesus on legal
grounds the Pharisees arrogate to themselves the position of legal judges in Jesus' case. They love to do
that sort of thing, deeming themselves the great
guardians of the law. Therefore, after establishing

his own competency as a legal witness, Jesus establishes the incompetency of these self-constituted
judges: "But you do not know whence I come, or
where I am going." Whether we read δέ or not, this
statement is not a continuation of the proof that Jesus
is a legally competent witness. The ignorance of the
Pharisees in no way helps to qualify Jesus as a witness. Such qualification inheres and must inhere in
Jesus alone; it cannot inhere partly in other men. Nor
does this statement about the ignorance of the Pharisees mean to say that because of their ignorance they
are dependent on Jesus for any testimony regarding
whence he comes and whither he is going. A thought
of this kind would be entirely out of line with what
Jesus presents. The statement about the ignorance
of the Pharisees is the preamble to their disqualifica-
tion as judges in Jesus' case. It goes together with
what follows on this point in v. 15. We see at a
glance that in the clause, "whence I come," ἔρχομαι
is identical in thought with the same clause that precedes, "whence I did come," ἦλθον. This is the aoristic
present, which expresses the fact in a timeless manner; R. 865, etc., calls it "the specific present." Here
Jesus uses "or" between the object clauses, drawing
separate attention to each of the two.

15) Since the Pharisees labor under this ignorance they are rendered totally incompetent to make
a legal pronouncement as judges concerning Jesus as
an inadmissible witness. **You are judging according to the flesh.** That is all they are able to do in
Jesus' case when they arrogate to themselves the position of judges. Note the article in κατὰ τὴν σάρκα. All
they see and know is "the flesh" of Jesus, his human
appearance. They have no other norm (κατά) for
judging him. Who this person really is, whence he
came, or whither he is going, is hidden from them.
This ignorance disqualifies them. Deprived of the real

data for pronouncing a valid judgment on Jesus, in particular as to whether he is a competent witness, they fall back on a superficial datum (his flesh) and thus render an invalid, spurious judgment, showing that they are unfit to serve as judges. These Pharisees, however, have had many followers. "The flesh" is specific and refers to the flesh of Jesus; without the article, κατὰ σάρκα, "according to flesh," would state only a general principle, that of customarily judging only in an outward way. How these Pharisees customarily judge is not the point here but how they judge in this specific case of Jesus.

The Pharisees made a profession of judging; see the shallow judgment in 7:15, and the intemperate judgment in 7:49. Jesus contrasts himself with them. **I judge no one,** ἐγώ in contrast with the preceding ἡμεῖς. But in the next breath he adds, "And if I do judge," etc. Many seek to remove what to them seems like a contradiction. So some add, "I judge no one according to the flesh," or "like you," which the very sense of the phrase forbids. Others stress the tense, "I judge no one now," meaning that he will eventually judge at the end of the world; but the following, "if I do judge," also refers to the present time. Still others stress the pronoun "I" and let it mean "I alone," "I in my human individuality," as if John had written ἐγὼ μόνος, which he has not. Finally, "no one" is stressed as a singular: he judges no individual but does judge "the moral state of the people." Those are right who supply nothing, find no appearance of contradiction, and stress neither one nor the other of the words. What Jesus says is this: "I am engaged in judging no one." The mission on which God sent him is not to act as a judge but as a Savior, 3:17. Here the context points to the contrast between judging and testifying. His great function is to testify to the truth and thus to save. He is the light of the world, sent to bless with enlightenment and salvation. Luther puts it tersely, "He here indicates his office."

16) But this very office with all its great saving purpose and in the very prosecution of that purpose necessitates the secondary function, a certain kind of judging. Luther continues: "If you will not have the Lord God, then keep the devil; and the office, which otherwise is not established in order to judge but to help and to comfort, this is compelled to judge." This does not mean that unbelief turns the testimony of Jesus into judgment for itself but that Jesus himself does utter judgment on certain men in the prosecution of his office. **And if, nevertheless** (δέ)**, I do judge, my judgment is genuine, because I am not alone, but I and the Father that did send me.** Here καὶ ἐὰν κρίνω is exactly like κἂν μαρτυρῶ in v. 14, present actuality (if subjunctive). The emphatic ἐγώ = "I," who am sent to testify not to judge. This moves δέ back to fourth place in the sentence, which is unusual; it marks the contrast with the previous statement. When this necessity of judging, nevertheless, arises, Jesus says, "my judgment (note the emphatic possessive: *my* in contrast with *your* judgment) is genuine," ἀληθινή, worthy to be called a judgment. His judgment will not be only ἀληθής, "true," rendering a correct verdict by some means or other, but "genuine," coming from one who is in every way competent to act as a judge, who does not only happen to hit the right verdict but penetrates to all the facts in the case and pronounces accordingly. That kind of a judgment is, indeed, genuine, far beyond the judgment of these Pharisees on Jesus, who saw only his flesh.

As Jesus has qualified as a witness, so he now qualifies as a judge: "because I am not alone," a mere man, as these Pharisees think, left only to the penetration and wisdom of his human abilities. Such a judge may err, even with the best intentions, and in many cases his judgment may not be "genuine," worthy of the name. When Jesus judges, sent as he is by his Father from heaven on his saving mission, his judging must be infallible, hence his qualification as a judge must be according, far above those with which we are satisfied in mere men. Jesus has this qualification: he is not alone, "on the contrary (ἀλλά after a negation), I and he that did send me, the Father" (πατήρ omitted in some codices), i. e., we two are always together. By thus pointing to his Sender in connection with his judging Jesus declares that his judging is in connection with his mission. We may compare 5:19 and 30, also 8:26. Also in his judging Jesus never acts apart from, or contrary to, his Sender. The judgments of Jesus are thus identical with those of his Father, unerring and divine. In all the verdicts of Jesus these Pharisees have the verdicts of God himself. A note of warning to the Pharisees lies in these brief statements which reveal the kind of judge that Jesus is.

17) What Jesus says of himself as a judge is only incidental, elicited by the action of the Pharisees in usurping judicial authority by calling the testimony of Jesus illegal and void in a court of law. Therefore, after briefly contrasting his genuine judging with the spurious judging of the Pharisees, Jesus reverts to the main issue, that of the legal competency of his testimony regarding himself. In v. 14 only the preliminary point is settled, that when Jesus does testify he testifies from actual and direct personal knowledge. Now the main point is taken up. **And in your own law, moreover, it has been written, that the testimony of two men is true.** Here καί . . . δέ is not the same as in v. 16; it is not "and yet," or "and . . . nevertheless" (with δέ adversative), but as

in 6:51 and in I John 1:3: "and . . . moreover"
— καί adds, and δέ marks the addition as something
different from v. 14. Jesus himself cites the law on
the point at issue, formulating it himself from
Deut. 17:6 and 19:15. He knows that law perfectly.
"It has been written" means that it stands thus indefinitely (this being the force of the tense). Jesus
pointedly calls it "your own law." Jesus thus points
these legalists to their own supreme legal authority.
But not with the implication: This is *your* law not
mine; for Jesus was put under this law (Gal. 4:4),
came to fulfill the law (Matt. 5:17), and did fulfill
all its requirements. Yet Jesus cannot say *"our* law,"
even as he must distinguish *"your* Father" from *"my
Father"* and can never say *"our* Father." His relation to the law differed from that of men. The law
bound all Israelites since it was given for them. Jesus
placed himself under this law only for the sake of
men; he was the Son, thus the lawgiver himself, and
the law was never given for him. This vital disparity
between Jesus and men is here brought out. Therefore, too, the possessive "your own" in no way dis-
parages the law; Jesus always honors the law.

Now in Deut. 19:15, etc., the law demands that
there be more than just one witness; there must be
at least two. Each must corroborate the other. Our
state laws contain the same proviso. Testimony by
at least two witnesses stands as "true," ἀληθής, must
be admitted as true. The fact that one of the two witnesses may be testifying in his own case makes no difference. When citing this law about legally competent
testimony Jesus uses the genitive: the testimony "of two
men," (ἄνθρωποι), whereas Deuteronomy has "of two
witnesses" (μάρτυρες). This difference in terms might
be only accidental, since Jesus is not actually quoting
the law in a set form, if the case at issue were one
involving only a man and ordinary men as witnesses.

Here, however, where Jesus is on trial and where
he and his Father are the witnesses, the change in
terms is evidently intentional. In any human court
"two men," two human witnesses, would be enough;
for these Pharisees Jesus adduces two divine witnesses. So fully does he meet the requirement of the
law that he greatly exceeds that requirement.

18) **I am he that testifies concerning myself,
and the Father that sent me testifies concerning me.**
In the Greek the statement is chiastic; the subjects
are placed first and last, and the predicates are placed
in between, an arrangement that is highly effective.
Thus, indeed, we have two witnesses as the law requires. Both testify to the same facts concerning
Jesus. This, however, shuts out the idea that the
Father's testimony is already contained in that of
Jesus, that when Jesus testifies, the Pharisees already
have also the Father's testimony. The two are independent witnesses and stand as two; otherwise the
provision of the law would not be met. Jesus does
not need to state what the Father's testimony is because he did this a year ago when the same point
was discussed, 5:31, etc., and the Pharisees have by
no means forgotten. But the question is raised
whether Jesus now includes in the Father's testimony
both the works which he gave him to do (5:36) and
the Old Testament prophecies concerning Jesus (5:37-
47), or only the former. The present tense $\mu\alpha\rho\tau\upsilon\rho\epsilon\hat{\iota}$,
"he testifies," is stressed as pointing only to the works.
Yet the perfect tense $\mu\epsilon\mu\alpha\rho\tau\upsilon\rho\eta\kappa\epsilon$ in 5:37, which is there
used concerning the writings, has a present implica-
tion. Here, where the Father's entire testifying is
summed up in "he testifies," the writings certainly
cannot be excluded; and this the less since the presentation of the Father's testimony made in 5:31,
etc., is assumed still to be in the minds of the Pharisees.

19) **They were, therefore, saying to him,
Where is thy Father? Jesus answered, Neither
me do you know nor my Father. If you knew me
you would know also my Father.** The imperfect
ἔλεγον may mean that different ones of the Pharisees
put this question at Jesus. Their "where" question
has a mocking tone. If God is, indeed, the father
and Sender of Jesus, and if this God is to be the
second witness, with his testimony to corroborate
that of Jesus concerning himself, then let Jesus
present this Father, that he may be interrogated as
a witness, so that these Pharisees may see whether
his testimony agrees with that of Jesus. A silly
shrewdness lies back of this question: the certainty
that Jesus cannot produce this second witness in the
way they intimate. In this demand on Jesus to present
his second witness these Pharisees repeat their proceeding of v. 13: they dodge the main issue by raising a minor one that is wholly immaterial. The main
issue is: Does God testify as Jesus says, or does he
not so testify? In 5:36, etc., God's testimony was
given to the Pharisees: the works of Jesus and the
Old Testament declarations concerning Jesus. This
double testimony is undeniable and incontrovertible.
These men brazenly set it aside and instead fasten on
the point that Jesus should produce this second witness
in person before them.

But by foolishly asking where this second witness
is these Pharisees betray a second piece of fatal ignorance. The first Jesus points out in the last clause of
v. 14; the second he now states in the same categorical
way: "Neither me do you know nor my Father," i. e.,
the true God. Their question is evidence for this
their ignorance. People who ask *where* the Father is,
who want him produced so that they can place him on
the witness stand, thereby demonstrate that they do
not know him at all, and no wonder, then, that they

also do not know him whom God has sent. God is always on the witness stand of his written Word, where all who will may hear his testimony in full and thus also learn to know him most intimately and adequately. Those who reject this testimony know neither the Father nor the Son — and the guilt of this ignorance is theirs alone.

In the statement regarding the ignorance of the Pharisees Jesus uses "neither . . . nor," disjunctives, placing each person by himself beside the other. In the following conditional sentence "also" (καί) connects the two persons. Why Jesus puts himself first and the Father second is apparent from the latter: "If you knew me you would know also my Father" (present unreality, εἰ with the imperfect followed by the imperfect with ἄν; ᾔδειτε, pluperfect, always used as an imperfect). If Jesus had placed the Father first he would thereby have pointed to the Old Testament revelation as the means of knowledge, i. e., that by showing us the Father the Old Testament shows us also the Son. This the Old Testament, indeed, does. By placing himself first a different thought is expressed, namely that Jesus is the medium for knowing the Father aright. For although the Father speaks clearly enough in the Old Testament, he speaks more clearly still through his Son (Heb. 1:1, 2), his person, mission, word, and work (14:6, 7). He who knows the Son, he, and he alone, knows als the Father. Thus these two, who may be placed side by side ("neither . . . nor"), belong together ("also," καί), 14:9. The question of Philip in 14:8 is only apparently like that of the Pharisees.

The conditional form of the sentence shuts out the possibility of regarding it as an inverse deduction, in the sense that ignorance concerning Jesus is conclusive evidence that the Pharisees are ignorant also regarding the Father. Such a deduction appears in 5:38, where not believing in Jesus proves that the Father's word is not in the Jews. If Jesus had desired a deduction of this type he would have said, "Because you do not know me, therefore also you do not know the Father"; or, "You do not know the Father, for you do not know me." What he does say is that knowing the Father depends on (εἰ) knowing Jesus. Where this condition is absent, the conclusion is also absent. The implication is that it should be easy to know Jesus, who also has come to show us the Father and in and through whom the Father reveals himself.

20) This ends the present clash. The Pharisees have no reply and possibly walk away. **These words he spoke at the treasury while teaching in the Temple; and no one arrested him because his hour had not yet come.** Just what place is meant by "the treasury" is disputed. In the court of the women stood thirteen treasure chests with funnel or trumpet-like receptacles, into which the gifts were thrown; while near the hall in which the Sanhedrin met was the room in which the Temple funds were kept. The purpose in mentioning the place is to indicate that it was public, under the very noses of the authorities. Moreover, Jesus made not only the utterances here recorded but was engaged in teaching. Yet (καί for joining an adversative thought) no one, not even these Pharisees, who had again been refuted in public, ventured to make a move to arrest Jesus. No secondary reasons are mentioned why he was let alone. The supposition that the consciences of the Pharisees had been touched, making them cowardly for the moment, is improbable. The primary reason is the same as that assigned in 7:30, which see.

21) A second and much sharper clash follows the altercation which John has just marked as being

finished (v. 20). There cannot have been a long
interval between the events recorded in these two
verses. **He said, therefore, again unto them, I am
going away, and you shall seek me and shall die
in your sin. Whither I go, you cannot come.** The
connective οὖν, "therefore," refers to v. 20: since no
one had arrested him, his hour not having come.
"Again," once more (compare v. 12) he thus spoke
to them, this time in most serious warning. The persons addressed are the same, although John now calls
them "the Jews," such as belong to the hostile ruling
class. Jesus reiterates what he said to these men in
7:33, 34, but with important modifications. He points
in warning to what their wicked unbelief must lead.
This time the preamble, "Yet a little while I am with
you," is omitted. In 7:33 it was added because the
police officers had been sent out to arrest him before
the festival was ended; no police are now watching
to effect an arrest. This time, however, an emphatic
ἐγώ precedes the verb: "*I*, of my own accord, am going away" entirely irrespective of what you Jews may
plot and plan. Jesus' mission is approaching its end;
then he will leave (ὑπάγω, the futuristic present, R.
870). There is no need to repeat from 7:33 that he is
going to the Father, his Sender. Then what about
these Jews who are now so keen to be rid of Jesus?
Strange to say, then when they have what they wish,
they will not wish what they have — then: "you will
seek me," too late, with the seeking of despair; compare the explanation of 7:34. When the calamities of
judgment will set in, the Jews will cry in vain for a
deliverer.

In 7:34 only the negative is presented: "you shall
not find me," i. e., I shall not deliver you; here the
positive is stated: "you shall die in your sin," ἁμαρτία,
the collective singular. To die in one's sin is to re-

ceive the eternal penalty of sin after death. For
to die in sin is to die without repentance and saving
faith. To die thus is to perish, 3:16. Wanting to
be completely rid of Jesus, these Jews shall be rid
of him forever. "Whither I go, you cannot come."
The blessed presence of the Father, to which Jesus
returns after he has completed his mission, will be
closed to his enemies after death overwhelms them.
This is what their unbelief will at last lead to.

22) This renewed, most positive warning the
Jews again answer with mockery. **The Jews, therefore, said,** not addressing Jesus but speaking of him
in the third person as in 7:35, 36, **Surely, he will
not kill himself since he declares, Whither I go
you cannot come.** They state the question with
μήτι as if they have in mind a negative answer yet see
no other way but to answer positively. The ears
of these Jews are keen in a certain way, for they catch
the force of the emphatic "I": *"I myself"* am going
away, and tack their answer onto that. This "I" is
absent in 7:33, which accounts for the fling the Jews
there employ, fastening it only on the verb ὑπάγω. In
the present case the thrust that Jesus must be con-
templating suicide is more vicious than the sneer about
his going among the pagan Greeks in 7:35. We may
here regard ὅτι as causal, "since," but compare the
ὅτι in 7:35. The Jews here persist in their trick of
catching at some one word or expression in the utterances of Jesus, turning their venom on that, and
blindly ignoring the grave substance of what Jesus
says. So here they are deaf to the warning that they
shall die in their sins with all the horror that lies in
this statement; they pick up only the expression that
Jesus himself is about to go away. The fact that a
man who kills himself lands in hell, and that these
Jews do not intend to go there, is not implied in their

mocking question, although some have thought so. If
this were the point in their sneer, something in the
wording would indicate as much.

23) Jesus pays no heed to the mockery just
uttered. To ignore is also to answer, and often more
effectively than to use words. **And he was saying
to them,** means that he added the following to what
he had already said: **You are from below, I am
from above; you are of this world, I am not of this
world.** This double contrast is only the preamble
to the warning, combined with the call of grace, which
follows in v. 24. Jesus thus repeats and expounds
more fully what he has said in v. 21. The four ἐκ
denote origin. "From below" = "of this world"; likewise "from above" = "not of this world." The contrast in positive form is elucidated by the contrast
in negative form. The origin of the Jews is *not* the
origin of Jesus. Moreover, the emphasis is on the
two second members of the contrast, i. e., on the
origin of Jesus. He and he alone is the exception.
That the Jews, like all men, are "from below," "of
this world," is an ordinary fact, universally acknowledged. That Jesus is totally different in his origin
is the exceptional fact, denied by these Jews but a
fact, nevertheless, and, as v. 24 shows, decisive for
these Jews, whether they shall die in their sins or
escape from this death.

While "this world" defines "below," the latter also
helps to define the former; the same is true of the
opposite phrases. This means that the Jews are of
mundane origin, but Jesus of supermundane, heavenly,
divine origin. In the Biblical concept "world" mankind holds the dominating place, and "this world"
indicates the present actual condition of the earth with
its human inhabitants, with its corruption of sin and
death. The effort to dissociate sin and death from
"this world" as used here by Jesus fails because both

are mentioned in the next breath (v. 24). Yet this is true, Jesus does not here operate with the contrast: the Jews are sinful, he is sinless. This would only place a gulf between him and them. To be sure, the Jews are sinful because of their origin, and Jesus sinless because of his. This goes without saying. But Jesus, who is from above, is now amid those who are from below in order to lift them to his side. He who is not of this world now stands among those who are of this world in order to deliver them from the sin and the death in this world and to raise them to heaven. This preamble, therefore, intends once more to usher in for the Jews the way of escape through faith in Jesus.

24) Now follows the main statement. **I said, therefore, to you, that you shall die in your sins; for unless you come to believe that I am (what I say) you shall die in your sins.** Here is the full presentation of the briefer warning of v. 21. Its main point is that a way of escape from death is open. Hence the weight of οὖν rests on the clauses about Jesus in the preamble: "I am from above, not of this world." Since Jesus is such a Savior he can help these Pharisees so that they shall not die in their sins. Only secondary weight attaches to the first clauses in the preamble, that the Pharisees are from below and of this world; for this is obvious and accounts for their state of sin. This made it necessary, in the grace of God, that Jesus should appear in their midst, he who is from above, not of this world, divine, with power to deliver from sin and death. The reason, then, why Jesus told these Pharisees that they would die in their sins is not that, like all men, they are sinners. Note the thrice repeated phrase: die "*in* your sin" or "sins" (spreading out the collective singular in the plural). Though they have sins, they need not "die in them," for here is the divine

Savior from heaven come on his mission to free them from their sins.

The explanatory γάρ thus puts the warning in this form: "Unless you come to believe, you shall die in your sins." The sins of these men will destroy them by robbing them of life eternal only if they refuse to believe in Jesus. The "if" clause is pure gospel, extending its blessed invitation anew. Yet it is again combined with the warning about dying in sins. This note of warning with its terrifying threat persists because these Jews had chosen the course of unbelief. Yet the "if" opens the door of life in the wall of sin. The divine threats are conditional. You shall die if you do not come to faith (πιστεύσητε, ingressive aorist), come to accept, trust, and cling to the divine deliverer. That is why in v. 24 ἀποθανεῖσθε, "you shall die," has the emphatic forward position while in v. 21 "in your sins" has this position. In v. 21 Jesus says, *the sins* will bring on death; now he says, *death* will be brought on by the sins. The emphasis is shifted to death because of the implied contrast with escape from death in the "if" clause. Unfortunately, this shift in emphasis with its important meaning is lost in translation.

Jesus might have said, "unless you come to believe *in me.*" Instead of the mere pronoun he uses the far more significant object clause ὅτι ἐγώ εἰμι with its strong emphasis on "I" — "I" alone and no other. The ellipsis in "that I am," the omission of the predicate, is idiomatic in the Greek and quite common; see 4:26; 6:20; 9:9; 13:19; 18:5, 6 and 8 in John alone. The Greek mind is nimble and finds no difficulty in each instance in supplying the predicate from the context. So here "that I am" means: "that I am, as I say, from above, not of this world," i. e., divine, the Son of God, come from heaven on the mission to save sinners who are from below and of this world.

This is the substance of the faith that affords escape
from death. Some would supply: "that I am the
Messiah," or "God," etc.; but this disregards the context which alone supplies the predicate that the
speaker has in mind. In English this Greek idiom
cannot be reproduced; we must in some way fill the
place of the predicate: "that I am he"; "that I am
what I say"; *dass ich es bin.* Note also that Jesus
uses ἐάν, the condition of expectancy, and not the condition of present unreality: "if you would come to
believe." He does not imply that he thinks they will
not believe but rather that he hopes and expects that
after all they may come to believe. Thus ἐάν has
the kindly note of grace, it is like an efficacious invitation.

25) The reply of the Jews pointedly repudiates
both the warning and the invitation. **They were,
therefore, saying to him, Thou, who art thou?** The
descriptive ἔλεγον bids us contemplate this reply. Its
tone is contemptuous. These Jews are not asking who
Jesus is; they are sneering at him for making such
claims for himself: "How dost *thou* (note the
emphatic σύ) come to assume a role like this?" B.-D.
300, 2.

The reply of Jesus constitutes one of the most disputed passages in the New Testament, on which much
research and ingenuity has been spent without attain-
ing anything resembling unanimity.

Without question, τὴν ἀρχήν is an adverbial accusative and because of its forward position strongly
emphatic. Aside from the possibility that τὴν ἀρχήν
ever means "from the beginning" (our versions) this
meaning is here excluded by the present tense λαλῶ;
the A. V. changes it to "said" (aorist), and the R. V.
to "have said" (perfect or possibly aorist). It is
also excluded by the sense of λαλῶ; we should expect
to find λέγω used here, or rather the aorist εἶπον. In

other instances where John desires to say "from the beginning," he invariably uses ἐξ ἀρχῆς, 6:64; 15:27; 16:4; and in the epistles. Finally, why the strong emphasis on a phrase like "from the beginning"? Luther's *erstlich*, "in the first place," "principally," is without another example in the Greek; nor does any other statement follow in regard to who or what Jesus is. The suggestion to draw the adverbial accusative to v. 26: "First of all, since I am still speaking to you, I have many things to speak and to judge concerning you," likewise attributes a wrong meaning to τὴν ἀρχήν and duplicates λαλεῖν in the same sentence in a helpless manner.

More prominent authorities propose "at all" as the translation. Thus the margin of the R. V., "How is it that I even speak to you at all?" B.-D. 300, 2 and R. 730, "Do you ask, why I speak to you at all?" or, "Are you reproaching me that I speak to you at all?" and Zahn's exclamation, "To think that I yet speak to you at all!" *Dass ich ueberhaupt noch zu euch rede!* The sense of these renderings is that by their hostile interruptions the Jews have about made it impossible for Jesus to go on speaking to them. But this leaves no adequate emphasis on τὴν ἀρχήν; in fact, this adverbial accusative should appear after ὅτι not before it. The thought, too, is unparalleled in the speech of Jesus. Aside from the fact that he goes right on speaking to the Jews, why should Jesus intimate that he is wasting his effort by saying anything further to these Jews when in a moment John reports (v. 30) that many believed on him?

Far more acceptable is the rendering, "Altogether (in every respect) I am what also I am telling you" (compare Thayer). The exact force of τὴν ἀρχήν is ὅλως, but in the sense of *ueberhaupt* (C.-K. 176): **In general (I am) that which (ὅ τι) I also am telling you**, καὶ λαλῶ, not holding anything back in silence.

Jesus thus meets the question, "Thou, who art thou?" This he invariably does, no matter how contemptuous or hostile the questioners may be. But Jesus cannot here allow any implication as though he has been silent on any vital point regarding himself. He has spoken fully and not kept silent, in fact, is now speaking clearly (καὶ λαλῶ), v. 12; 23, 24. And these Jews have heard his testimony, for they refused and still refuse to accept it (7:19, etc.; 7:30, etc.; 8:13, etc.). This same testimony concerning himself, Jesus intimates (λαλῶ), will go on — he will speak and not remain silent. By thus holding the Jews to what he is constantly saying concerning himself Jesus rebukes their question as being altogether uncalled for. Why ask a man who he is when he keeps on telling you? The claim that in this rendering εἰμί would have to be written out after τὴν ἀρχήν is invalid, for we do not really need it even in the English, "In general, that which I also am telling you."

26) With this reply the contemptuous question of the Jews concerning Jesus is both answered and dismissed as uncalled for. While Jesus will keep on telling these Jews in due order who and what he is, just as he has done up to this moment, he now informs them: **Many things have I to tell and to judge concerning you. Now he that did send me is true; and what things I did hear from him these I am telling in the world.** In 7:33, 34 and again in 8:21 Jesus tells these Jews something not only about himself, but also about themselves, something of a terrible nature, amounting to a prophetic judgment. Instead of heeding these utterances about themselves the Jews deliberately ignored them and by their contemptuous rejoinders tried to shift all the attention to Jesus. But Jesus has an answer for them. He has "many things to tell concerning them," using the same verb as in v. 25, λαλεῖν, things about which

he cannot keep silent. Significantly he adds, "to tell and to judge concerning you," the second verb being in explanation of the first. Their unbelief turns this telling into judging; compare v. 16. Jesus does not say "to tell *you*," he says only "concerning you." They may or may not hear this telling and judging, that makes no difference, Jesus will certainly not be silent.

As in v. 16, Jesus places his Sender back of everything that he will tell concerning these Jews. Here ἀλλά is not adversative, "but"; it adds only "an accessory idea": "and," "yea," "now," R. 1185, etc. First the preamble, "And he that did send me is true," ἀληθής, whose very nature is verity, and whose every word thus expresses reality and truth. Being what he is, he cannot possibly say anything false or untrue. The designation "he that did send me" connects Jesus and his entire mission with this supreme author of truth. This again appears in the main statement, attached to the preamble with καί, "and what things I did hear from him these I (ἐγώ, I myself, emphatic) am telling in the world." Compare 5:30. All that Jesus tells on any subject emanates not from himself but from the Sender. This, of course, includes the "many things" he has to tell and to judge concerning these unbelieving Jews. Let them understand that in every word of warning and of judgment from the lips of Jesus they hear the word and the verdict of his great Sender. Will their conscience still remain callous? The breadth of Jesus' statement covers also his offers of grace and escape from sin and death (v. 24). Back of these, too, is the Sender of Jesus. Will the hearts of these Jews still refuse faith? The aorist ἤκουσα is explained by v. 23, "I am from above, not of this world" (compare 1:18). The tense refers to the same time as that expressed by ὁ πέμψας. The Son heard when he received his great commission. We need not put into this tense the present constant communion of Jesus with his Sender, expressed for instance in 5:30, "as I hear," and in 8:16, "I am not alone." Since Jesus here includes all his speaking, he says, "these things I am telling in the world" and not merely to these Jewish rulers. We need not worry about εἰς and try to make it "into" or "unto." This is an ordinary case of the static use of εἰς, "in," on which see the discussion R. 591, etc.

The old idea that ἀλλά is always adversative, "but," has led to a complete misunderstanding of what Jesus says. He is thought to say, that, although he has much to tell and judge concerning the Jewish rulers, nevertheless (ἀλλά), he will refrain and restrict himself to telling what he has heard from the Sender. Instead of spending his time in rebuking these Jews he will devote himself to his real mission. The moment ἀλλά is properly understood (R. 1185, etc.) ideas such as this fade away.

27) In order that we may understand why Jesus continues his discourse in the way in which he does in v. 28, 29, John introduces an explanatory remark. **They did not realize that he was speaking to them of his Father.** The Jews must have indicated their ignorance by some exclamation or objection which John does not record, preferring to state what their minds lacked. In ἔλεγεν we have a case where the Greek, like the English, accomodates the tense of the indirect discourse to the secondary tense of the main verb, here using the imperfect ἔλεγεν instead of the present after the aorist ἔγνωσαν, R. 1029.

The point of John's remark is not that the Jews failed to understand the expression "he that did send me" as a designation for the Father. Verses 17-19 are too plain to be misunderstood; moreover, the expression itself would be clear to any Jew. Of course, the obduracy of the Jews blinded them, but not to the extent that they understood none of the references to the Father, for then John's remark about their ignorance should have been made much earlier. The ignorance here meant refers only to v. 26, and in this verse only to the one point in the mission of Jesus, that every word he utters (λαλῶ) is in reality the word of the Father himself and thus verity in the highest degree. The Jews, indeed, heard Jesus say this, and the words he uses were quite intelligible to them. What their obduracy hid from them was the force of these words as pertaining to the Father. The verb γινώσκω denotes an inner grasp and realization, which is often lacking even where the intellect is active enough.

28) Jesus, of course, perceived that his mighty word about the Father's relation to every one of his utterances had not registered with these Jews. In fact, obdurate as they are, it would not register; they would not "realize" even if he repeated this statement about his Father. Therefore Jesus turns to prophecy. **Jesus, therefore, said** (giving a prophetic turn to his statement), **When you shall lift up the Son of man, then you will realize** (what now your obduracy will not let you realize), **that I am (what I say), and that from myself I do nothing, but, just as the Father taught me, these very things (and only these) I tell.** We see that Jesus does not expect these Jews to realize just what the force of his words is even after this restatement. They will go on treating them lightly, as if no real verity is back of them. But the time will come when this will change. Not indeed, as some have thought, that finally their obduracy will cease and turn to repentance. They will remain as they are, but God will speak another language to them, one that will crash through even their hard hearts — crushing them in judgment. Yet the purpose of uttering this prophetic warning now is

still one of grace, that ere it be too late these Jews
may yet turn, realize indeed, and repent.

Jesus uses a condition of expectancy in pointing
to that future time, ὅταν with the subjunctive in the
protasis, and the future indicative in the apodosis.
His mind vividly conceives the coming time of his
crucifixion. The verb ὑψοῦν, "to lift up," refers to the
elevation on the cross, just as in 3:14; compare also
12:32. Since Jesus ascribes this act to the Jews, the
debate should end as to whether the crucifixion is
referred to or the exaltation in heaven, or possibly
both combined in some way. Moreover, the crucifixion is here brought in as the final act by which the
Jewish rulers will repudiate Jesus and all he came to
bring. Here Jesus once more calls himself "the Son
of man," using the Messianic title he loves: he who
is a descendant of man, the incarnate Son of God.
See 1:51. In the crucifixion of Jesus the doom of
the Jews would be sealed; not, indeed, in an absolute
way as by the perpetration of this act alone, but in
a factual way as the final rejection from which the
Jews as a nation would never recede in repentance.
Thus that act will open the floodgates of judgment,
bringing on the destruction of Jerusalem, the permanent exile of the Jews from their native land, their
miraculous preservation as a foreign element scattered among all other nations of the world as a sign
until the end of time. Then will be fulfilled what
Jesus says in v. 21, 24, "You shall die in your sins."

"Then," Jesus says, "you will realize." Some connect this "then" too closely with the "when" clause,
as if hard upon the crucifixion the realization of what
Jesus here says will break in upon these wicked Sanhedrists and the unbelieving Jews generally. We
must, however, abide by the context. Verse 28 is
an elucidation of verses 21 and 24. Every unbe-

lieving Jew, upon whom the fate of his nation makes
no impression when he finally dies in his sins, will
realize too late just what Jesus says. First, ὅτι ἐγώ εἰμι,
a repetition from v. 24 and to be understood in the
same sense, "that *I* (and I alone) am" what I tell
you, namely "from above not of this world" (v. 23).
We see how this reference knits the entire discourse
(v. 21-29) together as a unit. Too late all these ill-
fated Jews will "realize" by their own experience of
the divine judgment that what Jesus kept telling them
concerning himself is verity indeed. Secondly, they
will "realize" in the same way the verity connected with the Father, already stated in v. 26 and
now repeated and amplified, "and that from myself
I do nothing (5:19, etc.), but, just as the Father
taught me, these very things I tell (5:30, etc.)." Back
of every act and thus also of every word of Jesus is
the Father and his verity ("he that did send me is
true," v. 26). Word and deed of Jesus go together, although here the emphasis is on the word;
and this means the threat and the warning as well
as the call and the offer of grace (v. 24) at present still
held out.

"That I am" is a repetition from v. 24; and the
predicate that is to be supplied is the   same.   The
aorist "he taught" is historical, just as the aorist
"I heard" in v. 26; both refer to the time indicated
in ὁ πέμψας με, "he that did send me," in v. 26 when
Jesus went forth from God on his mission. We must
note that καθώς . . . ταῦτα correspond: "even as
. . . these very things"; and ταῦτα is resumptive
for the clause "even as the Father taught me." But
from the manner "even as" Jesus turns to the substance, "these very things," instead of keeping to
the manner, "thus also" (οὕτως). This is lost in
our versions which translate, "I speak these things,"
as though Jesus refers only to what he just now says.

29) Jesus prophesies that the obdurate Jews will come to realize too late what they ought to realize now, namely that Jesus is what he says, and that every word of his has back of it the Father and his verity. From the Jews he now turns to himself. They shall die in their sins, but Jesus, being what he is, doing and saying what he does, is sure of his Father and that Father's support. **And he that did send me is with me; he did not leave me alone; because the things pleasing to him I for my part am doing always.** The observation is correct that these three brief statements are closely united and are understood only when taken together. The first is positive: the Sender is with him whom he sent; μετά here conveys the idea of help or aid, R. 611. While Jesus uses the present tense "is with me," this tense receives its force from the subject, "he that did send me." For in the entire mission of Jesus from its start to its finish the Father is with Jesus.

The positive statement is followed by the negative, "he did not leave me alone." The absence of a connective lends it greater force. Here Jesus uses the aorist ἀφῆκεν, "he did not leave" me alone. Like the present tense "is with me," this aorist receives its force from the subject, "he that did send me." The sense cannot be that the Father did not leave his Son only at the moment when he sent him. Some regard this aorist as constative: from the moment of the sending up to the present moment the Father did not leave the Son he sent. This is conceived as an expression of the consciousness of the Father's presence which Jesus has enjoyed until this very time. That, too, we are told, is why the hostile Jews with all their number and their power were unable to destroy Jesus as they planned to do — Jesus was not alone. Only by way of a deduction the thought is added, that as hitherto the Father did not leave his Son alone, so also

he will be with the Son until the end. We need make
no deduction whatever, the aorist itself covers all that
is added by the deduction. The Father who sent
the Son on his mission "is with him" during that
entire mission and "did not leave him alone" during
any part of that mission. "He that did send me,"
repeated so often by Jesus, is true regarding every
moment when Jesus utters this designation, applies to
every moment until his mission is completed and he
returns to his Father.

Jesus is here thinking and speaking of the close
of his mission, "I go away" (v. 21) ; "When you have
lifted up the Son of man." The crucifixion is in his
mind. With that before his eyes he utters the words
of verity and assurance that his great Sender is ever
with him and did not leave him alone. This is substantiated by the reason which Jesus assigns for the
constant presence of his Sender in his mission: "because the things pleasing to him I am doing always."
Jesus is not speaking only of what he is doing at the
moment. "I am doing always," the adverb made
strongly emphatic by being placed at the end, covers
the entire mission of Jesus. Most pleasing of all, indeed, "an odor of a sweet smell" (R. V.) for his Father,
is his passion when he prayed, "Thy will be done!"
and drank the bitter cup of death. "Always" looks
also to the cross.

When in v. 28 (compare 5:19 and 30) Jesus says
that he does nothing "from himself," he means that
in his entire mission *he* never disowns but always
acknowledges his Father. The counterpart of this is
the fact that in his entire mission the Father is "with
him" and never "leaves him alone," i. e., *the Father*
never disowns Jesus but always acknowledges him.
Both thoughts meet in the expression "the things
pleasing to him," the adjective having "a distinct personal flavor," R. 537. Jesus ever pleases the Father,

and the Father is ever pleased with Jesus. Thus the
two are bound together with never a break in the tie.
This holds true even with regard to the agony on
the cross; in fact, holds true there in the highest
degree. For there, if anywhere, Jesus did not his
own but his Father's will; there, if anywhere, Jesus
did what pleased his Father; there, if anywhere, the
Father was pleased in his Son. "With me" and "did
not leave me alone" (οὐ ἀφῆκεν) holds true with regard
to the cross. And yet God forsook Jesus on the
cross. But the verb ἐγκατέλιπες, "Why didst thou for-
sake me?" (Matt. 27:46; Matt. 15:34) means something entirely different, namely that Jesus trod the
winepress alone, drank the cup of wrath for our sins
alone, paid the penalty for our guilt alone. This was
the Father's will; and Jesus did it. Yea, for this
he had come (12:27; compare 10:18) and, though
it wrung the bitter cry from his soul, he carried it
through. He could perform this part of his mission
only in this way — alone; no one could share the
extreme agony with him. But paying the ransom
(λύτρον) and the price (τιμή) alone does not mean that
at that supreme hour Jesus acted "from himself," disowning his Father and his Sender's mission, or disowned by his Father and Sender. In that very hour
the hardest part of his mission was accomplished
(Phil. 2:8).

We may say that the emphatic pronoun ἐγώ, "I on
my part," is in contrast to the Jews and to all of us
as sinners, for none of us do what is pleasing to the
Father. Yet this is a minor point. For "the things
pleasing to him" signify all that belongs to Jesus'
mission. These Jesus did "always" without a single
omission. While thus the reason for the Father's ever
being with Jesus can be called ethical, this reason is
not ethical in the usual sense as obeying the divine
law but in the far higher sense of voluntarily assum-

ing the mission of redemption and executing that
mission with absolute fidelity. The opposite of doing
"the things pleasing to him" is, therefore, not the doing
of some sin displeasing to God — a thought that is
foreign to the connection; but of after all giving up
the voluntarily assumed redemptive mission and of
thus allowing it to remain unfulfilled. The perfect
sinlessness of Jesus is only mediately involved in "the
things pleasing to him" as one of the personal qualifications (as, on the other hand, the divinity) for the
redemptive mission.

30) **As he was uttering these things many believed in him.** It makes little difference whether
we add this sentence as the close of the previous
paragraph or make it head the new paragraph.
"These things" points backward, yet v. 31 mentions
believing Jesus, and v. 30 accounts for them. The
aorist ἐπίστευσαν merely states the fact that many
"believed." Amid all the hostility that Jesus faced he
won this victory.

V. *Jesus' Testimony Culminates in an Effort to
Stone Him, 31-59*

31) **Accordingly, Jesus was saying to the Jews
who had believed in him, If you remain in my word
you are truly my disciples and you shall know the
truth, and the truth shall set you free.** When
editors of the text and commentators make a paragraph at v. 30 or 31, this does not imply that we are
to insert an interval, either of hours or of a day, between the paragraphs, as is generally done. John
connects v. 30 with what precedes by means of ταῦτα
and the genitive absolute, "while he was saying these
things," and v. 31 with v. 30 by means of οὖν, "accordingly, Jesus was saying" to these believers. Any
interval is shut out. John's remark in v. 30 and in

the preamble of v. 31 are merely explanatory of the words which Jesus now utters, for they are words intended only for believers, and we must be told that and how such believers were present. John's explanatory remark is exactly like the one he inserted a moment ago in v. 27 in order to make plain to us why Jesus turned to prophecy in v. 28.

Once this is clear, we shall not think that τοὺς πεπιστευκότας αὐτῷ 'Ιουδαίους is an exceptional expression in John's Gospel. It is as natural as it can be in this its proper place. Nor shall we place the emphasis either on the noun "Jews" or on the attributive participle "having believed," for neither term is emphatic. We shall also not entertain such notions as that John means to convey to us the thought that the people here named have a double naturo, the old Jewish nature still persisting beside the new nature of faith. This idea is introduced in order to explain v. 33, "they replied to him"; the unspecified subject of ἀπεκρίθησαν is taken to be these believing Jews, whose old Jewish nature is supposed to be cropping out in objecting to what Jesus says. But the moment this is done, all that follows likewise refers to these believing Jews. Jesus would be telling them that they are seeking to kill him, that they are of the devil, etc. In fact, then the most scathing utterances of Jesus in this entire chapter would be hurled at these believing Jews. But so monstrous a situation is incredible.

From v. 21 to the end of the chapter is one uninterrupted narration. The persons participating are the same throughout, Jesus and a crowd of Jews. At first all are hostile to Jesus, but by the time we reach v. 29 a goodly number are actually won to believe in him (note the statement of this as a fact by means of the aorist ἐπίστευσαν in v. 30), not through miracles, but through the words of warning coupled with grace which these men have just heard. In some way or other, not indicated by John, these believers manifest their change of heart. At once Jesus has a word for them in particular. No sooner does he utter it than the hostile crowd of Jews raises further objection. They act just as they did from the start: they pick at some point to which to object (compare v. 22 and 25; also v. 13 and 19). John does not need to say in v. 33 who these objectors are, for we have heard them from the very start, and their objection is of the same type as before. Jesus answers them in v. 34, etc. But they go on. The clash becomes more and more intense until these Jews take up stones, and Jesus leaves them.

The imperfect ἔλεγεν is like the imperfect in v. 23 and 25, little more than a variation from the aorist; note that in the following exchanges the aorists introducing them are interrupted by one present tense, λέγει, in v. 39. After faith has been kindled in the hearts of a goodly number of the present audience of Jesus, the great need is that they continue in the blessed course upon which they have entered. The condition of expectancy (ἐάν with the subjunctive), "If you remain (or shall remain) in my words," counts on such continuance as the normal thing. The pronoun ὑμεῖς is emphatic, "If *you on your part* remain," etc., i. e., "you" as having come to faith. This singles them out from the rest of the Jews. We must not overlook the implication in the verb "remain" in my word. Jesus acknowledges that these men *are* now in his word; in other words, that they now embrace his word by faith. He uses the aorist subjunctive μείνητε, actually and definitely remain, be fixed and established in his word. The opposite would be to drop the word they have taken up, definitely to leave it again, namely by a return to unbelief. Jesus also uses the strong possessive adjective "word of mine," which is weightier than the genitive pronoun.

This clause sheds light on the dative αὐτῷ: who believed "him." It indicates that these Jews now believed in what Jesus had told them; to believe "him" = to believe what he says. Theirs was the genuine type of faith, resting on the word. All they needed was to become permanently fixed in that faith.

The apodosis: then "you are truly my disciples," corroborates the implication in the protasis. Jesus implies that these believers are already his disciples; on μαθηταί see 2:2. Yet there is a difference between being disciples and being truly disciples. The preceding aorist subjunctive indicates what this difference is. All are disciples of Jesus who in any way believe his word, but those are truly disciples who once for all become fixed in his word. Hence also the "if." Beginners, however genuine their beginning, may drop off again; but once they become fixed definitely to remain in the word, they will never drop off again. Note, too, that Jesus uses the present tense: then "you are truly" my disciples; and not the future tense: then "you *will be* truly." This avoids the implication that only at some perhaps future time these believers can achieve the higher status. They can become fixed and established in Jesus' word in short order. No long apprenticeship is needed. To remain in Jesus' word (aorist) carries an intensive and not merely an extensive idea. Not the amount and quantity of the word makes us truly disciples but the fidelity and the firmness with which we hold the amount of the word which has been vouchsafed to us. While these beginners in the faith must learn more and more of the precious word of Jesus on which their incipient faith rests, and while all further portions of the word, such as the portion they already possess, will tend to hold them in the faith, for them to remain in the word of Jesus means primarily what Paul puts into the admonition, "Be ye steadfast, unmovable!" I Cor. 15:58.

The word of Jesus (λόγος) is his teaching, the gospel; most emphatically it is "his" word. The necessity for firm adherence to it is at once seen when we remember that this "word" and this alone is spirit and life, outside of which is spiritual death. Jesus identifies himself with his word, "If you remain in me, and my words (the one word in its different parts) remain in you," 5:7. The word is the vehicle of Jesus, bringing him to us, and us to him. An example of remaining in his word is seen in the case of the 3,000 at Pentecost: "they continued steadfastly in the apostles' doctrine," Acts 2:42. Compare Acts 13:43; Col. 1:23; Heb. 3:14; I John 2:28 (John loves the word "to remain," "to abide"); II John 9. Thus to remain is not only a mark of discipleship but its very essence.

32) "And" adds the blessed result that is immediately involved in truly being disciples of Jesus, first the proximate, next the ultimate result. The former is: "you shall know the truth," γνώσεσθε, "realize" it by your inner spiritual contact with it. Of course, intellectual apprehension is included, but much more is involved (7:17), namely the knowledge derived from a living experience with the blessed power of the truth. No man who rejects the truth can possibly attain this type of knowledge. The future tense is constative, R. 871, like that of the same verb in v. 28; it summarizes the entire realization following real discipleship. "Shall know" does not refer to a remote future but to one that begins at once and continues and grows.

"The truth" is the contents of the word of Jesus, the substance of what he conveys to our minds and our hearts. "I have given them thy (the Father's) Word," 17:14; "Sanctify them in the truth; thy Word is truth," 17:17 (see also 17:8). By "truth," ἀλήθεια, "reality," is meant, and the Greek article here indicates the specific reality and actuality that exists in God and in Jesus, and all that they give to us and do for us by divine grace. Compare the term in 1:14. It is not in any sense philosophic, so that the language of philosophy could define it. It is not an abstraction formed by operations of the intellect but divine and everlasting fact, which remains such whether men know it, acknowledge it, realize it or not. It is a unit: "the truth," although it consists of many united and unified parts. Thus also Jesus speaks of his "Word" and of his "words." It centers and circles about Jesus who, therefore, also calls himself "the Truth," 14:6. In his own person and his life Jesus embodies, incorporates the saving realities of God.

At once and in any measure that we realize the truth this follows as the next effect: "and the truth shall set you free," shall liberate, emancipate you. R. 872 calls this future punctiliar or effective. Yet we should not disconnect it from the preceding future tense, which R. acknowledges as constative. For by realizing we are set free; hence the more we realize, the more we are set free. The one action grows immediately out of the other. Any measure of inner penetration on the part of the truth produces a corresponding measure of freedom. Moreover, these results have already begun in the believers Jesus addresses; for to believe the word of Jesus ever so little means to realize the truth to that extent and to be set free correspondingly. Then, of course, to remain in the Word of Jesus, to be fixed and firm in that Word, means a realization and an emancipation fixed and firm accordingly.

This liberating effect implies that here "the truth" is viewed as an inward and spiritual power, one that

conquers an opposing, an enslaving power. The implication is also that only "the truth," or the Word of
Jesus, is able to crush that opposing power and to
set men free. Hence, all who bar out from their souls
this liberating power of necessity remain under the
enslaving power. The quick rejoinder of the unbelieving Jews prevents Jesus from adding what he
means by this enslaving power and by the bondage
from which "the truth" sets the believers free. Yet
the very implication that lies in ἀλήθεια as "reality"
reveals that the opposing power must be "the unreality," the power of spiritual lies, falsehoods, decep-
tions (all that in religion is not so), which fetter
and thus enslave the souls of men. A glorious prospect
is held out to the believing Jews by Jesus, one to
inspire them to ever greater faith in order to be free
from all delusion and spiritual bondage. Liberty!
Men have fought and died for it on the lower plane
of life; philosophers dream of it in the intellectual
life; Jesus assures it on the highest plane, that of
religion and the soul.

33) **They made answer against him, Seed of
Abraham are we and to no one have we been in
bondage ever. How dost thou say, You shall
become free men?** Instead of the regular dative
αὐτῷ (or the plural where required) John here writes
πρὸς αὐτόν, "against him," affording us this hint that
these objectors are the unbelieving Jews who again
seize on one certain expression (see v. 19, 22, 25) in
order to upset what Jesus is saying. See the discussion on v. 31. Those who assume that the believing
Jews here speak against Jesus must assume also (and
some actually do) that, believing in one instant, they
lose their faith in the next and in a moment become
more vicious than ever. One thing is beyond question,
we now hear the voice of open unbelief. Note the
passion displayed: haughty pride: "Seed of Abraham

are we!" etc.; open scorn in the emphatic σύ, as much
as to say, "Thou, who art thou!?"; resentment in
restating ἐλευθερώσει by ἐλεύθεροι γενήσεσθε, "you shall become free men." If the believing Jews could thus
pass over into passionate unbelief because of one simple
word of Jesus', he certainly made a mistake when he
held out to them the sweet prospect of spiritual liberty.
Had he here lost his power to see what is in men's
hearts (2:25)?

Besser's paraphrase is good: "If the truth you
speak of is good only for *slaves*, do not trouble us,
Abraham's seed, with it! We are a freeborn, royal
nation (Gen. 17:6, 7; 22:11) and acknowledge no
one as our master save God. To him we belong as
children (Deut. 14:1) and to no one else. This is
the *truth* which makes us free!" The reply is headed
by the emphatic, "Seed of Abraham are we!" This
shuts out the notion that these Jews refer to political
liberty, which also would contradict most flagrantly
the facts of history, the domination of the Jews by
the Babylonians, the Persians, the Seleucidae, and
the Romans (these latter at this very time). It
shuts out also the idea of social liberty, namely
that in this nation Jews were not made slaves.
"To no one have we been in bondage ever" asserts
unbroken religious liberty for all Jews as God's
own chosen people, compared with whom all Gentiles were slaves of idols. Talk of *them* becoming
free men! These Jews understand correctly that
Jesus is speaking of religious liberty, and what they
hurl against him (πρὸς αὐτόν) is meant in that sense.

The name "Abraham" here broached runs on
through the remainder of the conflict to the very end.
It constitutes the acme of Jewish assurance and pride
— does so to this day. The emphatic σύ gets its force
from the feeling of outrage that Jesus should presume
to say anything against *Abraham's* seed. Who art

"thou" to dare such a thing? In v. 48 these Jews disown Jesus as a son of Abraham by calling him a
Samaritan, the very antithesis of a child of Abraham.
What these Jews voice as Jews in the name "Abraham"
is found in all the sons of Adam, all of whom cling to
their unholy pride when the gospel comes to give them
true freedom.

34)   Calm, quiet, direct, crushing is the simplicity
and the force of the answer of Jesus. **Jesus answered them, Amen, amen, I say to you, Everyone
who does sin is the slave of sin.** The double
"amen" is the seal of truth for what Jesus says (compare on the term 1:51); "I say to you" is the voice of
authority based on absolute knowledge and truth.
This preamble marks the weight of what follows. It
is in the nature of a moral axiom: "Everyone who
does sin is the slave of sin." The truth of the statement is self-evident. The article in ὁ ποιῶν is needed
to substantivize the characterizing present participle
and thus does not affect πᾶς as meaning "every." The
article in τὴν ἁμαρτίαν is generic, everything that is
rightly termed "sin." The man so characterized, who
does what is sin, obeys the dictates of sin, cannot
break away from them — he is beyond question a
slave of sin, in the spiritual soul-slavery of the worst
kind. This is true of men everywhere, at all times.
The effect of sinning is as certain as the mathematical
law that two and two make four. Jesus does not say
outright that all men are sinners and thus slaves of
sin, but his application to the Jews includes that
thought. "Doing sin" is to be taken in the widest
sense, doing it by thought, word, and act. Compare
II Pet. 2:19; Rom. 6:16. Even the pagans voice what
Jesus says about this slavery. Seneca declares that
no bondage is harder than that of the passions; Plato,
that liberty is the name of virtue, and bondage the
name of vice.

35) A second axiomatic statement follows and in a surprising way opens up what lies in the word "slave." **Now the slave does not remain in the house forever; the son remains forever.** To be sure, the status of the slave is such that he may be sold. He is in no sense a permanent part of the family. This again is undeniable. Not "the slave" but "the son" (both articles being generic) remains forever, namely by virtue of his relation and position as son and hence heir. Probably in order to avoid an incongruity the genitive τῆς ἁμαρτίας in v. 34 was dropped in some codices, so that the clause reads, "is a slave," and not, "is a slave of sin." The idea of the codices seems to be the avoidance of two masters, first "sin" as the master of this slave, and secondly he who is the head of "the house" together with "the son." But no father or head of the house is mentioned. Jesus is not narrating a parable in which all the figurative details have their place. The illustration turns only on the correlative points: slave and son, or, we may say, slavery and freedom. We really do not need the usual explanation that this slave, made such by the domination of sin, would thus be nothing but a foreign slave in the house whose head is God, thus having even less right in the house. The figure Jesus uses is without such complication; for what would a native slave of the house be? All that Jesus uses is the status of a slave and the status of the son. In the phrase εἰς τὸν αἰῶνα the noun αἰών denotes unlimited time and thus eternity, here with εἰς eternity *a parte post* (from now forward), C.-K. 93.

36) What Jesus means appears in the application which he makes of the figure. **If, therefore, the Son shall set you free, you shall be free men in reality.** The application retains the figure, now plainly joining it to the reality. Jesus goes back to his first utterance concerning those who are truly his disciples and are

set free from bondage. He even combines his own
word "shall set free" (v. 32) with that of the Jews,
"shall become free men" (v. 33), for which Jesus sub-
stitutes "shall be free men." What Jesus said regarding the truth in v. 32 he now predicates of himself.
For the generic term "the son" (as opposed to "the
slave") in v. 35 is now turned into the specific "the
Son." This one and only Son is the embodiment of
"the truth" and as such the great Liberator in his
Father's house. For, not only are he and the Father
one, but into his hands is laid the entire administra-
tion of the house by virtue of his redemptive and saving mission. For this reason also nothing concerning
the Father needs to be provided for in the figurative
terms.

Who is pictured by "the slave" is also plainly
stated: "you," the unbelieving Jews. Note that the
believing Jews were already set free, needing only
to be fully established in their liberty. Thus Jesus
vindicates his implication in v. 32 that the unbelieving Jews need emancipation from slavery and that,
in fact, they are slaves, an allegation against which
their ire rises. Yet fine as the figure is for the main
point Jesus means to drive home, like so many other
figures and illustrations taken from merely human
relations, it falls short in picturing what Jesus does
for those who believe in him. When Jesus sets us free,
we, of course, are ἐλεύθεροι, "free men," and yet we
are far more than the so-called freedmen (liberated
slaves) in the old Roman Empire; we are ourselves
turned into "sons," adopted into the household of God,
children of the Father, joint heirs with Christ. Only
the emphatic adverb ὄντως, "really," hints at this
result of our emancipation by the Son. Perhaps also
ἔσεσθε, "you shall be" (durative), is placed in contrast
to γενήσεσθε, "you shall become" (punctiliar), used by
the Jews.

Glancing back from the application in v. 36 to the figure used in the axiomatic statements in v. 34, 35, we see that already there part of the reality is interwoven with the figure. "Everyone that does sin" is non-figurative, and in "a slave of sin" "sin" is literal. Thus the figure about the "slave" only helps to bring out the axiomatic character of the statements. In v. 35 εἰς τὸν αἰῶνα, "forever," might be considered part of the figure, simply meaning that the slave does not remain "always," only the son remains "always" (compare the phrase in 13:8; Mark 11:14; I Cor. 8:13; etc.). And yet where figure and reality are combined, as is the case here, and where the fate of souls is the subject, we may well prefer to take "forever" in the literal sense. "One thing have I desired of the Lord, that I will seek after; that I may dwell in the house of the Lord all the days of my life, to behold the beauty of the Lord, and to inquire in his temple," Ps. 27:4. Again, "I will dwell in the house of the Lord *forever*," Ps. 23:6.

37) First, the point that these Jews do need liberation; now, the point that they are not "seed of Abraham." The two belong together: true seed of Abraham would, indeed, be free; these Jews are not such seed, hence they need to be set free and thus truly become Abraham's seed. **I know that you are seed of Abraham,** namely his physical descendants. No question about this point, and also the fact that it constitutes a great advantage to have a forefather like Abraham. Jesus is speaking of spiritual relationship, something that is on an altogether higher plane. Hence he lays his finger on the moral nature and character of this physical seed of Abraham: **but you are seeking to kill me because my word has not free course in you.** The question is: How does this agree with your being seed of Abraham and thus really free sons of God?

How can they as sons so treat the eternal Son? Compare 5:18; 7:19 and 25; also 8:59. With ἀλλά Jesus merely holds up the glaring contrast between the proud claim to be Abraham's seed and the criminal determination to kill Jesus, the Son. One would expect of the physical sons of Abraham that they more than all men would turn out to be also Abraham's spiritual sons and thus enter upon the spiritual inheritance of their great father. With these Jews the contrary is the case. Their real character they themselves reveal ("you seek to kill"). The gravity of what they thus reveal lies not merely in the fact that they are base enough to plot murder as such but to plot the murder of the very Son, whose day Abraham desired to see (v. 56), for whom Abraham was made what he was, to whom the Father committed his entire house (v. 36).

The reason why these Jews fell so far from their Abrahamitic descent and heritage is presented in negative form, "because my word has not free course in you." Moreover, it assigns a fact which does not stop at a halfway point but goes to the very root of their defection. With this reason Jesus also returns to the vital point which he had emphasized for those who had begun to believe him (v. 31, αὐτῷ, believe what he said), namely "my word." Those believers, he said, must remain in "my word"; of these unbelievers he says: "my word" finds no place in you. The negation is in the nature of a litotes. Not to have free course = to be barred out. In the believers the word, having entered, must remain; in these unbelievers it has found no entrance at all. The word of Jesus would make these Jews believers and thus true seed of Abraham. Instead of criminal designs against the Son the result would be loyal attachment to the Son. These slaves of sin would be turned into sons of the Father to abide with the Son forever. Thus all that Jesus says from v. 31 onward turns on the one point of his word. Note how much weightier ὁ λόγος ὁ ἐμός, "this word of mine," is than ὁ λόγος μου, "my word." The word χωρεῖ is not transitive, for then we should have χωρεῖτε τὸν λόγον, "you make no room"; but intransitive and in the sense, "my word finds no room in you." Every effort of that word to enter leaves it outside.

38) The final statement is still about this word (λαλῶ), now tracing it back to its ultimate source and on this point placing it over against the ultimate source of the word which controls the unbelieving Jews. The text of the A. V. cannot be accepted. **What things I myself have seen with the Father I utter; and you, accordingly, what things you did hear from your father you do.** It is hard to pronounce on all the minutiae of the readings, some of which are altogether unimportant. The two statements are parallel but with marked differences in detail. The main thought is that Jesus' word has one source, and the actions of the Jews the very opposite source. The two relative clauses are prominent, being placed, as they are, ahead of the main verbs. But the emphatic ἐγώ is placed in the first relative clause, "I myself have seen," while the equally emphatic ὑμεῖς precedes the second relative clause and forms the subject of the main verb, "and you, . . . , you do." Thus the pronouns are in contrast, yet each has its own angle. Jesus was "with the Father" in heaven (the pronoun in the relative clause); the corresponding statement would not be true of the Jews, for they have not been with the devil in hell, their father, (hence the pronoun outside of the relative clause and with the main verb).

Jesus has seen the Father (properly with the locative, παρά and the dative); the Jews have not seen their father. He would not dare to show himself to them. They only heard from him (properly the ablative, παρά and the genitive, R. 614). He whispered insidiously to their hearts, not showing his real self but masquerading, just as in Eden. Even the tenses add a point, the extensive perfect indicating the prolonged seeing and association of the Son with the Father while in heaven, the effect of which is still present with Jesus; on the other hand, the aorist stating only the fact: "you did hear from your father." In other connections, where no such contrast is intended, Jesus uses the simple aorist also regarding himself, "I did hear," in v. 26; the Father, "did teach" in v. 28. In the phrase "with the Father" we do not need the pronoun "my," which is added in some texts; for only one Father exists, he whose Son is Jesus; but in the corresponding phrase "from your father" the pronoun "your" is in place. Its omission in some texts has led to a decidedly different interpretation: "Do you also, therefore, the things which you did hear from the Father!" (R. V. margin.) This would be an admonition addressed to the unbelieving Jews to follow the example of Jesus. But the Jews heard something far different, as their objection shows, namely an intimation in regard to their father, that he was evil. "The things which you did hear from your father" includes their plot to kill Jesus and thus intimates other deeds of this kind.

Jesus says, "I utter" (λαλῶ), because he has been speaking of his word and on this visit to Jerusalem had confined himself to speaking and presenting testimony, doing no miracles. With his utterances of the divine truth he was conferring the greatest benefit upon the Jews. Yet for this they wanted to kill him. Regarding the Jews, however, he uses "you do," or "you perform" (ποιεῖτε), referring to their actions, including especially their efforts to kill him, these actions so openly marking their spiritual parentage.

39) Whom Jesus has in mind when he so pointedly says "your father" he does not yet state. One thing is clear, namely that this is not the one whom he calls his Father; yet this, too, is a father in the sense that he confers a spiritual character that is like his own, the opposite of that found in the heavenly Father. Jesus thus strikes at the consciences of these unbelieving Jews, seeking thus to convict them of their sins. They are "in their sins" (v. 24), liable to die in them; they are "doing sin" (v. 34) and thus lie in slavery. It is thus that they are doing "the things they did hear from their father," thereby betraying their real parentage. This explains their reaction. **They answered and said to him** (the doubling of the verbs indicating the weight they put on their reply; see 1:48), **Our father is Abraham.** The observation is correct that by this reply these Jews are not attempting to make Jesus speak out more plainly in regard to whom he terms their father. They had an inkling whom Jesus had in mind. Their conscience was pricked. Therefore, to ward off the sharp sting they assert the more strenuously that they have no father, physically or spiritually, but Abraham. Note that this reply is purely defensive, and that all their previous replies are either altogether offensive or connect offense with defense. Their next reply (v. 41) is also nothing but an effort at defense; then comes vituperation, since defense fails (v. 48), and after that the preliminaries to murderous violence (v. 52, 53; 57 and 59).

Jesus is succeeding. The first sharp stab at the conscience is followed by a deeper thrust. **Jesus says to them: If you really are Abraham's children you would be doing the works of Abraham. But now you are seeking to kill me, a man who has been telling you the truth which he heard from God. This Abraham did not do. You are doing the**

works of your father. Note the vivid aoristic present
λέγει at this climax of the altercation and how it lends
a special touch to the reply of Jesus, just as the
double "answered and said" in v. 39 lends weight
to the reply of the Jews. The first sentence uses a
mixed condition, a protasis of reality and an apodosis
of unreality (the imperfect with ἄν, although ἄν may
be and often is omitted, as here). Mixed conditional
sentences are perfectly in order (in all languages),
according as the thought may require. Some texts
have ἦτε for ἐστε (and even add ἄν), merely changing
the form to an ordinary conditional sentence of
present unreality: "If you were . . . . , you
would." With ἐστε Jesus says: "If you, indeed, are,
as you assert, children of Abraham, you would," etc.
He here uses τέκνα not σπέρμα as in v. 37, with no difference in the sense. A generally admitted axiom
underlies the statement, namely that children are like
their father, disregarding the cases where abnormally
a child differs from his parent.

40) In v. 39 Jesus really lays down the major
premise of a negative syllogism. In v. 40, with the
logical νῦν δέ, he lays down the minor premise. The
conclusion of the syllogism is not stated. It is inevitable, left by Jesus for the Jews to draw for themselves, namely: "*Ergo*, you are not Abraham's children as you assert." This negative syllogism is irrefutable. Its effect is deadly for the claim of the Jews.
It stamps their claim as a brazen lie. In stating
the minor premise Jesus uses the specific act of the
Jews, their seeking to kill him. This act as such could
not serve as the minor premise. But the moment this
one act is placed in its proper category and is viewed
as marking that category, the minor premise is perfect. Therefore Jesus adds the simple apposition:
You are seeking to kill me, "a man who has told you
the truth which I heard from God," and sets over

against the action thus characterized and generalized the undeniable fact: "This Abraham did not do." When any man came to Abraham with the truth of God, Abraham did not try to kill him. This strong negative implies an equally strong positive: Abraham accepted that truth of God and the messenger who brought it to him.

This formulation of the minor premise lends terrific force to the entire syllogism by the simplicity with which the enormity of the crime of the Jews is indicated: trying to kill a man who brought them the truth of God! The greatest divine benefit — rewarded by the most dastardly human ingratitude! If the thing were not an actual fact, it would be utterly incredible. Just as the Jews, self-blinded and deaf to the truth Jesus brings them, know only the trick of fastening upon one certain word or expression of Jesus, perverting that into an objection to the truth, so later deniers of the Godhead of Christ fasten upon the word ἄνθρωπος here used by Jesus and try to prove by that that Jesus is not God. Indeed, Jesus is "a man," perfectly human, even "flesh" (1:14); but what a man? Why fasten upon "a man" and omit the relative clause, the final part of which repeats what Jesus constantly testifies to the Jews, for which also they first (5:18) resolved to kill him, that as God's Son he "did hear from God" and came down from God on his great mission. This divine Son is the "man" who here again testifies that he is God. Note that both λελάληκα and ἤκουσα are verbs in the first person: "I have told," "I have heard." In translation this "I" is lost in the first verb. What this "man" here says of himself applies to his person only. No other man heard directly in heaven from God and then came to tell what he thus heard.

41) But if Abraham is not the spiritual father of these Jews, then who is? To this point Jesus returns

by repeating with slight change the veiled statement
of v. 38. **You on your part** (ὑμεῖς, emphatic) **are doing the works of your** (ὑμῶν, correspondingly
emphatic) **father.** Now, however, it is clearer
what Jesus means, since he has instanced one of these
damnable works. Spiritually, then, these Jews can
claim only a father who approves and who impels to
such works.

The Jews are stung to the quick. The lash of the
law makes these sinners squirm and wince. That they
should, is just what Jesus intends, and we see that
he lays the whip on still more severely. Unless he
succeeds in crushing these hard hearts, the gospel
cannot enter them. Frantic under the veiled imputa-
tion of Jesus, they attempt no counterattack but only
hopeless defense. **They said to him, We, not of
fornication were we born   One father we have—
God!** The stress is on ἕνα, "one," followed by τὸν
θεόν, "God." The battle is far away from the question
of physical fatherhood, abandoned already in v. 37; it
is altogether on spiritual descent. Driven from the
claim of being the spiritual children of Abraham by
the inexorable syllogism of Jesus in v. 39, 40, the Jews
now seek cover behind the passionate claim of their
supposedly impregnable standing in the theocracy of
God. For who can deny that they and they alone
properly belong in that theocracy — all other people
and nations are here shut out. God and God alone
has placed them there — he is thus their one spiritual
father.

The negation of this relation would thus be
γεννηθῆναι ἐκ πορνείας, to be born of fornication, in the
sense of having two fathers: one their real father,
who actually begot them; the other their apparent
father, in whose house they are merely tolerated.
Their real nature would be inherited from the former;
and only outwardly and nominally the second would

be deemed their father. Is this what Jesus suggests, that, while these Jews are outwardly in the theocratic house of God, they are really the product of (ἐκ) fornication, illigitimately carried into that house? They do not indicate directly, as little as Jesus had done, who this adulterous real father would be. That he could only be evil is the implication which makes these Jews so passionate. Thus ἕνα is opposed to δύο.

Usually, since the Old Testament so frequently pictures the defection of the Jewish nation from God, their running after idols in the time prior to the exile, as fornication and adultery and thus the idolatrous Jews as "the seed of the adulterer and the whore" (Isa. 57:3), this reference to πορνεία is taken to mean: born of *idolatrous* fornication. The emphatic ἡμεῖς is then regarded as referring to the present generation of the Jews in the sense: "we Jews now," we cannot be charged with idolatry, for since the days of the exile our nation has been practically free of this type of spiritual fornication. The difficulty regarding this view is the fact that Jesus in no way charges idolatry against these Jews and that he speaks only of one evil father (the devil) not of many such fathers (pagan idols or gods). To defend a point not attacked is senseless.

42) Again Jesus crushes this new vain defense of the Jews; this time not by a syllogism (although he might have put his reply in that form) but by applying the most simple axiomatic test. **Jesus said to them, If God were your father, you would love me; for I came forth and am come from God; for not of myself have I come, on the contrary, he did commission me.** The conditional sentence is the ordinary type of present unreality, εἰ with the imperfect, the imperfect with ἄν. The test is simple: true children of God would at once recognize the Son of God and in intelligent love (ἀγαπάω) would turn

toward him; it is impossible that such children should not recognize and embrace God's Son. Whereas in v. 40 Jesus speaks of himself as a man and adds the mark of divinity, here he does the reverse, stating what makes him divine (his coming forth from God) and adding the mark of his humanity ("I am come," i. e., am here). The verbs ἐξῆλθον and ἥκω are not a mere duplication; both verbs are also modified by ἐκ τοῦ Θεοῦ. "I came forth from God" = the Incarnation, God's Son became man (1:14). "I am come from God" = the mission, Jesus is standing here before these Jews, engaged in his mission, (ἥκω, present tense from a root with the meaning of the perfect, R. 881). Doubly these Jews would recognize and love Jesus if they were God's children: once as their relative, come from their God to them; again as their benefactor on his saving mission from God to them. His very person and his very work so mark Jesus as "from God" that any contact with him at once opens the hearts of God's true children. Not one of them could possibly fail in this test. To fail is to demonstrate that those who fail, however emphatically they assert their childhood, are not children at all but — liars. For the coming of Jesus from God the Greek may use ἐκ, παρά (16:27), or ἀπό (16:30), R. 579.

The fact that "I am come from God" refers to the mission of Jesus, which he is now executing before these Jews, is explained by the second γάρ which elucidates ἥκω: "for not from myself have I come," not thus am I here, carrying out a plan conceived only by myself; "on the contrary, he (ἐκεῖνος, God, emphatic, R. 708) did commission me" with a mission from him. Compare 7:17 and 28, 29; 8:28 and 42; 10:36; 11:42; 12:49; 14:10; 17:3 and 8. While the going forth from God and the mission of Jesus cannot be separated, since the latter is the one and only purpose of the former, the mission from God with all the truth it brings from God well deserves especial emphasis in the present connection. For, certainly, true children of God must at once recognize and love him who comes with God's own truth and blessings.

As an affinity with Abraham would automatically show itself in doing the corresponding works, so an affinity with God would automatically show itself in loving him who came out from God and is sent by God. The claim of the Jews perishes under this natural test.

43) So far are these Jews from receiving Jesus with intelligent love (ἀγαπᾶν) that he appears as a foreigner to them. **Why do you not understand my language, seeing that you are unable to hear my word?** "You are not able to hear" is a litotes for "you are deaf." They are deaf to τὸν λόγον τὸν ἐμόν, this "word of mine" (emphatic), i. e., *my* meaning, what *Jesus* has to say. These Jews are not deaf to what others say, that goes right into their ears, they "are able to hear" just what is meant. The ὅτι clause, "seeing that," just states a fact, a strange fact but a fact nonetheless. Jesus may present to them all the truth he pleases; these Jews "are unable to hear" a particle of it. The explanation lies in the first part of the question: they do not even *recognize* what "language" Jesus is speaking. The emphasis is on the verb; also λαλιάν and λόγον are distinct, the language used in speaking and the meaning that is put into that language. The very language of the divine truth is foreign to these Jews. The evidence that the language is foreign to them is their inability to hear what is put into that language. Jesus may as well talk to deaf men. These Jews indeed claim that thy are God's children; but when Jesus talks to them in the language of God and of God's house, they act like deaf persons, his meaning is lost upon them. That fact has only one explanation: they do not even

recognize the language, that it is that of God. That proves that God is not their father. Children know their father's language, it is their mother tongue. These Jews belong to a foreign land, where a different mother tongue is used. No need to say what land that is.

The fact that ὅτι must be rendered as here indicated is established by the use of this connective in 2:18; 7:35; 8:28; 9:2 and 17; 12:49; 14:10 and 22; Matt. 8:27; Mark 4:41; Luke 4:36; 8:12; see the grammatical explanations in B.-D. 456, 2; 480, 6; R. calls this ὅτι consecutive, 1001. Yet the grammars say nothing at all about our passage, although this is the very passage most in dispute. Is it because many translators and commentators take ὅτι to mean "because"? This turns the passage into a question which is followed by its answer: "Why do you not understand my language? Because you cannot hear my word!" But the answer is wrong. It ought to be, "Because you have not learned that language!" Or things ought to be reversed. "Why are you unable to hear my word? (why are you deaf to my meaning?) Because you do not understand my language!" To escape the incongruity between the question and the answer λαλιάν is translated "speech" instead of language, and the emphasis on γινώσκετε is overlooked. Yet even then little more than a tautology results.

The Jews had been deaf to all that Jesus had said to them (his word, the truth). In view of this Jesus asks whether they even *understand* his language. The question is rhetorical; it answers itself.

44) Now comes the final crushing blow, striking home in the conscience. The name of the spiritual father of these Jews, withheld so long, is now hurled straight into their faces: **You, of your father, the devil, are you, and the lusts of your father it is your will to do.** Note the emphatic subject ὑμεῖς. There

are children of God, but *you*, you unbelieving Jews, are the devil's children. Of course, the devil did not create these Jews while God created those people who are his children by faith. The fact that moral and spiritual relationship is referred to the clause with καί places beyond question. The ἐπιθυμίαι of the devil are the evil desires, lusts, and passions that fill the devil himself and show that he is the devil. His children are naturally inflamed with the same lusts; they get or inherit them through their spiritual descent from him. And yet, since the entire relationship with the devil is moral and spiritual, these lusts of the devil find place in his children only by their own consent and will. Not unwillingly these Jews are what they are. Nor are these lusts merely passive or latent in their hearts. The devil's children always actually will and go on willing (θέλετε) to do or to carry into action (ποιεῖν) these lusts. The evil desire kindled in the heart gives birth to the corresponding deed. No evil deed is without this evil root. Thus the deeds are prima facie proof first of the lusts, secondly of the inward connection with the devil. With τοῦ πατρός we need no ὑμῶν; the article alone suffices, and really no more needs to be said. And τοῦ διαβόλου is the appositional genitive. Among the inanities of exegesis is the one which makes this genitive possessive: of the father "of the devil," turning the Jews into brothers of the devil, and Jesus and John into gnostics.

"The lusts of your father" is general, including all of them. Two of them are outstanding, as the history of the devil shows, and these two lusts reapppear similarly in the devil's children. Thus Jesus specifies: **He, a manslayer was he from the beginning; and in the truth he does not stand because truth is not in him. When he speaks the lie, he speaks from what is his own; because he is a liar and the father there-**

of. Here is the historical moral portrait of the devil drawn by Jesus himself. The subject ἐκεῖνος is emphatic. Murder and lying are mentioned as the devil's lusts because they are that, as history shows, and because his children, the very Jews to whom Jesus is speaking, display these identical lusts. The historical reference in "manslayer" is not to the killing of Abel by Cain (I John 3:12), but, as "from the beginning" shows, to the first introduction of sin among men, by which death entered and slew our race (Rom. 5:12). "Manslayer" attributes to the devil far more than the physical murders that are committed by men; it charges him with bringing death in all its destructive power upon the whole of mankind.

Because lying was the means by which the devil murdered our race, lying is mentioned as the second lust. For the text we must rely on the text critics. Since οὐκ is at times written also before a rough breathing, it makes little difference whether we agree on οὐκ or write οὐχ before ἕστηκεν. B.-D. 73 and 91, 1 prefers to read ἕστηκεν, but also as the perfect of ἵστημι and he explains the smooth breathing in 14. So this, too, is only a difference in writing and in pronunciation. Hort makes ἕστηκεν the imperfect of στήκω, but R. 224 and 1219 leaves this idea wholly with Hort. While an imperfect would in a way match the preceding ἦν, yet no phrase such as ἀπ' ἀρχῆς accompanies the second verb; and the perfect of ἵστημι (whether written with a rough or with a smooth breathing) is always used as a present and certainly matches the following ἐστίν, which is also more closely connected with it than the preceding ἦν. Thus Jesus says, "and in the truth he does not stand." Why not? "Because truth is not in him." Since ἀλήθεια is an abstract noun, it may or may not have the article. Truth and the devil are wholly foreign, in fact absolutely antagonistic to each other. Take the sphere of truth (ἐν τῇ ἀληθείᾳ) — the devil has no place in it anywhere. Reverse this and take the devil — truth has no place in him anywhere. The word "truth" is here objective truth, since the truth and the devil are wholly separated; but also all that we conceive as subjective truth is denied with reference to the devil by the verbs used ("does not stand in," "is not in") ; personally "he is a liar," etc. A wrong implication should not be inferred from οὐκ ἕστηκεν, such as "does not stand firm" (as though he does stand loosely in the truth), or "does not stand permanently" (as though he does stand temporarily in the truth). The verb is absolute: "does not stand in any way."

The statements that follow have no connective such as γάρ and do not mean to prove that such a gulf exists between the truth and the devil. Their purpose is much deeper. These statements reveal the origin of untruth, falsehood, lies, and place that origin in the devil. "When he speaks the lie he speaks from what is his own," ἐκ τῶν ἰδίων. This does not mean that he acquired or appropriated what is now "his own," for it had no existence before him or apart from him; "his own" is what he himself originated. In this sense Jesus adds, "because he is a liar and the father thereof" — a liar, not like others who learned lying from him, but unlike others, the parent of the lie itself. We find no difficulty in αὐτοῦ, which goes back through ψεύστης to τὸ ψεῦδος, B.-D.282,2;R.683. This pronoun is frequently construed without a close antecedent, merely *ad sensum*. To think of "his (the devil's) father" is untenable. To translate, "and his (the liar's) father," is impossible, for this would make him his own father since "liar" is the predicate of "he (the devil) is." The devil is the father of the lie; in this way he speaks "from what is his own" when he speaks the lie (for instance in Gen. 3:1-6; Job 1 and 2; Matt. 4:1-11).

Since ἡ ἀλήθεια denotes reality (that which is so), it exists by itself even apart from any created expression. Since τὸ ψεῦδος denotes unreality (that which only pretends to be so), it never exists by itself but only as some created mind may conceive it or give it expression. Hence "the lie" must go down before "the truth." The truth, however, is also the expression of the actual reality, as the lie is that of the pretended reality. Truth loves to express what it really is, the lie never dares to do that. The two are powers with no peace possible between them. Truth's power is eternal, because the reality cannot cease; the power of the lie is ephemeral, because its pretense is bound to be exposed. God himself is the essence of the truth; the lie is the devil's vain invention. To receive the truth is to connect with God; to yield to the lie is to be the child of the devil.

In the most decisive way Jesus here declares the existence, personality, character, and potency of the devil. Either these statements of his are "the truth," ἡ ἀλήθεια, or he himself is guilty of "the lie," τὸ ψεῦδος — no escape from this alternative is possible. To say that Jesus knew that no such being existed as he here describes, that his language is only an "accomodation" to the superstitious and false notions of his Jewish hearers, is to rob language itself of its meaning and to strip Jesus himself of his moral character. By making the devil the originator of sin the notion that evil is also an eternal principle is shut out. In the two types of evil made prominent as inhering in the devil Jesus recalls to the Jews the main chapters of Satan's activity among men as set forth in the Old Testament. Jesus has no occasion here to declare the fall of the devil. Those who think the devil's fall is implied in the tense of οὐκ ἔστηκεν misread the tense; it is a grammatical perfect but an actual present: "does not stand" in the truth. It describes the devil as he now is and says nothing about the fact that at his creation he was otherwise. The testimony regarding his fall is recorded elsewhere. How the devil could become the author of evil, or how evil first began or could begin in him, is one of the mysteries that are wholly impenetrable to the mind of man.

45) From the devil Jesus turns to the Jews, the devil's children. **But because I on my part declare the truth, you do not believe me** — proof positive that they are descendants of him who stands not in the truth, because the truth is not in him. Truth always demands faith; this is the very law of our concreated moral nature. To reject the truth because it is the truth is to turn devilish. These Jews, bent on doing the lusts of their father, the devil, trample truth under their feet. As sons of the father of lies their souls have an affinity only for lies; they believe only liars and lies (πιστεύετε, durative to express continuous conduct).

46) But this statement that Jesus "declares the truth" to these Jews must not be understood superficially as though he means only that what he tells them is true. This statement about Jesus declaring the truth is in direct contrast to what he has just said about the devil. As the devil's very nature is "the lie," so the very nature of Jesus is "the truth." When the devil opens his mouth (λαλεῖ), out flow "what are his own" — lies; when Jesus declares his thoughts (λέγω), these thoughts coming from *him* (emphatic ἐγὼ δέ) are the very expression of his being and his person — the truth. This is the connection for the dramatic and challenging question: **Who of you convicts me of sin?** *He* has convicted, is convicting *them* in the most crushing way with un-

answerable proof. He has done this by bringing "the truth" to bear upon them, the reality of what they actually are. He has specified, pointing to their murderous plot and to their open refusal to accept the truth, irrefutable evidence of their filial connection with the devil. By doing all this Jesus furnishes to the Jews equally irrefutable evidence that *he* is the very opposite of them and of their father, the *devil*, — his very nature is "the truth." And what are these Jews doing by way of reply? Is even one of them convicting Jesus in any way whatever? No, not one. Are these Jews then by their utter inability to convict Jesus in any way not furnishing the strongest kind of evidence as to the true character of Jesus?

To be sure, the challenging question of Jesus is an incidental part of the truth with which he convicts the Jews. But not the small part which some consider it, as if all that Jesus challenges these Jews to do is to convict him of the fact that any allegation he is making against them is untrue, or that any allegation he is making concerning himself is false. Then the challenge would have to read, "Who of you convicts me of a lie?" But Jesus uses ἁμαρτία, the generic term for "sin." He even omits the article, so that we are compelled to understand "sin" in the broadest sense of the word and not as restricted to some one sin which may perhaps be suggested by the context. The effort to reduce ἁμαρτία to "fraud" or "mistake"·in the indictment of the Jews by Jesus is misspent. "Sin" means any and every kind of sin. And ἐλέγχειν means to convict by proof, to furnish genuine evidence of guilt, not merely to accuse. An accusation may be false and lack grounds. The Jews accused Jesus violently enough, for instance at his trial, but altogether groundlessly. Compare Trench, *Synonyms*, 1, 31, etc., on the word. In a conviction it makes no difference whether the person himself is convinced and confesses his guilt or not. The Jews were convicted by Jesus although they scorned to confess and would not amend their ways. They stood convicted because neither they nor anybody else could possibly show that they were not guilty exactly as Jesus charged. Their sole defense consisted in lies; thus that they were not slaves (v. 33) when they were; that their spiritual father is Abraham (v. 39) or is God (v. 41), neither of which is true. So the challenge Jesus hurls at these Jews defies them to bring proof of anything in him that in any way is sin. Let them take the entire category of sin, on not a single point are they convicting Jesus, yea, can they convict him.

Some look at this challenge only in so far as it is addressed to the Jews: "who of you." This passage, we are told, cannot be used as proof for the absolute sinlessness of Jesus; for the inability of *the Jews* to prove some sin in Jesus certainly would not establish his entire freedom from sin. Many a criminal even, to say nothing of a common sinner, cannot be convicted by us simply because we lack the necessary evidence — the crime or sin is hidden from us. So this defiance of Jesus, challenging the Jews to prove sin against him, we are told, is sufficient to establish only a relative sinlessness for him not his absolute sinlessness. But this view leaves out the main fact, namely that it is *Jesus* who utters this challenge. Morally he would convict himself of inner falseness if he knew of any sin in himself and yet, counting on the ignorance of these Jews regarding himself, defied them to point out sin in himself. The fact that *Jesus* makes this challenge shuts out another mistake that is sometimes made when it is granted that in him was "no consciousness of sin." Not to be conscious of sin is not by any means to be sinless. Paul "knows nothing against himself" and yet adds in all honesty, "I am not hereby justified," I Cor. 4:4. With the same honesty David prays, "Cleanse thou me from secret faults." The case of *Jesus* is different, for not only does *his* consciousness reveal to him all that is in his moral being, leaving no secret recess hidden from his inner eye, as the very Son of God all possibility even of sin in any sense of the word was shut out for him, and this he knew with infallible knowledge.

The constant use which the church has made of this word of Jesus as an assertion of absolute sinlessness from his own lips is sound in every respect.

Since there is no sin in Jesus, everything that he says is and must be pure truth and verity. The assertion in v. 45, that the Jews do not believe Jesus just because he speaks the truth, is now turned into a question to strike once more and still harder at the callous conscience of the Jews, in order to crush them in repentance or to convict their obduracy by reducing it to impotent silence. **If I say truth, why do you not believe me?** The condition of reality implies that Jesus does say truth, never says anything but truth. Jesus has already given us one answer. Just because he presents truth, these Jews do not believe him. Their kinship with the devil is thus made evident. These Jews never dared to assert or to prove that what Jesus says is untrue. They do not spurn what Jesus says because they think it is not really true, or because they do not see that it is true. In their case the reverse is the fact: they see and know that what Jesus says is truth and for that very reason spurn it. The fault is not in Jesus, that he did not make the truth plain enough, that if he had done better in this regard, they would believe. The reverse is the fact. Aside from the fact that Jesus did his work of presenting the truth most perfectly, the more these Jews were made to realize that they were face to face with genuine truth, the more that truth stung them to rid themselves of it at all hazard. That is why the question of Jesus receives no answer. Any true answer would resemble v. 45. An unreasonable act cannot have a reasonable explanation. When truth is rejected because it is truth, all that can be said is that the act is the height of unreason, is vicious, and stands self-condemned. Refusing to give this true answer, these Jews are left dumb. On this silence compare Matt. 22:12, also 21:27; and Luke 19:20-22 for an attempted answer. Silence proves conviction.

47) The Jews dare not answer, hence Jesus answers for them. **He that is of God hears the utterances of God. For this reason you do not hear because you are not of God.** The verb ἀκούειν is used with reference to true inward hearing, one which perceives and believes. Even the ῥήματα of God, the expressions used for conveying the truth of God, will thus be received as holy vessels filled with holy contents by him who is of God, a true child of his. Jesus employs a regular negative syllogism (compare another in v. 30). Major premise: "He who is of God hears God's words." Minor premise: "You do not hear God's words." *Ergo:* "You are not of God." The conclusion is deadly in its grip. Here, then, is the real reason why these Jews refuse to believe the truth which Jesus declares. They are not of God and want nothing that comes from (ἐκ, out of) God. Even the bitter truth Jesus now tells them about themselves, doubly because of its bitterness, they refuse. The more complete is their conviction.

This conviction Jesus executes by the calmest, clearest, most deliberate and irrefutable line of reasoning — but one that presents nothing but the undeniable realities themselves.

48) The boiling rage of the Jews breaks out in vicious insults and vituperation — an open confession of defeat in their war against the truth and at the

same time an involuntary and unconscious substantiation on their part of all that Jesus has said about
them and their moral parentage. **The Jews answered and said to him** (1:48 for the use of the
two verbs), **Say we not well, that thou art a
Samaritan and hast a demon?** By the tense of
λέγομεν these men convey the thought that they have
right along been calling Jesus such names when speaking of him. They mean to say that by denying that
they are true children of Abraham and of God by
calling them the devil's offspring, Jesus, though he is a
Jew, speaks like a Samaritan, one of the hated race
who would reciprocate with equal hate; and, though
he is sane enough, he speaks like a demoniac, like one
possessed of an evil spirit that uses Jesus' tongue to
vilify these Jews, God's dear people. These vicious
insults intend to wound most deeply.

49) With the calmness of complete mastery Jesus
makes reply. **Jesus answered, I, I have not a
demon; on the contrary, I am honoring my Father,
and you, you are dishonoring me.** He simply puts
in glaring contrast what *he* is doing and what *they* are
doing; the pronouns are the pivots: ἐγώ . . . ὑμεῖς.
This contrast speaks for itself. Jesus touches only
the second epithet hurled at him, that of being
possessed by a devil, because that is enough for the
contrast he is bringing out between what he is doing
and what they are doing. Moreover, while these Jews
utterly despise the Samaritans, Jesus does not; but
to be a demoniac would destroy the force of every
word he has uttered. Even then Jesus denies the
latter only in passing. For the emphatic ἐγώ is to
be construed with τιμῶ, to match the emphatic ὑμεῖς with
ἀτιμάζετε: "*I* am honoring, *you* are dishonoring." The
implication is not, "*I* have no demon," meaning, "but
you have." "Who, when he was reviled, reviled
not again," I Pet. 2:23. The vicious outburst of the

Jews by which they dishonor him makes Jesus tell
these slanderers what he on his part is doing, namely
honoring his Father. Indeed, he honors his Father
most highly when he proves that these vicious Jews are
certainly not the Father's children and when he tells
them just what they are. A tongue governed by a
demon would never speak so.

By saying that they dishonor him Jesus means
himself as he is engaged in honoring his Father. The
dishonor heaped on Jesus thus falls also on his
Father, 5:23. Here again the Jews show how certainly they are not this Father's children but the offspring of an entirely different being. The exclamation in 7:20 should not be paralleled with the slander
that Jesus has a demon, for the former is mere
incredulous surprise, while the latter is deliberate
insult.

50) Jesus suffers the insult, he does not retaliate.
**But I seek not my glory. There is one who seeks
and judges.** Under this insult offered him Jesus
commits himself to him that judges righteously,
I Pet. 2:23. Again ἐγώ is emphatic. The matter of
maintaining and vindicating the honor of Jesus is in
other, proper hands. He uses δόξα, "glory," the highest
form of honor, not merely τιμή (see τιμῶ and ἀτιμάζετε
in v. 49). The person and the honor or glory of Jesus
are not cheap, for men to abuse at will; even though
Jesus makes no defense. A mighty Vindicator stands
behind Jesus, whom he describes only most briefly.
His name these Jews may tell themselves. He is the
one "who seeks" the glory of Jesus, i. e., who sees to
it that glory will be his. Most deeply is he concerned
as the Father about his Son, as the Sender about the
representative he has sent. He both seeks and he
"judges." He justifies Jesus, who upholds his
Father's honor; he condemns those who drag down
his honor by reviling his Son and messenger.

51)   Amen, amen, I say to you (see 1:51), **If anyone shall guard my word, death he shall not at all see forever.** This glorious gospel word, uttered with the assurance of verity and with the force of authority hard upon the stern words which convict these unbelieving Jews of sin, puzzles many of the commentators. Some assume that a pause occurred, after which Jesus begins anew; but John indicates no pause. Some think that Jesus turns from the unbelieving to the believing Jews and intends this word only for the latter. Those who think that the believers of v. 31 lose their faith in v. 33 and are called the devil's children in v. 44, also suppose that Jesus now desires to revive their faith. Still others think that Jesus here declares that his word, on account of which the Jews revile him, will be gloriously vindicated by the great Judge. Yet Jesus does not mention the Judge or any act of vindication by him in his great statement. What he does is to place the gospel beside the law, exactly as he does in v. 34-36. First he convicts of sin, then he opens the door of salvation from sin. In the wall of fire with which the law surrounds the sinner the gospel opens a wide gate of escape through faith in the Savior and his word. Never dare the law and the gospel be separated if their divinely intended result is to be achieved. In preaching either may come first; here law then gospel, but in 4:7-15 gospel then in 4:16-19 law. The two may also alternate as in v. 34-36 followed by 37-51 and further by v. 54-58 — three times law and gospel.

"If anyone" is universal and opens the door to all the sinners in the world. At the same time it is personal: each sinner must enter for himself. In the condition of expectancy (ἐάν with the subjunctive) Jesus sees that many will, indeed, guard his word and thus never see death. As in v. 32, it is *"my* word," or "*my own* word," (the possessive adjective added with the article) as against the word of anyone else. "*My* word" has this effect, mine alone. In substance "to guard" Jesus' word is the same as "to remain in" his word (v. 32). Both verbs are aorists denoting actual guarding and actual remaining in the word. Jesus loves the verb τηρεῖν, especially in connection with his word, his sayings, and his commandments (behests, ἐντολαί), 14:15-24; 15:10 and 20; 17:6. The picture in the verb is that of keeping an eye on the word, so that it is not tampered with but is kept inviolate. The English "to keep" has too much the suggestion of only retaining. Usually only two ideas are found in τηρεῖν, that of faith in the word, and that of obedience to the biddings of the word ("observe," Matt. 28:20). We should add a third, that of letting no one tamper with the word, guarding it against perversion.

He who thus guards Jesus' word, "death he shall not at all see forever." This again matches v. 32, "you shall truly be my disciples, know the truth, and the truth shall make you free." Save that v. 32 speaks of the proximate result (free from the bondage of sin), v. 51 of the ultimate result (eternal freedom from death). "Death" is made emphatic by position; οὐ μή, "not at all," is the strongest negation with a subjunctive (as here) or with a future, intensified in this case by "forever" and by the strong promise in the verb "shall see." So far and so completely shall he who guards Jesus' word be removed from death that he shall never even *see* it. Not to see death is the opposite of not to see the kingdom (3:3), the opposition being death and the kingdom. But "cannot see (ἰδεῖν) the kingdom" (explained by "cannot enter into the kingdom," 3:5) conveys the idea that the person in question shall not catch even a glimpse of that kingdom; while not to see (θεωρεῖν, to view) death conveys the thought that the person in question shall not view death as crushing and destroying him. He shall not view death by experiencing it, by partaking of it (Abbott-Smith, *Manual Greek Lexicon*). The negative thought here expressed is coupled with its positive counterpart in 5:24; see also 6:50. He who has the life (ζωή) which Jesus and his word bestow is free from death forever. Only by implication we gather that he who rejects Jesus' word shall, indeed, see death and see it forever. This negative fact Jesus here leaves un-said. On εἰς τὸν αἰῶνα see v. 35.

52) Once more the Jews justify what Jesus says about them in v. 45, that just because he tells them the truth they do not believe him. Their one determination is to repudiate whatever he may say. **The Jews, therefore, said to him, Now we know that thou hast a demon. Abraham died, and the prophets; and thou sayest, If anyone shall guard my word he shall not at all taste of death forever.** In ἐγνώκαμεν we probably have an intensive perfect, R. 893, "know beyond a doubt," now after this last statement of Jesus'. No man in possession of his own sound mind would say a thing like this; a lying demon must rule his mind and his tongue.

The fact that Abraham died, as well as the prophets, the holiest people named in the Old Testament, brands as a lie this assertion of Jesus, that one who guards his word shall not experience death forever. The verbal change from "shall not see death" to "shall not taste of death" is unimportant, as both alike denote the experience of death, C.-K. 231. The latter is analogous to the rabbinical Hebrew and Aramaic and seems to refer to the bitterness of physical death, perhaps also to the more extended figure of drinking the cup of death. "Abraham died" is the commentary of the Jews themselves on their

expression, "shall not at all taste of death." With
superficial blindness they substitute physical death for
eternal death and thus pervert the word of Jesus.
This is the more inexcusable since he had often told
them of eternal life, the opposite of the death of
which he now speaks. The perversion may even be
deliberate on the part of the Jews, an evidence of their
wicked intention *not* to understand whatever he may
say if it does not serve their purpose.

The attempt is made to deny this perversion,
whether blind or deliberate, and to have the Jews
and Jesus understand death in the same sense. The
souls of Abraham and of the Old Testament saints,
we are told, passed into the "realm of the dead"; in
this way they "saw death," "died," "tasted of death."
In this realm these souls remained until Jesus released
them. To the New Testament saints Jesus promises
a better fate: their souls shall not enter that dread
realm. That is what Jesus means to say, what the
Jews understand him to say and what they themselves have in mind. Their mistake, we are told, was
only this that they considered Jesus a mere man and
thus unable to give his believers what he promises.
But this "realm of the dead," identified with the *sheol*
of the Old Testament, is a fiction. The entire Bible
knows of only two places in the hereafter, heaven
and hell. Elijah was carried bodily into heaven;
compare Gen. 5:24 on Enoch. Moses and Elijah
appeared to Jesus and three of the disciples on
the Mount of Transfiguration (Matt. 17:3). Did
Moses come from "the realm of the dead"? And
whence did Elijah come? Read Acts 2:25, etc., "that
I should not be moved . . . my flesh also shall
dwell in hope." And why? "Because thou wilt not
leave my soul in hades," correctly rendered, "thou
wilt not abandon my soul unto the house of hades,"
οὐκ ἐγκαταλείψεις τὴν ψυχήν μου εἰς Ἅδου (supply οἶκον).

David knows that at death his soul will not be abandoned to hades (*sheol*). Ps. 16:10. The supposition of two compartments in this hades realm of the dead, one for the damned, and one for the saints, found even in C.-K. 80 and based on a misinterpretation of Luke 16:22, etc., only embellishes this alleged realm and is as fictitious as the realm itself.

53) In the original deduction that, since Abraham and the prophets are dead, a devil must wag a man's tongue if he talks of preventing death by his word, lies a second deduction, namely that the man who talks thus must imagine himself greater than even Abraham or the prophets. This is like the deduction made by the Samaritan woman in 4:12. Yet hers led to faith while this leads the Jews to violence. **Certainly thou are not greater than our father Abraham, seeing that he died? and the prophets died. Whom art thou making thyself?** The interrogative word μή shows how certain the Jews feel of a negative answer; and ὅστις has causal force, R. 728. The break in the construction: "and the prophets died," ending the interrogative sentence with a declarative clause, is both natural and effective, R. 441. The only thing wrong about this second deduction is the assumption of the Jews that it cannot be drawn in fact but only in the imagination of Jesus. That Jesus is greater, infinitely greater, than Abraham or any mere man these Jews *will* not believe, no matter what the evidence. All the previous proof Jesus has given them in regard to his deity is non-existent for them. In the pointed question, "whom art thou making thyself?" lurks the threat that the questioners attempt to carry out in v. 59. A question such as, "Who art thou?" asked with a real desire to find out the truth, might lead to faith; but not the question they ask.

54) Jesus starts with the base insinuation that he is ascribing a fictitious glory to himself, but he proceeds not only to say who he is but also to prove that what he thus says is fact. **Jesus answered, If I shall glorify myself, my glory is nothing,** without reality, empty, talk — "I," apart from God, like a man vaunting himself. The aorist subjunctive refers to some certain act of self-glorification which Jesus may perform. What Jesus here says of himself would apply equally to any boaster. **It is my Father that glorifies me,** and the present participle ὁ δοξάζων με includes all that the Father does in glorifying Jesus, past, present, and future. Here Jesus declares who he is, the Son of his heavenly Father. This Son the Jews may dishonor, God not only honors but glorifies him.

The relative clause is masterly in the highest degree. It is directed against the Jews and their false claims of honor and at the same time defines just who the Father of Jesus is and who Jesus himself thus is: **of whom you assert that he is your God, and** (coordinating the very opposite) **you do not know him** (proving that your assertion is false). Here again (as in v. 52) the perfect ἐγνώκατε seems to be intensive (R. 893), "truly know," with the sense of the present intensified. These Jews had the fullest means of really knowing God, γινώσκω, through actual experience and the realization it brings, through the Old Testament revelation. The evidence, proving that these Jews are strangers to God, is furnished in v. 47; so here only the fact is repeated. These Jews claim the great honor of being the children of this the true God. They are the ones who are making the empty boast. This very God is the Father of Jesus, Jesus is his Son.

Hence Jesus adds: **but I do know him, and if I shall say that I do not know him, I shall be like you, a liar; on the contrary, I know him and I am guarding his word.** Three times Jesus here uses οἶδα in declaring that he "knows" God, in marked difference from γινώσκω, which he uses regarding the Jews; a difference lost for us in translation. The former fits intuitive knowledge, the latter knowledge gained by experience; thus the former reflects the very presence of the Son with the Father in heaven, and the latter the experience with God through his Word. When Jesus says, "I know the Father (οἶδα)," he means that he has been with him; when he tells the Jews, "You do not know him (οὐκ ἐγνώκατε) although you call him your God," he means that they do not realize who God really is although he has revealed himself to them through his Word. This negation does not imply that the Jews followed idols instead of the true God but that their conceptions of the true God are in conflict with the revelation God made of himself in his Word. They have only a caricature of God. C.-K. 388 adds another point: οἶδα indicates a relation of the object to the subject, γινώσκω a relation of the subject to the object. Thus in Matt. 25:12: οὐκ οἶδα ὑμᾶς, *you* have no relation to me of which I know; but in Matt. 7:23: οὐδέποτε ἔγνων ὑμᾶς, *I* have had no relation to you of which I know. Likewise here, "You do not know him (γινώσκω)" because *you* are not his children but only call yourselves so; while, "I know him (οἶδα)" because *I* bear a relation to him, *I* am his Son, and he is my Father. The knowledge here expressed by οἶδα includes also that expressed by γινώσκω, hence the latter type of knowledge is also claimed by Jesus for himself in 17:25.

In order to drive home this contrast between the Jews and himself and, if possible, to pierce their conscience, Jesus adds, "and if I shall say, (εἴπω, aorist subjunctive: in some statement) that I do not know him, I shall be like you, a liar." The condition with ἐάν in the protasis, followed by the future indicative in the apodosis, conceives the thought in a vivid and realistic manner. Jesus minces no words when he says, "like you, a liar," thus calling these Jews liars to their faces. The vivid supposition would, indeed, make Jesus "like" these Jews. only in an opposite way: they claim to know God and yet do not; Jesus would claim not to know him and yet he does know him.

The repetition, "on the contrary (I am not a liar like you), I know him," is due to the evidential proof that is added by the coordinate clause, "and I am guarding his word." The contrasting comparison with the Jews is carried even to this vital point. The Jews do not even "hear" God's word (v. 47), to say nothing of "guarding" it (v. 51). That proves who they are. Jesus meets this axiomatic test: he is guarding his Father's word. Here τηρῶ evidently means not only to hold to that word and to obey it but also to keep guard over it, to defend it against attack, and thus to keep it inviolate. Jesus here refers to his office as the great Witness and Prophet, but to defend and keep God's Word inviolate is the natural duty of every true child of God.

56) The charge of self-glorification is answered first, by the facts of Jesus' relation to the Father, and now, secondly, by the relation of Jesus to Abraham. **Abraham, your father, exulted to see my day; and he saw it and was glad.** It is correct to say that "your father" here refers to the father of whom these Jews boast. Also that in regard to Jesus this father acted very differently from these Jews who claim .to be his children. We must add that when Jesus said, "this (seeking to kill me) did not Abra-

ham," Jesus had in mind what he now says about
Abraham. But apart from these points, Jesus cannot say "our Father," for even physically Abraham is
not the father of Jesus in the same sense as he is the
father of the Jews. Invariably Jesus marks this difference in his human descent.

Two things are said of Abraham: he rejoiced that
he was to see (ἵνα, subfinal, purport, not purpose,
R. 993) ; then that he did see and was glad. The first
is hope, the second realization. The object of both
is identical: τὴν ἡμέραν τὴν ἐμήν, "my own day." The
statement is evidently a *mashal* with a hidden meaning, like a riddle, which needs a key to solve it (like
2:19) ; for Abraham lived about 2,000 years before
Jesus came to earth. The two words Abraham
"exulted" and "was glad" intend to fix our attention
on the central occurrence in the patriarch's life,
Gen. 17:17; 18:12-15; 21:6-8, all marked by
"laughter," even as Isaac's name itself means
"laughter." The other two prominent verbs "to see"
and "saw" may intend to recall Gen. 22:14: "Je-
hovah-jireh," meaning, "In the mount of the Lord
it shall be seen." Moreover, it should be clear that
"to see the day" means "to live to see it" and
thus to behold the great event that distinguishes the
day referred to.

These observations put to rest the bizarre, un-
biblical notion that Abraham hopefully exulted during
his earthly life and then, when Jesus was born, in
some way saw this event in the fabled "realm of the
dead" (hades, *sheol*) and there was glad. Likewise
we must decline the view that Abraham "saw and was
glad" in paradise, "in the bosom of God," in heaven,
namely when the birth of Jesus finally occurred in
Bethlehem. Not only are all the aorists alike: "he
exulted to see," and "he saw and was glad," historical
aorists in the earthly life of Abraham, but also

"my own day" cannot mean "my own birthday," "seen" first in prophetic vision 2,000 years before its occurrence and then "seen" in some other supernatural way in hades, or in heaven, when it actually arrived here on earth. Abraham "rejoiced to see and saw" means: Abraham during this life.

Some seek the solution of Jesus' *mashal* in the typical nature of Isaac's birth. Accordingly, Abraham first rejoiced that he was to see, and then also he actually did see with joy in the birth of his son Isaac the future birth of God's Son Jesus. This sounds plausible yet proves unacceptable. Jesus does not in any way mention Isaac or hint at such a thing as type and antitype. He speaks only of Abraham and of two actions of Abraham, each of which is made decidedly emphatic by doubling the verb, and the exulting and being glad fixes the exact time in Abraham's life here meant. For the mysterious *mashal* in 2:19 Jesus gave the Jews no key; John gives it to his readers in 2:21, 22. Here Jesus furnishes the key, "Before Abraham came to be, I am." This key contains nothing of type and antitype. Such a thought would be wide of the point at issue, namely the greatness of Jesus' person as compared with Abraham.

With the key of Jesus in hand we can unlock the mystery. What caused Abraham to exult was the promise of the birth of Isaac as the son through whom the nations should be blessed. Abraham saw that son born and was glad. Then and there, in that event, Abraham saw with his own eyes what Jesus calls "my own day." Then and there the day of Jesus began. In that wonderful gift of Isaac the very person now speaking to the Jews began by an action of his a deed both astouding and infinitely blessed, his own saving manifestation. Promises had preceded, only promises. Here the first great fulfillment was wrought, a fulfillment that one could "see." It was as Jesus says, "my own day." Abraham, though a hundred years old, had lived "to see" it. He saw it and was glad. Was Jesus greater than Abraham? Is the incredulous question of the Jews comparing Jesus with Abraham answered?

57) The Jews ignore all that Jesus has told them about his divine sonship, about his having come from the Father, about having known the Father directly, etc., and regard his words as those of a mere man. **Thou hast not yet (lived) fifty years and hast thou seen Abraham?** The reading, "and has Abraham seen thee?" is discredited. We need not trouble about how old Jesus seemed to the Jews, or bother about the deductions based on the "fifty years," which are merely in contrast to the 2,000 years since Abraham lived. The question of the Jews rests on a correct conclusion, namely that if Abraham actually saw the day of Jesus, Jesus must have seen Abraham. Does Jesus actually mean to say that he is so old?

58) Not only does Jesus affirm what the question of the Jews asks, with the solemn formula of verity and authority he affirms vastly more. **Amen, amen, I say to you, before Abraham came to be, I am.** The aorist γενέσθαι (πρίν with the infinitive after a positive verb, R. 977, 1091) marks the historical point of time when Abraham came into existence as against the time prior to that point when Abraham did not exist. This aorist is in contrast to εἰμί; which Jesus predicates of his own person (ἐγώ), here a finite verb not the mere copula (R. 394). As the aorist sets a point of beginning for the existence of Abraham, so the present tense "I am" predicates absolute existence for the person of Jesus, with no point of beginning at all. That is why Jesus does not use the imperfect ἤμην, "I was"; for this would say only that the existence of the person of Jesus antedates the time of Abraham

and would leave open the question whether the person of Jesus also has a beginning like that of Abraham (only earlier) or not. What Jesus declares is that, although his earthly life covers less than fifty years, his existence as a person (ἐγώ) is constant and independent of any beginning in time as was that of Abraham. For what Jesus here says about himself in comparison with Abraham is in the nature of the case true of him in comparison with any other man, no matter how far back the beginning of that man's existence lies. "I am" = I exist. Thus with the simplest words Jesus testifies to the divine, eternal pre-existence of his person.

To speak of an "ideal" existence before the days of Abraham is to turn the solemn assurance of Jesus into a statement that means nothing. Unacceptable are also all other efforts to empty out this divine "I am" and to substitute for the fact and reality of existence before Abraham something merely mental, whether this occurred in the mind of Jesus or in that of God. Yet this "I am" is nothing new; by means of two tiny words it states only what Jesus has testified and continues to testify of himself in many other words in other connections. Thus, too, it forms the parting of the ways for faith and unbelief.

Yes, Jesus has seen Abraham — the deduction of the Jews is right in every respect, only it should go much farther.

59) As Jesus had made his meaning clear to the Jews in the first place, so also he did in this final word. They understand its full import, namely that, if the existence of the person of Jesus antedates that of Abraham in absolute continuation, he declares himself to be God. To them this is rank blasphemy. **They took up stones, therefore, in order to throw at him; but Jesus was hidden and went out of the Temple.**

672   *The Interpretation of John*

The Jews, with what they deemed blasphemy ringing in their ears, proceed to carry out Lev. 24:13-16 upon Jesus, and this without formal legal proceedings but by an immediate act of popular justice. This haste and irregularity is the expression of the murderous hate in the hearts of these Jews, rushing now that they feel they have caught Jesus *in flagrante delicto* to make short work of it and to be rid of him once for all. The stoning mentioned by Josephus, *Ant.* 17, 9, 3, is of quite a different type.

Parts of the Temple were in the process of rebuilding during these and many following years, so that pieces of stone could be obtained for the deadly work. Yet a brief delay ensued as some of the Jews ran to the spot where the builders were at work and "took up" the stones. During this interval, we may take it, Jesus "was hidden." The form ἐκρύβη, a second aorist passive, might be read in a middle sense, "hid himself," since the Koine increased the number of these passive forms and used them in preference to the middle (R. 349). But here the passive sense is entirely in place (R. 807): Jesus "was hidden" from the Jews so that they could not reach him. We may suppose that he moved aside, and that his friends massed around him, and thus "he went out of the Temple." The addition found in later texts: "going through the midst of them, and so passed by" (A. V.), must be cancelled as a combination that was added from Luke 4:30 and John 9:1. This addition is also untrue in fact. For nothing miraculous took place in the escape of Jesus. "He was hidden" and "he went out" are two facts placed side by side, nor can we follow B.-D. 471, 3 in the suggestion that the second verb is used in place of a participle: "by going out he was hidden."

Inwardly and outwardly the tension between Jesus and the Jewish leaders increases and approaches the breaking point. The realism of John's narration is perfect — we see and hear just what was said and done. Always and at every point the antagonism of the leaders together with their followers is revealed as unjustified, unreasonable, due wholly to their own ungodliness. With ever greater clearness Jesus reveals to them both their own character and state and himself as the Son and Savior. He never temporizes, compromises, hesitates, or hides. He is absolutely fearless, and his victory is complete at every step. The Jews are driven from argument to vituperation and finally to desperate violence — their defeat is complete.

CHAPTER IX

VI. *Jesus Attests Himself by Healing a Blind Beggar, 9:1-12*

1) All that John reports from 7:14 onward transpired in the Temple, and these Temple scenes are now ended. "Jesus went up into the Temple and was teaching," 7:14, begins what 8:59 closes, "he went out of the Temple." For the remainder of his present stay in Jerusalem we hear no more about his appearing in the Temple. Not until his next visit to the city is the Temple again mentioned (10:21). Yet Jesus remains in Jerusalem. Soon after the altercations in the Temple he attests himself by a remarkable miracle. By this *deed* he shows himself as the Light of the world, who bestows the light of life, just as he had showed it before by his *Word* (8:12). Those who reject him remain in darkness. In this instance the Jews do not pounce upon the Sabbath desecration (5:16-18) but endeavor, though vainly, to discredit the miracle itself. This effort marks their progress in hostility and hardening. We see how the breach continues to widen as Jesus proceeds with his self-attestation.

And in passing by he saw a man blind from birth on. "And" (καί) merely "hooks" the new account to the one that precedes (R. 1180) and does not mean that Jesus saw the blind man on leaving the Temple. Moreover, this is the Sabbath (9:14), hardly the same day on which the Jews sought to stone him. Somewhere in the city, while walking along, Jesus came across the beggar blind "from birth on," a classical phrase found only here in the New Testament in place of the more Hebraistic "from his mother's womb on," Acts 3:2. "From birth on" is

(674)

at once mentioned, because the question of the disciples turns on this point, and then also because the healing of such a case is astonishing in the highest degree. When Jesus saw the man he stopped, and very likely the beggar himself told that he had never seen during his life.

2) **And his disciples asked him saying, Rabbi, who did sin, this man or his parents, so that he was born blind?** Here for the first time in connection with this visit to Jerusalem John mentions the disciples (2:2). In the two chapters preceding this one their presence required no mention for what John records; but they must have been with Jesus all along, as they were closely attached to their Master, and a rabbi without disciples would have been unusual and not impressive in public teaching. The disciples are perplexed about this beggar's blindness. From the Old Testament the rabbis deduced that the sins of parents are punished in their children, yet the prophets said that each must bear his own sin. The disciples assume that a specific sin has been committed: "Who did sin?" ἥμαρτε, an aorist, to indicate a definite act of sin. They are at a loss in regard to the person who committed the sin. If the sufferer himself committed the sin, then, seeing that he has been blind from birth on, his punishment would antedate his sin. On the other hand, if the parents sinned and as a result had a child born blind, the worst part of the penalty for their sin would lie upon the poor child.

On "Rabbi" see 1:38. It seems needless for B.-D. 391, 5 to struggle against the idea that ἵνα expresses actual result. He even advocates a different reading in order to escape this finding. Here, beyond doubt, we have not merely contemplated but actual result: "so that he was born blind." See the confessions of J. H. Moulton and A. T. Robertson in R. 998. etc.

Even the A. V., "that he was," etc., while it is not decisive enough, is more correct than the R. V., "that he should be," etc. In noting the inroads that ἵνα has made on the infinitive we must accept the idea that it usurps the following uses and in this order: final, subfinal, consecutive (first contemplated, then also completed result).

3) **Jesus answered, Neither did this man sin nor his parents but in order that the works of God should be made manifest in him.** This, Jesus says, is not a case in which a specific sin either on the part of one or another person has produced a specific penalty. He corrects the general idea of the disciples to this extent that they must not consider every serious affliction the penalty for some equally marked and serious sin. At times this is the case (compare 5:14) but not always (compare Luke 13:1, etc.). Sin works out its painful and distressing results in many ways that are beyond our ability to trace. Jesus does not attempt enlightenment on this wide and intricate subject, either here or elsewhere. Instead, he opens up an entirely new view in connection with the particular case before him. The disciples are not in every case of suffering to look back to find a possible cause of sin but to look forward to the divine purpose which God may have in providentially permitting such suffering to come upon a person. To be sure, all suffering in this sinful world is the outcome of sin in some way or other, but this is only half of the story. The other half is that God governs even in this wide field, and in some instances we are able to trace his purpose, especially those of grace and mercy, in allowing certain afflictions to befall a man. Here, in the man born blind, we have a case of this kind.

The adversative ἀλλά is elliptical: "on the contrary, this man was born blind," etc. This time ἵνα is plainly final: "in order that," etc. For the aorist subjunctive φανερωθῇ indicates a future event: "the works of God should be made manifest"; and not like the aorist subjunctive in v. 2, γεννηθῇ, a past event: "was born." "The works of God" which Jesus has in mind are the ones now about to be wrought, not merely works of omnipotence over against human impotence, but blessed works of mercy and grace for the blind man's body and his soul. Moreover, these are to affect not only the blind man himself but are to shine out for many others to see. The verb "should be made manifest" implies that the works of God are so often hidden from general view; so this man's blindness is to serve God in making these works of his public before men.

4) **We must work the works of him who did send me while it is day: the night is coming when no one can work.** The reading ἡμᾶς δεῖ κτλ· is assured: "We" must work, etc., instead of ἐμέ: "I" must work, etc. Jesus thus includes his disciples: they, too, will have works of God to do. These "works of God" are wrought through agents, namely through Jesus and his disciples; yet they remain "God's" works. When they are now called "the works of him who did send me," we see that these are the works which comprise the mission of Jesus, for which he had appeared on earth. The share assigned to the apostles will appear after the resurrection of Jesus, on Pentecost. Here the reading is μέ and not ἡμᾶς: who did send "me." Invariably the distinctiveness of the sending of Jesus is adhered to: we have only one Redeemer. Always also the Father sent Jesus, and Jesus sends the apostles; a resemblance exists between the acts (καθώς, "as," John 20:21) but nothing more. Their sending is only an outgrowth of that received by Jesus, wholly subsidiary to his and nothing more. The idiom δεῖ is used to denote all forms of necessity, here according

to the context one that is involved in the Father's sending of Jesus. "To be working (present infinitive) the works," one by one as required, is to carry out the commission of the greater Sender of Jesus. And these works are "made manifest" (v. 3), displayed for men to see, when they are "worked," actually performed.

The emphasis is on the temporal clause, "while (ἕως, R. 976) it is day," for which reason also the thought of this clause is elaborated by pointing to the coming of the night when no one can work. The figure of the day which is terminated by the night must not be pressed beyond the point of comparison intended by Jesus, namely the time allotted to Jesus by the Father for accomplishing his mission. We may refer "the night is coming" to the death of Jesus, in harmony with his cry on the cross, "It is finished!" and with the word in his high-priestly prayer, "I glorified thee on the earth, having brought to a finish the work which thou hast given me to do," 17:4, etc. The figure is made general by the addition, "when no one can work," and thus includes also the apostles and the time allotted to them for their work. We must not bring in the work which Jesus does in his glorified state since his death, for this is of an altogether different type, a work which rests on the perfectly completed task performed here on earth. Moreover, Jesus combines his working with that of the apostles, and their work will cease at death with no continuation in an exalted form in heaven.

5)   Returning from the reference to all the works he must be busy doing in his mission to the one work which is now in order upon this blind beggar, Jesus adds: **As long as I may be in the world I am a light of the world.** The use of ὅταν, which generally means "whenever" when it is construed with the subjunctive, is unusual. To say that it has the idea of

duration (R. 972) is hardly to the point. The ἐάν in
the compound ὅταν rather points to the indefinite length
of Jesus' stay in the world. He expects to stay for
a time yet, but he withholds mention of how long this
will be. In 8:12 he calls himself "the Light of the
world" (subject and predicate being convertible,
hence the article with this predicate), i. e., "the light
absolutely and forever." Here he speaks only of the
brief time that yet remains of his visible stay in the
world of men. Hence the predicate is without the
article: "a light." It merely states that while he
remains as he now is he will shed light. As a light
in a dark place he cannot but send forth the radiance
of truth and grace. When he enters the glory of
heaven and there shines as "the light of the world,"
that activity will rest on what he now does and will
complete during his earthly mission.

6) At once suiting the act to the word, John reports: **Having said these things** in explanation of
what he intended to do, for the beggar as well as
for his disciples to hear, **he spat on the ground and
made mud of the spittle and put the mud of it on
the eyes and said to him, Go wash in the pool of
Siloam (which [name] is interpreted, Sent).** The
αὐτοῦ is to be construed with τὸν πηλόν and not with τοὺς
ὀφθαλμούς. For the sake of the blind man Jesus here
uses sign language. The only answer we know for
the question as to why Jesus proceeded in this fashion
(as also in Mark 7:33; 8:23) is that he knew best
how to obtain his object. By placing the mud from
his own spittle on the beggar's eyelids he lets him
know that the healing power comes from Jesus. The
beggar is not merely to wash off this mud, for which
any place that had water would suffice, but to wash
it off in the pool of Siloam, which word or name ὅ
(neuter) signifies ἀπεσταλμένος, "the One Sent." For
the beggar to act on this strange command with noth-

ing but an implied. promise, requires some degree of faith, which certainly also is intended to be aroused by Jesus as in the analogous case of the ten lepers, Luke 17:14. We may call these effects on the beggar psychological, if we will. Since the beggar is to cooperate in the procedure of his healing by going and washing in that pool, it is ill-advised to deny these effects on the score that they are psychological.

One is surprised at the strange ideas that have been connected with this proceeding of Jesus. One is that spittle was considered medicinal; but Jesus uses mud. Another is that Jesus wished to create a delay in order to let the crowd scatter; but no crowd is at hand. Still another is that Jesus meant to give the eyes time to develop sight, since this was a case where the man was born blind; but what about the man born with deformed limbs in Acts 3:2, etc.? Finally, we are told that plastering the man's eyes with mud was symbolical, adding an artificial to his natural blindness by making him close his mud-plastered eyelids over his sightless eyeballs. This is to symbolize that men, who are by nature spiritually blind, are to be brought to a realization of their sad spiritual condition. Preachers thus often allegorize the miracles of Jesus, because they have no other way of getting anything out of them for their hearers. To turn simple facts, infinitely weighthy as facts, into pictures and allegory is illegitimate in preaching and even worse in exegesis.

The indeclinable Hebrew name *Shiloach,* "Siloam," with its masculine genitive article τοῦ, is here translated by John for his Greek readers by the nominative masculine perfect participle ὁ ἀπεσταλμένος, "the One Sent," i. e., who, having been sent, has that character and quality. This, of course, is not merely an interesting incidental philological remark that John inserts.

On the contrary, John here asks his readers to substitute "the One Sent" for "Siloam": "the pool of the One Sent," the pool that belongs to him; for "of Siloam" is the genitive of possession. Both the spring and the pool it formed are called Siloam; but in the combination "the pool of Siloam" the genitive must denote the spring. In v. 11 the beggar repeats the significant name, this time applying it to the pool. What distinguishes this spring is the fact that it flows from the Temple hill and forms its pool at the foot of that hill. For this reason Isa. 8:6 uses Siloam and its waters as a symbol of the blessings that flow from the Temple; likewise, the water of Siloam was used in the sacred rites of the Feast of Tabernacles as we have seen in connection with 7:38. We must, therefore, say that just as Jesus used the Temple as his own Father's house, in which he has a Son's rights, so now he appropriates this Temple pool and its waters for his sacred purposes. How the spring and the pool originally came to be called "Siloam" need not be inquired into; they now became, indeed, the spring and the pool of Jesus, the One Sent. They were appropriated by him and used in his mission of making manifest the works of God and thus sending out light in the world (v. 3 and 5).

We cannot assume that Jesus selected this pool for the beggar's washing without himself being conscious of the meaning of its name. Too often he speaks of his Sender and thus designates himself as the One Sent. He never acts without the most comprehensive insight. In this instance even the disciples may well have caught the connection: "Wash in the pool of Siloam — of the One sent." Even the beggar does not afterward say merely, "Go wash!" but, "Go to Siloam and wash!" To apply the name Siloam to the beggar as being "the one sent" is beside the mark; likewise, that the pool is another "one sent," com-

pleting the work of Jesus as also being "One Sent."
To think of some medicinal power in the water of this
pool that was great enough to give sight to a man
born blind is ridiculous.   An elaborate allegory has
been attached to the name "Siloam."   The pool is
Jesus.   "Go to the pool!" means, "Go to Jesus!"   The
open, sightless eyes are closed with mud to impress
the fact that man born blind by nature cannot see.
"Siloam," Jesus, gives man spiritual sight.   Clay was
used because God's creative power used clay when he
made man in Eden.   Into this allegorical structure is
mixed another figure, namely that the beggar's sight
pictures that Jesus is the world's light.   Mud, water,
light — strange mixture!   This entire structure is
shattered at the start when we see that only the name
"Siloam" means "the One Sent" in the phrase, "in the
pool of Siloam"; the pool itself might have had some
other name.

Briefly John reports: **He went away, therefore, and washed and came seeing.**   "Therefore,"
οὖν, certainly excludes the notion that the beggar acted
on the word of Jesus as so many ignorant people do
who are ready to try any questionable means suggested
to them to remove some ailment.   All that really
transpired in his heart, who can tell?   Let us not forget that he heard what Jesus said to his disciples, that
the very presence and every word and action of Jesus
always make a deep impression, that he knew the name
of Jesus (v. 11).   Possibly he had heard of some of
the miracles wrought by Jesus.   The almighty power
of Jesus wrought the miracle the moment the man
washed in accord with the promise implied in the
command.   The beggar merely "washed," i. e., dipped
up some water and washed the mud off his eyes.   Because the use of εἰς with static verbs and verbs of
condition and being in the Koine has become known
only quite recently, the idea has long been entertained,

and some still hold it, that the beggar plunged into
the pool because Jesus says: νίψαι εἰς; or in some
other way the notion of "into" is retained. Jesus
said, "Wash *in* the pool!" and here εἰς means nothing but "in."

8) Naturally the man went home. Jesus, too,
had quietly gone on, and the beggar could not have
found him. Arrived at home, great excitement
ensued. **The neighbors, therefore, and they that
formerly saw him that he was a beggar were saying, Is not this he that was sitting and begging?
Some were saying, This is he; others were saying,
No, but he is like him. He was saying, I am he.**
The neighbors and others are here mentioned, because
of what some of these do, namely take the beggar to
the Pharisees (v. 13) ; we shall hear about the parents
later. R. 866 makes the present participle οἱ θεωροῦντες
gnomic (timeless), which is questionable; B.-D. 330
points to the adverb and to the following imperfect
ἦν as turning the time of the present participle back
into the past, which may suffice. Since the Greek has
no imperfect participle but uses the present instead,
why not apply that fact here as being the most natural
explanation? All the verbs of saying are imperfects
ἔλεγον, etc. When we are merely told that a statement
was made, the aorist is used, εἶπεν, "he said"; but when
we are to think of how the person was speaking (*Schil-
derung*), or when the statement of an indefinite number of persons is introduced, we have the imperfect,
B.-D. 329.

The question with οὐχ shows great surprise. "Why
this is the same man — incredible!" The two present
participles describe the beggar as they know him,
"the one sitting and begging," for which our idiom
demands the past tense. On the article in the predicate see R. 768.

9) Some are sure of the man's identity, others find only a resemblance to him. The beggar himself openly and joyfully declares that he is, indeed, the man.

10) Naturally these people ask, **How then were thine eyes opened?** and the beggar narrates the story quite correctly.

11) The previous imperfects of the verbs of saying are now repeated with the simple aorist: **He answered: The man that is called Jesus made clay and anointed my eyes and said to me, Go to Siloam and wash. Having gone away, therefore, and having washed, I got to see.** We see that Jesus was a stranger to the beggar, who had heard only his benefactor's name. Too much is read into ὁ ἄνθρωπος when this is thought to mean "the well-known man." The variation in quoting the command of Jesus is insignificant and negligible. The Greek would subordinate the subsidiary actions of going and of washing by using two aorist participles and employing a finite verb only for the main action. The English would not make the distinction, saying, "So I went away and washed and got my sight." The aorist ἀνέβλεψα is ingressive, "I recovered my sight" (ἀνά, after having lost it at my birth).

12) To the further question: **Where is he?** he is able to reply only: **I do not know,** this evidently also being the reason why he had gone home.

VII. *Jesus' Attestation Through the Beggar Nonpluses his Opponents, 13-34*

13) John devotes considerable space to the story of this beggar, whose name he withholds. In chapter five only the alleged breach of the Sabbath is charged against Jesus; here this breach is repeated, yet the Pharisees make no issue of that point but endeavor

to discredit the miracle itself. This marks the advance in their wilful blindness. In chapters seven and eight Jesus shines as the Light of the world by the testimony of his word against which the Jews deliberately close their eyes. Now Jesus shines as the Light by an astonishing miraculous deed. By this deed he "makes manifest the works of God" (v. 3). It is only incidental that this deed consists in the opening of the eyes of a blind beggar. Hence we should not carry allegory into the miracle. The final words of Jesus on spiritual sight and blindness in v. 39-41, are suggested by the restoration of physical sight to the beggar, yet constitute no allegory. The words are literal and matter-of-fact and, in fact, go far beyond any allegory that might be drawn from the blindness of the beggar and the miraculous gift of sight to him.

No connective joins this account to the preceding, which indicates a lapse of time. **They bring him to the Pharisees, him once blind.** Possibly several days elapsed. We must note that ἄγουσιν has no subject. It is rather hasty to conclude that the neighbors and others who used to see the blind man begging constitute the subject. Why should they bring the blind man to the Pharisees? To answer, because their opinions were divided, and because they thus sought an authoritative decision, is conjecture; for the only difference in opinion was as to whether this was really the blind beggar or only somebody who looked like him, who had never been blind at all and was posing as the beggar. This question the beggar himself settled from the start, and if any doubt were yet possible, the man's parents had certainly removed that. Moreover, the man's identity is not at all the question brought before the Pharisees. In their investigation no such question is even touched. The effort to read something hostile into the question of v. 12, "Where is he?" is also unwarranted. John records this question and its simple answer only to prepare for the next meeting of Jesus with the beggar, v. 35, etc. We are also to see how this insignificant beggar, who had come into contact with Jesus but once in his life, stood up before the Pharisees and defended his benefactor most manfully. The account would lose an illuminating point if John had not written verse 12.

This subjectless ἄγουσιν is like the German *man brachte ihn* — somebody or other did this. The most probable view is that one or the other of the Pharisees had heard about this beggar and had the case brought to the attention of others of his party. Thus we find a gathering of "the Pharisees." They came together in some convenient place in order to look into this case. Some commentators speak only of a meeting of the Pharisees for some unknown purpose or other. They met in order to investigate this case. This accounts for ἄγουσιν — being too important for any of their standing to go after a mere beggar, they have somebody else bring him before them. During the whole proceeding with the man we hear of no neighbors or others who ask to have any question settled for them by the Pharisees. These Pharisees are the only ones who show concern, and even they do not know just what they want; for presently they themselves are divided. These Pharisees do not act as a regular court, either as belonging to the Sanhedrin, or as one of the two lesser courts in Jerusalem, each constituted of twenty-three members, or as rulers of a local synagogue. They act only as an incidental gathering of men of the influential Jewish party, just Pharisees who are bent on making their superior influence felt.

14) **Now it was a Sabbath on the day when Jesus made the mud and opened his eyes.** John does not write γάρ, "for," as though this were a

charge brought forward by somebody or the reason
why the Pharisees called in the beggar; he writes δέ,
marking this statement as parenthetical, a point he
wants us to note so that we may understand what
follows.   On the phrase ἐν ᾗ ἡμέρᾳ, literally, "on what
day," for "on the day on which," see R. 718 "incor-
poration." To make mud on the Sabbath the Pharisees regarded as a forbidden work; to heal the sick
likewise, except in extreme cases, and this case they
would not consider extreme — it could wait until
Sunday.

15) **Again, therefore, the Pharisees were also
asking him how he got his sight,** just as the people
about the beggar's home did in v. 10.   The imperfect ἠρώτων is like those used in v. 8, etc.   Due,
no doubt, to caution the beggar makes his answer
brief.   **And he said to them, Mud he put upon my
eyes, and I washed, and I see.**   Note the present
tense: "and I see."

16) **Some, therefore, of the Pharisees were saying, This man is not from God because he guards
not the Sabbath.   But others were saying, How can
a man (that is) an open sinner do such signs?   And
there was a division among them.**   The imperfects
permit us to view the scene: Pharisees against Pharisees.   The conclusion of the first group is certainly
correct: one sent and commissioned by God (παρὰ
Θεοῦ, from his side) would certainly guard (τηρεῖ, as in
8:52) and observe the Sabbath law in his conduct;
but God never ordained the Sabbath traditions set
up by the Pharisees and regarded by them as more
sacred than the divine law itself.   The argument of
the second group is equally to the point.   A man who
is a ἁμαρτωλός, "an open sinner" in the sight of God
such as a breaker of the Sabbath would be, could not
possibly do such signs as this one wrought upon the
blind beggar.   In the ancient epitaphs found in Asia

Minor ἁμαρτωλός is used like ἐπάρατος, "cursed," and
ἔνοχος, "guilty," "let him be a sinner before the sub-
terranean gods," to be treated as one accursed by the
gods, Deissmann, *Light from the Ancient East*, 115;
sceleste, 322, 3. The first group of the Pharisees thus
questions the reality of the miracle. By saying that
this man who does not observe the Sabbath is not from
God, they mean that Jesus could not have wrought a
miracle — there must be something phony about the
case. This the second group contradicts, accepting the
reality of the miracle — and let us note — of others
like it in spite of the alleged Sabbath violation, for
which they have no satisfactory explanation. The
conclusion of neither group is decisive; neither one is
able fully to prove its contention. What is suspicious
about the case? How can the Sabbath violation be
denied? So the division remained.

17) Both groups are helpless to break the dead-
lock. They know of nothing else to do but once more
to turn to the beggar. **They say, therefore, to the
blind man again, What dost thou say concerning
him, seeing that he opened thine eyes?** It sounds
significant for John to designate the beggar as "the
blind man" in a connection like this — these Pharisees,
who considered themselves so far removed from blindness, asking the verdict of a blind man! There is no
need to refer λέγουσιν only to one or to the other of
the two groups indicated in v. 16. Both are helplessly
battling with a difficulty, and so they ask the beggar
"again." There is no need also to inquire what they
hoped to obtain from the beggar by asking him again
— they themselves probably had no clear idea. As in
2:18, we regard ὅτι as elliptical: this we ask "since,"
or "seeing that," etc. We must not regard "seeing
that he opened thine eyes" as an admission on the
part of the Pharisees that Jesus had actually done this
— John himself cautions us against that. This clause

is spoken from the standpoint of the beggar and merely repeats his testimony.

And he said, He is a prophet. It certainly took courage to give this answer before these authoritative persons. Here we begin to admire the man. He might have hidden his conviction by saying, "I do not know." He is honest and confesses. That Jesus must be classed as a prophet of God was beyond question to him.

18) Now that the Pharisees had the plain verdict of the beggar, they refuse to accept it and revert to their suspicion of some kind of a collusion between the beggar and Jesus. Their minds cannot let go of the thought that something must be crooked about this apparent miracle. Someone among them hit upon the bright idea of questioning the man's parents. This might not at all be their blind son, or they may know what is back of the affair. So John informs us: **The Jews, therefore,** in spite of the beggar's verdict, **did not believe concerning him that he was (formerly) blind and received his sight** (as he had testified) **until they called the parents of him that received his sight and asked them, etc.** John now writes "the Jews" instead of "the Pharisees," but only to bring out the hostility of these men. So often in this Gospel "the Jews" has this implication. On the tenses ἦν and ἀνέβλεψεν see R. 1029; we should write pluperfects: "had been blind," "had received his sight." Also ἕως ὅτου is merely a set phrase, R. 291. Not that the Jews believed the fact of the miracle after questioning the parents; for they got nothing whatever from them, and "until" never itself implies that the reverse follows afterward.

19) So the parents are brought in, and after the beggar had been ordered out of the room, the Jews **asked them, saying, Is this your son, of whom you yourselves say that he was born blind? How, then,**

does he now see? The point of the first question lies in ὑμεῖς (emphatic) λέγετε. The couple might, indeed, say that this is not at all their son; but for such testimony the Jews have little hope. Hence the stress on the other point: does this couple really mean to say that this son of theirs, if he is their son, was actually born blind? And if this too is true, then the most important point of all: How in the world does he now see?

20) The parents answer each point in turn.. They are most excellent witnesses, for they testify only to what they know at firsthand. John, too, introduces their testimony with two finite verbs (see 1:48). **His parents, therefore, answered and said, We know that this is our son and that he was born blind.**

21) On the third and vital point they are more explicit, for they answer with a double statement and even add a piece of pertinent advice. **But how he now sees we do not know; or who opened his eyes we ourselves do not know.** Note the emphatic ἡμεῖς, "we ourselves," in the second statement. They know no more than these Jews or anyone else. What they have *heard,* the Jews and others have likewise heard. So they add what is certainly to the point if these self-constituted judges desire firsthand testimony: **Ask him; he has age** (is a grown man); **he himself shall speak for himself.** To be sure, that is the only correct and sensible thing to do.

22) The carefulness of the parents in assuming no responsibility of any kind before these Pharisees is explained by John. **These things his parents said because they were fearing the Jews; for already the Jews had agreed that if anyone should confess him as Christ, he should be one banned.** To such a pitch the hatred of the Jews, namely the party of the Pharisees, had already risen that by a general agreement among themselves they had determined on

the severest Jewish measures against possible believers in Jesus who should dare to confess him as "Christ," the promised Messiah. These stern measures were to act as a deterrent. The Pharisees were numerous and powerful enough to carry out their threat. Subfinal ἵνα introduces the substance of the agreement; and ἐάν reads as though the Jews expected such cases to occur. John has two accusatives with ὁμολογεῖν, the second being predicative to the first, R. 480.

To become or to be made an ἀποσυνάγωγος does not refer to one who does not dare to enter a synagogue but to one who is expelled from the religious communion of Israel, cut off from all its blessings, hopes, and promises, like a pagan or Gentile. We have no assurance that the later double ban was known in the times of Jesus, a minor ban lasting for thirty, sixty, or ninety days, and a major ban for all time. The New Testament references read as though the expulsion was permanent. Grave civil and social disabilities were as a matter of course connected with the ban. The *aposynagogos* would be treated as an apostate who was accursed, under the *cherem* or ban. No wonder these parents were careful of their words. When they refer the Pharisees to their son they seem to have known that he would be able to take care of himself; at least, he here shows that he can do so.

23) **On this account his parents said, He has age,** is a grown man; **ask him.** They have no fears for their son. Thus John points out why they added just these words.

24) Having gained nothing by their second effort and being without any other prospect of success, the Pharisees would like to close the case. **So for a second time they called the man that was blind and said to him, Give glory to God: we ourselves know that this man is an open sinner.** In all due form as before a court of law the beggar is again

brought in. Expectantly he faces these Jews who pose
as a court, wondering what they had extracted from
his parents. It is John who calls him "the man that
was blind" (we should say, "had been blind"). The
investigation has ended, the verdict is now handed
out, and, though it deals with Jesus, is addressed to
the beggar. One of the Jews acted as spokesman.
"Give glory to God" is an adjuration (compare Josh.
7:19; I Sam. 6:5) to seal as the truth before God
the summary of the whole matter at which these
Pharisees have arrived and to which they demand
that the beggar should solemnly assent by himself
assuming the adjuration plus the finding to which it
is attached. The A. V. has, "Give God the praise,"
which is generally understood to mean, "Give the
credit for your healing to God not to Jesus." But
this is incorrect. In their verdict the Pharisees admit
nothing about the healing; they do not even say that
God wrought it; they ignore it altogether. What they
say is this: "Give glory to God by now telling the
truth, and this is the truth, which *we* now positively
know — and *we* are the people to know, ἡμεῖς — that
this man is an open sinner, ἁμαρτωλός (as in v. 16)."
They imply that they have sounded this thing thoroughly, that besides the man's testimony they have heard
that of others, and the only correct conclusion of the
whole case is what they now state. They count on
their superior authority to effect submission on the
part of the beggar. Many others have put forth the
same kind of authority and often enough have found
submission.

It seems that the second group mentioned in v. 16
yielded their opinion. The reference to Jesus is derogatory throughout, as here "this man," never deigning
to mention so much as his name.

25) But this beggar is a steady disappointment
and a growing surprise to the Pharisees. Trench calls

him ready-witted, genial, and brave. Really he is far more: honest, grateful, and entirely sincere — and this especially differentiates him from his judges. Not for one moment does he accept their finding as true. The fatal flaw in that finding is the omission of his healing. Instead of uttering the truth regarding that and a true conclusion based on it concerning the healer, it leaves out the healing altogether and from some other premises draws a conclusion that is wholly false. **He on his part** (ἐκεῖνος, emphatic subject), **therefore, answered, Whether he is an open sinner, I do not know; one thing I do know, that being blind, I now see.** Over against the emphatic *we know* of the Pharisees this beggar puts his own emphatic *I do know*; and in the clash the beggar wins because his knowledge is real, that of the Pharisees pretended. There he stands with his bright, shining eyes, looking right at the Pharisees. Can they not see those eyes of his? Here, right before them, just as Jesus said (v. 3) "the works of God are made manifest." But these men deliberately stultify themselves: they will not see what so magnificently challenges their sight.

An indirect question is introduced by εἰ, "whether." The action of the present participle ὤν is thrown into the past by the adverb "now" and becomes, as R. 892, 1115 says, a sort of imperfect particle. By their foolish proceeding these Pharisees start this beggar toward doing his own simple, straightforward thinking and toward drawing his own truthful conclusions. By trying to oppose the truth they only help to further the cause of truth. It is often thus. When the beggar says that he does not know whether Jesus is an open sinner he means that he has no knowledge on this point, so that he can testify as to that. In a moment we find him saying far more. We actually see him growing in courage and in conviction. "One

thing" he "does know" and again testifies: once
blind, he now sees. Facts are facts. And this one
is so patent that the Pharisees themselves dare not
deny it.

26) The verdict, with which these judges seek to
end the case, is smashed. They are back where they
were before and as utterly helpless; their state is even
worse. All they know is to ask the old questions over
again. **They, therefore,** not knowing what else to
say, **said to him** (whereas he had replied, they only
said), **What did he to thee? how did he open thine
eyes?** Are they parleying for time? Attempting
to sit as judges, they have plainly lost their hold.
Already they are admitting what they are determined not to admit, that Jesus opened this beggar's eyes.

27) The man takes full advantage of their predicament and of the weak questions they put to him.
He answered them, and his answer was an answer.
**I told you already, and you did not hear. Why do
you want to hear again? You, too, certainly do
not want to become his disciples?** This is a telling
thrust. The helplessness of the Pharisees emboldens
the beggar. Instead of allowing himself to be put
on the defensive by having to go over the story of
his healing again before these men, whose only purpose is to catch him up in some way, he puts them
on the defensive. The tables are being turned. They,
the judges, thought to question him, the defendant; he
now becomes the judge and probes them as defend-
ants with telling questions. God helps his own in the
tests to which they are put for Jesus' sake.

"I told you already" means that they already have
the truth. "And you did not hear" means that they
did not believe that truth. If, then, they did not
believe it the first time, why do they want to hear
("be hearing," present tense) it again? Judicial

reason there can be none. Is there perhaps another
reason? Two might suggest themselves. The one
would compromise these judges badly, namely that
they are trying to upset and confound that truth. To
the honest mind of this beggar this answer does not
appeal; at least he does not voice it. He takes the
other, namely that after all these Pharisees, impressed by beholding the eyes which Jesus had opened,
would also like to become his disciples. With μή
the beggar suggests that he can hardly think this
possible but — strange things happen. He is hardly
making only an artful thrust at the Pharisees; his
artless simplicity leads him to entertain the thought
that possibly these men are willing to change their
minds about Jesus. The suggestion about becoming
disciples of Jesus is something like an invitation to
join the beggar in this; for καί, "you, too," intimates
that he is ready to be such a disciple. Alas, their will
(θέλετε) is absolutely contrary.

28) **And they reviled him and said, Thou art
that fellow's disciple; but we are disciples of Moses.
We know that God has spoken to Moses; but as
for this fellow, we do not know whence he is.** To
revile is all that is left the Pharisees — a sign of
complete bankruptcy. They caught the force of καί
in the second question of v. 27 and charge the beggar
with being a disciple of Jesus. The genitive "of this
fellow," ἐκείνου, is highly derogatory. *Hoc vocabulo
removent Jesum a sese,* Bengel. By calling the beggar
Jesus' disciple these Pharisees imagine that they are
reviling and heaping shame and insult upon him;
in reality they could offer no higher testimonial of
honor and praise to him. With an emphatic ἡμεῖς
they place themselves over against the beggar with
the proud and lofty assertion, "*We* — we are the
disciples of Moses!" Here they pronounce sentence
upon themselves, and out of their own mouth the

Lord will judge them at the last day. Moses himself, on whom they set their hope, will accuse them,
5:45. There is, indeed, a difference between Moses
and Jesus; for "the law was given by Moses, but
grace and truth came by Jesus Christ," 1:17. But
all that Moses wrote he wrote concerning Jesus, 5:46;
even the law, of which he was the mediator, was to
be for us a παιδαγωγός, a boy's slave-conductor, to lead
us to Christ. These Pharisees were the disciples of a
fictitious Moses, whom they had invented for themselves, and who did not exist.

29) And now they imitate the beggar's own
words, "I do not know — I do know" (v. 25), but they
reverse the two, "*We* — we know (emphatic ἡμεῖς) —
we do not know." In the first assertion, "*We* know!"
speaks the voice of arrogant authority, seconded by
the other assertion, "We do not know!" spoken with
the same authority. What *we* know, that alone counts;
what we do not know, regarding that nobody dares to
pronounce. And knowledge is our personal prero-
gative; whoever does not bow to us and our knowledge
knows nothing, and whoever presumes to know anything we do not know is a fool. Even to this day the
skeptic, the agnostic, and a certain type of scientist
take the same attitude. It pretends to intellectuality,
but at bottom the intellect is made to voice only the
attitude of an ungodly heart.

These Pharisees claim that they know "that God
has spoken to Moses," for instance in Exod. 3:2-4 and
in other cases. They lack only the essential thing, a
knowledge of what God really said to Moses ("he
wrote of me," 5:46; the Scriptures "testify of me,"
5:39). Many even know much about the Scriptures,
and yet their knowledge is empty of the real substance. This the Pharisees themselves declare when
they add, "but as for this fellow, we do not know
whence he is." The scornful accusative τοῦτον, while

it is the object of the verb, is placed forward, almost as if it were independent; and in what respect they do not know "this fellow" is added by the indirect question, "whence he is," i. e., who sent him, or by whose authority he comes. The implication, however, is not that perhaps God after all sent him but that somebody else sent him, or that as an impostor he came on his own authority, certainly without God's commission.

30) Even the simple logic of the man whom the Pharisees seek to override pierces through this flimsy armor. The two verbs: **The man answered and said to them** mark the importance of the beggar's reply. **Why, just in this is the marvel, that on your part you do not know whence he is, and yet he opened my eyes. We know that God does not hear open sinners; but if anyone be a God-fearing person and do his will, him he hears. From eternity it was never heard that anyone opened the eyes of one born blind. If this man were not from God, he would be able to do nothing.** Boldly the beggar makes an actual speech. It is precipitated by the assertion of the Pharisees that they do not know whence Jesus is, meaning that he is certainly not from God, and that certainly God never spoke to him and gave him a commission, as he did Moses. Instead of bringing their awkward case to something like a satisfactory end, the Pharisees themselves, against their own intentions, stir the beggar up to make this penetrating reply. They have actually only furthered the beggar's thinking; for while at first he is not ready to discuss whether Jesus is an open sinner or not, now he proves conclusively that he must be the very opposite, "a God-fearing person" who does God's will. The logic of the little lecture is invincible. It deals with premises which are axiomatic to all Jews, hence the conclusion is inevitable. The beggar's parents were

wise, indeed, when they told the Pharisees, "Ask him,
he has the age!" The tables are completely turned.
The judges are judged — and by a beggar!

On the use of γάρ at the head of a new statement
see B.-D. 452, 2, and R. 1190. The thing itself is
very plain, and the beggar sees it. Jesus had opened
his eyes — that shows whence he is; it is a manifest
(v. 3, φανερωθῇ) proof that in some way he is from
God. The Pharisees refuse to see it, pretend even to
deny it. This is "a marvel," an astonishing thing,
indeed — although it has since occurred many times.
The beggar supports his simple conclusion by an
equally simple deduction.

31) This verse constitutes the major premise and
is put in popular form. The point to be proven is
that Jesus is connected with God. All present agree
that God does not hear flagrant sinners; in fact, the
Pharisees themselves had admitted this when they
asserted that Jesus is an open sinner (v. 24). A man
whose life and conduct are in opposition to God is not
heard even if he asks divine help for some work. If
God is to hear a man, he must be of a different kind,
namely a θεοσεβής (opposite of ἀσεβής), "God-fearing,"
and this in the sense that he occupies himself with
doing (present subjunctive) God's will. Such a man,
we may assume (ἐάν), God will hear. This is the
fundamental principle for deciding the case at issue,
so certain and simple that no one would dare to
deny it.

32) Now follows the minor premise, a statement
of the beggar's own case in all its greatness. It
declares not only that no sinner ever wrought a
miracle but that no man (τίς), *no* man of God even,
ever opened the eyes of a person born blind. A case
such as this is absolutely unheard of; even the Old
Testament reports no miracles of this kind. The beggar's argument grows in the very statement of it.

The more the man ponders the thing, the nearer he gets to the truth about Jesus, namely that he is not only one of a class (God-fearing and a doer of God's will) but one altogether exceptional, ἐκ τοῦ αἰῶνος, "from the eon on," since the world-age began, ἐκ to indicate the point of departure, R. 597. Jesus had restored to sight eyes that were born blind, whose defect was organic as when the optic nerve is ruined, that were absolutely hopeless and beyond human skill to cure. This is the astounding thing that Jesus has done.

33) Now follows the conclusion. As the minor premise offers far more than the syllogism needs, so the statement of the conclusion with its negative form claims far less than the beggar is entitled to claim. The effect of such a presentation is the more convincing, in fact, it overwhelms. The beggar does not say, "Therefore he is of God," as many a good logician would be content to say. Or, using the negative form, "Therefore, if he were not of God he would not have been able to open my eyes," which again is sound logic. With one grand sweep the beggar takes in the deed wrought upon him and all other godly deeds great or small: "If he were not of God he could do — nothing." The conditional sentence is one of present unreality, εἰ with the imperfect (protasis), the imperfect with ἄν (apodosis, often with ἄν omitted, as here).

This beggar never intended to set himself up as a teacher of men who were his superiors in education, social position, and dignity in the church; they have driven him to it. By trying to quench the light they only forced it to shine the brighter to their own undoing. And the brighter its rays, the greater their fault in not admitting them into their hearts.

34) Now at last the Pharisees make a strong reply, strong, alas, not in truth and logic but only in

vituperation and violence. **They answered and
said to him, In sins thou wast born altogether and
dost thou teach us? And they threw him out of
the place.** Thus they surrender the argument.
Since the world began, when men have felt the sting
of truth and refused to yield, they have taken their
refuge to personal abuse. What the disciples thought
possible, and what Jesus roundly denied (v. 2, 3),
these Jews make their shameful refuge, namely that
this man's affliction of blindness from his birth proved
his wickedness, and that even to the present time.
"In sins" is placed forward for emphasis. They call
it an outrage that such a man (emphatic σύ) should
pretend to teach them (ἡμᾶς, emphatic — all their
dignity being stressed in the word) anything. "Char-
acteristically enough they forget that the two charges,
one that he had never been blind and so was an impostor: the other that he bore the mark of God's
anger in a blindness which reached back to his birth,
will not agree together but mutually exclude one another." Trench. They have found a crime that is
greater than either of these two: his presuming to
teach *them* — who, indeed, were beyond teaching!
And so they threw him out of the building, ἐξέβαλον
ἔξω, "out," so that he landed "outside" (preposition
plus the adverb, idiomatic).

We have no reason to locate this incident in the
Temple before the Sanhedrin, nor in a synagogue
before a Jewish minor court. With others the author
in *The Eisenach Gospel Selections*, p. 864, held that
this throwing out was the ban mentioned in v. 22,
which would make a martyr of this beggar and
would lend itself to such reflections as Lightfoot,
Trench, and others make. We give this view up because the verb alone is insufficient to yield this thought
and because no distinctive term is added as in
v. 22. That the ban was inflicted a few days later

is, of course, only supposition. The beggar, too, must have seemed too insignificant a person to induce the Pharisees to begin pronouncing the ban on him, and such an act would only help to spread the news of his healing.

VIII. *Jesus' Testimony Concerning Spiritual Sight and Blindness, 35-41*

35) When the Pharisees quizzed the beggar, he came close to the confession that Jesus is the Son of God. Jesus himself brings the man to that confession. **Jesus heard that they had thrown him out of the place and, having found him, said to him, Thou, dost thou believe on the Son of God?** With an aorist verb and an aorist participle John merely reports the facts, that Jesus heard how the beggar had fared, and that presently he found him. That the latter occurred in the Temple is not indicated. Both the hearing and the finding would occur in a perfectly natural way, and yet there is a higher hand behind these acts. The contact would not end with the miracle; compare the case of the impotent man, 5:14. Jesus would finish the work he had begun. As far as John's report goes, Jesus proceeds in the most direct manner. It is taken for granted that the beggar knows that he is now looking with his eyes upon the man who had miraculously opened those eyes. The pronoun σύ is emphatic, *"Thou,* dost thou believe," etc., when so many important persons are not believing? The question sounds as though it expects an affirmative answer. Jesus knows the readiness of the beggar to confess, but he nevertheless asks him to make that confession.

"Dost thou believe," πιστεύεις, dost thou trust with thy heart? The beggar could no longer trust the Pharisees, though they were leaders in the church, for he had seen their deliberate blindness and falseness. Yet Jesus does not ask merely, "Dost thou trust me?" or use only some designation for the pronoun "me." He asks, "Dost thou trust in the Son of God?" While this question does not intimate that by "the Son of God" Jesus is referring to himself, on the other hand, it certainly also is not abstract as though it was without any vital reference to Jesus. Moreover, the question is deeply personal for the beggar, and is to be understood in the highest religious sense, a parallel to the question whether one trusts in God, relies on him for guidance, enlightenment, help, blessing, yea, heaven itself.

Did Jesus say, "the Son of God," or, as good texts read, "the Son of man"? In a way this is again a question for the text critics, yet we cannot leave it entirely to them. Neither term stands only for "me." Certainly, the beggar would trust a benefactor like Jesus — how could he help it? But this would be an inferior trust, dealing only with benefactions such as the one the beggar had received. A prophet (v. 17), a holy man of God (v. 31) might obtain such gifts by prayer to God. Jesus thus had to designate himself so that this beggar would drop all thoughts of a holy prophet or merely human messenger sent from God, so that he would at once lift his thoughts to the person of the divine Messiah, the very Son of God. For this purpose Jesus might have used "the Son of man" if this designation had been current among the Jews as a name for the Messiah, one that would at once have been understood by the beggar. But it is Jesus alone who uses this name, not even his disciples employ it (see 1:51). It has a mysterious sound, and its real import must be searched out by those who hear it without some previous intimation as to its meaning. However the text critics may ex-

plain its introduction in our passage, the internal
evidence is too strong for the reading "the Son of
God." This the beggar at once understood, just as
did the hearers of the Baptist when he called Jesus
"the Son of God" (1:34).

36) **He answered and said, And who is it, Lord,
in order that I may believe?** Although his knowledge of Jesus was limited, this beggar already trusts
Jesus to such an extent, that he is at once ready to
trust whomever he may point out as the Son of God.
The "and" with which the question begins is like the
Hebrew v^e and hardly connects with an unexpressed
idea. Usually it is connected with the question Jesus
has just asked. R. 999 makes ἵνα consecutive, contemplated result; B.-D. 483, a case of brachylogy, so that
we supply *antworte*, in order that I may believe. This
seems best, especially after a question.

37) **Jesus said unto him, Thou hast both seen
him, and he who is speaking with thee is he.** There
is no reason why the first καί should be "even"; "thou
hast even seen him." Why such stress, especially
when only ordinary physical seeing is in the commentator's mind? Here καί . . . καί is "both
. . . and." Jesus might have said quite simply,
"It is I." He has a better answer, one that calls
out and encourages the beggar's faith. But it would
certainly be inferior if the answer Jesus does give
means no more than, "Thou both seest and hearest
him." Either one would be enough. If Jesus meant
to refer to the beggar's newly opened eyes, "Thou
seest him" would have been the word. If Jesus had
in mind only his person, "Thou hearest him," or
words to that effect, might have done; "It is I," ἐγώ
εἰμι, would have been better. The answer of Jesus
contains far more than a reference to the physical
senses. Jesus tells the beggar that he has already

seen the Son of God; and then he tells him that the person now speaking with him is that Son of God whom he has already seen.

Some do not sufficiently note the difference between the two tenses which Jesus employs: ἑώρακας, perfect, "thou hast seen," and ὁ λαλῶν, present, "he who is speaking." But John uses many perfects, and always most carefully in the sense of perfects. To be sure, the Greek has a group of perfect forms which are always present in sense, but ἑώρακα is not in this group. If Jesus here means, "thou seest him," the present tense alone is in order. Jesus might say, "he who has spoken with thee," recalling to the beggar how he heard Jesus tell him to go and to wash; but as regards physical seeing the beggar has not seen Jesus until just now. Some find a present sense in ἑώρακας because they think of physical seeing alone. The Pharisees, whose physical eyes have always been good, see Jesus thus, but do not at all see "the Son of God," concerning whom Jesus is asking this beggar. In the very next verses (39-41), where Jesus continues to speak about seeing, not physical but spiritual seeing is the topic.

With the perfect "thou hast seen" Jesus reaches into the beggar's past when his eyes were opened by the divine power of Jesus — then the beggar caught the first inner glimpse of who his benefactor really is, namely "the Son of God"; and the perfect tense implies that what there dawned upon the beggar remained with him. To arrive at faith in the Son of God requires more than physical eyes with which to look at Jesus. After this significant reminder to the beggar, connecting the miracle at Siloam and what there took place in his heart with "the Son of God," Jesus directly answers the beggar's question by adding, "and he who is speaking with thee is he." This means more than, "I am the one." That seeing at

Siloam was a revelation of the Son of God by means
of a deed, to which Jesus now by speaking with the
beggar is adding a revelation of the Son of God by
means of his *Word*. This, then, is the answer of Jesus
to the beggar's question as to who the Son of God is:
The One whom the beggar has already seen in the
miracle, the One who is now speaking to him in his
Word.

38) The beggar also answers by word and by
deed. **And he said, Lord, I believe. And he worshipped him.** His act is a definition of his word.
The verb προσκυνεῖν means to evidence prostration and
adoration, here in the full religious sense of worship
due to God. Sometimes the verb means less, namely
to pay deep reverence to some man deemed worthy
thereof. A lesser sense is shut out where the act is
directed to "the Son of God." The significance of the
beggar's act cannot be reduced by our searching out
and weighing just what "the Son of God" actually
meant to him when he fell on his knees and touched
Jesus' feet. So much is clear, that this beggar was
a Jew with a knowledge of the true God which he
had gained from the Old Testament.

39) After calling himself the Son of God, Jesus
accepts the beggar's worship as intended for that Son.
In fact, he shows that he is deeply moved by this beggar's word and act. A remarkable word comes to his
lips, one which sums up all that has occurred in the
beggar's case and that lets us feel why John wrote
this story at such length. **And Jesus said, For judgment I did come into this world, that those not seeing shall be seeing, and those seeing shall become
blind.** No one is directly addressed. What Jesus
says is intended for all who are present. When he
says that he "did come into this world" he speaks as
the Son of God, as he who became incarnate (1:14)
and thus entered upon his redemptive mission in "this

world" (see 8:23) of sinful humanity. Already in 3:19 Jesus speaks of the judgment which results from his mission. There he calls it κρίσις, an act of judgment; now he uses κρίμα, a verdict of judgment. Both terms are neutral, including acquittal as well as condemnation. Yet only in a secondary way does the mission to save the world bring about a judicial verdict which divides mankind. It is only because so many reject the Son whom God sent into the world to save it and spurn the mission which brings them grace and redemption.

With a subfinal ἵνα Jesus states this judicial verdict. Here it is stated in the form of a striking oxymoron: "that those not seeing may be seeing, and those seeing may become blind." The former are all those who, although by nature they are without spiritual sight and light, let Jesus, who comes to them, give them the light of life by bringing them to faith. In them the saving mission of Jesus is accomplished. The latter are those, who by nature are equally without sight and light and who when Jesus comes to give them the light of life spurn him and his gift by the boast of unbelief that they already have sight and life. In them the saving mission of Jesus is frustrated. The wording which Jesus uses is suggested by the miracle which Jesus wrought on the blind beggar by giving him the sight of his physical eyes. Yet the miracle is not allegorized, for the Pharisees have not been made physically blind but are left to see physically as well as ever. Jesus is speaking only of spiritual blindness and spiritual sight. His words are formulated so as to fit the Pharisees most exactly as contrasted with the beggar. They are the ones who love to call themselves βλέποντες, men who see — recall their boast: ἡμεῖς οἴδαμεν, "we know." The beggar knows only what Jesus has done for him and what the

Scriptures say, besides that he humbly asks that he may know and believe.

Thus the verdict is: these "shall be seeing," βλέπωσιν, present subjunctive (durative), have and enjoy spiritual sight forever; those "shall become blind," γένωνται, aorist subjunctive (punctiliar), shall arrive at a point that fixes them as permanently blind. To begin with, all are alike in the darkness of sin, none see. All would remain alike if Jesus, who is "a light in the world" (v. 5), did not come to them. It is when Jesus comes as "a light" with his enlightening power that a difference results. Some are made to realize that they, indeed, are blind; these arrive at sight, a seeing that remains. Others will not realize that they are blind and boast that they see; they are left devoid of sight, and their blindness remains. It is bad enough that by nature all men are μὴ βλέποντες and that in the course of nature they would remain such; it is infinitely worse that, when the Light has come and shines over us and seeks to enter and to give sight to our hearts, we should so oppose that Light as to become fixed in blindness forever.

40) **Those of the Pharisees who were with him heard these things and said to him, Certainly** (thou dost not mean to say), **we too are blind?** Some of the Pharisees are at hand, dogging the steps of Jesus and keeping an eye on him. They feel themselves hit by what Jesus says, although he had not addressed them. With a scornful air they repudiate what they think Jesus says as applying to them. It seemed ridiculous to them, who imagined that they were "guides of the blind, a light to them that are in darkness, correctors of the foolish, teachers of the law" (Rom. 2:19, 20), to be called "blind," so that they must come to Jesus to receive sight. This they indicate with the interrogative word μή and its implication

of a negative answer, which, if Jesus in any manner denies it, will make his words meaningless. With τυφλοί the Pharisees refer to the class designated by Jesus as μὴ βλέποντες. If they referred to the second class whom Jesus himself calls τυφλοί, their question would have to be: Have we too "become blind"? It is conscience and the prick of Jesus' second statement which makes these Pharisees touch only the first statement. Added to this is their repudiation of Jesus as the one who makes the blind to see. For: "Are *we* too blind?" means also: "Must *we* too come to thee for sight?"

41) **Jesus said to them, If you were blind you would not have sin; but now you claim, We see. Your sin remains.** Jesus turns their own words against them. He takes the word "blind" as they use it and declares that they certainly do *not* belong to that class. They are perfectly right in assuming that Jesus would not place them into that class. For this is the class that comes to see — Jesus is able to give them sight. But if they do not belong to this blessed class, where do they belong, where are they placing themselves? Why, in the only other class that is left. There Jesus had placed them; and they had deliberately closed their ears to that part of his word. With a condition of unreality Jesus again tells them where they belong and at the same time exposes their fatal guilt. "If you were blind," blind only as not seeing, there would be hope for you; but now you are not any longer blind in that sense. Then "you would not have sin," sin such as the other blindness involves, the sin of deliberately rejecting the Light, the sin of sins, unbelief, which forever shuts out from light and life; but now this sin is upon you; you have it, and it has you.

Against the unreality (the class to which even on their own testimony they do not intend to belong),

Jesus sets the reality (the class to which they do belong, whether they intend to or not) : "but now you claim, We see." Here, too, Jesus lets their own testimony speak, λέγετε, "you claim, assert, declare." As they would not dream of it to be included in the first class, so they are proud to include themselves in the second. The asyndeton makes the final sentence stand out as a verdict by itself: "Your sin remains." The sin of rejecting the light, the sin of unbelief. It "remains" with all that it involves for their other sins, lies like a curse upon their souls because they want it thus and will not let it be removed from them. This is a fearful word, spoken in advance to these Pharisees by him who will at last sit on the throne of judgment again to render that verdict. Yet as he now utters it, it constitutes another penetrating call to repentance to these men and a warning to all of us who believe in him today. Note the syllogistic form of the κρίμα with the stringency of its conclusion. Major premise: "If you were blind," etc. Minor: "But now you claim," etc. *Ergo:* That you have no sin does not apply to you — "your sin remains." In this negative syllogism the conclusion may be stated either way, negatively or positively, either equals the other.

CHAPTER X

IX. *Jesus' Testimony Concerning His Flock, 1-21*

Without a break or a pause Jesus continues to speak before this audience, namely his disciples, the formerly blind beggar, the Pharisees, and other Jews. The connection of thought is close. Jesus has told the Pharisees in his audience that their wilful blindness entails abiding guilt. That statement deals with them as far as their own persons are concerned. But they posed as men who "see" and who "know" over against the common people (ὁ ὄχλος) who do "not know" the law, and whom they thus look down upon as accursed (see 7:49), among them being this wretched beggar: "and dost thou teach *us* (9:34)?" Thus these Pharisees set themselves up as the only true teachers and leaders of the people (Rom. 2:19, 20). In reality they were pseudo-teachers and pseudo-leaders. So Jesus continues and now treats these Pharisees in their damnable influence and work upon others.

But this time he employs a παροιμία (παρά, *præter*; οἶμος, *via*), for which term we have no exact equivalent in English: a mode of teaching deviating from the usual way; a kind of extended *mashal*, containing a hidden sense. In the strict sense of the term a parable relates a definite story or case, it may be one that is ordinary, and again one that is quite beyond the ordinary; while a paroimia describes actions as they are known regularly to occur (the shepherd always uses the door; the robber always avoids the door and climbs over the wall). Moreover, in a paroimia an allegorical correspondence appears between the realities presented and the illustrative features used; in a parable no allegory is found. In explaining his own *mashal* Jesus gives us the key-point in the allegorical statement, "I am the door of the sheep" (v. 7).

"We see!" say the blind Pharisees. Very well, Jesus puts them to the test. He presents a simple, lucid *mashal.* Do they see? Not in the least (v. 6). To tell them that they are blind makes no impression on them; perhaps this public demonstration of their blindness will accomplish more. To be sure, blind men cannot see, nor did Jesus expect these blind Pharisees to see what his paroimia means. Part of their very judgment is that they shall not see. Yet for such blind people the use of this uncommon way of teaching does at least one thing: by its very strangeness it remains in the memory and long after challenges the mind to penetrate to the true meaning. Perhaps thus at last the light will succeed in penetrating. In this case Jesus even condescends to explain his *mashal* and to elaborate it quite extensively (v. 7-18). In the case of many even this was in vain (v. 20), but others began to catch something of the light (v. 21). Read Trench, the first three chapters of *The Parables of our Lord.*

1)   **Amen, amen, I say to you, He who does not enter by the door into the fold of the sheep but climbs up elsewhere, he is a thief and a robber; but he that enters by the door is a shepherd of the sheep.** On the preamble see 1:51. It marks the weight of what is said. The brief *mashal* is perfect in every respect. Its obvious sense is quite axiomatic; so also is the higher reality which it describes. The picture is that of a sheepfold, a walled or fenced enclosure, where the sheep are kept at night, while during the day they are led out to pasture. The vital point is the action of the two persons in regard to the door of the fold. He who shuns the door and gets in some other way, such as by climbing over the wall or fence, that man (ἐκεῖνος, a word John loves) is a thief who means to steal what does not belong to him, or a robber who would obtain by violence what belongs to another. In

contrast to a man of this kind he who uses the door to get to the sheep is a shepherd of the sheep (ποιμήν without the article, like "a thief and a robber"; not: *the* shepherd, but merely a quality), his action shows that he stands in the relation of a shepherd to the sheep.

3)   At this point the paroimia might be regarded as being complete.   But Jesus extends the picture to make still clearer the great difference obtaining between the true shepherd and the man who is anything but that.   **To him the doorkeeper opens, and the sheep hear his voice, and he calls his own sheep by name and he leads them out.**   From the night we move on to the morning.   The door is naturally guarded by a keeper.   We now see why the thieving robber, who comes at night, avoids the door.   One who is a shepherd not only uses the door as a matter of course, he is also admitted there, known as a shepherd by the doorkeeper.   The sheep, too, know him; they "hear" (ἀκούει in the sense of εἰδέναι, v. 4), i. e., recognize, his voice.   In the early morning hour, when it is still perhaps dark, a shepherd, coming to get his sheep, calls to them as he enters, and they know him by his voice. Several shepherds use the fold for the night; so each one "calls his own sheep" in his own way.   A beautiful touch is added by κατ᾽ ὄνομα (distributive, R. 608), "by name," one name after the other; for he has a name for each of his sheep to which it trustfully responds. And so at early dawn he leads his own little flock forth. And the other shepherds who use the fold do the same.

4)   This action is more fully described.   **When he has pushed all his own out he goes before them, and the sheep follow him because they know his voice.**   As each sheep responds to its name, the shepherd takes hold of it, sees that it is his own, and pushes it out.   When all are out, he walks ahead, and the little flock follows at his heels.   This is how the shepherd uses the door.   It agrees with his shepherd relation to the sheep, a relation which is mutual: he

knows every one of them, they know him. More than
this: they know "his voice." See how this word "voice"
is repeated in v. 3, 4, and 5. How do we believers
know Jesus? By his voice as we hear it in his Word.

5) The contrast with any other man who is not
the shepherd is now brought out. **But a stranger
they will in no way follow; on the contrary, they
will flee from him, for they do not know the voice
of strangers.** What a stranger might want with the
sheep does not need to be said; but he could intend only
what a thief or robber would want. The picture is
now that of the sheep grazing, some being scattered at
a distance from the shepherd. The moment a stranger
approaches and tries to reassure them with his voice,
the sheep not only will not follow him, they will even
turn and flee from him. The future tenses are not
merely futuristic but volitive: they *will* not follow,
they *will* flee; and οὐ μή is the strongest form of negation with a future: "in no way." Jesus might have
used a conditional sentence; but the simple declarative
sentences are far more effective. Observe that the
shepherd goes to the door and uses the door to get his
sheep. The stranger tries to get in some other way,
without using the door. So the door is still the key.
Likewise, the last clause, "they do not know the voice
of strangers," is the direct opposite of v. 4, "they know
his voice," that of the shepherd. Of strangers, too,
there are many who seek to steal the sheep; there is
only one shepherd. As the shepherd's "voice" is
emphasized by three repetitions, so the fact that the
sheep "know" his voice is twice repeated. The two
correspond: "voice" — "know."

6) Now John adds in explanation: **This paroimia Jesus spoke to them; they, however, did not
realize what the things were which he was telling
them.** The subjects are abutted: "Jesus — they,"
and thus put in contrast. What Jesus meant by his
figurative language the Pharisees, who boasted, "We

see," failed completely to comprehend (aorist). The entire presentation is lucid; but, of course, it requires eyes to see through the lucid figure to the inner reality.

7) The first intention in using a *mashal* was to demonstrate to all present that the Pharisees were indeed utterly blind. Yet this form of teaching impresses itself upon the mind more than any other, and if there is any hope at all, it may eventually penetrate and enlighten. In so far as men will not see, they, indeed, shall not see, and this is a judgment upon them. For those who see, a *mashal* reveals the truth still more and by its very form enters more deeply and thus enlightens still more and opens the eyes of the heart more fully. A purpose of grace is thus combined with one of judgment. Which is to prevail in the end is decided by the heart of those upon whom the truth is thus brought to act with its power. So John writes: **Jesus, therefore, said to them again.** One purpose was already accomplished; a still greater purpose may yet be accomplished even in the blind Pharisees. More light is added. If this does not penetrate, the judgment on these men will be more pronounced. If it does penetrate at last, grace and truth will win another victory. The added light will, of course, still more enlighten those who see. So Jesus speaks "again." He interprets his paroimia and, as in so many instances, adds new features to the interpretation, intensifying the power of the light to the utmost.

Amen, amen, I say to you, I am the door of the sheep. Jesus begins anew, just as in v. 1, with the same formula for verity and authority. Here is another great "I am," ἐγώ εἰμι. In the very first brief statement, "I am the door of the sheep," Jesus offers the key to his entire *mashal*. Even a little spiritual sight should now see what Jesus really intends. The genitive is objective: the door "to the sheep," not subjective: the door "for the sheep," R. 501. The article with the predicate, I am "the door," means that the subject and the predicate are identical and interchangeable, R. 768. All who are really shepherds of the sheep (teachers, leaders, pastors) use Jesus as the one and only door to the sheep, are there admitted, acknowledged as shepherds, received as shepherds by the sheep, taking them out by the door, and as shepherds leading them to pasture.

When thus interpreting his own paroimia Jesus employs another type of teaching that is both highly interesting and effective, though it is at times misconceived and criticized. He weaves together the figure and the reality: "I am (reality) the door of the sheep (figure)." Trench calls this "Biblical allegory." A fine example is Ps. 23; another John 15:1, etc. As the figure illumines the reality, so the reality brings out the contents and the beauty of the figure.

8) Jesus now takes the key and himself begins to unlock the door, not waiting for his hearers to do this. **All, as many as came before me, are thieves and robbers; but the sheep did not hear them.** Here we learn what "thief," "robber," "stranger," and "strangers" signify in the paroimia. With the aorist ἦλθον Jesus speaks historically, but by adding εἰσί he brings the history down to the present Jewish leaders, some of whom stand before him at this moment. "All, as many as came before me," is certainly not absolute as already 5:39 and 45, 46; 7:19, sufficiently attest. Moses, the prophets, and other godly leaders used "the door," the promised Messiah. For Jesus that needs no saying. All efforts to change the temporal meaning of πρὸ ἐμοῦ to something else break down. Jesus looks back to the false Jewish religious leadership that had come into control since the second Temple and was represented especially by the Pharisees, beside whom stood the Sadducees. No special meaning attaches to ἦλθον, as though these leaders came by their own authority. This is true enough, but the verb means only that these self-seeking leaders appeared in

order to do their destructive work. Some have thought that Jesus here refers to false Messiahs who had come before his time. But this is historically incorrect and also untrue to the figure. False Messiahs would be false doors to the fold not thieves and robbers who fight shy of "the door." When Jesus adds that these "are" thieves and robbers he comes down to the present and includes the present Jewish leaders. All, past and present, "are" self-seekers.

All these are (reality) "thieves and robbers" (figure). They do not own the sheep and they are not shepherds. For their own evil purposes they attempt to get the sheep into their power. How ill the sheep would fare at their hands is left to the imagination. That they are, indeed, nothing but men who steal and rob is evidenced by the present representatives, who, like their predecessors, reject "the door."

Jesus can say, "but the sheep did not hear (figure) them" (reality), namely those who came thus. The true children of God ("the sheep") never do. Jesus does not complicate his figure by introducing people who follow false leaders: deceivers and deceived. These leaders rule by fear, 7:13; 9:22 and 34, the very opposite of the gentle care of shepherds. "Did not hear," as in the *mashal,* means: did not recognize the shepherd voice and thus gladly and trustfully follow; they only seek to flee (v. 5), lest they be hurt.

9) One point of the figure has thus been interpreted, that concerning the thieves and robbers who shun the door. The other point is now also interpreted, that concerning the shepherds who use the door. So again Jesus emphasizes the key: **I am the door** in the same sense as before, although "of the sheep" is now omitted because it is readily understood. **By me if anyone shall enter, he shall be safe and shall go in and go out and shall find pasture.** Here the reality ("by me," etc.) is again

combined with the figure ("he shall be safe," etc.). Jesus is speaking of the shepherds who use the door to enter the fold, who are thus entirely safe, go in to get their sheep, go out with them, and find good pasture for them. Whereas Jesus before speaks of the past as it extends to the present, he now starts with the present and looks into the future ("shall enter," subjunctive and thus future, from the present moment on; "shall be safe," etc., all future tenses, starting now). The past is done with and cannot be changed; what happens from now on is another matter, and Jesus holds it up like a delightful promise: "Use the door, use the door! — then all will be well."

The interpretation is upset at this point when the figure is changed from the shepherd to the sheep: "If *the sheep* shall enter, it shall be saved and shall go in and out and find pasture." What prompts this view is the verb σωθήσεται, which is referred to the reality instead of to the figure, in the sense of "shall be saved," i. e., rescued from sin and damnation. Under stress of this idea the words of the entire verse are scanned in order to find support for thinking of the sheep and not of a shepherd. Thus support is found in the fact that Jesus omits the genitive "of the sheep" and says only, "I am the door." Yet it is obvious that if he now intends to speak of the sheep and not of a shepherd, the addition of the genitive would be decidedly in place. Although Jesus again says, "I am the door" and then with emphasis, "By *me* if anyone shall enter," we are told that the figure is now expanded and becomes that of the Shepherd (Jesus). Going in and going out is made to apply only to the sheep and is denied to the shepherd by thinking that these verbs refer to a home, which the dweller enters and leaves at pleasure.

The verb σωθήσεται is part of the figure. This verb means not only to be rescued and delivered but includes the condition that results, to be safe. Here the context calls for the latter, and this is the case whether the shepherd or the sheep are referred to. For neither is rescued, either is said only to be safe. Once this is settled, our eyes will not be closed to all else that applies only to a shepherd, leaving nothing that can be properly applied to a sheep. The subject τὶς is masculine, "anyone" (a person), and cannot refer to a sheep, the Greek for which is neuter, πρόβατον. The figure has not become that of sheep lost and scattered, of which Jesus now says that, if any such sheep enters the door, it will be saved. How else but by the door would it enter the fold? And even if such a ridiculous thing could be possible as the sheep climbing into the fold over the wall or the fence, would it not be saved and safe just as well? The image is not that of the fold as a refuge to which a sheep may flee for safety, for in the next breath Jesus speaks of going out and finding pasture. Would the sheep then be exposed again? Moreover, the entire conception of a sheep going in and out of the fold at pleasure is wrong. No sheep does that. It is led in by the shepherd and let out by him. Nor does the sheep go out and seek and perhaps find pasture for itself. This is not at all the business of the sheep but that of the shepherd, and he always makes certain of the pasture. All is out of line if we regard "anyone" as a reference to a sheep; all is perfectly in line when we refer it to a shepherd.

If the shepherd uses the door, Jesus says, "he will be safe." The opposite of entering by the door is climbing up elsewhere (v. 1); this only a thief or robber does. When doing so the criminal is never safe but in the gravest danger of being discovered and punished. The shepherd uses the door for any business he may have in the fold, and thus he is, indeed, safe. The porter knows him and raises no alarm. He may go in and out whenever he finds it necessary. This suffices for the order of the two verbs: "shall go in and shall go out." Of course, this is connected with his shepherd duties. We find the same order in Acts

1:21, but reversed in Num. 27:17; Deut. 31:2; I Sam. 18:13 and 16, and I Kings 3:7, — all with reference to men attending to their duties. The order of the verbs is governed solely by the viewpoint. In the shepherd's case his going in and going out is not confined to taking the sheep into the fold at night and bringing them out again in the morning, for here no phrase is added such as "before them" in v. 4; the shepherd also has other occasions for going into the fold and coming out again. With all this the last clause agrees, "and shall find pasture" for his sheep. This is the final touch which marks him as a shepherd whose concern is the welfare of the sheep. The thief and robber act far otherwise (v. 10).

Yet σωθήσεται is misinterpreted even when all else is rightly interpreted. Jesus is thought to leave his figure by introducing the reality: this shepherd himself shall be saved from damnation. He has this in mind because he so uses this verb in 3:17 and 5:34. The answer is that these passages are literal and without a figure. In our passage the verb is embedded among figurative terms and is thus like them — figurative. When we are pointed to I Cor. 3:15 for a case where this verb is used literally in a figurative connection, the answer is that this is a mistake; I Cor. 3:15 is figurative throughout, verb and all, just like our present passage. The claim that σώζειν is always used in a literal sense cannot be upheld.

10) In order to throw the character and the actions of the shepherd who uses the door into bold relief, Jesus paints the black picture of the thief. **The thief does not come except to steal and to slaughter and to destroy.** No need to add that the thief is also a robber; no need to specify that he deals thus with the sheep. The three aorists in the purpose clause express actuality. He may kill the sheep right in the fold in order to stop its bleating. The last verb is added to bring out the disastrous effect upon the

poor sheep: it is destroyed. Surely a contrast to the shepherd — going in and going out and finding pasture for the sheep! In this dreadful work the thief cannot be safe (σωθήσεται).

Jesus now rounds out and completes his interpretation of the *mashal*. The coming of the thief for his nefarious purpose is contrasted with the coming of Jesus and his blessed purpose. **I** (emphatic ἐγώ) **came, in order that they may have life and may have abundance.** This statement is literal. The two plural verbs leave the subjects unnamed; they are the persons meant by the sheep. "I came" means: from heaven into this world (9:39; 8:23; 3:17). Others keep coming (the present tense used with reference to the thief for his coming to the fold) to destroy; the purpose of Jesus is to bestow life. On the expression "to have life" compare 3:15. Note the durative present tense ἔχωσιν and its emphatic repetition: have as an enduring possession. The repetition of the verb "may have" makes the second part of the purpose stand out more independently than if Jesus had said only, "may have life and abundance." The neuter adjective περισσόν is treated as a noun, "abundance" or "superfluity," namely of all the blessings which go with the true spiritual life; hence not, "may have it (life) abundantly" (R. V.), or "more abundantly" (A. V.), for this "life" has no degrees.

In this last statement Jesus tells us literally what he means by calling himself "the door" in relation to the sheep. He is the mediator of life with all its abundant blessings. We need not press this "abundance" to mean merely pasture for the sheep. It goes beyond that and includes everything connected with the door — and even this figure, as we shall see in a moment, is too weak to picture it all. All who approach the sheep by the door and remain in proper relation to the door are true shepherds, because they employ the mediation (δι' ἐμοῦ, v. 9) of Jesus; all others who reject this mediation are branded as thieves and robbers. At this point the interpretation of the paroimia (v. 1-6) ends. It intends to portray just so much, and what that is Jesus himself has set forth in clear and simple words.

11) The paroimia in v. 1-6 is a unit and its interpretation, v. 7-10, is another unit, the second exactly matching the first. Both pivot on Jesus as the door and distinguish the shepherd from the thief by the relation of each to the door. But what makes *Jesus* the door? In other words, why is the relation of any religious leader to this man Jesus so absolutely decisive, that if one uses Jesus he is, indeed, a shepherd, and if he rejects Jesus he is, indeed, a thief? The answer to this question lies in the conception which Jesus presents of himself as the door of the fold, but this conception is veiled in the image. In other words, this figure does not and can not reveal that vital point about Jesus. Therefore Jesus now draws this veil aside. He does this by means of a new figure. We hear no more about the door. A new picture is thrown on the screen. Its center and key is Jesus as the Good Shepherd. Around this center and, of course, in vital relation to it a new set of figures appears. While this new picture is different and thus distinct from the one first used, it is, nevertheless, related to the other. We now have the one Supreme Shepherd. We still have the sheep, but now the hireling is introduced, plus the wolf, and the vital point is the relation of the Great Shepherd and of the wretched hireling to the sheep, and of the sheep to them. Thus all that lies back of the figure of the door is now revealed by the allied picture. Again, as in the paroimia and its interpretation, law and gospel are combined in order to open the eyes of the blind and still more to enlighten those who see. This time the imagery and

its meaning are woven together, but in such a way that toward the end the language becomes entirely literal.

One interpretation starts with the observation that in the Old Testament kings are at times likened to shepherds and deduces that by calling himself the door and the shepherd Jesus here pictures himself as the true King of Israel over against the house of Herod as Idumean usurpers, the Asmoneans who also were illegitimate, the Sadducean high priests, and one or two pseudo-Messiahs; and the Pharisees are left out. This political conception, wholly foreign to Jesus, departs from the connection with the two previous sections which deal with the spiritual leadership of the Pharisees as teachers and say nothing about princely rule and princes. In the Old Testament no king is called "a door," to say nothing about the other impossibilities that result when princes and kings are found in the imagery of Jesus. In the Old Testament the figure of the shepherd is by no means confined to kings; in the New Testament it is certainly used only in a religious sense to refer to spiritual teachers and guides.

Twice Jesus says, "I am the door"; twice he now adds, **I am the Good Shepherd,** and the correspondence is not accidental. Here appears another great ἐγώ εἰμι, *I AM.* The linguistic points in the predicate ὁ ποιμὴν ὁ καλὸς are sufficient to free us from a number of fanciful ideas. When the predicate has the article it is identical and convertible with the subject, R. 768. Hence, this shepherd is absolutely in a class by himself; no other shepherd can ever be grouped with him. Thus we cannot attach to the article the idea of previous reference, for this Supreme Shepherd has not been mentioned before; nor the idea that this shepherd is now to be described, which is true but is not implied by the article; nor a reference to Old Testament prophecies (Ps. 23:1; 80:1; Ezek. 34:11-16; etc.), which nothing here indicates, as also the main point in the

description of this shepherd is entirely absent from the
Old Testament imagery of the shepherd.

Jesus does not add the adjective καλός predicatively;
for this would say only that "the shepherd is good" and
in the same class with other good shepherds. Jesus
says far more; he is in a class by himself. He does not
say ὁ καλὸς ποιμήν; for this would place the emphasis
only on "good" over against "bad," or on "excellent"
over against "inferior." Jesus does not here compare
himself with other shepherds; he asserts far more than
that he is relatively better than other shepherds, namely
that he is a shepherd in a sense in which no other man
can ever be a shepherd. This is the thought in making
the predicate read ὁ ποιμὴν ὁ καλός. By adding the adjective with a repetition of the article both the noun and
the adjective become strongly emphatic, and the latter
becomes a sort of climax, an apposition to the noun by
the use of a separate article, R. 776 and 468. Unfortunately, the English is unable to reproduce this weight
of meaning in translation. Jesus is *the shepherd,*
absolutely in a class by himself as the *shepherd;* and
he is *excellent* with an excellence unique and all his
own. *Der gute, der treffliche Hirte, schlechthin ge-
dacht, wie er sein soll; daher der Artikel und die
nachdrueckliche Stellung des Adjektivs.* Meyer.

At once the proof is added, the more effective because of the asyndeton: **The Good Shepherd lays
down his life in behalf of the sheep.** The expression
τιθέναι τὴν ψυχήν is peculiar to John who uses it repeatedly; M.-M. do not find it in the papyri. In order to
understand what Jesus means it is quite necessary to
take the entire predicate together: "lays down his life
in behalf of the sheep," as well as at once to add what
is made so emphatic in v. 17, 18 about his doing this
of his own accord and about taking up his life again.
One may, indeed, compare the laying down of a garment and taking it up again in 13:4 and 12, yet the
resemblance is only superficial. A better analogy

appears in 13:37 where Peter offers to lay down his life in behalf of Jesus, and in 15:13 where a friend lays down his life for his friends; but both of these fall far short in that neither has power to take up his life again as Jesus has. The act of Jesus is absolutely without analogy. Men may risk and even lose their lives for others, but that is all they are able to do; they cannot recover their lives. Jesus lays his life down "in order to take it up again" (v. 17). That is not merely an addition, a second act following the first; that shows that the first act differs essentially from any similar act of others.

This eliminates the idea drawn from v. 12 that Jesus, unlike the hireling, faces the wolf and lets the wolf kill him in defense of the sheep. Little good that would do the sheep, for after the shepherd is killed, the poor sheep would be utterly at the mercy of the wolf without a single hand to interpose. The only deliverance of the sheep would lie in the shepherd's killing or driving off the wolf, himself retaining his life for their benefit. Jesus is the one and only shepherd, who saves the sheep by laying down and then taking up his life again. We see that this is another case in which the human figure is too weak and small to cover the divine reality. The reality should not be reduced to the small dimensions of the figure. Where the figure gives out, we must do as Jesus does (v. 17, 18), proceed without figure, with the reality alone.

The meaning of Jesus is lost because of a limited view of the preposition ὑπέρ, of which it is said that this preposition cannot designate substitution, and that only ἀντί can mean "instead of." A study of R. 572, etc., on ἀντί and R. 630, etc., on ὑπέρ clears up the matter completely. We note that Abbott, *Johannine Grammar*, p. 276, finds that in almost all instances in John ὑπέρ denotes the death of one for the many. Robertson, *The Minister and his Greek New Testament*, 35, etc., has an entire chapter on ὑπέρ as designating "in-

stead of" in the ostraca and the papyri. We quote:
"When we turn to the New Testament from the papyri
there can, of course, be no grammatical reluctance to
allowing the same usage for ὑπέρ if the context calls
for it. Theological prejudice must be overruled." "It
is futile to try to get rid of substitution on grammatical arguments about ὑπέρ." "The grace of our
Lord Jesus Christ appears precisely in this, that,
though rich, he became poor that we, through his poverty, might become rich. That is substitution. The
one who knew no sin God made to be sin in our stead
(ὑπέρ) that we might become God's righteousness in
him (II Cor. 5:21). All this and more Paul poured
into the preposition ὑπέρ. The papyri forbid our
emptying ὑπέρ of this wealth of meaning in the interest
of any theological theory." Moulton, Deissmann, and
other authorities on the ostraca and the papyri in
relation to the language of the New Testament agree.

In brief, ἀντί really means "at the end of" and thus
suggests contrast, succession, substitution, opposition,
as the case may be; while ὑπέρ means "over" and thus
comes to mean "concerning," "beyond," "in behalf of,"
"instead of." The context invariably decides. We
may translate ὑπέρ "in behalf of," but this is no more
exact than "instead of." When Jesus dies ὑπέρ the
sheep and then takes back his life again, the only sense
in which this could possibly benefit the sheep is by way
of substitution — he dies in their stead. An ordinary
shepherd might die in defense of his flock, but this
would not benefit his flock in the least; after he was
dead, the flock would become a helpless prey. Jesus
came that the sheep may have life and may have abundance (v. 10). This is achieved, strange to say, by
his vicarious and substitutionary death and by the still
stranger act of again taking back his life out of death.
How this death serves in winning life for the sheep is
seen in Matt. 20:28 and Mark 10:45, "he gives his life
as a ransom for many," λύτρον ἀντὶ πολλῶν. The idea of

a ransom is not brought in here where the imagery of the shepherd and the sheep is used. But it is in vain to argue that the sheep already belong to the Shepherd and thus cannot yet be acquired by him; or that his ideal possession of the sheep cannot here be turned into a real possession. All such stressing of the figure in order to bar out the idea of substitution in ὑπέρ is beside the mark, for it bars out much more, namely the entire idea of this Supreme Shepherd with his power to lay down his life and to take it up again — something that is utterly beyond anything we know of human shepherds. When saying that he lays down his life "for the sheep," the sacrifice of Jesus, which is for the world and all men, is viewed with reference to its actual final result, which appears in the saved. This view is taken repeatedly in the Scriptures and never furnishes the least ground for the idea of a limited atonement.

The astonishing realities here clothed in the figure of the shepherd and the sheep are chiefly two: first, that instead of some sheep of the flock serving as a blood-sacrifice for the shepherd, here the very reverse takes place — the shepherd makes himself the blood-sacrifice for the sheep; secondly, that whereas all other blood-sacrifices yield their lives in sacrificial death never to regain them, this marvelous shepherd does, indeed, like them also yield his life but, absolutely unlike them, takes his life back again. A third point may be added: all other blood-sacrifices die without volition of their own, this shepherd of his own will dies for the sheep. And a fourth: no other blood-sacrifice by its death brings forth and bestows life upon others, but this is exactly what the blood-sacrifice of the Supreme Shepherd does. Only Jesus has ever used a human figure in this divine manner, and unless we rise to the realities thus actually pictured by him, we ourselves, like the blind Pharisees, remain in the dark.

Here Jesus prophesies, for only in the light of his actual death and resurrection can these realities be understood. None of the hearers of Jesus understood the full import of his words at the moment. He speaks for the future, just as he does in so many other instances. After the brief space of six months all will be plain. That too, we may take it, is why Jesus uses this figurative language with its astonishing relation to the realities, language which by its very form is bound to embed itself in the memories of his hearers, on which they will ponder until the final actualities reveal all its divine meaning.

12) **The hireling, not also being a shepherd, whose own the sheep are not, beholds the wolf coming and leaves the sheep and flees; and the wolf snatches them and scatters — because he is only a hireling and is not concerned about the sheep.** It lies on the surface that the negative picture of the hireling is intended to throw into full relief the positive image of the Good Shepherd. Some think that this is all, and thus make their task of interpretation very easy: the hireling is an imaginary person, intended to portray nobody in particular, and the drama of the wolf is a mere embellishment without reality back of the picture. It has well been objected that this view cannot be correct, because Jesus describes the hireling at such length. Everybody also, at least as far as the author has found, forgets about the true and faithful human shepherds, so beautifully and completely pictured to us in their relation to the sheep in v. 2-4, who most certainly must be placed between the Supreme Shepherd on the one hand and the hireling on the other. These true human shepherds are not imaginary but godly teachers and guides of the flock; hence also the hireling cannot be a mere shadow but must be the opposite of the true human shepherds, a picture of all false prophets, teachers, and guides, those of the days

of Jesus and of all other days. As the godly teachers resemble Jesus in their love and care for the flock, so the hireling is their very opposite. And this, too, Jesus brings out in his picture of the hireling, and it helps us not a little in understanding his meaning.

We should not think of the human shepherd and teacher portrayed in v. 2-4 as being the actual owner of the sheep, for no human teacher owns the children of God over whom he is placed. This aids us in regard to the hireling. We are not to think of him as a hired hand employed for wages by the owner of the sheep and thus serving as a substitute shepherd in care of the sheep, let us say at least temporarily, perhaps only for a day. He is not hired by the owner of the sheep, he has no connection with him in any way. This becomes clearer when we note that even Jesus is not the real owner of the sheep. They belong to God. Only because he is sent by God on the great mission of redemption is Jesus placed over the sheep. "Thine they are, and thou gavest them to me" (17:6). Only thus does Jesus "have" the sheep (v. 16) and does he call them "mine own" (v. 14). Then as the Father sent Jesus to be the Supreme Shepherd, so Jesus in turn sends all true teachers also as shepherds under himself (17:18). This helps to show who the hireling really is. Jesus never hired, employed, or sent him in any way. "Not also being a shepherd," καὶ οὐκ ὢν ποιμήν, means that the name "shepherd" does not in any sense include him. We cannot translate, "He that is a hireling and not the shepherd" (A. V.), or "a shepherd" (R. V.), because ὁ μισθωτός is definite, "the hireling," and the subject of the sentence not a predicate after ὤν. The ὤν is merely attributive to μισθωτός (R. 764), and καί is "also"; a hireling, as such "not also" like Jesus and the teachers sent by Jesus, in any manner to be classed with them as a shepherd. Observe that οὐ with the participle ὤν makes the negation clear-cut (read R.

1136 and 1163) and means that as a hireling he is the direct opposite of a shepherd.

"Whose own the sheep are not" thus has nothing to do with real ownership but denies only the delegated ownership such as a shepherd has (v. 2-4) to whom the sheep are entrusted by the owner. Jesus never sent him or entrusted him with a single sheep. How the hireling managed to get hold of the sheep is left unsaid yet with the plain implication that it was done in an illegal way. He usurped the place of the shepherd; he stole the sheep in some way. Here the figure of the thief and the robber amalgamates with that of the hireling, and the latter amplifies the former. Neither thief nor hireling cares for the life or the welfare of the sheep, as we see this primarily in Jesus (v. 10b), and secondarily in those sent by Jesus (v. 2-4). All the hireling-thief wants is sooner or later to kill the sheep, in order to enrich himself with the flesh, hide, and wool of the sheep. In this process the poor sheep perish; they lose everything in order that the hireling-thief may gain something.

Now we see why the man thus described, first by a participial modifier and secondly by a relative clause, is termed a μισθωτός or "hireling." We must drop the meaning "hired servant" (Mark 1:20) and any hiring by Jesus. The μισθός or "pay" this man expects is not derived from Jesus, but consists of what the fellow is able to extract from making away with the sheep he has stolen. If he were a hired man with legitimate wages and thus connected with the sheep, he would in some sense at least be a shepherd, an unfaithful shepherd, indeed, for running off in the hour of danger, yet even then a shepherd; but this he is not, οὐκ ὤν. Due to the portrait here drawn by Jesus the term "hireling" has come to stand for a base type of character, one that is venal, mercenary, utterly selfish. In the portrait drawn by Jesus we have this type of character in its most fully developed form. This hireling is a hireling through and through. In actual life we often meet men who exhibit only some one hireling trait, but this does not affect the picture here drawn by Jesus, which has often enough found its complete counterpart in real life.

Beyond question, this hireling portrays all false religious teachers found in the visible church. The portrait is extreme in order to include also the worst teachers of this type. The lesser and partial types are thereby not excluded. Jesus undoubtedly had in mind the Pharisees as a class, some of whom stood before him at the moment; he had in mind the Sadducees as well, for their influence on the people was equally pernicious. The hireling character of the Sanhedrin and of its leaders is plainly brought to view in 11:48; even Pilate saw it, Matt. 27:18; Mark 15:10. Other figurative portrayals of it are found in Matt. 22:38; 24:48, 49. The objection that, if Jesus intended the thief and the robber to apply to the false Jewish leaders, the hireling, because it is a different figure, cannot also apply to them, is groundless. Not only are the two figures related, as has been shown, their very difference brings out two allied wicked features in these Jewish leaders, showing in two ways what their true character is, how far they are from God and Jesus, and how ill God's children fare at their hands. Moreover, does not Jesus also use two figures with reference to himself: the door and the Good Shepherd?

Some commentators do not seem to understand what the wolf is really intended to picture. It is true that the wolf is the natural enemy of the sheep, and that thus we here have the wolf and not the lion or the bear (I Sam. 17:34-37). If, however, the sheep signify the actual children of God, then their natural enemy cannot be a mere figure of speech without substance. This wolf does actual damage to God's children, and actual damage to actual people is not wrought by mere embellishments of rhetoric. These ways of interpreting the wolf are unrewarding.

Another way is to parallel the wolf with the doorkeeper in v. 3. Since nobody in particular is prefigured by the latter, nobody in particular is said to be prefigured by the former. True, the doorkeeper is only incidental to the door of the fold, for the thief would even prefer an unguarded door to climbing the wall, and thus the door and its keeper come to con- stitute a unit image. Jesus is not the unguarded door by which anybody may reach the sheep at will; he is the guarded door of the fold, and only as the guarded door does he reveal who the shepherds and who the thieves are. Let us also avoid the thought that the guarded door actually protects the sheep against all harm. The thief gets to the sheep in spite of the door and does them harm. But where is there anything that is in any way like the door, with which we might combine the image of the wolf and thus eliminate any special interpretation of the wolf? The search reveals only the more that the wolf is an independent figure and therefore portrays an actuality.

More promising is the reference to Matt. 7:15, where the false prophets in sheep's clothing appear as rending wolves, and to Acts 20:29, where false teachers as grievous wolves spare not the flock; for here the devil and his agents are identified. Yet they are not always thus identified; see I Pet. 5:8; Eph. 4:27; 6:11; James 4:7; Rev. 20:2 and 10; and other passages. The argument that, since the Pharisees are identified with the devil (even called his children, 8:44), the devil cannot here be opposed to the hireling, unless forsooth we mean to chase the Pharisees by the Pharisees, thus proves untenable. Such refer-

ences to the devil only obscure the main point of the
figures of Jesus, which unquestionably centers in the
sheep. From the door down to the wolf the life and
the welfare of the sheep are the pivot on which everything turns: "that they may have life and may have
abundance." Yes, when the sheep are obscured, we
see only the hireling running away from the wolf.
But Jesus says that the hireling runs away from the
sheep: "he leaves the sheep and flees"; Jesus makes
the wolf attack, not the hireling, but the sheep: "he
snatches them and scatters." Always, always the
sheep are placed in the center. Thus the hireling
and the wolf actually cooperate in the hurt to the
sheep: the former contributes his part by running
away from the sheep, and the latter his part by pounc-
ing upon the sheep.

Surely, we all feel a tacit implication at this point.
If, instead of this hireling, one of the true shepherds
of Jesus were with the sheep, he would attack the
wolf, if necessary, yield his life in the combat and thus
prove himself a genuine shepherd. The church has had
such noble undershepherds, who had learned well
their role in the school of Jesus.

Many are agreed that the wolf does denote a reality.
Those who deny the existence of the devil bar this
being out on *a priori* grounds. They reconstruct the
sacred texts according to their own assumptions, not
only on this but likewise on many other points. To
them the debate is no longer on exegetical questions.
They are free to discard the entire Gospel of John. In
seeking for the reality intended by the wolf many good
Bible scholars decline to admit that this reality is the
devil. They admit the devil's existence, even as the
Scriptures teach, but when it comes to the wolf, without assigning any actual reason, they simply say that
the devil is out of the question. They prefer some
tool or tools of the devil, even saying that the devil

is behind these tools. They think of the Roman power, or more indefinitely of the anti-Christian world power, of the heretics, or quite abstractly of the principle of evil. It is certainly true that the devil works through many agencies in seeking to destroy God's flock. Yet, as in this case, the Scriptures frequently leave these agencies unmentioned and speak of the archenemy of the church himself. Until sounder reasons are offered why the wolf here prefigures, not the devil himself, but only his tools, we are constrained to hold that the wolf is the devil. Nothing also does he like better than to find a hireling with God's sheep instead of some shepherd sent by Jesus and made courageous by him. Then he can complete what the hireling has begun: snatch with his fangs and kill by destroying the faith in the hearts of God's children; scatter helplessly those not at once spiritually crushed by making them shift for themselves in the wilderness of this world until he either snatches them too or until their spiritual life faints and dies out of itself.

13) Twice the wolf is mentioned; twice the hireling; even as Jesus twice declares, "I am the Good Shepherd." Note also the arrangement: in the center: "wolf . . . wolf"; on either side of the wolf: "hireling . . . hireling"; on either side of the hireling: "I am the Good Shepherd . . . I am the Good Shepherd." This pattern is by no means accidental. By the fact that they are mentioned, all three are made important. So we now revert to the hireling. Why does he act as just described? Because he is what he is: "a hireling." The word is now the predicate, whereas before it was the subject; hence we now have no article, thus stressing the quality expressed in the term — a base, abominable hireling.

When first mentioned, the hireling is characterized by his relation to the sheep; in the second mention likewise, but with a marked difference: first, Jesus never made him a shepherd and never placed him over any of his sheep; secondly, in his own heart he has no love for the sheep. Two things mark the true human shepherd: Jesus places him in charge of some of his sheep; he himself is filled with concern for the sheep in his charge. As the hireling has no inward relation to the Supreme Shepherd Jesus, so also he has no inward relation to any of the sheep for which the Supreme Shepherd Jesus lays down his life. These two negatives really are one; neither exists without the other. So the opposite positives are also one, neither being found in a man without the other. The hireling is centered only in — himself. Let the wolf rend and scatter, just so the hireling saves his own hide.

14, 15)   **I am the Good Shepherd** — this testimony rings out for the second time. More sharply even than before the pure white image of the Good Shepherd stands out against the black background of the hireling. Yet this is by no means all. Jesus is contrasting himself with the false teachers and leaders of the Jews. It is their own black image that stands out the blacker against the pure white of Jesus. This contrast, terrible as we look from Jesus to the Pharisees and their allies, blessed as we look from them to him, Jesus leaves in the memories of his enemies there to do its work; to act, if possible, as a blow to crush the conscience and then as a balm to bind up and to heal; and if this be not possible, to act as a sentence of judgment and doom. They will remember — this they cannot help; they will question again and again what he meant. In six brief months the actual death and the actual resurrection of the Good Shepherd, now foretold so clearly, will re-enforce every word they have heard. No; none of these words are mere rhetorical embellishment; all of them reveal vital facts.

We have two parts, each headed, "I am the Good Shepherd." The first shows him to be that by his relation to the sheep (v. 11-13); the second, by his relation to the Father as well as to the sheep (v. 14-18). The first presents only the main act, laying down his life; the second again presents this act (v. 17, etc.) more fully and adds its connection with the Father as well as its result for the sheep (v. 14-16). The first remains on earth, the second joins heaven and earth. The wolf, the hireling, the door, the Good Shepherd are each mentioned twice, the latter two with the mighty *I AM* emphasis. The Father is mentioned three times and each time in connection with the Good Shepherd's office; the Father gave him that office (v. 18, last sentence), loves him for executing its supreme part (v. 17), knows him as owning him for his own (v. 14) — these three stated in reverse order.

I am the Good Shepherd and **I know mine own, and mine own know me, even as the Father knows me, and I know the Father; and my life I lay down in behalf of the sheep.** The very name "Good Shepherd" connotes "the sheep" that belong to him and for whom he is such a shepherd. So here again everything circles about the sheep. The figure is retained throughout, for τὰ ἐμά is neuter, not "mine own" (persons) but "mine own" (sheep, πρόβατα); but, as now used, this figure becomes completely transparent. "Mine own" sheep are all who in heart and soul, by living faith and trust belong to Jesus who dies in their stead and rises again. "Mine own" is in silent contrast to others who are "not mine own," all those who refuse to yield heart and soul in trust to Jesus and his sacrifice. Nothing further is here said con-

cerning these others, simply because they are away
from the line of thought.

Four times Jesus uses the verb γινώσκειν in its pregnant sense, which has been well defined as *noscere cum
affectu et effectu*, to know with love and appropriat-
tion as one's very own and to reveal that loving ownership by all the corresponding actions. Not to know
thus is to realize what is not one's own and to repudiate what is thus not known. When the verb is
used in this intensive sense, we must be careful not
to eliminate the idea of knowing with the mind and
intellect, for to this basic meaning the thought of
ownership, appropriation, love, and all the manifestations of love are added. While the added thought extends to the affections and the will and thus intensifies
the concept, this added thought does not eliminate
the knowing of the mind and turn it into an act of
the will. Compare II Tim. 2:19, and for the negative
Matt. 7:23. In this affective and effective way the
Father "knows" Jesus and Jesus "knows" him.
After the same manner (καθώς) Jesus "knows" his
own, and they "know" him. The latter can, of course,
be only "as" the former, because of the disparity in
the persons. The divine persons are equal, and they
know each other accordingly. The Good Shepherd
and his own are not equal; his own are only men with
such spiritual abilities as they have acquired. Yet the
relation between the divine Savior and the human
souls he has saved is a lovely reflection of the supreme
relation between the Father and the Son. Always
and always Jesus "knows" his own and in countless
blessed ways manifests that he knows. And always
they "know" him, their Good Shepherd, and all that he
is to them. In this life their knowledge of him is
still imperfect and must constantly grow; but even in
the life to come their knowledge of him will be that
of finite creatures, while his knowledge of them is

divine. Here is the place for many comforting applications. The neuter plural τὰ ἐμά is here used with the plural verb γινώσκουσι, showing that the Koine has broken away from the Attic rule of construing neuter plurals only with singular verbs. This is done not merely because persons are referred to, the rule as such no longer holds, and liberty prevails. R. 403, etc.

The effort to connect the γνῶσις of which Jesus here speaks, together with the γνῶσις which Paul expounds in First Corinthians, with that of the pagan Hellenic mysteries, or at least to draw light from the latter for the true understanding of the former, has proven abortive. The two move in mutually exclusive spheres. The pagan idea is pantheistic, mingling him who knows with him that is known; the Christian idea is theistic, never mingling the two. Paul even ranks γνῶσις far lower than ἀγάπη and πίστις — spiritual fields into which pagan thought never entered. The character of the pagan γνῶσις is magically physical, and it is doubtful whether it ever rose to something even mental; the character of Christian γνῶσις is spiritual throughout and personal in the highest degree. The more we trust and love Jesus, the more we know him and realize just who he is and what he is to us. C.-K. 244.

While it is true enough that the hireling does not "know" the sheep, since they are not even "his own," even as the sheep do not "know" him, it is more than doubtful that Jesus still has the hireling in mind. Instead of looking downward to illustrate by means of a contrast, Jesus now looks upward to illustrate by a similarity: "even as the Father," etc. The tenses used are present, and yet they evidently refer to no specific time, being true for any and all time. Let us call them gnomic (R. 866).

When Jesus adds with καί, "and my life I lay down
in behalf of (instead of) the sheep," this repetition
from v. 11 is made coordinate with the preceding
and must not be made subordinate even in our thought,
as if Jesus means, "I know mine own, etc., *because*
I lay down my life," etc.   The true connection is:
"I am the Good Shepherd": first evidence: "and my
life I lay down," etc.   The sense of the repetition
is the same as in v. 10.   The subject lies in the verb
τίθημι and is thus in the first person, a merely formal
change.   The emphasis on "my life" (nothing less!)
is the same as in v. 10.   In both verses we have the
present tense, "I lay down," which, indeed, is futuristic, "I am laying down," i. e., will do so presently;
but not as R. 870 suggests, "covering the whole of
Christ's life viewed as a unit (constative aorist)."
This would mean that Jesus "lays down his life" for
the sheep by living his life for their benefit, whereas
what Jesus means is that he lays down his life by
dying, for he takes it up again (v. 17) by his resurrection from the dead.

16)   Because they are general and thus indefinite
the gnomic tenses in v. 14 require that something more
should be added.   After saying that Jesus knows his
own (sheep), and that they know him, he now adds
that he is thinking of all his sheep throughout all the
ages of the world.   **And other sheep I have which
are not of this fold; them also I must lead, and they
will hear my voice.   And there shall be one flock,
one shepherd.**   The word "other" is defined by the
relative clause, "which are not of this fold."   Yet
the implication is not a second fold in which these
other sheep exist.   Jesus knows only of one church or
kingdom of God.   When he spoke, this existed in the
form of the old covenant originally made with Abraham and embraced the true children of God in the
Jewish nation and the few Gentiles who had come to

the true faith and had identified themselves with this
true Israel of God. Paul knows of only *one* olive tree
in Rom. 11:7, from which the unbelieving Jews were
broken out and into which the believing Gentiles shall
be grafted. In Eph. 2:12 he writes of only *one* household and city, into which the Jews and the Gentiles
are equally admitted, being not any longer two classes
but one. These "other sheep," then, are the hosts of
future Gentile believers.

Jesus says only that they "are not of this fold,"
that they did not grow up in the old covenant. He
does not say that he will "bring" them into "this fold,"
i. e., as this is now constituted in the old covenant.
The verb is ἀγαγεῖν, "to lead" as a shepherd leads
his flock, not συναγαγεῖν or προσαγαγεῖν. The Gentiles
are not to become Jews in order to become members
of the flock. What he says is that he will lead them
as the Shepherd just as he leads the believers of
Israel. A new era and covenant is thus in prospect,
which will be consummated under Jesus when his
redemptive mission is accomplished. He speaks of
these "other sheep" as already being πρόβατα or "sheep"
and even says that "I have" them. It has rightly
been urged that this is not a mere prolepsis; "other
sheep" might possibly be, but certainly not the verb
"I have." Compare similar statements in 11:52 and
Acts 18:10. "I have" denotes divine foreknowledge
and, we may add, predestination; but the latter not
in the sense of an absolute decree, or a decree according to some mysterious principle which simply selects
some and passes by others. Just as Jesus foresaw
the existence of these other sheep as men, born into
human life, so he foresaw the success of his saving
grace in their hearts, the birth of their spiritual life
as children of God. As far as predestination is
concerned, this embraces all in whom the grace and
gospel of Jesus succeed to the end. These God chose

for himself as his own elect even before the world began.

With the hosts of future Gentile believers before his prophetic eyes, Jesus says not only, "them also I must lead," but adds the counterpart, "and they will hear my voice." As their Shepherd Jesus will lead them, and as his sheep they will hear his voice. The verbs "must lead" and "will hear" correspond so closely to shepherd leading and sheep hearing and following their shepherd, that ἀγαγεῖν cannot mean "bring" or "feed." How these Gentiles become believers is not indicated. Why should it be, when it is in the same way as Jews come to faith? Jesus portrays these Gentiles as his sheep, following him as their Shepherd, just as his Jewish believers now follow him. The conversion is taken for granted where faith and trust bind to Jesus. The force of ἀκούσουσιν is not merely futuristic: "shall hear," but volitive: "will hear." It is not that Jesus and his voice bring about the hearing, but that these sheep, always listening for his voice, are willing to hear so that they may follow. Jesus says, "them I must lead" (δεῖ). Why "must" he? Because this is his office as the Good Shepherd. His redemptive mission will then be accomplished and at an end, but he will remain the Good Shepherd. His very death and resurrection a brief six months hence will usher him into his world-wide shepherd work during all the coming years. Brought from the dead, he will still be "the shepherd of the sheep" in connection with (ἐν) the blood of the eternal covenant, Heb. 13:20. Years after his glorification Peter calls him "the Shepherd and Bishop of your souls," I Pet. 2:25.

Thus Jesus adds, "and there shall be one flock, one shepherd." Eph. 4:4-6: One church, one Lord. Whether we read the singular γενήσεται, "there shall be" (impersonal), or the plural γενήσονται, "they shall be," makes but little difference, although the singular seems better. All racial, national, social, educational, and other differences are abolished. The R. V. translates "shall become," in distinction from the A. V.'s "shall be." The former may refer to a process that will not be completed until the consummation. All believers in Christ have ever been "one flock" under "one shepherd." Not in the sense of the Roman Catholic Church, one outward, visible organization but in the far deeper and truer sense of one communion of saints, all being brethren by faith under one Master, one spiritual body, the *Una Sancta.* This is the essential unity of the church. All who have faith, all who are justified and pardoned, are in this unity; all others are outside of it. "There shall be" is definite and decisive, with no degrees and nothing halfway. For this oneness Jesus never prays. It exists and needs no prayers, and it exists as perfect, with no rent or breach. In his high-priestly prayer (17:17, etc.) Jesus prays for a different oneness, namely that all his believers, who are one by faith in him, may also be one in the Word of truth (I Cor. 1:10), holding the divine truth with one mind, one in doctrine, free from all error. For every error means danger to the spiritual bond that joins to Christ and joins us to each other. Only by guarding his Word are we his disciples indeed, 8:31, 32.

A dangerous misconception in regard to "the other sheep" makes these "the God-seekers" in the pagan world, who, when Jesus comes to them, "shall hear his voice" and join his flock, while the rest turn a deaf ear. Entrance into the one flock is not thus decided in advance in pagan hearts. Some that we might call "God-seekers" spurn the gospel, and some that we may think utterly depraved in superstition and vice yield to the gospel. None are shut out in advance. As none are shut out in advance by a divine abso-

lute decree, predestinating them to hell, so none are
shut out in advance by their own sinful and depraved
state. The gospel is full of the *gratia sufficiens*,
not merely for a certain fortunate class but for all
men alike. This grace is not dependent upon a certain amount of aid in man, so that without that aid
it fails; its efficacy and power to save lie in itself
alone. Rom. 1:16.

17) The act which both makes and reveals Jesus
as the Good Shepherd has already been impressed upon
us by two statements: he lays down his life for the
sheep. Due to this act he has the sheep whom he
knows and who know him (v. 14), also the other sheep
who together with the first shall constitute one grand
flock under him as the Supreme Shepherd. This great
act of self-sacrifice is so important that he elucidates it
most fully. **For this reason the Father loves me
that I lay down my life in order to take it up again.**
It is true, the various forms of οὗτος (here διὰ τοῦτο)
often refer back to what has just been said. Here,
however, this is not the case because ὅτι follows and
as an apposition states what "this reason" is, R. 965.
The attempts to make "for this reason" refer back
to v. 16 end up by after all making ὅτι refer to διὰ τοῦτο.
This connection lies in the very nature of the statement made about the Father's love for Jesus. Whatever may be said of love in connection with the sheep
gathered into one flock by Jesus is bound to involve the
great sacrifice by which this gathering of the sheep is
accomplished. The Father loves Jesus, not merely because of all these sheep, but because of the sacrifice by
which he wins these sheep.

The Father, of course, loves Jesus as his Son irrespective of his mission in the world. Not of this love
does Jesus here speak but of the love which Jesus
wins by voluntarily assuming and faithfully executing
the Father's plan for bestowing. redemption on the

lost world, a task to be accomplished only by the sacrifice of himself. Here the verb ἀγαπᾶν is fully in place, to love with complete understanding and with a purpose to match that understanding. The Father's whole heart goes out to his Son as he lays his human life down in the sacrifice of death. The Father knows all that this means for Jesus, prizes his act as he alone can prize, and uses it for the glory of himself and of his Son.

The emphasis on ἐγώ should not be overlooked: "I, I myself" lay down my life, I of my own free will. In a moment this will be made still plainer. And the act of which Jesus speaks is not merely his death. Like other blood-sacrifices to die and to remain dead, would avail nothing, would, in fact, be less than nothing — at best a heroic effort that ends in abject failure. Jesus lays down his life for the very purpose of taking it up again. Both acts are his; the two are halves of one whole. Only thus will he be the Good Shepherd his Father intends him to be; only thus will he be the one great Shepherd of the Father's one great flock; only thus can and will the Father's great plan be realized for the world. Therefore, neither grammatically nor merely in our thought dare we separate the laying down from the taking up. We must not translate, as S. Goebel points out: "The Father loves me because I lay down my life — (but I do it only) in order to take it up again." This sacrifice is like none that ever occurred before, because it indeed effects what all others could not effect, what they could only foreshadow. This sacrifice actually atones, actually redeems, and, doing that, the life laid down is not forfeited but is to be taken up again as freely as it was laid down. The human body and life, once laid down as a ransom for us, are now enthroned in glory at the Father's right hand.

18) Voluntary in the highest degree is the act
of Jesus in laying down his life and, therefore,
it merits the Father's love in an equal degree.
**No one takes it from me, on the contrary, I my-
self lay it down of myself.** We need not trouble
about the reading with the aorist ἦρεν: "no one took
it," etc., R. V. margin, as this lacks both sufficient
authority and harmony with the thought. "No one"
has no reference to the Father but only to hostile
powers. His enemies will, indeed, crucify Jesus, and
it will seem as if they take his life from him; but this
is not the fact. The very contrary is true: it is Jesus
himself who of himself by a free volition of his own
yields himself to their hands (18:4-11 and Matt.
26:52-54; 19:28-30 and Luke 23:46). Jesus makes
this so emphatic, first for his believers, that they may
remember it when the time comes; secondly, for the
Jews who are so anxious to kill him, that they, too,
may remember when the time comes. Both are then
to recall that by his voluntary death Jesus wins the
supreme love of his Father.

But this emphatic statement calls for further
elucidation. Did not Jesus say in 5:19 that the Son
is able to do nothing "of himself," ἀφ' ἑαυτοῦ? How,
then, can he now say that he lays down his life "of
himself," ἀπ' ἐμαυτοῦ? Here is the answer: **Power
have I to lay it down, and power have I to take it up
again. This commission I received from my Father.**
Both are true: first, that Jesus can do nothing of himself, i. e., without the Father or contrary to the
Father; secondly, that he can of himself give his life,
i. e., as a free and voluntary act carried out by him
alone. In the loving behest with which he sent his
Son on his redemptive mission the Father himself gave
him right, authority, and power to follow his own
will. No one English word has the exact meaning
of ἐξουσία here used in diverse connections; hence the

difference in translation, which seeks to keep the same word for the two connections. "Power" fits well for taking up the life but not well for laying down the life; "right" or "authority" fit the dying but hardly the rising. What Jesus means is entirely plain: he is free to do both, lay down and take up his life again. Note that ἐξουσία is derived from ἔξεστι, which means "it is free"; and thus the noun shades from the idea of the right and authority to act to that of the power to act. While Jesus uses two parallel statements to express his thought, it would be a mistake for us to separate them in our minds by speaking of his liberty to do the one act and yet *not* the other. No such choice presents itself to his will as to lay down his life and not take it up again; but only to lay it down in order to take it up again (v. 17), or to do neither. In these matters it is idle to raise hypothetical questions, and it is worse to raise them while splitting normal units by abstractions.

Jesus must go one step farther and state how he comes to use his ἐξουσία as he does, how he makes the choice, instead of keeping his life to lay it down in order to take it up again. This is due to the "commission" he has received and accepted from his Father. The ἐξουσία resides in Jesus himself as God's Son — no one could compel him to lay down his life. The Father, of course, would be the last to think of such compulsion. If Jesus, then, lays down his life in order to take it up again, i. e., to go through the bitterness of death in our stead, it is, and in the very nature of the case can be, only by his own free volition. But something induces him to use his free volition in this way. We might say that it is his love for us, his desire to save the world. His motive is far higher. It is one which is so high that it includes anything he might say regarding his love for

us. He decides as he does because he desires to please
his Father. He and his Father are one in their will to
save the world. Thus the Father gave him this ἐντολή
to lay down his life and to take it up again in order
to redeem us, and Jesus accepted it from his Father.
By pointing to his taking this commission from his
Father, Jesus reveals to us his deepest or, let us say,
his highest, motive.

The translation "command" may mislead. Commands are peremptory, issued by a superior to a subordinate. Commands are compulsory and shut out
free volition. No command of that kind prompts the
act of Jesus. Such a command would rob his act of
the very thing that makes it so pleasing to his
Father (Eph. 5:2). Nor is this ἐντολή a moral obligation and a "command" in this sense, something
that Jesus ought to do, as we ought to obey the
Decalog and, failing which, he would in some way be
morally remiss. Jesus is under no moral pressure
whatever, either in the matter of passing through
death for us, or in the first place accepting his
Father's commission. He was just as free to decline
as to accept. This ἐντολή is a commission which the
Father requests the Son to assume and which he
freely assumes because he and his Father are one
in their desire to save the world. When offering this
commission to his Son the Father appeals to love;
by accepting that commission the Son responds with
his love. Both the offer and the acceptance lie on
the highest possible plane. And now we know how
Jesus became our Good Shepherd by giving his live
for us, and what it is that makes him such a shepherd.
We have looked into both his heart and into that of
his Father.

19) These wondrous words had their effect. **A
division again arose among the Jews because of**

these words, just as happened temporarily in 9:16, and more decisively already in 7:40-44.

20) **And many of them were saying, He has a demon and raves. Why do you listen to him?** Compare 7:20 and 8:48. These are the majority and find no reply except to revile. That is the easiest answer, even if it is quite irrational to attribute such words of Jesus to a demon using his tongue for mad raving. The real intention of this majority comes out in their question. They evidently see that Jesus is making an impression on some of his hearers. This provokes them. They seek to turn everybody against him.

21) But their effort only provokes a telling reply from the minority. **Others were saying, These are not the utterings of one demon-possessed.** No; not the least resemblance could anyone note — only the absolutely opposite. First, an assertion like that of the majority; then, a question again like them. **Can a demon open eyes of blind people?** He certainly cannot! He could and would do only the opposite. The plural "eyes of blind people" generalizes from the one notable case, 9:6, etc. The minority is impressed by both Jesus' word and his act. And thus this visit of Jesus to Jerusalem (7:10, etc.) closes. The two imperfects ἔλεγον leave the situation hanging in the air; John lets it hang thus without adding a final aorist of any kind.

X. *Jesus' Attestation as the Messiah at the Feast of Dedication, 22-42*

22) **And it was the Feast of the Dedication in Jerusalem. It was winter.** This festival, called *Chanukah,* was instituted by Judas Maccabaeus in 167 B. C. in commemoration of the cleansing and re-

dedication of the Temple after its profanation by Antiochus Epiphanes. The annual celebration lasted eight days beginning the 25th of Chisleu (about the middle of December) and was observed throughout the country, a special feature consisting in illuminating the houses, from which fact the festival was called τὰ φῶτα, "the Lights." When John adds to the mention of the festival the phrase "in Jerusalem" to designate the place, this would be superfluous if Jesus had spent the intervening two months (7:2, end of October to the end of December) in the city. He left shortly after the October celebration and had now returned. This is substantiated by what is now reported. The new situation and the new testimony Jesus utters connect directly with the last that he spoke before leaving the city (10:1, etc., in regard to his sheep). Where he broke off two months ago there he now begins. The situation, highly strained during that last visit (chapters 7-10:21), now reaches its climax (10:39), and Jesus leaves the city for good, not to return until the Passover in the spring, when he will enter upon his passion and his death. Quite in the same way the miracle recorded in 5:2, etc., for which the Jews resolved to kill Jesus (5:18), is taken up again after the lapse of an entire year on the return of Jesus to the city (7:10) in his very first clash with the Jews (7:19 and 23).

We cannot assume that Jesus spent the two months in the city, either hid away from the Jews, or teaching in public. If he had appeared in public, the situation would have moved on of its own momentum, and 10:26, etc., could not connect, as it does, with 10:1-18. Where Jesus spent the two months after leaving the city John does not tell us. All that we have is recorded in 10:40: "he went away again," ἀπῆλθε πάλιν where the adverb intimates that he returned to the place beyond the Jordan, i. e., that this was the locality to which he had retired.

The remark that it was winter is, of course, not intended to inform us about the season of the year but to explain the next statement that Jesus was walking in a sheltered place in the Temple.

23) **And Jesus was walking in the Temple in the porch of Solomon,** the covered colonnade that offered some protection from the weather on that wintry day. Josephus, *Ant.* 20, 9, 7, informs us that this portico was the only part of the old Temple of Solomon left standing after the destruction wrought by Nebuchadnezzar, and was thus named "the porch of Solomon." Here Jesus "was walking" to and fro for greater comfort in the cold. John again says nothing about the disciples, and the opinion is offered that Jesus is alone at the moment. This would make the ensuing encounter still more dramatic; but it is better to assume that the disciples are walking with Jesus as usual, and that John omits mention of them because they play no part in what transpires.

24) **The Jews, therefore, surrounded him and were saying, How long dost thou hold us in suspense? If thou art the Christ, tell us openly!** The connective οὖν indicates that the Jews see their opportunity and embrace it. Here Jesus suddenly again appears in their midst; he is alone except for his disciples; now they can have it out with him. By a concerted action they surround and enclose him, meaning that he shall not again get away. No friendly multitude is at hand to support him and to stay their hand. Jesus is suddenly face to face with his bitter enemies, who are now bound to force the issue. The moment is charged with the gravest potentialities.

The passion of the Jews flares out in their accusing question coupled with the decisive command. The two together act like a challenge. The Greek of the question is idiomatic: ἔως πότε, "till when" = how long; τὴν ψυχὴν ἡμῶν αἴρεις, "art thou lifting our soul," lifting or raising it in suspense. But ψυχή is not our English word "soul" but a designation for the person: "our soul" = "us" (C.-K. 1141) as animate beings subject to tension. The question charges Jesus with keeping the Jews on tenterhooks by not coming out fairly and squarely on the main question. What that question is their demand states, "If thou art the Christ," etc. "Tell us plainly" ("with openness") means: then we shall know how to act. The implication is by no means that these Jews would believe if Jesus would say in so many words, "I am the Christ." Nor is the idea this that the Jews would use such a plain statement as a political charge on which to bring Jesus to trial. Still less may we assume that the Jews are seeking to ease their own consciences in regard to their treatment of Jesus by casting the blame on him for not speaking out plainly. They are long past such scruples. The suspense to which these Jews object is that of thrusting the fact of his Messiahship into their consciences in such a way as to cause divisions in their own ranks (9:16; 10:19) yet without giving them the chance they are determined to have to bring him to book for his claim. They mean that this is now to end; *they* are determined to end it right here and now. "Art thou or art thou not the Christ?" If he says, "I am," the stones will fly.

25) The first two words of Jesus: εἶπον ὑμῖν, **I did tell you,** is a perfect master stroke. Here they are demanding a thing with such a show of suspense — and it has been told them long ago! Where had they their ears? Here they are now trying to force an issue — why, they should have forced it long ago when Jesus first told them! Why all this show and demonstration now? — they know well enough, and Jesus lets them know that he knows. More than this: Jesus

right here and now is again telling them with his first two words just exactly what they ask. So far is he from evading the dangerous issue thrust upon him that he meets it squarely and directly in his very first utterance. This quick, unexpected directness takes the Jews quite off their guard. The question is asked when Jesus had told the Jews that he is the Christ. The answer is to be found in every one of his discourses. We single out 5:17, etc., where the Jews first resolve to kill him for "making himself equal with God."

The trouble lies not, even in the least, with Jesus but with these Jews: **and you do not believe.** After all his telling, including the present word, they do not believe (durative present). All his telling is in vain — in vain through fault of theirs; is so even now.

In order, once and for all, to settle the question of his telling them properly Jesus points to that most convincing form of his telling, which is not merely by words but by deeds which substantiate his words in the highest degree: **The works which I am doing in my Father's name, these are testifying concerning me.** Words alone, mere verbal statements ever so plain and direct, however valuable and necessary they may be, could not suffice. A fraudulent Christ might say with his mouth, "I am the Christ." We know that false Christs did arise and so declare; but their works proved them liars. The works of Jesus substantiate every word of his concerning his person and his office as the Christ of God. These works Jesus is still engaged in doing, ποιῶ, their number and the force of their testimony is increasing. They not only tell, they "testify" concerning Jesus and do this right along (present tense). Like witnesses who have seen and heard personally, these works emanating from Jesus himself speak intimately and truly of him who wrought them. And this testimony we must have. If these witnesses were silent, or if they gave a different testimony from the one they so clearly and unanimously utter, then, indeed, we might be in doubt. But now doubt is folly.

Jesus says far more than that he is just doing these works; he is doing them "in my Father's name." This reference to his Father again tells these Jews that Jesus is the Christ. Once more he asserts his mission from the Father, the mission which makes him the Christ. The ὄνομα is not the authority, so that we should understand, "by my Father's authority"; nor representation, "as my Father's representative." It denotes revelation, "in connection with my Father's revelation," i. e., the ὄνομα or revelation given by God to Israel, by which they should know the Father and be able to recognize any works that emanate from him. God's revelation displays his omnipotence, grace, and mercy, these especially. And in every one of Jesus' miracles these divine attributes shine out with utmost clearness. By aiding the body they seek to lift the soul, too, to life eternal. Compare the two notable works which Jesus set before the eyes of these Jews, 5:2, etc., 9:6, etc. The cry of these works was even now ringing in the ears of these Jews.

26) How are they treating this double testimony? **But you — you do not believe because you are not my sheep.** Mark the strong adversative and the emphatic pronoun, also the repetition, "you do not believe," which places the blame entirely on them. True and sufficient testimony ought to be believed; not to believe it is both unreason and guilt. He who refuses to believe such testimony convicts himself. "Because (ὅτι) you do not believe" states the intellectual reason which explains the Jewish unbelief, not the effective cause which produces this unbelief. It brings the plain evidence, it does not indicate the secret source. The sense is, "Since you are

not my sheep you do not believe"; and not, "Since you are not my sheep you cannot believe." The preposition ἐκ is partitive. The reference to "my sheep" connects directly with the discourse spoken two months ago in v. 1-18.

27) Jesus even repeats the particular characteristic of his sheep which here comes into play and which the Jews utterly lack. **My sheep hear my voice, and I know them, and they follow me.** Always they hear, always he knows, always they follow. Trustful hearing is meant; they know not the voice of strangers (see v. 5). Jesus says "my voice" and not "my word." The "word" signifies the contents, the "voice," the tone, sound, personal peculiarity. Both are inseparably bound together. In the shepherd's word, wherever and whenever it is spoken, the sheep hear the shepherd's voice, and it is inexpressibly sweet and attractive to them. "This lovely, delightful picture you may, if you wish, see for yourself among sheep. When a stranger calls, whistles, coaxes: Come, sheep! come, sheep! it runs and flees, and the more you call, the more it runs, as if a wolf were after it, for it knows not the strange voice; but where the shepherd makes himself heard a little, they all run to him, for they know his voice. This is how all true Christians should do, hear no voice but their shepherd's, Christ, as he himself says." Luther.

To those who are not his sheep Jesus speaks of his sheep. This is the gospel call to become his sheep. It is combined with a hint as to what those must be who will not be such sheep. Thus, too, Jesus once more tells these Jews, not only what they asked, who he really is, but also what they had failed to ask, who they are, and what they ought to become if they desired salvation, and what will become of them if they remain what they are.

The first four tenses are gnomic presents and thus
timeless. What they relate is true irrespective of
time. Note how these four statements intertwine:
they hear — *I* know — *they* follow — *I* give. In four
short master strokes the relation between the shepherd and his sheep is pictured. Something vital would
be left out if one of these four were omitted. Note
that all four are simultaneous, not successive; and
that while they are twined together, we still have
two pairs: to hear and to follow, likewise to know
and to give. The emphasis that is strongly brought
out in the two κἀγώ: "I myself know . . . I myself give," runs through the entire description: *"My*
sheep hear *my* voice; *I* know them; they follow *me*;
I give to them, etc., and no one shall pluck them
out of *my* hand." On the statement, "I know them,"
compare the comments on v. 14, in particular also
on the verb γινώσκω. "I know them" simply asserts
the great fact and stops with that. This is the point
these Jews are to note when Jesus is compelled to tell
them they are *not* his sheep. He knows all who are
his sheep. The fact that his sheep know him in turn,
while it is true enough, is not pertinent here.

Hearing the shepherd's voice is an inward act,
following the shepherd is both inward and outward.
This time the verb is plural, as in v. 14 (R. 403, etc.).
"They follow me." I call, they come; I choose the
path, they trust and come after; I lead, they are safe
in my care; I command in love, they respond in
obedience and love. If this at times means the cross,
they do not waver. One cannot hear without following, nor follow except he hear. It is all so simple
and natural — just as in the case of sheep and their
shepherd.

28) As the two actions of the sheep correspond,
so the two actions of the shepherd, each with its
emphatic ἐγώ: **and I give them life eternal,** the life

already described in 3:15 (which see). This is the very principle of life which flows from God, is grounded in God, joins to God, and leads to God. Born in regeneration, it pulses in every believer, becomes stronger as faith increases, and reaches its full flower in the glory of heaven. Temporal death merely transfers this life from earth to heaven. Itself invisible, this life manifests itself in a thousand ways and thus attests its presence and its power. When the day of glory comes, its manifestations shall be glorious altogether. No earthly shepherd is able to give life to his sheep; Jesus "gives" life eternal to his sheep. By way of gift alone this life is ours — free grace alone bestows it, and by free grace "without any merit or worthiness on our part" it is our possession. This verb δίδωμι reveals all the richness, greatness, and attractiveness of our Good Shepherd. The incomparable Giver stood there before the Jews and was actually offering them his divine gift of grace. But they would have none of his greatness and riches.

The four present tenses are now followed by two futures, both negative, but with their opposite positives shining through. **And they shall in no wise perish forever, and no one shall snatch them out of my hand.** This is a double and a direct promise; the doubling increases the emphasis. "To perish" is to be separated from God, life, and blessedness forever. John and Paul use especially the middle voice of this verb in this sense, C.-K. 788. It is the opposite of being saved. Here we have the second aorist middle subjunctive ἀπόλωνται, with οὐ μή as the strongest negation of a future act, and the aorist because the act necessarily would be only one and as such final. "Shall in no way perish" would itself be enough, the modifier "forever" is added pleonastically: this dreadful act shall never occur. This promise does not refer only to the time after the believer's death, implying that then he shall be forever safe; this promise holds good from the moment of faith onward. The verb "to perish" never means "to suffer annihilation," or to cease to exist.

The first part of the promise is stated from the viewpoint of the sheep: they shall never perish. The second part is from the viewpoint of Jesus and of any hostile being that might attack his sheep: no one shall snatch them out of his hand. This promise, now stated with the future indicative, is intensified in a moment: "no one is able to snatch them out of the Father's hand." First the fact then the possibility is denied. The two promises, one referring to Jesus, the other to the Father, indicate the equality of the two persons (5:18). The blessedness of the sheep is not only great and sweet, it is also sure and certain, not like that of the world, which is bright today then gone forever. The phrasing οὐχ ἁρπάσει τις recalls what is said of the wolf in v. 12. The "hand" of Jesus is his power. His gracious power is all-sufficient to protect every believer forever. Even at this moment Jesus and his disciples are surrounded by the Jews who are bent on violence, but the hand of Jesus is mightier than they. However weak the sheep are, under Jesus they are perfectly safe. Yet a believer may after all be lost (15:6). Our certainty of eternal salvation is not absolute. While no foe of ours is able to snatch us from our Shepherd's hand, we ourselves may turn from him and may perish willfully of our own accord.

29) What lies in and back of these words of Jesus (v. 27, 28) regarding the entire relation between him and his sheep and their complete safety in his hand, is now stated most clearly and fully. In his entire reply to the Jews, from v. 25 onward, Jesus proceeds, not as the Jews demand, by simply declaring, "I am the Christ," but as he has proceeded all along, by do-

ing such works and offering such testimony that those
who see and hear must be stirred in their own hearts
to confess of their own accord, "Thou art the Christ."
If this method of procedure has put the enemies of
Jesus in suspense, that suspense is now driven to the
limit; for instead of changing to the method they propose for their murderous end, Jesus for his own purpose of grace carries his own method to the climax.
Back of all that he does for the sheep is his Father.
**My Father, who has given them to me, is greater
than all; and no one is able to snatch them out of the
Father's hand.** The Greek does not need to name
the objects "them," which the Greek reader automatically supplies from the context. Therefore the absence of the two "them" is no warrant for converting
the statements into abstract assertions by supplying
"aught": "who has given aught to me," and "to snatch
aught," etc. (R. V. margin).

The variant readings turn on two points, whether
we should read ὅ for ὅς, and μεῖζον for μείζων: "That
which my Father has given to me is greater than
everything (now also neuter) ; and no one is able to
snatch it," etc., (R. V. margin). This and any similar
reading has little textual support, which fact already
settles the case. In addition, it introduces a thought
that is wholly untenable. For this reading which
draws ὁ πατήρ μου, placed in front of the relative clause,
into that clause, throws a peculiar emphasis on "my
Father": "What *my Father* has given me," etc., and
thus injects the implication into the clause that besides
what his Father has given him Jesus has something
that is not so acquired. This is not true; *all* that
Jesus has comes from his Father. In addition, this
reading produces the strange thought that the sheep
are greater than everything else and on this account
are held firmly by the Father's hand. In what respect
are they "greater?" one is moved to ask. In v. 28 it

is the power and the greatness of Jesus that protect
the sheep; and so again in v. 29 it is the greatness and
the power of the Father, exceeding that of any possible
foe, that safeguard the sheep.

The Father, who sent the Son, works through the
Son, whom he sent. It is·thus that he has given the
sheep to Jesus: "which thou gavest me out of the
world; thine they were, and thou gavest them to
me," 17:6; compare 6:37. This shuts out the notion
that the Father merely employs Jesus to take care of
the sheep. Likewise, it shuts out the thought that
the old keeper of Israel (Ps. 121:4, 5), who neither
slumbers nor sleeps, has gone to rest, and that
Jesus is now his successòr in office. When Jesus says
"my Father" he denominates himself as "the Son,"
and it is thus that these two are equally concerned
about the sheep: the Father through the mission bestowed on the Son, the Son in the mission received
from the Father. "Has given," the perfect δέδωκε,
has its usual force: a past act when the Son entered
on his mission and its abiding effect as long as that
mission endures. This Father is "greater than all,"
μείζων πάντων, and "all" must be masculine and denote
persons, for it includes the masculine τίς in v. 28 and
οὐδείς in the present verse. While "greater" is broad,
here it must refer especially to power: the Father
exceeds in power every being arrayed against the
sheep (Satan, demon spirits, human foes however
mighty).

After thus declaring the Father's might, it might
seem superfluous for Jesus to add, "and no one can
snatch them out of the Father's hand," for this is
certainly self-evident. The reason for the addition
lies far deeper. Jesus deliberately parallels what he
says of himself, "no one shall snatch them out of my
hand," with what he says of his Father, "no one can
snatch them out of the Father's hand." The fact that

he mentions the detail ("shall snatch") with reference
to himself is due to his being on his saving mission;
that he mentions the possibility ("can snatch") with
reference to the Father is due to the Father's institution of that mission. Both thus belong together:
Father and Son, fact and possibility. Does the
promise of Jesus, standing there in human form before the Jews, sound preposterous, that no one shall
snatch his sheep out of his hand? To snatch them
out of *his* hand is the same as snatching them out
of *the Father's* hand. Remember the relation of these
two hands, as this relation centers in the sheep.

30) What is thus prepared is now pronounced in
so many words: **I and the Father, we are one.**
The equal power to protect the sheep is due to the
equality of these two persons. This makes the mighty
acts of equal protection perfectly plain. "We are
one," therefore, cannot be reduced to mean only one
in purpose, will, and work. This, however true it
may be in itself, does not suffice; for the reference
is to power, namely almighty power, against which
no other being, however great his power may be,
is able to rise. To deny that equality of power is
here expressed is to deny just what is asserted. This
denial resorts to the faulty reading μεῖζον instead of
μείζων, and places the power in the sheep instead of
in the Father. Another way to reduce what Jesus
says is to point to ἕν and to assert that, if identity
is meant by "we are one," we should have εἶς, a masculine instead of a neuter. Augustine has answered
that: ἕν frees us from the Charybdis of Arianism,
ἐσμέν from the Scylla of Sabellianism. If we had εἶς,
this would mean that the two are one and the same
person, producing patripassionism and other extravagant fancies. Jesus says, "we are ἕν," "one thing,
one being, one God, one Lord," Luther. The two persons are not mingled, for Jesus clearly distinguishes

between ἐγώ and ὁ πατήρ; but these two, while they are two in person, are ἕν, one, a unit substance, or, as we prefer, a unit in essence.

It is fruitless to bring in analogies for ἕν in order to reduce this oneness to something with which our minds are conversant, which they are able to grasp intellectually. Thus Paul says of himself and of Apollos, "He that planteth and he that watereth are one," I Cor. 3:8. Here, however, not persons as persons but their activities, planting and watering, make them one. It is certainly unconvincing to point to I Cor. 12:12: one body composed of many members; and it is an actual descent into filth to think of I Cor. 6:16. When Jesus prays that all who will come to believe through the Word of the apostles (17:20) may be one, this is so manifestly the increasing oneness of conviction and confession regarding the one truth of the Word that it seems strange to adduce it in this connection. Eph. 2:14 and 4:4, as well as Gal. 3:28 speak of the spiritual oneness of the *Una Sancta* or Communion of Saints, in which any number may be joined. Acts 4:32 is merely the accord of thought and will. Efforts will constantly be repeated to follow some such analogy in thinking of the oneness of the Father and the Son. But all these human and earthly analogies are really not true analogies. Among them all no oneness exists which can be placed beside this expression of Jesus, "We are one." Nor is this strange, for each of the different lower types of oneness is peculiar and unique in itself according to the subjects which it embraces. The resemblances are only formal. Once this is perceived, we shall drop the effort to classify the oneness of Jesus and the Father with some other oneness of which we know.

As high and as absolutely singular as are the Father and the Son, so high, so absolutely singular

and unlike any other oneness is that of him who is
the one eternal Father with him who is the one
eternal Son. Only he who has sounded the depths
of the godhead of this Father and this Son could
grasp what their oneness actually is. The ancient
church defined the ἕν of Jesus by the great term
ὁμοουσία, which retains the supreme credit of rising
above all earthly categories to the actual numerical
ἕν of the οὐσία (being or essence) eternal in the Son
as in the Father. No truer, higher, or more adequate
term has ever been furnished by the mind of the
church. Unsatisfactory by comparison is the idea of
a oneness of several joined merely in action or suffering (Zahn). Paul wrote Col. 2:8, 9: "Beware
lest any man spoil you through philosophy and vain
deceit, after the tradition of men, after the rudi-
ments of the world, and not after Christ. For in
him dwelleth all the fulness of the godhead bodily."
Before the divine oneness of these infinite persons we
bow down in childlike adoration and worship. As
regards 14:28, this passage refers only to the human
nature of Jesus.

31) **The Jews again took up stones in order to
stone him.** They picked them up where the building operations of reconstructing parts of the Temple
were going on and brought them to the Porch of
Solomon as they had done once before (8:59). This
their action is their answer. The aorist records only
the fact.

32) As Jesus met their challenge (v. 25, etc.) un-
flinchingly, so he now stands his ground as the stones
arrive. **Jesus answered them,** namely this action of
theirs, **Many excellent works did I show you from
the Father. On account of which of those works
are you trying to stone me?** The pertinency of the
assertion and the question of Jesus is lost when the
emphasis is placed only on the object "many excel-

lent works" and not equally on the modifier "from the Father." The point is not merely that these many works are καλά, "excellent," *praeclara*, and that Jesus showed these works to the Jews, so that they could not but see this excellence; but that by their very excellence these excellent works show that they are and must be "from the Father." In other words, these works reveal in an actual, visible manner, that Jesus and the Father are one, just as he has said. This oneness of himself with the Father is manifested not only in the one work by which Jesus and the Father equally keep the sheep in their hand against any possible foe, it is manifested in every work of Jesus; for every one of these works wrought in his great mission, while it is done by him as the Son coming from the Father, is done equally by the Father through the Son. This is the point which makes the preamble so vital for the question. John has recorded two of these excellent works at length (5:1-9; 9:1-7), to the rest he refers in 2:23 and relies on the records of the other evangelists.

With ποῖον Jesus asks the Jews to point out a quality (R. 740) in any one of these many works which shows that it is not "of the Father," does not originate (ἐκ) from him and reveal this its origin to them. What Jesus asks is this, "Does any work that I have shown you contradict my assertion that I and the Father are one," so that this assertion of mine must be ranked as blasphemy deserving the penalty of stoning? The question is directly to the point. Those who think that Jesus is shifting the issue from his words (which sound like blasphemy to the Jews) to his works (which the Jews must acknowledge as "excellent"), miss the very point that is emphasized in "from my Father." The present tense λιθάζετε is inchoative, "begin or try to stone me," R. 880. The question of Jesus contains no irony,

which would only the more enrage the passion of the
Jews. It calmly asks them to stop and to think, to
make sure of their ground, and lays the finger on the
one decisive point. Jesus never asks anyone simply
to assent to the abstract metaphysical proposition
that he and the Father are one in essence. That would
be a serious mistake and would call out equally abstract denials. What he does is to show us the quality
of his words and of his works; these are the true
mirror of his person. He who looks into this mirror
will confess with John, "We beheld his glory, glory
as of the Only-begotten from the Father."

33) The Jews do pause and feel that they must
justify themselves. **The Jews answered him, Not
for an excellent work are we trying to stone thee
but for blasphemy, namely that thou, being a man,
makest thyself God.** Since this is nothing but
defense and self-justification, we are not to think that
the Jews here admit that all the works of Jesus are
"excellent," or that they have forgotten their deduction that, because he did some of these works on the
Sabbath, he could not be of God. All they say is that
they are not considering any work of Jesus, whether
it is excellent or not, when now proceeding to stone
him (λιθάζομεν, again inchoative present) but his
blasphemous utterance — that being more than
enough and coming squarely under the law set down
in Lev. 24:15, 16. Bent only on justifying their
action, these Jews separate the words and the works
of Jesus, whereas Jesus demands that they be combined. Never having seen the Father (whom they
did not even know, 8:19) in any of the works of
Jesus, nor heard the Father's voice (which was wholly
foreign to them, 5:37, 38) in any of the words of
Jesus, they now again are wholly deaf to the decisive
phrase: many excellent works "from the Father,"
and judge both Jesus' works and words without

true reference to the Father, who is so foreign to them.

This, however, the sharp ears of these Jews at once caught, that by saying, "I and the Father, we are one," Jesus was making himself God. They caught this because it was exactly what they wanted, a word on which to base the charge of blasphemy and thus full justification for the summary inflection of the death penalty. The fact that this penalty should be decreed only by a legal court after a fair and honest trial counts for nothing in their passionate hatred once for all to be rid of Jesus. They intend to dispense with legal formalities and to lynch this flagrant blasphemer on the spot. This Jewish charge of blasphemy must stand against Jesus to this day if he, being nothing but a man, either by implication or by some direct statement (here or elsewhere) made himself God. He could be exonerated in only one of two ways: first, by proving that he never said what all sacred records state that he did say — that these records are spurious; secondly, by proving that what these records state is not what the recorded words mean. Both methods are hopeless as far as fact and any legitimate proof of fact is concerned. If, nevertheless, we choose the first, we end by having no historical knowledge of Jesus — with the records we completely wipe out "the historical Jesus" and retain nothing but myth and legend. If we choose the second method, then no recorded word of Jesus can mean what it says — we ourselves make these words mean what we think they should mean, and again a "historical Jesus" becomes vapor.

34) Only in one way can the charge that Jesus, being nothing but a man, makes himself God be refuted: he must prove that he calls himself God because he is actually God. This is exactly what Jesus does. By taking up stones against an alleged

John 10:34 765

blasphemer the Jews appeal to their νόμος, "the law."
By use of this very law Jesus begins his refutation
(v. 34-36) and then completes it by the appeal to his
works (v. 37, 38). In this refutation Jesus not only
repeats the assertion, "I am God's Son," but defines
with simple clarity how he as the Son is one with the
Father. **Jesus answered them, Has it not been written in your law, I myself said, Gods are you? If
he called them Gods, to whom the Word of God
came — and the Scripture cannot be broken — do
you say of him, whom the Father sanctified and sent
into the world, Thou blasphemest! because I said,
Son of God am I?** The force of the circumscribed
perfect is: "it is on record" in Holy Writ. The term
νόμος need not here be restricted to "law" in the
sense of norm according to which one forms his judgments. While "law" often designates the Pentateuch, it is likewise used as a brief title (*Torah*)
for the entire Old Testament. This is the case here
where Jesus quotes Ps. 82:6. On the possessive "your"
law see 8:17.

The refutation is accomplished by means of a syllogism. Major premise: The Scriptures cannot be
broken; minor premise: The Scripture calls men
commissioned by God "Gods"; *ergo*: Jesus, sanctified
and sent into the world by God, is rightly called "God"
in a correspondingly higher sense. This syllogism
operates *a minori ad majus,* and is the more convincing because of this very form. It is hasty to
call this refutation an *argumentum ad hominem.* This
would be the case if by "your law" Jesus referred to
a law which he for his person does not accept; but
he accepts this law as fully as do the Jews. His
major premise is the fact that this law cannot be
broken, i. e., set aside in any way or by any person.
Nor is this an *argumentum ad hominem* by claiming
for Jesus as a mere man the title "God" in the way

in which the human judges in the Psalm have the title *Elohim* or "Gods." The contrast between these judges and Jesus is entirely too strong for this: they, to whom only the Word of God came; he, the one and only one, whom the Father sanctified and sent into the world. This mighty contrast *a minori ad majus* destroys any *argumentum ad hominem.* The supposition that Jesus states the *ergo* in the form *a majori ad minus* is untenable. While he might say, "I am God," he says only, "I am God's Son." In the passage from the Psalm the title "Gods" is synonymous with "children (literally: sons) of the Most High." The fact is that Jesus never calls himself simply "God," ὁ Θεός or Θεός, but always far more precisely, "the Son of God," as in all the instances where he speaks of "my Father" (never using the plural "our"). So in the present case "Son of God" denotes the Second Person of the Godhead as compared with the First.

The Psalm deals with judges and rulers of Israel, scoring them for judging unjustly. God tells them that although he himself called them Gods and children (sons) of the Most High, yet because of their wickedness they shall die like common men. Jesus quotes only these words from the Psalm: "I (Yahweh) said, You are Gods." He at once explains in what sense Jahweh called these judges *Elohim.*

35) It is because "the Word of God came to them," but not in the sense that God granted them certain revelations to communicate to Israel, or gave them his laws to administer in Israel. The Word of God that came to them is the one that appointed them as judges and placed them in their high and holy office. They were judges in a theocracy, in which Yahweh himself was the supreme ruler and judge. Though they received their office through human mediation, they actually held it by divine appointment as God's

own representatives among his people. In this sense, Jesus says, Yahweh himself called these judges *Elohim*; they were appointed by Yahweh's own word. In this respect they resembled the kings and the prophets of Israel. On the latter compare Jer. 1:2 and Ezek. 1:3; to them the appointive word came immediately, just as this afterward was the case with the Baptist, Luke 3:1.

Before Jesus brings in the conclusion he adds parenthetically, "and the Scripture cannot be broken," i. e., in any point or any statement which it contains. While it is only a parenthesis and is like a side remark, this is really the axiomatic major premise of the entire syllogism. Without it the conclusion could not possibly stand. Note that Jesus does not say οὐκ ἔξεστι λύειν τὴν γραφήν, "it is not lawful (not allowed) to break the Scripture." This would be only a subjective Jewish valuation of the Scripture. Any deduction resting only on this premise would be nothing but an *argumentum ad hominem*, binding only the Jews not necessarily Jesus or us, who might hold a view of the Scripture differing from that of the Jews. The axiom in this parenthesis is objective and absolute: οὐ δύναται λυθῆναι ἡ γραφή, "the Scripture cannot possibly be broken," no word of it be dissolved; compare 7:23; Matt. 5: 19. Every statement of the Scripture stands immutably, indestructible in its verity, unaffected by denial, human ignorance or criticism, charges of errancy or other subjective attack. Thus in the present case no power or ingenuity of man can alter Ps. 82:6, and the fact that Yahweh called his human judges *Elohim*.

36) On the premises thus laid down Jesus rests the incontrovertible conclusion. But in doing so he lifts himself far above the human judges and the reason why they were called gods. Over against the relative clause which declares why Yahweh could and

did call these judges gods, Jesus sets the relative clause
which describes the supreme nature of his own office,
"whom the Father sanctified and sent into the world."
In a broad way, like those judges of the Psalm, Jesus,
too, has an office from God and can thus be classed
with them. But the moment his office is compared
with theirs, a tremendous difference appears. This
centers both in the designation of the person who
placed Jesus in his office and in the action by which
this was done. It is "the Father" who sanctified and
sent Jesus. As "the Father" he did this, which
means that the one sanctified and sent is the Son, and
that for this office and work he could use none other
than his own Son. Judges in Israel there could be
many, but only One could be sanctified and sent into
the world from heaven itself for the actual redemption and salvation of the world. To such judges (and
any other men commissioned by God) he could send
his appointive word at the proper time in the course
of their lives; not so in the case of Jesus, his mission
began in the counsel between the Father and the
Son in heaven. His very person and the work he
was to do necessitated this course, and this very course
reveals who Jesus is and what name properly designates him.

Both aorists, "he sanctified and sent," are historical. In the nature of the case both acts precede
the coming of Jesus into the world. Because they
take place between the Father and the Son in
heaven, we are able to conceive of them only imperfectly. Whether the sanctifying and the sending are
distinct, or whether they are simultaneous is hard to
determine. If we may judge from the analogy in
Jer. 1:5, the former is the case, and the act of sanctifying would consist in designating and setting apart
the Son for the blessed mission. Yet, as taking place
between the Father and the Son, this sanctifying

would exceed that of any human prophet or apostle
(Gal. 1:15), even as the Son stands infinitely above
them. As regards the sending itself a similarity
exists (Isa. 6:8, 9; John 20:21, καθώς "even as");
yet of no man do we ever read that God "sent him
into the world" on a mission. The verb ἀποστέλλω
means to send away for a definite purpose or on a
specific mission, and thus differs from the wider term
πέμπω, also used regarding Jesus, which denotes only
transmission, C.-K. 1018. The accusative after
ἀποστέλλω only occasionally indicates what the person
sent becomes by being sent; thus in Mark 1:2, "I
send my messenger." Quite generally the accusative
states who the person is that is being sent, Matt. 21:1,
"two disciples"; 21:34-37. This is especially clear
when a second accusative indicates what the person
sent is to be in his mission: "The Father sent the
Son to be the Savior of the world," I John 4:14. Thus
the claim is answered that the Son became the Son and
is called the Son only by virtue of the sending, i. e., is
the Son only as having become man.

Again, this sending is not merely *"to* the world"
and to be dated from the time when Jesus began his
public work; but a sending *"into* the world," to be
dated prior to the Incarnation: "I came forth from
the Father, and am come into the world; again, I
leave the world, and go to the Father." The fact that
God's Son is thus sent reveals the greatness and the
value of his mission: *Ratio sub qua Jesus Christus
agnoscendus est; missio praesupponit Filium cum
Patre unum,* Bengel on 17:3. Having come thus from
heaven to earth on his great mission, Jesus rightly
confronts the Jews with the question: "Do you say
of him, whom the Father sanctified and sent into
the world, Thou blasphemest! because I said, I am
God's Son"? When our excellent grammarian Robertson ventures into the field of exegesis with a reference

to υἱός without the article and has Jesus claim that he is "a son of God" by way of an *argumentum ad hominem* (781), he contradicts himself when he admits that υἱὸς ἀνθρώπου in John 5:27 may mean either "*the* Son of man" or "*a* son of man." But the matter is not determined alone by the absence or the presence of the article. When Jesus calls himself, "*the* Son of man" some eighty times and then in one instance omits the article, this exception means only one thing — he now says, "*a* son of man." And when Jesus places "Son of God" beside "Father," and does that after a relative clause as plain as the one here used, by "Son" he means *the* Son beside whom no other such Son exists. See above on 5:27.

37) The Jews may well have been startled to learn that God himself called men appointed to office by him "gods." If Jesus should claim no more than that he belonged to this class, their charge of blasphemy against him would already be refuted. It is overwhelmingly crushed by the evidence that the office of Jesus is one that is infinitely above all such judges or any other representatives of God who in the course of their lives receive their appointment only by some word of God. This evidence Jesus now once more lays before them in a manner so clear that any doubt or denial is utterly in vain. **If I am not doing the works of my Father, do not believe me,** i. e., do not give me credence in what I say of myself. In conditions of reality the negative is alway οὐ, R. 1011. Note the present ποιῶ, which is not timeless but durative: Jesus is still engaged in doing these works. He has pointed to them in v. 25 and 32. In the latter passage he does it to shame the ingratitude of the Jews who seek to stone him; here he does it to show the wrong nature of their unbelief, making him a liar and a blasphemer. Jesus here refers to what he did in 5:31 and 36, and again in 8:13, etc. These Jews

claim that the testimony of Jesus is unsupported and that, therefore, they are right in refusing him credence. They can do this only by completely shutting their eyes to the works of Jesus, which absolutely substantiate his verbal testimony concerning himself as God's Son.

"The works of my Father" are the miracles of Jesus. Whether we make the genitive merely possessive: which belong to my Father; or subjective: which my Father does through me, these works show beyond question that he whose mission includes such works is the very Son of the Father who sanctified and sent him on his mission. Any other estimate of these works is inadequate and wrong and, therefore, untenable. We see this right along in the way in which these works worry the Jews. They are compelled to shut their eyes to these works (9:41); they try to pick some flaw in them (9:16; 5:18 and 7:23, 24); they never attempt a real fathoming of these works. The denial of the deity of Jesus has never progressed beyond this attitude of the Jews in regard to his works. The imperative, "do not believe me," i. e., what I say of myself, is not categorical but permissive. We must recall 4:48 with its complaint that men will not believe unless they see signs and wonders; likewise 8:14, where Jesus asserts that his word-testimony is true, irrespective of any further testimony. Thus Jesus does not forbid faith in his words alone, apart from his works. His words alone are enough for faith. In a large number of instances we do not require the legal two or three witnesses; one testimony is ample to convince us. Only where men refuse credence, the second and the third testimony, by corroborating the first, compel credence; so that, if it be still refused, the refusal is full of guilt. It is thus that Jesus here appeals to his works: "If I am not doing — actually doing — my Father's works, then you may claim that you are not bound to believe what I say to you about myself."

38)   On the other hand: **But if I do them, and if you believe not me, believe the works — in order that you may come to realize and may go on realizing, that the Father is in me, and I am in the Father.** By making both conditions conditions of reality: "if I actually do not — if I actually do" my Father's works, Jesus puts the alternative squarely up to the Jews.   They must choose either the nay or the yea — a third does not exist.   To refuse to make the choice is to condemn themselves.   That the choice must be yea, since the works are being done and cry out their testimony to all who see them, Jesus does not even need to intimate.

This time the imperative is categorical, "believe the works!"   That this is the case we see from the preamble, "and if you believe not me," namely my words about   myself.   This condition of expectancy points to   the refusal of   the Jews to believe Jesus' words.   At the same time   it implies that the person and the words of Jesus are themselves enough to receive credence without the works; compare 6:63, etc., and 68, etc.   Note the contrast between the two datives ἐμοί and τοῖς ἔργοις, the faith-inspiring personality of Jesus as it reaches out to men's hearts in his works.   On "and if," in preference to "even if," see R. 1026.   The thought is that the more one may hesitate to believe Jesus' words, the more he is bound to believe the works, which as actual works admit of no legitimate denial; compare 14:10, 11.   The words one may connect only with Jesus, since they fall from his human lips; the works are so connected with both Jesus and the Father who sent him to do these works that he who will not believe the works sets himself in antagonism against the Father.   "Believe the works!" means, "Fly not in the face of these!"

The battle of Jesus with the Jews most certainly turned on the truth and the trustworthiness of his statements, here especially the two that he and the Father are one (v. 30), and that he is the Father's Son sent into the world (v. 36). The use of πιστεύειν with the dative by no means reduces the verb to mean only assent to what Jesus thus declares concerning himself. A study of C.-K. 902-905 on John's use of this verb is highly profitable. To receive the testimony of Jesus concerning himself as trustworthy always involves on the part of him who so receives it a personal relation to Jesus in accord with that testimony accepted as trustworthy, i. e., a personal relation to him as God's Son who is one with the Father. This C.-K. define, "to acknowledge Christ and therefore to cling to him." The moment the Jews would admit Jesus to be what he said of himself, that moment their entire attitude toward him would accord with their admission. A glance at M.-M. 514 shows that in the pagan world πιστεύειν moved on a far lower plane, substantiating the abundant references in C.-K. to this effect.

This aids in understanding the purpose clause, which really modifies the entire previous statement. Jesus points to the works he is doing and calls on the Jews to believe at least these works, i. e., that they are indeed — as they can see for themselves — the works of the Father. The moment they thus believe these works as being most certainly connected with the Father, they will believe what Jesus testifies to them concerning his connection with the Father when he says that he and the Father are one and that he is the Son of God come into the world from the Father. The full profundity of this connection will

not at once be clear to them. But this faith will effect
the purpose of Jesus and of the Father who sent him:
"in order that you may come to realize and may go
on realizing that the Father is in me, and I am in the
Father." The verb γινώσκω, here used twice, (this
being the assured reading) means far more than intellectual knowing. It denotes an inner spiritual realization due to the inner contact of faith with Jesus and
the Father. C.-K. 244 are right in stating that
γινώσκω predicates an inner relation of the subject to
the object, one involving the essentials of salvation.
The aorist is ingressive: "may come to realize"; and
the present is durative: "may go on realizing" with
deeper, fuller personal insight.

The object that will thus be realized is "that the
Father is in me, and I am in the Father." The great
fact and reality is meant, not the mode and manner
of these persons being the one in the other. The
latter will always be beyond our mortal grasp, the
former will grow clearer and more self-evident as
our relation with Jesus and the Father becomes more
intimate. It should be plain that Jesus here defines
what he says in v. 30, "I and the Father, we are
one." This means far more than that the man Jesus,
who stood before the Jews, is in intimate communion
with God, that God merely fills his heart and mind;
or that as an instrument of God Jesus is in all his
official work moved by God's power and grace. This
communion and cooperation of the Father with Jesus
is something visible to faith from the very start,
apparent in all the words as in all the works of
Jesus. Even the beggar in 9:33 at once saw this.
The realization of which Jesus speaks follows this
basic perception of faith and is its result. It is
summarized in the statement, "Son of God am I."
The oneness we behold in Jesus and the Father is
by no means merely "dynamic," even though a meta-

physical basis for it is acknowledged. Jesus is not merely "the effective organ," and the Father "the determining potency." This might fit "the Father in me"; it would leave untouched the second and equal statement, "I in the Father." For exactly as the Father is in the Son, so the Son is in the Father. And these two are persons, hence their oneness is that of being. This is the ineffable mystery that Jesus, God's own Son, is in essence one with his Father. "He that hath seen me hath seen the Father," 14:9. The relation of these two is an indissoluble interpenetration, equally from the Father to the Son, from the Son to the Father. For it the ancient church coined the term περιχώρησις *essentialis,* than which term no better one has yet been found. That this essential interpenetrating oneness of the divine persons should manifest itself dynamically goes without saying. An additional part of the mystery is the place of the human nature in this divine oneness. All that we may venture to say is that its part in this oneness is wholly passive and receptive through its union with the person of the Son.

39) **They were trying to arrest him again; and he escaped out of their hand.** The supposition that when Jesus concluded by saying, "The Father in me, and I in the Father," he toned down his statement made in v. 30, and that thus the Jews mitigated their violence and instead of stoning him at once sought only to arrest him, is untenable. The closing words say more, and say this more pointedly than v. 30. What stopped the immediate stoning was most probably the effective reference to Ps. 82 and the refutation of the charge of blasphemy. The Jews felt less sure on this point. So they closed in on Jesus to arrest him and to bring him to formal trial before the Sanhedrin, where the exact measure of his guilt could be determined. The imperfect ἐζήτουν = "they tried to

arrest him," and the following aorist records the outcome, in regular Greek fashion; "again" recalls 7:30 and 44.

All that John records is that Jesus escaped their hands. How he succeeded in doing so has called forth various conjectures. Those that assume some kind of miraculous action are least probable, as John would probably have indicated as much if Jesus had escaped in this way. He escaped — that is all.

40) **And he went away again beyond the Jordan to the place where John was at the first baptizing.** The final break had come — Jesus did not return to Jerusalem until Palm Sunday and the final Passover. The adverb πάλιν would intimate that Jesus went back to the place from whence he last came to Jerusalem (v. 22), where thus he had already a short time before spent about two months (the interval between the last two festivals). John does not again (1:28) name the place, but he indicates that the Baptist did much of his work here "at the first," τὸ πρῶτον, adverbial accusative. That is how the people came to make the comparison in v. 41, with the result that many came to faith. **And he remained there** until he was called to Bethany by the death of Lazarus (11:7), after which he retired to Ephraim (11:54).

41) **And many came to him and were saying, John did no sign, but all whatever John said concerning this man was true.** Only a glimpse at the activity of Jesus here in Perea is afforded us. The people flocked to him, and he must have taught them as usual. These people, in a way, compare Jesus with the Baptist, the memory of whom was still vivid among them, for they remark that the Baptist did nothing (οὐδέν) in the way of a sign, implying that Jesus did signs also in this locality. At the same time they connect Jesus and the Baptist and quite in the right manner when they remark that literally

everything the Baptist had told them about Jesus "was true," i. e., when he told it, as now they are able to see for themselves. The testimony of the Baptist was thus bearing its fruit.

42) **And many believed on him there.** The aorist may be ingressive, "came to believe," or simply historical, just reporting the fact. What the rulers at the capital reject with violence these simple people receive for their salvation. John says nothing about them and thus leaves the impression of great success in this corner of the land. Stones for Jesus in Jerusalem, faith for Jesus in Perea. With this bright picture the dark and ugly story of this part of John's Gospel (chapters 7 to 10) ends.

41860568R00434

Made in the USA
San Bernardino, CA
06 July 2019